KU-267-549

SWANSEA LIBRARIES

6000358823

Frank Lloyd Wright ®

ALSO BY PAUL HENDRICKSON

Hemingway's Boat:
Everything He Loved in Life, and Lost

Sons of Mississippi:
A Story of Race and Its Legacy

The Living and the Dead:
Robert McNamara and Five Lives of a Lost War

Looking for the Light:
The Hidden Life and Art of Marion Post Wolcott

Seminary: A Search

Plagued by Fire

Plagued by Fire

The Dreams and Furies of
FRANK LLOYD WRIGHT

Paul Hendrickson

THE BODLEY HEAD
LONDON

1 3 5 7 9 10 8 6 4 2

The Bodley Head, an imprint of Vintage,
20 Vauxhall Bridge Road,
London SW1V 2SA

The Bodley Head is part of the Penguin Random House group of companies whose
addresses can be found at global.penguinrandomhouse.com.

Copyright © Paul Hendrickson 2019

Paul Hendrickson has asserted his right to be identified as the author of this Work in
accordance with the Copyright, Designs and Patents Act 1988

First published by The Bodley Head in 2019

www.penguin.co.uk/vintage

A CIP catalogue record for this book is available from the British Library

Hardback ISBN 9781847923103

Printed and bound in Great Britain by Clays Ltd, Elcograf S.p.A.

Penguin Random House is committed to a sustainable future for
our business, our readers and our planet. This book is made from
Forest Stewardship Council® certified paper.

For Tim Samuelson,
who took me to a stone

CITY AND COUNTY OF SWANSEA LIBRARIES	
6000358823	
Askews & Holts	29-Oct-2019
720.92	£25.00
SWOY	

The true poem is the poet's mind; the true ship is the shipbuilder.
                                    —Ralph Waldo Emerson, "History"

Do I contradict myself?
Very well then I contradict myself,
(I am large, I contain multitudes.)
                                    —Walt Whitman, "Song of Myself"

The world asks us to be quickly readable, but the thing about human beings is that we are more than one thing. We are multiple selves. We are massively contradictory.
                                    —Ali Smith, in an interview in *The New York Times*

You shouldn't judge the artist for the art.
                                    —Sally Mann, in an email to the author

And so, by a long detour, we come back to the original question, whether character and art are correlated. The answer is that they are, but in a complicated fashion. Masterpieces can be produced by saints of art or of the church; they can be produced by rascals or crazies or even, at times, by accident; but I refuse to think that they can be produced by genuine scoundrels, "men without honor or virtue." The artist, no matter what his sins may be, is bent on giving himself away ...
                                    —Malcolm Cowley, —*And I Worked at the Writer's Trade*

Contents

PART V End Story: 1950–1959

Plagued by Fire

On the crawlingly slow way home to Spring Green that night (it was the Saturday local, a milk train, all he could get out of Chicago, and the thing seemed to buck to a halt at every two-bit town and junction and siding), he had sat nearly catatonic in a compartment in the buffet parlor car as newsboys in their woolen tams and plus fours kept running along the platforms at the larger stops, thrusting through the hot open windows their penny sheets with the big black banner headlines on them. Then, too, there were the reporters, those twenty-dollar-a-week parasites, hopping aboard all along the roughly one-hundred-and-seventy-five-mile route with their brutish cameras and those yellowed cards that barked PRESS slanted into the headbands of their bashed fedoras. They were coming down the aisle in almost frantic search for him, trying to shag a quote for the morning's edition. If they couldn't shag one, though, they'd make one up, no problem. This damn story had everything: an inferno fire right out of the Old Testament; people's brains said to have been sliced open or crushed to pulp with some kind of hand axe or shingling tool; a Negro manservant in a white coat said to have been subserviently ladling the midday soup but who'd somehow up and gone berserk; even—and this was the juiciest part—all that innuendo and whispered rumor and barely suppressed gloating, its own kind of midwestern wildfire, about retribution, divine retribution, the Lord's own justice against libertines, adulterers. Hadn't the wages of unrighteousness come home to roost for Frank Lloyd Wright, even if he'd been personally spared from the flames and butchery? Maybe it was somehow better this way. Let it work on him for the rest of his days.

Prologue

Out of the Old Testament: August 15, 1914

Frank Lloyd Wright, with Taliesin Fellows, November 1937

I n a way, this is a book about standing at stones.

Frank Lloyd Wright was born two years after the end of the Civil War and died not quite two years after the launch of Sputnik—ninety-one years and ten months on the earth. In the approximate middle of that near-century span, on August 15, 1914, when he was forty-seven, the greatest architect America has yet produced suffered a personal catastrophe that would have destroyed a man of lesser will and lesser ego, although perhaps that is just saying the same thing twice. A crazed black servant named Julian Carlton set fire to Wright's home, Taliesin, in Spring Green, Wisconsin, and went about murdering or fatally wounding seven people, one of whom was the woman Wright deeply loved and had been living with "indecently" for the past several years, even as his own decent (and denying) wife, down in Oak Park, Illinois, kept praying he'd somehow come to his moral senses and return to his family. "Now a blow had fallen like the lightning stroke," Wright wrote years later in his autobiography, which is one of the great memoirs of the twentieth century even if you must distrust it on every page. "In thirty minutes the house and all in it had burned to the stone work or to the ground."

Five years before the blow fell, in the fall of 1909, having already revolutionized American architecture and produced what other artists might have considered a lifetime's worth of work, Wright had abandoned his practice and gone off to Europe with the freethinking Mamah Borthwick Cheney, who was both his Oak Park neighbor and his client. (Their homes were six streets apart, and the two families had mixed socially and in other ways as well.) It was not just a local scandal, condemned from pulpits and on editorial pages, but a regional outrage and in some ways a national one. She had forsaken her spouse and two little children, as he had forsaken his spouse and six children, the youngest of whom was a five-year-old. He said he was on a "spiritual hegira." And now, after some relative quiet in their lives, and after fitful efforts at rebuilding a suspended career, on a late-summer Saturday afternoon, just as a world war was about to break out in Europe, in a stunning home cantilevered into a Wisconsin hillside, forty-five-year-old Mamah Borthwick (since her divorce, she had dropped her married name) was dead, no, not just dead, but slaughtered, in the most gruesome way, and so were those two children on whom she had earlier turned her back to go away with the man she loved.

BATTLE COMING WHICH WILL SHOCK WORLD, blazed the *Chicago Sunday Tribune* the next morning on page one in an eight-column headline, and right below, in a typeface not quite as black but nearly as large and going the width of the page: AWFUL CRIME IN WISCONSIN COTTAGE. Other papers couldn't keep out of their headlines the words LOVE BUNGALOW or LOVE COTTAGE or LOVECASTLE.

Thirteen days before, John and Martha Cheney had come from Illinois for a month-long stay at Spring Green with their publicly scorned mama. (Their father, who had since remarried, had their custody.) Nine people were attacked that day, but the famous, or notorious, person to whom the house belonged wasn't one of them. Frank Lloyd Wright was in Chicago on business. He had left Wisconsin four days before, intending to be back on the weekend. If the slayer had had his way, there would have been no survivors and nothing to be back to. As it was, in what was perhaps no more than ten or twelve or fourteen minutes of frenzied work, the small-boned and medium-sized and quiet-seeming and place-knowing Julian Carlton, about whom history is still confounded, managed to pour lines of foamy-looking gasoline, strike the matches, and, with his weapon, abruptly end seven of those nine unsuspecting lives. (They'd all just sat down to their noon meal, which was his job to put before them.) That's not quite accurate: three of the seven died at his blurring hand more or less instantly, while the other four lingered for a few hours or days in separate agonies.

He had used a hand axe, in some cases used both ends of it—almost arbitrarily, or so it seems, from all that can be reconstructed. More technically it was a roofer's shingling hatchet, which meant it had a specially weighted iron head and an elongated wooden handle, giving it more swinging power, torqueing force. On one end of the slender head was a knife-edge blade, for sizing and cutting shingles, and on the other was a square knob of hammer, for pounding the shingles in place with nails. In some grotesque sense, you could say it was an inspired choice of weapon: double lethality, with all the weight front-loaded. On the other hand, maybe it was just the tool lying around, available, in place of, say, a double-barreled shotgun. No one really knows. A shotgun, though, would have been a lot more obtrusive than a shingling hatchet, which you could bring into an eating area concealed under your white serving tunic or maybe holding it low against your trouser leg, its head pointed downward. Not that this is how it happened, necessarily. Because for as much as this moment has been chronicled, pored over, dreamed into by what is now three generations of Wright biographers and historians, dreamed into by playwrights, by newspaper feature writers, by documentary filmmakers, by a handful of novelists, by conspiracy theorists, even as it's been dreamed into and performed onstage by an opera company, there is still so much about it that has to be imagined, conjured. Which is to say we know so much and simultaneously so little. Which in a way is its own definition of Frank Lloyd Wright himself.

Riddles wrapped up inside of riddles, triangles drawn inside of circles drawn inside of squares.

About the shingling tool: The previous night, in his servant's quarters, raving paranoid things to himself and his woman (who was either his lawful wife or his common-law wife—no one has ever been able to pin it down), the slayer is said to have gone to bed with it beneath his pillow. For a couple of nights before that, he kept it in a sack with a drawstring by his side of the bed. Carlton's companion, whose first name was Gertrude, and about whom history knows even less than it does about Carlton, testified to this after the rampage was over.

Various newspaper accounts—but not the several that managed to get their bulletins and EXTRAs out on the street within a couple hours of the slayings—had this dazed woman speaking like a female Stepin Fetchit: "I dunno what took him. Dis noon he was all upset. De las' I seen he was runnin' roun' de house actin' crazy and talkin' 'bout killin' folks. Den I run out an' hid myself. An' when I seen de smoke I run away."

Julian Carlton. God knows how the name, never mind the act, has been mangled down through the decades. It was mangled at the time, which is understandable. But even latter-day Wright scholars have mangled the spelling. It's as if the simple inability to get a name right is its own proof of our inability to penetrate the life itself, to ever really know what took him. One photograph of him is known to exist. It's a head-and-shoulders shot, a splash of light on sensitized emulsion, a bit out of focus, with watermarks and creases and chemical white spots. It was snapped in his jail cell (or possibly in the hallway outside) a day or two after his capture. The capture had come about five hours after the killings, after he had apparently swallowed a bottle of poison. He looks—dare it be said?—poetic and haunted and moody. He looks so *slight*. His hair is close-cropped, and he's got on an old muslin-looking work shirt, and he is staring downward, as if in contemplation of what he's done. His lids are mostly closed and his lips are pressed in a thin, flat line. I have been in that below-the-ground county jail cell in Dodgeville, Wisconsin, where Julian Carlton lived for fifty-three days, wasting toward his death, his throat gutted out, his tongue swollen, most times refusing to eat, speaking in cryptic sentences, or not at all. I have traveled some fair distances from that dank, dirt-floored, and no-longer-in-use space next door to the Greek Revival–styled courthouse to try to discover something, anything, about his life. And I have found out some unexpected things about that life, not to say some provocative things about the outward-spreading and concentric-circle consequences of his act. But I will hold them back until later, when it will make more chronological sense—and perhaps will be less provocative—to relate them. But it almost goes without saying that Julian Carlton, who may have been only twenty-six when he did what he did, and who was reported to have been from Barbados or Cuba (he was from neither—he was from Alabama, one of at least thirteen children, with parents who may have been born into slavery), and who probably never weighed more than one hundred and fifty pounds in his life, is the greatest mystery in this mystery, at least if we're speaking only of August 15, 1914. And, of course, we're not.

Stepin Fetchit. The press, onto one of its more sensational stories in years, portrayed him in this way, too—when they weren't portraying him as the articulate opposite. The next morning, *The Milwaukee Journal* ("Daily 1 c; Sunday, 2 c.") had him saying, upon his capture, "Ah's gwine to die, ah is. Ah's done took poison. Ah's dyin' right now. Youall doan' need to kill me." But the *Journal's* rival paper, the *Milwaukee Sentinel*, always thirty or forty thousand readers behind the *Journal*, had him speaking of an "altercation" he'd recently had with another employee in the house, which has always been just one more unproven (if widespread) theory of why it happened.

The capture: its own slice of freighted myth. They found him hiding in the furnace below the house, in a part of the building that hadn't been destroyed. More accurately, he was in the asbestos-lined boiler attached to the furnace. He must have worked himself in feetfirst. When the sheriff, trying to stave off gathering lynch mobs, heard a noise in the boiler and opened the door about 5:30 p.m., there he was. The sheriff and his deputies pulled him out by the head. "Acid," he is supposed to have moaned, supposedly still clinging to his brains-smeared weapon. "Drink of water." Another account had him saying, as if he was a hobo alighting from a boxcar and doffing his hat after the railroad dicks had slid open the door to discover him: "It's muriatic acid, boys—muriatic acid." Muriatic acid is what we know today as hydrochloric acid.

But go back to approximately 12:20 p.m. If there are some known facts, they are asbestos-sealed inside scores of questions that can never be answered. For instance, one of the abiding if lesser mysteries (lesser in the scheme of things) is the almost supernatural energy and speed which one man would have had to summon: a kind of white-jacketed dervish swinging a tomahawk-like thing. It seems impossible Julian Carlton could have acted alone—except he did. Nine people took their seats that noonday: a group of three was at a table in one room, a group of six at a table in another. The two eating spaces were on a diagonal from each other. One was on the northeast side of the house, the other on the southwest side, and they were separated by other rooms and doorways. The group of three was on a porch, or terrace, just off the living room and family dining area. The second group was in a somewhat smaller room inside the house that had been fashioned into a dining space for workmen, for this is who they were: people in Wright's employ. They were laborers and draftsmen. Some did chores around the house and on the grounds, others were working on design projects that Wright had under commission. One was a child: thirteen years old. The boy was there with his father, a master carpenter. Ernest Weston, in whom Frank Lloyd Wright had taken an interest, was hoping one day to become an architect, to raise himself a notch above his daddy's life. Early that morning, the two Westons had pedaled their bicycles from their own home over the moist country roads to Taliesin. It was threshing time in the county. By mid-morning, when the dew was off, farmers would be cutting alfalfa fields, perfuming the Helena Valley.

Taliesin: It's pronounced Tallie-ESS-in. It is Welsh for "shining brow," and it's also the name of a sixth-century Welsh bard. Taliesin was three years old then, and it was made of wood and plaster and yellow limestone hauled by teams of horses from a quarry a mile away. Everywhere in the house there was wood, especially cypress, a recent favorite of its owner, giving the interior, the more so in the lamp-lit evenings, a kind of pumpkin gleam. Wright had built his sandstone-colored home into the not-quite-top of a green hill overlooking a looping bend in the Wisconsin River. You never build on top of the hill, Wright would preach to his acolytes. You do that, you lose the damn hill. You build on the crest, on the brow. This hill and this valley were Wright's ancestral country on his maternal side, and he had known it and loved it since boyhood, and family members (including one sister) lived all through these whale-humped parts.

Taliesin yet sits on the brow of that green hill, on the south side of the Wisconsin River, rebuilt and rebuilt yet again. Six decades from Frank Lloyd Wright's death, Wright worshippers from around the globe come to this bluffed and still rural and sweetly rolling neck of southwestern Wisconsin to marvel at the thing he made. As various critics have said, the house is his autobiography in stone and wood, endlessly revised. Others have called it his "wet-oil canvas." One of the marvels is the way Taliesin seems to be growing out of the hillside, as if nature, not Wright, had nestled it in, or, better said, as if house and hill somehow came into existence together several ice ages ago. One of Wright's lifelong dictums was that his buildings were like plants and trees that grow from inside out and come up from the earth craving the light. It was part of his gospel of "organic architecture," even if his definitions of that concept were always shifting around, like verbal tectonic plates, and sometimes seemed to mystify even him. It was as if he knew what he meant, or at least felt, even if *you* didn't know, and even if in some ultimate spiritual and intellectual sense he didn't really know either. He didn't need to know. He just needed to conceive the thing, draw the thing, and make the thing. "The thing had simply shaken itself out of my sleeve," the old shaman liked to say, ever his own best publicist. In a seventy-two-year career as an architect and egotist, Frank Lloyd Wright shook more than eleven hundred things from his sleeve, a staggering number by any artistic measurement. They were churches, schools, offices, banks, museums, hotels, medical clinics, an automobile showroom, a synagogue, a mile-high skyscraper—and one exotic-looking Philips 66 gas station in Cloquet, Minnesota. Overwhelmingly, though, they were houses, residences, shelters for mankind. Not quite half of all his drawings and designs and studies were realized, and about four hundred still come magically out of the American ground looking for the light: Fallingwater near Pittsburgh; the Guggenheim on Fifth Avenue; the Johnson Wax Building in Racine, Wisconsin; Unity Temple in Oak Park; Robie House on the campus of the University of Chicago—to cite just five masterworks by their vernacular names.

At approximately 12:20 p.m. on August 15, 1914, a wholly different kind of thing is rising up from nowhere. The draftsmen and workmen have come in to eat. Imagine straw-hatted laborers in their cross-strapped overalls, having rolled their denim sleeves to the elbow and washed up with lye soap at chipped porcelain basins and having now toweled themselves off and horsing around a bit as they find their seats, just hungry as hell, all of them, including the boy. In the country, lunch is known as "dinner." Let 'er rip, bring it on, that fresh-picked corn and sweetened tea and fried chicken and collards and platters of just-sliced beefsteak tomatoes. (It's often been said soup was the first thing served—and the last thing, too. Nobody seems to know what kind of soup, though—and wouldn't the idea of soup, in the heat of August, be suspect? It all sounds bogus.)

On the terrace, Mamah (her name was pronounced MAY-muh) and her son and daughter, having taken the leisure of a country Saturday morning, are perhaps hoping to pick up a stray breeze. Actually, I picture them sitting there stiffly. It's known that neither of her children particularly liked Wisconsin: too remote.

Although some latter-day Wright chroniclers have tried almost forensically to reconstruct the following ten or twelve or fourteen minutes (as if doing so would really explain anything), the truth is no one will ever be able to know the exact sequence of events or precise time frames. But it is generally believed that the servant-turned-mass-murderer struck first at the three on the terrace, after having set the food, or some of it, before the workers in the other room. If that is so, Julian Carlton must have left that room quietly, as if intending to go back to the kitchen for more food. But instead, once out of sight, he must have raced to the terrace, done his work there, raced back to the other space, where he splashed ropes of fuel beneath a doorjamb, lit the fire, and sought to do additional killing and maiming as his victims clawed for escape. It's long been part of popular myth—handed along in books and articles—that at some earlier point Julian Carlton had soaked a rolled rug and bolted all doors and windows. There's no evidence to support this.

On the terrace: It is believed Mamah was the first person to die that day. He drove the blade through the back of her head, and apparently with a single rounding swing, so that it came through her brain and out nearly on the other side, just above her forehead. "Head cleft in twain" is the way several newspapers put it the next day. There were no surviving witnesses to what happened, but that fact didn't stop a fevered scribe from writing: " 'O Mama, look at Julian,' exclaimed John Cheney, the 13 year-old son of the woman, as the negro crept up behind Mrs. Borthwick and raised his weapon." John was twelve, not thirteen, and his mother wasn't a "Mrs.," not for the last several years.

It is thought that Carlton killed her and then drenched her body with gasoline. In all probability he didn't do this immediately—he must have circled back to the terrace, once again, six or seven or eight minutes later. When the rescuers draped a sheet over her later that afternoon, Mamah's clothes and wavy dark hair and fair skin (she never liked the sun) were mostly gone, and what wasn't gone had gone black, in the way even the tiniest insects will go coal black in a burned-over forest. This is why it is believed he'd saturated her corpse: the extent of the burning, as if she hadn't ignited but combusted, into a fireball; as if he wished not to kill her, but to erase her.

Of her son, who seems to have been next, and who also may have died instantly from the same kind of over-arcing blow, and who seems also to have been soaked with fuel, there was nothing left but some blackened bones among a lot of ashes.

But it was John's little sister, Martha Cheney, due to turn nine in September, who suffered the cruelest death, even though she didn't get incinerated. She had a helmet of boyish hair. She liked dime-store rings and other fancier rings that she would importune from her doting father. She was known for a small spoiled fussiness. When she saw what was happening, she apparently bolted up and took off running through the living room and dining area. Carlton chased after her. Perhaps because he was running, he couldn't get off a clean swing. This must have frustrated him terribly. He caught up with her. What can be said is that he hit her at least three times from behind with the blade end, each slice a little higher than the last. Perhaps he had already hit her once or twice before she was down. But now, over top of her, he decided not to use the blade end, but the pounding side. From the way she was hit, she had to have been facing up at him, although perhaps she had shut her eyes. Why would he have decided in those half-seconds of wildness to flip the instrument to its hammer side? Maybe the flipping just happened in the still-unexplained way of the flipping of his mind.

In any case, Julian Carlton struck the girl so viciously, straight down, that when they found her, they also found an impression of the poll of the hammer in her partially caved-in face. And, somehow, Martha Cheney still wasn't dead, although he must have thought so. She apparently crawled a little further on from the spot where he had left her. She made it out into the sunlight, onto the uneven flagstones of the loggia and the inner court. When the rescuers came, she was gasping and bleeding badly and most of her clothes were burned off. She was able to hang on for about two and a half more hours, until somewhere past 3:00 p.m. They touched her lips with water. They wrapped her wounds. They stood over her and knelt around her, perhaps holding hands and singing prayers. At some later point that afternoon or evening, before she too was placed beneath a sheet, a doctor or a magistrate or a coroner or maybe just one of the hundreds of local farm folk who had rushed in to help and to put out the fires and to search for the murderer wrote down this clinical-sounding note, which appeared in its own cool, clinical way in several of the newspaper accounts:

"Three wounds back of right ear, one above the other; the upper one penetrated the skull. Imprint of head of hatchet under right eye."

Dreaming in. A decade ago, the fiction writer T. C. Boyle in his novel *The Women* found the poetry of gore for what took place in those several porch minutes.

And then he came through the door, moving so swiftly he surprised himself, and she looked up this time, this time she saw him, this time her eyes locked on his at the very moment the hatchet came in one savage furious stroke that went in at the hairline and let loose all the red grease of her brains, gray grease and pink grease, and it was on his bleached white jacket like a kind of devil's rain. The boy was next. Before he could react, before the knowledge of what was happening there in front of him could settle into his eyes, the hatchet came down again, twice, and he was dead and twitching even as the girl jumped up and ran till he hit her just behind the right ear, one time, two, three, until she was down on the stone crawling like a grub and her face turned to him now, grub-pale, with her eyes open so that he had to hit there again with the flat of it to crush the cheekbone and shut them for good.

But that's more or less historical invention. Compulsively readable as Boyle's novel is, he managed, like many others (whose business isn't making things up from reasonably accepted fact), to misspell the killer's name. (He has it as Carleton. That's better than Carlston or Carliton or Carlson, to cite three variants.) But it's okay.

What's also okay, maybe better than okay, is to cleave it off at this point. You've heard enough, at least for now. No need to tell what happened in the other room—you can imagine. Cleave it off and leave the victims where they lay in this ruined, fire-shooting home, so the story can change focus, to its center of gravity. Which is to say: What was it like for the one who wasn't there? What was it like about 1:00 p.m. on August 15, 1914, when an aforesaid forty-seven-year-old arrogant and narcissistic and egotistical and morally rebuked genius picked up a phone to hear the first staticky report of some incomprehensible news? What must it have been like for him for the rest of that day?

He was not quite two hundred miles southeast of serenely named Spring Green.

———

On the South Side of Chicago, in an un-serene urban neighborhood called Woodlawn, between East Sixtieth and East Sixty-First, there is a parking lot that serves a medium-rise apartment building and a smaller residential facility for the elderly. Until very recently (as I am writing this), if you had come in off East Sixtieth Street, and had gone through a gate between the two buildings, and then walked to the southeast corner of the lot and edged your way behind a tangle of bushes and weeds that used to grow tall and thick in the summer months, and had kicked away the latest refuse that may have accumulated there—old cigarillo wrappers, flyblown sales receipts from Burger King, Styrofoam takeout containers, maybe a spent condom—you would have seen a piece of buff-colored stone. It was about ten feet long and about seven or eight inches high and roughly half a foot across. The texture of it was pebbly.

It almost looked to be erupting from the earth, but in another sense it's as if it was erupting from time: this wedge of poured concrete, which must have been part of a foundation for a wall or a terrace or possibly a staircase, had existed at this spot for more than a century. It seemed to be the last visible trace of a buried and bulldozed moment of quixotic Chicago civic history called Midway Gardens. Midway Gardens was an indoor-outdoor entertainment complex. If you imagine a Munich beer garden, but multiply that by about a hundred in terms of grandness, exotica, you'll get something of the idea that must have been in the mind of its creator. Think of *Arabian Nights* married to visions of "Kubla Khan" under the middle-western stars. Think of cubed abstractions. Think of the geometric interplay of the circle, the square, and the triangle. The place was roughly a football field by a football field, which is to say three hundred feet by three hundred feet: large, but not *that* large for all that was trying to go on there. It had ornate sculpture, polychromatic murals, lantern-lit promenades, fountains, roof gardens, sunken gardens, belvederes, arcades, reflecting pools, overhanging balconies. There was a large music pavilion and a stage. There were formal and informal dancing and dining spaces. (The formal indoor dining facility, the centerpiece of the "winter garden," had thick white monogrammed tablecloths, and specially fired glazed ceramic plates, and custom-designed teapots, napkin rings.) For outside dining and dancing, there was the "summer garden," with its five levels of flowered terraces. Everything—the leaded-glass windows, the chairs, the tableware, the cigar stands, the casino, the cloakrooms, the concession areas, the public tavern, the private club, even the toilets themselves—was meant to be part of a single harmonious interflowing space. There were nights when full orchestras played, and there were Sunday afternoons when dance combos got everybody out on the floor, even the kids. It was as if all the entertainment arts for public pleasure, high and low, for the masses and the bluebloods, had been brought together into one improbable whole, taking up a large part of a city block of the South Side.

The National Symphony Orchestra performed the prelude to Wagner's *Die Meistersinger* on the opening night at Midway. Anna Pavlova of the Imperial Russian Ballet danced at Midway. Wop Waller and Murphy Steinberg and Benny Goodman later tooted at Midway. And yet:

Within four months of the opening—which was in the early summer of 1914, the day before Archduke Franz Ferdinand of Austria was assassinated by a Serbian nationalist—there were already stories in the local papers about Midway's possible foreclosure. The place had been badly underfinanced from the start, it turns out. It continued to operate under severe economic stress (and to grateful if spotty crowds) for something like two more years before it slid into receivership. Still, the gardens limped on, for another decade or so, with other proprietors and in various entertainment guises that had little to do with the original concept. Ultimately—this was in the late twenties, and by then Prohibition had come in—the wrecking balls and the salvage companies dumped the whole shebang into Lake Michigan for breakwall and landfill. (Injury to insult: part of the site, later on, at least for a time, turned into a gas station and car wash.)

The whole shebang, that is, but for one little slice of pebbled and lightly colored concrete that got passed over, inadvertently left behind, like a piece of the True Cross, up against a metal fence, in the southeast corner of that paved parking lot behind a seventeen-floor apartment building and a five-story residence for the elderly at the head of an old and rehabilitating Chicago neighborhood called Woodlawn. Cottage Grove Avenue borders one side of where this stone was, and Langley Avenue the other, and in the middle distance, off to the northeast, the stately gothic outlines of the University of Chicago.

In the years of working on this book, I found myself coming to this lot, this spot, this stone, fairly often, but not because I wished to pay homage to an architectural relic (which very few people seemed to know about). I came when I was trying to feel Frank Lloyd Wright's humanness again. As you have figured out, he was the creator of Midway Gardens. And as best I can determine—and I have consulted a lot of experts, at least one of whom has given over much of his scholarly life to a study of Midway Gardens—he may have been standing no more than a hundred or one hundred and twenty-five feet from this chunk of worthless-looking and now-gone rock when he pressed the telephone receiver to his ear and got the first word from Wisconsin of what had just happened. He may have been half that distance. That part doesn't matter. He was somewhere nearby. Which is why I always came, on reporting trips to the Midwest, more or less to just stand there, be there, minding my business, kicking away trash, sometimes feeling foolish, but trying all the same to imagine a man's dizzying shock, his instinct to disbelieve, his fear, his need to reach out and grab hold of the nearest solid thing. In front of this stone I could find Frank Lloyd Wright's humanity again, which, as a matter of fact, I contend was large—no, greater than large, in fact, immense. The problem is, when you are in search of that humanity, wish to make a case for it, you have to be willing to keep kicking away with your shoe a lot of refuse, dross, under which, behind which, the humanity and vulnerability will lie—every time. That's part of what this book is about, hopes to say, although that is trying to define it from the top down, when the Wrightian building principle is to work from the bottom up, and from the inside out.

The creator of Midway Gardens was at the site that day because, although the facility had opened to the public on June 27, it wasn't nearly done. Wright was forever putting finishing touches on his projects, but in this case there were significant things left undone. He was there with his second eldest child, John Lloyd Wright, who was twenty-one and just beginning his own career in architecture and who had begun working for his father with a certain fear and loathing but longing, too. Wright's relationship with his children would make its own large book and will loop in and out of this one. It's enough for the moment to say that the overpowering and self-absorbed and neglectful father—who, although he had left his family five years before, was still in his limited emotional ways trying to be a parent to four sons and two daughters, whose ages just then ranged from twenty-four to ten—had come down from Wisconsin on the train on Tuesday evening and had arranged for his second son to meet him at the depot.

He had met his boy—whom he had made a kind of on-site superintendent of the South Side project—and the two had gone in a taxi to Midway. For the last four nights they had supposedly slept side by side on a pile of shavings in one corner of the property so they could keep an eye on the small crew of overnight workers. (It wasn't an unknown thing for him to do, especially as a younger architect: to just show up unannounced at an out-of-town project and inspect the work and goad it onward and find sleep that night on a pallet or a blanket or whatever else was handy.)

Now, Saturday, early afternoon, the two are in the tavern, which is in the northeast corner of the gardens, next to the main public entrance, fronting Cottage Grove Avenue. It rained yesterday, and the temperatures are moderating toward the first real hints of autumn. The son is up on scaffolding, painting a mural on one of the tavern's walls. His father has drawn the sketches for the mural. The son is using oil stains and gold leaf. His father is at a table at the far end of the room, eating a sandwich, inspecting the job. Maybe the morning papers are strewn on the table and he's glancing at the increasingly scary news from overseas: a huge force of Germans advancing across Belgium, the Japanese navy said to be sailing to join the British fleet.

A female stenographer or office clerk walks in. "Mr. Wright, you're wanted on the telephone." In a small, strange book, entitled *My Father Who Is on Earth*, published in 1946, not quite a biography and not quite a memoir, untrustworthy on the facts, full of passive-aggressive anger and deep filial need, John Wright describes this moment. (His book, starting with its title, is an admixture of all these things, yes, but at the same time it's a crucial account simply because he was there. But it requires cross-checking at every turn, which is next to impossible in some instances.)

He remembers his father following her out of the room. When Wright comes back, John is facing toward the wall with his brushes and trying to manage a sandwich as well. There's an unnatural silence except for his father's labored breathing. John looks down. His father is trying to steady himself against a table. John monkeys down from the scaffolding. "What's happened, Dad?" he says. "John—a taxi," Wright whispers. "Taliesin is on fire," he whispers again. The son quotes his father as saying about Mamah and her children: "Why did I leave them today?" (That obviously makes no sense.) "What if they're hurt?" he quotes his father as saying. "His voice broke, his lips were parted and pale," the son writes.

The clear implication is that he doesn't yet know the worst of it. Only the fire.

John remembers that he helped his father into a taxi and together they tore uptown to the station and caught the first available train to Wisconsin, and that it wasn't until that long rail ride home in "that feebly lighted compartment" that his father began to learn the "ghastly details from the reporters and heard them shouted from the throats of newsboys along the way." He reaches into his memory and manufactures a headline sitting there: TALIESIN BURNING TO THE GROUND, SEVEN SLAIN. (No. As earlier noted, seven of nine were slain, but not all died that day. By late Saturday, five were dead, but it took two more days and nights for Julian Carlton's final two victims to die.)

Except: The real story is grainier, ruder. The real story of that afternoon and evening has about it the drip-drip-drip of reducing a haughty man to his near-nakedness.

If the next morning's *Chicago Sunday Tribune* is to be believed (of all the metropolitan dailies in the Midwest, the *Tribune* did the most reporting on the story, or at least devoted the most coverage to it, that day and for days after), the first person to reach Wright was a man named Frank Roth. The *Tribune* had him calling from Madison, the state capital, but that seems doubtful. (How would someone in Madison, a good hour away, have gotten the word so quickly?) The paper had him as a friend of Wright's, but there's no evidence for this. Who "Frank Roth" was, if that is even how his name was spelled, is just one more mystery in the mist. (There's no such name in the Madison city directories of that entire period, although there are individuals named Frank Ross.) Was Frank Roth, or Frank Ross, or some other sound-alike variant, not from Madison at all, but was he rather a minor public official in the Spring Green area? That would be a logical thought, except that all this time his identity has never been determined. I have done my own trying, believe it.

Wrote the *Tribune,* after bungling about a dozen other facts in earlier paragraphs: "Mr. Wright almost collapsed when the news first reached him. He got the tragic long distance telephone message while at Midway Gardens, the new south side amusement park, which he designed. 'This is Frank Roth at Madison,' came a voice over the wires. 'Be prepared for a shock. Your wife—that is, Mrs. Cheney—the two children, and one of your draftsmen have been killed by Carleton. Carleton set fire to the bungalow and got away. He must have gone crazy. A posse is chasing him. You'd better get to Spring Green right away.'"

We know from other sources that there were some panicked calls back and forth after the first call, and that there was trouble getting through. Wires were sent and a wire or two reputedly came back— but none has survived. Wright called his lawyer, Sherman Booth, who, since it was the weekend, wasn't in his office in the Borland Building on LaSalle Street in the Loop, but at home, in Glencoe, a suburb on the North Shore, about an hour from downtown. Wright reached him and asked if he'd be able to go to Wisconsin with him on a train as soon as possible. Wright also apparently spoke with one of his young drafts-men, Herbert Fritz, who'd escaped the shingling hatchet. (He'd hurled his lit body against a bank of low windows in the men's dining area and had fallen onto stone, crushing his arm, and then went rolling, as if propelled by gravity and blind instinct, down a steep hill toward a small creek and a dammed-up pond.) It has never been recorded what Fritz told Wright, from a neighbor's phone, but it had to have been about more than just the fire, however terrifying in itself that would have been.

At some point, perhaps within an hour or so, father and son got into a taxi and directed its driver not to the depot but to Wright's office in Orchestra Hall, on South Michigan Avenue, in the Loop. In trying to reestablish his practice after the scandal of his family abandonment, Wright had decided he must once again set up a Chicago office, even though his home and principal studio space were now in Wisconsin. He was in one of the city's more cultural addresses, across the street from the Art Institute, a small suite on the eighth floor, the rent on which he was forever trying to duck.

The *Chicago Daily News* reached him there in mid-afternoon. Maybe the editors were tipped and had rushed a reporter to Midway Gardens and had stationed another in Orchestra Hall's ornate lobby. If so, Wright must have hurried past him to the elevators at the south end. Upstairs, in number 810, the phone rang. It wasn't someone from Spring Green; it was the city desk of the *Daily News.* He was caught.

"Have you heard that there has been a murder at Spring Green?"

"I have just heard by long-distance telephone that there has been a terrible catastrophe at my country home. I cannot talk about it now. I am going up there as soon as I can get a train."

"What information have you of the crime?"

"I cannot talk about it."

"A *Daily News* correspondent has reported that Mrs. Borthwick and the others were struck down by someone who stood at the door of the house while it was burning."

"Yes."

(The story soon to be out on the street has him "low and tremulous" at the "yes.")

"It will do no good for me to discuss it at this time. I am going up there this evening. I shall probably catch a train about seven o'clock. I was just trying to find when the first train leaves."

By suppertime, these hot quotes, scooping the competition, are being hawked on Chicago corners. The story containing them has made it into the "box score edition." It's the paper's last SPORTING EXTRA, the tenth edition, recapping world and national and local headlines and, not least, all the ball games. At the top of the page, a two-column headline: MRS. CHENEY, "MATE" OF F.L. WRIGHT, SLAIN; TWO MEN MURDERED. And just to the left of that, under LATE NEWS BULLETINS: "John Cheney, son of Mrs. Mamah Borthwick Cheney, slain by a madman at Spring Green, Wis., was found dead in the ruins of the house late this afternoon."

The *Chicago American* is all over the story, too, with at least four EXTRAs coming off the presses through the afternoon as fast as the Linotype machines can spit out the hot metal. KILLS THREE IN 'LOVE HOUSE' is the first headline the paper manages, before some of the afternoon's ball games are even a quarter over. 3 KILLED IN "LOVE BUNGALOW" comes the header in another press run, maybe forty-five minutes later, with updated scores. Then a double-decker in another press run: TRIPLE TRAGEDY IN "LOVE BUNGALOW" WRIGHT'S SOULMATE KILLED! The text is goofy with spelling: "A number of persons were wounded by the negro wren he started on his mad career." Nine paragraphs down: "The story of the terrible tragedy enacted in the Wright 'love bungalow,' where for some years the celebrated architect and the former Mrs. Cheney had been living in open defiance of the conventionalities, was a grewsome one as it came today." In the "FINAL Box Score" edition, with the VERY LATEST NEWS: "Carlton is twenty-eight years old. He is married. His wife lived with him at the Wright home. He had been employed by Wright for six months. He was formerly employed by John Z. Vogelsang, proprietor of Vogelsang's restaurant. He is five feet eight inches tall, of medium build and light in color."

Father and son discovered there was a train leaving at 5:45 p.m. It was a local, to Madison, operated by the Chicago, Milwaukee & St. Paul Railway. There was nothing else going—they had to get on it. At Madison (if their Chicago train was running on time) they'd be able to connect to another CM&SP local that would deliver them to Spring Green, thirty-seven rail miles west, before midnight.

They got over to Union Station, probably by taxi (have newsboys stuck papers at them as they've come off the elevator in Orchestra Hall?), alighting at the depot's main entrance on Canal Street. Wright wanted to find his lawyer; what he found was a scrum of pushing and shoving reporters. There were detectives there, too, from the city's homicide division. John Wright remembered that he shouldered his father into the train car, but it wasn't quite so. Wright made a statement before boarding, possibly trackside at gate five. The *Tribune* would say the next morning that Wright was so distraught he couldn't speak coherently, but his quoted remarks were not incoherent and sounded almost composed. Several of the city's other dailies also quoted him, and while the quotations vary, they are similar enough that they can be assumed to be fairly accurate. But in a larger way, the remarks Wright made before departing are deeply troubling—that is, they raise their own issues—in regard to some crucial unknowns that will always plague this story, but especially this unknown: Were Julian Carlton and his wife about to leave Wright's employ, and had they given notice on their own, or, alternatively, had they been dismissed a couple of days before? If the latter was true—again, long part of popular myth—it could obviously speak to the question of possible motive. A huge if.

The *Chicago Sunday Herald* quoted Wright as saying: "Both were the best servants I had ever seen. The wife cooked and Julian was a general handy man. They were Cubans, and Julian especially seemed to have intelligence above the average and a good education. They had not been engaged permanently and were to leave today. They planned to come to Chicago and get their money. Three days ago when I last saw him Julian appeared perfectly normal. He must have lost his mind."

There is much more to say on all this, again, because it's very tangled.

Focus instead on the distraught man, just trying to get home, just trying to take his wicker-back seat in a compartment in the buffet parlor car of Train Number 143. One of the reporters from the *Herald* is already in that car. (Did he slide a sawbuck to a CM&SP porter to find out which car Wright was due to enter? Probably every daily in town had put four or five of its bashed-fedora boys on the story. On the other hand, maybe not: it was a weekend, and there would have been relatively few available bodies in city rooms. The story in tomorrow's *Herald* won't carry a byline, but the word BULLETIN in place of where a staffer's name would go.)

Wright's asking the train attendants if anyone has seen Sherman Booth; his lawyer must be in one of these cars. (He is, and they'll find each other.) Wright gets into his seat and the *Herald* man is within hearing distance, to scribble down any scrap. "I simply can't believe it," Wright is quoted as saying, almost as if speaking aloud to himself. "It is too horrible. I first received the news by long-distance telephone. I wired back for confirmation because I could not believe it. The answer was that it was true. She was such a good woman—the best on earth. She stood everything so bravely. Now the rags will smirch her memory with their vulgar ink. Will you please use her name right?"

Three days from now, on Tuesday the 18th, this particular rag, one of the city's most reliably vulgar (that is, when the *Herald* isn't climbing on its moralizing horse), will run a long editorial on page 8, rather crudely illustrated, and headlined THE END OF LAWLESS LOVES. It will start: "There was a woman and her husband and the other man." And it will close: "But violent and lawless loves have violent and lawless ends. . . . Why or how, no one knows, but a retainer of the 'love castle' among the Wisconsin hills fell into a murderous frenzy. . . . An old Greek dramatist would have said that the insane servant was the instrument of the gods for avenging the 'violence' of the decency-defying adventure. Those who believe that the moral verities still exist will find in it a tragic confirmation of the truth that 'the wages of sin is death.' "

Say this, though: the besmirching sheet will have used her name right—mostly.

The train pulls out. First stop is Western Avenue, three miles from

Union Station. Number 143 isn't even to the edge of the city and it has already bucked to a halt, after twelve minutes. And Christ almighty: Who gets on and enters the buffet parlor car?

Edwin H. Cheney. Decent and churchgoing and affable and boring Ed Cheney, bald, round-headed, middle-aged, the former cuckolded spouse of Mamah Borthwick, the father of John and Martha. He'd been out playing golf this afternoon when someone apparently walked onto the course to let him know. He must have gone home and thrown some clothes into a valise and had somebody hurry him here, to Western, which is the closest stop to Oak Park, where he still lives in the Prairie-style home on East Avenue that that bastard Frank Lloyd Wright began designing for him and his former wife in what seems like a lifetime ago, but, in fact, was only eleven years ago, in 1903. And now not only his purloined ex-wife gone, but his children butchered? (It's impossible to say how much he knew when he boarded; one would guess nearly all.)

The *Herald* reporter has Cheney coming to Wright's seat. Wright looks up.

"Ed!"

"Frank!"

According to the *Herald:* "They grasped hands. Then each put a hand on the other's shoulder. They withdrew to the end of the car. Instead of talking they sat facing each other in silence for some time. Afterward their conversation was brief."

To study old CM&SP timetables is to get an appreciation for the crawling agony of that evening. It was twenty-one stops just to Madison, counting unscheduled flag stops. The train was due at Long Lake, Illinois, at 7:05 p.m., milepost 46. Another two miles, another halt: Ingleside. Two more miles (actually 1.7), another halt: Fox Lake. Another four miles: Spring Grove, by which point Train 143, still in Illinois, would have crept not quite fifty-four miles, with still another eleven stops (and more, if there were any signal stops or mail drops) once it had crossed over into Wisconsin: Zenda, Walworth, Janesville, Milton Junction, Lake Kegonsa. It was as if the pace itself was its own punishment, never mind the hopping-aboard reporters, the thrusting-in newsboys, the lurching, the grinding gears, the groaning metal, the garish lights, the glancing-over faces, the general noise, the heat. And the worst of it still to come—by far.

That night, deep after midnight, Sunday now, twelve hours after first hearing, on the point of collapse, at his sister's nearby home (which he had designed), he would turn his head when he was aided past the candlelit space where the sheeted bodies were. They'd been brought there from the fire.

"All I had to show for the struggle for freedom of the five years past that had swept most of my former life away, had now been swept away," he would say in his autobiography, eighteen years from this moment.

————

This book isn't intended as a Frank Lloyd Wright biography, not in any conventional sense. Depending on how you count, there are about eight or nine of those, and never mind how many hundreds of historical studies, monographs, coffee-table treatments, scholarly examinations of specific Wright buildings or houses or periods. (No, he didn't go through as many artistic periods as Picasso; it only seems so.) The Wright industry, from calendars to placemats to bathroom glow lights to key chains to reproduction end-table lamps with their rice-paper shades and cherry-wine finishes to books themselves (whether pop-up books for kids or heavy academic tomes), just churns on, year after year.

Rather, this book is meant to be a kind of synecdoche, with selected pockets in a life standing for the oceanic whole of that life.

The aim is to move the narrative backward and forward in time, through these non-linear pockets, or storytelling boxes, trying not to confuse you, while also taking things in a general chronological direction and arc from east to west: that is, from June 8, 1867, when Frank Lloyd Wright was born, in Richland Center, Wisconsin (it's about twenty-five miles northwest of Spring Green), to April 9, 1959, when Frank Lloyd Wright died in his sleep one morning two months from his ninety-second birthday after a hospitalization and risky abdominal surgery near Scottsdale, Arizona. As any serious Wright student knows, Scottsdale is where Taliesin West comes magically up out of the Sonoran desert, in the foothills of the McDowell Mountains. Even though he was in his hospital bedclothes (at St. Joseph's Hospital in nearby Phoenix, where they'd taken him in a rush five days before), I nonetheless like to picture him there at the last, 4:45 a.m. that Thursday, as the great silver-haired dandy with the swept side bangs, as vain about his dress as he was about everything else, a week and a half after Easter (always such a big celebration at both Taliesins), fitted out and all set to go in his rolled-brim porkpie hat and Dracula cape and herringbone jacket (gardenia boutonniere and folded pocket square) and high white collar and fluttery scarf and absurd pants (almost pantaloons) that are pegged at the ankles and the chalk-white shoes with their one-and-a-half-inch heels and, best accessory of all, his water-smooth, curl-handled, Malacca wood walking cane with which he used to stroll along Fifth Avenue in Manhattan, shooing away reporters and pigeons. The legend is he just sighed and floated off on the coolish air of that fine desert spring morning.

Poof. Perfect. Gone.

But possibly not before he had slipped into the left side pocket of his jacket one of his soft black drafting pencils, along with a pocket knife for sharpening it, so that he might polish off a drawing or two in heaven. Nothing so seductive in this life, he once said, as the prospect of sitting down to a blank piece of saffron-colored onionskin paper with a stubby, coal-black, newly sharpened, soft-leaded pencil. "There is no being lonesome after that," he said. It's almost hard to imagine, but in the last decade of his life, Wright designed nearly a third of his total output—he just kept rising and going to his tilted board. With his T-square, triangle, and scale. With his fading eyesight and periodic Ménière's disease. (The inner-ear disorder could make him so dizzy and nauseous he'd have to crawl around on all fours like a blind man.) "That is what it means to be an artist—to seize this essence brooding everywhere in everything, just behind aspect," he once said, beautifully, mysteriously, Wrightianly.

So this book seeks to be a biographical portrait more than true biography. But it's also intended as group portraiture, with a central figure—who, on the tallest day of his life, even in elevator shoes, never saw more than five foot eight and a half—prowling every page, even when he's pretty far off the page. And, for a cluster of reasons, and not without recognition of the risks, I have decided to start the narrative with this extended look at the most mythic moment in Frank Lloyd Wright's myth-laden life. And I am hardly done with it.

Yes, August 15, 1914, has been extensively peered into and dreamed over. But to my way of thinking, we can't dream ourselves into it enough. Why? Because August 15, 1914, can seem to stand for so much else, is so emblematic, is its own exasperating definition of the exasperating man himself: which is to say, no matter how much we look, we'll never really know, not conclusively. The moment, that day, is too shape-shifting, too protean. Also too alluring. It has the emotional content of a novel.

All of which could be said of Frank Lloyd Wright himself.

No question that the gothic aspect is part of the cluster of reasons. Call it the profane against the spiritual. (That could also serve as a work-ing definition of the man.) You can't begin to drill down into Wright's life without coming face-to-face with a blunt fact: so much of his history was attended by the gothic and the tragic, encircled by it, pursued by it. No one has ever quite been able to explain this. Frank Lloyd Wright was an artist, arguably one of America's four or five greatest artists ever, who spent a lifetime conceiving sublime and supposedly safe spaces for our aesthetic contemplation (although, really, for *his* aesthetic sat-isfaction and contemplation, to hell with us, and to hell with those for whom the spaces were supposedly being built and for whom he was allegedly working) but who lived a life largely of seeming Old Testa-ment disaster and disarray, plenty of it of his own making. If harmony and order were his great artistic ideals, he could find little of them in his own debt-plagued, scandal-wracked, death-haunted history. In a way, it's the oldest artist's story there is, except in this case the story seems multiplied exponentially. "You would not dare invent Wright's life; it is too melodramatic," is the way one of his more recent biogra-phers, Ada Louise Huxtable, has put it. (Her 2004 study, *Frank Lloyd Wright,* is one of the most perceptive short treatments we have, even if it's far too unwittingly reliant on his lies.) Maybe there is another way of expressing this thought: Why would you ever wish to make up anything about Wright's life, even if *he* spent almost his entire life mak-ing things up about it? If he is hands down our greatest architect, he is also hands down one of our gold-standard artist-prevaricators. He was such a fantastic fabricator, on any subject under the sun, that it's become something of a cliché among his chroniclers to say he barely grasped the basic concept of truth telling. I don't believe that. I think he understood precisely—and went ahead anyway, willing to pay the internal cost. Which, it nearly goes without saying, makes for the more human story: he knew.

But just on this idea of the gothic, the tragic, the darkly improbable: You could take one full step away from Wright's own life—which is to say, toward the lives of his clients and patrons—and find yourself coming face-to-face, sooner than later, with this same phenomenon. It is not always there, or even predominantly there, but when it's there, it's startlingly there: a woman accidentally falling (or rather did she hurl herself?) down an elevator shaft on the third floor of her much-loved Wright home on South Woodlawn Avenue on the South Side of Chicago in the fall of 1909, twelve years after she and her meatpacker husband had moved in. (The legend around Hyde Park is that Ida Heller, that woman, was in love with her architect, and that there may have been some recent infidelity, but when he ran off with Mamah, that did it.)

A three-year-old named Ned Pope, stepping outside into a Virginia wood on a May afternoon in 1941, having momentarily gotten loose from his overjoyed parents (overjoyed with their little Ned, of course, who was their only child, but overjoyed as well with the snug little $7,000 haiku of a one-floor L-shaped "Usonian" wooden dream that the great architect from Wisconsin had designed personally for them and into which they had moved not even two months before), and, somehow, the profane against the spiritual, the inconceivable against the incontrovertible, escaping down the slope and into the neighbor's pond, where he drowned—in shallow water, inside of two minutes of being out of sight. I talked to Ned Pope's father, Loren, about this tragedy many years after. I was writing a Wright story for *The Washington Post*. Loren, a small man, was old then. He was hunched forward on a sofa. February sunlight was streaming the room. "Well, that was my day off," he said. "I was walking outside, digging on something. He just sort of got away. I wasn't paying attention, I guess." He began to square the edges of some stacked books on his coffee table. One of the books was titled *A Natural History of the Senses*. Another was titled *Emerson: The Mind on Fire*. "Let's see. How can I talk about this? I haven't cried recently. I haven't cried for the last three or four years. I'm not sure why. Ned. What can I say? He was a lovely kid. Sweet and bright child. It was such a small pond—if he'd been five or six, he probably wouldn't have died. I blame myself for his going down there. I just instinctively ran to the pond. I was the one who found him."

Some of these stories will appear in fuller detail as this book travels in its zigzaggy path from "east" to "west." Seeking to reveal Frank Lloyd Wright partially and not quite in mirror-like ways and yet on oddly parallel axes through some of the lives of the people who actually lived in his houses is a neglected theme in Wright studies, in my view. It'll play itself here in a minor key. And at least one part of it will be in some sense personal: a particular gothicism happened in and around a Wright house—a hugely important Wright house—on the street that I grew up on, in the fifties, in Kankakee, Illinois. This macabre story—which has to do with a botched burying alive for ransom money of one of the town's wealthiest citizens—happened years after I was gone, but its shock waves reverberated to where I was then living. It's as if I had my own Julian Carlton mystery. I used to bike past that Wright house as a nine-year-old on my J.C. Higgins three-speed. I'd stare at it from the sidewalk. It was so otherworldly.

But the most important reason for having started this book with a deep first glimpse of August 15, 1914, is to try to knock back, from the outset, a wrongheaded misperception already alluded to: namely, that the stainless-steel armature of Frank Lloyd Wright's ego and arrogance allowed him to ride through the world for nearly a century without pain or remorse and with little compulsion to ever look back, unlike Lot's wife in the Bible. "He lived from first to last like a God: one who acts but is not acted upon," wrote Lewis Mumford, the great mid-century historian and sociologist and architectural critic for *The New Yorker*, who knew Wright for something like three decades and wrote about him perhaps more penetratingly than any other single critic for a newspaper or magazine. But on this I say Mumford was flat wrong. (For starters, wasn't Wright pretty acted upon, in absentia, by Julian Carlton in those few minutes on that August Saturday at Taliesin?)

And as long as I am disagreeing with established authorities, here is something pithy and lyrical—and as flatly wrong, at least in its conclusion—that the late, magisterial teacher-critic Vincent Scully of Yale once said of Wright: "I think of him always as the great American confidence man, who's changing the world according to his own images, who's wearing many disguises all the time. He's right out of Mark Twain, he's right out of Melville. He's the man, you know, in his rebuilt Lincoln Continental, in which he's taken out the rear window because, he says, 'I never look behind.'"

He was always looking behind, however surreptitiously. There's too much evidence otherwise. It's there at the margins, ghosting at the edges, sometimes not ghosting at all. Sometimes the cues and clues are hiding in plain sight. This is especially true at the back of his life—the comments he made, the odd things he did, the places he sought out. But, really, the phenomenon is present from the beginning, too, and in the middle. On the other hand, it's absolutely true we can collectively squint and see him, at the back of his life, the great television gadfly, ready to say nearly any outrageous, puffed-up thing to the interviewing likes of Mike Wallace or Dave Garroway or Charles Collingwood or Hugh Downs or Alistair Cooke. (Did any American celebrity of the 1950s adore more or colonize better than Frank Lloyd Wright that rectangle of silver glowing in all our living rooms?) But two things can be true at once. You can be so self-satisfied and full of yourself, and also secretly shamed by things, quietly haunted.

"In my own life there is much that is complex, at least. Life is not the simple thing it should be if within myself I could find the harmony that you have found. It is difficult for me to square my life with myself, and I cannot rest until it is done or I am dead," he wrote in a letter to a patron, his most long-suffering one, Darwin Martin, in 1908. Three decades later, after Martin had died, Wright said to his widow: "I only wish I had been less taking and more giving where he was concerned but character is fate and mine got me into heavy going—and no safe harbor yet in sight."

"Ugly things happen. I've said that the best and the worst of everything came to me," he said in a letter to another patron, eight years later, with whom he was having titanic fights about the building of the Solomon R. Guggenheim Museum. He didn't go on to say in that letter: *And why?* Nor did he have to.

In the days after Julian Carlton's act, when Wright's back and neck were sprouting with hideous boils, when he couldn't sleep or eat and was rising in a little back room in the saved part of Taliesin to take ice baths and to go out on the hills in the moonlight or to gallop across the valleys on his horse, he said to his baby sister (she was ten years younger, and her name, Margaret Ellen, got contracted to Maggie Nell, which got further contracted to Maginel): "You know, you told me once when I was reaching so high, that someday I would pull something down that would destroy me."

A quarter of a century later, in 1938: "I have found that when a scheme develops beyond a normal pitch of excellence the hand of fate strikes it down. The Japanese made a superstition of the circumstance. Purposely they leave some imperfection somewhere to appease the jealousy of the gods. I neglected the precaution."

Ten years before that, on December 5, 1928, in a letter to his first cousin for whom he was building a house in Oklahoma and, naturally, having nasty fights about its design, he reflected on how "I've met with terrible misfortunes and accidents. . . . There is a good deal of sadness back of all the bravado and though you may not know it, I too have fought a good fight." This cousin's name was Richard Lloyd Jones, and he and Wright had grown up together. Jones, a hotheaded and pharisaical and ruinous newspaper publisher, will have his own huge role to play when the events of August 15, 1914, lead narratively to some outward-spreading chains of moral consequence.

Reference has already been made to Wright's autobiography, and of how it must be distrusted on every page. It's titled just *An Autobiography,* which is the only thing simple about it. It will figure much into this book. It was published in 1932, and then significantly expanded and subtly revised a decade later. (The original had sold right out of its modest first printing.) It's such a mirror to Frank Lloyd Wright himself: inspired, lyrical, empurpled, self-dramatizing, self-pitying, heroic, prolix, boastful, untrue, even as it's gorgeously true (as opposed to factually true) in all the larger ways. If there is a bald lie or canny distortion or unintentional misremembering in nearly every other paragraph, there is also in and about the whole of it an amazing truthfulness—call it honor, call it integrity—constantly trying to pound up, leak out, filter through. Sometimes this queer and beautiful honesty is ghosting at the edges, and at other times it is sitting right in black ink and plain sight. "Memories would haunt the youth as they haunt the man . . . ," he says, the ellipsis seeming almost more revealing than the words. Three pages over: "He never got the heavy thing straight." It's an oft-quoted line. The antecedent of "thing" is multi-layered, although specifically he is referring to the divorce of his parents, though also, I think, to a terrible lie in that regard that he told against his father, whether he even fully realizes that. Many pages later, in another context: "Shame to me too—an unfamiliar moral cowardice. . . ." And five paragraphs onward: "Dissension and discord had shamed the peace. . . ."

Remorse, much less shame, much less secret haunting: these aren't ideas we associate with Frank Lloyd Wright. But what if our ideas are wrong, have long been wrong, or at least not wholly correct?

There was something, in some sense, always haunting the day—so I contend. Something about the artist, no matter his sins, always bent on giving himself away.

Oh, yes, one other large reason for having begun with a long look at August 15, 1914: fire itself. If Frank Lloyd Wright has seemed to resist true explanation by his uncounted chroniclers (probably all for the better), this can be said: he lived his preposterous life in a kind of beautiful rage, and flames ran through it. It's just a fact, and you will know it by the end of this book. I was once having this conversation at Taliesin West with one of his old apprentices, Arnold Roy, who'd come as a nineteen-year-old from Boston, and gotten mesmerized, and who was now past eighty and suffering his various ills. He had kindly hobbled out of his room into the fire-like heat of an Arizona noon to make time to meet. He was seated at lunch with other old apprentices and current staff and architectural fellows. When the subject of fire came up, something flint-struck. It was as if six or seven decades of his life had just been lopped off.

"Frank Lloyd Wright *attracted* fire," he said, leaning across the table.

Pause. Beat. Almost a fiery gleam.

"And then I suppose the next question is, Why?"

But he just let it hang in the tinderbox desert May midday air.

PART I

Longing on a Large Scale
1887–1909

Longing on a large scale is what makes history. This is just a kid with a local yearning but he is part of an assembling crowd, anonymous thousands off the buses and trains, people in narrow columns tramping over the swing bridge above the river, and even if they are not a migration or a revolution, some vast shaking of the soul, they bring with them the body heat of a great city and their own small reveries and desperations, the unseen something that haunts the day.

—Don DeLillo, *Underworld*

At the back of his life he was visiting London, something he'd done on and off since 1910. The head of the Architectural Association School of Architecture had lured him over with a telegram attesting to his greatness, and then had made better on the bet by saying at a reception on the first or second night of the visit that there was only one really great architect in the world, and that was obviously Mr. Frank Lloyd Wright, and thus it had seemed imperative for Europe's best budding architects to have the experience of this great man in the flesh, even if the school could ill afford to have him come. It had all worked: he'd bit. It was a pretty good visit: the great man charged many top hats in St. James's Street. In the company of his wicked and scheming last wife, Olgivanna (nearly as vain and paranoid as he was, but without as many of the competing redemptive qualities), he made a side trip to Wales, land of his maternal forebears, relieving himself against the wall of a not-yet-completed modernist icon called the Brynmawr Rubber Factory (designed by a co-op group of the architectural students he'd come to visit). Back in London, one evening in a studio in St. John's Wood, a group of students and elders and a stray reporter or two and several critics were hushed around him. There he sat at the head of the sofa with his own beautifully sculpted head and that Roman (or maybe Druid) face in perfect profile. Time ticked. Everyone leaned in. "It all started in the long grass of the Prairies," he said in his deeply musical voice.

The Enigma of Arrival

Frank Lloyd Wright, Chicago, 1887

Mother-fueled, father-ghosted, here he comes now, nineteen years old, almost twenty, out of the long grasses of the Wisconsin prairie, a kid, a rube, a bumpkin by every estimation except his own, off a Chicago and North Western train at the Wells Street Station on the north bank of the Chicago River, into the body heat of this great thing called Chicago, on a drizzly late winter or early spring evening in 1887. It is about six p.m. Supposedly he has never seen electric arc lights before. Supposedly he has seven bucks in his pocket.

(To get most of that, he has sold off, at old man Benjamin Perry's pawn-shop on King Street in Madison, some of his departed father's library, including a calf-bound copy of *Plutarch's Lives*. He's also hocked a semi-ratty mink collar of his mother's that was detachable from her overcoat.) Supposedly he has managed his secret escape from his broken home on this mid-week afternoon without his two little sisters, who adore him, or his loving, divorced, and impecunious mother knowing. And now, with his pasteboard suitcase, and in his corn-pinching "toothpick" shoes, he's made it to what he's so long imagined as the Eternal City of the West.

He's just one part of this disembarking, suppertime crowd, these narrow tramping columns, anonymous thousands (well, hundreds), drifting out of the depot's great clock-towered front entry (after having checked his bag at the overnight luggage hold). He's turning south with them onto the Wells Street Bridge, which is a swing bridge directly outside the front door, not quite knowing where he's headed, not willing to ask, just surfing along on this strange inland sea, possessed of his own small reveries and desperations and unseen haunts, longing to make history on a large scale, propelled by a "boundless faith grown strong in him. A faith in what? He could not have told you." So he will write, in the next century, on page 60, of his first version of *An Autobiography*.

The boundless belief is that he will somehow turn himself in short order into a world figure on architecture's stage. It's not only going to happen, but in not much more than a decade. Frank Lloyd Wright—who will later wish to claim that he was seventeen, not nineteen, at this arrival moment; who wishes to profess to any would-be employer that he's finished three and a half years of college but has decided to skip his final several months before obtaining his degree because it was all bunkum anyway; who has an extraordinary gift for thinking in three dimensions—has just stepped out into one of the great building laboratories of the globe. Stepped out into a rude, teeming, black-sooted, horse-carted, Bible-belted, prostitute-prowling, not exactly cosmopolitan and nowhere close to eternal metropolis that has been remaking itself since October 1871, when an apocalyptic fire, burning for thirty-six hours, took almost a third of its whole, something like 17,450 structures, practically down to weeds and the sands of Lake Michigan. Stepped out into a city that, in this decade alone, 1880 to 1890, has been doubling over on itself in population—from half a million souls to more than a million. Chicago, which incorporated itself only fifty years ago, is now the most explosively growing place on earth. Because of the circumstances and geography of its location it has also become a world center of architectural innovation and experimentation, not to say a world center of transportation, on both land and water. (There are six major rail depots here—no other American city has anything like it.) It's a horse-collared city whose tight downtown building core is hemmed in on three sides by a small river and a great lake: it must go up instead of out, at least inside the horse-collar. In the *Lakeside City Directory* there are 187 listings for architectural offices—from one-man ops to firms with rows of draftsmen and delineators. Some of these names are already entering American myth: Burnham & Root, Holabird & Roche, Adler & Sullivan, William LeBaron Jenney. This small-town boy, with his large imagination, has struck Chicago, has hit architecture, the mother of all arts (so he believes), at its seeming ripest moment.

It's such a grand American story: the lowly arrival, the startling *becoming*, and practically every Frank Lloyd Wright book that's ever been written, not least his own, has wanted to deal with it in some way or other. Even accounting for all the luck and seized opportunity, no one has ever quite been able to explain how it happened, the realizing part, because artistic genius of this sort, or maybe any sort, doesn't have real explanation.

Except what if it didn't happen, not nearly, not even by half, in the way he himself later told it? Meaning: the arrival itself and the landing of the first job, but more than that, too. Wright chroniclers have pretty much known for years that so much of the arrival story and the first-job story, no matter how rich they are as stories, are, well, bunkum. Almost from the first sentences, the artist was once again giving himself away, leaving unwitting little breadcrumb clues as to some of his absurd falsehoods and myth-makings. I wish to try to take the bunkum a whole step further from what's been previously reported, but not just for the sake of doing it.

Never mind that now. Let's keep falling in step with him, pretending we believe it all, as he leaves the depot and turns right and crosses the bridge from the north bank into the city proper, gazing down at the "mysterious dark of the river with dim masts, hulks, and funnels hung with lights half-smothered in gloom—reflected in black beneath. I stopped to see, holding myself close against the iron rail to avoid the blind hurrying by." Three pages later, in *An Autobiography:* "The gray, soiled river with its mists of steam and smoke, was the only beauty. That smelled to heaven."

Not that he knows, but he's arrived at a part of the city called Wolf Point, where the river's north branch joins with the south to make the main stem. During the day this is the busiest trade spot in Chicago. The Air Line Elevator, over his right shoulder as he's exiting the depot, holds 700,000 bushels of grain. By day Wolf Point is lumbermen and wharf-men and bargemen and cursing teamsters, but at this hour, the evening hour, it's turning back into what everybody knows as "The Shadows." Wolf Point is emptying out, and he with it. Soon there will just be the forests of the tall-mast ships bobbing in the turgid stream—and the stray, odd prostitute in a darkened doorway.

When you get across the bridge (it takes less than five minutes), you're at the junction of Fifth Avenue and South Water, where the wholesale grocers of the city do their cursing and trading; and if you were to turn west from there, and walk along the south bank, to where South Water Street unites with Lake Street, at Market, you'd be at the site of the old Wigwam, where Abraham Lincoln got nominated in 1860. But he's going straight ahead, which is to say south, into the heart of the commercial business district. This century and some later, you can track the pilgrim's progress, squint and imagine him jaunting along, look down Loop alleyways and see the exposed brick sides of old nineteenth-century buildings, the ones he would have seen.

However, before he's across, while he's holding himself close against the rust-red iron railing, in the center of the span, above the green-gray soiled stream, peering down at its mysterious dark, trying not to get pitched over the side: look again at the photograph that begins this chapter. It's thought to be one of the first photographs taken of him after his arrival in Chicago—maybe three months in. Don't be fooled, such finery is part of the mask, real and not real. And yet what utter seeming sense of himself, at least on the exterior, with that slight-tilted head, those just-flared nostrils, that purposed jaw. Did he rent the duds? What's that little pin or medallion edging from beneath his waistcoat?

In any case, he has gotten himself down to Matthew J. Steffens's portrait studio on Twenty-Second Street—it's one of the best in the city—
where maybe Commodore Steffens himself has disappeared under a
black hood behind a large-format wooden bellows camera on a tripod
to memorialize young Frank L. Wright onto a plate of ground glass. (A
not incidental question: How did he pay for the session?) The portraitist
may have printed his work on albumen and toned it with gold chloride
crystals, bathing it in brown, the way Eugene Atget did, about a decade
later, when he started catching, with his large-format view camera and
its rectilinear lens (like this one), the hues of those perfect, empty, early-
morning streets in Paris. I'll stretch things here a tad and say that the
warming hues of this old first or second surviving photograph are the
prefiguring hues of all those Wright interiors not yet born but somehow alive in him all the same. Even on the hottest day of summer,
his interiors can make you pine for a crackling fire in a great brick or
stone hearth. He made hearths the centerpiece of nearly every home he
ever drew. They stood for probity, protection, family security, this from
someone who once said, almost blithely: "Is it a quality? Fatherhood? If
so, I seemed born without it. And yet a building was a child. I have had
the father-feeling, I am sure, when coming back, after a long time, to
one of my buildings. That must be the true feeling of fatherhood? But I
never had it for my children." (How did that make them feel?)

Okay, what remarkable sense of self, at least on the surface, but a
telltale clue as to the mask part: he hasn't quite decided what to call
himself or how to sign his name. Sometimes it is "F. Wright." Sometimes
it is "F. L. Wright." Sometimes it is "Frank L. Wright." And sometimes
it is "Frank Ll. Wright," with the double "l" (a cap and a lowercase)
representing the name Lloyd, which is the common name of all his
pious, maternal, clannish, prideful, Unitarian, Wisconsin-out-of-Wales
people—the "God-Almighty Lloyd Joneses," as even they like to think
of themselves, never mind their semi-disdainful farming neighbors.
(It's the family's infernal ego and self-righteousness, principally.) But it's
a supposed fact that he was born "Frank Lincoln Wright," not "Frank
Lloyd Wright," and that his middle name was given to him by his now-
spurned father. In any case, he's in the process of shifting his way of
identifying himself, but he hasn't quite figured it out yet. (Sometimes
he has been initialing himself "FLlW.") The use of *Lloyd* in his profes-

sional life won't come for almost a decade. It'll happen as he's finishing the last set of drawings for one of his early and important transitional houses to his fully arrived Prairie Period. Then he'll be "Frank Lloyd Wright" for the ages.

A bell is clanging. People are starting to run. Oh, goodness, the provincial's been in Chicago ten minutes and he's getting "bridged." The Wells, one of thirty-five bridges over the river, is swinging out. (The bridge sits on a pier, or piling, and a bridge-master in his little stall makes it pivot lengthwise, parallel to the shore, so that the tall ships can get through.) He locks his knees, holds on, rides it out, takes the swing, and damn if it isn't kind of fun. From *An Autobiography*: "Later, I never crossed the river without being charmed by somber beauty." Moments like that tend to get sealed in muscle memory.

God, he's starved. Somewhere near Fifth and Randolph, which is five lines deep of horsecars, buggies, hansom cabs, every pedestrian for himself, the drivers larruping their nags with furious swearing, he ducks into a cheap eating joint and gives up seventy cents—ten percent of his entire stake. Back out onto the street, the rain harder now, shivering, drifting south again, no idea where he'll stay tonight, turning east, coming down Washington Street: the monolith of the courthouse on his left, the lights of an opera house on his right. It's the Chicago Opera House, magnificent palace, with its big canopy out front. Beneath the canopy, nearly life-size cutouts of dancers hold their painted colors against the gloom and the wet. He goes in. The booth man tells him the cheapest seats range from a quarter to a buck fifty. (He doesn't tell us this per se, but the prices are checkable in John J. Flinn's *Standard Guide to Chicago*, and it tracks with his narrative.) He parts with a dollar. The performance—it's a ballet called *Sieba*—won't start for an hour. Fine by him, he can dry out. He watches the place assemble. Say this, his deserter of a father gave him the lifelong gift of loving classical music. It's thrilling listening to an orchestra tune up. Even if this is sentimental music, it's orchestral music all the same. Suddenly he's sad. What must his sisters and his sainted mother back in Madison be thinking? His heart is aching for what he's done. But he wouldn't not have done it.

Back out onto the street, drifting with the crowd eastward again, to Wabash. He boards a cable car—supposedly he's never been on a cable car—and takes a seat up front by the grip-man, so he can understand how the thing works. But it's a short ride: the car is going to the barn for the night. Everybody off. He catches another car, headed back north, assaulted even more by the phantasmagoria of saloons and eateries and dry goods places, all with their signs and lurid lighting. This is the glorious Chicago? He gets a bed at the Briggs House, on Randolph and Fifth, not far from where he'd started out about four hours ago. It's a good hotel, nothing like a flophouse. His bag's still at the depot, so he wraps a sheet around himself and surveys himself in the mirror. "A human item—insignificant but big with interior faith and a great hope." Tomorrow, he'll attack Chicago.

Which he does, finding a city directory, making a list of firms he'll call on. In his pocket, after the thinnest breakfast, the thin jangle of three silver dollars and a dime. It's a Thursday (he doesn't tell us this, but if you follow the logic of the narrative, it has to be), and the response is the same at every firm he steps into: no drafting work at present, young fellow, try us again down the road, won't you? Down the road? Don't they get it? "University man, eh?" a bigwig asks. Would that be Ann Arbor? "No, University of Wisconsin." As he exits and enters offices, he's starting to sweat. His feet are killing him in these stupid toothpick lace-ups. Back in Madison, they'd seemed so smart. But he's not above critiquing for his own amusement the architectural landmarks of the city. There's the Palmer House, supposedly one of the great palazzo hotels of the west. Looks "like an ugly old, old man whose wrinkles were all in the wrong place." That night, again at the Briggs, he asks meekly for a cheaper room, and the clerk takes pity with a seventy-five-center nearly as good as the one he paid more than two bucks for last night. Earlier, supper was twenty cents at Kohlsaat's Bakery, on Clark, a spot he'll grow to love in all the Chicago years ahead.

Friday, second full day from home, third day out if you count the escaping day. Skipping breakfast and lunch, he buys ten cents' worth of bananas. (If you do the math, he must have a buck forty left.) Five other firms today: nada. He has fetched his suitcase by now and so has a few things to show from college drawing classes. Still nada.

"Awakened rudely to the fourth day," he tells us. It's Saturday. "Got started again, pavement-sore, gaunt. Something had to happen today." Eureka: with twenty cents left in his pocket, and after three more rejections on the front side of noon, he lands a job. (There is so much building work in Chicago that the larger firms are generally open until six p.m. on Saturdays.) It's in the well-regarded concern of Joseph Lyman Silsbee, at 53 Lakeside, southwest corner of Clark and Adams. Prominent address. Actually, his extended family has a connection with Silsbee, and not a small one. Pride kept him from coming here straightaway the other day. But he has no choice now. People in the Silsbee shop are getting hungry for lunch, while the applicant is getting ravenous, but for more than lunch. Silsbee, transplant from the East, out of Harvard, in his forties, tall with an imperial air, a freehand sketching marvel with a soft black pencil, has been specializing of late in the half-timbered, Queen Anne "shingle style" of housing for the upper middle classes. He can sit down and deliver you turrets and inglenooks and oriels and bays and gables and the most seductive fenestrations. He's wonderful with angles. He likes playing with the surface of walls, recessing them, pushing them outward. But is he a truly serious man who wishes to rebuild the world in his own image? He's got a gold pince-nez attached to a gold chain running down into a watch fob pocket. He comes out of a door marked "Private" and through the swing-gate. He glances over with disdain. And yet he has seen the work. If you're willing to believe the autobiography, which reports the bulk of what you've been reading here, including the bit about being down to dimes and bananas on the third and fourth days, then J. L. Silsbee apparently hasn't made the connection of the connection. Nope, it's just the work. From *An Autobiography*:

"'All right,' he said, 'take him on. Tracer's wages—$8.00.'"

He has said it, boomingly, not to the supplicant, but to the twenty-six-year-old chief draftsman who's standing alongside, Cecil S. Corwin, who, a minute ago, when the boy came in, had looked at his drawings, and possibly something more, and had decided, almost on the spot, to take up for him with the Old Man himself.

––––––––

"Exactly when Wright went to Chicago is the kind of question that tantalizes scholars, but the best guess is that he was working for Silsbee by February 1887," Meryle Secrest wrote in her 1992 *Frank Lloyd Wright*, the most in-depth biography we have: the life of record, prodigiously researched. Secrest:

No one believes that Wright's account of his hiring at Silsbee's, in which he slipped in through the back door, not letting his identity be known, can possibly be true. . . . The most puzzling issue is why Wright should be at pains to present himself as a struggling outsider, hired on merit alone, with no strings pulled by anyone. The account he gave was published in 1932, when he was in his sixties and, one believes, bent on fashioning a legend. By then he was unwilling to concede that he had ever been helped, or that anyone whose ideas predated his own could possibly have influenced him. He came from nowhere and out of nothing, a full-fledged genius.

Exactly, and always one of his more unattractive qualities. Two years before he died, in 1957, the great unacknowledger wrote: "To cut ambiguity short: there never was exterior influence upon my work, either foreign or native. . . . My work is original not only in fact but in spiritual fiber." I've heard such a condition described as "the anxiety of influence." Yes. Rank egotists need to think—need the world to think—that they've descended directly from the right hand of God.

What if the boy off the train not only went straight to Silsbee, as practically any Wright chronicler now believes, leaning on family connection (to be explained in a moment), and that thus there had been no romantic pounding of pavement, but more than this, he came *twice*? That is, he came to Chicago for the first time in the late summer or early fall of 1886, more or less in haste and secret, to try to check things out and line up possibilities of future work, before returning home to Madison and the start of another semester in college—which, as it would turn out, was going to be his "final" semester, not that he knew so at the time, and with the word "final" here not being the one you may be imagining. And he then came back to Chicago for the second time, the staying time, in the winter of 1887, soon after Christmas, possibly as early as the first week of January, or perhaps even in the last days of 1886—which is to say, about four months later.

In other words: There had never been any kind of real runaway. That was just part of the bilge and bunkum. He didn't light out eastward for the big city as much as he had sought to pre-arrange it all. His family knew, even if they didn't like it. And the capper: Wright pretty much stole wholesale the telling of it—meaning the way he spun it all into myth in his autobiography—from his celebrated author friend, Hamlin Garland, in an 1895 novel called *Rose of Dutcher's Coolly*.

And you might be asking: What does any of this even matter? Doesn't the becoming, the realizing, which is to say the work itself, no matter how precisely it happened, make everything else beside the point? Yes and no. The question matters for two reasons: First, it reveals the gift to myth-make so early, even if he didn't set down the story in print until late middle age. But far more important, it matters because, within all his prevaricating about how he arrived in Chicago and obtained his first job, there is, conversely, if you study what seems to be hiding in plain sight, a revelation of Wright's deeper character, of his fundamental decency as a person, of a certain kind of protective tenderness. And those things are tied up intimately with the name said just above: Cecil Corwin. But his story, in all of its homoerotic implications and complications, and in its essential sadness, and in its redemptive and beautiful aspects too, can't quite be told yet.

———

Start with checkable fact—with *Sieba*. Inadvertent time clues hiding in plain sight: the Kiralfy Brothers' "magnificent spectacle" of three interwoven ballets, of which *Sieba* was the principal offering, played at the Chicago Opera House for fourteen days, from Sunday, August 29, through Saturday, September 11, 1886. So, if Wright's late-middle-aged novelistic memory brought up a faded old minor classic that was part of *The Ballet of Laces,* then he could have seen *Sieba* only between these dates. I believe his memory did bring it up in the way it brought up that he apparently got "bridged" the first time he ever crossed the Wells. Muscle memory.

The time window for his seeing *Sieba* lines up neatly with the time frames for his getting back to Madison for the start of the fall term at the University of Wisconsin.

College. Every serious Wright chronicler now knows Frank Lloyd Wright barely attended college at all. No matter what he claimed throughout his life, the fact is that he was enrolled at the University of Wisconsin for a total of two semesters, and barely that, with the whole of his college career amounting to twenty-seven weeks, a little more than six months. In those two semesters, he received two grades. He had been admitted in the first place as a "Special Student," since he had not achieved enough credits to graduate from Madison High School. His two semesters, closer to a part-time status, took in parts of two academic years.

Wisconsin's proud and progressive state university sat around the curving shore of beautiful Lake Mendota about a mile west from where Wright and his mother and sisters lived in the frame house with the milk cow in the shed out back. He was a day student, and his family could barely afford that. The University of Wisconsin—UW is how it's better known—operated then on a three-term academic year: fall, winter, spring. University records show he took one class in the winter semester of 1886—or enrolled for it. That term began on January 6 and ended on March 31. The course was French, but he received no grade, or at least no grade was registered, so it's not clear he even stuck out the course. His freshman year transcript has him in the scientific curriculum. It's possible he audited one or more courses, but there's no record.

He was not enrolled for the spring term of 1886, which ran from the beginning of April into June.

His "final" term in college was in the fall of 1886, in his so-called sophomore year. The semester began on September 8 and ended on December 22. He registered for two courses—descriptive geometry and mechanical drawing—and received a C in both. These courses were as close to an architectural program as UW had; as close to a college transcript as Frank Lloyd Wright would ever have.

A question: Did a boy off a train in the late summer or very early fall of 1886, between these two spread-apart semesters, pay a dollar on a rainy Wednesday evening to see a performance of a ballet at a gilt opera house? If so, there could have only been two Wednesdays possible: September 1 and September 8. By the second one, though, as I said, school would have just started up in Madison. Even for a disinterested student, the first Wednesday seems more likely. Just for the sake: What was the weather like in Chicago on those two Wednesdays? On September 1, the skies were mostly clear but there was a shower or two late in the day. Even more so on the following Wednesday: scattered patches of rain after intense heat. So, yes, there could have been a remembered glaze of gloom and wet in the million-footed city. Within the fictions, little facts, or factoids.

It's hilarious to watch him dissemble about his college career. Here he is at Music Hall, in Detroit, on May 14, 1951, an old man now, speaking to a packed audience, including almost the entire student body of Lawrence Institute of Technology. A typed transcript of his remarks survives, and apparently the organizers had sent it to him afterward for publication purposes, and so the prevaricator edited his own lines—and you can fairly see him penciling in new lies over the typed copy in his handsome hand:

"I studied engineering myself, and if I had had more patience, if I had stayed in school three months longer, I could have had a degree as a civil-engineer. I walked out. I was not getting architecture, and I wanted it. Col. Lindbergh and I attended the same school in Wisconsin. He got fired. I walked out." (The type-scripters had entered the word "Laughter" after the Lindbergh line.)

From *An Autobiography*: "So the University training of one Frank Lloyd Wright, Freshman, Sophomore, Junior, and part Senior was lost like some race run under a severe handicap. . . . The feeling about this best period of youth, lasting three and one-half years, is not so much that it was wasted. . . . Mother would never consent to his giving up so near the time for graduation—only another winter and spring term. . . . But the fall term of his senior-year was just ended. Why go on with it. . . . Why not go to Chicago . . . ?"

Even several of the early biographies and historical studies raised questions about how much time he'd actually spent in college, including Grant Carpenter Manson's *Frank Lloyd Wright to 1910: The First Golden Age*, published in 1958, the year before Wright died. But it wasn't until the late sixties, nearly a decade after his death, and thirty-five years after the publication of the first version of *An Autobiography*, that someone teased out the bogusness all the way—along with so many other untruths about the growing up, about the divorce of the parents, about the year he was born. A doctoral candidate from Mississippi in American history at the University of Wisconsin, Thomas S. Hines, Jr., who was working part-time on the staff at the university archives, got an assignment to prepare a research memorandum about Wright's time in Madison. So he went looking for documents, which happened to be hiding more or less in plain sight, in registrar files and in old drawers at the Dane County Courthouse in downtown Madison, and what the grad student found were all manner of lies Wright had told or intimated through the years. Hines published his discoveries in the winter 1967 issue of the *Wisconsin Magazine of History* in an article carrying the innocuous-sounding title: "Frank Lloyd Wright— the Madison Years: Records versus Recollections." It was a crossing over for all future Wright scholarship—and not a little embarrassing one as well, for so much had been earlier swallowed. I called up Hines. He was in Los Angeles, still active as a scholar. "I just got the assignment from my boss," he said modestly. "I did what I was told. I followed the paper trail. It was all lying there, once you started looking." The word "lying" made both of us laugh a little.

Breadcrumb clues: In addition to the time frames of *Sieba*, lying in plain sight in old newspaper ads and theater reviews, there is another time giveaway arguing for the idea Wright first went to Chicago to look around and to call at Silsbee's office in either late August or early September 1886. I deliberately didn't give the background of it above when we were jaunting with him across the bridge in the shivering rain and as he supposedly went tramping for the next three days in his college "toothpicks." This time clue connects centrally to "Uncle Jenk," about whom every Wright student knows: Jenkin Lloyd Jones, one of Wright's many uncles on his mother's side, and a significant influence on his life. (Uncle Jenk was also the father of Richard Lloyd Jones, Wright's first cousin, whose name was mentioned above in connection with ruinous outward-spreading consequences of August 15, 1914.) Uncle Jenk was the core family connection to the firm of J. L. Silsbee. He was a man of God, a Unitarian minister, a Civil War veteran, who'd enlisted in the Union army as a teenager and fought at Missionary Ridge and Chattanooga and Vicksburg and Atlanta. (He was a Wisconsin private, got wounded, and thereafter walked with a cane.) Uncle Jenk owned a mellifluent preaching voice and knew how to present himself with unconventional dress and flowing hair. He was a large man besides. (All Wright's uncles on his mother's side were big-shouldered manly men; how he must have loathed it, having inherited his own far punier physique from his father's people.) Uncle Jenk, who was to become an avowed pacifist, was the dominant figure in the leadership of Unitarianism in its westward liberal spread from its more conservative and upper-class New England roots. A radical theist, he wished to move

Unitarianism away from a Christian focus toward a more nonsectarian engagement with all the world's religious people—Jew, Buddhist, Muslim, Hindu, it didn't matter. To Uncle Jenk, the Bible was only one path to God. From his pulpit he was as apt to evoke Emerson or Whitman or Goethe or Thoreau or John Ruskin as to quote scripture itself. What he espoused was the divinity of man and the humanity of God: the kind of slyly egotistical, nature-based pan-belief that a nephew could fully embrace, and would.

More to the point, Uncle Jenk had engaged J. L. Silsbee to design and build a new church for him on the South Side of Chicago—right in the period when a recalcitrant student was aiming for the lights of Chicago. This church was known as All Souls Church, and for decades it was a famous spiritual and social services outreach center in the greater Midwest, as well as a place of social and intellectual refuge for Wright himself in his earliest days in Chicago. (Wright would meet his nearly child-bride first wife, Kitty, at an All Souls social function.) All Souls amounted to a large commission for Silsbee, his first institutional job since arriving from upstate New York a few years before. Obviously, Silsbee would have been beholden to Uncle Jenk. And even if Uncle Jenk wished his nephew to stay in school and not come to Chicago—which, no question, he did—it seems ludicrous to think that the headstrong boy, determined to come anyway, wouldn't have tried to exploit his uncle's relationship with Silsbee's firm, or that his uncle wouldn't have given in and obliged, whether he quite wished to or not. So when Wright writes in *An Autobiography* (he's wolfing down his seventy-cent supper that first night in a joint near Randolph Street), "As I ate, I was sure of one thing, never would I go near Uncle Jenkin Lloyd Jones nor ask his help nor use his name," what he is really saying is: *I'll go straightaway to Silsbee in the morning and I'll use Uncle Jenk for all I can use him.*

All Souls, an unchurchy-looking Queen Anne shingled building, sitting squat on the corner of Oakwood Boulevard and Langley Avenue, was built in the early and middle months of 1886. (It no longer exists.) In *An Autobiography,* Wright writes of getting his first look at the handsome building when it was "nearly completed."

The construction was essentially done by late summer 1886. On September 12, Uncle Jenk and his family moved into the parsonage, which was part of the church itself, along with a school and large social function room. The dedication came the following month, on October 12. So if a nephew saw his uncle's new house of worship for the first time in its "nearly completed" state, it could not have been in the late winter or early spring of 1887. It would have to have been in and around the time of *Sieba*.

Something more: It's long been known Wright had been involved in minor ways in the building of a small family chapel on the Lloyd Jones home ground in Wisconsin, close to Spring Green. Silsbee designed this country chapel, probably as a favor to Uncle Jenk and as part of the bargain for the much larger and more financially important commission down in Chicago. Unity Chapel still stands, in its simple brown-shingled lyric beauty, forty yards in from the asphalt, on County Highway T, in a grove of old trees, next to the Lloyd Jones family cemetery, just across the cornfields from Taliesin. It had been built in the early months of 1886, and its dedication had come that summer, in the middle of August (two weeks before *Sieba* opened). A church magazine, co-edited by Uncle Jenk, told of how "a boy architect belonging to the family looked after the interior." The boy architect was Wright, and he was far from a real architect, even if he knew things about engineering and drawing. Wright's first published rendering of any building we know of was of Unity Chapel—so an historic document. He apparently drew it freehand from Silsbee's design and signed his name, "F.L. Wright Del." (The "Del" was for delineator.) It was published in Uncle Jenk's church annual in early January 1887. Historians believe Wright could have shown the rendering to Silsbee as another way of importuning himself into a job. It's very possible he had even met Silsbee in Wisconsin.

Question: Why is it (above, Secrest was quoted on this) that Wright historians and biographers believe that the best guess as to when Wright made his supposed secret escape from home and began working for Silsbee was sometime in, say, late February or early March 1887? Principally, it's because of several letters to Wright in and around this time. There's a letter from his Aunt Nell, his mother's sister and Uncle Jenk's sister, who was a devoted Wisconsin schoolteacher. On March 9, 1887, she wrote to her nephew and asked: "How is it with you in the great city? Homesick, just a little? I want to hear all about it, my dear boy—how you like it, how you live, what it costs you and everything."

Yes, the letter implies he's recently left home. But there's nothing in it to suggest he's slunk off one afternoon without telling his family. There's no rebuke per se.

There's also a letter from Wright's mother in the same time frame. Same thing. In her passive-aggressive way, Anna Wright communicates how much her dear boy is missed by his family, but again no real tone (let alone words) of recrimination: *How could you have done this to us? How could you have gone off without telling us?*

I contend Wright arrived in Chicago earlier than has long been believed, and that his family knew he was going, even if they didn't like the fact. He was settled in the city by at least January 6, 1887. Why? Because in the church annual for All Souls, published on that date, he's listed as an active member, boarding with a parish family at 3921 Vincennes Avenue, just around the corner from All Souls. There is another book of record for the church, dated February 6, 1887, and his name is inked there—"F. L. Wright"—in what is known as the "Bond of Union." The words are exactly what they imply: a pledged involvement. Aunt Nell's March letter notwithstanding, his mother's letter notwithstanding, I believe, if cannot prove, he was in place right after the New Year, if not right after Christmas, and was shortly working for J. Lyman Silsbee.

But a second and far more crucial question, hinging to the above: Why would a boy, albeit a boy already profligate with other people's money, decide to get initiated into a college fraternity in the late fall of 1886 if he knew he wasn't going to stay in college? Even for Wright, that would seem unconscionable, given the fact that fraternity fees at UW were costly then, probably double the regular college costs, even for a day-hopper. But on November 13, 1886, a little more than a month before the term ended, Wright became the eighty-first member to be inducted into the oldest fraternity on UW's campus, Phi Delta Theta. There's his name, on page 125 of the red-bound, gold-leafed, six-inch-by-eight-inch university yearbook: F. L. Wright. Soph.

Could the (provocative) answer be that Wright didn't know he was going to drop out of college, not when he got initiated? He knew he was headed for Chicago, just not this soon. Was he being pulled back, at least partially, and right after the Christmas holidays, at the dreary turn of the New Year, by something he couldn't quite understand, much less articulate? My hypothesis is that the something wasn't inanimate, but a flesh-and-blood vision perhaps of a pair of muscular arms in sleeves rolled above the elbow that were "thickly covered with coarse hair, but I noticed how he daintily crooked his finger as he lifted his pencil. He had an air of gentleness and refinement. I told him my trials."

That would be Cecil S. Corwin, in Silsbee's office, and we will return to him shortly.

But first, one small piece of unfinished business: It seems clear that Wright appropriated key parts of the novel *Rose of Dutcher's Coolly* from its author, Hamlin Garland. Now thought of as an eclipsed literary son of the middle border, Garland was born in Wisconsin seven years before Wright. (*A Son of the Middle Border* is the title of his fine auto-biography.) The two came to know each other in the decade or so after Wright moved to Chicago. In 1907, Garland founded an arts and culture society that within a few years became known as the Cliff Dwellers Club. (Its kiva powwow room was on the top floor of Orchestra Hall.) Wright was a charter member of the Cliff Dwellers. Two years after the club's founding, when Wright startled Oak Park (not to say the world) by running away to Europe with Mamah Borthwick Cheney, and then got found out by the press, Wright's long-suffering wife, Kitty (about whom you'll hear more), was quoted in the *Chicago Tribune* as saying that only a very few of his close friends "are able to understand him," and one of those was Hamlin Garland.

In 1895, Garland published a bold if awkwardly written novel about a girl running away from her Wisconsin farm home to become a "poet-ess" in Chicago. There are unmistakable undertones and overtones of sexual awakening. Rose, who has grown up in Dutcher's Coolly, arrives about 6:30 p.m. off a train from Madison (where she's gone to college), and she's being pushed along with the crowds through the depot (it has to be the Wells Street Station), searching for a Chicago friend who's due to meet her. "[S]he moved on mechanically with the rest. . . . It was terrifying, confusing. Shrill screams and hoarse shouts rose above a hissing, scraping sound. . . . A train of cable-cars came nosing along like vicious boars. . . ." Peddlers cry, there's the assault of laundry wag-ons and vegetable wagons. That evening, in a rooming house, her eyes brim with tears when the "figure of her lonely old father came before her. She saw him sitting beside the kitchen table, his head on his palm, and all the new house empty and dark."

No, Rose didn't get bridged on that first night inside the beast. Nor did she duck in out of the rain to see a ballet. But she knows what she's done: fled home, loved ones.

There's mention of Garland's novel in the best study that's yet been written about the epic of Chicago in the years when Frank Lloyd Wright first lived there: Donald Miller's 1996 *City of the Century*. When I called up Professor Miller, he said he hadn't quite realized the extent of some of the parallels in the two works, and of how Wright almost couldn't not have known of the existence of Garland's novel, the more so for its notoriety when it was published. So: Roughly three decades after *Rose*, in the middle and late 1920s, when a genius with an outsized anxiety of influence, and a gift for assimilating things and making them far better than their originals, began to set down his own life story, with its elisions and made-up truths, its slipped time clues, its own unmistakable undertones and overtones of sexual awakening, especially in the parts having to do with his first days and weeks and months in Chicago, and with the first true friend he ever made there, why couldn't he, why wouldn't he, have reached back and pulled up an old remembered novel and begun to light-finger certain parts of it for his own uses? By then Hamlin Garland and Frank Lloyd Wright were out of touch, and the former was about to forsake the long grasses of the Midwest for the orange groves and dream factories of Southern California, where he'd have about a decade left to live. No letter between them about *Rose* has ever surfaced. Who knows, maybe Garland read *An Autobiography* and saw the appropriating and just kind of grinned appreciatively.

In 1991, the American Institute of Architects named him the greatest American architect of all time, and also that year Architectural Record published a list of the one hundred most important buildings of the twentieth century. Twelve of his were on it. Had he been alive, he'd have demanded a recount. His roofs were legendary for leaking. Why wouldn't they have leaked? He was always pushing the limits of materials, straining against the form. "I don't build a house without predicting the end of the present social order," he once said. "Every building is a missionary." (There is that famous story—maybe it even happened—that when a much-favored client, giving a dinner party, called him up and yelled that he was getting puddles on his dining room table and drips on his bald noggin, he replied: "Well, move the table.") What's not apocryphal—there is documentation—is that he liked letting himself into "his" houses to begin rearranging the furniture while the owners were out, moving books and photographs and putting their ghastly trinkets in bottom drawers. He once—it was 1940—went into a tiny "Usonian" he'd built for a family named Jacobs in Madison, Wisconsin, four years after he'd created this perfect wooden jewel box on the corner of Toepfer and Birch. He got in through the carport. Frank Lloyd Wright more or less invented the carport. He despised garages and basements and attics: too dark, too cluttery. For as florid, even garish, as he could sometimes be, he was constitutionally a prophet of minimalism. Like Thoreau, like Jesus, he thought too many material possessions an unhealthy thing. (Possibly the only thing he had in common with Jesus.) He had along with him at the Jacobs House that day his young and fairly new personal photographer, Pedro Guerrero. Once inside, according to Guerrero, "He was brutal. He declared that, if I thought I could get away with it, I should destroy any of the unauthorized objects." Then he went off to run some errands.

The Lost Architect

Frank Lloyd Wright and Cecil Corwin in Chicago,
circa 1888

The interiors of Frank Lloyd Wright houses are about many things, but at the center of each one is the intertwined idea of openness and flow. No matter what else he did with the design of a home in his nearly three-quarters of a century as a revolutionary architect, whether hanging it on the lip of a waterfall in Pennsylvania or sticking it mirage-like in the middle of a desert in Arizona, Wright was out to "break the box," to destroy forever those tight, draped, dark, horse-hair, closed-off Victorian rooms of our nineteenth-century forebears. He wanted to let light and space in, air in, *life* in. And he did so, radically. Evangelically. It was a way of thinking and feeling he never let go of. He did it initially, and most radically, in his Prairie houses, in and around the turn of the twentieth century, which alone are enough to have made him immortal. The esteemed contemporary architecture critic Paul Goldberger once put it this way in regard to Wright: "He really did feel that America, as this new democratic country . . . needed a new architectural expression . . . that was horizontal, open in plan, open across the landscape, a sense somehow that it was connecting to that great open American land. . . . He saw that American landscape, the openness of it, the sense that it was always moving across the land, pushing westward."

Throughout his life Wright himself tried to articulate what he was doing or what he had already done in terms of this interlocking idea of openness and harmonious flow as it connects to the larger idea of freedom and indeed to the still larger idea of America herself. Six years before he died, he wrote:

> To say the house planted by myself on the good earth of the Chicago prairie as early as 1900, or earlier, was the first truly democratic expression of our democracy in Architecture would start a controversy with professional addicts who believe Architecture has no political (therefore no social) significance. So, let's say that the spirit of democracy—freedom of the individual as an individual—took hold of the house as it then was, took off the attic and the porch, pulled out the basement, and made single spacious, harmonious unit of living room, dining room and kitchen, with appropriate entry convenience.

It's almost impossible to step inside any Wright building, but especially his houses, and not get something of this ineffable feeling of openness and freedom that somehow seems greater than the (beautiful) building itself. There are certain moments, standing in such spaces, if the light is falling right, when it will begin to seem as if Whitman is singing to Emerson, or vice versa, channeled through an ego that could see both of theirs in the great stakes game of fame and self-love, and raise it by half. There are also moments when what comes, as others before me have said, is the wonder of a religious feeling.

I wish to propose that an almost entirely forgotten American architect, whose name we probably wouldn't know at all were it not for some sexually freighted passages in Wright's autobiography, whose talent was a fraction of Wright's, and knew it was, whose life, like Wright's, bridged parts of two centuries but, unlike Wright's, ended in near-oblivion and apparent failure, had something vital, if ineffable, to do with this literal and figurative opening up and letting in of the light—and thus deserves our homage, our honor, our attentions paid.

His name was Cecil Sherman Corwin. He was not only Wright's first and truest Chicago friend and earliest professional associate, but he was probably the greatest male friend of Wright's life, period. (Wright himself said this four months before he died.) He and Cecil had only a decade together, and barely that, before their lives went apart and never came back together, except once, many years later, and not in person. (It was in a poignant and coded exchange of letters, forty-six years after they met.) But they never forgot each other, and Cecil—I am convinced if cannot really prove—never quite got over his unrequited romantic love for the infectiously alive and preternaturally gifted boy off his suppertime Wisconsin train. If indeed that love was unrequited.

Prurience isn't the least point or interest here. The point is the opposite of prurience, which is to say tenderness and protectiveness and decent-heartedness. Which, again, aren't words leaping to mind when we say the words "Frank Lloyd Wright."

The freighted sentences: You can't miss them, although, curiously, almost all of Wright's biographers, and Wright historians as well, have seemed to wish to steer clear of them, and, in a sense, to steer clear of Cecil himself. In any case, the freightedness begins on page 67 of *An Autobiography*, immediately after the lost architect—who was far from lost at that point—walks onstage. In fact, make it the other way around: Wright, not Cecil, is the seemingly lost Chicago soul (a "human item—insignificant," to use his own words) who's doing the walking onstage on page 67. Or at least he's walking unannounced through the outer door and into the main room at J. Lyman Silsbee's modest-sized architectural firm on the fifth floor of a large office building at Clark and Adams—where Cecil is the suave top-kick.

These are his first two words about Cecil, whom he spies almost as soon as he enters: "Liked instantly." (He also likes the sketches on the walls.) Is he instantly directing us how to think about himself and

Cecil? The rest of that sentence: "... the fine looking, cultured fellow with a fine pompadour and beard, who quietly came forward with a friendly smile."

In no particular order, here are some other sentences the reader encounters in the next half-dozen or so pages, which represent perhaps six or so months in Wright's life and Cecil's life in chronological time:

"'Come home with me tonight and we'll concertize with my new grand-piano.'"

And: "He looked me over. 'I believe we could get along,' he said."

And: "'No!' said Cecil, 'he's going to stay with me tonight.'"

And: "Cecil was often taking me home and we went to the Apollo Club concerts or other concerts wherever we could find them. And we went to the theaters sometimes."

And: "Cecil and I were still together noons and evenings."

And: "I preferred Cecil's company. If I couldn't have that I would find something to do."

And: "Cecil and I went dancing around the big table in the center of the room in a friendly tilt."

And: "During these later months at Silsbee's Cecil and I were inseparable. Discussed everything in the heavens above, the earth beneath and the waters thereof."

And: "We would go to Madame Galle's, Italian table d'hote, or various other cozy restaurants. Or, if we had a little money, to the 'Tip-Top Inn' in the Pullman Building. . . ."

And: "But Cecil was already more in himself than I could have imagined. His culture similar to mine, yet he was different. And so much more developed in it than I."

And: "I began to go to school to Cecil."

And: "We were soon together everywhere."

Stop it here. *And so much more developed in it than I:* What is the antecedent of "it"? Is it "culture" in the previous sentence, and, if so, isn't that sometimes employed as a code word for homosexuality? But if the answer to that is yes, and if the author is telling us he began to go to school on this culture ("similar to mine," although not quite) and on Cecil himself because Cecil was so much more developed "in it" than he was, then couldn't the sentence, couldn't the passage, be construed to read and mean that the author himself, not just Cecil, is also gay, or might be gay, only not as far along in his homosexuality, or the possibility of his homosexuality, as Cecil? Is this why Wright made a key but almost unnoticeable syntax change in the next edition of his book, published in 1943? (It grew by almost two hundred pages.) He took out the words "in it," so that the sentence reads "And so much more developed than I." That sort of open-ends it, generalizes things (although not if you're a careful reader). But, once you compare the two editions you begin to get it all the way: he's working to protect them both.

Which has to be the operative word: protecting. It took a long time to grasp what Wright is really doing in his autobiography in evoking his old lost comrade, who I am convinced was a mostly closeted gay man: signaling complex truths even as he's tenderly taking care. The more you look at the Cecil passages—and there are more than what's been quoted here—the more you can feel a certain honor for Wright, admiration. The notorious American lothario, not to say supposed shameless adulterer; the thrice-married biological father of seven (Wright's seventh child was born out of wedlock in December 1925, when he was fifty-eight, which was about eleven months before he began drafting the early sections of *An Autobiography*); the tabloid celebrity who once got jailed in Minnesota under the federal Mann Act for transporting a female across state lines for alleged immoral purposes (they were trumped-up charges and didn't last long, but, oh, the smudgy photographs and black, blocky headlines again), is unafraid, in his Cecil remembrances, to employ the language of lovers, to "implicate" himself, to allow—no, to encourage—any old damn suspicion to come forth that might wish to come forth.

Far from being unaware of what he's doing, he's absolutely aware. And at the core of the awareness is something decent, kindly.

It's his own form of homage, his own expression of solidarity and kinship and gratitude. Gratitude for all that Cecil gave him, back there, when he'd been so young and inexperienced and know-nothing hungry. Cecil helped open him up to the wider world and all its sensuous big-city possibilities and opportunities. Cecil introduced him to a kind of sophistication he'd never known. It was art and music and theater and dance. It was late-night dining. It was outings to galleries and museums. It was, perhaps most of all, one-on-one conversation on a hundred topics, including philosophy, religion, and man's higher purpose, which included the wish to conceive dignified human shelters that would be around long after the two of them were not. And I am proposing that this intellectual and spiritual and emotional opening up, in all its forms and phrases, with Cecil showing the way, and never more so than in their first days and weeks and months together, had its own unquantifiable influence on the creation of some opened-up and aired-out buildings that, within little more than a decade, would be standing American architecture—world architecture—on its drawing head. Wright, destined to shoot right past Cecil as an artist, never forgot Cecil's early generosities to him. And wished, eventually, in his own way, to repay them in kind. This is the way I understand their joined story, brief as it was in actual time. This is the way I understand some freighted language in *An Autobiography.*

Would Cecil have had his own mixed motives in the bargain? It would seem naïve to think he didn't. But that doesn't take away the generosity and kindness.

Is it possible they *were* lovers? Is this what Wright wants us to know, or at least wonder about, for whatever welter of reasons? Anything is possible. Human beings can be hard-wired in their sexuality in unknowable ways—and thank God for it. But the guess here is no, they were not lovers in the physical sense. The guess is that Wright's feelings toward Cecil, right from the start, were something powerful and equivocal and disconcerting all at once, but not quite acted upon. Disconcerting in the sense he'd possibly never had such feelings inside him before for another male (a subject that will be revisited). And Cecil's feelings for Frank? From all that can be gathered about this shadowed, alluring figure—and I've gone some ways to try to gather it—I can only believe that his was an erotic desire unfulfilled. And that Wright himself sooner than later came to understand it as such. And it isn't necessary to look again at the grainy and lovely old photograph at the top of this chapter to fortify the belief—even though you're invited now to take another look.

Isn't it a picture of homoerotic longing, from the right side of the frame? That's Cecil's curled right hand—thumb and first two fingers— resting lightly on Frank's left shoulder. (It almost looks like he's wearing a kid leather glove, but it's probably an optical illusion.) And from the left side: Is this boyish man, with his scrubbed face and slightly tousled hair, in his fine overcoat and tightly buttoned waistcoat, with his right thumb hooked at the corner of his pant pocket, oblivious to the longing practically breathing at his neck? That's probably just proof of the way a photograph, any photograph, is able to lie. As it turns out, the picture has its own equivocal and grainy history. The image has turned up in many places over the years, not just in Wright biographies. It's on Ancestry.com under Cecil's name. For a while the picture had its own Facebook entry. It keeps cropping up and out.*

"I learned a good deal about a house from Silsbee by way of Cecil," Wright says in his autobiography.

"[W]here people were concerned, I had nearly everything yet to learn," he says.

"I began to go to school to Cecil," he says, in the passage quoted and parsed above. And so did I. I almost felt I didn't have a choice. It was as if Wright was baiting me, egging and begging me, to go find Cecil. The story I found, even if I could find only fractions of it, edges and pieces, was one rich for its own sake. But that isn't why it's being told here. It's being told for what it reveals about the Rubik's Cube named Frank Lloyd Wright. Which insofar as Cecil is concerned is something all to the good.

————

Is it a version of the Salieri and Mozart story? Yes and no, even if the Salieri-Mozart story is a largely misunderstood myth, thanks to that wholly seductive 1984 movie *Amadeus*. You remember its theme: mediocrity in the face of genius, with the envy-mad Salieri ending up in an asylum because of a prodigy's effortless musical gifts. That part isn't the Frank and Cecil story at all.

Arc of a life, snapshot of a life, some facts large and small in a life:

He lived from the eve of the Civil War to the eve of Pearl Harbor. He died a month shy of eighty-one, fairly broke (in several senses of the word) in an upstairs room at his kid sister's home in Buffalo. His death notice in the local paper went to five lines of tiny type and didn't mention he'd been an architect for six decades—at least in name. He

---

* More about this in the endnotes. The reader should be aware that specific citations for this book, as well as some background and/or anecdotal material that couldn't fit into the main text, can be found there, in the Essay on Sources.

was gifted at lettering and freehand drawing. He was devoted to nieces and nephews. He dressed impeccably. In middle life, he had a mustache that went straw-white and that he kept thick as a shaving brush. (He was also handsomely bald by then and filled-out a little, but still trim.) He was born in Hawaii (on February 26, 1860), in what was then better known as the Sandwich Islands. He attended three Midwest colleges and graduated from none. At age fifty-six, in 1916, in the mountains of North Carolina, he got more or less abruptly married to an old and land-rich family friend from Racine, Wisconsin. (She was an author of middlebrow novels, seven years his senior.) The marriage seems to have been made out of compassion and a mutual desire for companionship and maybe also a small opportunism on Cecil's part, no matter (or even) that he continued living in New York City for most of the marriage with another man, an artist named Howard White McLean, who seems eventually to have dumped him for someone younger, a theater person. He was the sibling of overachievers: a partner in a noted Manhattan law firm; a muralist and painter who taught at the Art Institute of Chicago and was on the staff of the Field Museum of Natural History and who'd once occupied a studio with Whistler in London; a specialist in laryngology and pulmonary diseases who was widely celebrated for his poetry. (There were seven children in the Corwin family, and Cecil was in the middle.) So even within his own family there must have been the constant burden of comparison and competition, and perhaps the more so for someone who seems always to have been, as was noted above, only semi-open in his gayness, if gayness is what it truly was, for I'll acknowledge here that I have no hard proof of it, only my instincts, and a fair amount of circumstantial evidence (from various kinds of documents), and the hedging belief of several of Cecil's relatives many times removed, and, not least, what Wright himself seems to be signaling to us from the page, however protectively. (As for the semi-openness: probably ninety-nine percent of America's gay men and women living in the late nineteenth and early twentieth centuries had no choice but to be closeted, or mostly closeted.) You can go around Chicago, the North Side, the South Side, and some neighborhoods in between, and find sturdy and handsome Cecil Corwin houses—not so many, but they're there, their own legacy and witness. Most of the occupants—or the ones who've let me in off the sidewalk for a quick look around—have no clue as to who he was, much less any knowledge of his once-intimate connection to Frank Lloyd Wright. He was seven years and three months older than Wright, but in another way he was older by several light-years. And not least must Cecil S. Corwin—who liked to sign his name that way—have seemed so on that day in the Lakeside Building when the hungry boy in the toothpick shoes and with semi-shaggy hair and the sheaf of drawings under his arm showed up without an appointment at Old Man Silsbee's and won a tracing job, with some crucial midwifery by the firm's head draftsman, at a wage of eight bucks a week.

(And just to reprise: When was this? Impossible to know for certain, but the wager here is that a general offer of a job, helped along by Uncle Jenk's influence, whether active or passive, was made in the last week of August or in the first part of September 1886, when a ballet was playing at the city's main opera house, and as Uncle Jenk's new church was finishing up. But the actual work didn't begin until some four months later, after the turn of the year, or even before the turn, when the UW dropout showed up back in Chicago a bit earlier than expected. And asked for the job again. And got it. And found his desk. And began to draw—or trace.)

That supposed Saturday noonday: Cecil comes through the gate in the outer office railing. He's humming several bars of Handel's *Messiah*. Right off the applicant recognizes them. Right off: something artistic and musical and kindred. The instant attraction seems mutual: as Cecil comes, he calls out a hearty hello—"as though he knew me." How can that be?

Nervous small talk is breaking out. Cecil sits down beside Wright, and it's then that Wright first notices the sleeve-rolled arms with their coarse and thick and black hair—but offset, as it were, by the "daintily" bent pinkie as Cecil takes up his pencil.

They discover they're both the children of clergymen. Cecil has just intuited this, and it fairly astonishes Wright. How did he know? Oh, just something about your manner, Cecil allows. He nods his head toward the Old Man's office behind him and says that Silsbee is one, too: son of a minister. In fact, so are two others in the office—if Wright should get to "come in here, there would be five of us." More laughter, a stammer: "Well . . . could I by any chance come in?" To which Cecil proceeds to look him over, and to suggest that, yes, he believes they could possibly get along, yes, and "Let me see your drawings." Almost sounds like a line from Mae West.

The chief draftsman is up from his chair. He disappears with the work behind the "Private" door. And then Cecil and the Old Man emerge, although the Old Man only hangs in the doorway with something like disdain on his face, and then comes the offer, and then, just as abruptly, the shutting of the door. As Wright puts it a couple pages later: "Isn't the opening to 'the way' usually as simple?"

Cecil, sensing the disappointment about the amount of the offer, insists on taking the boy to lunch. "Come with me." Out the door, down to the first floor, across the street, and over into the middle of the next block to Kinsley's: one of Chicago's kitschiest-cum-beautiful eating joints, five stories tall, many dining rooms, done up in vaguely Moorish style, reputed to be patterned after the famous Alhambra at Granada. Nothing will do, says Cecil, but that you have black coffee and Kinsley's famous corned-beef-hash. From *An Autobiography*: "And ever since, when feeling hungry, nothing has tasted so good to me as browned corned-beef-hash." (The recipe was so celebrated that it got write-ups in local papers and eventually made its way into the archives of the Chicago History Museum. The key ingredient, apparently, was the three drops of Tabasco sauce.)

On the black coffee, though: Uh, no, thank you, don't drink it, he says.

From *An Autobiography*: " 'Well then,'—amused—'milk?' " It's as if Cecil, subtly, charmingly, knowingly, is working his age cards, his worldly cards.

He wants to know if Wright has any money left? Oh, for sure. How much? Uh, well, maybe twenty cents. Mmm, had anything to eat since yesterday? From *An Autobiography*: "This was getting rather too personal so I didn't answer." Cecil answers for him, with the line that was quoted above: "Come home with me tonight and we'll concertize with my new grand-piano."

He does, they do. Wright reports that he got his bag from the Briggs House and they went to Cecil's place (they doubtless took a streetcar), where Cecil lived with his widowed ministerial father and younger sister, Marquita, who looked after them all—but this isn't so. It's only a misremembering. Cecil's father, Reverend Eli Corwin, an itinerant pastor and missionary, who for four decades had been serving Presbyterian and Congregational flocks from upstate New York to California to Hawaii to downstate Illinois, was, at this moment, still the minister of First Presbyterian in Racine, Wisconsin—about an hour-and-a-half train ride north of Chicago. And Reverend Eli's wife, Henrietta, was still much alive and living with him in the parish house, along with a grandchild and their youngest daughter and last child, Marquita. The fact that Wright misremembered must only have been a homesick boy indulging in some wishful thinking—or, more accurately said, a late-middle-aged autobiographer incorrectly recalling how he'd sat around with Cecil's big happy family, concertizing in the parlor. In the coming years, Wright would come to know members of Cecil's family quite well, just as Cecil would come to know Wright's immediate family—his mother and two sisters. By then both families would be living in the Chicago area. But on that first night Cecil took him home, they had to have gone, according to what old city directories and other Chicago public documents reveal, to 256 Ashland Avenue, about two miles straight west of downtown. For several years Cecil and several siblings had been boarding in this row house owned by an extended family member on his mother's side named Francis S. Collins, soon to retire as a Chicago butcher. Collins had his own family, so a full house.

After the music Cecil leads him upstairs to a spare room. Cecil, seeming to wish to linger, and also gauging the homesickness, produces a sheet of stationery and an envelope and pen and ink. Wright, grateful for such tacit understanding, asks if he might borrow ten dollars to send to his mother with the letter. He promises he'll start paying it back two dollars at a time for the next month.

From *An Autobiography:* "He said nothing, took a ten dollar bill from his pocket and laid it on the table." There's an odd ring to this sentence. Almost as if some kind of sexual transaction has been made. Perhaps it's the "said nothing" and the placing of the bill on the table rather than handing it to Wright. Yes, the awkwardness of lending money to a newfound friend: but still. An undertone. Whether intentionally placed there or not.

The letter done, the two go straight to the nearest postal box. Who cares if it'll sit there in the overnight? This friendship is already more than made.

Next day: They decide, after the Sunday noon meal at home, to go down to the South Side, to the corner of Oakwood and Langley, where Uncle Jenk's church is all but completed. Cecil, it turns out, is the one at the firm personally charged by the Old Man to look after the construction of All Souls. They're down there, and Wright is on an opposite corner, wanting to view the building in full, while Cecil is tending to something or other, and, suddenly, from behind, this fairly rude grasping of the boy's collar.

Uncle Jenk! Anna Wright's brother reproves the boy: his mother has been worrying her head off about him, doesn't he know? He'll wire her that he's been found and is okay. But it *is* okay, Uncle, Wright says, I am okay, truly. Already have a job, and even wrote to her last night and sent money.

A job? Where could you have gotten a job this fast?

Why, at Silsbee's, he says.

From *An Autobiography:* " 'Silsbee's? Of course. That was mighty good of him. Told him who you were I suppose?' "

Oh, absolutely not.

Uncle Jenk informs his nephew he'll be coming to the church parsonage with him tonight—" 'where I can keep an eye on you.' "

Cecil has just walked up.

To repeat a line quoted above, but now with its context: " 'No!' said Cecil, 'he's going to stay with me tonight.' " (He's in "astonishment" to find that the two are related.)

If Wright is inventing and embroidering the "facts" of his history, he is also, as said before, relating larger truths. I am willing to believe that actual remembered lines here had lived for decades in his inner ear like little novels. And that he was willing to give himself away in more ways than he knew.

———

Cecil Corwin comes in and out of *An Autobiography* for sixty additional pages. And then, on the bottom of page 128, following a pent-up confession about the worth of his own architecture (meaning its *non*-worth), he's gone, he has disappeared, with this haunting final sentence from the author: "Cecil went East and, God knows why—never have I seen him since."

In these sixty-one pages, Wright is telling the first ten years of his Chicago life, although he isn't worried about chronology (or accuracy). He jumps far ahead, circles back, trombones his narrative in and out. So many things, personal and professional, streamed in on Wright in the period from 1886 to 1896. But here are the essentials of what you need to know, before Cecil's story can go on:

- Wright had worked at Silsbee's for something like a year—before quitting to join another architect, W. W. Clay, who had offices on Dearborn Street. (The quitting had been over money. Silsbee had elevated him to a draftsman pretty quickly, but he had wanted more than he was making, and pride was at the bottom of it.) He had come back to Silsbee's after a short while, with his hat not quite in his hand, but contrite all the same. Silsbee had listened and then called out into the other room: "Corwin!" We're taking Wright back, he said, and, oh, yes, we're boosting him to $18 a week. The re-hiree had shut the sanctum door as he'd come out, and then he and Cecil—who'd never really been apart, even in the apartness—had gone tilting around the main room in their impromptu polka. In those eight or nine or ten months at Silsbee's, which architectural historians have probably undervalued, Wright had learned a great deal about flow, and Cecil had been the facilitator of technical aspects of the learning. After work they'd go to music and art and whatever cozy-cornered or noisy restaurant struck their fancy. The music was best. "Loving concerts," Wright calls them. The talk had so often been about the work. From *An Autobiography,* and this is Cecil speaking: "'But *whom* are you going to build homes for? If you go against their wishes and try to give them what *you* think right and not what they think they want?'"
- He (Wright) had met and started courting the barely sixteen-year-old high school girl who, in the early summer of 1889 (so roughly two and a half years after he had arrived in Chicago), became his (barely) eighteen-year-old spouse. Her name was

Catherine Tobin. Everybody called her Kitty. She and her family
lived in a handsome South Side neighborhood called Kenwood.
Wright had met her—it seems to have been somewhere in those
first six or seven or eight months—at a study–cum–social club
at his uncle's church. It was at a costume party dance celebrating
the end of the Novel Club's reading of Hugo's *Les Misérables*. He
had run her over by accident on the dance floor, had knocked her
down. Cecil had helped him prepare his absurd costume. (A saber
that kept getting in the way as he tried to walk.) Kitty Tobin had
blue eyes and ruddy curls and was about the same height he was.
She could affect tam-o'-shanters and plaid walking jackets and a
sweetly bossy little manner, as if she were an only child. (She was
the eldest of four children.) At the wedding, performed by Uncle
Jenk, Wright's mother had theatrically fainted and Kitty's father
had copiously cried. Anna Wright, fierce infighter that she was,
having long made her son the center of her universe, had tried
hard to stop the courtship, never mind the marriage itself; had
come temporarily down to the Chicago area from Wisconsin
with one daughter, once she'd gotten wind of such ridiculous
(and threatening) puppy love; had enlisted Cecil's secret help
against it; and, when none of this worked, had relocated with
both of her daughters to Oak Park, first suburb due west of the
city, eight miles from the Chicago River. Oak Park's leafiness and
churchgoing ways ("Saints' Rest," it would come to call itself,
for its banishment of saloons and for its everywhere houses of
God, sometimes several on the same block) had reminded Anna
a bit of Madison, and also it was just far enough away from the
wicked city. Anna had gotten her son to leave the South Side
and come out to Oak Park to live with her—again it had been
a bid to stop the romance, which hadn't stopped. Oak Park is
where the eventual newlyweds would build the first edition of
their first home, a small, gabled, and shingle-style house (with
Mother Wright and her girls living right next door, same lot, in
a white clapboard). Cecil is said to have liked Kitty fairly much
from the beginning, even as he had understood she was just a
child, even as he had understood Wright was all but an emotional
child himself, even as he must have been harboring so many

ambiguous personal feelings. Kitty used to come to pick up her
boyfriend at the office. One day after work, when things were
pretty far along, Frank had said: "She's awfully fond of me, Cecil."
From *An Autobiography:* " 'Well,' he said, 'so am I.' " And then,
as if quickly to recover: "So is your mother. So are your sisters."
Cecil had asked if he had so much as ever kissed another girl. But
how do you know I've kissed Kitty, Wright had answered. From
An Autobiography: " 'I'm clairvoyant,' he said, 'didn't you know?' "
You can practically hear the hurt and peevishness radiating
off the page. Toward the end of this exchange, during which
Wright discovers that Cecil and his mother have been conspiring
against him, Wright has Cecil saying, "Well, let's not quarrel."
Earlier, Wright more or less turns to the reader and says of Cecil,
disingenuously: "He himself knew few girls. They were much
older than I. Uninteresting, I thought. He was such an attractive
person I often wondered why he didn't know more interesting
ones." He knows exactly why. At any rate, against all seeming
collected wills on two sides of a family, except for the wills of
the two principals, the marriage had happened (on June 1, 1889,
with a pouring rain outside), seven days before Wright turned
twenty-two. Wright doesn't tell us whether Cecil had attended
the wedding, but doubtless he did. After the wedding, and after
the move into their new home (early months of 1890), Wright
and his wife had apparently been thought by more temperate
Oak Parkers to be breeding offspring in almost heedless fashion:
three of their eventual six children would arrive in the first four
and a half years of their marriage. (Kitty had become pregnant
within a month of the wedding.) There had never been enough
money in these years (or any years, really), and the spendthrift
head of the house had been determined to keep living high above
his means: dandy clothing, subscription tickets to the opera and
symphony, Oriental rugs, books, Japanese prints, state-of-the-art
camera, and, not least, a horse he would saddle up and canter out
onto the open prairie beyond the Des Plaines River, in his girly,
balloonish riding breeches. There is a famously quoted Wright
line from *An Autobiography:* "So long as we had the luxuries, the
necessities could pretty well take care of themselves." Who cared

if poor Mr. Gotsch, the village grocer, had had to come round begging for payment on his months-past-due $850 bill? Actually, the luxuries/necessities crack, not to say such a cracked way of thinking, has everything to do with the next (and last) bullet point here, and indeed everything to do with Cecil himself, in a kind of "bearding" role.

- In either the final months of 1887 or the early part of 1888, Wright had gone to work at the firm of Adler & Sullivan, and specifically gone to work for his *lieber meister* ("beloved master"), the great, gifted, prideful, riddle-filled, and ultimately tragic Louis Sullivan. Louis Sullivan, so-called father of the American skyscraper. Louis Sullivan, promulgator (if maybe not precise originator) of one of the most famous phrases in all of modernism: "form follows function." Louis Sullivan, who probably has never had an equal in America in the art of the exquisitely drawn geometric ornament. Louis Sullivan, with his huge brown eyes and small athletic stature and that passive-aggressive habit of coming up behind his draftsmen and scratching his flaky scalp with the sharpened point of his lead pencil. (When his dandruff fell on their work, he'd lean down and blow it off.) If Frank Lloyd Wright is the greatest American architect, then his Boston-born mentor, Louis Henry Sullivan (who, it is often forgotten, was only eleven years his senior), cannot be far behind him—perhaps in the top three or four architects of our history. Wright had gone over to A&S, whose offices were then on the top floor of what was called the Borden Block, at a wage of twenty-five dollars a week. He'd been hired for a specific job, not necessarily for permanent employment—although he'd ended up staying until 1893. The specific job was to help complete interior drawings on what was then the largest piece of architecture in Chicago civic history: the Auditorium Building. It was being put up on a prime site at Congress Street and Michigan Avenue, and construction had started in the summer of 1887. It was a multi-use, monumental mega-structure: 4,200-seat auditorium, 400-room hotel, and 136 business offices. No matter how badly he had wished for a spot at A&S, and a chance to work on the Auditorium, Wright had nonetheless worried about Cecil and himself. From *An*

Autobiography: "Then I thought of Cecil. It would mean leaving his daily companionship." But Cecil had urged him to go ahead and try, and that "we won't get lost." On his first day at his new drawing board, he'd had "a notion to call up Cecil to say 'hello' and hear his voice. But did not." In no time he'd become "a good pencil in the Master's hand," to the envy—better to say hatred—of many of his co-workers. He'd earned one promotion, and then another, and then, by mid-1890—which is to say roughly a year after his marriage to Kitty Tobin, and soon after the move into the newly built Oak Park home, and maybe a year and three-quarters after he had begun at the firm—there he was, Frank Wright (the middle name still not in any kind of permanent use), supervising the entire drawing staff at A&S, something like two dozen draftsmen and delineators and tracers. Sullivan had moved him into a semi-private office right next to his own. The firm, by now one of the most noticed in the country, at the peak of its (relatively short-lived) history, had relocated to the top two floors of the Tower atop the Auditorium, so Wright had one of the best views in the whole city. But one crucial thing to note here, and this is where Cecil is directly connected: in the late spring of 1889, not long before his wedding, Wright had gone to Sullivan and declared his intention to get married. Could the firm guarantee him greater job security? Sullivan had listened and then had called for Dankmar Adler, who was the senior partner and the engineering genius of the firm who'd helped make the auditorium portion of the Auditorium, with its ornate and elliptical ceiling arches, into such an acoustic wonder for performance. Not wanting to lose the star pencil, and especially Sullivan not wanting to lose him, the partners had proposed a five-year contract worth $5,000, which, according to Adler, would make Wright the highest-paid draftsman in the city. But Wright, typically, had had a different money idea: If they wished him to work for the firm for at least another five years, could they not pay him the agreed-upon salary, but also loan him an additional $5,000 right away, so that he might build his own home in Oak Park? Could not weekly deductions be taken from his paycheck until the note had been

satisfied? The partners had agreed. Now there was enough money
for Wright and his mother to pool their funds and buy the large
tree-filled lot on the corner of Chicago Avenue and Forest
Avenue—and this Anna and her son had done, on May 5, 1889,
three and a half weeks before the wedding. Sullivan had gone out
to Oak Park with Wright and had walked the proposed building
site. And he had arranged for the loan from his own funds. He
would hold the deed. So there'd been much personally at stake,
and, really, it had pretty much been this way from the start. A
contract had been drawn up, and one of the conditions to the
agreement (it seems not to have been written down but implicitly
understood) had been that Wright would do no moonlighting on
his own residential commissions, a practice then common among
young architects on the Chicago rise. Wright's honor had held for
about a year and a half. But the reckless spending habits, not to
say the arrival of children in stair-step order, had caught up. He'd
needed more money. Thus Wright had begun drawing and then
building on the nighttime sly what we know today as his famous
"bootlegged houses," as he later termed them. Between 1891 and
1893, more than half a dozen of his "boots," each with its
modernist effect and his distinct experimental stamp, even if cast
in more or less traditional architectural styles, had begun to
appear in and around Chicago, not least on the South Side. Several
of these boots were within blocks of where Louis Sullivan was
living. And where does Cecil fit into this? The South Side bootlegs
had been announced in the various building trade publications—
and in some of the regular Chicago newspapers, too—as the
projects not of Frank L. Wright but of Cecil S. Corwin. So Cecil
had been the supposed architect of record, Wright's beard and
credible cover. Had Cecil's best friend importuned him? Had he
exploited what he might have perceived as a certain emotional
vulnerability? Had he paid him a fee? Had Cecil agreed to lend his
name out of a combination of love and friendship and need—or
did he need no persuading at all? Perhaps parts of all of these
possibilities obtain. It has been wrongly reported by historians
and Wright biographers that Cecil, too, had been working for

Adler & Sullivan, which would have made the betrayal that much worse once Sullivan discovered it. It's not so. In the late summer or early fall of 1889, Cecil had left his job as Silsbee's chief draftsman to enter into a loose partnership with another rising Chicago architect named George W. Maher; the two ran a successful practice out of room 925 at 218 LaSalle Street. The story of Wright and Sullivan and Cecil and the bootlegs (and the boots will come up again, because they are formative houses) is far more complicated than what history imagined for a long while. Sullivan seems to have known about them for at least a year before the confrontation occurred. His so-called discovery of the boots seems to have been only the pretext for something deeper, and maybe some of it was this: A son was passing up the father, and the student had overtaken the teacher. In any event, a bitter fight broke out. A relationship of not quite six years shredded itself. From *An Autobiography:* "I threw my pencil down and walked out of the Adler and Sullivan office never to return." This was in early 1893. Years later, long after the master was dead, in a kind of public apology to Sullivan (who died in squalor in April 1924), Wright wrote of their blowup: "Swallowing my shame hard I went back to see him. I was astonished to hear him say, 'Wright your conduct has been so perfidious there is nothing I care to hear you say.' . . . I went home, my shame doubled. Although I often felt drawn to him in following years, I never went near him after that. It was nearly twenty years before I saw him again." If Wright's arithmetic is off, his emotions aren't. And that word again: "shame." Doubled down.

————

Cecil and Frank were soon back together. Sometime in the first half of 1893, Wright leased offices at the top of the magnificent Schiller Building on Randolph—designed by Adler & Sullivan and worked on by Wright himself. (Is it easy to read some of the not-so-secret shame just in this? From *An Autobiography:* "Accustomed to the view from a high place and feeling nearer Adler and Sullivan by being there, I suppose, I wanted that space.") They yanked out the door panels and put in a clear plate of glass and had a sign-maker stack their names one atop the other in gold leaf: *Frank Lloyd Wright, Architect. Cecil Corwin, Architect.* From *An Autobiography:* "You notice the order? By seniority Cecil should have been first but he wouldn't have it so." They weren't partners, but they were sharing office space and ideas, each with a drafting room, and common reception room, close again on a daily basis, just like the old days, not even seven years before. Much in the world, not to say in the world of building, had changed.

There is a specific date—symbolic, metaphorical, and, in another way, almost literally exact in its historic significance—that could be said to represent a kind of hidden symmetrical moment when the fortunes of two men, who cared for each other deeply and in complex ways, began to go irreversibly in opposite directions. The date is April 15, 1894. For a year, Frank and Cecil have been officemates in suite 1501 in the Schiller, helping out each other, scrabbling for their separate commissions. Wright is almost twenty-seven, Cecil's age when they'd met. The now independent architect is the father of three, including an infant born three months and three days ago. (Her name is Catherine Dorothy Wright, and she will grow up to marry a man named Kenneth Baxter, and one of her children will become a Hollywood star named Anne Baxter.) Wright's wife, Kitty, social matron of Oak Park, is starting to fill out in matronly ways. Cecil? He turned thirty-four about six weeks ago. He lives in the city, at 1066 Warren Avenue, in a row house he designed and that's been paid for with his own money and that of his family. His father, the Reverend Eli, having left First Presbyterian in Racine, lives there, along with Cecil's mother, Henrietta, and several of Cecil's siblings. It must not be easy for a thirty-four-year-old unmarried son, never mind one with secret yearnings, to be still living at home— a pious home, in fact.

April 15, 1894, is the day an eight-line notice appears on page 29, in the Sunday real estate section, column six, small type, three items up from the bottom, of a Chicago newspaper called the *Inter Ocean.*

Cecil S. Corwin has designed for H. G. Mitchell and construction is under way for a two-story, attic and basement residence at Racine. It will be in the colonial style of architecture with gambrel roof. The first story will be constructed of broken ashlar stone. The interior will be finished in hard wood and will be heated by hot water. It will cost $12,000.

This is the greatest house Cecil Corwin will ever design—and the fact that it is being announced "today" to the general reading public in a general-interest newspaper is the symbolic and metaphorical part of the hidden historic symmetry. The notice is correct in its description: the style of the house is Colonial Revival with a hint of Romanesque. The house is there today at 905 Main Street in Racine, still lived in, occupied by one family, beautifully preserved, sandstone in color, just solid as hell, more than 120 years old, two blocks in from Lake Michigan, having survived who-knows-how-many fierce wintry gales and just-as-fierce summer lightning storms, with a carriage house and one-time stable out back (they're like houses unto themselves), with art-glass windows and a semicircular porch off the front that takes in your eye in its understated classicism that's marked by five white columns. The gambrel roof also takes in your eye. (A gambrel roof is a roof with two sides, each of which has a shallower slope above a steeper one.) Inside there's a remarkable twisting-back-on-itself staircase, off the reception room, lined with 159 spindles carved from high-grade Santo Domingo mahogany. Any kind of mahogany will gleam when it's polished, but the Santo Domingo variety seems lit from within. Twelve decades after the carpenters fitted the delicate spindles in, the grain of the wood can fairly astonish, and likewise the same gleaming Santo Domingo trim in the various and airy downstairs rooms, with an intricate beading effect set into the board-and-batten walls. A description of this house could go on, but you get the point.

Cecil drew it in early 1894 and oversaw construction in the spring and summer of that year for Henry and Lily Mitchell, who were members of one of Racine's wealthier families in a turn-of-the-century town wealthy due to all of its manufacturing. The Mitchells were members of Reverend Corwin's church, which was two blocks up and two blocks over, at Seventh and College. So, in all probability, it was the church connection that had helped Cecil secure the commission. Indeed, the Mitchell House, as it is still known by Midwest architecture buffs, stands about 150 yards south, on the same street, from the spot where Reverend Corwin had lived with his family in the 1880s. That was the parish house. (It is gone now.) The address was 810 Main. Cecil had lived with his parents and some of his siblings in the parsonage in parts of 1881 and 1882, while he was a college student. It's easy to imagine the Mitchell and Corwin families, neighbors and friends, picnicking out on the lakefront on weekends.

And not quite a decade and a half later, having become a moderately successful Chicago architect in his own practice, having served as draftsman and then head draftsman for J. Lyman Silsbee, having been in semi-partnership with the respected George W. Maher, and then working out of the Schiller Building in loose association with his best pal Frank Wright, the middle child in this family had achieved—or, more accurately, was in the process of achieving, as of the date of a public announcement in the real estate section of the *Sunday Inter Ocean*—his one small certifiable masterpiece. Call it the Last Fine Building Moment of Cecil S. Corwin. As of the spring of 1894, with construction on the Mitchell about to start, Cecil had not quite another five decades to live, and his trajectory from there, or here, would be more or less steadily downward.

Before delineating the other half of the hidden symmetry, it has to be noted that there was a period, about two decades ago (as this is being written), when several Wright historians were trying to make the case that the Mitchell isn't Cecil's house at all. *He wasn't up to it. It is too fine a building. His imagination couldn't have conceived of something like this.* This handful of historians had begun to claim it was really Wright's house, another bootleg, in effect. But that argument has been generally cast aside, and the consensus among the scholars seems to be that, yes, it was and is Cecil's house, Cecil's commission, if with some significant design input and attention to detail by Cecil's officemate and best friend. There are no surviving signed drawings with Cecil's name on them that would put the argument to rest for good. But it's important to note that the Frank Lloyd Wright Foundation in Scottsdale—which has the last word on the certification of all Wright projects—has never recognized the Mitchell as a Wright house.

But as a matter of fact: Why wouldn't Cecil's officemate have leaned over a drawing board in the Schiller Building and offered suggestions to help turn his friend's largest hometown commission into a small marvel? Wouldn't that be his decent side rising again? It's unarguable that design elements of the Mitchell have counterparts in some of the actual bootleg houses and in two other houses Wright worked on for Adler & Sullivan during regular business hours.

Here's the other side of the hidden equation and the sad symmetry: At almost the precise moment—that is, in the early months of 1894— when Cecil, in the Schiller, would have been working up the presentation and final drawings on the Mitchell, Frank Lloyd Wright, in the Schiller, would have been doing the same thing on not just his first realized commission as an independent architect but on what turned out to be a world-class house that was going to take him forward to all the houses of the next five and six and seven years, not to say to all the work in the decades beyond. Its name, which any Wright student knows, is the William H. Winslow House. Like Cecil's house, it's there today, in River Forest, Illinois, one town over from Oak Park, in all its horizontal-cum-vertical orange-and-cocoa classical beauty. It's stunning to approach it for the first time, as opposed to seeing it in a photograph. It's a St. John the Baptist house: a precursor to an art that would soon overtake the world yet it stands so grand in its own right. Indeed, once you've experienced the Winslow, have come off the sidewalk and made the almost imperceptibly rising approach toward its wide wooden front door with its decorated stone frame and foliate panel, you almost can't go back to look at the Mitchell. (On page 96 there's a photograph of the Winslow House, so you can glimpse some of its power on your own.)

If the Mitchell was a cresting moment, the Winslow was a blossoming moment—but who could have understood it that way then?

Time went on. Two best-friend architects in a city of hundreds of architects kept up their figurative dance around a big table in the center of the room, even as they seemed to be slowly starting to go their own ways. From *An Autobiography:* "I did not see so much of him now for I was intensely busy, and meantime he had found some new intimates." Then one day—it seems to have been in the fall of 1896—Cecil came into the office. They sat talking. He'd been working on new additions to Rush Medical College—it must have been bringing in decent money. But he was visibly dejected. His pal asked him what was the matter.

From *An Autobiography:* " 'Not much, in general, Frank, except, in particular, I don't believe I'm an architect, that's all.' " Wright: But what's wrong with the stuff you're doing for Rush? From *An Autobiography:* " 'You know. Why ask me?' " Wright: But it's good work. From *An Autobiography:* " 'Is it architecture?' he said quietly."

Several lines down: " 'I've found there's no joy in architecture for me except as I see you do it. It bores me when I try to do it myself. There's the truth for you. You *are* the thing you do. I'm not and I never will be. And worse than all I'm not sure any longer, lately, that I want to be.' "

Several lines down, the author: "I had lost sight of him. He had been lagging behind. Dear old Cecil."

Several lines down, Cecil: " 'I'm going East, Frank.' "

Several lines down, the author: "This was unbelievable. I reproached Cecil because I had an uneasy sense of having betrayed him and so— inclined to blame *him.*"

Several lines down, Cecil: " 'I might as well make a clean breast of it, Frank. I don't want to go on seeing you do the things I can't do.' "

Several lines down, the author: "It flashed through my mind that I was right, this abnegation on his part was genuine discouragement due to my own neglect—and felt ashamed of myself. Why not take him in with me. But that was not what this meant. And I knew he wouldn't come."

Several lines down, Cecil: " 'You do need me for a friend, and I'll always be one. You are going to go far. You'll have a kind of success; I believe the kind you want. Not everybody would pay the price in concentrated hard work and human sacrifice you'll make for it though my boy. I'm afraid—for what will be coming to you,['] he added."

Several lines down, the author: "Cecil was something of a prophet."

And then that last sad Cecil sentence in the book, the one quoted earlier: "Cecil went East and, God knows why—never have I seen him since."

———

After. It's a forty-seven-year history. I'll tell it in telescope. In a sense that's all that could ever be done anyway, for what you mostly get (or I could get), as earlier said, are glimpses, fractions, edges, and pieces of a life. Cecil's there, findable—even though he feels like a shadow inside an echo. You get a sense of a man straining for his dignity, and trying in his way to be generous and kind. Most times.

It turns out he didn't leave the profession. An architect does his architecting, or seeks to.

Here he is, one day in early August of 1899 (about three years after he's left Chicago), writing in handsome penmanship to two close Racine family friends, Herbert and Flora Miles. It's about an addition they want to do on their home on Washington Avenue. (They've just had a child and among other things need a nursery.) Again, there's a family-church connection. It's a four-page letter, along with an exterior sketch and floor plans. "You doubtless have been looking for my obituary which might have been a reality so far as possibilities might have rendered it. The toils of a summer cold have circled me and if my supply of lungs hold out till I am rid of this cough all right. If not good bye Cecil. But let us not anticipate." The letter goes on, with the same sense of formality and self-deprecation and soft wit. He hopes they'll choose him for their architect, but if not, fine. He wishes to get out to Racine, possibly in the fall. "I am anxious to see that child and chiefly your own good selves." He signs it, "I am most sincerely, Cecil S. Corwin."

He didn't get the job. The Mileses decided not to do anything just then. And a footnote: Two years later, Wright himself drew up a set of plans to remodel the Miles home. Apparently they'd contacted him in Chicago. But they ended up not going with his suggestion, either. Did Wright know about Cecil's earlier presentation sketch? That sketch, which is in an archive at Northwestern University, is a beautiful rendering of the house, and it's also, it has to be said, pretty ordinary in its architectural ideas.

A March 30, 1901, story in *The New York Times:* Grant Brothers Stockbrokerage on Broadway has gone bankrupt, leaving many unsecured creditors in its wake, among whom is Cecil S. Corwin, who has lost $9,600. Is this practically his entire stake? (It would have represented more than $250,000 in today's money.) Not two months later, his name is in the legal print of a Manhattan publication called *The Real Estate Record and Guide.* He's trying to collect a judgment of $1,246. (A balking client?)

Monday, April 7, 1902, column two, a four-paragraph story in *The*

New York Times under the headline: CONFIDENCE VICTIM HIS OWN DETECTIVE. (This would be almost exactly a year after the loss of his money in the collapse of Grant Brothers.) The story is about a man named James A. Donovan, a businessman from South Framingham, Massachusetts, who'd come to town to see the sights and to have an innocent good time. Instead he claimed "he had been flim-flammed out of $75 by Cecil S. Corwin, who told the police that he was a masseur from Honolulu." The flimflammery involved the defendant allegedly taking the out-of-towner to a back room of a saloon in Greenwich Village called J.J. Kelly's. The story made three New York dailies—in fact, it got onto the front page of *The Morning Telegraph* with a two-column headline and a story going all the way down the right side of the page. It made two publications in Boston, including *The Boston Daily Globe*. The stories contradict themselves in the finer points, but the general narrative is the same, and the more you compare the accounts, the more it begins to sound like the plaintiff was a possibly closeted gay man who'd come to the city to seek out its sexual underworld. He'd booked a room in a midtown hotel, had gotten picked up on a bench in Madison Square Park at Saturday midday. The defendant had allegedly told him that he, too, was an out-of-towner and so why not spend the day together? By evening, having been joined by another party or two, they'd all drifted down to the Village, to the corner of Hudson Street and Perry Street. Part of the bunco had to do with making bets about who had the most money in his pocket. The language in several of the stories seems almost comically freighted, as if the scribes were having their own kind of homophobic sport: "His two companions, after a time, pulled out rolls of bills, and made bets as to who had the bigger roll. Donovan, not to be outdone, pulled out his $75. Just then a waiter ran up and cried out, 'No gambling here!' There was a scuffle, and when Donovan finally emerged from a pile of tables and chairs, his two friends, the waiter, and his $75 had all disappeared."

I tried to find out if J.J. Kelly's Saloon (the five-story brick building is still there) was a known gay bar at the turn of the century. The hedging answer from several Village historians was that it probably was not an exclusively gay bar—which wouldn't disallow for illicit things to have gone on in back rooms. Most of the Village gay bars were down on Bleecker Street, eight or ten blocks away. That's where the most notorious of them all, the Slide, had been located, before the fathers of probity had shut it down in 1892.

And what was the upshot? Cecil got locked up and put in a cell in the Tenderloin. His name's there in the massive Second District Magistrate's Court Docket Book. The charge was felonious larceny. His age was listed as forty. (He was forty-two.) But the lower courts of that era have retained only their docket books, not the proceedings. According to the "disposition of case," entered by hand, the defendant was held for three nights and two days and then released. When I queried a New York City municipal archivist on this, he said it seemed odd, considering the charge that had been made, that he would have been just set free. The archivist guessed that possibly there had been some benevolent intervention. Could that have come from Cecil's brother, eldest in the family, John Howard Corwin, almost eight years Cecil's senior, partner in a sizable Manhattan law firm with a house in Yonkers? No way to know, but it doesn't take a lot of imagination to wonder about the humiliation that Cecil must have felt.

And isn't there the possibility that it wasn't Cecil at all who was behind the fleecing? He insisted at the time he was a victim of mistaken identity. There was a twenty-four-hour gap between the swindle and his arrest, and supposedly by then he'd shaved off his beard. There isn't doubt that a "Cecil S. Corwin," born in Honolulu, was the person who got locked up—but was he the one who "masterminded" (as one paper had it) the saloon robbery? If he was, then it was possibly the lowest moment in a life, owed, at least in some measure, one would guess, to financial desperation. I've never found another New York misdemeanor or criminal court record with his name in it.

Edges and pieces: Starting along about 1908, Cecil's name begins to appear in various Manhattan general directories; he's usually listed as living on the Upper West Side. He puts down his profession as architect. But he is never listed in any of the city's business directories. Possibly this means he is trying to survive as a freelance, working from home, which seems in most cases to have been no more than a room. Possibly it means that he is working at a level below that of "architect" at one of the hundreds of New York City area architectural firms—which is to say at the level of draftsman, or even at a level below a draftsman. Thus, he wouldn't have needed or even wished to name himself in the business directories, and the firm where he might have been employed wouldn't have done so, either. There is an authoritative two-volume reference directory compiled by the Committee for the Preservation of Architectural Records. One volume is entitled *Architects in Practice New York City, 1840–1900,* and its companion is *Architects in Practice New York City, 1900–1940.* (The compilers claim to have researched every known business directory in the history of the city.) Cecil isn't listed. According to New York City historians, what this suggests is that he existed—it seems the proper word—at a level below the threshold of any kind of archival preservation of his work. Thousands of people in the New York building trades and designing arts would have been in similar circumstances. In not a single historical record having to do with building or architecture or real estate in New York City have I been able to find a single surviving Cecil Corwin architectural drawing. I have to believe in my ganglion such drawings exist. Maybe someone else will find one somewhere down the line.

Here he is in the 1910 federal census, at 223 West Eighty-Third Street, in what is described by the census taker as a two-person household, living with Howard W. McLean, who is roughly two decades younger. Cecil is listed as the head of the house, McLean as the lodger. Half a dozen other adults live in the building, so perhaps the two have their own modest space. McLean, from Virginia, is a painter of impressionist landscapes, Central Park scenes, and not a bad one at all.

Saturday, August 12, 1916, a small story in *The Charlotte Observer* beneath this headline: NOTED AUTHORESS WEDS ARCHITECT. The wedding was two days before, in the mountains, at a church in Asheville, North Carolina, with only immediate family of the sixty-three-year-old bride in attendance. Her name has just become Emma Payne Erskine Corwin, although her literary name will continue to be Emma Payne Erskine. A few years back she had a couple major commercial hits, including her romance novel, *The Mountain Girl.* (*Ladies' Home Journal* serialized it.) But her career is on the downslide. The fifty-six-year-old groom is Cecil S. Corwin of New York City, and there's little question his career is on the downslide. The basic track of the narrative: Emma and Cecil had known each other from the 1880s, in Racine. Once again, the connection is the church—Cecil's father's church. Their families had remained distant friends all this time. Decades before, Emma had married an executive of one of Racine's largest manufacturers—the J.I. Case Threshing Machine Company. She and her husband had raised six children. With their wealth they'd begun to steal away from the bitter Wisconsin winters, eventually establishing a home on the southern slope of the Blue Ridge, in Tryon, North Carolina. In 1908 Charles Erskine had died. Afterward, Emma, who was a painter as well as a writer, who had become a buxom woman with thick wrists and thick arms and a kind of mannish self-confidence, had grown increasingly lonely. She had kept at her work. In April 1916 (eight years after her husband died), there'd been a huge fire at the family's mountain estate, named Lyncotte. Much was lost. On a consoling trip to the Northeast—to Connecticut and to New York, to visit several of her grown children and their families—she ran into her dear old family friend from Racine, Cecil. Four months after the fire, the two were wed.

Contrary to what the world (and perhaps Cecil, too) might have believed, Emma Payne Erskine was land-rich, yes, but surprisingly cash-poor. Following her husband's death she had inherited all of their joint property, but the money got divided seven ways between herself and her children. Despite her iron will, Emma was wildly impractical when it came to business things. At the insistence of her children, a trust had been set up to help manage her affairs. Not long after Cecil came into the picture, the original trust was expiring, and, by 1918, two years into the marriage, there was much pressure among family members to get Emma to sign on to a renewal—which she did, to her everlasting sorrow and agitation. A banker and two trustees (who were her children) effectively held all the purse strings and doled out the cash crumb by crumb—at least in her view. This was complicated by the fact that, also in 1918, Emma suffered a stroke. Her mental faculties were only semi-impaired, but the emotional and physical anxieties were severe. She became a semi-invalid—and a major handful.

Cecil, who had lived in North Carolina with his wife on and off for the better part of those two years, seems to have been itching to get back to New York City. In some ways, he must have been itching to get away from "Nan," as the family called Emma, given how difficult things had become, financially and otherwise. Emma, despite her stroke, had many real estate schemes, and these schemes and dreams involved Cecil's architectural expertise. But none of it really panned out. Until she died (six years after her stroke), Emma kept trying to get the family trust voided. There are letters in which she is politely haranguing her grown children, knocking them in a ladylike murderous way on their damn traces.

One might think Cecil had been gold-digging in the first place when he married Emma. But a stack of letters (and other documents, too), saved by the Erskine family, argues for the idea that Cecil was proceeding far more honorably than others in similar circumstances might have done. Did he have mixed motives in the bargain? As was said earlier, in regard to his almost instant and long-ago bonding with a boy from the provinces off an evening Wisconsin train, it would seem naïve to think that he *didn't* have mixed motives. Was there romance there? There must have been some kind of romance. I wouldn't exclude the possibility of some kind of sexual relationship there either. When I went to North Carolina to meet extended members of the Erskine clan, I did so with half-dread, wondering if Cecil's name had passed down through the generations in an ugly way. It hadn't. One of the people who greatly helped was Emma's great-grandson, Andy Haynes. He is a respected attorney in Tryon. He's also the informal family historian.

"Here's what I know," he said. "Cecil was basically a good guy. He married a rich old lady, at least rich in land. He could have, if he wanted, mined that gold for all it was worth. I never knew him, of course—he was dead before I was born, and Emma too. I'm quite sure a lot of people wondered about it at first, wondered about him. He could have looked out for number one in all kinds of ways. He didn't. Even if they didn't really live together as husband and wife very long, maybe about two years, he and Emma were very fond of each other—the letters bear it out. And, listen, don't you think this tough old gal Emma would have greatly appealed to this fey, soft, artistic guy from New York—and vice versa? She's grateful every time he comes to visit. Basically, Cecil went back to New York and lived his life. And I think the family more or less understood."

Maybe the understanding on the part of Emma's family represented a kind of implicit quid pro quo: Emma's children felt Cecil wasn't fortune hunting, and in return they were willing to accept his eventual need to return to the life he had previously led—even as he remained kind and solicitous toward his wife (and their mother).

Andy Haynes knew about Cecil's connection to Wright, but he was surprised to learn how close they'd once been. "Wow," he said. "This boarhog guy Frank Lloyd Wright with the ego that won't stop stooped down so many years later to remember beautifully in his book this nonentity Cecil Corwin. So some decency there, too, eh?"

From a Cecil letter to one of Emma's children in July 1918: "Nan has had another of her painful attacks, but she has pulled through with her usual fortitude and resiliency, however I feel rather anxious that she should have no further recurrences of it, as it no [doubt] is brought about partially by a tense mental state." He's still in Carolina with her.

When Cecil returned to New York, more or less for good, he moved back in with his old housemate, Howard W. McLean. Maybe McLean had kept a place for him all along. It can't be said if Emma knew about McLean, or even knew about her husband's gayness—but wouldn't she have known about it in visceral ways? From a letter, dated March 13, 1920, from Emma to one of her children who lives in the East: "If Cecil has no telephone at 55 west 70th Street, can't you drop him a line? . . . I think just a line denoting interest would reach his sensitive and affectionate heart and do him good as he is very fond of you. It would please me also very much for he is sweet and dear to me." In 1920, Cecil and McLean, along with seven other roomers, are listed as living at 55 West Seventieth Street. Are the two wedged into one room?

One could take a harder view here: Cecil was acting selfishly (and hardly as a husband) in returning to New York, the more so when his wife needed care. But what the letters also suggest is he felt he had no real way of making a living in North Carolina.

A time or two, despite her infirmity, Emma traveled to New York to visit her children and Cecil. But she apparently didn't stay with Cecil. From an undated letter (probably written in 1920) to one of her children: "To be alone in New York in a hotel is to an elderly country woman rather an appalling thing. . . . I know I could call a taxi when I wished to go to you, or Cecil or Harold, but there is the expense to consider."

Emma died on March 4, 1924. It isn't clear if her husband was with her in her final illness, which lasted about a fortnight. She died without a will—or at least no will was ever filed in a Carolina probate court. The family trust remained intact. Two years before, when her finances were at their lowest point, she had sold her main property, Lyncotte, to one of her daughters, so that the once-baronial but now-ruinous estate could remain in the family. Her real estate holdings had once encompassed nearly seven hundred acres. In her last years, still painting, she lived in a Tryon cottage with a series of female attendants and companions. Very little of what remained of her estate had passed to Cecil. But he seems to have had little or no bitterness (or even interest) and stayed on affectionate terms with Emma's six children, who eventually drew up an agreement whereby Cecil was granted a small house and barn, known as Wayside, on about an acre of land, where he could live out his life, if he chose to, with the taxes and repairs and other upkeep borne by the Erskine family trust. But he never moved back to Carolina.

From about 1920 on, Cecil earned his living working for a Manhattan interior decorator named William Rau. It seems to have been at scraping-by pay. Rau Studios were noted for their cinema interiors. The New York City directories are sporadic in this period. The last published directory of this era is in 1933–34, and this is how he appears: "Corwin, Cecil, drftsmn Rau Studios Inc 100 W 42nd." It's as if, literally, they're abbreviating his life. Three years before, in the 1930 federal census, he is living—apparently alone—on West Seventy-Seventh. He is listed as "roomer" and "widowed," and there are twenty other adults and one child living at the same address. Howard McLean? By the 1930 census, he is living ten blocks away, in a two-person household, with Reynolds Sweetland, who is involved in theater and cultural journalism. As McLean was about eighteen years younger than Cecil, so Sweetland is about a decade younger than McLean. They'll be together until McLean's death, two decades hence.

Sometime after 1936, with America still deep inside the Great Depression, Cecil's little sister, a decade younger, came down to Manhattan and gathered him up and brought him to her home in Buffalo, where Marquita Corwin Beach lived with her husband and a grown son. The family legend is that he was all but destitute, but it wasn't precisely true. He lived with his sister's family until the end. On January 31, 1941, at 267 Norwalk Avenue, Cecil Corwin, on the other side of eighty, died of arteriosclerosis and senility and acute dilation of the heart. Under "Usual Occupation" on the death certificate, someone typed in "Retired Decorator." He was cremated. That summer his remains were shipped to Chicago, where he was put in a plot with other family

members in Graceland Cemetery on the North Side. When they probated his one-page will in a Buffalo court, the worth of his real property
was listed at $250, and his personal property the same. Half a dozen
nieces and nephews received a dollar each. A favorite niece, whom he
had kind of looked after emotionally through the years, received a little
more. His kid sister Marquita, who'd rescued him, tended him, got the
rest.

Back to Frank Lloyd Wright and the coming back together of two lives
that went in such opposite directions. There is the sense of redemptive
beauty here, even amid such sadness and seeming objective worldly
failure. It happened, the coming back together, just once, eight years
before Cecil died. As noted earlier, it wasn't in person, but in a coded
and poignant exchange of letters—on both sides.

In both letters there seems so much being written below the surface
of the actual sentences themselves. In both letters you can hear a certain
longing—or I can.

The context: In March 1932, an aforesaid boarhog of an American ego had published his life story to surprising sales and acclaim—
and had proceeded to act pretty much as a boarhog about it, not least
on the lecture tour, where he was happy to insult his audiences to their
faces. Later, when we're more chronologically there, more will be said
about the publication of *An Autobiography,* which had much to do
with helping bring its author back into the public eye after a long, long
drought.

Cecil had read the book soon after it was published. (A highly successful New York architect, a friend, gave him a copy.) He had a feeling
he was going to appear in it, but he had to have been deeply gratified
to find that he'd been written about so prominently and generously. He
would have instantly understood how the author was signaling complex
truths to his readers, even as he was tenderly taking care. But Cecil
hadn't tried to get in touch with Wright, or, more accurately, perhaps,
he hadn't tried very hard. Maybe the gulf was too wide. They hadn't seen
each other in thirty-six years, although unbeknownst to both of them,
there had been occasions in those thirty-six years (it can be tracked)

when they'd passed within almost figurative feet of each other: Wright staying over, for instance, in a New York hotel or giving a talk that was within blocks of where Cecil was then living.

Seven months after the book came out, on the evening of November 9, 1932, Cecil's sister Marquita and her twenty-four-year-old son, John (and possibly Marquita's husband, Ernest Beach), attended a Wright lecture at Buffalo's Albright Art Gallery. Back in Chicago days, Marquita had known Wright well. Cecil wasn't at the museum talk that evening—he was still living in New York and working for Rau Studios. But before the event, or, maybe afterward, Wright and Cecil's sister had been able to speak to each other. Wright was apparently generous and warm and nostalgic and stressed how much he'd like to see Cecil. Within a day or two, Marquita's son wrote to his uncle and reported this.* It broke the psychological logjam. On the stationery of his employer, Cecil hand-wrote a four-page letter full of his old formality and self-deprecation, his pride but not his pridefulness, his apparently unembittered heart. He seemed to wish for Wright to know certain things—that he'd been married and that he had a grown daughter, true facts as far as they went. (In fact, he had six stepchildren, but the daughter to whom he is probably referring—but whose name he doesn't mention—was Emma's youngest child. Her name was Susan Erskine Rogers, and she and Cecil were particularly close.)

"Dear Frank," the letter begins.

A letter from my nephew states that he had a most delightful interview with you in which you expressed a desire to hear from me. While in Chicago some weeks ago on a brief visit I took the

---

* In the late summer of 2013, nearly eighty-one years after John Beach wrote to his uncle—his letter hasn't survived—I went to Rochester, New York, and spent a weekend with John Beach's daughter and her family. Her name is Cynthia Beach-Smeltzer. In the way that Andy Haynes in North Carolina is the informal historian of the Erskine clan, so Cynthia Beach-Smeltzer has spent half a lifetime acquiring Corwin family documents. She never knew "Great Uncle Cecil" or even her grandmother Marquita. But she pulled from drawers—and allowed me to make copies—so many articles, photographs, journals, diaries, genealogy charts, and other family memorabilia that it almost began to seem as if Marquita, not to say Cecil himself, had entered the room. Some powerful emotional things happened between Cynthia and myself that weekend in regard to her understanding—and misunderstanding—of Cecil and his story, as his story had passed down to her, and as it had connected to Frank Lloyd Wright's story. But rather than trying in a truncated way to say those things here, I have put them in the Essay on Sources.

liberty of looking you up and found that you were at "Taliesin." Had I the time to call upon you there I should most certainly have done so. No! I have not lost track of you, but followed you through all the intervening years. I have never been able to forget our early friendship.

Two paragraphs down:

Our ways have been diverse and divergent. You have made a name for yourself of inestimable value. I have only made friends and a living.

In the next paragraph:

Your book has given me a deal to think upon and revived the pleasant recollections of the interesting characters whom you recalled. Uncle Jenkin Lloyd Jones, your wonderful mother and sisters and the aunts and cousins whom I had the pleasure of knowing and loving.

In the next paragraph:

I suspect you are a very busy man, but I should be delighted to hear from you and have you call upon me if you ever find the time when in town. I am in the decorative field. Are you amazed that I am as my daughter humorously observes, "making nice attraction" [and I] have had much to do in the line of cabaret and theatre work. Have been for the past dozen of years associated with Mr. Wm. Rau. We have pulled through these hard times to-gether and are still pulling and probably shall for some time to come. He is an artist, and more or less temperamental. But we understand one another, which is something. I married an artist and know the nature.

At the close:

Be sure I shall be very glad to hear from you and glader [sic] to see you.

He signed it: "Very sincerely your friend, Cecil."

The reply was dated November 20, 1932. It's a typed letter, which means it was dictated. It is one page. From external evidence, it seems as if Wright answered on the day he read Cecil's letter. "My dear Cecil," it begins.

More of the fatal procrastination that has marked me for its own. I was more than glad to hear from you again and if we can ever get out of the ruts in which we have been running and get together once more I'm sure we will go on again, as ever. It is not so long since we were Damon and Pythias, and those old days were romance. Much has come in between. I tried, in the Autobiography, to recreate you as you were, not verbatim but in character. I feel that I succeeded and everybody likes the figure of "Cecil" in that work. I haven't changed much since "our time," haven't learned very much—battered up somewhat but as young as ever where foolishness is concerned.

He invites him to Taliesin. He mentions seeing Marquita, and how well she'd looked. He mentions Cecil's younger brother, Arthur Corwin, a Chicago doctor. And then, at the close, inviting him again to Wisconsin, this, with its odd seven-dot ellipsis: "Your friends the[y] . . . . are nice people. They might like to come too."

Cecil never did get to Taliesin. And this was their last known communication.

In Greek mythology, the legend of Damon and Pythias is about trust and loyalty and the Pythagorean ideal of male friendship, even to the point of offering up your life for the other. The myth also can be understood—and has been interpreted as such by artists in different mediums down through the ages—as a story of deep homosexual love. In 1889, about two years after Frank and Cecil met, a writer named Alfred J. Cohen published, under a pseudonym, a novel entitled *A Marriage Below Zero*. The two gay men at the center of the story (one is foppish and married) like to call themselves Damon and Pythias. So do their so-called friends in upper society, but with the common knowledge that they intend it more or less in thin code as a homophobic slur. It's not a very good novel, though—overwrought and heavy-handed.

A generation later, in 1925, a young and unknown would-be southern writer named William Faulkner published a New Orleans sketch entitled "Damon and Pythias Unlimited." It, too, was shaded with gay-love themes. Affectionately. Humorously.

———

Cecil Corwin had the extreme good fortune and uncommon bad luck to know an artistic genius. There is a line in a story by the late and great William Maxwell of *The New Yorker* that I think about every now and then when I think about Cecil: "I had inadvertently walked through a door that I shouldn't have gone through and couldn't get back to the place I hadn't meant to leave."

This book is dedicated to a man named Tim Samuelson. He is a big, bluff, eccentric, obsessively curious, and extraordinarily giving individual who works for the city of Chicago, functioning as its cultural historian. If we have had one conversation about Frank Lloyd Wright, we have had one hundred. He has spent a lifetime combing old building sites and poring over late-night microfilm reels, hoping to find one more fact or artifact having to do with Wright, but, of course, not only Wright. It sometimes seems as if he's on some endless search for lost brass doorknobs, circa 1902. He loves them all—Louis Sullivan, Dan Burnham, Mies van der Rohe—but in a way, he cares most about all those gone Chicago builder-dreamers whose names will never be lodged on the back of our cultural eyeball. One bitter cold January afternoon we got into my rental car and drove out to Graceland Cemetery on Irving Park Road to hunt up Cecil Corwin's grave. We found the little wedge of gray stone in Lot 850, Section C. We scraped the snow off its surface with our gloves. We didn't say much. After about ten minutes, we went back and sat in the car and dialed up the heat. Tim said: "I feel sorry for him. It makes me sad. He tried to get there on his own and he knew he couldn't. He didn't have the gift of three dimensions. In a sense, he's all the rest of us. He's the basis of everything I've ever tried to research. He made his contribution. To me it was an important one. He must have died not believing that. As it is, we just have him in and through Frank. But I'll take that, if that's all that's being offered to us."

Tim sighed. "You see, for me it's that last line, '—never have I seen him since.' "

In his great 1936 documentary work about the lives of Alabama sharecrop-
pers, Let Us Now Praise Famous Men, *James Agee writes of pulling up to*
a backwoods, clay-scoured, single-spired, white-clapboard Negro church
and being nearly overcome as the building "powerfully strove in through
the eyes its paralyzing classicism."

You can get that same kind of feeling at first sight of the William H.
Winslow House at 515 Auvergne Place, River Forest, Illinois.

Wright himself, years later, called the Winslow his first "prairie house,"
although God knows it doesn't, at first glance, or even second, look like what
we commonly think of when we use that term in an architectural context,
in a Wright context. The true Prairies (scholars tend to capitalize the word),
with their long horizontal lines and cantilevered balconies and low terraces
and ground-hugging roofs and sequestering gardens and sheltering eaves
and narrow bands of glittering art-glass windows—they were still something
like six and seven years off in Wright's imagination and pencil. When they
came, they seemed to come from his drawing board in dizzying waves of
design and variety. From the sidewalk you can look at any one of them now
and instantly get what is meant by the descriptive word itself: prairie. "The
horizontal line is the line of domesticity," Wright once said, poetically, mysti-
cally, with his weird ability to get across something even when it makes no
literal sense. That line, he added, with his own quirky use of the comma, is
"the only one here worthy of respect,—the prairie." In another place, with-
out any opaqueness or poetry or faulty punctuation, he wrote: "I loved the
prairie by instinct." He meant its birds and trees and creeks and grasses and
hillocks and wildflowers. He meant its openness, its lack of confinement,
its sense of freedom, even as it was enfolding him in its bosom. But he also
meant its flatness—in literal ways. Where others saw dreariness in that fact,
he could see the beauty—yellow waves of grain, fitted field-sheets of summer
corn. He meant the prosaic thing beneath your feet if, say, you're standing
in the middle of Oak Park, Illinois, gazing at one of his Prairies with your
trusty Frank Lloyd Wright field guide: flat earth, so flat sometimes that the
horizon can seem as true and straight as a carpenter's level. He hadn't come
out of the Rockies, he hadn't been born into the desert, he didn't grow up at

the cannonading seashore. No, "I was born an American child of the ground and of space," he said. So he would make of that geologic necessity and bio-graphical birth-fact a sublime virtue. So it would come to him, eventually, as an architectural idea and a building principle that every house "should begin on the ground, not in it." A radical thought and so difficult to compre-hend in its ultimate logic: make the thing of the thing. Not in the thing but of the thing. It's the Louis Sullivan idea of form following function—or, as Wright would prefer to say, form and function: he would give to his houses the sense and feel and look of the very ground the buildings were sited on, so that all of it would become an organic, harmonious, aesthetic, and, not least, American whole. And right along with this idea, the corollary idea of shelter. "An idea (probably rooted deep in racial instinct) that shelter should be the essential look of any dwelling," he said. And how was he going to make that happen? With the so-called horizontal line of domesticity. Let verticality be for the city—he would go out instead of up. "I began to see a building primarily not as a cave, but as broad shelter in the open related to vista—vista without and vista within," he said.

Say it this way: The land had to do its own work before he imposed his will on it.

So the Winslow: You drive up to it and it's as if it has powerfully strove in on all your senses with its formal, paralyzing, almost classical façade. The word "almost" is important. It is classical, but not quite. It is horizontal, but not quite. There is the gently sloping and overhanging hipped roof, which is key to the coming Prairie principle: something wide and open and long and yet simultaneously sheltering. There is, in the center of the roof, a massed, stone-capped chimney. It's broader and lower than you would expect to see, and thus has the instant visual and metaphorical effect of further tamping down the already tamped-down roof. There are the double-hung first-floor windows—they aren't holes cut in a wall, rather, they are precisely placed openings, providing, again, a subliminal sense of domestic order and propri-ety. The three spaced windows on the second floor go up to the eaves—they almost seem to be reaching under the eaves, to what architects call the sof-fit. A window in a normal house would stop a foot or two below the soffit. Again, the subliminal suggestion is that the windows are part of an organic whole instead of sawed openings in a wall for air and sight and light.

Best of all, there is, on the first floor, going across the width of the house, the yellowish and buff-colored brick face. Not regular brick, but what builders know as Roman brick. It's a greatly elongated brick that gives the house, despite its two floors, its essential horizontalness. That the colors are of slightly different hues (which has to do with how each brick came out of the kiln) only enhances the naturalistic, earthlike feel.

Then, too, there is the approach itself. Although Wright placed the wide, wooden front door (with its ornate but not too ornate foliate design) squarely in the middle of the house, it's a fact that you can't walk directly up to it, at least if you don't intend to trample through a planting bed. You have to go either to the left or to the right, around the bed. (In 1894, the planting bed was a reflecting pool, so you'd get your shoes wet if you were intent on going in a straight line.) In the true Prairies to come, Wright will go to great pains to conceal his entryways—putting them most often at the side of the house. The hiding has to do with deliberative approaches as well as with ideas of security and family privacy. But also the artist wishes you to be making a kind of pilgrimage into his piece of art—call it the "ceremony of entry." He wants nothing to happen abruptly. He is working toward the totality of an artistic experience. Give him all of that. In another way, call it just rank Wrightian ego. You must earn your way to his doorway—and it is his door, even if he's drawing it for someone else. But that point's already been made.

Once, the Winslow sat nearly alone on a large tract of gradual sloping land at the edge of an Illinois village, in a bend of the sluggish Des Plaines River, which Marquette and Joliet paddled in 1673. In 1894, the house must have seemed truly part of the American prairie, and once you were on the other side of the river, on the west bank, there must have been the illusion the earth was going off westward, ribbon-straight, pancake-flat, uninterrupted, save for wagon-wheel ruts of the pioneers, all the way to Colorado. The house is hemmed in now by suburbia and exurbia. Doesn't matter. It's there, and it's as if it's going to be there, as William Faulkner once said in another context, until "the last ding-dong of doom."

Haven't even spoken of the back of the house, which is radically different from the formal front. Haven't even mentioned the interior, which is even more of its own breathtaking thing. Enough: You can turn the page and see for yourself, if only in photograph, this cream and tawny and dark brown precursor, this St. John the Baptist, to all of the actual Prairies up ahead. By the way, the term "prairie house" wasn't even around when Wright was beginning to draw them. That label came much later.

Ships on the Prairie

William Herman Winslow House, 515 Auvergne Place, River Forest, Illinois

t's as if the words are standing up on the page. You know instantly they're from a child's hand and head, even before you've read the sentences themselves, some of which are non-sentences, at least in terms of grammar and punctuation. The letter is two pages long, with a kind of formal closing on a third and stand-alone page that seems immediately suspect, as if an adult with a not-too-secret agenda is hovering nearby. On the envelope, bearing a crookedly affixed two-cent stamp with George Washington's bust on it, a half-dollar-sized circular postmark: "10 00 AM OAK PARK ILL. OCT 21 1911." The envelope is addressed, with the same absurd, gargantuan, cursive letter-loops, to "Mr. LL Wright, Hillside Wis."

The author is a curly-banged and sweet-natured little boy named Robert Llewellyn Wright, born on November 15, 1903. He's the last child of Frank and Kitty Wright. In three weeks he'll be eight, and a party is planned. Two years and one month ago, when he was five, soon to be six, his daddy went away on a long trip with another lady, not that he knew that or understood all its meanings at the time, or that he truly gets the situation now. (He must understand parts of it; children live mystically and they live deep, even or especially in their inabilities to articulate their understanding.) What he knows is the fact of the absence, the fact of the missing. It's true his father had come back home from that long trip after about a year. (The lady had stayed on in the place they'd gone to.) But then he'd packed up and left again. Now his papa lives in a new house somewhere up in Wisconsin, not that Robert Llewellyn necessarily knows where Wisconsin is (one state north of Illinois) or that the lady is again with him there.

"dear papa," his letter begins, and then, on the same line as the greeting, no comma, going straight in, its own kind of urgency, taking up the next two sheets, fifty-eight words, looking two feet high on the page, as if conveying everything and nothing about the inner mysteries of a ruptured family:

how are you I am feeling sad with out you I love you very much. My room is suny and pretty. I like my misic lessons. I wont to play like you some day. James has gone home is it raining at Hillside now? I like to write you tomorrow is play day these are good night kisses oooooooo

On the third sheet, standing apart from the two pages, in more ways than one, this:

"from your loving little boy Llewellyn Wright"

Had Kitty Wright importuned her son to write to his father as part of her (doomed) campaign to win him back from Mamah Borthwick Cheney? Historians and biographers have suggested that, and it seems more than likely. But the longing here—isn't that something unimportunable? Unmanipulatable?

Three weeks later, on his birthday, November 15, 1911, another letter from the same hand and head. Same sense that someone nearby, much bigger than Robert Llewellyn, may be seeking to puppeteer the whole thing. He begins on a small sheet, illustrated with a mama pig and her dancing baby pigs. Twelve words on the first page:

Dear Papa
This is my birth day. I miss you very much

On the second:

Will you please eat thanksgiving dinner with us. We are lonesome with out you. We are afraid you are sick. We have snow now and sliding.
 I hope you are warm as we are in the house. I am eight years old. good bye from your loving son.
 Llewellyn Wright

On the third page, two words: "birthday kisses," followed by eight zeroes, darkened in with his pencil: "ooooooo."
So what happened to this curly-banged and sweet-natured little boy, victim, in a sense, of not just one parent but of two? (Of Wright's six children by Catherine Wright over the space of thirteen years, their youngest was said to be the most naturally quiet and docile and easy to get along with.) Did Robert Llewellyn turn eventually into a homicidal maniac, a serial adulterer? Then how about just a deeply embittered malcontent, cursing lifelong the cards fate dealt him? No, Bob Wright, or Robert Wright, as his friends knew him, grew up to be a successful lawyer, spending most of his career in Washington, D.C., in and out of the federal government. (At one point he was a high official in the anti-trust division of Attorney General Robert F. Kennedy's Justice Department.) He was skilled at both litigating and trial work. He fathered three children and they turned out fine (more than fine; professionally accomplished), and he was married, if not quite in true happiness, at least in stability and harmony, to the same good woman for half a century, and he loved chess and tennis and baseball, and in middle life he moved into a house outside Washington that his father designed for him (it's in the family yet, a lesser if still amazing Wright work), and he died, at eighty-two, on February 22, 1986, more or less

peacefully, of congestive heart failure, with his debts paid and his affairs in order, having made, early on, it seems clear, and clear not least to his children (who are now up-in-age people themselves, each having been generously open to personal questions about their emotionally distant father), a conscious turn away from, a deliberate rejection of, the vulgar narcissism and arrogance and bombast and egocentrism and reckless financial—not to say moral—ways of his transcendently gifted father.

When he was in his seventies—somewhere in the 1970s—the emotionally cautious Robert Llewellyn Wright sat down and wrote a handful of essays about his life. He called them "Letters to His Children on His Childhood." One of the essays was a ten-page single-spaced piece entitled "Your Father's Recollections of His Father." He might have titled it "Your Father's Non-Recollections of His Father." The essay is remarkable, not for its modesty or eloquence (it has some of both), but for its emotional flatness, which might sound harsh, except it isn't meant that way. Yes, there is an arresting anecdote or two about Frank Lloyd Wright, most especially this one: "I remember visiting him in his Chicago hotel room when I was about twelve—he never returned to the Oak Park house, even for a visit—and seeing him stave off an insistent creditor with jocular excuses. When the man left he turned to me, all smiles, and said, 'Son, that's the way you handle creditors.' I didn't think so then and still don't. To me he had just gone through such a humiliating experience that I have been afraid to buy anything on credit ever since. To him it was all a joke—on the surface."

But what the document mostly seems is its own sad proof for the kind of damage Frank Lloyd Wright inflicted on his children. The creditor story notwithstanding, it's as if a son is straining terribly just to fill up ten pages. This is how he ends:

> Well, that's about it and I hope it hasn't bored you. I have dutifully restrained myself from a chronological account of all our many brief contacts. Unfortunately we never had any real rows or any especially tender moments. He was always kind and affectionate with me; although frequently impatient, and seldom used on me the kind of sarcasm I have employed in dealing with you. The sad truth is that we were friendly strangers and almost any of his favorite clients could tell you more about him than I can.

So a question, which in a way is probably this book's first and final (and unanswerable) question: Would the world possess something as soul-touching and seemingly imperishable as the William H. Winslow House in River Forest, Illinois, had its creator managed also to have been an even halfway selfless presence in a boy's life?

———

Looping back to a different longing: to Frank Lloyd Wright's first decade in Chicago, when, as was earlier said, so many things, personal and professional, were streaming in on him from every side. Looping back to pick up some strands in the narrative necessarily left out previously—or, if not left out, brushed past.

One strand has to do with what might be called the mystery and good fortune of Chicago itself, in and amid a history of terrible misfortunes, not least its biblical burning of 1871, a decade and a half before Wright arrived. Tim Samuelson once explained the luck of his hometown to me this way: "It comes out of a mud hole, a perfectly located mud hole. Because of its geography, certain things seem inevitable. You can connect to the Mississippi. Water is the center of commerce, so this frontier settlement, heck, not even incorporated until 1837, becomes the perfect place for a nation moving west. Almost simultaneous to the development of the water commerce, the railroads come in. Ergo, the water can meet the rail. You can come here and try out things to make a buck. There's nobody to stop you. It's all about opportunity. Then, jumping ahead, there's this little incident everybody knows called the Great Fire, supposedly caused by Mrs. O'Leary's cow kicking over a lantern in a barn. Well, that's folklore. The fire is devastating, it takes down the central business district, it becomes one of the great myths of American history, but, guess what: it doesn't destroy the water, or the wharves, or the railroad tracks, the trunk lines that connect Chicago to the world, the lumber yards, the stockyards, the heavy industry to the west of the loop. In other words, in all the terrible loss, there's so much that gets saved. So the city can start rebuilding almost before the ruins cool—everything is in place to make it happen."

Historian Donald Miller, in his *City of the Century,* describes how the rebuilding from the rubble was really a double rebuilding. "This is what is amazing about Chicago's post-fire recovery," he writes. "In less than two decades, not one but two new cities were built." The first stage, in which little thought was given to the quality of the architecture itself, lasted something like two years. Then had come an economic depression, halting things for the rest of the decade. The second rebuilding stage began in 1880 and ran through that whole decade, and into the early nineties, when an even greater recession hit the country. The architects managing the second phase were astonishingly young— according to Miller, their average was a bit under thirty. It was as if this new generation of builder-dreamers had no precedents to worry about—just relying on their swaggering and almost naïve sense, in Miller's words, "that they were making history in a part of America only recently claimed from the wilderness and in a city not much older than they were." So the old saw somewhat obtains: their ignorance was their bliss. Miller: "By 1886, Chicago—a place almost without architecture in 1880—was the world center of architectural experimentation." Eighteen eighty-six? Isn't the back half of that year, give or take a few months in either direction, just when a nobody from Wisconsin with a longing to make history on a large scale emerges from the Wells Street Depot in wan light with his supposed seven bucks and pasteboard suitcase? He's nineteen, soon to be twenty, a decade younger than the (astonishingly young) architects making over the Eternal City of the West. The emeritus Harvard scholar Neil Levine, in his 1996 book *The Architecture of Frank Lloyd Wright,* an indispensably rich study, put it this way: "For someone with virtually no training or experience, Wright could hardly have picked a better place or a better time." He almost could have said: could not have picked a literal, luckier *minute.* What Levine seems to be suggesting is that if there were luck and seized chance on Wright's end, there was just as much on Chicago's end. City and boy came together like a hammer hitting a nail square on. Power of place met power of person.

Not least among the architectural experimentation going on in 1886 was something called the "skyscraper." The American skyscraper wasn't invented in Chicago—New York is its true birthplace—but that's a little like trying to insist that the distance from Key West to Cuba, through that mythical slice of fast-moving blue water known as the Straits of Florida, isn't actually ninety miles, but rather closer to ninety-nine nautical miles. What's the point of arguing for the actuality? The distance from Key West to Cuba in popular culture will always be ninety miles. So, too, with any argument about Chicago not being the fountainhead of the tall building. The truth is that Chicago perfected the tall building. The new breed of engineers and architects had to discover ways of anchoring tall buildings in Chicago's squishy soil, and what they came up with, at length, was a fireproof, steel-skeleton construction. Eventually, tall buildings in Chicago and everywhere else turned into all steel-frame ideas. Exterior load-bearing walls, sometimes six feet thick on a building's lower floors, became a thing of the past. The concept, not to say the availability, of metal framing materials at the end of the nineteenth century eliminated the need for massive load-bearing walls.

Again, Tim Samuelson: "Why does the skyscraper start in Chicago—all right, get developed here? Easy. You have a lake on one side, you have a river that loops in the other two sides, and on the fourth side, which is to say the South Side, the railroad eats up your available building space. You can't go east—you'll be in Lake Michigan. You've got this tight downtown building core. You're inside the horse collar. You've got no choice but to go up. But you've got to figure out a way to do it, to support all that weight, and the answer is the metal frame, not masonry. They did it here because they had to. You wouldn't really improve that many technologies unless you were forced to."

As Miller notes in Century, the most important theorists and practitioners of the skyscraper were gathered in Chicago at the right moment (but why this was so, no one can really say), and chief among them were William LeBaron Jenney, John Wellborn Root, Dankmar Adler, and Louis H. Sullivan. Sullivan's reddish, squareish, Palazzo-styled, ten-story Wainwright Building, at 709 Chestnut Street in downtown St. Louis, with its lightweight steel-skeleton structure, is commonly regarded as one of the world's first true skyscrapers. In fact, there were plenty before. The Wainright is the first in terms of defining modern skyscraper form from an aesthetic standpoint. It was put up between 1890 and 1892, when Wright was enjoying maximum influence with and access to his lieber meister. Decades later, in a lecture at Princeton, Wright called the Wainwright "the very first human expression of a tall steel office-building as Architecture." And yet, years before, he wasn't above trying to take credit for the building himself in an attempt to secure clients. You can go to St. Louis now and stand in front of Sullivan's Wainwright and be awed by its harmony and uniformity and dignity and intricate sandstone ornamentation running from top to bottom—while trying to ignore the Hooters across the street.

Mysteries of luck: In the long view of history, Silsbee and Sullivan, in that order, seem to have been almost the perfect mentor-employers for the aforesaid arriving nobody. J. Lyman Silsbee wasn't really involved in reconstructing the Loop—his boutique firm specialized in residential work, which of course was the work where Wright would find his first true stroke and more or less reign supreme for the rest of his life. As was earlier noted, Silsbee taught him how to create flow, and he shortly took that lesson over to Adler & Sullivan, where, in something less than six years, he would metabolize even greater lessons about unity and organic principle. To oversimplify: If Silsbee showed him the art and idea of not getting hemmed in, Sullivan would show him how to bring everything together, and to provide a philosophical underpinning, so that the design emerging from his drawing board with a T-square and triangle could become a single architectural idea: the all-inclusive struc-ture of utility and beauty. And, as long as complex notions are being oversimplified, let this quickly be noted: Sullivan, from whom Wright would learn more about architecture than from any other person in his life, was always way out ahead of the pupil on the gospel of creating an *American* architecture for Americans. Frank Lloyd Wright gets way too much credit for that idea, not that he didn't believe in the gospel to his toenails or understand it in deeper ways than Sullivan or raise it to far more brilliant levels. But the dream didn't originate with him: just one more instance of the smooth appropriating. The historians know the truth.

In *An Autobiography,* Wright seems to be expressing authentic remorse about the way he up and left Silsbee in a matter of months. The old man had taken him back in, but then there had been the open-ing at A&S, and the boy out for the main chance was gone. Yet, looking back, so many years later, Wright is able to use the words "anguish" and "regret." Is this the hidden self again? But the words don't seem very hidden: "I left him like any tramp draughtsman when he had been really handsome toward me. . . . I never saw Silsbee again." Again, as with Cecil Corwin: the emotion, ringing true, of never again seeing some-one he truly cared about. (Except with Cecil, the caring was magnified tenfold.) Just ahead of the never-seeing-again sentence, this: "If he can see into my heart now, he will see what he saw in my face then."

But now the main chancer's over at A&S, at the peak of the firm's fame. Naturally the other draftsmen can't stand him. It's the way he's so quickly insinuated himself with the master. Doesn't help that he seems to have contempt for his co-workers and keeps his hair long and wears such strange clothes—one day he shows up in tight black knickers, another day in what appear to be felt slippers that he claims cost twenty-five dollars and that were fashioned by Chicago's best shoemaker. He's a sissy, and a shrimper to boot. At noon, some of the draftsmen go into a back room to box. They're itching to get him in there. What they don't know is that he has boxed a bit in his life, and that, despite his puny size, there is a deceptive strength in him, owed to boyhood years of working dawn to dusk on the summertime Wisconsin farms of his Welsh uncles. There is this particular odious taunter in the office, Henry L. Ottenheimer: a "heavy-bodied, short-legged, pompadoured, conceited, red-faced Jew, wearing gold glasses." (*An Autobiography* is pockmarked with its casual anti-Semitism, but Ottie, as people called him, apparently *was* a coarse-grained type who wasn't above spanking children who weren't his own. Such an incident, involving legal action, even made it into *The New York Times* a couple of years before Wright landed in Chicago.)

One noonday, when the office has emptied out for lunch, Ottie says to the new boy: "You're just a Sullivan 'toady' anyway, Wright. We all know it." That does it. The new boy sets down his pencil and pivots on his drawing stool and walks over to Ottie's board and strikes him flat in the face, knocking him to the floor. His specs splinter. (Wright will later try to say he didn't realize his opponent was wearing glasses.) Ottie rises and crouches and comes at him "with a peculiar animal scream," and also with an arrow-shaped steel scratcher-blade (it's a draftsman's tool), with which he supposedly slashes Wright in eleven places right to the bone on his shoulders and in his neck. Wright picks up a T-square and fairly brains him with its broad blade end. Wright's shoes filling with blood, Ottie splayed on the floor—is he dead? (No.) When the thing is over, Wright has one thought: *Get hold of Cecil.* Cecil, gotten hold of by phone, rushes the five blocks straight north from Silsbee's office at Clark and Adams to the Borden Block at Dearborn and Randolph. He pulls off his friend's coat, folds his shirt down over his waist. What a sight. Cecil does a makeshift bandaging and leads Wright out the door and over to Rush Medical College to find Arthur Corwin, a doctor in training. (Wright has it that Cecil's little brother has finished med school and is already in practice—not so.)

An obvious question, given an autobiographer's compulsion not only to misremember events but also blithely to make them up: Did any of this even happen? It turns out it did. In addition to the combatants, one other person was in the room that day: George Grant Elmslie, who almost couldn't have been more different in temperament from Wright. He was a couple of years younger than Wright and ended up having a long career—his name would be well known to any halfway serious student of Midwest architecture of the latter part of the nineteenth century and early decades of the twentieth. He was a self-effacing Scotsman who longed for the old country. He had worked as a draftsman at Silsbee's with Cecil and Wright, and then Wright was instrumental in getting him hired at A&S, where the two worked together on various buildings, and where Elmslie stayed on, long after Wright had departed in disgrace. He became Sullivan's chief draftsman and did ornamental detail on some of the master's great projects. He is another Prairie practitioner and member of the so-called Chicago School, or New School of the Middle West, who, later, on his own and in partnership, built beautiful Prairie-styled houses (and modernist commercial buildings too, not least Merchants National Bank in Winona, Minnesota, in 1912, with its stunning terracotta and ornamentation). But his name, like the scores of Chicago others, tends to get bull-horned out of history, or at least out of popular culture, by the name "Frank Lloyd Wright." (Like Cecil, his career ultimately went bad, ending in widowed loneliness and financial ruin.)

George Elmslie thought Wright an architectural genius possessed of an appalling character. In the fall of 1932, seven months after Wright published his autobiography, he wrote a five-and-a-half-page, typed, single-spaced letter to Wright, refuting stories in the book (and taking exception to a few of Wright's gratuitous swipes at him), and yet in the process verifying (for posterity) the brawl with Ottenheimer. A decade and a half after that, in 1946, in a private letter to his architectural partner, he again verified the incident, even if he called out its exaggerations.

Life magazine had recently done a piece of semi-puffery about Wright, calling him the "Titan of Modern Architecture." *Reader's Digest* had picked up the story, and this is apparently where Elmslie saw it—and his goat was a little too much gotten. From the piece: "He [Wright] engaged in herculean brawls with Sullivan's other apprentices who objected to his flowing tie and artsy attitudes. One of these nearly ended in tragedy when a fellow apprentice, whom he later beat to insensibility, slashed him in eleven places with an open clasp knife." Not quite, Elmslie said. Not an actual knife (as Wright described it), and hardly eleven cuts to the bone, or a bucket of blood, or a beating to insensibility. But still: the thing had happened, which is something. Elmslie's setting-straight letter found its way into a university archive in Minnesota—which would have likely mortified him, since he was such a discreet and mostly quiet man.

Summer, 1890: an office schematic, with its apparent unarguable facts, and a family photograph, with its seemingly unwitting transmitted messages. The schematic: It's a rendering of the new offices of Adler & Sullivan. It's published on June 7, 1890, a Saturday—the day before Frank Lloyd Wright turns twenty-three—on page 5 of a national weekly trade publication called *The Engineering and Building Record*. Wright's been at the firm for more than a year and a half. He's the straw boss of all the draftsmen, who sit, garter-sleeved, head-bent, on unpadded stools, in seven rows outside his door. He's married to Kitty now, has a child. A&S is located on the sixteenth and seventeenth floors of the tower in the Auditorium Building. In the schematic, "Mr. Sullivan's Room," labeled that way, is located in the southeast corner of the sixteenth story, and, immediately adjacent: "Mr. Wright's Room," somewhat smaller but with what might be the best office view of Lake Michigan. More to the point: Could anyone argue with such intimacy to the master?

Intimacy. In 1987, Brendan Gill, the late prolific *New Yorker* writer, published a semi-controversial Wright biography entitled *Many Masks*. Of the many Wright portraits over the decades, whether partial or full accounts, and whether essentially life-based or work-based, Gill's is easily among the more readable and discerning—except that it too often gets its facts wrong, and, to some scholarly tastes, veers too close to psychobiography; also it sometimes seems to be going out of its way to put its subject down, as if there might have been some unsaid personal slight for which the author had never quite forgiven Wright. (Gill knew Wright at the back of Wright's life.) If there's truth in all that, the book is also damn good. Nonetheless, an arguable and characteristic passage: "Sullivan's graphic work seems charged with a frustrated sexuality; some of his designs, in their twisting, anguished exuberance, appear to be making love to themselves. This sexuality threatens to break through at any moment into some sort of figurative equivalent of a primal scream." Gill entertains the possibility—his book wasn't the first and won't be the last—that the riddlesome Sullivan's love of the American skyscraper ("every inch a proud and soaring thing," he once famously called it) may have had something a bit too obvious to do with phallic preoccupations, with autoerotic ideas. If it's a bit too obvious, the speculation may also be a bit too facile. (Sometimes a cigar is only a cigar.) It's known that Sullivan, who married in midlife (the marriage ended badly, only piling on to his general misery and final squalor), had a long history of hiring female prostitutes. It's been theorized that Sullivan was really a repressed homosexual—or, in another way, not repressed at all, in that we have the proud and soaring things themselves. The truth is, no one knows, and the further truth is his sexuality may have been a many-splintered thing (not unlike Wright's seems to have been), and the ultimate truth is that it doesn't matter in the end, because we have the work itself, the ornament, not least the ornament on the first two floors of what used to be known as the Carson, Pirie, Scott department store at State and Madison streets in the heart of the Loop. All you'd ever need do to appreciate the master is go stand in front of the main entry of the old Carson's (now a lowly Target), where the corners of the two streets come together and where the iron facing still looks intricate as lace filigree.

Gill's book suggests a homoerotic attraction to Wright on Sullivan's part. It's a fact they spent long hours together after work, discussing the dream of architecture. This was a wholly different relationship than Wright's with Cecil: father to son as opposed to brother to brother. Was Wright unaware there may have been something erotically charged from the "father" side? In *An Autobiography* Wright says: "Ah, that erotic supreme adventure of the mind that was his ornament!" Well, it was supreme, his mind.

The photograph: It was taken in the early summer of 1890, the exact date unknown. Then let it arbitrarily be stipulated that it was framed on Sunday afternoon, June 8 (the day after the office schematic appears in national print), because, for one thing, there is the look of something festive and dressed-up here—so why not a birthday celebration? Nine people are on the front steps of Frank and Kitty Wright's new Oak Park home. An oriental carpet has been dragged out from indoors and folded into the steps. Uncle Jenk's on the far left—he's brought his family out from the city, probably by rail and trolley. His wife, Susan, holding up the stagey-prop racket, as if to signal the good air and robust life of the suburbs. Then Wright's sister Jane; then Kitty Wright bearing Frank Lloyd Wright, Jr. (born barely two months before, on March 31, the infant has bobbed his head right at the shutter-snap, blurring his features); then Anna Wright; then Wright's adoring kid sister, Maginel; then the mustached master of the house; then Wright's first cousin Mary, the daughter of Jenk and Susan. (It is thought that the person who took the picture was Richard Lloyd Jones, son of Jenk, who, as already hinted, would one day, a few decades later, become a prime player in a great racial and moral tragedy in America.)

Is it only a circumstance that Kitty leans ever so slightly to the left,

away from her husband? And is it the same kind of randomness that her husband is the only one of these posing nine (excepting the newborn) who isn't looking into the lens, as if to signify his mind could be somewhere else? And is it only chance, pure chance, that the steel-haired and steel-willed and grimly divorced and dark-clad fifty-two-year-old Anna Lloyd Jones Wright—tilted four degrees to the fore with her characteristic, unnerving, flat-lipped smile—is poised (maybe inter-poised is better) almost exactly halfway between her son, who can do no wrong in this life, and her daughter-in-law, whom, it is clear by this point, one year and seven days into the marriage, she holds in a not-subtle contempt? To quote Meryle Secrest's fine Wright biography: "One of the most difficult aspects of marriage for Kitty must have been living next door to the one person who (as everyone knew) would always try to drive a wedge between her son and any woman perceived as a rival." Here, "wedge" seems more than metaphor. From infancy on—no, from conception on—Frank Lloyd Wright has been his mother's one consuming passion. Psychically, that bathing belief has given him what he has needed to go out and slay the world.

Anna's son is nineteen years away from abandoning his family. He's a couple years away from the bitter break with *lieber meister*. He's not quite four years from working up plans on the Winslow. He's roughly a decade from becoming a world-recognized artist. But, in some faint sense, thin as photographic paper, is it possible to imagine the canker is already in the rose? To quote a photography critic named Mark Stevens: "Every great photograph has a secret. Something mysteriously and tantalizingly withheld, even when the world seems laid out as plainly as a corpse upon a table."

————

As it turns out, the precursor had its precursors. Which is to say: If the 1894 Winslow stands as Frank Lloyd Wright's first great domestic work once out on his own, there were a handful of critical earlier houses making the Winslow House possible, and all the greater greatness to follow. We are talking primarily about the aforementioned "boots," the nominal cause of the break with Sullivan.

Adler & Sullivan's fame (and the firm's vision of itself) rested on commercial work. Houses were thought too small in several senses of the word. Most ambitious-minded architects wish to make their bones with the grand commercial or civic commissions. "Monumentality," it's sometimes called, which is a word that could apply to the egos of the creators. The few domestic projects A&S took in were more or less favors to important clients, and the supervision of the jobs seems to have been handed off to Wright, in addition to his other duties, as a way of feeding his own special interests and also allowing him to earn over-time pay—at least this is Wright's telling of it. Among the most impor-tant projects he worked on that could be said to be aboveground—even if he reportedly did the work nights and evenings at home—was the 1891 James Charnley House at 1365 North Astor Street, just north of the Loop, close in to Lake Michigan, in what Chicagoans know as the Gold Coast. It's a radical-looking building that resembled nothing in the neighborhood—still true. The first instinct is to say it's not even a house, maybe a museum of some sort. (In a way, that's true, too: the building is the longtime national headquarters of the Society of Architectural Historians.) It fills up its tight urban site at Astor and Schiller. In his autobiography, Wright said that with the Charnley he "first sensed the definitely decorative value of the plain surface . . . of the flat plane as such." Historians have had a hard time agreeing on whether this beau-tiful, modernist thing is wholly Wright's—and probably it's not. What seems closest to the truth is that it's a Sullivan design, with many of the astonishing details worked out by an astonishing twenty-four-year-old. As others have noted, on the inside of the house it's clear that a head draftsman is already tearing down the solidity of the mass.

But then below the pavement: the bootlegs. As was earlier noted, Wright's honor (not to stray into moonlighting) seems to have held for about a year and a half past the five-year agreement negotiated with the firm around the time of his wedding in June 1889—and this can be tracked from the published announcements in the trades and in the dai-lies of some key houses bearded by Cecil. On July 12, 1891, in a regular Sunday listing in the *Tribune* called "Among Architects and Builders": a seven-line notice that plans are now complete for a fifteen-thousand-dollar house for Dr. A. W. Harlan on the South Side. (Dr. Harlan was a professor of dental surgery, and his dwelling, with its fairly princely price tag, is alas long gone.) Two months later, in mid-September, the building permit gets issued to the supposed architect of record, last name of Corwin. It would have taken at least six months or so to get things to this point—thus, the actual architect must have been meeting with his client, sketching out plans for him, on the Oak Park sly, back in the winter, say, in January and February. The moonlighter's firstborn would have been not quite a year old then, and his second child (John Lloyd Wright, whom you've already met, so to speak, from events on the early afternoon of August 15, 1914) was still a little while from coming into the world—but not that far off. So the money pressures are already there. Incidentally, among his other semi-modest claims to fame, in a life spent fighting for its own worth, John Lloyd Wright grew up to be the inventor of the children's building toy Lincoln Logs.

But something not incidental: The Harlan House, with its pyramidal roof and overt stylistic references to Sullivan, with its distinctly horizontal and ground-hugging look amid its far more conventional neighbors, was built on a site just a couple of blocks from where Sullivan was then living. The Harlan was in the 4400 block of South Greenwood Avenue, and *lieber meister* was residing with two married friends named Lewis just a little bit south and west, at 220 Forty-Sixth Street. The house wasn't, as some have claimed, in his direct line of sight. But it was close enough that it seems impossible to think he wouldn't have taken notice on his evening walks, one of the ways he liked to unwind. Was Wright doing something self-destructive? Or was it just plain arrogance?

And then, the following year, middle of 1892, the announcement of two more boots (obviously not referred to as boots), sitting side by side, as if to up the dare of being caught: the George W. Blossom House and the Warren McArthur House. They were also on the South Side, in the Kenwood neighborhood (where Kitty Wright had grown up), a little north of Hyde Park and the University of Chicago, still in the evening walking range of Sullivan. (He had relocated with the Lewises early in 1892.) On June 19, the daily *Inter Ocean* told the world, or the Chicago building world, that "C.S. Corwin is preparing plans" for two eight-thousand-dollar houses at Forty-Ninth Street and Kenwood Avenue. Wright had been at the firm for something like four and a half years. Could his mentor and employer have been fooled, once he saw the rising and beautiful siblings themselves? One, the hipped-roof Blossom, is in the style of a Colonial Revival, and its sister, the gambrel-roofed McArthur, six yards north, is cast as a Dutch Colonial.

They're there today. There are no historical markers in front of them. They've both endured ignominies and torments, many of which, in recent years, have had to do with neglect. Of the two, the larger Blossom has suffered more, although a rescue effort has come at last. I have been there in years past when rain was sheeting through the gaping hole in the hipped roof, which a flapping and loosely tied-down blue tarp could do nothing against. (A hipped roof is typically a single sheltering unit without dormers or gables and where all sides slope downward to the walls, usually at a low angle.) I have been there when the projecting terrace on the Blossom's south side, with its wooden balustrade and spindles, was caving in on itself and with shards of the spindle lying out on the sidewalk, as if free for the taking.

One of the things you notice when you get up close is how its author is experimenting with the surface of the exterior walls—in seemingly precise mathematical academic geometries. In fact, the entire house is highly symmetrical. There is its recessed front entrance with a semicircular projecting porch. The sides also feature recesses where roughly the center third of the mass is set back from the portions on either side of it. And so forth. Inside, more surprises. The immediate feeling of openness. Also strong hints of what historians and builders know as the cross-axial, or cruciform, floor plan—anticipating every Prairie of the next decade. On the southwest side, the first floor ends in a sunlit and glass-enclosed half-circular dining area described as "the conservatory."

Tim Samuelson: "If you look at the corner eaves on the Blossom, you'll get the slightest Prairie feel, but it's true no one would ever call this a Prairie house. Still, what pushes out, what recesses in, this is clearly someone thinking in three dimensions. If you really want to know what's going on, this is a classically based and Sullivan-derived adaptation of a Colonial Revival, but with all of Frank's imagination applied. It embodies all the indecisions of where he wanted to go, who he wanted to be. And almost nobody has wished to speak for this house. It's like an orphan in the Wright universe. Yet in some ways it can tell you more about him than some of his greatest houses ever."

He didn't say it, but what Samuelson must have meant is the fact that, not ten blocks almost straight south of the Blossom, right at the edge of the campus of the University of Chicago, sits a Wright wonderwork—

one of his greatest houses ever—that Wright-goers can't get enough of: the Frederick C. Robie House. There it is, at 5757 South Woodlawn Avenue: "magnificently poised," as it has been described, "like a great steamship at anchor," with its brick overhangs supported by a series of hidden steel girders, some as long as sixty feet. You tour the Robie and you'll never have to wonder again at the word "Prairie," much less the concept of the horizontal or the cantilevered. The Robie, looking impossibly cantilevered, and worked on at the very end of Wright's Prairie Period, in 1908 and 1909, when he was fleeing everything, overturning everything, ranks in reputation with the Guggenheim and Fallingwater and the Johnson Wax headquarters and Unity Temple and the two Taliesins. But to Tim Samuelson's point: What fraction of the yearly thousands who travel to Hyde Park to see the Robie (and part with money afterward in the gift shop for calendars and key chains) have ever heard of the George W. Blossom House at 4858 South Kenwood, right up the street from the Robie, let alone ever want to visit it?

So he got found out and got dismissed—or that is the leaky legend, which seems to grow leakier with the decades. (From Wright's side, one of the supposed great grievances was that, when Sullivan found out about the boots, he refused to sign over the deed for the Oak Park house. Since the deed was paid off, Wright grew enraged.) So he reunited with Cecil and reestablished himself in the Schiller Building—that's a checkable fact. It was mid-1893 now, and, as also earlier noted, much in the world of building, not to say in the world itself, had changed. One of the largest things to happen in America—you could say the world—in mid-1893 was the opening of the World's Columbian Exposition, nominally to celebrate the four hundredth anniversary of the discovery of America. Forty-six countries participated. The neoclassic "White City," a term that has worked its way past myth and into the vernacular, occupied almost seven hundred glittery-pooled acres in the newly created Jackson Park on the South Side. According to Miller's *City of the Century*, the event "drew an estimated 27 million people, 14 million from outside the United States, making it the greatest tourist attraction in American history." There were twenty-four railroads serving Chicago at that moment—it was as if the city was the country's magnet. But far beyond turnstile facts, the fair changed the look and direction of much of architecture in America. In essence, the Beaux-Arts temporarily won, or at least won in what you could call the civic wallet. Into the new century, large American cities and little county seats would begin casting their downtown public faces—on banks and courthouses and libraries and museums—in the neoclassical revival mode, with Greek or Roman façades. As historian Neil Levine has put it, out of the fair emerged "a new urban vision of classical order"—except that the new was old. Best-selling books have been written about the great Chicago fair of 1893, and more will probably come. As critics have said, the fair is the principal reason why the National Mall in Washington, D.C., looks as it does, which is to say a monumental kind of architecture unimaginatively if beautifully copied from our supposed betters in the old world. The White City—accomplished by steel frames done in lath and staff, with a mixture of plaster, cement, and jute—all but put an end to the short-lived fame of Adler & Sullivan, an end (for the moment) to the dream of an American architecture for Americans. In a figurative sense, Louis Sullivan died, and died bitterly, at the hands of the Columbian Exposition. Like Cecil, after the Mitchell House in Racine, only more dramatically and consequentially, *lieber meister*'s career and life began afterward to drill downward: alcoholism and financial ruin. That, too, is only the barest synopsis of a long, sad story. In his life story, entitled *The Autobiography of an Idea,* the first bound copies of which came to him right at the moment when he was dying (in the spring of 1924), and which would be almost totally ignored by the reading public after he was dead, Sullivan remembered the fair as a "lewd exhibit of drooling imbecility." A great, supposed part of his story is that he couldn't adapt swiftly enough to the changing moment. It was his pride. And he wasn't as smooth with clients, although there are those who would argue that. Unlike his protégé, he lacked the charm, the grace, the natural guile, the wile.

(Footnote of a sort: Do you know where the term "the midway" comes from as it relates to all those county fairs you went to as a kid? Yes, the Chicago world's fair. The Midway Plaisance is today a slightly raised strip of green, 220 yards wide and a mile long, between East

Fifty-Ninth and East Sixtieth, along the southern rim of the University of Chicago. During the fair, the Midway Plaisance connected Jackson Park to the east with Washington Park to the west. The Plaisance, which people soon started calling the Midway, is where the fair's amusements were put. And a footnote to the footnote: If you went now to the westernmost tip of the Midway Plaisance, to Cottage Grove Avenue, right where it begins to merge into Washington Park, but turned south instead of north into the park, and proceeded along on the western side of the street for about forty yards, you'd be at the approximate long-since-bulldozed main entrance of the afore-described and long-since-bulldozed Midway Gardens, where, one seemingly calm late summer Saturday in 1914, a forty-seven-year-old arrogant man, about to suffer the shock of his life, had just paused in his work to take a sandwich and glance over the dailies.)

If Louis Sullivan died symbolically at the fair, Frank Lloyd Wright more or less sought to give the fair the back of his hand, not altogether successfully. It's true he scented the air and recognized the coming changes, and in this respect he put himself in for a competition to design the monumental Beaux-Arts-inspired Milwaukee Public Library and Museum. (He didn't win.) It's true also that the great Daniel H. Burnham (of Burnham & Root), who'd been put in charge of the fair and had willed it into existence in something like twenty months, had afterward tried to convince Wright to come to work for him. The story, burnished into legend, not least by Wright himself, was that Burnham, having been hugely impressed by Wright's Winslow House, was willing to underwrite a kind of all-expenses-paid, six-year, postgraduate education in Paris and Rome. Wright turned him down. He would stake his chances on his own visions.

As was earlier noted (and brushed past), the country in the mid-1890s, after the fair, entered an even worse recession than that of the 1870s, following the great Chicago fire (after the initial building burst that had taken place after the fire). But there will always be people of means to pay for what they desire, recessions be damned. The newly independent architect got his commissions, the first of which—at least in terms of a realized work—was the Winslow House. As historians have written, it was as if William Winslow was paradise-sent: a thirty-six-year-old Republican and suburban businessman with progressive bents in religion and social causes willing to grant his architect creative license. From a well-known passage in *An Autobiography*: "The Winslow House had burst on the view of that provincial suburb like the Prima Vera in full bloom. It was a new world to Oak Park and River Forest. That house became an attraction, far and near. Incessantly it was courted and admired. Ridiculed, too, of course." The wealthy Mr. Winslow, who dealt in ornamental iron and brass, reputedly had to slink to his morning commuter train to the city by alleyways, to avoid being laughed at by his neighbors.

———

Wright's own home, that wooded lot at the corner of Chicago and Forest, was expanding upward and outward as well—and suffering ridicule, too. Its first edition had been a tiny two-floor thing that pinwheeled around a central chimney core. When it was completed, in the early months of 1890, Forest Avenue had only recently been paved. Chicago Avenue, running east and west—east toward the city, west toward a seeming infinitude—was a dirt road. Beyond Chicago Avenue, to the north, were fields and farms and the occasional house: so the "suburb" of Oak Park was hardly what we regard today as a suburb. Despite how small the original house—six rooms—its owner had designed a grand hearth, with an inglenook, featuring cushioned benches on either side of the fireplace. The inglenook could be closed off with thick olive drapes, on wooden rings, hooked to a horizontal wooden bar: room within a room. There was also a well-lit studio upstairs, where the head draftsman for A&S did his nighttime and weekend work.

Other jobs came, in and around the city, in and around Oak Park. Other ships on the prairie began quickly to rise. Quickly? In the fall of 1895, just past the sixth year of his marriage, Wright's fourth child, a boy christened David Samuel, arrived. (He'd make 102, and be married three times, and, like his siblings, carry lifelong father wounds.)

By 1895, now two years on his own, work and kids seeming to arrive fairly nonstop, he had somehow wangled the financing and added an east wing, and designed a new kitchen, and remodeled the dining room, and, the pièce de résistance, had built up on the second floor a barrel-vaulted playroom that tourists from around the world now make pilgrimages to Oak Park just to see, because it is such a structural tour de force: a kind of miniature auditorium sitting on the top of a house. The kid in him had built this whimsical and wonderful thing. It was a gymnasium, a music room, a theater, and a kindergarten wrapped in one—with a span of eighteen feet at the top of the barrel. A small child could heave a ball in its arc and might not hit the ceiling. He inserted a grand piano in the wall and held it up with an iron belt. Over the playroom's huge hearth was a mural inspired by the *Arabian Nights,* something about a fisherman and a genie.

When you study photographs of the interior of the entire house in this period, it is surprising to see how much Victorian clutter there is, especially downstairs: a lot of fringed brocaded cloth and velvet coverings and potted plants and gaudy-looking lamps.

But there is another photograph that strikes in a different way. He is not in it, so possibly he made it. (Wright developed an early passion for photography and expensive cameras, just one more thing he couldn't afford.) It's a picture of his three children and expectant wife—so it had to have been taken sometime before September 26, 1895, when David Wright was born. Perhaps it's late winter 1895. The snow is piled outdoors. Kitty, who would have just been turning twenty-four, is in the south bedroom with the children. Her husband, soon to be twenty-eight, has turned this second-floor room into her dayroom. The room has wonderful light, owing to the way he has created a two-level ceiling, with a south bay, under a low soffit, with much glass. As historians have noted, there seems a delicacy in this room that's not quite duplicated anywhere else in the house. This seated and round-faced woman, a shawl around her, has a book in her hands. She's reading to her kids. Something far away and a bit older-than-her-years in her, as if lost in the fantasias of the story, even as she must be trying to do likewise for her kids. (Who knows, maybe it's Robert Louis Stevenson's *Treasure Island,* published about a decade before.) Sons John and Lloyd lean in close, propping themselves against their mom. Baby Catherine is a couple feet away, in the family crib, which is ornately tooled and spooled. Such a homely moment, time trapped in a rectangle, as if to testify: All is serene here. And yet the more you look, the more you sense, within the delicacy of this room, this moment, a kind of inexplicable sadness. Emily Dickinson: "There's a certain Slant of light, / Winter Afternoons— / That oppresses, like the Heft / Of Cathedral Tunes—."

————

Certain slants of mystery: Two years after the Winslow (and the year following that photograph), Wright designed in the Hyde Park/Kenwood neighborhood what is known today as the Isidore Heller House. It's a couple of blocks down and a few streets over from the Blossom and the McArthur. Like those two houses, not to say like the Winslow itself, the Heller House is another crossing point of who he was just about to become. Isidore Heller, born in Hungary, was part owner of Wolf, Sayer, and Heller, packers and suppliers for the Chicago butcher industry. He and his spouse, Ida, born in America, a decade younger, had acquired a narrow lot at 5132 South Woodlawn Avenue, and in 1896 they commissioned the Oak Park architect to build for them and their three children a three-story residence with multiple bedrooms and baths. On the rather severe-looking outside, Wright used yellow Roman brick, and he filled the warming inside with quarter-sawn white oak, waxed to a high gleam. Although it was unquestionably vertical, the house ended up looking somehow horizontal at the same time. In the words of Henry-Russell Hitchcock, an early-twentieth-century architectural historian and important critic of Wright's work, "the cross-shaped main rooms reach out toward one another," with the effect being that the "space of the rooms seems to break out of the long oblong mass into a cross axis." If that sounds like architecture-speak, the point is that the artist had created an open and flowing thing out of a trench-like property, on the exterior as well as the interior. But there are two larger points to make about this semi-famous house, constructed in 1897. In a sense, both of these larger points are written in stone: firstly, there is a Beaux-Arts frieze crowning the house, sculpted by an artist named Richard Bock, and these sensual winged maidens, up on the third story, are more than a little suggestive of the sensual ornament of *lieber meister*. Were they Wright's way of saying goodbye to Sullivan? Tim Samuelson has suggested that, as well as this idea: although the Wright archives contain various Heller plans, the drawings have suffered fire and other damage through the years, and it is hard to fix timelines. But if you study the plans, you are struck, as Samuelson notes, by the fact that the early ones are signed "Frank L. Wright, Architect, Chicago." But the later ones are signed just "Frank Lloyd Wright." Not only is the three-part name now more or less in permanent use, from this point forward, but it's as if someone is declaring to the world, *I am set in stone: FLW.*

I said two larger points—but, actually, three. Call it the cross-axial and free-flowing urban legend of Ida Heller, who died suddenly, at apparently fifteen minutes to midnight, on October 10, 1909, seventeen days after Frank Lloyd Wright ran away to Europe with Mamah Borthwick Cheney. *Apparently* fifteen minutes to midnight on that Sunday night, because the ink on the death certificate is a little rubbed out, and so you can't quite tell for certain whether she died at 11:45 a.m. or 11:45 p.m. That might partially explain the confusion in the five or six Chicago dailies that ran their death notices in the two days following: several indicated that she died on Sunday the 10th while several others, publishing their notices that Tuesday, reported that she had died "yesterday," meaning Monday.

The legend is that a striking, preserved, unhappily married, and perhaps sexually unfulfilled fifty-one-year-old housewife and mother of three threw herself in a fit of late-night love depression down the new three-story elevator shaft that had been built onto the north side of the house. Did that happen? It seems impossible to know. What is known is that the man who had designed the house twelve years before had recently returned to South Woodlawn Avenue to attend to the elevator addition as well as to other alterations. (A few years before, circa 1906, the Hellers had acquired extra footage on the north side of the property.) Ida Heller was roughly a decade older than her architect. But had something developed between them when he'd come back into her life in 1909? Had it been there in some form from the time when the house was first designed? And did word that Wright had suddenly abandoned his family and gone to Europe with his Oak Park lover take Ida under—and down? "Cause of Death" on the certificate was listed as "Valvular Heart disease and shock," and beneath those five words, an additional nine, indicating the contributory factor: "shock due to accidental fall at home of deceased." No mention of an elevator, much less of a hurling down.

There was no autopsy. The family physician, Dr. Filip Kreissl, reported her death to the coroner, and the coroner's report is there in the state archives, but it's brief and essentially repeats what's on the death certificate. The funeral service was held at the family home on Wednesday the 13th. In the obituary notices, most of the papers mentioned Ida's heart troubles, and one paper said she'd "recently returned from a European trip made in the hope of bettering her health." An intriguing sentence.

I decided to see what I could find out within the family. I had to go three generations down—the earlier generations were all gone. A great-granddaughter was in Old Greenwich, Connecticut. Her name is Dana Heller Whamond. We spoke on the telephone for about half an hour, and while she was not at all unfriendly, it was a mostly stilted conversation. She professed to know almost nothing, and I believed her. And yet the more we spoke, and the more I heard the "nothing," it was as if I was hearing everything I was awkwardly inquiring about.

She said she had never been to the house. She thought it had been torn down. Although she knew that the Heller was a Wright work, she knew little of its historical significance. She said that her father (his name was Peter E. Heller), who'd been raised in Chicago (whereas she had been raised in the East), had never wished to talk of his growing up, of his parents, of his grandparents, of the Heller side of the family. "It was just something that wasn't talked of, he didn't want to talk about it, he always made that clear," she said. But why? "I don't know," she said. Ida would have died well before Whamond's father was born, and her father had not grown up in that house. Her father's father—his name was Walter E. Heller, and he became a wealthy investment banker and semi-famous philanthropist—was an almost-nineteen-year-old son still living at home when Ida died. She hadn't known that fact. "You'd have to understand something about our family," she said. "Nobody wants to talk about the past. A strange family that way." She said that whenever she had traveled back to the Midwest with her father—Peter E. Heller died in 2012—there was always a certain awkwardness.

Before hanging up, Dana Whamond repeated that she'd never heard the story. But could she imagine it being true? Haltingly: "It fits." And then, politely: "But, if you don't mind, I'd just like to leave it where it lays."

Fine, except that this next part cannot be left where it lays.

Sometimes, in spooky ways that could never be explained, it almost seems as if the histories of certain Frank Lloyd Wright houses are trying to reproduce his own history of calamitous fall, improbable comeback, lurid headlines, quiet beauty, incalculable sorrow, financial desperation, sexual intrigue, unsolvable riddle, and, not least, the determination to survive—no, to triumph. There's even fire, not to say front-page suicide and murder of a ghastly kind, attached to the story of the long-lived B. Harley Bradley House, which sits now, as it sat then, in my parochial fifties childhood, at the very bottom of the same street I lived on, South Harrison Avenue, in the downstate river town of Kankakee, Illinois. Kankakee: an old Indian name, possibly from the Pottawatomi, said to mean "swamp country." It fits. There's been a lot of sinking in this house. And yet it's here, or maybe better said, "she's" here, for there's almost a palpable feminine quality to this magnificent great ship on the prairie that has lasted, a century and more, in spite of all. You could make the case she looks better today than she ever did.

It's been said this is the first Frank Lloyd Wright house that looks like a Frank Lloyd Wright house. You'll get the truth of that on the next page. The Bradley, so huge then, so huge now, came right at the tick of the new century, 1900; or, more figuratively, came out of Wright's head just as the second hand was sweeping toward midnight, taking him to a new place and level and fame. More than the Winslow or any other FLW thus far described, this is the key and penultimate transitional work to all of the full-bloomed Prairies immediately ahead. But I had no clue of that then. I wonder if I'd even heard the name "Frank Lloyd Wright." I was just a Catholic kid on my three-speed, gazing over at the thing he'd made, a little afraid of it, terribly pulled to it.

Attended by the Gothic

B. Harley Bradley House, 701 South Harrison Avenue, Kankakee, Illinois

First, architecturally:

He built it in the cruciform plan, and he made the main axis of the cross the living room and the kitchen. To situate you: The living room is located on the first floor directly beneath that low projecting gable at the front, on the second floor, with its deep overhanging eaves. Even on canvas-dreary February midwestern days, there can be wonderful light in this room, which is the central room of the house, and it filters and fractures through the polygonal bay windows (they're on both the first and second floors) that are tied together with cocoa-colored bands of wood trim. The ribbon art-glass casement windows offset the pale stucco exterior walls: so a kind of stark simplicity in and amid the daring, in and amid the instant strangeness to the look of the whole. (Did it come down from Mars?)

When you're on the inside, looking out, this curve of windows that fills up nearly the entire first-floor bay gives the effect of being in a modernist stained-glass chapel—or almost so.

But the cruciform design just spoken of: on either side of the living room and the kitchen—to achieve the two arms of the cross—the architect placed a reception room and a dining room. Except that he did one brilliant thing more: he elongated both arms of his cross by designing a carriage entry on one end (look to the far right, beneath that jutting-out cedar-shingled roof) and a screened porch on the far other end. No photograph, including this one, can capture that great stretch-out quality. For that, you must stand in front of it, or "her," on the sidewalk, perhaps from across the street, as I used to do, leaning on my handlebars. Then you'll get the full wide measure.

To further orient you: The carriage entry, or porte cochere, as the architect labeled it in his drawings, is at the north end of the property, and the screened porch, which has long been enclosed, is on the south end, just feet from the sloping bank of the Kankakee River. You can barely see the river but it deceptively curls behind. The Kankakee, gray and swollen in the winter, steelish-blue in the summer, has unseen undertows, a fact that seems to fit in metaphorically. In my timid altar-boy childhood, there were always stories of pleasure-boaters or fishermen or ice skaters or swimmers who'd gotten careless and lost their lives in the river, and once, I remember, *Life* magazine came to do a report.

We lived five blocks north from the extreme right edge of this photograph, at 230 South Harrison Avenue. The address of the Bradley is 701 South Harrison. In those five blocks, you pretty much got the economic demographics of a town of about twenty-five thousand people: upper crust to middle strivers. Our house was up where the ordinary folk lived, close to the courthouse and the town's shopping district, a rangy old three-story stucco that my barely middle-class parents rented for a hard-won seventy-five dollars a month. Down here, at the river, on the cluster of streets fringing what was then called Riverview Park, were where nearly all of the town's wealthy lived. Kankakeeans still speak of it that way: "at the river."

The extreme right edge of the photograph: What's also just out of sight here, immediately to the north of the carriage entry (where, incidentally, Wright also placed, or hid, the main entry), is the Bradley's sister house. It's known as the Warren R. Hickox House. Yes, two Frank Lloyd Wrights sitting side by side, in a little rust-belted and once-agricultural and long-economically-threatened but still-handsome Illinois town roughly sixty miles south of downtown Chicago. The Hickox is smaller than the Bradley. It has always been a private residence. But the Bradley, now a Wright public site, is the sibling that takes your eye. It's the one that pulls in Wright-goers off the interstate to take the tour. And yet there are scholars willing to make the case that the less elaborate Hickox is the more radical architectural work. In some uber-scholarly sense, that might be true.

The Bradley had a riverfront sitting area, a great hearth of Roman brick, a sleeping porch on the second floor. The Bradley had a separate staircase for the servants. The Bradley had five horse stalls and a kennel and a hayloft and a chauffeur's quarters in the stable/carriage house in the rear. The Bradley had more than one hundred art-glass windows and light screens. The Bradley had specially designed furniture, both freestanding and built-in pieces. The Bradley had a butler's pantry and a first-floor "dressing room." The Bradley had a front terrace with low walls that seemed to be reaching right out to the sidewalk. In a way, it was like some manor house out of the English Tudor countryside—in Kankakee, Illinois.

Even the carriage house and stable were outsized in its creator's imagination: three thousand square feet, on two floors. (The main house is six thousand square feet.)

In 1988, before the saving began, when many art objects in the house had been plundered, sold off piecemeal to antiques dealers and other speculators, when raccoons had been eating through the roof for several years, an agent for megastar Barbra Streisand bid $176,000 at Christie's auction house in Manhattan for a long, low, brass-handled, desk-table from the Bradley. The price hit more than twice the estimate.

Years before that, just at the point when this house would have been first stoking my wonder (and also my vague fears, which must have had to do with all those layers of overhanging and brooding-seeming roof and those stark colors on the exterior), the Bradley had converted itself into an inn called Yesteryear. This was 1953, five decades after its birth. Grand people dined in there, on white tablecloths and with pressed napkins. They were eating by candlelight on the other side of those glittering ribbon windows. I would have been a fourth-grader at St. Patrick's Elementary, which was one block over and three blocks up from the Bradley. One of my classmates was Burma Mathews. Her family was Catholic and middle class, too, and I'd bet they also never got to eat at Yesteryear. She has long given tours at the Bradley as a volunteer docent. On one visit there, as I was awed again by the interior gleams and quarter-sawn-oak angularities and interflowing spaces, Burma and I, out of earshot of the other tour-goers, whispered about what an egotistical jerk he could be. Then she said, "But look at this thing he made."

Yes, take a look at it again. If the point to be stressed here is the feeling of utter horizontality, the more so when you see it from the outside and in its so-called flesh, then what to make of that aforesaid imposing and low-hanging and deep-eave gable at the front? Doesn't this second-floor gable, not quite in the center and projecting out toward the sidewalk, sort of wreck the horizontal effect? In a sense, yes, because the front gable, no matter its lowness, gives an undeniable vertical accent, even when you are standing fifty yards off and nearly gasping at the kind of north-south stretch-out Wright simultaneously achieved. So to experience the house for the first time (although maybe not as a child) is to imagine someone's interior torment—and perhaps to feel a little of your own. It's as if something schizoid was going on in him, some kind of unresolved artistic torture, as if teams of mules were pulling the house and the house's creator in opposite directions. As if that creator sensed that he was almost there, to his next level of purity and abstraction, but that he couldn't quite yet make it, couldn't quite find it yet, couldn't quite get over the transom of his own imagination. The full getting-over wouldn't happen until the following year, 1901, in a wealthy North Shore suburb called Highland Park, Illinois, when Frank Lloyd Wright began designing the Ward W. Willits House. Architectural historians seem in general agreement that the Willits stands as the first unadulterated Prairie. Is it a greater house than the Bradley? No doubt. And yet the argument might be made that this house, in economically hanging-on Kankakee, is the far worthier study, because it's the one that came just as the clock was closing in on twelve.

Let someone else tell the full tale of the B. Harley Bradley, architecturally and otherwise. It could easily make its own book. All there's room for here is the more or less capsule version, which might still suggest the truth, or near-truth, of a proposition that's never been explored enough: that there are particular FLW houses, for whatever reasons, that seem bent on writing their own versions of his own byzantine history. It's as if it's all there, or here, his whole up-and-down life, in a kind of weird, mirroring miniature.

————

In the middle years of the nineteenth century, a plowman out of the East named David Bradley, with a knack for tinkering with farm equipment, imported pig iron into Chicago, which was his new home. He worked at a foundry. He partnered with a man who made wagons and buggies, and eventually he bought out that man and gave the concern his own name. He invented something called the Diamond Breaker Plow, which won prizes at the 1893 Chicago world's fair, and he also did innovative things with horse-drawn manure spreaders. In 1895 his Chicago manufacturing plant, needing room to grow, relocated downstate, to North Kankakee. In gratitude, the financially pressed city fathers changed North Kankakee's name to Bradley City, and then the next year just to Bradley. Bradley's sons worked for him in the David Bradley Manufacturing Company, and the next generation did, too, and one of these grandchildren, apparently less striving, perhaps because of a lingering, lifelong infantile paralysis, was named B. Harley Bradley. (The "B" stood for Byron.) On January 6, 1897, in the town's Episcopal church, twenty-six-year-old B. Harley Bradley, who'd gone to Amherst College, married Anna M. Hickox, a native Kankakeean four years his senior. Anna and her brother, Warren Hickox, Jr., had inherited from their recently deceased father (whose wealth was in the real estate and loan business) a wooded site at the river, bottom of South Harrison. Two families, the farm-implement Bradleys and the long-prominent Hickoxes, had joined, perhaps the closest thing Kankakee then had to aristocracy. Three years later, in the winter of 1900, Anna and her brother took a train to Oak Park and engaged Frank Lloyd Wright to build for them and their families adjoining if not quite equal-sized houses.

But something went wrong on the Bradley side, or maybe it was many somethings. B. Harley and Anna, and their adopted daughter, Margaret, lived in the house that they'd named Glenlloyd for about eleven and a half years—from the spring of 1901 until the fall of 1912. After B. Harley was dead, after he had shot himself through both temples one summer Monday morning in 1914 while still in his pajamas in a room at the LaSalle Hotel in downtown Chicago, there were stories—in

Chicago dailies and passed around orally in Kankakee—about a previous suicide try with ether, about the reemergence of the polio, about "the mystery woman." Here is the basic narrative of what seems to have taken place, and at least some of it is documentable, in and amid the many conflicting news reports: the patriarch of the Bradleys, the one who'd started the company, had died in 1899, and afterward his descendants had tried to carry things on—until Sears, Roebuck & Company bought out the firm in 1910, keeping the name but otherwise wresting control, even if certain family members were allowed to stay on. Was there enough money to go around among the family heirs? It can't be said precisely. What is known is that B. Harley's finances began seriously to dwindle. In September 1912, he and his wife—whose name the house was in—deeded Glenlloyd to a wealthy Iowan named A. E. Cook. They did so in trade: for one dollar and also 522 acres of Cook's western Iowa holdings, which were vast. So B. Harley and Anna and their daughter—as well as his retired parents, who'd been living with them in the house at the river—moved to Onawa, Iowa, hoping to start anew.

But things hadn't worked in Iowa, and money pressures seem to have been a lot of the reason why. Two years later, in July 1914, forty-three-year-old B. Harley left for Chicago on a business trip. The trip didn't go well. At three a.m. on a Saturday morning, on hotel stationery, he wrote a letter to Anna in Onawa and essentially said he was going to do away with himself. "Dearest Anna, You perhaps don't know that I love you and I am a coward to get out of it all and leave it up to you to make so good." Toward the end he said, "I know you will expect me home on the 7:30 train and I am going to disappoint you just this once more. Forgive me if you can, and don't forget that I love you." He posted the letter in a box later that morning. He'd already purchased a .32 caliber automatic pistol for ten dollars at a Loop sporting goods store. The letter arrived by train in Iowa on schedule, at 7:30 p.m. on Sunday night. Anna was waiting trackside with a horse and buggy. Thinking her husband would step off, the death letter, in effect, stepped off instead. Terrified, she wired a family member in Chicago. Meanwhile her husband, having been out for much of that day, came in at ten o'clock in the evening, placed the revolver under his pillow, and went to bed. He awoke about nine on Monday morning, lay thinking, propped himself up with two pillows, pulled the trigger. The shot blinded him. Somewhat later, a maid at the LaSalle, finding his room locked, sent for the house detective. The detective hoisted himself up and peered in through a window slit above the door. When the detective and the house doctor broke in, there he was, mortally wounded, strangely calm. "I have a few lucid hours left," he reportedly said. "Send for a *Tribune* reporter." The next morning, the *Chicago Tribune*, wishing its readers to think it had an exclusive, put the story at the top of page one, column three: BUYS DEATH GUN WITH NO PERMIT. But the city's other sheets were trying to own the story as well. In most of them, B. Harley's quotes strain credulity. To the *Tribune*, he was able to speak in rounded paragraphs about coming to the city "expressly for the purpose of committing suicide. My health hasn't been good and business reverses caused me to shoot myself." Not to be outdone, the *Chicago Examiner* wrote: " 'Got a cigaret?' the dying man said. But he was too weak to smoke. He lay quietly for a moment. Then a look of disgust came on his face. 'To h——l with it,' he muttered and became unconscious again." He lasted until five o'clock that afternoon. By then, Anna had received a wire that her husband was dying at the city's St. Luke's Hospital. With her nineteen-year-old daughter she rushed for the overnight six o'clock train, not knowing he was already dead by the time they'd boarded. The two arrived in time for the Tuesday morning inquest at a morgue on North Clark Street. The verdict: temporary insanity. B. HARLEY BRADLEY SUICIDES was the headline in the *Kankakee Daily Republican*, but only on page 11 in its first-day report. The paper had been occupied with the Interstate Fair taking place in Kankakee.

Not that it's been commented on much (or maybe ever), but these headlines—in Chicago, in Kankakee, in western Iowa—came almost exactly a month ahead of some other (and much larger) headlines about a noonday rampage in a place called Spring Green, Wisconsin. In the Chicago papers, the page one stories about B. Harley appeared on Tuesday, July 14, the day after his suicide. By the next day, the story was essentially over for Chicago readers, consigned to the inside pages, and by then, too, the question of a so-called mystery woman in the case had all but vanished, like the supposed mystery woman herself, who was said to have been in a Chicago boardinghouse, awaiting some kind of contact from B. Harley. That part of the story seemed to fall away pretty fast.

In Kankakee, on July 15, a story headlined DEATH LETTER OF LOVE ran on page one, the headline sounding eerily similar in tone, if not in content, to some Taliesin headlines that would be appearing in EXTRA EXTRA afternoon editions one month later.

Did Frank Lloyd Wright see any of the Chicago stories, and, if so, did he quickly connect B. Harley's name? It can't be said. His name wasn't mentioned in the Chicago dailies in connection with the death, or at least none that could be found. (Even in Kankakee, Wright's name didn't come up in most of the coverage.) But it seems possible, if not likely, that he would have seen at least one or two of the Chicago stories. He was in and out of the city in this period, working intensely on Midway Gardens. He enjoyed turning through the papers. It relaxed him.

Anna Bradley? She and her daughter and in-laws came back to Kankakee. The woman who'd grown up in privilege (as a schoolgirl, her parents had sent her off to Miss Bliss' School for Girls in Rochester, New York) opened the Tea Room, on Court Street, in downtown Kankakee, where she did the cooking and lived above the store with her in-laws. (They later left town.) Anna lived in her hometown for another twenty-four years, a faithful communicant at her childhood church, until April 1938, when they buried her beside her husband, out at Mound Grove Cemetery. She had died at the modest home of her brother Warren, who had been earlier forced to give up *his* fine Frank Lloyd Wright home down at the river. Yes, he, too, had lost his fortune.

Capsuling the next six and a half decades, up to the critical saving year of 2005: First came the Birdman (who had taken up the house from A. E. Cook, who, incidentally, himself later lost his fortune but who didn't shoot himself or come otherwise to a page-one end). That's how Kankakee historians affectionately refer to him: the Birdman. His name was Joseph H. Dodson. He held the property for the next thirty-four years. For many years he'd been a member of the Chicago Board of Trade. But his first and last passion was for birds. At one point he served as vice president of the American Audubon Association. In Wright's ornate stable, he began manufacturing Dodson Bird Houses, distributing them nationally. He published pamphlets with such titles as "Your Bird Friends and How to Win Them." He planted trees and shrubs, put out dozens of birdbaths and feeders, bought suet by the carload. By his counting he had three or four hundred species living with him and his wife, Edith, every spring and summer: robins, scarlet tanagers, orioles, cardinals, brown thrashers, warblers, flickers, rose-breasted grosbeaks, hummingbirds, juncos, wood thrushes, vireos. They were his surrogate children, turning the property sweet with song before daylight, but from other points of view (the neighbors') infernal with noise. His Martin Apartment House, more than five feet high, had a ventilated attic and ninety "rooms" for his nesters. It was made of cypress and redwood with a bright copper roof. It was like a tiny Frank Lloyd Wright production.

In the peak of a Kankakee summer, you could anchor a boat in the river opposite the landing dock of the B. Harley Bradley House and look through the tall trees and make out the peaks of the gables and imagine a one-acre aviary without walls. If the Birdman of Kankakee, wandering the grounds in a straw boater, in his dress shirt with sleeve garters, is said to have taken reasonable care of Frank Lloyd Wright's near-masterpiece, at least until the last years, he loved his birds far more, and apparently didn't mind saying so.

He died at the property, which he had long named Bird Lodge, in the fall of 1949. He was a widower of eighty-seven. His spouse had died five years before, and after her death and before his own he had deeded the house to his secretary, Lida Nelis, who was almost three decades younger than he was, and who had long served him in the birdhouse-building business, and possibly other things, too, not necessarily of a business nature. According to city records and collective memory, she lived in the house with her own spouse in the final year of the Birdman's illness. Did she tend him in his dying? Was she cynically after his money when his mind may have been befogged? Was there always more to the story than that of bird boss and loyal young secretary? The legends float.

Next, an interim owner, a local car dealer and his wife, Ed and Alice Bergeron. Then, in January 1953, the transition to Yesteryear. The new proprietors were two men, in their middle and late thirties, who met in the military during World War II, where at least one of them had worked as a cook. Their names were Marvin Hammack and Ray Schimel. They ran a colonial inn in St. Joseph's, Michigan, and had been induced to come to Kankakee to repurpose Wright's increasingly famous building. They liked going around in three-piece suits with tea roses in the lapels.

They didn't go around holding hands, but the citizenry knew about them, or thought it did. (In fact, they *were* a gay couple. These decades later, a family member expressed astonishment, and also gratitude, that Kankakee had seemed to accept them so quickly into its midst.) It was as if these cultivated gentlemen, known to be kind to neighborhood children, were giving Kankakee a fresh cut of class. Soon restaurant-goers were driving down from Chicago and even up from St. Louis to try the prime rib and steaks, the baked Indian pudding, the fudge pecan cake balls. For meals catering to businessmen at midday, the innkeepers set up what they called their "Ballerina Room." Not an immediate hit.

Hammack and Schimel watched over the house for the next three decades, a difficult proposition when diners were coming in and out six days a week. (Sometimes they arrived in chartered buses.) And then the restaurateurs got sick—cancer for the one, a condition akin to Parkinson's for the other. They had property in Fort Lauderdale and had long wished to get out from under the daily grind and hard winters. The house was starting badly to show its age, and along with this had come declining reviews and falloff of trade. In April 1984, after a year and a half of trying, the ill couple negotiated a sale with a local businessman and his out-of-state partner. Reportedly, only three pieces of Wright's original furniture remained. Half a dozen colored glass ceiling-screens and other custom furnishings had been recently stripped out and sold for cash. There seemed new hope for the restaurant, but not even ten months after acquiring it, the owners filed for bankruptcy. Still they tried to keep the doors open. In March 1985, during the Friday lunch hour, Commonwealth Edison shut off the electricity. Six months later, a reporter for the *Tribune* drove down from Chicago and looked around and wrote that the B. Harley Bradley had "deteriorated into a vacant, cold and musty-smelling building," with first, second, and third mortgage holders fighting among themselves. On the tables, brown and pink folded linen napkins stood upright between silverware furred with dust.

And then, in 1986, Stephen Small entered the frame, and there came the strangest turn of all. His family had long controlled a conglomerate called Mid America Media. *The Kankakee Daily Journal* was one of its properties, which included broadcasting and print groups across several states. Forty-year-old Steve Small, who'd been a high executive in the company, until its recent sale, tooled around town in a maroon

Mercedes. He was a family man, a nice guy. He and his spouse intended a full restoration, starting with the caving-in roof. But on September 2, 1987, with scaffolding up and the work under way, Small got lured from his own nearby home in the middle of the night. (The voice on the other end of the line told him the Bradley was being burglarized.) His captors, who were after a million dollars in ransom, put a stocking cap over his face and handcuffed him and drove him to a wooded area about twelve miles southeast of town, where they buried him alive beneath three feet of sandy earth, in a homemade box six feet by three feet. They gave him five candy bars, a jug of water, a flashlight, a package of gum, and another light hooked up to two car batteries. For his supposed breathing, they rigged a length of PVC plumbing tube that stuck up through the sand and the top of the box like a periscope. The PVC tube didn't work. The media heir suffocated to death as he apparently kept trying with muffled screams to jam at the ceiling of his shallow grave. At the trial, the medical examiner testified that he'd probably survived for no more than three or four hours. About seventy-two hours after he'd been taken, the police and the FBI were led to the box and his body. By then they had the kidnappers in custody: a thirty-year-old local cocaine trafficker and his twenty-six-year-old girlfriend, who'd been a cashier at Kroger. (The ransom demands had been haplessly made from pay phones at local gas stations; the police had little trouble tracing them.) The nationally covered trial was in the Kankakee County Courthouse, and Frank Lloyd Wright's name and house came up in some of the stories. The trial didn't quite last two weeks, and on the first day the state wheeled into the courtroom, and kept it there, the plywood box that the ringleader had built in his garage. (His name was Daniel Edwards, and he had sealed the seams with white caulking, but had left in the trash a pair of gloves with the caulking on them.) The jury listened to a recording of Small's voice from his grave; it also saw a videotape of his body. Edwards was convicted of first-degree murder; a few days afterward he got the death penalty. His accomplice-girlfriend, Nancy Rish, tried separately, got life. (In 2003, the governor of Illinois, who was from Kankakee, commuted all death row sentences to life imprisonment.)

In 1990, Frank Lloyd Wright's hard-luck house, which by now, at least to some, was an object of almost macabre curiosity, came into the hands of its ninth set of owners: a firm of Kankakee lawyers and an architect. They turned the Bradley into offices, doing what they could to restore things, even if their agenda wasn't necessarily that of Wright purists. Their restorations didn't include the stable/carriage house, and when the building seemed about to cave in on itself, they applied for a permit to demolish it. "Wrong on Wright," the *Daily Journal* editorialized in 2001. "Kankakee has always seemed to be a community that has struggled with its past." Maybe that sentence threw down the gauntlet. A few years later, in 2005, a vice president of a Chicago acoustics design firm, along with his wife, acquired the Bradley. It was as if Gaines and Sharon Hall were the true inheritors at last. Relying on Wright's original drawings, the Halls set to work rescuing the entire property, but first the stable. In the house they painted the walls in shades of mustard and green and deep burgundy, using a technique called scumbling, popular at the time the Bradley was built. (You soften the colors by applying thin coats, as many as four, ending up with a delicate mottling effect.) The old house, against every reversal, every injury of time and weather, every gossip and bad headline, was coming back, if not to what it once was, then to something trying to honor what it once had been.

Except not quite: *fire.* On a Friday night in early January 2006, after the Halls had been living in the Bradley for a year, with the work going on around them, the couple was having dinner with friends at the Kankakee Country Club, which is in the river district, about five minutes from the house. An assistant manager came over and whispered into Hall's ear: "Sir, your house is on fire." He jumped up from the table and ran to the parking lot. Sharon Hall said to the server: "What's going on? Where did my husband go?" Someone drove her over to the house, where ladder trucks were shooting towers of water onto her home's new roof, with the sky weirdly lit up in arc lights. The fire had started in the attic near or in an air-conditioning unit—which, of course, wasn't on in January—and had begun to work its way down the chimney, through the master bedroom on the second floor. If the fire had come a few hours later, the Halls might have died in their bed. Sharon Hall found her husband at the ring of the shooting sprays. He was shaking his head while the firemen put out the last flames. She said, "That's it, I'm done." Her husband turned to her and said, "Okay, but will you take me with you?"

They were out fourteen months (the damage was said to be two hundred thousand dollars), but started in again, and over the next four years brought the house up to a kind of shine and artistic integrity it had almost never known, except at the start of a previous century. These days the B. Harley Bradley, which has been on the National Register of Historic Places since 1986, is under the stewardship of a nonprofit organization called Wright in Kankakee. They take extremely proud care. I've been on the tour with Kankakee historians and with my old first-grade girlfriend, Burma Mathews. I've been through the Bradley's thirteen light-refracting rooms with Gaines Hall, retired now from his Chicago architectural practice and also from a late-life stint as a professor and associate dean at the University of Illinois. Some days it seems quiet as a church in there. "This is the house that changed the face of American architecture," Hall likes to say. If the sentence isn't literally true, it's true enough. Leave it where it lays.

———

Right at the tick of the new century: In the early summer of 1900, at about the point when contractors would have been getting set to break ground on the Bradley and Hickox (building records haven't survived, but this is the timeline), a puzzlingly generous man named Robert C. Spencer, Jr., published, in a widely respected and large-format professional journal headquartered in Boston, a twelve-page article about Frank Lloyd Wright. It put him on the architectural map—in national and international ways. It was the first serious piece about Wright's work, and it was remarkable for its unstinting praise and graceful (if semi-florid) writing and, not least, for its apparent lack of professional jealousy on the part of its author, for he, too, was an ambitious architect on the Midwest rise. It was lavishly illustrated with line drawings and floor plans and photographs. (At the back were foldouts with exquisite renderings of the Winslow House and Heller House.) The article was entitled "The Work of Frank Lloyd Wright," and it was as if the editors of the June issue of *Architectural Review* (not to say the fellow architect himself) had sat down and agreed: Okay, if we're going to feature this guy, let's take it over the top, him over the top. "Few architects have given us more poetic translations of material into structure than Frank Lloyd Wright," Spencer wrote, going on to say in the next sentence that "this young man, whose career has but begun" was providing his profession "the cause of independent architectural thought and original native effort." The houses he was building "embody new thought and new ideas. They have life. They express clearly and consistently certain ideals of home." They represent the best hope for "a real basis for a great national architecture." When the dreary rest of "the middle-class houses of the west were honeycombed with the box-like compartments which were considered necessary, his houses were pioneers in the broader appreciation of 'home.'" If his work showed "an evident love for the horizontal dimension and the horizontal line," it was never the horizontal for the horizontal's sake.

Did Wright himself write this lavish thing, under the ghosting of Robert C. Spencer? And who, by the way, was Spencer?

Unlike Wright, he was well educated. Unlike Wright, he was tall and slender, with silvery-gray hair. He was three years older, having been born in 1864. He and Wright had become close friends. In fact, Spencer may have been Wright's closest friend in the period after Cecil Corwin, up until the early 1900s. Unlike Wright, Spencer was from a well-off family, in Milwaukee, and had graduated from the University of Wisconsin in mechanical engineering (again, unlike the person he was writing of, who'd barely stopped for a cup of coffee there and would prevaricate about it ever after) and had then enrolled in architecture at Massachusetts Institute of Technology and had then gone to work for two of Boston's best firms. (J. Lyman Silsbee was also educated at MIT, and Louis Sullivan had attended for a year in 1874.) He had won a fellowship, which allowed him and his wife to travel through Europe for two years, studying architecture. Then Spencer had landed in Chicago, where he worked for the Midwest branch of a prior Boston employer, and then in 1895 he had started his own practice in an office in the tower at the Schiller Building, right across the hall from where Cecil and Frank had happily stacked their names on a plate of clear glass in gold leaf two years before. In the following year, over the winter of 1896–97, with Wright's best pal having peremptorily gone away, it seems to have been the decent Robert Spencer who'd convinced Wright to join him and two others in a loft space at Steinway Hall.

Steinway Hall: one of those iconic place-names in the history of Chicago architecture—at least iconic to anyone who's ever tried to understand what's been variously and imprecisely called, at one time or another, the Chicago School and the New School of the Middle West and the Secessionist and the Protestants and, not least, the Prairie School, which is the name that exists in popular imagination but in truth came into more common use only in the 1960s. Strictly defined, "Prairie School" refers to that loose association of architects who worked in the middle of America from roughly the turn of the century up until about 1920. The group's spiritual mentor was always Louis H. Sullivan. In Chicago, Steinway Hall was one of the group's earliest homes.

It was on "piano row": on Van Buren Street, between Michigan Avenue and Wabash Avenue, very close to the lakefront. The eleven-story building housed a concert hall and offices and a big showroom for the grand-piano maker to exhibit its wares in competition with other manufacturers. At the top of Steinway, in a kind of attic space, under a peaked roof, too cold in the winter, too hot in the summer, Robert Spencer and Frank Lloyd Wright and Dwight Perkins and Myron Hunt formed the initial core of what we think of today as the Prairie School. That's where they did their drafting. Apparently, the four shared a receptionist on the eleventh floor and put up wall screens and luxuriated in their cheap rent. At noon they'd take a sandwich and maybe go out on the roof and talk about the future of American domestic architecture. Not particularly theory-minded, they looked nonetheless for certain inspiration to the international Arts and Crafts Movement, promulgated by such British thinkers as William Morris and Charles Robert Ashbee. Its American adherents wished to make beautiful things, and, like their English arts-and-crafts counterparts, they wanted to make them with traditional craftsmanship, with respect for materials, and with simple forms: brick, plaster, stained wood. But, as various scholars have pointed out, to think of the Prairie School as only architecture is missing the point—its makers, and none more so than Frank Lloyd Wright, were after a totality of art experience. As the preeminent architectural historian Richard Guy Wilson has written: The so-called school (it was never really that) wasn't "a movement about style as much as a movement about an ideology of independence."

Wright was a founding member of a kind of non-club luncheon club of these Chicago arts-and-crafts independents. They named themselves The Eighteen. They took up leadership roles in the Chicago Architectural Club, the successor of the Chicago Architectural Sketch Club. The

CAC, in turn, helped establish, in 1899, the Architectural League of America. These organizations were a way and means of proselytizing their work. Wright, pretty much the lifelong non-joiner, nonetheless participated in some CAC events over the years, and indeed was showcased far above his colleagues in several group exhibitions at the Art Institute of Chicago: the first among equals, except none of the others were even close to his equal in his own mind—and, in fact, he was right.

Over about two decades, turn of the century through the First World War, maybe as many as sixty or seventy architects worked in the Prairie style throughout the greater Midwest: Minnesota, Iowa, Wisconsin, parts of Illinois. But the nucleus of the movement was always Chicago. One of the floaters in and out of the Prairie dream was George Elmslie, spoken of earlier. And as was also said earlier, and is self-evident, but is worth contemplating again: not one of these other Prairie practitioners has ever been able to endure on the lid of our national cultural eyeball, even if books have been written, separately or collectively, about the work of Irving and Allen Pond and Walter Burley Griffin and Marion Mahony and Barry Byrne and Thomas Talmadge and William Gray Purcell and all the rest. They are famous men (and several women) who aren't at all famous. A certain American boarhog saw to that. Okay, he saw to it with his greater giftedness, his ability to move mentally through space (and, in a way, even time) as he envisioned something he hadn't yet drawn. But he also saw to it with something else that is hard to pin down: force of personality, preposterousness of life story, rankness of ego, rage of ambition, all of it. In a way, it's like trying to figure out how one starting-out American writer named Ernest Hemingway, sitting around the café tables of Paris in the early and middle 1920s, turned himself almost three-dimensionally, as if moving through space and time, into something that a hundred others near him could not. Yes, his genius (at least genius then), but something else that seems uncircumscribable. And yet, bringing the riddle and the matter back not to words on a page but materials rising out of the ground, the fact remains that you can go seek out Robert Closson Spencer, Jr.'s work today—say, the Edward W. McCready House at 231 North Euclid Avenue in Oak Park—and fall in love with its simple, declarative Prairie beauty, even as so relatively few seem to know of its existence. (Any serious student of Midwest architecture knows it.) Spencer and his partner built this house in 1907. Its yellow-orange brick seems in perfect harmony with its deep-set door and its art-glass windows. There is such a subtle balancing of details. It has a kind of Palladian formality. As it happens, the McCready is next door to a fairly early and ungainly Hansel-and-Gretel-looking Wright work (1897) known as the George W. Furbeck House. Hands down, the McCready wins, at least on this Oak Park corner. If Spencer couldn't think in three dimensions in the way of Wright, he created something fine and lasting. In a way, it's the Cecil story, but without the tragic echoes. (Spencer had a long, good career, as a writer, architect, and businessman, and taught at two universities, and retired finally to Arizona.)

And yet none of this addresses the question suggested above with an adverb: *puzzlingly*. What was in it for Robert Spencer to write such a self-effacing and map-placing piece of architectural criticism about a friend and younger colleague? (Spencer was such a prolific writer for popular and professional magazines that you'd almost want to call him an architect-journalist, or vice versa.) Some pages ago, in regard to Wright's bootleg houses, bearded by Cecil, the question was raised whether Cecil's best friend had importuned him, or seized on what he might have recognized as an emotional vulnerability, or paid him a fee?

According to Prairie scholars whom I've queried on the question, the answer mostly seems to be that, no, Spencer was just a generous-minded guy not unstrung by someone else's greater abilities. He recognized he was part of a movement, and he wanted to get the word out. It may have been that simple. But Wright's great charm must have come into play, too. You can picture the sly and not-so-sly egging. You can also not picture Wright doing any such thing for Spencer, were the tables turned. Yes, he could be surprisingly generous—his protective tenderness toward Cecil in the autobiography is a case in point—but not this kind of generous. Hemingway was much the same way: great, surprising, hidden streaks of decency, but not when it came to the work itself, or any work perceived to threaten his.

It is thought that Wright may have had a direct role in the production of Spencer's article. He may have designed and laid it out, and it has also been speculated that he even had a hand in writing parts of it (which, to my mind, would raise ethical-cum-journalistic issues).

Spencer worked on the piece in the final months of 1899 and into the early months of 1900, readying it for June publication. In his soaring last paragraph, the author gives Wright's real age. This is how that paragraph ends:

> Here, in this condensed monograph of a young man's work, a boy's work, perhaps, as he is but thirty-two, the best obtainable that he has done during an independent career of seven years has been concisely presented for the thoughtful consideration of the architects of America. . . . Youth admires courage. Enthusiasm is contagious. Youth wants to be free and exults in the use of its own untrammeled power. As a leader of revolt against dead custom Frank Wright has come into touch with the younger spirits because of his own youth and because his work has varied from the humblest cottage to the largest project,—because he has entered into every part of it with a zeal and courage which are a perpetual inspiration to those who understand and know him best.

He *was* thirty-two, in those early months of 1900, since he was born on June 8, 1867. Clearly, he told Spencer the truth. (As a rule, you don't find the consistent age-fudging for about another decade and a half, at which point he starts to shave off two years—though not always. You can track this on passport applications and ship passenger lists—he left us a documentary trail.)

That issue aside, my own belief is that Wright must have had some kind of serious hand in the piece, from early stages to completion. Consider, just as a small matter, the idiosyncratic punctuation—a comma, followed by a dash—after the words "largest project." That's Wright's style all the way.

Eight months after the Spencer article, in February 1901, at just about the time when B. Harley Bradley and his wife and daughter would have been getting ready to move into the nearly completed Glenlloyd, *Ladies' Home Journal,* the largest mass-circulation magazine in America, ran the first of two articles under Wright's own name. This put him on the architectural map in another way, in a publication with more than a million readers. They are historic pieces in their own right. The first was called "A Home in a Prairie Town," and the second, published in

July of that year, was entitled "A Small House with 'Lots of Room in It.'" Both were one page long and included drawings and floor plans. What Wright essentially seems to have done was to rework what he had done on the fly for his two Kankakee clients. He was trying to show the homemakers of America that an indigenous and new American style of house could be had at reasonable prices. Actually, all this had been the idea of the editor of the *Journal*, Edward Bok—as early as 1895 he had been seeking articles from builders and designers on "model suburban houses at moderate cost." The two cruciform plans Wright presented have been called prototype plans for all his great Prairies that followed in the next eight or nine years—but that isn't precisely accurate. The real prototypes were already in the ground, at Kankakee. The two magazine plans seem to have been a bettering in his own mind of what he might have done had he had a little more time, even as he suggested less expensive materials to keep down costs (for instance, Georgia pine floors instead of quarter-sawn oak). In the words of historian Neil Levine: they were houses that showed something "even more extended, open, and spatially dynamic" than what he'd done on South Harrison Avenue. His "Small House with 'Lots of Room in It'" looks a lot like the Bradley House. Wright didn't call his offerings "Prairie Houses" (as some have suggested), but it's true that, in the first article, the words "Prairie" and "Home" appear in close proximity in the headline—which he very possibly didn't write. Editors tend to write the headlines. (For the record, the first known time, at least in print, Wright seems ever to have used the term "Prairie School," uppercasing it, putting it in quotes, was quite late, in a July 30, 1936, essay in the British periodical *Architects' Journal*. In this same professional publication, two issues prior, on July 16, 1936, he spoke of the Winslow House as the first of his "prairie houses," lowercase. He didn't use quote marks.)

Proximity: There is a boomeranging sentence in the text of the first *Ladies' Home Journal* piece—the one published in February 1901. He said, in regard to his open floor plan, with all of its airiness, that he was trying to present "the least resistance to a simple mode of living in keeping with a high ideal of the family life together." That's his writing voice. He was speaking architecturally, but in another way, whether he knew or not, and maybe he exactly knew, or somehow knew in his glands, he was writing a kind of epitaph for his own life story, and its coming crash.

He *wasn't* going to keep his family together, not this one. In the way that the words "Prairie" and "Home" had been more or less conjoined, the words "family life" and "together," although next to each other on the printed line, amounted to a beautiful lie. Tragic lie. Prefiguring lie. And, as a matter of fact, that was also going to hold sadly true for the three-member family just getting set to move into the big fine Frank Lloyd Wright house on the north bank of the deceptively treacherous Kankakee River.

The inner mysteries of a ruptured family: No biographer or historian or critic or journalist or novelist or playwright or filmmaker or opera librettist or just half-interested passerby with a Frank Lloyd Wright field guide could ever hope to pierce the whole truth of that. That kind of truth is God's truth. But from the outside of things, skein of the story, this might safely be said: They had gotten married way too early and young. They had slowly begun to grow apart. He had his work and his ego. She had the children. The children had come too fast—at least the first four had. It was the lovers' profligacy and passion and free-spiritedness—for a time. As time went on, it was as if their common interests got all bollixed up, the one against the other. It wasn't that she was anti-intellectual or uninterested in things artistic—she was interested in them—it was more that Kitty Wright had no need to be invested in the life of the mind to the degree her husband did. Then, too, there was his growing eccentricity and unconventionality and narcissism, almost, or so it seems, in inverse proportion to his auburn-haired wife's growing conventionality and quiet, matronly, suburban ways. Kitty was like the town itself: utterly proper, at least on all the surfaces. Ernest Hemingway, a generation behind Wright, grew up in Oak Park in the first two decades of the twentieth century with five siblings and with his doomed stern bipolar father and his impossible and vain and competing mother. Their large house with its faint Prairie touches, at 601 North Kenilworth Avenue, was in the near shadow of where the Wrights lived, on a diagonal northeast of them, across Chicago Avenue. Of Oak Park, Hemingway is famously supposed to have said, after he was gone, that it was a town of broad lawns and narrow minds, but there is no evidence that he ever got off that good line. At any rate, the righteous odor of the place, all that sobriety, all those church spires poking above the treetops, seems eventually to have galled them both, in their separate ways and times, and there was no recourse but to flee.

In Wright's case, there were other issues, too, not least the work itself, and where he felt it was leading him: nowhere.

"This absorbing, consuming phase of my experience as an architect ended about 1909," he wrote in a section of the autobiography called "The

Closed Road." He said, "*I was losing grip on my work and even interest in it.*" He said, "*Every day of every week and far into the night of nearly every day, Sunday included, I had 'added tired to tired' and added it again and yet again.*" He said, "*I could see no way out.*" He said, "*Because I did not know what I wanted, I wanted to go away.*" Even when you know the larger story, it's hard to read such sentences and not feel a little moved by them. There's almost a childlike simplicity about such blank, needy admissions, recalled from late middle age.

Similarly, on the following page: "*Everything personal or otherwise bore down heavily on me. Domesticity most of all. What I wanted I did not know. I loved my children. I loved my home. A true home is the finest ideal of man, and yet . . . [the ellipsis is his] to gain 'freedom' asked for a 'divorce.'*"

The only problem is that the memoirist has finessed a central fact: that he has fallen in love with another woman. He more or less wants to leave that part out. You'd have to read on into the following pages to really get it. And even then he won't say it directly so much as lapse into loftiness: "*I, too, sought shelter there [he means Europe] in companionship with her who, by force of rebellion as by way of Love, was then implicated with me.*" Only once in the entire book does Wright say her actual name—and that comes when he is burying Mamah in the family churchyard across the fields from Taliesin, on the rainy Sunday evening a day after Julian Carlton has split her head in two and tried, not quite successfully, to incinerate her. "*No monument marks the spot where 'Mamah' was buried,*" he says on page 190. (This is quoting from the 1932 edition.) In every other reference, oblique or direct, it's just "*her*" or "*she.*" It would be possible to read psychological meanings into that. And maybe the meanings would be wrong.

He speaks of his "*persecution.*" But then, a page later, this sentence, impossible to parse, and yet, at the end, its sudden clarity and self-awareness: "*So, when family-life in Oak Park in that spring of 1909, conspired against the freedom to which I had come to feel every soul entitled and I had no choice would I keep my self-respect, but to go out, a voluntary exile, into the uncharted and unknown deprived of legal protection to get my back against the wall and live, if I could, an unconventional life—then I turned to the hill in the Valley as my Grandfather before me had turned to America—as a hope and haven—forgetful for the time being of grandfathers' 'Isaiah.' Smiting and punishment.*"

Smiting and punishment: He knows, even as he rejects his grandfather's prophet.

"I loved my children," he says. But he clearly didn't love them enough. In an earlier section of An Autobiography, *he speaks of his inadequacy as a father, and, once again, no matter the compulsion for evasions and half-truths and omissions and distortions and self-justifications and self-pity, the sudden counter-compulsion to seek the truth, as if he can't stop that part of himself, either: "The architect absorbed the father in me—perhaps—because I never got used to the word nor the idea of being one as I saw them all around the block and met them among my friends." In setting off "perhaps"—with dashes—isn't he suggesting the possibility it wasn't the work at all that drew him away? It was his cursed selfishness. He knew, he knows.*

On the previous page, four quick un-lofty sentences: "I am afraid I never looked the part. Nor ever acted it. I didn't feel it. And I didn't know how." The I-didn't-know-how has nearly the same childlike plainness and plaintiveness of "Because I did not know what I wanted, I wanted to go away."

Just ahead of this, he relates a not-quite-believable story (which many chroniclers have taken for apparent fact). One Sunday, Warren McArthur—for whom he had designed and built on the sly, under Cecil Corwin's bearding, the gambrel-roofed bootleg at 4852 South Kenwood Avenue in the Kenwood district on the South Side—came out to Oak Park to visit. Maybe Kitty had made him breakfast. Maybe the kids in their knickers were screeching around and bouncing rubber balls from the balconies. He seems to be suggesting that all six were born by this point. So if the moment occurred somewhere around, say, 1905 or 1906, which is to say three or four years before he left, then his six children would have ranged in age from about fifteen or sixteen (son Lloyd) to two or three (baby Llewellyn). He says that McArthur "caught one of the children, and called to me—'Quick now, Frank, . . . what's the name of this one?' It worked. The 'father,' surprised by the peremptory request gave the wrong name. Hard to believe—but true."

In the 1943 edition, he omitted the last sentence, leading one to think: Could he have invented a story out of whole cloth at his kids' expense? Sure he could have. The story does him no credit but in perverse ways serves his agendas.

Unity and Mamah

The Sacred Against the Profane

951 Chicago Avenue, Oak Park, Illinois

ecause he did not know what he wanted, he wanted to go away. . . . This stretched-out rectilinear photographic moment is taking place on the Wright family terrace. That's his studio right behind, and behind that is Chicago Avenue. The leaded-glass, diamond-paned open window on the right is in the north bay of the living room. You can go and stand in this spot today and things look exactly the same, including the brick wall with its concrete cap. Only the people are missing.

Several shots were made that sun-squinting day. If you were just looking casually, you might not even notice the differences. One or two of the kids fidget a bit before the next exposure, turning this way or that. One or two decide to change places in the lineup. And yet if you were to look more closely and train your eye only on the mother and father (Kitty, hard to see at first, almost blending into the foliage, is second from the right, behind her oldest son and next to her sister-in-law; and—it hardly needs be said—that's Frank at the far left, in his rather girly-looking work smock), you might be struck by several thoughts. For instance, why is it that Kitty doesn't look at the camera, but keeps her head down? Or why is it that the head of the house seems to have separated himself by a literal foot or two from his mother-in-law (her name is Flora Tobin, she is a starchy woman, and she is minding baby Llewellyn) but, in another sense, separated himself by a football field from the whole homely scene? Several Wright commentators through the years have pointed out how he seems present in the moment and also removed from it. But none, so far as I am aware, has commented on the way he is holding his head, which to me offers the most tantalizing possible clue: slightest tilt upward, barest trace of knowing smile, as if he knows something no one else on this terrace knows. Photography is such a strange art, able to capture both the utterly mundane and the inadvertently revealing. It can tell you a lie as quickly as it can provide a documentary fact. You can invest a lot of time in "reading" a photograph, only to discover—perhaps through a piece of outside evidence you've later come on—that you've read the thing wholly wrong.

Outside evidence. It might further help to decipher the codes, or the seeming codes, if we knew for certain the date. We don't, but we have an approximate one. In the summer of 1969, a decade after his father's death, and three years from his own, John Lloyd Wright (he's in the middle, floppy hat, perched on the wall, as if to imitate the father from whom he can never get enough attention) sent a print of this picture to the archives of the Oak Park Public Library. He intended it as a gift. He asked that a copy be sent over to the town paper, *Oak Leaves,* with the idea that the editors might like to run it in an upcoming issue, which they did (far in the back). On the rear of the image, John, who was then seventy-six, identified the ten people in the picture. He got two of them wrong, including his mother. He provided a date: "June 1904."

No matter that Wright's second son can never quite be trusted in regard to any so-called fact about his family, this time frame would seem to fit. (The moment cannot be June 1903, as several Wright commentators have said, because baby Llewellyn wasn't alive yet.) Let's say that it *is,* in fact, June 1904 and, in fact, let's up the ante and say it's June 15, 1904. Why? Because that's the day Frank Lloyd Wright's own father died: after breakfast on June 15, 1904. Not that the son knew, which is pretty much the point of why this is being belabored. Wright hadn't talked to or seen his father since 1885 (or at least not that anyone knows). His father died on the east side of Pittsburgh, apparently having just come back from the corner drugstore, where he'd gone to buy the morning paper. Suddenly, William Carey Wright, who'd spent the last nineteen years moving from place to place in America, something like nine or ten residences across at least four or five states, was grabbing at his throat, trying to yank off his shirt collar. "Cardiac insufficiency," someone wrote, three days later, on a "Registry of Deaths" form. The dying was over in a matter of minutes, apparently. He was seventy-nine. So much of Frank Lloyd Wright's life seems a novel of improbabilities and a parable of coincidences that you can imagine the gods seeing to it that a rebuked and cast-off and falsely accused father fell to a floor on the same day, same morning, same *hour*, in fact, that a black box on a tripod was making a series of small white puffing noises on an Oak Park veranda.

Except, no: Things could never be quite that neat, even in the riddle inside of the rhyme named Frank Lloyd Wright. The evidence of the shadows suggests this is not eight thirty or nine o'clock in the morning but somewhere toward mid-afternoon. The sun would have arced over the top of the house by then and would have been slanting back across Forrest Avenue toward the not exactly blissful group assembled here.

On the tilt of head and trace of smile: Although it's doubtful that anyone will ever precisely be able to say when it started, I believe Wright's fatal relationship with Mamah Borthwick Cheney took hold—in its first incarnation—somewhere in late spring or early summer 1904, right about *here,* maybe exactly *here,* if not yet sexually then romantically. Took hold, say, about five or six months after the building permit had been issued to a local contractor for the six-thousand-dollar, two-story, mostly walled-in Prairie bungalow that Wright had conceived for Mamah and her decent and steady and methodical and engineering-minded spouse, Edwin H. Cheney, at 520 North East Avenue in Oak Park. That old building permit, a shard of documentary detail, specifying the lot number and some other technical data, is dated January 14, 1904, and it's still around, preserved, retrievable, in an Oak Park municipal archive. Not that it reveals anything more than the raw data itself. Still, there comes a small, visceral feeling, just from staring at it.

Data alone could never tell this story, but some numbers all the same: From 1899, when his commissions began gaining speed, to the back part of 1909, when he seemed, at least on the surface, to be willing to give it all away—his work, his life, his reputation, his family—Frank Lloyd Wright executed 114 designs out of something like 208 projects. Between 1902 and 1906, he and the half-dozen or so draftsmen and artists in his employ at his home studio worked on more than seventy-five buildings. Speaking purely of houses: Between 1903 and 1909, Wright oversaw the construction of at least forty-five residences and designed some twenty-five others that never got to the point of being built. In terms of just Prairies: From 1901 to 1909, he is said to have conceived them at the rate of about twelve a year. As was said at the outset, for any normal artist, normal human, these figures—heroic figures, really— would represent a lifetime's work, more than a lifetime's, but what isn't even underscored in this tally is the fact of two of his greatest non-residential buildings ever: the Larkin Administration Building in Buffalo (long since gone) and Unity Temple in the heart of Oak Park, still gloriously standing. Both were built in the decade. (For a discussion of these numbers, and their sources, and the scholars to whom I am indebted, see the Essay on Sources.)

So picking up—selectively—the over-arc of the narrative from, say, late winter or early spring of 1901. Think of B. Harley and his family moving into Glenlloyd at the river. Think of America's homemakers studying plans for an elongated house on page 17 of *Ladies' Home Journal*. A career is starting to explode with jobs and possibilities and acclaim. And in a different sense of the word, it'll explode again, eight years hence, on a Thursday afternoon in late September, when the country's most celebrated architect will seem inexplicably to have walked away from his family, just as his own deserting father had supposedly once done.

"The Art and Craft of the Machine," Hull House, Jane Addams: to any Wright student—or, really, to any student of the history of turn-of-the-century Chicago—these words and names carry resonance. On March 6, 1901, thirty-four-year-old Frank Lloyd Wright, in his sonorous and still-youthful voice, delivered to the Chicago Arts and Crafts

Society, at newly founded Hull House on the Near West Side, what would become one of the most famous—and visionary—speeches of his career. Hull House—started in 1889 by social worker and suffragist Jane Addams and partner Ellen Gates Starr—was a settlement center providing political and social and educational support to its immigrant and working-poor neighbors. Many famous Americans would come to be associated with Hull House, or give talks there—John Dewey and Clarence Darrow and Susan B. Anthony, to say three. (Uncle Jenk—Jenkin Lloyd Jones—was long associated with Addams and her mission.) In "The Art and Craft of the Machine," Uncle Jenk's nephew called for acceptance, not rejection, of the new century's machines entering the old world's garden. If the talk in many ways was a Whitmanesque song of himself, it was beautifully expressed. "If the artist will only open his eyes he will see that the machine he dreads has made it possible to wipe out the mass of meaningless torture to which mankind, in the name of the artistic, has been more or less subjected since time began," he said. Allow us to "learn from the Machine. It teaches that the beauty of wood lies first in its qualities as wood." And this sentence, layered, lyric, boomeranging in its ironies, if not quite yet: "Cut the primitive bed of a river abruptly, with a canal hollowed out beneath its level, and the river will desert its bed."

In Oak Park, in 1901, the visionary man was setting to work on what would become known as the Frank W. Thomas House. (There are Wright scholars who wish to claim it as the first Prairie.) It was on the same street as his own home, down at the far corner, closer to the center of town: he could walk to the building site in about four minutes. The lot was only one hundred feet wide, and he filled it up, north to south. He gave the house no basement as such, no attic, and put the main rooms on the second floor, illuminated by a string of in-line windows with a mirrored gold-glass effect. The look was almost Viennese, the more so at night. The clients were characteristic: upper-middle-class local professional folk (in this case a family of stockbrokers) who were interested in art and willing to take a dare. Part of the dare was finding your way in: the entry was through an arch at the front, and then up to the left, and then doubling back to the right and through a room of full-height art-glass doors.

It was more or less that way, too, maze, that is, on entering the front door of his home studio. He had begun building it in 1897 and completed it in June of the next year. Although he kept an office in the Loop (principally to meet clients and to keep his eye on his own fame), the real work was now being done in this two-story addition, hinged on to the east side of his home. The entire studio complex included a library/reception room and his office. (His office manager, Isabel Roberts, who also worked on designs, tended to use the latter space.) The drafting room was a large, square, vaulted room, and over top of it was an octagonal balcony (with clerestory windows) suspended from the ceiling rafters by huge iron chains. It was both a functional and aesthetic space.

He had designed the entry to the studio complex so that it took a visitor something like five right-angle turns to move from the wooden sidewalk out on noisy, dusty Chicago Avenue into the serene, narrow, darkened reception hall. The distance was only about ten feet but you would never feel that, making the tight turns. If he was at work in the drafting room, Isabel Roberts would likely fetch him to announce a client had arrived.

On the outside wall, facing the street, he put up a limestone plaque with hand-hewn letters cut out of the stone, in relief: *Frank Lloyd Wright, Architect.* Below, his logo: cross within a circle within a square. In the interior of the complex, he used a richly stained dark basswood. The woody unified glow. His draftsmen sat on stools sans backs.

Within a year, 1902, he was working on one of his most magisterial Prairie houses ever, and this one was even closer to him than the Thomas: the Arthur B. Heurtley House. It was (and is) only a few houses south of his. You can go up and down Forrest Avenue today and see many stunning houses with broad lawns: great Victorians, his own works, the works of his contemporaries. But this house, so monolithic, so beautifully scaled, built almost entirely of brick and concrete, with its great piers; with its low, hipped roof; with its two shades of brownish-orange brick set in alternating sequences. The mortar in the vertical joints between the bricks is the same color as the brick itself, so that your eye is able to sweep the surface in almost one glance, even though the house, sited well back from the curb, seems as massive as a city hall or a great post office from FDR's New Deal. The chimney is low and wide, as if pressed down onto the roof. But best of all, in terms of both aesthetics and an architect's unrelenting ego (both of which you're able to sense, if not fully grasp, when you are first taking it in), is that this is a house without downspouts. Downspouts would give the work such an unseemly vertical element. No, no. Downspouts not allowed. Let the rainwater just course from the brown and barely glimpsed gutters at the corners straight down into the hidden ground drains. In a summer squall, the Heurtley can be its own "Fallingwater," and in a January ice storm of a hard Illinois winter she's been known to produce some beautiful if scary four-foot-long stalactites. Hell with it. Let the aesthetics trump.

In April 1902, *he* trumped, at the fifteenth annual exhibition of the Chicago Architectural Club at the Art Institute. His work so overlorded the proceedings that a critic from New York's *American Architect and Building News* wondered about "the professional ethics" of "such a pronounced personal exhibit" favoring one individual. More than 115 architects and firms were represented—and Wright with his own room within the galleries and a special section in the printed catalog devoted to him. He presented drawings, photographs, art pieces, furnishings, floral arrangements: sixty-five items, including doors from the dining room at the Warren McArthur House (Cecil's bootleg), electro-glazing models for the Luxfer Prisim Company, a scale model of the River Forest Golf Club. "Why in an architectural exhibit, the chief one in Chicago for the year, why should Mr. Wright's tables and chairs, and his teazles and milkweeds and pinebranches cover so much space?" asked the reviewer for the *AA&BN*. That's easy, he'd have replied: first among non-equals.

Came the commission for Buffalo's Larkin Building—this was late 1902, and it would occupy him on and off along with other work until 1906. In the world of Lost Wright, the Larkin is now regarded (it wasn't always) as one of the most painful losses of all. (The building was demolished in 1950.) The Larkin's business was mail-order soap, and its success at the turn of the century was enormous, just like the headquarters Wright conceived for its progressive managers and eighteen hundred employees. On the outside, the five-story building seemed Egyptian tomblike—or, as the architect put it, a "simple cliff of brick hermetically sealed," purposely so, against the smoke and grime and general ugliness of its industrial neighborhood. Inside the sealed vault there was a magnificent sky-lit atrium court, with the floors forming wraparound galleries. On the top level there was a restaurant, and a conservatory overflowing with ferns, and a brick-paved exercise promenade. Far down below, rows of Lilliputian-seeming workers sat at their desks lined up edge to edge, filling the orders while organ music played softly in the background. There were noonday concerts and lectures. Photographs survive: the men in their suits, the women in their white blouses and put-up hair. Ada Louise Huxtable, in her Wright biography, wrote that this temple to mail-order commerce and efficiency looks "at once futuristic and old-fashioned, like something out of a retro *Star Wars*." That could be a description of the architect himself: Han Solo by way of Henry David Thoreau. In 1987, a Wright historian named Jack Quinan published the definitive account (*Frank Lloyd Wright's Larkin Building: Myth and Fact*), reproducing images of the sculptures and inscriptions and biblical quotations placed throughout the building with their FLW signature lettering: "INTELLIGENCE, ENTHUSIASM, CONTROL." Or: "THOUGHT, FEELING, ACTION." Or: "ASK AND IT SHALL BE GIVEN YOU."

In mid-November 1903, Robert Llewellyn Wright, the last child of a paling marriage, entered the world. Sometime in here, too, a handsome Oak Park couple, four years married, casual acquaintances of the Wrights, approached the architect and asked him to build them a house. They lived at 316 South Oak Park Avenue, below the railroad tracks, so it was a little bit of distance from where the Wrights lived, on the north end of the village. Theirs was a three-story, high-peaked, not-quite-Victorian house, and they seemed to be wishing for something a little more daring. The lot they'd secured was up on the north side, where some large and daring houses had lately risen, not that they particularly wanted a large house. This couple had a one-year-old son named John, who wasn't going to live past twelve. The couple had a niece named Jessie, whose mom had died two years earlier in the aftermath of childbirth and whom they'd brought into their home to raise as their own. The couple was hoping for at least one more child—maybe she'd be a girl—as a growing-up companion to their son and his first cousin. The couple's name was Cheney. (They pronounced it CHEE-nee.) They arranged a meeting with the architect at his home office and were apparently swallowed up by his charm and eruption of ideas. First plans were drawn in mid-December 1903, and were fussed over between January and early

March 1904, and Mrs. Cheney was said to be in on almost every stage of the deliberations. The architect produced seven drawings for the living room, and these have passed down through history.

Picture Mamah and Edwin arriving at the studio complex one dreary Oak Park fall afternoon. The architect sweeps into the reception hall, where the couple is seated stiffly along the north wall in capacious chairs. (Isabel Roberts has greeted them and taken their coats and sat them down in this low-lit space.) He's in his shirtsleeves. He gathers them up and leads them by the arm along the hall toward the westward end of the house into what he calls "the library," where there is a burst of light. It's a library with damn few books. It's really a presentation room, a winning-over room, a seduction room. He has built it in an octagon. Plenty of light streams in, but it's from overhead, not quite at the ceiling, rather, in a series of six diamond-paned casement windows that he's positioned up close to the ceiling: clerestory. The ceiling itself has a skylight. You'd have to crane your neck to see sky. The shafts are coming down, angling in, arcing through. He has set up the room to concentrate your gaze right here, eyes downward, on this nearly square oak table, and these unfurling sheets of drawings, prospective plans, he has ginned up for your visit. Well, he'd like you to focus on him a bit, too. With his great charm he smooths out the drawings, which are maybe only rough sketches, weighting the corners with small iron ornaments. "Now what can I do for you, or perhaps you for me?" he says with a kind of unctuousness slaughtered always by the great charm, smile, guile.

———

If something like seven drawings for the living room of the Edwin Cheney House have survived, what has passed down through history in a different way is a question to which there will probably never be a satisfying answer: Who *was* Mamah Borthwick Cheney? In the universe of Wright, she isn't as shadowy a figure as, say, Julian Carlton, but she remains frustratingly obscure all the same. Until modern times she was almost literally mute to historians, which is to say there were apparently no surviving letters or diaries or apparently any other self-written trace of her. In that sense, she could be whatever the world wished her to be, or wished to project onto her: unfit mother abandoning her children, proto-feminist in a soulless marriage trying to keep herself from strangling—and all possibilities in between. And then (first in 1995 and then more prominently in 2002) ten of her letters were found in a Swedish archive, and brought to light and placed in context by separate scholars. This gave biographers and historians something fairly priceless (if also tantalizing and incomplete): a sense, at last, of Mamah's own voice in the final three or four years of her life. (There will be more about this cache of letters and its discovery later.) Yes, there has also been in these latter years a fine historical novel about Mamah, Nancy Horan's 2007 best-selling *Loving Frank,* which has allowed us to dream a little further into her inner life. But that's fiction, with made-up characters and scenes and invented writings from Mamah and Wright, even if it's also true that Horan adroitly used whatever historical record she could gather. (She wasn't always perfectly faithful to that record—it was her prerogative.) The plain truth is that the real woman, the *factual* flesh-and-blood woman, remains to this minute held behind all our would-be storytelling curtains. She's quicksilver. It's the Frank Lloyd Wright story again, but reduced in scale. Only three or four photographs of Mamah as an adult have ever surfaced, and each looks different from the other. The one presented here was taken, apparently at Taliesin, in the early summer of 1914, so maybe something like two and a half months before a man in a white serving tunic went berserk for unknown reasons. This portrait, apparently the last we have, was meant as a gift for her partner's forty-seventh birthday. She's not quite forty-five years old, sitting in a straight-backed chair, in quarter-profile, as if someone has just spoken to her and she's quietly turned her head. Leaning slightly forward. Her delicate necklace, her white shoulders. The just-flared nostrils of the fine-boned nose, and the pursed lips, and the imperfectly brushed hair, but mostly, mostly: Mamah's deep-set eyes. They seem not sad so much as . . . wondering. What color? Only one of a hundred things history doesn't know. Was she taller than Wright? You'd think so. Something almost ostrich-like about her body mass.

––––––––

Pausing here: She was born on June 19, 1869, in a little rural Iowa place called Montana—it later changed its name—in Boone County. It's in the center of Iowa, just west of the state university of Ames, America's

first land-grant institution. Maybe that fact has something to do with the larger family fact that all three female offspring of the far-from-wealthy Marcus Smith Borthwick and Almira Bowcock Borthwick were educated women.

Mamah was the youngest of the sisters. Was she born Mary or Martha? Numerous accounts have it as the latter—with Mamah becoming the corruption that stuck for life, both legally and informally—but the federal censuses of both 1870 and 1880 have her first name as Mary. (Census takers are known to get things wrong, but it seems unlikely that two census takers, a decade apart, would get her first name wrong—and, besides, all the other names and ages in the family roughly track.) Boone County itself cannot help: its courthouse records of births and deaths don't begin that early. In all probability she was born at home, and the details would have been inscribed in the family Bible. But where is that Bible? So put her down equivocally as either Mary Mamah Bouton Borthwick Cheney or Martha Mamah Bouton Borthwick Cheney. A mouthful, either way. The belief here is that "Mary" became "Mamie" (you see that in places, along with "Mame") and "Mamie" became "Mamah." To remind you once again of the pronunciation: MAY-muh.

What you chiefly hear about are the three accomplished sisters in this family: Jessie, Lizzie, Mamah. But, in fact, there was another sibling: Frank Lindsay Borthwick. He was the eldest child, born in the second year of the Civil War. He has mostly disappeared from history. After his eighteenth year (he's there in the 1880 federal census) there seems but one trace in the public record. In 1888 (he would have been about twenty-six), he suffered a ghastly work-related railway accident in Dixon, Illinois, with "his abdomen nearly crushed to bursting," according to the local paper. So far as I know, his name has never even come up in any published Wright account, or even Borthwick/Cheney account. It isn't clear if he survived. No death record seems to exist. And why is this being brought up? On the idea of early and middle sorrow in this family.

Boone County was coal, and then it was the railroads, specifically the Chicago and North Western Transportation Company. Marcus Borthwick built carriages and then he gravitated to working on railway cars. He must have been pretty mechanical-minded. By at least 1880— Mamah would have been eleven—he had taken his family to Chicago, where he worked in the C&NW repair yards and rose to foreman. In 1880 the family was living above a store, at 95 North Wells Street, about three blocks from the yards and the depot where, six years hence, the quick-striding hayseed from Madison would emerge into evening Chicago light. Eventually the Borthwicks moved out to Oak Park— a smaller house, and then a larger one. Marcus seems to have worked right up until practically the day of his death, which was April 21, 1900. He was seventy-one. By then he was the assistant superintendent of the repair yards and one of the longest-tenured employees in the company. Again, why is this worth mentioning? Only on the idea that perhaps Mamah—who waited a good while to marry and who then seemed to marry someone not at all like her in character or interests—had been predisposed in half-known ways toward dependable, hardworking male figures with engineering-like brains.

Between 1888 and 1893, the youngest and perhaps most questioning and questing daughter had attended the University of Michigan, where she'd earned both a bachelor's and a master's degree. (She had majored in Greek and French and had studied two or three other languages as well.) After, Mamah had moved to Port Huron, Michigan, where for about three years she taught high school courses in the liberal arts. One of her best college friends had been there with her, Mattie Chadbourne.

They had lived in a boardinghouse for young professional ladies on Seventh Street. There weren't a lot of eligible suitors. It has been reported that she eventually took a job at the public library, but records don't seem to support it. But in any case, by then an eligible suitor whom she'd known casually at college (they were both in the class of 1892) had been making rail trips to Port Huron, which is northeast of Detroit, on the eastern edge of the state, just across the border from Canada. His name was Edwin Henry Cheney. He'd been born in Detroit, and at Ann Arbor he'd studied electrical engineering and pledged FIJI and sung first tenor in the glee club. And now, living in Chicago, ardently professing his weekend love for the brainy and artsy Mamah, he was making damn good money at Chicago Edison. (He had begun as a chief draftsman but had recently taken a large role in the company's construction department.) He was nothing if not persistent, earnest, a bit plodding. The two were married on June 15, 1899. (Mamah seems to have moved back to Chicago for a while before the marriage.) They were both thirty. Edwin was six days older. Thirty was old enough for him, but almost dangerously old (which is to say getting close to spinsterish-old) for her. Small, curious fact: Mamah's big sister, Jessie Octavia Borthwick, who had worked for a while at the Art Institute, got married seven days ahead of Mamah. Jessie was thirty-five: seriously old for a woman of that time. She had married a middle-aged son of a prominent Oak Park family named Pitkin—and she wasn't going to live to see her second wedding anniversary.

Which gets back to the idea of early and middle sorrow, and of how such sorrow may have effected—we'll never really know—some eventual fatal life choices. How it might have given the youngest child a heightened sense of her own mortality and the fleetingness of time. But past the speculation, this fact: Between 1898 and 1901, there were three deaths, at least three, in quick succession in the Borthwick family. The first was Mamah's mother, who died on January 28, 1898. (Almira had turned fifty-nine nine days previous.) Then, twenty-seven months later, her father's death, a long life, yes, but maybe with too much hard work in it. The funeral was held at the family home on South Oak Park Avenue, into which Mamah and Edwin had moved after Almira's death. (Edwin had become treasurer and manager of the Mutual Electric Company of Chicago.) Then, almost exactly a year after her father's death, the hardest death of all: that of her sister Jessie Octavia. The eldest sister succumbed at 9:30 at night on April 16, 1901, in her Oak Park home. She was thirty-seven. Had there been a deathwatch? Had she been okay but then fell ill? Was the death childbirth-related? The swirls of what isn't known. In the local paper: "Death was caused by paresis of the bowels, and a little daughter scarcely a week old survives her."

Another kind of swirl, the swirls of *what if*: What if Jessie Octavia Borthwick Pitkin's daughter, born on April 10, 1901, who was meant to live when her mother wasn't, and who was given in her mother's honor the name Jessie, and who was raised in the home of Mamah and Edwin, had been at Spring Green, Wisconsin, on August 15, 1914, seated with her two first cousins on a terrace, waiting to be served lunch? She very likely could have been sitting there. The summer before, this Jessie—who grew up to be Jessie Borthwick Pitkin Higgins—had visited at Taliesin with Martha and John Cheney. On at least two or three occasions between 1912 and 1914, Mamah had brought her adoptive niece to Wisconsin along with her own children for brief stays as part of the custody visits agreed to by her former husband. But Jessie, who would have been thirteen in the summer of 1914, wasn't at Taliesin that day. Which is one reason in the great chain of reasons why *this* Jessie lived to make it three days past her eighty-third birthday. She had grown up to marry an English teacher at Phillips Academy in Andover, Massachusetts, and bore by him a child named Haydn Higgins, who became known to the jazz world as Eddie Higgins. In the 1950s and '60s, pianist Eddie Higgins, the grandchild of Jessie Octavia, the great-nephew of Mamah, was a fixture at the London House, Chicago's greatest jazz club, sharing the marquee with Oscar Peterson and Stan Getz and Dizzy Gillespie and Erroll Garner. He gained a wide following, especially in Japan, where he did much recording. I talked with Higgins's widow, Meredith d'Ambrosio. She, too, is a noted jazz figure. I stumbled around on the phone. She said quietly, "Yes, I know what you're asking. And I think he thought about it a lot."

The namesake Jessie, who was raised on South Oak Park Avenue and then at 520 North East Avenue, grew to have deep love for Mamah. The surrogate mom's leaving happened when the child was eight. It happened when Mamah's own children, John and Martha, were respectively seven and just turned four. The namesake Jessie, no less than the biological Martha and John, apparently also grew to have an abiding love for their Aunt Lizzie. Lizzie (born Elizabeth Viletta) was the middle sister of the three Borthwick girls, two years younger than Jessie, three years older than Mamah. She had moved in with Mamah and Edwin to help raise the children—first at the Oak Park Avenue house and then to the new one designed by the man who wore such strange-looking clothes. Lizzie, who never married, was an elementary schoolteacher. In the years after the Borthwicks came from Iowa, she took a job at Washington Irving School, on the Near West Side of Chicago, not far from where Cecil Corwin's family had once lived. She rose to become head assistant to the principal at Irving. At one point after her retirement she moved to the Hotel Kenwood on the South Side, about a block and a half north of Wright's two bootlegs, the McArthur and the Blossom. Later she moved to Andover, apparently to be near the niece she had long ago helped to bring up. Lizzie's seems to have been a modest life, an out-of-the-public-eye life, and also perhaps a somewhat lonely life, adjectives you wouldn't associate with the mother and spouse and kid sister who went away with Frank Lloyd Wright.

———

So back, back to the arc and the slide of time between 1901 and 1909: The architect seems to have thought a lot about the house he designed and built for the Cheneys. (The house is in the first block north of Chicago Avenue, on the east side of the street, about a twelve-minute walk from the Wright home and studio.) Architectural historians have appeared confounded about the Cheney even as they have admired it. It is not quite like any other Wright Prairie. It sits over top of a basement constructed at half-level, almost like a concealed tent. From the street it's still hard to get a true visual sense of this smallish brick building with its wood trim, even though some of its once ten-foot-high walls have long since been removed. If you stand directly in front of it, the semi-shrouded house looks like a single-story home when, in fact, it is two full stories. Inside, the space is continuous—almost a single room made up of a living room framed on either end by a dining room and a library. For the fifty-two windows on the main level, the architect used art glass. The confounding part has to do with the seeming contradictions between inside and outside. It's as if the walls were meant to suggest metaphorically the role of a housewife and mother kept secluded from the outer world. To quote Wright scholar Neil Levine: "Inside, it is low, dark, snug, and cozy at the same time that it is spacious, light, airy, and open. Outside, it is a mysterious combination of belvedere and bunker, a balance of opposites impossible to define in any more singular way."

As I said, it's unlikely anyone will ever be able to fix precisely when their relationship first took hold, but possibly it can be dated from the general time of the photograph on the terrace in the squinting summer sun. In *Loving Frank,* the author creates a scene where Mamah, having just discovered she is pregnant, stands at the screen door of her new home and tells Wright the news. She won't be able to see him again. The vague time frame seems to be the back of 1904. There is no suggestion by the novelist that the coming baby is any other than Edwin's, and I also believe that to be the truth, although who really knows. The view here is that the deep physical intimacy between them didn't begin for another two or three years; and that in between was a suspension of their longing gradually becoming known to all parties, including, perhaps, on some inchoate level, child parties. But in any case, if Mamah did tell Wright, whether standing at a screen door or not, that she and her husband were going to have a baby, and told him soon after she had found out, then this moment probably would have occurred before Christmas 1904, about six months from the rectilinear moment on the terrace—say, in the second or third week of December. Why? Martha Cheney was born nine months later, on September 10, 1905. And in that wheel of time you can find some exhilaration and ennui and distraction and fury in Frank Lloyd Wright.

———

In late 1903, a twenty-seven-year-old architect left Burlington, Vermont, to work as a draftsman in the home suburban studio of the architect he regarded as the great new artist of the "west." The young man's name was Charles E. White, Jr. He would make his own mark as an architect, and his work stands today in Oak Park and other places, but his lasting gift to history is the lengthy, talky, keenly observant letters he sent back home to a fellow architect and former employer. They are a glimpse from the inside. Here he is, writing on November 16, 1903, shortly after his arrival, speaking of his employer as "W." (W's last child by Kitty has been born the day before, not that this gets mentioned.)

W has told him "to stop reading books for a while, and do nothing but study nature and sketch." W has told him that he is so "thoroughly saturated with the spirit of the prairie" that he "doesn't think he could easily design work for a hilly country." W is maddeningly—maybe inspiringly—"the most impractical man—is way behind in his work, but calmly takes seven weeks to alter his office, and lets the work wait. The Buffalo drawings are not even completed, and they are hammering him all the time!" W has reminisced to the apprentice on his university days at Madison and how "[a]fter three years, he made a head for Chicago (did not get his diploma) with seven dollars in his pocket. After tramping about several days, got a job in Silsbee's office at eight dollars."

Three decades from publishing his autobiography, the fabulist is already working up the fable.

Six months go by in the employ of W, and the rookie understands a little more about how things work: the boss tends to "develop his unit first, then fits his design to the requirements as much as possible, or rather, fits the requirements to the design. I do not mean by this that he ignores the requirements, but rather that he approaches his work in a broad minded architectural way, and never allows any of the petty wants of his client to interfere with the architectural expression of his design. The petty wishes are taken care of by a sort of absorption and suppression within the scope of the plan as a whole, and are never allowed to interfere with the system or skeleton of the house."

That letter is dated May 13, 1904. Summer is coming to Illinois. The maples and willows have budded out, and the draftsman from the East is surprised at how beautiful spring is in these parts. In another month or so, Kitty Wright and her husband, in his girly-looking work smock, will gather their kids and his mother-in-law for a couple of poses on the front veranda—not that White has any idea of that.

One more: It's written about nine months later, on February 13, 1905. Tomorrow Frank Lloyd Wright and his wife are leaving for a trip to Japan—his first. The letter covers many topics and goes to many handwritten, hard-to-read pages. A couple of sentences at the end seem to leap off the page, in terms of possible over-themes and concealed under-themes. Again, not that the letter writer could know about the latter—he's just putting down what he observes, and what he observes, apparently, is how his employer has "become so sort of petered out this last year. For the past three months it has been almost impossible to get him to give any attention to us. As he expresses it he 'has no appetite for work,' and I think the reason is that he has taken no period of complete rest from his work in several years."

For the past three months. For all history knows, it may have been somewhere in the same general time frame that a client, who was more than a client, living in her walled new home, informed her architect, who was more than her architect, that she was pregnant. Maybe it happened, maybe it didn't. But it seems likely, more than likely, that the news, changing everything, would have been communicated to him in one form or another. The only thing that can be said for sure, however, is that, on February 13, 1905, the questing spouse of Edwin H. Cheney was inside her first trimester.

————

The trip to Japan was thrilling for Wright and lasted from Valentine's Day to the middle of May. (He would have set foot on Japanese soil in early March and left it at the end of April.) Wright and his wife were in the company of Mr. and Mrs. Ward Willits, for whom, as was noted earlier, he had designed a huge home in Highland Park, Illinois, the year after the Kankakee houses. The Willitses were friendly enough with the Wrights to intuit that things seemed wrong with the marriage—and maybe this trip would help. They are said to have paid for a lot of it. The couples took a train to San Francisco and sailed onward to Yokohama. For the next two months they were up and down the skinny misty island nation. Wright shot many photographs and bought all the woodblock prints he could beg, borrow, or barter for. He seems barely to have slept. There is a legend (as an adult, Robert Llewellyn Wright told the story to various interviewers, and somehow you'd want to believe it, just because of the source) that Mrs. Willits collared her husband out of a bathhouse tended by geishas—to which Wright had taken him. That peremptorily ended the Willits part of the trip, and, supposedly, Wright never saw or spoke to his clients for about the next forty years, until, once, when he and an apprentice (who was also his son-in-law), having discovered themselves in Highland Park, decided on impulse to go up and ring the doorbell. An elderly woman answered, in curlers and an apron, took a quick look, turned, and shouted into the living room, "Ward, Frank's here."

What isn't legend, but has rather been a thorny scholarly question, argued for much longer than forty years, is the extent to which Wright's architecture is indebted to Japanese culture. In his own lifetime the architect himself always denied it, of course: the odor of his ego, the anxieties of his influences. You might say he protested too loudly. He once said (rather wittily, in 1936, in London's *Architects' Journal*), "No, my dear Mrs. Gablemore, Mrs. Plasterbilt, and especially, now, Miss Flatttop, nothing from 'Japan' had helped at all, except the marvel of Japanese colour-prints. They were a lesson in elimination of the insignificant and in the beauty of the natural use of materials." Japan didn't inspire his thinking about organic architecture, but, rather, *proved* the ideas and ideals already in place. Okay. But even his pal Robert Spencer, in that map-setting piece in *Architectural Review,* wrote of how Wright looked first and last to nature, but appended: "If not to nature at first hand, then to those marvelous interpreters of nature, the Orientals and the Japanese." Most Wright historians point to the Japanese pavilion at the 1893 Chicago world's fair as the epiphany moment for Wright, particularly a temple called the Ho-o-den. The Japanese government had sent traditionally trained wood craftsmen to build the $650,000 piece on-site. But even before the fair, Wright, through Silsbee and Sullivan, would have likely marveled at the seamless joinery and rice-paper delicacy of all things Japanese. Both employers were known admirers.

The Wrights returned to their home and children in budding-out Oak Park in the third week of May. (It is a little startling to think of them having gone across the Pacific, for three months, leaving all of their kids behind, when their youngest was only fifteen months old. Yes, upper-middle-class parents, who had servants and relatives willing to step in, did such things then.) His spirits, if not his marriage, seemed restored. And then, three weeks later, about five o'clock on Sunday morning, June 4, 1905, lightning and fire struck in his direction—except that they struck with unexpected fortune. Meaning that out of a violent thunderstorm (and the reducing to ashes of a conventionally built nineteenth-century Unitarian Universalist house of worship called Unity Church, of which he and his family were members) came one of his greatest masterworks of all. Many critics would place it in the top four or five of not just the four-hundred-plus Wrights still standing across America but of everything he ever drew. This is Unity Temple, on the southeast corner of Lake Street and Kenilworth Avenue in downtown Oak Park. It was his first solo public commission. (The Larkin, while a public building of sorts, was a commercial commission.) From the first, Wright was fighting for it to be called a temple, not a church. It was the least of his battles.

Pausing again. No single piece of Wright architecture moves me more. I haven't seen all of his extant buildings, but I've seen plenty. Long before I started this book, well before I started the last, which was about Ernest Hemingway, I was going to Unity Temple whenever I could, to sit in one of its old smooth wooden pews, with all its light and silence and seeming saving grace pouring down. Going to Unity, during the years of the work on Hemingway, so I believe, helped me to begin to understand things about him I wouldn't have otherwise remotely understood. Similarly, sitting these days in Unity (no less than standing now and again at a stone on the South Side of Chicago) has helped me to find, or re-find, the person who I think Frank Lloyd Wright truly was.

I submit that there is a strange and beautiful convergence between the art of Hemingway in general and the art of Unity Temple in particular, and that the convergence meets at the simple-seeming word "space." "Space" is the word Wright himself used at various times in his life to try to explain what he had accomplished with Unity. Seven years before he died, he said of Unity: "[T]here is where you will find the first real expression of the idea that the space within the building is the reality of that building." What did he mean, exactly? That space itself, air itself, invisibility itself, not borders, not walls, not pulpits, not altars, not cloisters, not pews, not organ pipes, but something you couldn't actually *see* was what he aimed to make people see—and to feel? His "little jewel box," he called Unity. As for Hemingway, it's easy to think of early little three- and four-page jewel-box stories, or even fragments of stories, inter-stories, inter-chapters, where the white space on the page seems almost equal to the print on the page. Wright once said of his work on Unity that it "looks easy enough now, for it is right enough," words that might also have been said by a kind of autodidact, shed of Oak Park, living impecuniously in Paris in the mid-twenties with his wife and baby boy above the now-so-mythic whine of the sawmill at 113 rue Notre-Dame des Champs and trying to do something he didn't fully understand. It was essentially about elimination. It was a notion of a new kind of writing in which you purposely leave things out, create white space on the page. The art of omission, of trying to make the reader feel more than he necessarily understands. His "iceberg theory," he later called it, noting that the "dignity of movement" of an iceberg owes to the fact that only one-eighth of it is above water. In the fall of 1905, when a full-fledged genius named Frank Lloyd Wright began working on what would become Unity Temple (it would take him thirty-four studies and more than three years of elimination to get it all down right), a sturdy little incipient genius named Ernest Hemingway was in short pants and in first grade at Oliver Wendell Holmes School catty-corner across Chicago Avenue from the architect's home studio. He probably seemed unremarkable, except maybe for that disconcerting grin, parts of it aggressive, parts warming.

So a try, however inadequate, at saying a little of what Unity is. He conceived it as a cube. It's a kind of cubed cube. In a way, it's as if seven-eighths of it cannot be seen, floats beneath the surface. Regarding the metaphor of water: It's possible to feel almost a sense of weightlessness when for the first time you enter the central space, or sanctuary, with

Unity Temple, Oak Park, Illinois

its two levels of balconies that enclose three sides of the room. The room, in its pale-yellow and pale-green and yellow-gray color schemes, draws you up and up, right to the clerestory windows and the stained-glass skylights, which wash and cone the room in amber. It's as if all the details of the architect's design have been left out, all the interior structure deliberately destroyed, so that the only thing remaining to experience, if not understand, is this vaulting and intimate and light-filled room itself, so full of space. The great and late Yale critic Vincent Scully, already referenced, once said: "It's not a big building, but I think it's the biggest space in America." Neil Levine has spoken of the perfect square of Unity's main room as a "raised platform." A platform with the sensation of floating. You're "on this raised plane with space dropping away from you on every side." Levine has also written that it is as if the room is somehow "free of material constraints." Yes, water; yes, the seeming weightlessness.

I have been in acoustically magical Unity, on the second tiered level from the main floor, high up, close to the ceiling, when two-year-olds on their mothers' bosoms were hacking all around me—and it was as if the minister was still whispering in my ear. What was the theme of the homily on that particular Sunday? Wasn't it about humility, and didn't the minister talk about "giving life to the shape of justice"?

The temple seats roughly four hundred worshippers, and yet no seat is more than forty-five feet from the pulpit. How is that possible?

I have been in Unity with a retired Chicago architect named Jack Lesniak. He had a long, good career, mostly in architectural administration. He is a humble man. He has served on early preservation and restoration committees for Unity. It was a winter day. Just the two of us. He wore an old tam, like something a cabbie might have worn in Al Capone's Chicago. He removed it when we entered. He kept wringing it in his hands, like a man trying to squeeze water from a chamois cloth. "I'm an architect and yet I have a terrible time trying to understand what he did here," Lesniak said. "It keeps changing in spatial dimension. The planes on the wall become almost like folded paper. He does it with the color, with the trim, with the banding. The wood is folding across the corners. At night, the building glows from the outside. Think about when this was built. This is the beginning of the century. This is a spaceship. Nobody has ever seen anything like this."

From its tight lot, and taking up nearly every foot of that lot, Unity looks on its exterior like a fortress—a cubic and forbidding-seeming monolith of stone gray, something the Mayans must have left behind. (In some real sense, the Larkin Building is Unity's St. John the Baptist.) It was as if the architect was bent on breaking apart all the conventions of American religious architecture. Wright used poured concrete: Portland cement and crushed red granite set into forms erected on site. He did it to save money, but he grew to love the look and texture of it. He used pea gravel or crushed stone aggregate to give the surface a pebbly feel. Unity is one of the first examples of the use of reinforced concrete on a large scale in America. The building committee's contracted budget, once construction began, in May 1906, not counting the cost of the lot, was for $32,000—and by the time the work was mostly done, toward the back of 1908, he'd run it over by almost twice that. He'd run *them* fairly over—and to distraction. But they were grateful—in the main.

In a letter of March 4, 1906, Charles White, working in the runner-over's office, said: "The chief thing at Wright's is of course Unity Church, the sketches of which are at last accepted, after endless fighting. We have all pleaded and argued with the committee, until we are well nigh worn out. All hands are working on the working drawings."

To get fully inside Unity, from the sidewalk out on Lake Street, which is still Oak Park's main east–west thoroughfare, you have to make at least six right-angle turns. When Unity went up, there were clanging streetcar tracks out on Lake and two railroad lines behind. Lesniak and I began making the turns together from car-honking Lake. "It's a way to get you to be one with the building," he said. "I think Wright said something to the effect that each turn was a chance to change your mind, transform your consciousness from walking down the loud, dirty street to coming inside the peace of the sanctuary."

You enter on the side. First, you pass through a low-ceilinged entrance hall. On the right is a meeting-cum-social-space called Unity House—its own part of the complex. The place of worship is on the left. You turn instinctively in that direction, but it turns out that the only way you can get there, from either side of the sanctuary, is to descend some stairs and go along darkened corridors parallel to the sanctuary. Wright named the corridors "cloisters." From these below-the-ground passageways you can see the slats of light burning up above, but it isn't until you make another ninety-degree turn and ascend one of the small stairways and enter the chamber itself that you get to experience the full explosion of light. In a way, it's like emerging from the tunnels of an old ballpark and feeling overwhelmed by the sight of the perfect napkin of clipped sunlit green before you. Only it's as if the "diamond" has somehow been suspended in air.

All of the boggling geometries and interconnecting forms of the room are there, but they will have striven in on you only viscerally: from the darkness to the light.

Earlier, there was mention of a fellow Wright Prairie School architect, George Elmslie, and of how, after *An Autobiography* appeared, he wrote a long letter to Wright to both congratulate him and to chastise him on his ego and prevarications. He said, "[I]t may amuse you to have recalled to your mind a comment you made to me, long ago, in connection with Unity Church in Oak Park. I made some general comment about the use to which the building was to be put, and your reply was, 'I don't give a damn what the use of it is; I wanted to build a building like that.'"

Wright attended neither the informal opening of Unity in October 1908, nor its formal dedication a year later. For the second, he wasn't invited. They wrote him out of the program—literally. Four days before, he had left Oak Park to meet Mamah Cheney in New York. By then practically the whole village, not just the decent stewards of Unity Temple, knew he was an adulterer of no shame. But this jumps ahead of the chronology.

He kept turning out Prairies, and this was part of the problem: it was leading not just to exhaustion but also to boredom. He'd hold office hours in the city and rush back to Oak Park on the Elevated to do late-afternoon work with his associates in the home studio. He often worked alone on Sundays.

He had designed a library in Springfield, Illinois. He had built the E-Z Polish Factory in Chicago. He had agreed to participate in the Chicago Architectural Club's twentieth annual exhibition at the Art Institute. The show had run from late March to late April 1907. Once again (as in 1902) he'd fairly hogged the whole thing, with thirty-eight pieces and his own separate exhibiting space.

He'd begun again with Mamah, and doubtless now in a sexual way. Probably by at least mid-1907.

September 1907: *Oak Leaves*, publishing every Saturday, runs a news item: on alternate Thursday mornings this fall, Scoville Institute will be hosting a series of book talks on famous poets as part of the cultural programs of the Nineteenth Century Woman's Club. Enlightened Oak Park housewives had begun the Nineteenth Century club in 1891 to serve educational and charitable and civic missions. Anna Wright was a member. Mamah Cheney was a member. Kitty Wright was a member. (Hemingway's mother, Grace Hall Hemingway, was a member.) Through the years Kitty had chaired various arts and education committees. And so this three-line item, halfway down page 4, in the September 21, 1907, issue of the town's weekly:

> November, Goethe. November 7, "Life and Short Poems," Mrs. Cheney and Mrs. Frank Wright.

The program following this, on November 21, will be devoted to a discussion of Faust.

Nothing would have seemed off about this item. The Wrights and the Cheneys were known to be quite friendly by now, occasionally going to the theater in the city, dining in each other's homes. Mamah and Catherine, although quite different, were nonetheless surprisingly close. There is a line from Nancy Horan's *Loving Frank*. The novelist is dreaming herself inside Mamah's mind: "How had she come to a point where she could so easily tell herself that adultery with a friend's husband was all right?"

In March 1908, *Architectural Record*, a monthly published in New York, turned over practically its entire magazine to Wright—as if in a kind of Faustian bargain to lure more readers that month than its Boston competitor, *Architectural Review*. Four years earlier, the *Record* editors had offered to devote the entire issue of January 1904 to his work, with Wright free to name the author of his choice. But it hadn't worked out. The following year, the magazine had written about him glowingly in an unsigned piece. But now, for the March 1908 issue, they'd apparently told him *he* could write whatever he wished to write at practically any length, and they'd run it. In the lead-in, the editors said: "The sentiment for an American architecture first made itself felt in Chicago twenty years ago. Its earliest manifestation is the acknowledged solution of the tall office building problem. An original phase of that early movement is now presented." The piece was sixty-seven pages long and took up about eighty percent of the issue. There were fifty-six pages of photographs and drawings. "In the Cause of Architecture" has since been recognized as one of Wright's most enduring statements. (Over the next couple decades he would use the same lofty title for additional essays on the subject.) He had written drafts in longhand, and then had them typed, and then revised further. Some of his drafts are in the Library of Congress. In one beautiful passage, he writes of his hope that "some day America may live her own life in her own buildings, in her own way," and then strikes the next words ("turning to Nature for the guiding principles of my own inspiration"), adding instead: "that is, that we may make the best of what we have for what it honestly is or may become." But the sentence doesn't end there: it keeps rolling on and down, for another forty-three words, the waters of his ego and conviction.

In an earlier passage: "Buildings like people must first be sincere, must be true."

In a passage before that: "We of the middle west are living on the prairie. The prairie has a beauty of its own and we should recognize and accentuate this natural beauty, its quiet level."

In terms of where his life was, where his marriage was, by March 1908, it seems possible to hear double echoes in the opening paragraph. He's talking about American architecture, obviously, not about a person constructing interior arguments for following out his "conscience" when he feels the life he's in is dead. Okay. But.

> Radical though it may be, the work here illustrated is dedicated to a cause conservative in the best sense of the word. At no point does it involve denial of the elemental law and order inherent in all great architecture; rather, it is a declaration of love for the spirit of that law and order, and a reverential recognition of the elements that made its ancient letter in its time vital and beautiful.

When did Wright make a declaration to his wife of his love for Mamah? No one knows for sure, but possibly right in this period, in May or June 1908, which is to say about sixteen months before he went away, and two or three months after the publication of "In the Cause." There seems a *Sieba*-like time clue hiding in plain sight in *An Autobiography*. The passage was quoted earlier, and a portion of it again: "So, when family-life in Oak Park in that spring of 1909, conspired against the freedom to which I had come to feel every soul entitled and I had no choice would I keep my self-respect, but to go out . . ." Since he didn't "go out" until fall, this at first seems just another careless recollection— but, in fact, maybe it's the opposite. What's clear is that Kitty refused him a divorce. According to Wright, she said that if he still felt the same way in a year, she would consent. If their strained talk did occur in the late spring of 1908, say, in late May or early June, and the waiting period of a year afterward began, it lines up generally with other events.

Had Mamah made the same open declaration to Edwin? No one really knows.

What would it have been like for the kids in those two households, supposedly being held in the dark? Don't the children in some sense always know, long before the adults have any idea? Their intuitions, their secrets, are closer to the ground.

There is an obscure book, a family memoir published in 1976 by a member of the Belknap family, who lived next door to the Cheneys. It is entitled *Family Memories of Four Sisters*. The author, Margaret Belknap Allen, one of the four sisters, got some things factually wrong in the several pages she devoted to Wright and Mamah, although perhaps she remembered this precisely, for it seems the kind of memory that would have burned into her brain cells: "Mr. Wright not only built their home, but he fell in love with Mrs. Cheney. When we children became aware of this drama, we would stand up on dollie trunks stored away in [sister] Helen's closet with its high windows, and look down into the Cheney living room below to watch the two of them making love." She says that one Sunday morning—the secret no longer a secret—Wright came over to the Belknap house to borrow some cream. He spoke to the family's maid. The girls' mother, overhearing, rushed forward and said, "I would not tarnish the Sabbath by giving you cream. You who are breaking the Ten Commandments every day of the week!" No time frames are given.

His work, too, is paling now, in its own way, and, in fact, for three or four years past, although maybe still a secret to the outside eye. Much of 1908, as well as parts of 1907, had been financially "lean," to use Wright's word. But it's also true that large (and subsequently some of his best-known and -loved) residences were under design and construction in these same years: The Avery Coonley House in Riverside, Illinois. The Meyer May House in Grand Rapids, Michigan. The Frederick C. Robie House in Hyde Park. But, in a way, it was as if these were culmination houses, not fulfillment ones, or at least not fulfill*ing* ones. To quote an early Wright biographer named Robert Twombly: "It was as if he sensed the prairie genre had reached its limits, that he had explored all its possibilities, that he had reached a logical and successful conclusion, and that nothing was to be gained from further effort." No great public commissions were on the horizon. Several other hoped-for residential projects had also fallen through, including an immense one (the size of the house, that is, and the possible money) for Harold F. McCormick, the heir to a Chicago farm machinery fortune. After Wright had put in much work on the project, and seemed to have the all-clear sign, McCormick's wife, who was a daughter of John D. Rockefeller, rejected his plans in favor of a classical Italianate villa by an eastern architect.

Mixed in with this creative torpor and professional disappointment was the always chronic overspending: the excess of the one perhaps a response to the flattening other. On December 2, 1908, feeling broke, surely in more ways than one, Wright wrote a letter to Darwin Martin in Buffalo. Martin's name was referenced previously—he was one of the high executives of the Larkin Company, and over time he became Wright's longest-suffering client, benefactor, confidant, correspondent, and moral goad. (He was a strict Christian Scientist, two years older than Wright. His brother, also a Wright client and long-sufferer, lived in Oak Park.) It was through D. D. Martin that Wright had been able to make entree into the Larkin Company. In 1903 and 1904, Wright had designed a huge house for Martin—really, an estate—and, later, a Buffalo house for Martin's brother-in-law, and then another for another executive at the company. (Buffalo is rich Wright country.) In his letter of December 2, six years into their three-decade, quasi-father-son relationship, Wright said: "I suppose Mrs. Wright has written you that it is impossible for us to come to you just now. My affairs are not in good order. This year has been a great disappointment so far as opportunity to work is concerned from any present outlook. . . ." Just that layered word: "affairs."

To point again to that layered, childlike sentence in his autobiography: "Because I did not know what I wanted, I wanted to go away." The sentence following that is "Why not go to Germany and prepare the material for the Wasmuth Monograph?" The author puts in an ellipsis. Then: "I looked longingly in that direction."

He's referring to the fact that the renowned European art publishing house of Ernst Wasmuth had invited him to come to Berlin with the intention of publishing a full portfolio of his work. Most Wright historians believe that a German-born Harvard professor named Kuno Francke was the link to the offer. Francke had visited Wright in Oak Park in early 1908 and the two had become quick friends. He'd urged Wright to show his work abroad. This may have been how things developed at Wasmuth, and Wright suggests so in the autobiography. But a scholar named Anthony Alofsin—in a groundbreaking 1993 work entitled *Frank Lloyd Wright—the Lost Years, 1910–1922: A Study of Influence*—has raised some doubts. But he doesn't raise doubts about the deep longing to escape, extricate, flee. Alofsin points out that something like half of Wright's other designs in this period, both residential and public, had fallen into the limbo of "unexecuted."

Go back to the stretched-out photograph at the start of this chapter. Couldn't he almost be the eldest child? Kitty has her hands full with six kids—but he could nearly make her seventh. (In some ways, Wright almost *was* one of his own kids. He was a terrible disciplinarian. He'd just as soon turn the hose on his boys out in the yard or have pillow fights up in the playroom, leaving the cleanups and rebuke to his spouse. This is probably one reason why his children, for all their rage against him in their adulthood, seemed to bear an odd, muted, concomitant affection for him.) Keeping that earlier image to one side of your mind, consider this one. Five or so years later now. Where has the exuberance gone? No knowing sliver of smile, just the seeming wreath of gloom. As with the photograph of Mamah, isn't it his eyes that haunt most of all?

Well, only a photograph, circa mid-1909. (So he's either forty-one or just forty-two.)

At Christmas 1908, the Ashbees of the U.K. had come to visit: C.R. and his wife, Janet. Much has been written about this odd international arts-and-crafts couple, heirs to the philosophies and social reform crusades of the great William Morris of Britain. Charles Robert Ashbee, a gifted architect, an unhidden homosexual, had somehow gotten married to an astoundingly insightful woman whose own reputation as a writer and thinker has come to the fore only in the last few decades. She was a prolific diarist. Her husband had met Wright in 1900 and they'd kept in touch and found reasons to both admire and disagree with each other's work and beliefs. Late on the evening of December 21, in the playroom, Janet Ashbee sat down and wrote eleven pages of impressions in an elegant ink and hand. It was as if, knowing little, she saw everything.

These have been quiet happy days in the circle of this beautiful family. Lloyd Wright is a strange delightful soul—a radical original thinker working out his ideals consistently, as an artist. . . . Much of his building is, to me, too bizarre & away from all tradition to be beautiful; & the decoration of squares & geometric lines I find fussy and restless. But he has big ideas & is gloriously ruthless in sticking to what he believes. He has the head of a musician—a sad thought-

worn face, that smiles whimsically between almost fanatic earnest-
nesses. He is only 41 now & his beautiful wife 37—& they hardly
seem like the parents of their 6 splendid children. . . . There is something wonderfully tender & loveable about Mrs. Wright. With so
many other of the best & finest American women she has an abiding
youngness—a suppleness of gait, gesture & smile—combined with
that maternal gathering-in elderliness which always brings tears to
my eyes. . . . Every tone of her voice rings with fearless honesty—
almost a defiant cry against sham—compromise & all disloyalty—
& all cruelty. I feel in the background somewhere difficult places
gone through—knocks against many stone walls—& brave pickings
up from sloughs of despair. . . . And I am certain I hear too beginnings of a different kind of sadness—a battling with what will be an
increasing gloom & nervousness (spite of success) in her husband.
If her children do not comfort her, she will be hard pressed. As yet
she is almost the girl still—slender & lovely—but strongly built—
& when she laughs you forget the tragic lines round her mouth.

But people do not kiss one in that way unless they are lonely in
the midst of plenty.

Ashbee, too, had urged Wright to come to Europe. But a batch of
work had surprisingly appeared for him at the back of 1908. On January 3 of the new year, Wright wrote to Ashbee that "I must make hay
while the sun shines, particularly as this year has been a lean one." But
next paragraph: "No temptation to 'desert' was ever so difficult to resist
as this one from you and I shall only postpone the visit—surely I shall
join you in England within a year." "Desert": a word resonating in him,
in father-ways, since 1885. No wonder he has put it in quotes. Did he
even know? Was it a reflex?

The longing to escape: There is a great myth about Frank Lloyd
Wright, in the several years before he left Oak Park, in relation to automobiles, notably his brass-trimmed, leather-upholstered, straw-colored,
four-cylinder, forty-five-horse Stoddard-Dayton rumble-seat roadster.
The thing was known as the "Yellow Devil." (It was said to be one of
the first three cars in Oak Park, but that isn't remotely true.) There he
supposedly was, from about 1905 onward, crazy and incorrigible Frank
Lloyd Wright, the genius-juvenile, with his brown wavy hair stream-

ing in the wind, tricked out in an ankle-length white linen duster and a driving scarf and a pair of absurd saucer-eyed goggles, roaring down Oak Park Avenue or Lake Street at sixty per, when the posted speed limit was twenty-five. Beside him, holding on for holy life, was some hat-flying married woman of the town who'd momentarily taken leave of her senses and fallen into the arms of her architect's charms. While slices of this legend are apparently true, it's an inconvenient fact that Wright didn't even get his first automobile until somewhere in the early or middle months of 1909. So the gleeful terrorizing of the natives at the hands of the Yellow Devil had to have been a fairly short-lived phenom-enon. By the time he would have adjusted his goggles and clambered in for a momentary escape from all his problems, Oak Park was fairly lousy with cars. Just ask the city fathers at their village council meet-ings. It was a source of local pride and angst, all those belching open-air machines. It was a terrible worry about how to keep their children safe. Someone had even formed a How to Cross the Street Club.

Another part of the Wright car legend, and this one is true: He owned eighty-five automobiles—and one motorcycle—in his life. He got started late but damn well made up for lost time. He had a Bentley, four Cadillacs, three Jaguars, five Lincolns, three Mercedes-Benzes, at least one Packard, two Cord L-29s, six Hillman-Minxes, two Jeeps, a Crosley Super Roadster—and sundry others. His relationship with gas machines seems to have been nearly an erotic thing. Like all else he could ever ill afford, he seems to have loved them almost for the fact that he couldn't afford them. More later on Wright and cars. Right now the darker note has to keep being struck.

Eight days after writing to C. R. Ashbee, on January 11, 1909, Wright spoke to the Nineteenth Century Woman's Club. It was a Monday after-noon. Mamah was there. Kitty was there. His mother was there. His baby sister was there. The subject was ornamentation—the sins of it, the ignorance about its true uses. In *Loving Frank,* Horan rearranges the date: she has this lecture occurring in 1907, just as he and Mamah are falling in love again, this time all the way. She has the lecturer sail-ing into the room, throwing off his Dracula cape. I picture it just the opposite. I picture the gloom, the anger. The words "lust" and "stupid" and "ugly" and "masquerade" and "pitiful" and "burlesque" studded his text, which *Oak Leaves* published on the following Saturday. (The paper called him "one of the most famous architects in the world.") Perhaps only this passage needs be quoted: "We are living today encrusted with dead things, forms from which the soul is gone, and we are devoted to them, trying to get joy out of them, trying to believe them still potent." Did those words stab Kitty Wright to the core?

Early March 1909. A national trade publication has announced that Edwin H. Cheney is the new Chicago district manager of the Wagner Electric Manufacturing Company of St. Louis. Ed's now working out of the Marquette Building in the Loop and rides the "L" in every morning. A few days later Unity Church (the faithful persist in calling it a church, not a temple, to Wright's annoyance) holds its annual meeting. As earlier noted, Unity had held its first service in the new building back in the fall, but the formal dedication is still a few months off. The minutes run to seven pages, and about 115 of the faithful are present, and the gratitude is effusive: "Because of its uniqueness in style and construction, it is set apart as a thing by itself. . . . We extend to the architect, Mr. Frank Lloyd Wright, our most hearty congratulations. . . . We believe the building will long endure as a monument to his artistic genius and that, so long as it endures, it will stand forth as a masterpiece in art and architecture."

By September this same genius will be a non-person in their midst. But a question: Don't many of them know *now*? Isn't the adultery out in the open?

In late June, Mamah told her husband she was taking her children (although not her niece) to Boulder, Colorado, to stay with her old college pal, Mattie Chadbourne, now married with a family. (What kind of tension must there have been in *this* house? A whole other question.) Mattie had recently given birth to a third child, and the half-plausible excuse for going was that Mamah could help out with the new arrival, and her own children could have the good mountain air of the West. But did both Edwin and Mamah understand she wouldn't be back, or at least not ever to live under his roof again? It seems so, at least from what Edwin testified at the divorce proceedings (which Mamah didn't attend) several years later. In any case, the timing of Mamah's June leaving coincides with the expiration of the one-year waiting period Kitty Wright had imposed—assuming that she'd imposed it in June of the preceding year. What's known is that Mamah stayed out west for the summer, while Wright seems alternately to have fumed and dithered.

It had to have been a terrible time for the Wright children, the older four of whom were in their teens. Surely their mother and father were sleeping in different rooms, had long been doing so. How much fighting in front of the children? What does Anna Wright think? She is still right next door. Is she secretly pleased?

In his final weeks before escape, Wright sought to close his office—or, rather, to find a competent person to assume control of his ongoing projects, one of which was the Robie House in Hyde Park. The Robie? Another Wright wonderwork with its own seeming attendant curses and reversals of fortune—certainly for its namesake first owner. Frederick C. Robie, twelve years younger than Wright, cocky young man, had studied engineering at Purdue and was involved in his family's manufacture of automobiles and bicycles. He invented something called the "Robie Cycle Car." But then his father died in 1909 and the thirty-year-old took over the company, which owed much money to lenders. He and his wife, Lora, and their two children moved into the great house on the corner of South Woodlawn Avenue and Fifty-Eighth Street. The company failed. Robie's marriage began to disintegrate. He tried to settle the debts as a promise he'd made to his father. His wife accused him of adultery and of visiting whorehouses. She left with the children in April 1911 and sued for divorce. Robie was forced to sell—he'd been able to live in the house for not even two years. He went to New York, where he again failed. He came back to Chicago, but couldn't find work. And yet, other side of the story, he endured into old age. And yet there the Robie stands today, on its corner, a not-quite-reddish, stained-glass ocean liner of a Prairie house that seems almost to be swaying imperceptibly at anchor: repointed, rehabilitated, with shrine-goers at the ticket counter in the gift shop every day of the year that the place is open. Neil Levine: It's the "house that can be considered the final outcome of the process of abstraction and analysis begun in the Winslow House." Wright himself once called it "a source of world-wide architectural inspiration." And he was right.

The man who, because he did not know what he wanted, just wanted to go away, sold off Japanese prints. He arranged to borrow money. He worked on a contract regarding the turning over of the office to an MIT-educated architect named Hermann V. von Holst. Eleven of his projects were under construction, and there were also prospective ones in the pipeline. Wright wasn't about to give all this away, myths to the contrary. He negotiated a detailed contract with von Holst on September 22, 1909.

Six days earlier he had written to D. D. Martin in Buffalo. He had lately designed a gardener's cottage for the Martin estate. He said, "Let the bill rendered you cause you no emotion. If it is more than you think it worth amend it as you wish and send what it may be, or, nothing—to the office—the matter is not worth the agony." Next sentence: "I am leaving the office to its own devices, deserting my wife and the children for one year, in search of a spiritual adventure, hoping it will be no worse." What was the antecedent of "it"? The office? His family? His life? Everything?

He went off the day after signing the contract with his office-keeper. The leaving seems to have been in the afternoon. It was Thursday, September 23, 1909. (He possibly rode the L into the city where he probably caught an evening Pullman for the East. We don't have the record.) Was his family standing there waving as he went out the door with his luggage? Doubtless not a pasteboard suitcase in his freckled paw this time. Many stories have grown up around the gothic going. His eldest son, Lloyd, is said to have attacked him on the way out. (I have my doubts, for several reasons, and one of them is that Lloyd was away at college that fall, in Madison. Yes, he could have come quickly home at his mother's beseeching.)

An unpaid grocer's bill for $900 is said to have lain on the kitchen table as he walked out. Two days later, *Oak Leaves* publishes a six-line item. It's on the back page, page 32, squeezed in with other items about a fire alarm going off and somebody headed for the Seattle Exposition: "Frank Lloyd Wright left Thursday for Germany to superintend publication of a book to contain his architectural work. He expects to be absent a year, and the work may take even longer."

Four days after his departure, and one day after the Saturday publication of the six-line piece of gossip-news that, in some sense, the whole town already knows, Unity Temple holds its formal dedication ceremony. A dozen Unitarian ministers participate, one of them being Uncle Jenk. There are five or so speakers. The son of a former president of Harvard gives the main sermon at both the morning and evening services. *Oak Leaves* provides page-one coverage. The paper seems to be going through contortions to avoid saying his name. There are sentences like these: "The house was filled with members and others who came to worship and to see the interior of the building that has pro-voked so much comment." The printed program is the same: written off, written out. Nowhere in the program's two pages of background notes are the words "Frank Lloyd Wright" to be found. He's apparently in New York (settled into the Plaza Hotel) on this placid Sunday, September 26, 1909, awaiting his lover from out west. She'll leave by rail tomorrow, Monday, having put her children in the care of her friend Mattie and her husband, and having placed—perhaps on a dresser by the bed in Mattie's guest room—a letter of so-called explanation to her spouse. We don't have such a letter. But this part is fact: Decent Edwin Cheney rode out on the train in early October to collect John and Martha and bring them home. And this, too, is fact: Mamah's dear friend Mattie Chadbourne Brown died that fall. Mamah found out in Europe. How could Mattie have died? She was only thirty-eight. Made no sense. It was almost as if her sudden dying (on October 14, 1909) was some sort of proxy sorrow for someone else's moral selfishness.

Coda. Frank and Mamah are on the ocean bound for Europe about a week after they reunite. That would put the timing in early Octo-ber. Which means that it is about five weeks later that the Chicago press will find them in Berlin and begin filing lurid stories about the adulterous "elopement." But these stories, no matter their luridness and lip-smacking glee, will be as practically nothing next to the lurid and thinly concealed glee that will appear in many places in America five years from now, following a burning and a butchering of seven people by a small, black madman on a Wisconsin hill. For instance, here's what Utah's *Ogden Standard* will have to say to its Mormon readership on September 5, 1914, beneath the full-spread headline: THE TERRIBLE FATE OF MAMAH BORTHWICK IN HER BUNGALOW OF LOVE.

A new-made grave in a lonely Wisconsin wood is all that is left of the Kingdom of Love, which Frank Lloyd Wright, world-famed architect, established a few short years ago when he threw aside the conventions of the world, man-made conventions he called them and left his wife and family to be with his "soul mate," wife of his neighbor.

It was easy enough five years ago for Wright to talk of his idealism, but today with the new-made grave up in the Wisconsin wood, it is a different tale. Not only does that one grave refute his arguments, but two urns of his soul mate's children in a Chicago crematorium and the other dead deny his declarations.

The old law "Thou shalt not covet thy neighbor's wife," was so much trash to Wright. It hadn't been proven to him, and he could out-argue those who found fault with his course and who not only condemned him, but also condemned Mamah Borthwick Cheney for leaving her husband and going with Wright. Wright and Mamah Borthwick were governed by a law made by themselves. They refused to be bound by any provisions of others and therefore established a kingdom of their own in the land of their own, where they built their own "Love Bungalow."

It'll go on from there, five columns of copy in all.

And *Oak Leaves*? It will avert its eyes five years hence. The only thing the paper will do as regards August 15, 1914, is run a three-paragraph editorial, in which the editors will again artfully find a way to not even utter his name, Mamah's name. Instead, they'll speak of the "awful tragedy at Spring Green," and of how it had brought "death to two bright Oak Park children, known and loved by many," and of how "*Oak Leaves* can only bow its head in silence." Except that the paper won't be able to resist this coda: "At a time when even those who are farthest from the old orthodox tenets are wondering if after all there is something in the doctrine of providential retribution, it behooves us more than ever, perhaps, to have resort to the Christian virtues of charity and brotherly kindness. It may be true that 'God moves in a mysterious way,' but we are nevertheless under the injunction to 'Judge not, that ye be not judged.'"

These many years later, a century later, to go to the third floor of the beautiful public library in the beautiful broad-lawned town (it's just down the street from Unity) and to squint on microfilm at that old pharisaical editorial—because of course they were judging, and judging terribly—is enough, almost enough, to make you wish to take his side, her side. Feels surprising to have this sudden, strong, urgent feeling on both their behalves, although in another way not at all.

PART II

Chains of Moral Consequence
1914–1921

Most of the time (although I do not choose as I once did to deny the violence of my days by ignoring it) I am not so overtly violent. I remember that I am invisible and walk softly so as not to awaken the sleeping ones. Sometimes it is best not to awaken them; there are few things in the world as dangerous as sleepwalkers.

—Ralph Ellison, *Invisible Man*

Not a house in the country ain't packed to its rafters with some dead Negro's grief.

—Toni Morrison, *Beloved*

As long as there is earth under your feet
someone must dig into it.

—Philip Levine, from his poem "Naming"

I believe that in the search for the answer lies the answer.

—Frank Lloyd Wright

Going back to where it got cleaved off, many pages ago: that other room, and what happened in it. Think of this as stopped motion coming to life, a reel from an old sixteen-millimeter movie starting to flicker through a projector again. But keep in mind, as was said before, that no one really knows how it happened, or how long it lasted, first bludgeon to last slicing, or what the precise sequence of events was, or how in the world one relatively small person, flowing between two eating spaces, in different parts of the house, could do so much harm in so brief a time. In some ways, it is all conjecture.

Five men and a boy had just begun to eat in the compact dining area in the southwesterly corner of the residential wing. But to complicate that fact: the southwesterly corner was, in another (and literal) sense, in the true southern part of the compound, the entirety of which (the compound) took in work courts and barns and stables and other sleeping quarters, the whole of the place elongating itself in a northerly direction. One of the reasons it's so hard to fix coordinates for Taliesin generally is because, over the years and decades, Wright, in various remodelings and wholesale rebuildings, pivoted the house on its foundations, so as to have it pointed in off-kilter ways in respect to the Wisconsin River. The river, according to any map, lies to the north of the property—or, to say it another way, the property is on the south side of the river. Except what Wright called "north" was never true North. A Taliesin cultural historian named Keiran Murphy, who has probably studied the history of the house more closely than anyone else, and who seems to have much humility about all she doesn't know, much humility in the face of the bigness of August 15, 1914, once said to me: "The problem, essentially, is because the house was more or less turned on its axis through the years. What was South then is East today, and what was North then, or called North, is West today. And even then it wasn't a true South or a true West or a true North. So when you're trying to figure who was sitting where, and where these rooms were in relation to the compass, never mind how Julian Carlton did what he did, it can drive you fairly nuts. It only took me five years to get it."

Only another metaphor for the puzzle palace of Frank Lloyd Wright's life.

Apparently, the six were seated at two tables in this room, which is labeled in one Wright drawing as "Men's Dining Room." On one side was a bank of low windows, a few feet off the floor, looking out onto a walled-in garden. Immediately beyond the garden was a stone wall and some jagged rocks and a fairly steep hillside that led to a small dammed-up pond or lake feeding into a creek. Down this hill and toward the water, the Wright draftsman Herb Fritz, mentioned many pages ago, went instinctively rolling with his badly broken arm in the maybe forty-five seconds after the room—and his clothes and some of his skin—had become an envelope of flame. The draftsman, twenty, a favorite of Wright's, a go-along, get-along sort of person, had crushed his arm from the fall after he had thrown himself through the bank of windows. But he was destined to survive. He would later testify that he was not quite halfway down the hill when the flames died out, or at least died out enough so that he could slowly stop rolling and get up on his knees and then to his feet and then start running back up the hill while cradling his shattered arm (he had to have been half in shock) in time to see a fellow draftsman named Emil Brodelle—who may or may not have said a dirty racist thing three days before to Julian Carlton, and who was not a go-along, get-along sort of person at all—get his head split nearly in half.

The other side of the room looked out onto a flagstone court and the main entryway/driveway to the house. There was a door there, at the northeast corner. That would have been a primary means of escape. The door led to an inner court, through which a server (or any other person) would need to go if he wished to return directly to the kitchen. The kitchen was something like fifty paces away, in a straight line east of the eating space. The door is said to have had a lock on its outer side. (Just to further muddy: On the east side of the room there was another exit—not a door, but a passageway leading to a bedroom and to other interior parts of the house. This obviously would have been an escape route, too, but, so far as I know, it's something that's been paid scant attention to in terms of trying to figure out what happened.)

It isn't known if the murderer had locked the door leading to the inner court, once he had set down the initial serving of food, and just before heading back toward the kitchen, presumably to pick up more food. (A *tragically wrong presumption.) If he did lock it from the outside, he almost certainly didn't try to light the room, not at that moment. As was said earlier, he must have departed quietly, with no hint of his intentions, and then, once out of sight, perhaps begun to trot, or even broken into a run, in a straight path northward, toward the kitchen, but not stopping there, instead going through another interior door, and then skirting the edge of the living room, and then going around the large wooden dining room table and out onto the porch.*

Where Mamah and her two children were waiting in the sun to be served.

With his weapon now out of his tunic and held aloft.

Perhaps swinging it as he came.

After he had finished the first part of his killing on the terrace, but apparently having not yet set Mamah and her son on fire, and having also chased Mamah's daughter through the house until he'd caught her from behind, he then must have torn back to where the men were waiting for the next serving. He must have been full out now, crazed with his mission, understanding that he had only minutes to accomplish what he intended: destroy everyone on the premises, and roast the place to cinders besides. It seems fairly certain that this is the point when he would have poured the fuel under the doorjamb and tossed the match.

Apparently, he never tried to re-enter the room. His plan, inasmuch as he had a plan, seems to have been to get them from the outside as they tried to escape.

But he must not have counted on Herb Fritz and two others crashing through the bank of windows on the opposite side of the room. It was impossible for him to be in two places at once. So what he seems to have done in the next several minutes was to run around the outside of the building, one outer wall to the other outer wall, back and forth, swinging and pounding and slicing at whoever was in his line of sight. With fire and a choking smoke everywhere.

This must be the reason why not everybody in that tight eating room died. He got as many as he could. He got four of the six. It is hard to imagine that kind of fury and speed. It's hard to imagine that kind of resolve. Yes, he had the element of surprise on his side. Yes, all six were doubtless trying to shield their faces from the flames and so perhaps couldn't see him until he was on top of them. Still, you keep thinking there must be some other explanation. There must have been an accomplice no one has ever known or found. Something seems not quite right here. Something seems definitely off. Except that there has never been any other explanation, no credible piece of evidence has ever come forth to suggest that anyone else was involved in those ten or twelve or fourteen minutes of chaos, in which nine people, in two eating spaces, the spaces separated from each other by maybe eighty feet at most, got attacked by one man with a crudely efficient weapon, and in which seven of the nine (not instantly) lost their lives.

Not possible. Only it somehow was.

There are stories about him pouring the fuel and coolly taking up his stance outside the door, but not before retrieving his pipe from his pocket and clamping it in his teeth. There are stories of how he poured the gasoline, took out a match, lit the pipe, and then used the same match to start the explosion. That seems almost a cartoon, a cartoon of madness. There couldn't have been anything cool about it.

In any case, he got Brodelle, who seems to have been about thirty, and who lived in Milwaukee, and who'd recently become engaged, and who had come through the splintered bank of windows after Fritz, and whom the killer seems to have hated more than he hated any of them. (More on this later.) It was a clean hit, almost clear through, catching him at the hairline by his left ear and going deep into his brain. He died fairly close to the spot where he was struck.

He got thirty-five-year-old Billy Weston, who'd also crashed through the windows on that side of the room, and who'd gotten separated from his son, next to whom he'd probably been sitting at the table. Billy Weston had built a lot of Taliesin. He was known all over that region as a master carpenter. Wright loved his skills. The killer didn't get Weston fatally, though. His blows glanced off the mark. Weston's body was on fire, and he fell to the ground, and he was bleeding badly, but he, along with Fritz, was the only other one of the nine who would survive. For the rest of his life, Weston would wear long-sleeve shirts, to hide his burns.

On the other side of the room (so, again, picture the killer running in a half-loop around the building, one outside wall to the other) he got three more, all fatally, and perhaps in this order: Tom Brunker, David Lindblom, and Ernest Weston, Billy's son.

He got Tom Brunker, who would have turned sixty-six in September, a widower with many children, most of them grown, a devout Catholic, and who served as a foreman around the place, and got him with such a terrific blow that the old man's brains were said to have nearly spurted in his attacker's face. He'd live for another two days.

He got, and got from behind, David Lindblom, who seems to have been in his mid-forties, and who was an immigrant from Sweden, and who was the landscape gardener. By the time he hit Lindblom, the gardener's flesh was close to being burned off. He lived until the middle of the night on Monday, which is roughly how long Brunker lived. On Tuesday they buried Lindblom in the Lloyd Jones family cemetery across the fields at Unity Chapel.

He got the boy, Ernest Weston, thirteen, who sang in the choir at the local Methodist church, and who, although mortally hit, also didn't die right away. That took approximately two and a half more hours. They buried him on Monday, with his mother and five siblings in the front pew. His father, recovering, couldn't attend. During his son's dying, his father said (or at least you can find these quoted words in an oral history by one of Wright's neighbors): "[T]hat nigger up there. He killed my boy. He laid there right where he hit him."

"The black butcher," he was being called in the first flashes in the newspapers—and in later ones, too. "The black beast." "The Negro fiend." And, in a few places, worse than that.

And Frank Lloyd Wright, who was present for none of this, what did he have to say? Five days afterward, in his local paper, Spring Green's Weekly Home News, in an open letter to his neighbors, in which he was by turns contrite and grieving and humble and haughty, he spoke of "the black cunning face" that "the negro wears as it comes before me in my dreams."

But who really was this person? It's as if we've always had the act and none of the life. What follows is an attempt to say something about who Julian Carlton actually was. But there are other related things to be said, and the truth is they are just as important, if not more so. But, first: Julian, grainy as his photograph, the only one we have.

Coming Before Him in His Dreams

Notes on an Alabama Native Son

Julian Carlton, August 1914

I flew south one day...rented a car, and drove for a month
or so around Louisiana and Mississippi and Alabama, saw no
spokesmen, covered no events, did nothing at all but try to find
out, as usual, what was making the picture in my mind.

— Joan Didion, from *South and West*

I t can't be proven, not in any rock-solid way, not by me, that his mother
(and likely his father too) was born a slave child on a Deep South cotton plantation, and that he therefore was just one notch up from his
own chains, literal or metaphoric—I only strongly believe so. But even

if I could somehow document it beyond a doubt, would that fact have anything direct or even indirect to do with what occurred at Spring Green, Wisconsin, on August 15, 1914? Maybe, and maybe a whole lot more than maybe, but only a fool would try to push that argument very far. There had to have been ten thousand things burning in Julian Carlton's chaotic mind when he did what he did that noonday. Let that event, that moment, stand unopposed in its meanings and mysteries. And yet, to paraphrase the person who wasn't there, and around whom this entire work is trying to revolve and shadow and time-bend and breathe: Isn't there a kind of answer, if only threadbare and provisional, just in the act of searching?

———

Notes are all these can ever be. He's too hidden, his family's too hidden. So form will try to follow function and make a half-virtue out of necessity.

Sometimes he jumps right out at you—the picture forming itself in your mind. Here he is, page 269, halfway down the column, in the R. L. Polk and Company's official *Birmingham City Directory* for the year 1906. It's a one-line entry. "Carleton Julian, bellman The Birmingham." There's a tiny indentation in the line with an asterisk in front of it. It was the city's way of denoting "colored." Yes, they've misspelled his name, but it's him, has to be, because he's cross-listed in other directories for the same year, and he's registered in those as living at an address with his parents, along with some of his many siblings, whose names are identifiable from other sources. So, yes, it's him, if not in the flesh, something that feels almost palpable, as if having him momentarily back from the lost.

The Birmingham? One of the city's better hotels then. It was built in the 1890s and was six stories high and was on the corner of Eighteenth Street and Second Avenue North, near the heart of the downtown business district, when Birmingham was growing exponentially (a 245 percent increase in its population in the decade between 1900 and 1910, which is the period when this family, his family, having experienced its own exponential increases, had migrated there). The hotel got a lot of commercial trade. But touring theater people, even a few folks from Broadway, were also known to stop over—so maybe he rode up in the elevator a time or two with somebody white and famous, looking straight ahead, and put down the bags and waited around by the door, hoping to be flipped a nickel. Did he have a red uniform with blue piping and three rows of gold buttons down the front and one of those little cocked black helmet-hats with a chinstrap like the kid in the Philip Morris ads? Don't think so. The hotel had class, but not that kind of class. If the Birmingham was less than an architectural marvel, its builders had tried to accentuate its strengths with its faintly modernist look: tall windows with eye-catching orna-ment, making the building appear on its surface actually taller than it was. An octagonal tower on the top floor supported an observation perch. Down on the street was a long façade featuring a stepped gable with deep cornices and pseudo-ornate grillwork. Louis Sullivan would have likely turned up his nose, because it was the inorganic approach, with form hardly following function, and Frank Lloyd Wright would have doubtless hooted as well, but the question here has nothing to do with architectural principle or organic ornament or forms follow-ing function: Could Julian Carlton have landed such a job in the first place if he were some rude bumpkin up from the country? Which, essentially, is just what he was. All I can think is that he must have learned fairly early to accentuate his own strengths, and that some of the accentuating, the disguising, the seeking to seem something other than who he really was, layering it smoothly atop, must have started with trying to get rid of any traces of the country and backwoods speech.

One more note about the Birmingham: In June 1935, two decades after Julian Carlton was dead, a nighttime fire took a lot of it down. Didn't destroy it altogether. Some years earlier, the place had changed its name to the New Florence and then later to just the Florence. By the time of the fire, the hotel had gone semi-seedy and was serving tran-sients and long-term residents. A lodger was suspected of setting the blaze, which caused two deaths, including that of a seventy-two-year-old man on the third floor. The newspapers described female residents leaping from windows. There was a lot of screaming. The police could never quite figure a motive.

It isn't easy to know how the story first got started that he had come from somewhere in the West Indies, but it hardened soon enough into myth, and it has stayed that way for a century. "A Barbados negro with a handax yesterday" were the first words in the first sentence in the next morning's *Chicago Sunday Tribune.* Frank Lloyd Wright himself was under the mistaken belief his gone-mad employee had been born in Cuba or Haiti or Sint Maarten or Barbados or some other exotic Caribbean place. He told reporters that on the day of the murders, and he said it nearly twenty years later in his autobiography (he wrote of "a thin-lipped Barbados negro"), and he apparently believed it until the day he died, not that he ever spoke of it much. In all these years since, Wright biographers and historians (never mind how many acres of newspaper feature writers, and an opera company, too) have only helped to perpetuate the myth. Which is what it is: myth.

Did Julian Carlton himself insinuate—or outright claim—to Wright, and to his several Chicago-area employers before Wright, that he had come from an island in the Caribbean? It can't be said, but it's a reasonable assumption. And why would he have wanted people to think this? Again, unable to be answered, but possibly in his mind an Afro-Caribbean heritage would have suggested that he was distinct from and maybe morally superior to an ordinary American black person, that he was on a higher intellectual plane. Also, such an ancestry might have emphasized, but with slyly positive rather than negative connotations, the idea of a mixed-race background. Why, yes, of course, there was doubtless French or Spanish or Dutch or British blood in him—and might you not get a sense of that just from looking at his light-colored skin and thin lips and not particularly large nostrils? (It's instructive to go back and read some of the old first news flashes, and so many of the later ones too, and discover the casual implied racism in the reporters' physical descriptions of him. It almost seems as if the descriptions were unthinkingly more than maliciously written, which, in a sense, only made them more pernicious. Of course, there were all those other screaming descriptions of him: beast, fiend, savage, animal, brute, devil.)

Julian Carlton was from nowhere near the Lesser Antilles or the Greater Antilles or anywhere else in the tropics. His origins were far less exotic—and, in a whole other way, far more exotic, not to say far more complicated. He was from Alabama—firstly, the remote and rural and semi-rolling and clay-scoured and deeply green and red-dirted and night-ridered and semi-tropical and loblolly-pined parts of Alabama. Specifically, a place called Chambers County, and, more specifically, a little back-beyond-the-moon clot of Chambers life named Cusseta. And then, later on, he was from the so-called metropolitan parts of his native state, where supposedly there were more freedoms and opportunities for people of his race. And then, finally, a little further on from there, possibly somewhere around 1907 or 1908 or 1909, Julian Carlton was from the South Side of Chicago. No, that's not quite right. The "finally" part would have to include an earthen-floored and below-the-ground Wisconsin jail cell where he had one high window and a straw bunk and a straight-backed chair, and where he starved himself to death in a mostly glowering silence for seven and a half weeks—until about one o'clock on the afternoon of October 7, 1914—following his act at Taliesin.

This is his trajectory, his narrative arc, no matter how many lacunae exist in between.

If the surviving record of Julian Carlton's life in both the backcountry of Alabama and then up in Birmingham, in the years before he left his native state altogether, is frustratingly thin, full of gaps and omissions and confusions and questions, it can nonetheless be said without contradiction that he was born and grew up in a region of America where the question of light skin color and not particularly Negroid features is something freighted and layered with its own special grainy sexual implications. In the Deep South, issues of mixed-race ancestry, of white-blood ancestry, tend to speak in subterranean ways to the idea of sexual power, to the idea of one human being's coercion of and dominion over another. The history of race relations in the South in and of itself is exactly about that idea. But sex has always added the extra layer of implication, of haunt, of guilt. (You could argue—critics have—that the taboo of sex between master and slave is the central brooding preoccupation of William Faulkner's greatest novels.) The same kind of tensions would obtain in the Caribbean, with its long history of a colonized, subjugated people, but what went on there was *there*, foreign, not occurring on native ground.

So, is this why he reinvented himself—if he did—as having come from outside the United States: to blur those ghosts? It can't be said. But other things can—provisionally, speculatively.

———

His mother's first name was Mariah. (Sometimes you see it spelled as "Maria.") She may or may not have been mulatto but, at minimum, I believe her to have been descended from mulattos. She may also not have had a last name until after she was freed from slavery (she would have been roughly ten at the end of the Civil War), and then the family name she took was that of her masters—or, more accurately, was that of her mistress. I'll repeat that I cannot prove these things in an unassailable way. What I have are bits and pieces of compelling circumstantial evidence—I'll risk calling it haunting evidence—and I'll present those bits and pieces shortly.

But what *is* true, what *is* fact, is that Julian Carlton's mother lived into her eighties and more than a third of the way into the twentieth century. Mariah Diana Frederick Carlton—this was her full and married name, which she seldom seems to have used—died in Birmingham on June 24, 1939. There would probably be several ways to think about this date (you can find it in half a dozen records, and so I am convinced of its accuracy or near-accuracy), but one way to think about it would be that she lived for twenty-five years past the impenetrable thing that her child Julian—who had arrived toward the back of the astonishingly long ladder of kids—did in far-off Wisconsin. Had the woman who lasted until she was about eighty-four (she is reported in several sources to have been born in January 1855) long ceased thinking about it, or was it something living with her always? I have no knowledge one way or the other, but I prefer to believe the latter. Why? Because there *is* some fairly strong evidence that this was a faithed and churchgoing family, maybe not all of them, but certainly some. The Carltons—and there may have been as many as seventeen members in the original nuclear unit—seem to have been Methodist-Episcopal by way of Southern Baptist.

———

Notes. His father's first name was Galon, although, not unlike the name Carlton in various Wright books, you can find it spelled in almost every conceivable way: Gitlin, Galen, Gallon, Garland, Galeton, Gollin, Galing. This last is how it was recorded in the 1900 federal census. The family was living then in Birmingham's ninth ward, precinct 37, in a little rented space on Sixteenth Avenue, in the northern section of the city. (They moved frequently, sometimes only a door or two down, a block or two over, from where they lived the year before. This may have been their first Birmingham address.) Perhaps less than half of all the Carlton children were living under the same roof with the parents (several of the older ones were married by then, with the beginnings of their own families, and at least one child in the family was deceased), but Julian was there. If the census taker got it right—something that must always be considered—he was twelve and was working (along with a ten-year-old brother) as a "grocery porter," which possibly meant that he swept floors or held open doors for people of relative privilege (which is to say Birmingham people of the right color). He must not have been in school, but it was reported that he could read and write. The enumerator put down his date of birth as February 1888, which would make him about four or five years younger than what history has always thought. If he was, in fact, born in 1888, then, as was suggested in the opening pages of this book, he would have been about twenty-six and a half, and not thirty or thirty-one, on August 15, 1914, which are the ages that get cited in Wright books and articles. (And, by the same math, he would have been eighteen when he bell-hopped at the Birmingham, which also seems about right, and also seems to have been his last job in the city before he traveled further north.)

Pausing here. One of the chief reasons why thirty or—more commonly—thirty-one has long been given for his age at the time of the Taliesin murders is that the sheriff at Dodgeville, Wisconsin, wrote in the latter number on the death certificate on October 8, 1915, the day after his prisoner died. (It's possible that someone else made out the death certificate, but it doesn't seem so.) So that age, which was also in many of the newspapers, started to carry downward through the decades. The sheriff's name was J. T. Williams, and, from everything that can be gleaned about him, he was a decent man and conscientious lawman who served the county for only one two-year term and did what he could in those seven last wasting weeks of his prisoner's life to keep him alive and protect him and to pry from him whatever information he could. Curiously, what Wright historians and biographers seem almost willfully to have ignored for all these years and books is that the sheriff wrote the word "Alabama" and then put a question mark beside it in the box on the death certificate asking for place of birth. For me, the question mark was a first hint, instant hint, or at least first search-point for who he might truly be. That question mark took me to Alabama: to Birmingham, and to the place of his birth, which is also the place where his parents were married. (I will say more about Sheriff John T. Williams, who, like so many others in this story, not least Julian, not least the central figure of the entire narrative, seems only to want to lurk about in confusing shadow.)

To go on with what can be more or less reliably said. His father, Galon: He may have pronounced it as Gah-lawn. It's Hebrew in origin, for "wave of courage" and "heap of power." The patriarch of this astonishingly prolific family seems to have been born in Macon, Georgia, about 1845 (that year is listed on both the 1900 and 1910 census, again, suggesting that it's probably accurate, or close to accurate, and the Georgia reference also appears in other records), meaning that he would have been in his middle teens at the start of the Civil War and about twenty at its end. Because we don't have *his* father's name, his ancestry is much harder to trace. But, as with Mariah, we do know when he died, the day and year, and that's because of several surviving records, not least a remarkable twelve-page legal document: Galon Carlton's probated will and settlement of his estate, such as it was.

He died in Birmingham on February 21, 1918, so roughly three years and four months past what his son did. He was somewhere around seventy-three. He was still working. The death was not of natural causes. It had been some kind of work-related accident. He had spent his life as a laborer, and he was employed then as a porter for Birmingham Railway Light and Power, which operated streetcar lines and supplied gas and electricity to the city. He died, in the words (and the spelling) of the document, with an estate "consisting chiefly of house hold goods and wearing apparell," but a small amount of cash, too, with the whole of his worth put at $150. But two months after his death, in April 1918, his family received, or at least received in escrow, a check from his employer for $400. That would have been a lot of money, obviously, although in another sense maybe nothing at all in terms of a life wrongly taken, or that was apparently wrongly taken. (Was the company trying to avoid a lawsuit, or would that have been a laughable thought?) In the documents, there is this note accompanying the payout: "Received from B-Ham Railway Light & Power Co, as damages for causing death of decedent."

It took until 1926, eight years past his apparently wrongful death (to use a legal term), for time and the money collectors to catch up to and dispose of much of that held-in-escrow $400. After various bills and parties were paid off, including what seems to have been a pretty high bill from Welch Brothers Undertaking—a noted black Birmingham funeral service—there was a balance remaining of $165.95. Galon's widow—to whom he had been wed for just under half a century, and who had borne him all those children in a span of something like twenty-five years, and who seems herself to have been not quite fifteen years old when she got married and not quite sixteen when she had her first child—ended up with $33.19. The rest was divvied up among ten surviving Carlton children, each of whom got either a check or cash for $13.27. (When you do the math, it seems they collectively got cheated out of six cents.) Several family members signed a piece of paper agreeing to the final disposition. Mariah Carlton put down an X, and someone—probably one of her children—wrote above and below it the words "her mark." John T. Carlton, one of the elder children, who seems to have spent part of his life in Atlanta, and who, for a time, may have been a self-employed small businessman, and who must have been one of the family's larger successes, had acted as the executor.

When you read this document, much of it typed, perfectly preserved, you almost can't help getting a feeling—or I couldn't—that it had willed itself to hang around into another century just to be able to relate its own little family truth. About what? Maybe this: The less empowered you are in this life, the more the world will try to take advantage of you. Sometimes.

Julian Carlton's parents, of whom I have never been able to find a photograph, lie in Grace Hill Cemetery in Birmingham, along with some of his siblings and other relatives, close and far. Not that you can see any of their stones, or at least I have never been able to find a stone. Grace Hill is one of Birmingham's better-known and historically black cemeteries. (It is no longer an all-black cemetery.) It's pretty large. You can get a map at the office and walk the grassy slopes and try to imagine some of the unfamous lives beneath your shoes. Not all of the Carlton plots, including those of the parents, sit alongside or even near one another. Mariah Carlton is in Section C, block 72, lot 4, not quite under the shade of a fine old oak tree. Her husband is across the road, up near an old fence.

And their famous, or notorious, son, who put them on a certain map of immortality, except that that map, as a map, has long been dead wrong? He doesn't lie in Grace Hill Cemetery. His body was given over to pathologists and laboratory technicians at the University of Wisconsin for reported dissection of his brain, and afterward his remains were delivered in an unmarked panel truck to a campus crematory.

Not a house in the country ain't packed to its rafters with some dead Negro's grief.

Once you start spading into, and turning over, or trying to, the earth of this family's buried history, you come on a fact—call it a truth, even— that you almost cannot help but be stirred by, almost in spite of yourself: that the Carlton narrative arc as a whole, not just Julian's narrative arc, lines up with one of the largest (if still not known enough or appreciated enough) stories in the four-century history of Americans as a people: the Great Migration. Which is to say the journey outward from the baking fields of home to the tenement dreams of the urban North (and, in some cases, Far West). Which is to say that sea-movement myth and semi-hidden passage that took place in America between approximately 1915 and 1970 and that involved something like six million people. The Carltons as a family would have been in the first waves, or, really, pre-waves, of this tidal event. If the parents themselves didn't get past Birmingham, some of their children—who had scant formal educations, when they had any at all, and none of those educations, so far as I can determine, having gone past the middle grades of elementary school— made it, in the first decades of the century, to places like Anderson, Indiana, and Binghamton, New York, and Louisville, Kentucky, and Detroit and New York City. Not that they stayed for their lifetimes.

In the end, a number of them seem to have gone back south, to sweet home Alabama, with all its attendant curses and deep claims on their attachments. In Great Migration lore, Harlem and the South Side of Chicago are the two meccas, magnets, most iconic passage-places of all. (Chicago offered all that big-shouldered promise of the steel mills and the slaughtering houses.) Whether Julian got to the South Side by himself or with a sibling or a second cousin or a wife or a lover, and when exactly he came: one more thing that doubtless will not ever be known.

What did those many dispersed siblings think when they found out about August 15, 1914? It's something I've thought a lot about. Is it possible they never knew? Possible, but it seems unlikely. Wouldn't word have seeped through, leaked out, even if only in capillary ways, no matter where they'd gone in their separate migrations, diasporas? Were they deeply ashamed? Wouldn't they had to have been? Was he their lone bad seed? What made him turn?

You could get curious about this family as a family almost by names alone. There were Hosea and Major and Milton and Floyd and Lamar and Josie and Deliah. It almost seems as if two illiterate parents (on the 1900 federal census, the enumerator put down both Galon and Mariah as being unable to read or write), whose own given names were unusual and alluring, had been resolved, starting with the names they picked for their children, to try to differentiate themselves as a family. Most of the family's given names are religious in their roots. Julian is an unusual name, almost with a faint feminine quality, or it seems so to my ear, perhaps the more so for a black male born in the rural Deep South. It's a Hebrew name, or has Hebrew origins. The last pagan Roman emperor was named Julian. Several early saints of the Church were named Julian. The name is said to stand for "soft-haired," "youthful," "patient," "unobtrusive."

On names and naming practices in African-American families in the Deep South: another highly complicated and even contentious issue. But, in general: Research by latter-day historians has shown that for people born into slavery, their masters seldom picked the names. The enslaved families on the farms or plantations almost always selected the names for their offspring. In some cases, not all, first names were the only names that slave families possessed in the eighteenth and nineteenth centuries, or at least the only ones they possessed in

the eyes of their owners. (In the eyes of their owners, they were property; they didn't require last names.) Later, after they were freed, they
took up surnames, and often—certainly not always—those last names
came from the people to whom they'd been formerly indentured or, in
some cases, for whom they still found themselves slaving in the decades
after emancipation, still indentured by any other name or condition
or circumstance. No one has ever distilled this sad fact of our history
into a line of poetry better than the great W. E. B. Du Bois (first African
American ever to earn a doctorate from Harvard), who wrote that, in
the years after emancipation, "The slave went free; stood for a brief
moment in the sun; then moved back again toward slavery."

I don't pretend remotely to know where all of Galon and Mariah's thirteen or fifteen children went after they left the South, or how they subsequently lived their lives, but I have tried to follow out a few of their
stories, if only superficially, even as I have tried far more obsessively to
follow out Julian's story.

For instance, he had a brother named Solomon. Solomon M. Carlton, who ended up out west, may have been born in the fall of 1870,
and in that case he would have been about seventeen when Julian was
born. Solomon, who may have been the first of those thirteen or fifteen,*
was married for sixty-one years. According to several census records,
his highest attended grade in school was the second. In the 1940 federal census, he reported owning a home worth $2,500 and working for
more than sixty hours a week. He would have been either sixty-nine
or seventy.

Years before, perhaps somewhere around 1910, he'd gone out to California with his spouse, also a native Alabamian. Her name was Addie
and they seem to have spent the rest of their lives in and around San
Bernardino County. They had one daughter and they named her Virtue.
For a time, Solomon owned his own barbershop. He later turned to shoe
repair. He lived deep into his eighties, dying on September 12, 1956. At

---

* In studying the 1900 federal census, the key census and core document that we have in terms
of establishing basic identity facts about them as a family—and more on that in a moment—it's
hard to tell whether the enumerator wrote down a 13 or a 15. You look at the page one way, and
the 3 looks like a 5, and then you turn it sideways and you begin to think, no, it is a 3, after all.

his service at Tillie's Funeral Home Chapel in San Bernardino, with an AME (African Methodist Episcopal) minister presiding, a soloist sang "It Is No Secret" and "The Last Mile of the Way." His modest marker, with his dates cut in, is in Pioneer Memorial Cemetery. I tried to get in touch with Solomon's descendants—to no avail. I couldn't trace the line past Virtue Brown, who was born back in Alabama in 1896, meaning that Julian became her uncle at the age of eight. In just these bare bones of Solomon's story, I can't help feeling a little moved, the old idea of the extraordinary existing within the utterly seeming ordinary, the old notion of the far distance someone can come with apparently so little.

One more brief sibling story, and in this one there is some small avail: Julian had an elder sister named Minnie. Her married name was Strother. She died on January 7, 1968. She seems to have been born somewhere around 1880, about eight years ahead of Julian. That would have made her about eighty-eight when she passed on that Sunday night in Lee County Memorial Hospital in Opelika, Alabama. (She seems to have tried out the North for a while, but then come back home.) Three days after her death there was a notice in the *Opelika Daily News* under "Colored Deaths." Two brothers were listed as survivors, as well as a grandson. His name was Adolphus. He had gone up to Inkster, Michigan, to work on the automobile assembly lines, but when I tried to locate Adolphus Strother, it turned out that he, too, had been dead for several decades, and that he had no descendants, or none findable.

But one hot airless summer weekday Alabama night, I sat in a Bible-study class at Minnie Strother's old church and afterward spoke to some elderly members of the congregation who sought to remember her for me. I had gone fairly tremblingly to Ebenezer CME Church in Loachapoka, Alabama. (CME stands for Christian Methodist Episcopal. In the old days, the denomination was called Colored Methodist Episcopal. Loachapoka is about an hour by car southwest of the family's home ground.) I was trembling, not because of my skin color, but because I didn't quite know what I wanted to ask, or, more accurately, how to ask it. But I was also trembling because it seemed that a flesh-and-blood relative—a *sister*—of Julian Carlton was only one membrane of memory beyond me. Something about it seemed almost fantastical.

About a dozen people, most of them women, most up in age, all of them African American, all of whom had their book of scripture sitting out in front of them, all of whom had earlier parked their cars on the browned-out church lawn under fine old trees, sat at long cafeteria-like tables under fluorescent lighting in a spick-and-span utility room that was attached to the side of the handsome red-brick church. The pastor, who was using a PowerPoint presentation, who was in a short-sleeve dress shirt with a red tie, was teaching 1 John 3:15: "Anyone who hates a brother or sister is a murderer, and you know that no murderer has eternal life residing in him." I seemed to be the only person in the room perspiring. Everyone was almost too kindly, even if it seemed that no one had a precise idea of why I was there. (The week before I had spoken by phone to a parishioner and said I was coming to Alabama and was curious about a long-dead member of Ebenezer. If I was generalizing about my intentions, I didn't tell any untruths. Irene Dowdell seemed almost uninterested in what my intentions were. "Sure you can come to Wednesday Bible study," she said. "Just come along.")

When the hour was over and I had been introduced, I stood up in front of Irene and Luvenia Barnes and Imogene Crittendon and Mary Kay Stephenson and the others in the room. I told them the thing that Minnie Strother's little brother had done in 1914, and then went into some of the details. I told about the shingling hatchet, not holding back. No one in the room seemed particularly shocked. Several looked down. Several nodded. Several murmured things I couldn't catch. But it was as if they were embarrassed for my sake, for my perspiring, and not because of anything that was being relayed. No one had heard of Julian Carlton. As for Julian's big sister, their memories of Minnie had been disappointingly vague. I left a little disconsolate.

But then the next morning, my cell phone rang. It was a church member named Linda Henry. I didn't remember her from the night before. "Miss Strother came to me in my dreams," she said. "I didn't speak up last night. This morning I could see her again. I didn't have the picture in my mind for you last night. I would have been just a little kid when she passed, a teenager. I don't know if I ever even talked to her. Back then you didn't speak to your elders unless you were invited to. But I can see her there in her white gloves. She wore a hat. Purse. Very light skin, not a big woman, almost skinny, you'd want to say. Definitely thin, small. Snazzy-looking. Caramel-colored. She knew how to carry herself. She had an air. She's up there in what we used to call Amen Corner, backing up whatever the pastor preaches, with my grandmother and all the other Eastern Star ladies, men on one side, women on the other."

Linda Henry paused. "Isn't it strange how families do? She had to have carried that pain in her heart. I think I'll get down and say a prayer for her right now. And him too."

The journey outward from the baking fields of home. This is the hardest part to write, only because it is the opaquest part, and simultaneously the most tantalizing part.

Chambers County, where Julian Carlton's family began as a nuclear unit 150 years ago, is still a remarkably rural American place. Interstate 85 slices on an angle through the southern tip of it, but you can get off the highway, at, say, exit 70 and make a left turn, and then another left and in two more minutes be on a washboard gravel road with the only things in sight being stands of second- or third-growth trees, and beef cattle, and rolling pastureland, and crumbling foundations of what may have been an old plantation smokehouse. You might see a hawk riding the thermals.

The county—covering six hundred square miles, sparsely populated, except for its eastern border, where it is semi-industrialized—snugs up to the Georgia line, in the far east-central part of the state, close to the wide Chattahoochee River. Chambers is roughly 120 miles south by southeast of Birmingham (and about 95 miles southwest of Atlanta). The famous Alabama college towns of Auburn and Tuskegee aren't far away in either driving time or miles (they're in nearby counties), but those names, if Julian had even heard of them when he was growing up, would have been as distant and unobtainable to him as Mars. Tuskegee—an iconic name in black higher education, and practically synonymous with the name of its founder, Booker T. Washington, who, as it turns out, will have an uncannily large role to play later in this story, in terms of what I have spoken of as chains of moral consequence.

Cusseta, the spot within Chambers County where the Carltons began life as a family, is a dozing-in-the-sun little village. It is pronounced kuh-SEE-tuh, and it derives from an old Indian word, from the Creek Nation. Cusseta is less than fifteen minutes off the interstate, on a two-lane blacktop, through the rolls and dips of the landscape, but it still feels about fifty miles from anywhere. I have spent some pleasant if fruitless hours, driving up and down fragrant and overhung back roads in the environs of Cusseta (its population is said to be about 125, but that must count dogs and cats), looking for something I knew I'd never find: the *exact* spot, patch of scrub earth, old sharecropper cabin, tarpaper plantation shack standing up on cinderblocks, where Julian Carlton and his siblings might have blinked themselves into the world. That's a dream, a mirage. That ramshackle cabin or raw-board shack or whatever it was—which they may not have thought of as ramshackle in the least—must be decades long gone. With the wind.

Although there are still beautiful antebellum houses in Chambers County, there aren't any real cotton plantations here any longer—no, they, too, are all gone with the wind, although a little cotton does still get produced on local farms, and you can see it growing in snowy patches along red-banked county roadsides in the late summer and into fall. These days the diminished agriculture in Chambers County is mainly about timber products, about beef cattle and corn and peanuts and soybeans. But there was a time in the history of the state when this corner of eastern Alabama was one of the golden buckles on the belt of King Cotton. It couldn't begin to compete with the dark, alluvial riches of the Mississippi Delta, no, but Chambers knew its cotton glories. And, in fact, itty-bitty Cusseta itself knew its glories. It was one of the largest points of commerce in the county. The railroad came through and made its planters rich. There were once hotels here, and saloons, and academies for young (white) gentlemen and ladies. Around the time of Julian Carlton's birth, Cusseta had six general stores, five cotton gins, two gristmills, a shoemaker, a blacksmith, a railroad agent.

Charming and beautiful: This tucked-away place, down now to a few houses and no traffic lights and a one-room post office ("PLEASE GET MUD OFF SHOES / BOOTS BEFORE ENTERING THIS BUILDING"), is unquestionably that. But, as has been noted by others long before me, beauty and charm and rural quaintness can sometimes be a terrible mask for all kinds of ugliness. I am speaking historically, perhaps the only right with which I have to speak.

There are communities in Chambers County named Clackville and

Doublehead and Red Level and Rock Fence and Tiller Crossroads and Sparkling Springs and Hickory Flat and Shiloh and Marcoot and Sturkie and Fredonia. The unwitting poetry of American place-names.

Lawman Pat Garrett, who shot outlaw Billy the Kid in the New Mexico territory, came from Cusseta. Joe Louis, the great brown bomber of the heavyweight ring, was born in this county. (There's a statue of him in fighting trim on the county courthouse lawn.) One of the last battles of the Civil War was waged here. The movie *Mississippi Burning* was filmed in Chambers County. "Cotton Tom" Heflin, a turn-of-the-century white supremacist who made his mark large in Washington, D.C., first as a congressman and then as a United States senator, came from this corner of Alabama. "I believe as truly as I believe that I am standing here, that God almighty intended the negro to be the servant of the white man," Heflin orated in 1901 when the state was hammering out its bigoted constitution. (The newspapers, quoting him, made sure to lowercase.)

During Reconstruction, and in the years afterward (when the so-called white Redeemers came in and took back what they knew, as if handed from God, was rightfully theirs), there was plenty of Ku Klux Klan activity in and about Chambers, in and about Cusseta, as there was in almost every other part of the state. On the other hand, the night-riding and terrorizing were apparently never quite as bloody or as violent here in the years after the Civil War as they were in some of the neighboring counties—Talapoosa County, for instance, just to the west of Chambers. But Chambers had its share of burnings, whippings, and lynchings, and to be convinced of that all you need to do is consult an 1872 congressional hearing on the Klan quixotically entitled *Testimony Taken by the Joint Select Committee to Inquire into the Condition of Affairs in the Late Insurrectionary States.* The multi-volume document makes scary reading, even now.

In 1898—which may have been around the time that Julian Carlton's family left east-central Alabama for Birmingham—there was a killing in this county, an account of which appeared in many northern newspapers, including *The New York Times.* Early one Sunday a mob seized a black man named John Anderson from his cell (he was accused of killing a white farmer, for whom he cropped on the share) and lynched him. (They did much more than that to him, but the gore didn't get printed in the *Times* or the *Chicago Daily Tribune.*) But within a day or so it was pretty much admitted, even by the lynching mob, that they'd strung the wrong man.

The core problem in trying to unearth the Carltons as a family in Chambers County is that they are unexplainably missing from two documents that would do much to shed light on their lives: the 1870 and 1880 federal censuses. The 1870 federal census, undertaken only a few years after the end of the worst crisis in our history, was the first census to try to provide systematic information on the country's black population. Mariah and Galon had recently been married at the home of her father, and their first child was due within three or so months. So why don't they appear in the record? Impossible to know. Were they in the fields when the enumerator came?

Same disappointing story for the next census—1880. Missing. Just for the sake, I have tried to search for them in other parts of Alabama— and outside of Alabama. No luck.

And the next census? The 1890 federal census was largely destroyed by fire in the Commerce Department building in Washington in January 1921. Professional genealogists, especially those who specialize in the history of African Americans, regard that loss as nearly incomparable. So effectively, sadly, Mariah and Galon and their children all but disappear from documentary view for something like three decades before they can be picked up again in historical real time and in fairly fleshy ways—which is to say in Birmingham, in 1900.

Except no. There are some touchstones and traces. For instance, you can go to the beautifully restored red-brick 1899 courthouse in the county seat at LaFayette (it's a few miles up County Road 83 from Cusseta, and they will regard you funny there if you don't pronounce it in the correct Chambers way: luh-FAY-ette) and take down off a roller bar on a shelf in the deed room of the probate office a large red-bound book and turn to the correct page and there, on fragile paper, written in quill pen, in light-gray ink, between red-ruled lines, will be sitting, perfectly preserved, not unlike a probated will in a Birmingham drawer, the record of an application for a Chambers County wedding license, as well as the record of the marriage itself, both documents bearing witness to the fact that a young and doubtless extremely impoverished black couple named Mariah Frederick and Galon Carlton were legally wed, at the home of the bride's father, on November 19, 1869.

The bride's father's name was John Frederick, and I am convinced he'd once been the property of prosperous cotton-plantation people named Frederick. As had his daughter.

The volume is entitled *Marriage Record 1865–1872.* To slide the book off the shelf and to open it and hold the page lightly in my fingertips for as long as I wished was to arrive at a strange, comforting feeling, at once quite small and painfully obvious and impossibly huge. It was something along the lines of: *They weren't a figment of some novelist's imagination, after all.* This family (and in particular one of its members, still eighteen years and ten months away from getting born at the time the document was inscribed in a book) was *actual.* They lived, and they separately died, some much sooner than later, some with grace, some not, and here was the evidence, or evidence of a certain kind, of where and how their entire story as a family began.

Who was John Frederick, in addition, that is, to being Mariah's father (and the unborn Julian's maternal grandfather)? I think I have an answer, or at least a plausible answer.

———

There was once another family in these same regions with the name Frederick, born, you could say, on the seeming right side of fate and color. They were originally out of the Eastern Shore of Maryland and the Carolinas, and some of their people stretched into Virginia and even Tennessee. They could trace their roots practically to the *May-flower.* They were prosperous, if not extravagantly wealthy. They were planters and semi-industrialists—tobacco and cotton and pitch tar and turpentine—but they had professional and civic aspirations, too. A man named William Kenan Frederick, who became the first postmaster of Kenansville, North Carolina, and who also got trained in medicine, who also had served in the House of Commons in the North Carolina legislature, had a deed in which he received more than one thousand acres of prime Duplin County, North Carolina, real estate. *His* father, William Frederick, who was a Carolina planter, deeded him, in 1826, tracts of land on Back Branch, and the father and the son deeded and sold slaves back and forth and also with other family members. William Kenan Frederick's mother—her name was Nancy and she, too, came from plantation people—also was in on the deeding of land and slaves. In an 1832 will, she made provisions for real property and personal property and livestock to be divided among her children and grandchildren, those alive and those not yet born. She deeded to her descendants "the following Negroes to wit," and provided their names: Daniel, Nancy, Susa, and Andrew. Were these the forebears of Julian Carlton? I believe so.

In 1818, in Turkey, North Carolina, Doctor William K. Frederick married a fellow North Carolinian named Mariah Diana Hicks, who became, of course, Mariah Diana Hicks Frederick. The couple produced ten children, most of them born in their native state. (Their last child, born after they'd relocated, they named North Carolina, perhaps only indicating how badly they missed their original home.) In the mid-1830s, Doctor Frederick and his wife and their brood (along with his mother, Nancy, and some other relatives) picked up and moved three states southwest to the almost primeval-seeming wilderness of east-central Alabama. The clan settled in and around the new village of Cusseta. They carried their slaves with them. Alabama had been admitted to the Union in 1819, but Chambers County was only three or four years old. It had once belonged to the Creek Nation. Just a few years before, the county was still oaks and virgin pine and basswood and ash. There weren't any fields for row crops. You can guess what happened: The Creeks got forcibly removed and their lands confiscated. All the treaties were broken. By 1836, roughly when the Fredericks were arriving at Cusseta, federal troops were driving the Native Americans westward from Chambers, beyond the Mississippi, where many died along the way. Trails of tears.

In the newly created county of Chambers, the virgin timber got cleared and the fields got broken. Again, you can guess: The breaking got done on the backs of human property. The red-dirt soil and moist climate proved prime for the money crop of cotton. For almost the next one hundred years—in the three decades before the Civil War, and for six or seven decades after—cotton would stand at the heart of all agricultural production in the county, even though, it is true, the textile mills (they first came to Chambers right after the war, in 1866) would bring a new way of life, a semi-industrial way of life to Chambers, trying to prop up a ruined economy, trying to prop up a people spiritually and morally devastated from having lost the Cause.

Doctor William K. and his wife, Mariah D., had been among the most prominent newly arrived settlers to Chambers County in the mid-1830s. Their holdings of human property seem to have been fairly modest—maybe about a dozen slaves altogether at first. But as their children grew up and married local people, the slaves in those families got traded back and forth with the slaves of the Fredericks, so it is hard to know exactly how much human property they owned, or exchanged with their in-laws, or rented out for a farm season. In the decades before the war, some of the Cusseta neighbors of the Fredericks were known to have had thirty and forty and fifty and sixty slaves working in the fields.

Things went along—only they didn't. In 1839, perhaps not even three years after they'd come to their new home, Doctor Frederick, fifteen years older than his spouse, died. His widow was forced to assume a larger role in both her family and the community. She had to oversee plantation work and manage young children besides. She became the matriarch of a proliferating Chambers County clan in even larger ways than the word "matriarch" might imply.

Young female black workers on her family's plantations took her name.

Mariah, and at length some of her older children, became forces in the financial well-being of Cusseta Baptist Church, the most socially prominent place of worship in the town. (It had started life as Bethesda Baptist Church.) Many of her children ended up getting wed under the auspices of the church. A curiosity about Cusseta Baptist, hard to understand from the outside, is that the slaveholders often brought their slaves to church along with them and allowed them to become "full" members (even if they didn't participate in church voting and also sat in their separate pews). In the pre–Civil War records of Cusseta Baptist Church, the membership rolls tend to get listed this way: white family's last name, enslaved person's first name. With an apostrophe, for possession. For example: "Dowdell's—Mary." Or: "Carlton's—Fanny."

"Fanny" was the first name of Galon Carlton's mother—there isn't doubt of that (although you can find her name spelled as "Fannie"). As was said earlier, in general there seems scant genealogical or other information available for the paternal side of Julian's family.

Except: An expert county archivist named Robin Brown located a startling document regarding Galon—the more startling when you start to think about its possible implications. The document seems to date from the years right after the Civil War, perhaps 1867 or 1868, and concerns a state "Registration Oath" for both whites and blacks to obtain the right to vote. There's his name, if misspelled, in the right-hand column, very legible, three up from the bottom of the page: "Galin Carleton." A county clerk would have written it in. That Julian's father might have been able to go to the courthouse and take an oath to vote, in the violent Reconstruction South, in such a remote Alabama county, seems a little miraculous. Theoretically, the Registration Oath and the Fourteenth Amendment to the Constitution in 1868 cleared the way for a person to cast a ballot—but, of course, it almost never worked out that way for any black in the South, right up to and through the civil rights movement of the 1960s. What I am saying is that Galon's registered name doesn't seem to appear on any actual voter *lists* in Chambers County. There must have been swelling pride just in being able to take the administered oath. But, conversely, and this is the question that is hard to get out of the mind, once it has formed itself: Could the manipulated denial of Galon's right to vote, after he had been allowed to take the oath, have caused a deep suppressed anger—that might have passed down? It doesn't seem a stretch to imagine so.

And while I am imagining: Could Julian's parents have met in church, at Cusseta Baptist—two young backwoods freed people falling in love in the shadow of their Lord? Just speculations.

———

Professional genealogists warn of the hazard of being overly name-reliant in trying to determine whether someone was the owned property of someone else. To put this another way: Just because you encounter a black person who has the same name—even the identical name, in this instance—of a white slaveholding person who lived within the same small community, it doesn't follow automatically that the former was once owned by the latter. It can only be suggestive. At the outset of this search, I had been more than ready to make a false leap: that because Julian Carlton's mother, at her marriage, four years after the end of the war, perhaps now for the first time in her life having a full name, bore the identical first and middle and last name of one of the most prominent white women in her community—then, ergo, Julian's mother must have once belonged as property to Mariah D. Frederick and to her late physician husband.

Genealogists insist what a researcher must do is try to gather evidence from every possible source and then try to make reasonable guesses and hypotheses. Family Bibles, cemetery records, diaries that might have been kept secretly in an enslaved African-American household: these are among the tools. The greatest tool, which is also one of the most frustrating tools, is the so-called slave schedules that were made part of the 1850 and 1860 federal censuses.

The problem is that the slaves on these schedules do not appear by name (except in the rarest instances). They are numbered and listed by age, sex, and color only. Often the information was taken down inaccurately (the slaveholder didn't know or didn't give a damn, or a combination of both). Sometimes the listings in the schedules appear to take the form of family groupings, but mostly the slaves are just listed from eldest to youngest with no real effort by either the enumerator or the slaveholder himself or herself to suggest family structure.

Nonetheless, I have found what I feel is strong circumstantial evidence that Julian's mother, Mariah (as well as Julian's grandparents on his maternal side), belonged to the extended family of Mariah Frederick and the deceased William K. Frederick. On the 1860 slave schedule, there were several possibilities that suggested a person—only a child at the time—who could have been the same person who got married nine years after that census (while still in her early teens) and who ended up over the next quarter century bringing thirteen or fifteen children into the world, one of whom would be marked for history and given a soft-sounding name.

For instance, in the household of Peter Coffee Frederick (he seems to have been a favorite son, at least for a time, of Doctor William Frederick and his wife, Mariah) there is a listing for a six-year-old female slave. If this unnamed child was six, or thereabouts, in 1860, she would have thus been born around 1854—roughly the time of the birth of Julian's mother. Similarly, in the household of Peter Frederick's younger brother, Albert H. R. Frederick, there is another female slave child whose color is also given as black and whose age is recorded as seven. I found at least three additional such enumerated female child slaves belonging to various in-laws of the Fredericks whose ages would roughly match Julian's mom.

To my mind, even if it can't be proven, any one of these slave children, all belonging to the Fredericks of Cusseta, could have been Julian Carlton's mother—eventual mother.

Like his father, Albert H. R. Frederick, who'd been born back in Carolina in 1835, about a year before the relocation to Cusseta, grew up to be both a plantation master and a physician. He later left Alabama and went to Florida to continue a medical practice. But in the first federal census taken after the war, he was still living in Chambers County. The blacks working for him were no longer his slaves, not legally. In that census, two things jump out: Every employed worker on his place now has a last name of Frederick, and the color of each is given as mulatto.

Was Doctor Albert a benevolent master, even if the word "master" might have had lesser connotations at this point? If there were an old Frederick slave diary extant, it might say.* For all I know, the Fredericks of Cusseta were half-kindly to their black workers—before and after the war. Or, said another way, they were perhaps only half-brutal to them. Or put a third way, in the form of a question: Does relative decency or brutality make much overall difference in a system that was built and maintained on the exploitation of other human beings for profit?

In 1860, the year before the start of the War Between the States (which is what I've heard it called in Chambers County), Mariah Frederick (Doctor William K.'s widow) went to the courthouse and made out her will. (Quirkily, she registered it under the name Diana M. Frederick, and far more quirkily—or vengefully—she worded it to make it seem as if she had only three children, to whom she was leaving everything.)

---

* For what it is worth: In the middle of the Depression, the Federal Writers Project, which was part of the Works Progress Administration (WPA), compiled a multi-volume work of oral-history slave narratives. The former slaves, having lived into another century, were listed as "informants." Some of their stories make all-too-caricatured and painful reading now. In the Alabama portions, there is an interview with a man named Bert Frederick. The interviewers keep referring to him patronizingly as "Uncle Frederick." He was living in Opelika when the two (possibly white) interviewers drove up to his home and engaged him in conversation. From the internal evidence, it seems virtually certain that Uncle Frederick, who claimed to have no real idea how old he was, had once been attached to the Fredericks of Cusseta, and thus, in some way, near or far, must have been related to Mariah and her family. This exchange: " 'Did you enjoy the old slavery days, Uncle?' " Answer: " 'Yes, chile, day was good days. Some of de white peoples was bad to niggers, but my Ol' Master warn't dat kind. Dat de reason he would let all de niggers sit aroun' whilst he was singing'; an' he *could* sing.' "

The document is beautifully penned, and, in its own way, beautifully worded. She professes that she is of sound mind "and memory, and considering the uncertainty of this frail and transitory life, do therefore"— and it goes on from there. She makes provisions for all her land. She makes provisions for her bedding. Apparently, even though her grown sons have now taken over the family plantations, she has retained for her personal use two slaves, and at her death she wishes them to be sold at auction and the money to be equally divided "between my three children." She states the names of these two personal slaves: Valentine and Jack.

Is it possible to think that this first-name-only Jack—who, perhaps, after the war, when he is a so-called legally free man, will become Jack Frederick, or maybe, with an even more formal feeling of pride, will think of himself not as Jack Frederick but as John Frederick—is the *same* John Frederick who, on November 19, 1869, will preside as the host of his daughter's wedding, that daughter, just as he now is, having become a free person on God's earth?

It's possible for me to think that—no, believe that. Without any more proof than that.

I once presented some of this data—and other like it that I won't go into here—to a genealogy specialist named Hollis Gentry. She lives in Washington, D.C., and works at the Smithsonian Institution's National Museum of African American History and Culture. She has helped out on this puzzle on her own time; she's been a kind of intellectual and moral conscience to it. In one of our conversations, she said she has spent years in searches of her African-American ancestry, and that her own bloodlines include some white people. "You can only march it so far back," she said.

She looked at what I had almost feverishly spread out on the table. She said: "If you were on a deadline and had to have an answer right now, I would be willing to give you a 'possible.' I might even say more than possible—might be tempted to give you a 'likely.' But I can't sit here and give you what you want to hear: an 'absolutely.' Maybe your Julian Carlton did come straight up out of slavery, and his mother born a slave child." In the greater scheme, what did it really matter, she said. Because they were all oppressed people in one way or another from the time they were born, just because of their color, and isn't that sort of the point of why I went down there anyway—"just to convince yourself a little more of that?"

———

To finish it fast. So they came those 120 miles to Birmingham. In and of itself that fact seems, not least for the parents, like a leap through time and space. How did they come and when did they come? It cannot be said, but I believe they left Chambers County as a family sometime between the birth of the last child—Lamar, reported to have been born in 1895—and 1900. After 1900, older members of the family begin appearing in various listings and directories. Birmingham: It had come into being at roughly the same time this family did—early 1870s. It was once antebellum cotton farms. But then the Louisville and Nashville Railroad began helping turn the former crossroads into a Pittsburgh of the South: iron, steel, metalworking, coal. By 1900, when the Carltons were providing their first data about themselves as a family to a federal census enumerator, the city had a population of 38,415—and by the next census the population had jumped to 132,685. In this deeply segregated metropolis, black families located themselves in clusters, and one place they begin claiming for their own is Smithfield. The area lies to the west of the city center on the flat land and hills north of Village Creek. Even before the nineteenth century ends, the tracings of a black middle class are emerging here, along with desperately poor families. The former live higher up in Smithfield, away from the mosquito-infested lowlands of the creek and the railroad, while the latter—such as the Carltons—are down near the tracks, the bottoms. But the fact that this family has managed a roof over its head in Smithfield at all (which will one day be regarded as one of Birmingham's more historic districts, worthy of plaques and civic tours)—doesn't it once again say something about their sense of self, their collective pride?

They work at a laundry, in the Birmingham Saw Works, at the Moore & Handley Hardware, as dishwashers, at the Alabama Saw Repair, in the rail yards at the L&N. Julian, in 1902 (he's fourteen), is employed as a porter at W.B. Leedy & Company, on Twenty-First Street North, in the center of the business district. It's an insurance and real estate company, with one of the best client reputations in the city. (Again, could he have landed such a job, no matter exactly what the job was, if he had hay in his hair and couldn't speak with a sense of presence?) He lives at home, listed as 510 Martha Avenue in Smithfield. The Carltons have just relocated to this Smithfield address and will be here a couple of years until they move down the street. Maybe he rides the streetcar to work—there's a line that goes straight downtown. On the other hand, maybe lacking the fare, he has to walk both ways. What kind of clothes do you wear to this job, and what exactly do you do as a porter there? Sweep out the joint after hours? Run errands? Deliver packages? Maybe even greet customers (or at least open doors for them) as they come in off the street? It seems a higher-grade job than those held by some of his brothers and sisters.

In 1906, he steps up once more: to the hotel job. The brother right behind him—Milton, about twenty-one months younger—must be following his lead, because he soon gets a job bell-hopping at the Hotel Hillman, an even more upscale place than the Birmingham. Milton is married by 1907, and will eventually find his way to New York City.

After 1907: Julian's gone, or at least he's no longer listed in any directory. Is this the year he takes a train to Chicago? Did he even take a train, and was Illinois his first destination? It can't be said, but within half a dozen years there will be tiny glimpses of him in Chicago. More on this in a succeeding chapter, but right now, a small story, just one more Frank Lloyd Wright irony, riddle within the riddle: Julian Carlton's last known place of residence on the South Side in the spring and early summer of 1914, just before he and his wife (or woman) Gertrude left for Wisconsin, was at 4733 Evans Avenue. It was a brick row house carved up into rooms and flats, and all of its lodgers were from the Deep South. If you had a very large ball of string—say about a mile's worth—you could stretch it in a straight line for thirteen blocks, north to south, almost a plumb line, from the sidewalk in the 4700 block of Evans to the spot at a long-bulldozed-over fantastical sort of entertainment place called Midway Gardens where I calculate that a forty-seven-year-old artistic genius all too full of himself was approximately sitting or standing as he took time out for a sandwich and maybe a glance at the day's war headlines about one o'clock on the slightly cooling afternoon of August 15, 1914.

I have stood at both places numerous times, trying to dream myself into the moment. In the one spot: a wedge of old pebbled stone, up against a fence, hidden by underbrush and refuse, at the edge of a parking lot serving an apartment building and a residence for the elderly. In the other, only a paved alleyway, leading to a Walmart grocery center. The row house at 4733 Evans is gone, although its twin next door, at 4735 Evans, still stands. (Building records confirm they were twins.) I was in this alleyway once with Tim Samuelson, whom I introduced earlier. As was said, he knows about all things Chicago, and serves as its cultural conscience and walking encyclopedia (and God's giving man to researchers). It was a cold, cruddy Chicago day. Tim stopped halfway down the alleyway and went up to the side of the twin and lifted his arm and touched the outline of a slightly raised surface. I hadn't even noticed it. "See, this is a trace of the house that isn't here. This was the common brick wall. They used to call it the party wall. This raised surface in the old stone face has to be part of the main stack for the boilers of the houses. When they tore down the house where Julian lived, they just sort of sheared off the wall, and put in the alley, but if you take a look, you can make out the shadow of what had to be the flue to the furnace. Those were big furnaces in those days, had to be, to fire up good-sized row houses and keep them warm over these kinds of winters."

I said, "And they found him hiding in the furnace boiler that day at Taliesin, didn't they?"

"There you go," Tim said, maybe having momentarily forgotten.

Traces—not of an old boiler in an alleyway leading to a Walmart grocery, but of Frank Lloyd Wright's humanity. My contention is that the traces are always there, visible and yet not visible, hiding in plain sight, going away fast, coming back when you least expect it, sheared off, as if from a brick face, and all because of so much damnable ego and arrogance. The dilemma with Wright is that you have to keep lifting your arm and trying to brush your fingers across the raised surface of the stone monument of his pride, hoping that if you do this lightly enough and well enough you might be able to find—what? That essential thing trying to get out. The quality trying to show through, from underneath, like pentimento. It's true, of course, you can go to almost any building he ever drew, and his humanity will be right there on the surface of all your senses, the building itself fairly inebriating you with its natural beauty. (Okay, he drew some buildings, especially at the end of his life, that are pretty weird and ugly.) Fallingwater, on Bear Run, in southwestern Pennsylvania, receives almost two hundred thousand visitors a year. The docents of the Western Pennsylvania Conservancy have watched Japanese tourists stepping cautiously along the gravel trail in the woods on the left side of the stream, and then stopping at a turnaround maybe 150 yards below the house, so they can look back and catch her in full glory with their Nikons. Down there, at what's known as "The View," and the more so, if it's late autumn, when the forest has gone hues of yellow and red, it's possible to sustain the split-second optical illusion that she has disappeared. Fallingwater has returned to the ledges and crags and rocks and water-spray mists, out of which she erupted a couple of glaciers ago. "Cantilever slabs overhanging each other leaping out from the rock ledge behind"—that's how Wright described the house. He wrote that as she was nearing comple-tion. This disappearing effect, or going-back-in effect, or leaping-forth effect, whereby house has become waterfall and waterfall has seemed to become house, all of it one, has, in fact, happened to me: Blink, and the damp and structurally perilous and almost unlivable old girl is there in all her sublim-ity, her unmatched-ness. Blink again and she's gone, at least fractionally. Tour guides have told me they've witnessed Japanese visitors down at "The View" turning around to face her and then bursting into tears.

Connective Tissue: One

Forsaken: Catherine Tobin Wright, 1908

races, rubbings, pentimenti.

T At the end of *An Autobiography*—the edition published in 1932, the leanest and most beautifully written of the various versions—the author begins a brief section with the words "I remember." He tells four stories, each starting with those two words, placing them on a separate line, with a colon, and following with the memory itself. Each little self-contained piece after the mnemonic *I remember* is elegiac, pointillist, regretful. Each is about his family, or, more accurately, about his children. There's no way you could despise Frank Lloyd Wright's ego, or maybe anything else about him, at least on this page, which is all it is, all they are, one page, four memories, tucked at the back of his book, like outtakes or afterthoughts or leftovers, except that each is so artfully rendered. With so much seeming honesty, vulnerability, plainspokenness.

The first is about a night in Paris in the early winter of 1910, roughly four months after he has abandoned his family. (He dates the incident three weeks after he was gone from Oak Park—but that's okay.) He doesn't say so, but he and Mamah have temporarily parted. Nor does he say that his eleven-year-old daughter Frances (second-to-last born of his six by Kitty, who won't make sixty-one, and who will marry twice, and who, like all the others in her family, will carry around with her for life a trunkful of love-hate tensions with her father, and whose death, on February 11, 1959, as if in foreshadow, will occur almost exactly two months before his own) has just written to him, to ask him about the Arc de Triomphe and the "champ Elysees" and the "Louver" and the "Garde of the Tuileries," as the child spells them out in her sweet round Palmer Method penmanship. She has just learned from her mother that her father is in France. In school this year, her class has been studying the maps and monuments and museums of Paris, and she'd be very happy if her "Papa" (as she addresses him) "could give me any information." On the second page: "Don't forget to come home. I hope you will get some house to build." She signs it "always your's Frances Wright." Followed by: "p.m. Write soon."

No, he leaves all that out. But what he tells us, in another way, has all that in it. It's the seven-eighths of the iceberg floating beneath.

I REMEMBER:
The third week after I first left my first home in Oak Park the misery that came over me in a little café somewhere in Paris. Caring neither to eat or drink, I was listening to the orchestra. It had been a long depressing rainy season, the Seine most of the time over its banks. And it was late at night.

The cellist picked up his bow and began to play Simonetti's Madrigale. Lloyd had played the simple antique melody often. I would sometimes play with him, on the piano.

The familiar strains gave me one of those moments of anguish when I would have given all that I had lived to be able to live again.

The remembered strains drove me out of the café into the dim streets of Paris with such longing and sorrow as a man seldom knows. I wandered about not knowing where I was going or how long I went, at daylight finding myself facing a glaring signboard— somewhere on the Boulevard St. Michel.

All that I had lived to be able to live again: In later editions, he will try to water down this emotion, mollify it, extenuate it. He wishes to exculpate, inserting sentences like "It was not repentance. It was despair that I could not achieve what I had undertaken as an ideal." *No.*

The other stories in the *I remember* sequence are just as jewel-like. He tells of going on trips to Chicago, after Taliesin was built, in its first several years, pre-1914, when "all was well" there (we know what he means), and of slipping out to Oak Park after dark, hoping he won't be seen, and of looking in the windows of his home, which isn't his home any longer, "to reassure myself that all was going well, too, with the children." He sees the glowing light, sees a child at the piano, sees a child singing, sees a child calling out to another child. "And I would turn away to town again. Relieved."

Did this ever happen, even once? I am willing to suspend disbelief entirely.

In another *I remember,* he writes of Baby Llewellyn, softest in the family, who by this time may have been eight or nine, and of his coming down to the Loop on his own to stay for an overnight with his father at the Congress Plaza Hotel. The boy would bring his mandolin to play. "It gave me pleasure to see him fold each garment neatly and put it carefully on a chair when he went to bed. And I would tuck him in. The 'deserted' child." Something about the lugged mandolin, and the pleasure of neatly folded garments, makes it ring true.

Wright ends this page with a stand-alone sentence that seems much larger than itself. Just on the level of sentence-making, it is something to admire—no, envy: "So, I will remember to forget most of what I intended to write." *Remember to forget:* a formulation worthy of Hemingway, or maybe of Isak Dinesen, the great Danish author of *Out of Africa,* who said once that "all sorrows can be borne if you put them into a story or tell a story about them."

―――――――

This chapter is called "Connective Tissue," because that's all it's meant
to be: a kind of capsuling and bridging of the years 1909–1914. Without
doubt they were pivotal years, but they are also essentially outside the
lines, beyond the frame, of the story this book is trying to tell. The
most in-depth treatment, hands down, of this five-year period is a work
already cited: Anthony Alofsin's *Frank Lloyd Wright—the Lost Years,
1910–1922*. This next handful of pages, mostly in the tense of pluperfect,
are a grateful nod to Alofsin, as well as to others, although with some
specific slants and interpretations and modest new pieces of information being offered.

   Yes, the press—specifically one of the European-based correspon-
dents for the *Chicago Tribune*—had found him out, found them out, in
Berlin, approximately six weeks from the day he'd left Oak Park. He and
Mamah had been staying at the extravagant Hotel Adlon in the heart of
the city. The story, in the paper's Sunday editions, scooping all the Chicago competition, had appeared on November 7, 1909, column three,
top of page one: LEAVE FAMILIES; ELOPE TO EUROPE. The first
paragraph had told, no, sung of "two abandoned homes where children
play at the hearthsides," of a "wife pledging faith in a husband gone with
another woman," of an "affinity tangle of character unparalleled even
in the checkered history of soul mating." No matter that most of her
Oak Park neighbors had been aware of the basic story, such purple-ink
coverage had to have been deeply humiliating for Kitty Wright (not to
say for Anna Wright, still living next door). The article had quoted Kitty
at length, and she'd come across as an admixture of rage and denial and
a more-than-slightly-unbelievable forbearance. (She'd been quoted *too*
much at length, you'd say—whole paragraphs of smooth thought. Had
she actually said about a fourth of what they'd attributed to her?) The
correspondent in Berlin had filed his dispatches, and the home office
had camped a reporter on the steps of the Wright home on Saturday
afternoon, so that her comments could be folded in. Kitty had supposedly said: "It appears like any ordinary mundane affair, with the trap-
pings of what is low and vulgar. But there is nothing of that sort about
Frank Wright. He is honest and sincere. I know him. I tell you I know

him. I have fought side by side with him. My heart is with him now. I feel certain that he will come back." As for Mamah, Kitty had been quoted: "I have never felt that I breathed the same air with her. It was simply a case of a vampire—you have heard of such things." ("Vampire": that word would get a lot of traction.) The *Trib* had also gone to Edwin Cheney's house on Saturday—he wasn't home. But another reporter for the paper had managed to buttonhole him downtown at Orchestra Hall that evening. (Lizzie Borthwick, Mamah's older sister, was at home with John and Martha Cheney and little Jessie Borthwick Pitkin, the child whose mother had died in the aftermath of childbirth eight years before.) He'd kept trying to get away, and the reporter had kept right on asking, maybe following him down the aisle as he'd been taking his seat for the symphony. Edwin had been identified in the next morning's story (and would continue to be identified in the days following, as well as in many books in decades up ahead) as the president of the Wagner Electric Manufacturing Company. But, as was noted earlier, he was actually the Chicago district manager of the St. Louis–based company, having taken the position the previous winter. (How painful must all this dirty laundry have been for him just in the context of his new bosses at the Missouri headquarters?) In subsequent days, reporters would be hounding him at his office in the Marquette Building, located at Adams and Dearborn (an 1895 Loop landmark designed by the firm of Holabird & Roche). And the centerpiece himself of this hung-out two-family wash? Wright had been pictured in the first-day story, and in the follow-up ones, as an eccentric and spoiled and selfish and hedonistic and maybe slightly mad genius in the grip of his libertine impulses and helpless infatuation. Well, some of this was about half-right.

For, in fact, what the available record shows is that the elopers in the clutches of their supposed wild passion had actually been struggling at times, separately and jointly, with the decisions they'd made. The *I remember* moment from Paris certainly suggests this, but there is much other evidence, too, even if there are also many gaps in their known whereabouts, at least in the early stages of their "hegira." This isn't to suggest they'd been miserable in Europe, and wished to undo, no, just that all of it was complex and that there'd been times when the doubts and fears had seemed to have overtaken them both. Perhaps no Wright biographer has summed up the situation from Wright's side better than

Ada Louise Huxtable: "It was not pure romantic passion . . . or sinful lust, as the newspapers whipped up the story with prurient glee, or his unfailing instinct for drama, as some have speculated, that inspired Wright's exodus. It had as much to do with his priorities as artist and architect and the single-minded pursuit of his own potential, as with the crisis in his personal life."

Had they quarreled badly with each other? You could surmise that between the lines.

In any case, after being found out, Wright and Mamah had lain low. (To throw the press off his scent, he'd announced they were headed to Japan.) So it's hard to track them for the first several months. It's known that he'd signed a contract on November 24 with Ernst Wasmuth, his Berlin publisher. There were to be two publications—a large monograph of his drawings and a smaller book of photographs of the actual built work. It's known that by at least late January he'd gotten to Paris, and Mamah seems to have been with him for at least part of the time. Somewhere in here Mamah had discovered the writings of a prickly and self-involved Swedish philosopher, feminist, socialist, and child-educational theorist named Ellen Key—who'd almost immediately become a lifeline against her doubts. An advocate for women's rights as spouses and mothers, Key had much to say about families but also about the suffocation of loveless marriages. As was noted in a previous chapter, ten of Mamah's letters to Key (her dates are 1849 to 1926) have survived and have been brought to light by latter-day scholars. The letters, found eight decades after Mamah's death, in the archives of the National Library of Sweden in Stockholm, have allowed us to hear Mamah speak for the first time in history, and the voice that comes forth is anything but strident. It is a questing and determined voice, placating, passionate, selfish and idealistic, independent, a little unrealistic, a little importuning, sweet, always self-questioning and doubt-filled. It is the voice you hear in Nancy Horan's novel, *Loving Frank*. It is a voice that would have greatly appealed to Frank Lloyd Wright: a partner, and yet perhaps not quite a full partner.

Eventually Key and Mamah had met. (Scholars disagree exactly when the first meeting had occurred.) Afterward, Mamah, with her great proficiency in languages, had been anointed as Key's English-language translator. Six of the earliest letters to Key are undated, but a scholar named Alice T. Friedman has placed the first one in the spring of 1910, perhaps May, so approximately eight months after the lovers had gone abroad. If that is so, and it's an "if," it is an important date to think about in trying to understand Wright's own doubts, for the evidence is clear that he also had been struggling greatly in this same period. Had they reinforced each other's doubts? Perhaps. Probably. In any case, Mamah had written in what may have been her first letter to Key: "Trying to live, at a frightful cost, what I believed to be the only truth and light, groping in perplexity and darkness, with my poor, little dim light 'close to my breast,' suddenly in my darkest hour I found you. . . ." She'd gone on: "Still however my perplexity and doubt is great that perhaps that path was not after all the one I should have taken— perhaps it is not mine—Your torch however will also light me to the truth path—the true path for me—if I have mistaken it."

By May 1910, her lover had gone to Italy, had been there since sometime in March. At first he'd been in Florence, without Mamah, and then he'd relocated to a bucolic little spot in the hills and mountains above Florence called Fiesole. He'd gone to both places to work on the drawings for the Wasmuth portfolio. After the stay in Paris in January, it's known that Mamah had gone back to Germany to associate herself briefly as a teacher of languages at the University of Leipzig. It isn't clear when he and Mamah had reunited, but sometime in that late spring or early summer. What is known is that in Florence, and then in Fiesole, as the end of winter was trying to find spring, Wright had had the help of two draftsmen for the work on the portfolio. One was a man named Taylor Woolley, twenty-six, who'd been one of the last members of the design staff in the Oak Park studio before things had busted up. The other was his own son, Lloyd Wright, just turning twenty that spring, who'd been willing to suspend his engineering and landscape/design studies at the University of Wisconsin (he was in his third year) to come to Italy to help his father on the project. (The family genes had clicked in: Lloyd was already a skilled pencil in his father's hand, just as Wright had long ago been the skilled drafting pencil in Louis Sullivan's hand.) At Fiesole, in what Wright would describe in his autobiography as a "little cream white villa," no rugs on the cold stone floor, fired-up braziers to try to keep their freezing fingers warm, Wright and his two workers had labored on the outsized Wasmuth renderings with quill pens on tracing paper. They'd worked intensively, and for Wright it must have been a stay against loneliness. Work had always been that.

On March 31, 1910, he'd written from Fiesole to his friend C. R. Ashbee, the great British architect and theorist, described earlier. By turns shame-filled and self-justifying, this letter alone would fly in the face of anyone who wishes to think of Frank Lloyd Wright only as an egoist, incapable of self-examination, of looking back, of regretful reflection, a person whom ordinary life never touches. In fact, as is the central argument of this book, it was always touching him, haunting him, visibly and not.

It was a three-page fold-over letter addressed to "My dear Ashbee," and his first aim seems to have been to confess his adultery to someone whose opinion of him mattered much. It seems clear from the letter's underlying tone that Mamah wasn't with him. He'd said: "I have believed a terrible thing to be right and have sacrificed to it those who loved me and my work in what must seem a selfish, cruel waste of life and purpose . . . what a traitor I seem to the trust that has been placed in me by home, friends, and not least the cause of Architecture. I know the bitterness of it all. . . ." He'd said he'd never loved his wife, Catherine, as she had deserved, that "for some years" he'd loved "another." He'd said that, although both were married, and with children, only for a brief while had there been "anything furtive in it. It was open to all whose real concern it was and with their knowledge I took her with me when I sailed for Germany. . . ." He'd said that he knew now that his old life, as he had once lived it, "is broken—maimed, at best." And yet, in the next breath, defending himself: "I wanted to square my life with myself." And in the breath after that: "I want to live true as I would build true. . . ." And two beats away from that: "Life is living and living only brings the light. If I can live I will see the true way through the stress and wreck. . . ." Stress and wreck: When you study the letter, those words look just slightly fainter on the page, as if he'd been whispering them to himself, and his ink pen had unconsciously pressed down a little lighter. This letter also reveals that he and Kitty had been in touch—or at least that he had received a letter from her. And there is other evidence beyond this letter that suggests there'd been strained communication between them.

Other evidence: In almost the exact time frame of Mamah's first undated letter to Ellen Key—assuming that May 1910 is the correct date—Wright had received a letter from a clergyman named William Norman Guthrie. Guthrie lived in Sewanee, Tennessee. He and Wright had become friends—Guthrie, in fact, was a client. The letter was a reply to a letter that Wright had written to him, perhaps around the same time that he'd written to Ashbee, end of March. We don't have Wright's letter to Guthrie, but in his May 1, 1910, answer, Guthrie had referred to it, and it seems clear that Wright had stated his situation frankly and had asked Guthrie for his counsel and to not hold anything back. Guthrie hadn't. He'd been kind and brotherly, but blunt as well. He'd told Wright in an eight-page letter where his duties lay: "You have a wife & children. The ties that bind your soul to them will grow stronger as they should."

For his part, Charles Ashbee had written his own brotherly reply to Wright's letter of March 31. It had relieved Wright but hadn't helped him to resolve his family dilemma. By early summer, he and Mamah were at their hideaway villa, with Florence spread out below in the thin morning fog like a wicker creel of flowers. But no matter the romantic beauty, and their apparent happiness and doubtless sexual passion (he would lyricize about the former in his autobiography and hint vaguely at the latter), he had continued to wrestle with himself—as she had with herself. For Wright, the doubts seemed to have been centered on the responsibility of fatherhood: once again, not exactly the Wright that forges itself in our imagination.

On the fourth of July, from Fiesole, he'd written to his mother. The letter, handwritten, is quite long and parts are hard to decipher.

> I have been so troubled and perplexed that I have not known what to write. It might be one thing one day and another thing the next. . . . I dread the aspect my return must wear. I am the prodigal—whose return is a triumph for the institutions I have outraged—A weak son who infatuated sexually has had his passion drained and therewith his courage, and so abandoning the source of his infatuation to whatever fate may hold for her. . . . While I return to my dear wife and children who all along "knew I would" and welcomed by my friends with open rejoicing and secret contempt. . . . Anyone who lets, by his acts, the outer world touch in any way his affections must

submit to having them vulgarized, brutalized and spit upon by the mob. . . . You knew and Catherine knew that I was going to take her away with me as soon as I could, as I had declared openly to you both and to her husband a year before I did take her. There was no deception that makes the "runaway" match of the Yellow Journal anywhere. . . . She told her husband one year before she went away with me that she would go with me married or not whenever I could take her. . . . I may be the infatuated weakling, she may be the child-woman inviting hard to herself and others—but nevertheless the basis of this whole struggle was the desire for a fuller measure of life and truth at any cost. . . . I am a house divided against itself by circumstances I cannot control. . . .

Four days later, July 8, 1910, he'd written to Ashbee with the news: "The fight has been fought—I am going back to Oak Park to pick up the thread of my work and in some degree [the thread] of my life where I snapped it. I am going to work among the ruins—not as any woman's husband but as the father of the children—to do what I can for them." He'd continued: "But I have been cruel. I have hardness in my soul. I have destroyed many beautiful things. . . ."

Sixteen days later, on July 24, another letter to Ashbee. Again that word, "cruelty," and this time he had put it in quotes, as if it had been sitting on his neck in beautiful Fiesole. It was a cruelty that had "its basis in other hearts," and realizing this "clutches at mine when I see its bearings—as I see it now—eventually—Its price must be paid. . . ." By "other hearts," he had to have meant his family.

Does all this seem uncharacteristically introspective, sensitive to others? Hold on. The other side of him (or, better, one of his many other sides) was about to click in, and click in just as repellently, luridly, deviously, not unlike the all-over-again lurid and repellent coverage in the *Tribune*, and in the other Chicago dailies, which, of course, were only too happy to take up again the chase, the case, his case, the news, the delicious news, delicious for the newsboys hawking on corners, that the Oak Park reprobate was returning home, tail presumably between legs. Hardly.

He had come into New York Harbor on a Thursday in early October on the S.S. *Bleucher*. Mamah had stayed behind in Europe to work on

230 | PLAGUED BY FIRE

the Key translations and doubtless to try to keep on sorting out her own emotions and put-off decisions. By five o'clock on Saturday afternoon, October 8, his Pullman had slid into Union Station in Chicago. He had gotten off the train in leather knee trousers, long stockings, a rough English tweed jacket, a gray chapeau, and the strut of a monarch—or at least this is how it had gotten reported. He had a cane, not for aiding in his walk but for aiding in the strutting. His hair, a touch of gray in it, hung down over his ears and touched his collar. One story had reported that he'd taken a taxi out to Oak Park, but a revision of that account the next day had him riding the local commuter the eight miles out home and then sailing through the station on Lake Street and jumping into a cab. But if he'd been without any shame, why then had he apparently sat in that taxi until it was dark and then told the driver to take him to Chicago and Forest avenues? (Actually, he could have walked to his home.)

That evening he'd sat in a back room while the younger children had played in other rooms, probably the barrel-vaulted playroom on the lid of the house, giddy to have their father back, and while Kitty had carried into him the questions of the mad press on the doorstep. It's by turns comic and macabre to read the *Tribune*'s account: " 'Mr. Wright says that it is none of the public's business and that he has nothing to say.' This was the first message Wright sent out from a secluded corner of his home."

The press boys had kept demanding. According to the *Trib*: "Mrs. Wright again went to her husband and was in conference with him several minutes." He'd sent out another *no*.

That was Saturday night, like a kabuki or a little pantomime at the opera. At eight o'clock the next morning, the forty-three-year-old returnee of no seeming shame (but if that is so, why had he been hiding out in a back room?) had called up an old client, William Martin, who lived in town, and who was the brother of Darwin Martin, in Buffalo, who, as has been previously said, seemed to exist in some ways for the sole purpose of being Wright's easiest money touch and softest-hearted client if also ongoing moral scourge. That morning, Wright had wanted the Martin brother who lived locally to come by in his car and fetch him back downtown to the depot, because he hadn't been able to get his luggage the night before. From a long letter by William Martin to his Buffalo brother: "He called . . . in almost as matter-of-fact way as though it was but yesterday that he had seen me. . . . His nerve was staggering and I could not for the moment know what to say." But Martin had given in, as the Martins were wont to do. (At least the male Martins; the wives had long seemed another story.) Wright had appeared in much the same getup as the day before. ("W. was dressed to closely resemble the man on the Quaker Oats package," Martin had written.) He'd brought along Llewellyn. He'd told Martin as they motored on their luggage errand (had the child heard it from the back seat?) that he had come back "not as a prodigal son or a repentant sinner, but I am here to set up my fences again, not as they were—that perhaps will not be possible—but will do it the best I can. I admit I have done wrong, but I am not sorry for myself. I am only sorry for my family, my children, and my clients."

At roughly the same hour, an Oak Park pastor was denouncing Wright from the pulpit of First Presbyterian. He'd told a reporter later that day that such a man as Wright had "lost all sense of morality and religion and is damnably to be blamed."

A question that perhaps has not been considered enough: Could some of this strut and apparent non-repentance have been a form of almost childlike acting out? Acting like a truant child, tantrum child, had long been a part of Frank Lloyd Wright's character. He'd known what nasty copy he was going to make in the dailies, so why not serve it to them all the way up? A mask for all his feelings of humiliation?

Kitty Wright had told a *Tribune* reporter on Sunday (or the *Tribune* reporter had put the words in her mouth): "As you see, we are together again. Our family is reunited. I knew he would come back. He is the soul of honor."

But three days later, Wednesday, in a letter to Janet Ashbee (Charles Ashbee's forbearing, gifted spouse), who was in England, Kitty had told the truth:

Mr. Wright reached here Saturday evening, Oct. 8th, and he has brought many beautiful things. Everything but his heart, I guess, and that he has left in Germany.

I believe I could be more brave if I felt any justice in the present arrangement, but as near as I can find out he has only separated from her because he wishes to retain the beauty and ideality of their relationship and feared by staying with her that he would grow to loathe her.

Each morning I wake up hoping it to be the last and each night I hope may prove to be eternal.

The hardest part to read of this hard letter was that her husband had apparently told his wife, maybe on that first night back, that he had no intention of resuming his marriage. "And he seems to be so anxious to be sure I have no doubts about it," Kitty had written. Yes, cruelty.

———

What essentially happened between late fall of 1910 and late summer of 1914 was that a moral pariah and professional outcast named Frank Lloyd Wright extricated himself from Oak Park (again) and slowly reestablished his life and career on an ancestral hillside in southwestern Wisconsin. It didn't happen without much deception on several levels. In many ways, his character was on its worst display in this period, and for certain in the first thirteen or fourteen months. His life was "a skein of deceptions," as one Wright historian has written. Historian Anthony Alofsin: "Wright was now obliged to lead a double life, a life of denying his love for Mamah while planning his future around her." Which is to say he remained in his Oak Park home, with his family around him, fires lit, with no idea of being a husband again, and, apparently, with no idea of remaining in Oak Park for very long. He and his wife lived separately in the house, and Wright quickly came up with plans to split the property, if not quite in half, at least into two dwelling units, one that might be used for rental income down the road. What about his concern for his children? Where did that all go?

One of his chief deceptions was to convince his chief benefactor, Darwin Martin, that the Mamah business was over. The nut of it was that he needed Martin's money, to begin building Taliesin, in Wisconsin, which he would portray, certainly in the beginning, as a "cottage" for his mother. He wheedled $25,000 out of Martin under false pretenses.

Wheedling: Seventeen days after he came back, he wrote to Martin and said: "At least I will know who my friends are now—anyway. They are surprisingly few. Never in any sense popular, always an affront to the intelligence of the plain man, I have finally kicked the props from under what tolerance he ever had for me, and nothing but some extraordinary virtue can save me for my work. . . . As it is, I can tell you, my dear friend and client, it is bitter." He spent the rest of the letter wheedling Martin to intervene for him in securing a possible client in Detroit.

In late January he went abroad again (there were disputes with the publisher connected with the publication of the Wasmuth portfolio), and the trip was financed with Martin's money. He was away until the end of March. He must have seen Mamah on the trip, although there's no record of it (to repeat: in all these decades, not a single piece of correspondence between Wright and Mamah has ever surfaced, or at least that I know of), but this may have been the moment when they saw clear to try to make the rest of their life together. She did not return with him to America. (She came back in June and went about obtaining a divorce from Edwin.) In early April, determined to secure property in the Helena Valley of Wisconsin that would mark the start of this new life, he wired Martin that he had needed to step in as a son "to help my mother out of a tight real estate situation." And one week after that he deceived Martin again by saying that "I helped mother buy a small farm up country on which she had a contract for purchase," and that as the good son he'd gone with her to Spring Green "to close it and see about building a small house for her." Anna Wright was involved in all this, but, really, he was deceiving her, too. What he was going to build, start building, with money he'd gotten falsely, was his lifelong wet canvas on the brow of the hill that he'd loved from boyhood. As he saw it, Taliesin was the fountainhead of all his future plans: a home, a studio, a farm, a way of life. In his *The Architecture of Frank Lloyd Wright,* previously quoted, Neil Levine devotes a full chapter to "The Story of Taliesin," breaking down with evenhandedness the complex weave of deceptions.

Construction began in May 1911, and was effectively finished by December. That month Mamah wrote to Ellen Key: "I have as you hope made a choice in harmony with my own soul—the choice as far as my own life was concerned was made long since—that is absolute separation from Mr. Cheney. A divorce was obtained last summer and my maiden name is now legally mine. Also I have since made a choice in harmony with my own soul and what I believed to be Frank Wright's happiness and I am now keeping his house for him." She also said, rather chillingly, in two senses of the word, one being her own priorities and the other being what the future unwittingly held: "My children I hope to have at times, but that cannot be just yet. . . ."

The complex weave, complex skein: Along with lifelong cunning, there was always a strange, lifelong, and almost balancing-out naïveté in Frank Lloyd Wright. No one has ever adequately explained this, and it won't be explained here. The naïveté was mixed in and mixed up with all of his arrogance. It was as if he could never see through to the other side of self-caused consequences. It was as if he just had to blunder on instead of trying to think something through. Psychiatrists say that a large part of behavior is what you think you can get away with, and that seems yet another definition of Frank Lloyd Wright. In any event, at Christmas 1911, the Chicago press gang discovered that he'd moved his mistress into his new home. So a salivating on its part all over again. On Christmas Eve he was quoted in the *Tribune* as saying "Let there be no misunderstanding, a Mrs. E.H. Cheney never existed for me and now is no more in fact. But Mamah Borthwick is here and I intend to take care of her." On the twenty-fifth, the naïve-cum-arrogant man, who wished to get away with what he wished to get away with, paced back and forth in his living room, lecturing on his and Mamah's moral integrity, and why laws for ordinary mortals needn't apply. From the *Tribune*'s account the next day: "Apparently Mr. Wright did not feel any regret he was not present in the Oak Park house where his lawful wife and their six children were spending their Christmas, and Mamah Borthwick seemed to have forgotten the Christmases of the past which she had spent with her husband and children." For the next several days he issued statements to the press—raw kerosene on the fire. His morally pinched maternal relatives, having lived in these rural Wisconsin valleys for several generations, some now holding important positions in the community and others working at prominent jobs in Madison, were aghast at seeing their holidays thrown into this kind of tawdry upheaval. Some of them had let it be known that they were disowning him. On December 28, this headline on page one in the *Chicago Record-Herald*: WRIGHT KIN GATHER TO "TRY" ARCHITECT. Not exactly, but there was some truth in it.

On December 30, blundering naïvely on, self-righteously on, the child-man handed out another signed statement to reporters, several of whom had come to his door on horseback through the weather to see what their latest present from him would be. Quieter now, his statement said, with tinges of resignation, at least momentarily: "I am tired. The woman is tired. We are living the life that truth dictates. Our desire is to harm nobody. Our hope is that we may benefit humanity, our determination is to be true to our ideals at all costs."

And, in time, it all blew over. And, in time, his relatives took him back. And, in time, like a forest regenerating itself after a scorched-earth fire, the work took him back.

Which is only to say: Against all seeming odds, Wright's career over the next two or three years would slowly begin to uptick, with the best years—best decades—still in front of him. The Seven Ages of Frank Lloyd Wright. Yellowstone National Park renewing itself. Statistics, as I've said, can never tell the story, but a numerical context all the same: In 1909, the last good year of his practice before he became a national disgrace, Wright had twenty-seven commissions and projects under consideration—twelve of which were executed, or in the process of being executed, including the landmark City National Bank and Hotel in Mason City, Iowa, and the even more landmark Avery Coonley House in Riverside, Illinois. (He was doing additional work on this magnificent Prairie, which could be talked about for pages.) Two of those twenty-seven projects have since been demolished. By comparison, in 1912, finding his way back, he had a total of twelve commissions, four of which were built. Two of those have since been demolished, but one, a home on Lake Minnetonka outside Minneapolis, the Francis W. Little House, or Northome, as its owners lovingly called it, would find another life: in New York's Metropolitan Museum of Art. Or at least the living room of Northome has found another life. It's there now, installed, regenerated, with its bands of art glass and clerestory windows and strips of "back-banding" on the ceiling: not a room so much as a series of horizontal levels in a long tunnel of space, sealed in wood and glass, bouncing magic light from deep inside a museum.

In 1911, Wright had quietly taken a small office on the sixth floor of Orchestra Hall. The idea was to live in Wisconsin but to make periodic trips down to the city to meet new clients and old. Eventually he built up a small staff there, in rooms 600–610, including—at least for part-time drafting work—his two elder sons, Lloyd and John. The sense was that things were smoothing out, and maybe its relative quickness surprised even him. In January 1913, he and Mamah left on a trip to Japan—his second. They were gone until May. The chief purpose was to try to gain the commission for the design of a new Imperial Hotel. He would eventually win it, after protracted negotiation. It was to be the most consuming architectural project of his life up to that point, and would take ten years to complete, and require much travel to Japan, much staying in Japan, much frustration—and much final triumph. The first part of 1913 marked the start of his decade of on-and-off preoccupation with the Imperial and Japan. In the back part of 1913 came unexpectedly a commission for a multi-purpose entertainment plaza, with a summer garden and winter garden, to be built on the South Side of Chicago, at Cottage Grove Avenue and Sixtieth Street. He poured in all his exotic ideas. In not even a year's time—on June 27 of the following summer— the fandango of a dream palace named Midway Gardens opened to the public, even if it wasn't fully finished and thus required his presence that summer, summer of 1914, whenever he could find time to slip away on a train from Spring Green. Sometimes he slept at the site, sometimes he slept in his office in the Loop at Orchestra Hall. He'd moved two floors up now, top of the building, number 810.

———

To go back to that thought-provoking quote from Ada Louise Huxtable: that perhaps it wasn't pure romantic passion (for either), or heedless lust, as the press craved it, or his need for attention and a constant living on the edge (so as to fuel his work in some strange manner) that drove him away from his wife and children and the stability of Oak Park. No, the closer truth may be that the leaving was some complex weave, skein, of all of these things, and more besides, not least among them his vision of himself as an artist and the pursuit of his own ambitions.

I, too, have sometimes wondered how deeply he was in love with Mamah, at least in the middle goings, and whether or not in some sense he was using her—and maybe vice versa. Did they both need to escape Oak Park, and so became each other's aiders and abettors? To revise that thought a little, and in a more positive if painful light: Was he perhaps able to grow into a committed love for her only over a period of years, a process of years, from, say, about 1904 onward, and was that love—

on both their parts—coming to its best and most committed Spring Green place eleven years later just at the point when it got taken away? Had the gods seen to that? Who can really say, but I for one do not subscribe to the proposition that Wright was always too much of a narcissist to be able to give himself over wholly to another human being. I think it's a far deeper story than that.

Story. In place of knowing, what we so often seem to have with the life of Frank Lloyd Wright are the stories themselves. You've already heard the story of Ida Heller, who may or may not have flung herself in unrequited love-grief down the three-story elevator shaft of her South Side home in October 1909, a little past a fortnight after her architect had gone to Europe with Mamah Cheney. Was there a connection between her death and Wright's going? It'll doubtless never be known. But the stories of an illicit love between them float, or at least they do in certain quarters of Hyde Park/Kenwood. Similarly, if you travel to Rochester, New York, to see an incredibly beautiful (and mint-condition) Prairie house, the Edward E. Boynton House (it isn't open to the public, but you could at least stand on the sidewalk, and put yourself at the mercy of the owners, who are gracious people), you'll sooner or later come in contact with another unverifiable story about Wright and a supposed love affair. If Ida Heller was much older than Wright, Beulah Boynton was much younger. The love affair would have happened during the year 1907, when the Boynton was being built. Earlier in this book as regards the year 1907, I wrote: "He'd begun again with Mamah, and doubtless now in a sexual way. Probably by at least mid-1907."

Construction on the Boynton House began in June 1907.

It's the easternmost Prairie house Wright ever built. (Not too many literal prairies in upstate New York.) Edward E. Boynton was an industrialist, a partner in the Ham Lantern Company. His partner was Warren McArthur, for whom Wright had built, in 1892, on the bootleg sly (with Cecil Corwin's name out front), the gambrel-roofed Dutch Colonial on South Kenwood Avenue on the South Side, next door to the bootleg Blossom House. Boynton had lost three children to early deaths, and then he'd lost his wife, but he had his spirited and doted-on daughter, Beulah. In 1907 she was twenty-one. (Wright turned forty that year.) She took a keen interest in the building of the house on East Boulevard and followed the architectural plans. The architect, prone to showing up from Illinois unannounced to see about the work, took many suggestions from Beulah, not his characteristic stance. (For her bedroom, to store beloved dresses she didn't want to fold, she asked for six-foot-wide drawers that would pull out, like giant map drawers, on specially made ball bearings—and she got them.) There are stories about the local contractors leaving the job site at dark—and finding Wright there in the morning. He had taken a late train and had arrived at midnight and gone to the house. He would end up staying for two or three days. At least once he is said to have camped out back under some kind of thrown-up tarpaulin, although most times he slept in the house while it was going up. When she was in her late sixties, a widow, years away from having lived in the house (she had married a Rochester stockbroker, and they had eventually made their home in Manhattan), Beulah verified this last fact (about his sleeping in the house) for a Rochester reporter who was doing a piece on the Boynton House. He had sent her typed questions by mail, and she'd answered, and he had then gone to Manhattan to interview her in person. This was in late 1954 and early 1955. About a decade and a half after that, in the mid or late 1960s, now in her eighties, not too long from her own death (she lived to be almost eighty-eight), Beulah Boynton was interviewed by a historian from the University of Michigan, who was at work on a book about Wright and another Chicago architect. She remembered her architect as "extremely good-looking, had a keen sense of humor, and a light in his blue eyes." Wrote the professor, seemingly afraid to drop any shoes on the reader, even if he may have been hearing them when he'd interviewed her: "She found him very pleasant. . . . Obviously they got along well together. . . . Evidently she became quite interested in the process of construction, since she learned to read both working draw- ings and specifications while the house was being built." He described Beulah as the "vivacious young daughter."

Was Daddy snoring blithely down the hall while his daughter was entertaining Wright in her own rising boudoir? I wouldn't doubt it.

These years later, the stories float. Although perhaps they're leaky vessels.

Beulah and her father moved into Wright's beauty in early March 1908. In Illinois, the architect was making love to another man's wife, who'd once been his client, and he was just about to publish a beautiful sixty-seven-page article in *Architectural Record* in which he spoke of his hope that "some day America may live her own life in her own buildings, in her own way, that is, that we may make the best of what we have for what it honestly is or may become. . . ." Yes, above all, trying to live a life with honesty and moral authenticity. By one's own lights and definitions.

His sister's house, known as Tan-y-deri, which he had designed and named and built, not quite seven years before, in the ancestral Lloyd Jones family valley, became a makeshift morgue that night, and also a temporary medical facility for ministering to the dying and the burned. The covered corpses—it seems there would have been four at this point— are said to have had candles flickering around them. Either they were in a far corner of the living room or, more likely, they'd been placed out on the large, open, seven-sided veranda that vaguely resembled the prow of a ship. The veranda, with some distinctly Wrightian touches, was immediately off the living room, on the north side of the house. It looked over, across the valley, half a mile or so away, to his own much more elaborately designed home, now just a smoking ruin. A charred scent from the still-smoldering Taliesin was said to be riding in on the moist air.

There were hints of coming rain. God knows the farmers needed it. It had been so matchbox-dry of late. Earlier in the evening there'd been stray forks of noiseless lightning.

If he first saw them, the sheeted bodies, or caught a trace of them, with a kind of third eye of glancing horror, at about one o'clock in the morning of Sunday, August 16, 1914, maybe a minute or so after he had gotten into the house from that torture of a train ride from Chicago, wouldn't there be some poetic harmony, neatness, in it? For it was almost exactly twelve hours before, at Midway Gardens, that Frank Lloyd Wright had heard the first staticky word. And here he was now, the clock having gone around once, his world upended, staggering in, maybe being half-carried in, having just come from the station platform in town, having been transported to Jane Porter's house in the back seat of a car. What would that have been like, to have gotten out of the car and come in through the rear (where, in his perverse design genius, he had decided to locate the front entryway) and gone through the small foyer and then up the several steps, into the living room itself, and encountered this Kafkaesque sight?

The dead and dying, and perhaps some of those who'd been only marginally wounded in trying to fight the flames, would have been straight *ahead of him, maybe thirty or thirty-five paces away. Even if he closed his eyes, he still must have seen them.*

Although apparently no photograph survives, the semi-darkened first floor of Tan-y-deri (it's Welsh for "under the oaks") must have seemed something like a Red Cross nursing station at a battlefront. There's another image in my head: catacomb of the wailing.

Probably four bodies covered with sheets. Old Tom Brunker was still alive and fighting for his life, and so was David Lindblom. Young John Cheney, Mamah's twelve-year-old, was said to have been reduced to little more than some blackened bones and hanks of hair—so almost nothing to put a sheet over. That then would have left Mamah, her eight-year-old Martha, young Ernest Weston, and Emil Brodelle. Could Wright have understood that Mamah's was one of the silhouetted forms in front of him? He must have understood it viscerally, no matter how dumb he was with his grief and shock.

If you come into this space in the daytime, if it's any kind of ordinary daytime, summer or winter, but especially in the afternoon, you'll likely be struck by the way light, whether unfiltered or overcast, angles in through the six diamond-pane leaded glass casement windows on the left—the western side of the living room. The architect designed this Prairie house in simple fashion, letting nature do a lot of the job. It's a boxy, upright, woody, foursquare kind of Prairie, the more beautiful for its rustic simplicity. It has been kept that way.

Immediately to the left, in the southwest corner, the architect had arranged for a Steinway grand piano. He had told his sister—even though her name was Jane, he liked to call her Jennie—that this was the perfect spot for a piano. And Jennie, two years younger, a loyalist all her life, had agreed. The Steinway is still there, same spot in the living room. There is something seemingly odd that happened that night, in regard to Wright and the piano, or you can find accounts of it in at least one oral history, and the story has also passed down by word of mouth: At some point, after he had gotten in, perhaps taken off his coat, perhaps had sipped slowly from a glass of water, he went over, lifted the piano's lid, sat down on the small stool that was covered with brocaded cloth, gathered himself, and began to play Bach. He played the music over and over. Supposedly, he played through his crying. No one disturbed him. It went on for a long time. But if you knew something about his family history, this wouldn't have seemed so odd. Back in Madison, in his unhappy childhood, he used to watch his beaten-down father, William Carey Wright, who'd been beaten down yet another time by his relentless spouse, Anna Wright, and also beaten down by his own impractical dreams, do the same thing: fold himself, almost disappear, at moments of great stress and disappointment and frustration, into his beloved Bach and Beethoven and Brahms on the brocaded piano stool at the family piano in the parlor of the torn house on Gorham Street.

There is another story. It's about Jane and Andrew Porter's youngest child. His name was Franklin Porter. He was four that night. His parents had tried to keep him upstairs. Apparently for the rest of his life (he lived a long life), Wright's nephew could never quite get out of his mind and inner ear the moaning of the burned and the dying. The cries were coming in through his bedroom window and were somehow mixed in with the call of a whippoorwill. Decades afterward, he told Wright biographer Meryle Secrest that his bedroom was almost right above the open-air veranda.

There is a photograph of Franklin Porter on that veranda, taken maybe three summers later. Everything seems so back in order. Oriental carpet on the wooden deck. Wicker rockers. A goldfish swimming in a bowl on a table. His grandmother Anna is there, in a shawl, looking both forbidding and grandmotherly, and his own mother, with a book, and his older sister, with her knitting. The boy is in short pants and has one foot balanced atop the other. He seems happy. In the background, the faint blur of the hills and of Taliesin, fully rebuilt by then.

And destined to burn down again in less than a decade.

Frank Lloyd Wright slept, or tried to, in one of the four upstairs bedrooms that night. So did Edwin Cheney. There are stories about sobs coming from behind Wright's door. The next day, which was really the same day, Sunday, he buried Mamah.

But I want to tell of something that happened maybe thirty minutes before he would have entered the house and encountered that scene— something that had happened back on the station platform. (The old repurposed depot, as well as the half-rotting timbered platform, with its overhang, are still there, in the middle of downtown Spring Green. You can stand under the overhang and try to imagine.) Reference has already been made to John Lloyd Wright's unreliable and strange hybrid memoir-

cum-biography, My Father Who Is on Earth. *No matter its untrustworthiness and deeply conflicted tone, the book must always be paid attention to. As you recall, the son was on the train from Chicago with his father. He describes the scene upon arrival. I am willing to believe he got at least the spirit of it right.*

> *Spring Green at last! The night wind thrashed the smoke-filled countryside. Shadows of men taking on exaggerated proportions in the darkness . . . rays from flashlights darted here and there— lanterns swinging in mid-air detached from the bodies who supported them. The kindly blackness of the night saved him in some degree from the morbid curious—ghouls—who swarmed about, waiting as they had been for hours. . . . These were the good people of the town whose so-called religion manufactured in the main by their own intelligence caused them to nod their heads significantly, even wisely, as they exchanged glances. But all the while they pushed madly to see how one looks when he suffers. Pharisees— Sadducees—sadists, standing in huddled groups whispering. . . .*

Pushing through the crowd—or at least I imagine him pushing and elbowing his way through, possessed of his pharisaical righteousness and massive ego and proprietary family relationship—was Frank Lloyd Wright's first cousin, Richard Lloyd Jones, younger by six years. He is the most morally repugnant character in this book—by far. As you recall, Jones was the son of pious and right-living Uncle Jenk. For the past three years he'd been owner and editor of the Wisconsin State Journal. *It was one of the most important dailies in the state. If his ruinous story— ruinous to so many people, through several generations—has been only hinted at thus far, it's going to assume center stage in the pages that immediately follow.*

Through the afternoon, Cousin Richard's newspaper in Madison had been putting out bulletins and extras. Apparently, he'd rushed to Spring Green late in the day. He was there to meet the train. It may have been his car that carried Wright the three and a half miles out from town to Tany-deri. According to John Lloyd Wright, on the platform Jones got hold of his collapsing relative by the coat collar, pounded his back, shook him,

and cried: "*Stand up, Frank! It couldn't be worse, get hold of yourself!*"
That quotation has appeared in many Wright books, at more or less face
value. I have another interpretation, and it has everything to do with the
inappropriate-seeming words themselves, and the character of the man
who spoke them.

The Man on the Station Platform

Richard Lloyd Jones, in his Madison, Wisconsin, newspaper office,
August 19, 1916

We are speaking now of the Tulsa Race Riot of 1921. Yes, something that sounds absurdly far afield. And isn't.

You are gazing at Frank Lloyd Wright's first cousin on his mother's side. You are gazing at the man—or, to say it in reverse, he's staring at you, almost unnervingly, through the gelatin tones of this remarkably preserved old silver-print—whose pandering Oklahoma newspaper baited into being one of the worst racial burnings and large-scale decimations of a black community on record in America. And who, this same man, Richard Lloyd Jones, in the days after that decimation, not so much history's verdict as an unassailable fact, decided, as was one of his worst character traits, to double down. Meaning that he wrote and published racist screeds on his editorial page and in other places in his paper, too, saying, in effect, that the "bad niggers" of the town had it coming to them. Give a "bad nigger" (as opposed to a "good Negro") his dope and booze and his guns and his liquor and his loose women and his dirty gambling holes, and you've got a lethal and combustible mix that must be eradicated. For the civic good. For God's good. America's good.

The record of it is there, in black-and-white.

The real—and lethal—combustible mix was Richard Lloyd Jones's reactionary, black-and-white, either-or, self-righteous, Manichaean temperament and personality, and thus his way of viewing the world and most things in it. In that sense, Tulsa was just the catastrophe and sorrow waiting to happen. This quality of erupting, absolutist, impulsive, unyielding, hot-tempered, I-know-better character seems never to have left Jones, up to and including the day he died. He never apologized for his role, at least not publicly, and he lived into his tenth decade. Lived four decades past the grossly misnamed event that we know in history—to the extent we know it at all—as the Tulsa Race Riot. Kept on (at least for a time) with his mistress, enjoyed the friendship of presidents, held high national positions in his profession, was a devoted churchgoer (at the huge Unitarian Universalist Tulsa church he co-founded in the same year as the riot), got laureled with honorary doctorates (he apparently made up one of them on his résumé and *Who's Who* entries), grew far more prosperous, had grandchildren and great-grandchildren.

And what does any of this particularly have to do with Frank Lloyd Wright himself, other than the obvious fact that Jones was his close relation and someone with whom he more or less grew up? What does any of it have to do with the central themes and swirls of this book?

Only everything. So I contend. Which is why, ultimately, this isn't even a story about Frank Lloyd Wright's morally ruinous first cousin on his mother's side at all. And why the story, which isn't a detour at all, cannot be left out, even though there is a strong sense in which I wish it could. It would be easier to avert the gaze.

"Ruinous": a word that's been used three or four times to describe Richard Lloyd Jones—and needs to keep on being used. If it were just his life, his history, it would be one thing.

I wrote earlier in passing of my going down into the nearly lightless, below-ground, and long-out-of-use old county jail cell in Dodgeville, Wisconsin, where Julian Carlton wasted through the last seven weeks of his life, trying to fathom his act. But, in another sense, what I've really tried to fathom, or at least tried to fathom just as much, in that sealed-off space (you have to get someone from the county clerk's office next door to retrieve the key to the padlocks and take you down) is something broader, scarier. Namely: Is there a connection, and not a tenuous one, between what happened that summer afternoon in Wisconsin and another biblical fire, in Tulsa?

To begin with, the Tulsa Race Riot wasn't a riot; it was a race massacre, a kind of instant and unplanned pogrom. If the misnomer of a name rings only a small bell in you, you're not alone. Even now, a century later, after books have been written about it, documentaries made, studies undertaken, reparations demanded, granite memorials erected, the hiddenness of the Tulsa Race Riot, or semi-hiddenness, is a perverse part of the mystery of it all—maybe a perverse part of the mystery of *us*. For decades it was an event largely erased from classrooms and history books, not least classrooms and history books in Oklahoma. Oklahoma averted its gaze, in a way no less than America perversely did. Call it, for want of some better explanation, the phenomenon of memory blocking, of historical amnesia, of willful forgetting.

It happened on May 31 and June 1, 1921, from the middle evening hours of the first until the early afternoon hours of the second. Local white mobs reduced mostly to rubble something like thirty-five blocks on the downtown edge of Oklahoma's second-largest city. These mobs, and fragments of mobs, which in many cases seemed to consist of no more than just ordinary Tulsa citizens, which is to say fathers, husbands, wage earners, and churchgoers, seemed to rise up and then fall back in waves of terror. The community they leveled, or sought to, in their gasoline frenzy, was on the near-northeast side of the city, just across the tracks from the Frisco Line that ran from St. Louis to San Francisco. Those tracks, as they cut through that district of the city, essentially marked the color line in a still-raw frontier boomtown where oil was like gushers of black gold. (The actual line of segregation was a street named Archer. Everything north of Archer could be said to be black, everything below white.) The community that the mobs destroyed, or tried to, was known as Greenwood and was considered one of the most affluent if not quite self-contained African-American neighborhoods in the country. It was also known, by some who didn't live there, as "Little Africa." It was also known by some as "Niggertown." Its commercial district, comprising of hundreds of prosperous black-owned businesses, flowing out of and around the intersection of Archer Street and Greenwood Avenue, was known with great pride and large justification by many of its own residents, and also across what might be termed the Underground Negro United States, as "the Black Wall Street of America." It was Oklahoma's own miracle.

Upward of nine thousand black Tulsans were left homeless in that overnight of torching and looting and killing. More than a thousand Greenwood residences were lit. Churches, theaters, barber shops, shine parlors, doctor's offices, law offices, rib shacks, dry cleaners, hotels, cafés, corner groceries—gone, or mostly so. The Stradford Hotel went. So did the Hotel Gurley, and the Red Wing Hotel, and the Midway Hotel. So did the Dreamland Theater, and the East End Feed Store, and the West Archer Lunch Room, and A. S. Newkirk's photography studio, and the Tip Top Grocery, and Mabel Little's Hairdressing Studio, and the Johnson Undertaking Company, and the Blue Goose Tailoring Shop, and Ben Rickett's Restaurant, and the Colored Insurance Association, and Osborne Monroe's Roller Rink, and Metropolitan Baptist Church, and Mount Zion Baptist Church, and North Greenwood Church of God. Something like six thousand men, women, and children were put into temporary internment camps around the city. Part of the leveling, decimating, impromptu pogromming, however you wish to describe it or name it, may have been carried out by air, in civilian aircraft, with homemade firebombs dropped on rooftops. Only one of the things still being argued.

To this day, no one has ever been prosecuted.

And the full count of the dead, some of whom, it needs quickly be said, were white? No one can say for sure. There are credible reports—not least from an official riot commission that got sanctioned by the state of Oklahoma almost eight decades after the fact—of anywhere from 75 or 100 to 300 dead. (Official estimates at the time of the riot were far lower.) On February 28, 2001, the governor's commission handed over its nearly two-hundred-page "final report" of findings and recommendations—as if there could ever be anything "final" about an event so massive. You can go to Tulsa today and hear stories about at least one never-found mass grave on the edge of town, where the bodies were dumped in. I've been to Tulsa five times. I keep hearing that story, among so many stories that lead to further undocumentable stories. As two scholar-historians put it in one of their overview essays submitted to the then-governor as part of the *Final Report of the Oklahoma Commission to Study the Tulsa Race Riot of 1921:* "History knows no fences." Which is only an eloquent way of saying that the riot, which wasn't a riot at all (even though, no question, the residents of Greenwood, outnumbered at something like twenty to one, had fought back, had risen up to try to defend themselves, and, earlier, had grouped at the courthouse, with guns and clubs, to try to prevent a lynching of one of their own), will just keep smoldering, pooling, incandescing. And the names, and the count, of the dead will always be a part of that.

The names of some of the dead: Reuben Everett, a fifty-cent day laborer. Doctor A. C. Jackson, said to be the "most able Negro surgeon in America," shot in the stomach while reportedly running through his front yard with his hands up. The names of some of the survivors, almost all gone now, although some lived deep into their Oklahoma old age: John Melvin Alexander, Essie Lee Johnson Beck, Blanche Chatman Cole. She was seventeen when it happened. In an oral history, she said: "We found that we had lost everything. Everything we owned had been stolen or burned. I wondered why we had come back. There was nothing to come back to." And then there are all the others whose names we don't quite know—an old black couple reportedly shot in the back of their heads as they held hands and knelt, praying. To borrow from Ernest Hemingway's savage passage in his great World War I novel, *A Farewell to Arms:* There will always be things, certain words, that you cannot stand to hear in connection with certain obscene events, and sometimes it's as if only the names of the places themselves, of the people themselves, "had dignity."

A mother had given birth to a stillborn. She had placed the child in a shoebox. The burial was to be in the morning. But then the torching and the shooting and the wild running. The air so thick you couldn't breathe. Somehow, in the fury, this young mother, who could not have been in a healthy state, let go of the shoebox. "Where's my baby?" she screamed over and over, in the trampling, while others, of another color, were screaming, "Get the niggers, get the niggers."

And why and how did this thing happen in the first place? It's an excessively complicated story, and in another way not at all. Ostensibly, the Tulsa Race Riot happened because a local black teenager named Dick Rowland (he was nineteen) had supposedly attacked a seventeen-year-old white girl named Sarah Page in an elevator in a downtown commercial building the day before, which was a national holiday in America. He worked at a white-owned shoeshine parlor catty-corner across the street. "Shines," which is what the shoe-shiners were generally called in Tulsa, could make a dime a job, and they tended to get tipped a nickel. In a day's work a bootblack could make as much as two bucks: hot money. Sarah Page, who lived in a rented room on North Boston Avenue, operated the elevator wheel from her little stool behind the sliding iron grate in the bumpety shaft that went up to the top floor of the Drexel Building, which was at 319 South Main. The shine parlor lacked bathroom facilities for Negroes, but there was a washroom on the Drexel's top floor. The judgment of history is that the alleged assault, the attempted rape of the building's lone elevator operator in broad daylight (no one else was in the elevator, nor in the immediate vicinity, although a white store clerk did come running when he reputedly heard a scream), didn't occur, wasn't true, or, at best, it can't be proven that it was true. Like Julian Carlton, Dick Rowland has slipped into the margins of history—and yet there are some eerie similarities between their lives. Sarah Page? She fell off history's ledge, too. There are so many stories just about *them,* not the least of which is that they were secret lovers who'd had a spat.

But the real reason it happened is that Tulsa's afternoon white daily—its name was the *Tulsa Tribune,* and its editor and owner was the forty-eight-year-old recent transplant from Wisconsin, Richard Lloyd Jones, and the paper's offices were five blocks from Greenwood—stoked the fires of racial hysteria, mob panic, sexual rage. Played to the lowest common Tulsa denominator. Published, at minimum, a baiting six-paragraph article on its front page of May 31, 1921, regarding

Dick Rowland's arrest earlier that day by two Tulsa police officers. The story came out in the city edition, which was off the presses about three o'clock that afternoon.

The judgment of history, not to say the conclusion of the governor's final commission report: Had it not been for the *Tribune*'s "coverage" of the incident, there likely never would have been a Tulsa Race Riot, not then, not in that overnight. The adjutant general of the National Guard, who led troops from Oklahoma City into Tulsa, was quoted as saying the thing had its origins in the (non) thing that had happened in the Drexel Building and in "the fantastic write-up of the incident in a sensation-seeking newspaper." If that's true, and it indelibly is, it's also true that there were a thousand other parties attending this shame—law enforcement, the lathered mobs, those who just blithely and blindly turned their heads and went to church the following Sunday. And still do, this century on.

The write-up in question was headlined NAB NEGRO FOR ATTACKING GIRL IN AN ELEVATOR. The assumptions of Dick Rowland's guilt were there. All the tropes and loaded words and undertones having to do with the worst taboo about black men and white women were there. The fourth paragraph began: "[H]e entered the elevator, she claimed, and attacked her, scratching her hands and face and tearing her clothes." The sixth paragraph: "Tenants of the Drexel Building said the girl is an orphan who works as an elevator operator to pay her way through business college." The fuse had been lit. By three thirty, newsboys on corners were shouting, "A Negro assaults a white girl." Within a couple hours, mobs, or beginnings of mobs, were gathering.

Three documentable facts: First, the original bound volumes of the long-defunct newspaper no longer exist, at least not in their entirety. They were apparently purposely destroyed. Second, a microfilm version of that day's paper exists, but not with that article in it, not in the city edition. Someone tore it out before it was filmed, leaving, as more than one chronicler has said, a literal hole in history. But you can't "disappear" certain things from a people's memory. You can try to suppress and tear out and call back and otherwise eradicate bad things from the record, but it won't work, not finally. Those things live on, in cellular ways. Fact three: That brief front-page article, down on the lower right, in column eight, with its racial tropes and guilt presumptions, *did* eventually turn up—in a later edition of the paper that got distributed in the city and also by rail throughout parts of the state. We have extant copies of the state edition today, with that story in it. I have held it—the crinkly, actual page itself—in my fingers. I will explain more about that and the sequence of all this, because so many people, even scholars, have gotten the basic facts wrong. There has always been so much misinformation.

But there is another element to put immediately into the confusing mix, something far more inflammatory, never proven, haunting, scary, indicting: namely, that a *second* article is said to have appeared in the same early edition, possibly on the editorial page, which far more blatantly race-baited the citizenry to come to the courthouse for an evening lynching. It was supposedly headlined: TO LYNCH NEGRO TONIGHT. But that alleged article, if it existed, if it did appear on the editorial page of the afternoon edition, amounts to another literal hole in history: it, too, got ripped out and disposed of. It has never been found, in any edition, although at one point a $5,000 cash reward was offered. That editorial or article remains the holy grail of the Tulsa Race Riot. You keep thinking it exists in someone's attic, that it will float up somewhere in a bottle in the Philippines. It's unclear how many copies of the first edition got out on the streets with that alleged editorial or article in it—maybe several hundred. You can go to the microfilm reels of the *Tulsa Tribune* today and what you'll see, going across parts of the editorial page of the city edition for May 31, 1921, is the jagged hole. Looking at the hole itself, with parts of the next page leaking through from underneath (want ads and comics), is its own small cultural shock. And yet that alleged and missing headline, never mind the lost piece itself, remains a deep part of the folklore of the black community of Tulsa. Through the years, Oklahoma historians have taken testimony from numerous African Americans—and, in fact, from some white people, too—willing to swear on the family Bible that such a headline and such an article, or editorial, ran in the pages of the *Tulsa Tribune* on May 31. They remembered seeing it themselves; they heard about it from a grandparent or a great-grandparent. What the story actually said beneath the headline is just one more argued and apparently never-to-be-settled thing floating in the Great Plains mist.

Let's remove the words "alleged" and "reputed." For the sake of argument let's stipulate categorically that there was such a headline, and that

it said exactly that in large type (TO LYNCH NEGRO TONIGHT), and
that the piece of "journalism" beneath it was filled with the worst kind of
no-pretense, egging-on language. (Almost every serious student of the
riot I've spoken with believes there must have been *some* kind of inflammatory second article that day.) So a question, to which the answer at
first might seem more than self-evident: Would such a thing have been
put out on the street because the people who ran the newspaper, not
least the man who owned it and edited it and treated it as his God-given
bully pulpit, reviled all black people and wished to see them done away
with? Actually, I don't believe that for a second. Actually, his whole history would argue against it. This whole semi-hidden stain in American
history would be so much easier to come to terms with if that were the
case—then, it would just be a tale about Evil with an uppercase "E." But
I believe the real and difficult story of what happened here, the real and
difficult explanation here, insofar as Richard Lloyd Jones's part of it is
concerned, amounts to something far more insidious, tragic, and that
to understand it, or to make an attempt to understand it, you have to
leave Oklahoma. You have to go back to Wisconsin. In a way, you could
go straight back to the image at the top of this chapter, glimmering with
its hubris. Hubris has an awful lot to do with this parable.

The uncanny fact is that the photographer's lens is catching the
hubristic and morally hypocritical man at a hinge-point in his history—
and, of course, not only his. A hinge-point of hardening, turning. It's
been going on for several years. There have been many contributory
factors, meaning that it's cumulative, as is the way of most of our lives.
But the thing is in motion now, and, like a Newtonian law of physics, it
doesn't seem able to stop. This is sure: In the turning's wake, eventual
wake, will lie the ashes and corpses of Tulsa.

———

Consider him. Regard him. The editor and president of the *Wisconsin
State Journal* is in his office. Actually, regard all that's around him. Such
a textured photograph.

Thanks to that clearly caught little flip-over day calendar toward the
left of the frame, we're able to know the date the shutter is snapping: it's
August 19, 1916. (The date can be verified in ways outside the frame as
well.) More than that, and thanks again to the camera's crisp capturing

of that little wood-encased clock sitting on the cluttered shelf just above the calendar, and beneath the portrait of a headless Abe Lincoln (one of Richard Lloyd Jones's largest heroes), we're able to say the precise time: three minutes past one o'clock in the afternoon. (You might need to get a magnifying glass.) It's a broiling, cook-an-egg-on-a-Madison-sidewalk kind of day, a Saturday. The upper Midwest isn't accustomed to furnace fires like this. The mercury's going to top out at 109 today. If it's that outdoors, geezes, what can it be in here? See the way that thinning old canvas blind is pasted against the tilted-open window behind him? The breeze, such as it is, must be only making things worse. Hot sucking wind.

That's one of the kinder things Richard Lloyd Jones's journalistic and political enemies, of whom he has made almost too many to count in the past five years, since he's taken control of this newspaper, would be happy to call him. Hot sucking wind.

Speaking of pasting (the blind against the window, that is), speaking of all the appealing and journalistic kind of clutter in this frame and in this room—which, incidentally, is on the second floor of a blocky red building at the sloping corner of Carroll and Doty streets in downtown Madison, just a football throw or two away from the great dome of the Wisconsin state capitol—focus on just one item: that gloopy-looking, half-filled jar with the long-handled stick in it, next to a pair of scissors, in the center of the editor in chief's desk. The jar is a paste pot. The stick is really a narrow brush. Crucial items to get a newspaper out. In this heat, the jar's contents must be congealing into an icky white mess. That brush must be stiff as wood. Anyway, the way things work at a newspaper, any newspaper in America, as regards the paste pot, is that the copy boy of the operation (at a paper of this size, there were probably three or four, earning not much more than pennies, but hoping one day for their own journalistic glories) rushes in with a paragraph or two of a story-in-progress. The copy has been ripped right out of the carriage of some reporter's typewriter in the next room. The cruel and know-nothing editor waiting to massacre the reporter's prose does precisely that: marks it up unmercifully and scissors off the part he deigns to keep, and reaches for his pot, and glues the saved graph or two onto a half-sheet of newsprint that's cheaper than toilet paper, rolls up the sheet, pushes it into a cylindrical container, slaps the container into a pneumatic tube. Closes the lid of the tube and trips a switch. With a great vacuuming sound, the tube's compressed air sucks the scribe's copy on his running story, being written and edited in "takes," down to the composing room, where some greasy, bored, overalled Linotype operators stub out their Luckies, put away some girlie pictures, and start slinging more hot metal.

The "daily miracle" of producing a newspaper is in progress, at the second oldest newspaper in the state. These days the *Wisconsin State Journal* is reported to have something like a two-to-one advantage in subscribers over its sleepy and once-dominant conservative competitor, the *Madison Democrat.*

One last thing in regard to the paste pot: The crucial function that *we* rely on these days to move around paragraphs and sentences at will and whip-second speed on our computer screens? That ability, function, term, to "cut and paste," owes everything, metaphorically, spiritually, almost literally, to the old, laborious scissors-and-glue-pot ways of getting out a newspaper. The ghost of the paste pots made it to the cyber revolution.

Richard Lloyd Jones, a hands-on dandy of an ink-stained wretch, has probably been cutting and pasting copy all morning. He's the chief here, but he still pushes things down the pneumatic tube—or sends a copy boy racing down to a lower floor with the latest part of the story. He's known to work six days a week. He's between editions. He's put the thin Saturday sheet to bed; he's got the work of the fat Sunday paper to deal with, before he puts on his chapeau and suit jacket and heads out the door to his handsome home on the north shore of Lake Monona. He can take the car or hoof it in twenty minutes. Pretty good life, when you add it all up. He has no idea on August 19, 1916, at three minutes past one on an inferno Midwest Saturday, about the inferno waiting not quite five years off and 752 miles southwest of here. I'd be willing to bet—without any absolute proof—that Dick Jones (it's what his friends and extended family call him) has no idea that a few years hence he will even be relocating with his family (and his mistress) to Oklahoma, having sold off his business interests here and bought a new property in the Sooner State (for a mortgaged-to-his-eyeballs $300,000) because his Wisconsin newspaper fortunes will have turned against him, most of that being due—you could guess—to his own intemperateness, hard-headedness, hotheadedness.

Inferno. To time-frame this instant in the other direction: Julian Carlton's act at Taliesin was two years and four days ago. It was two years and three midnights ago that a first cousin was shouldering and elbow-ing through the Spring Green dark to meet a sagging first cousin under the eave of a train platform, telling him, *Buck up, Frank, it couldn't be any worse for you.*

Consider him, the man on the station platform, now sitting in his sweltering office. So confident and cocksure. Semi-turned now to stare at the camera's eye dead on. With barest hint of belly. In summer whites with a white leather belt. With hand-tied bow tie snugged up to the starchy-looking collar of the broad-striped dress shirt. (Hell with the record-setting heat.) With that semi-ridiculous-looking pompadour of pomaded hair. (Since babyhood he's had a profusion of curls, and for a long while now has enjoyed flaring them up in little poofy wings at either side and also raking the part straight down the middle of his wide forehead.) With that almost fey-looking signet ring on the pinkie of his right hand. (Again, you might have to take up a magnifying glass, but the ring is there, along with a stubby editing pencil and a pair of flimsy wire spectacles that he's holding lightly between thumb and forefinger of the same hand, having apparently just removed them, the better to stare unblinkingly at the photographer.) With that knot of dangling white rag half-concealed in his other hand. (It looks like a bandage, but the bet here is that he's using it to mop his forehead between pho-tographic takes.) With his secretary and mistress sitting ten feet away, in an anteroom, at a typewriter, in her modest collared dress and with her ankles demurely crossed. Her name's Amy Comstock. She's a col-lege grad. She's a dozen years younger. She comes from proper people in Milwaukee. Her boss has her on the masthead now as assistant editor and secretary. She's just outside this frame, waiting to take down his dic-tation or whatever other job or role comes up. (The photographer, who was from a local portrait studio, got a couple of shots of her that day, too, in the foreground, with Jones in the background, visible through the doorway, hunched at his desk, and these pictures are also preserved in the archives of the Wisconsin Historical Society at Madison.)

258 | PLAGUED BY FIRE

Keep gazing, holding him steady. I wish to relate a few key biographical and other crucial facts about Dick Jones, currently forty-
three. Some of the facts are likely to surprise.

———

He didn't grow up an only child—it must have just seemed so. His one
sibling, older by several years, was born mentally handicapped, with her
IQ never to rise above that of a twelve-year-old. So perhaps only half-
consciously did his strong-willed parents, but especially his mother, lavish far too much attention on him—and in another way put the burden
of too many expectations on him. You know who his father is: Uncle
Jenk, Frank Lloyd Wright's favorite uncle and largest family influence
outside of his own parents. Uncle Jenk, the bushy-bearded and orating
Civil War vet and pioneering Unitarian minister who resembled an
Old Testament prophet—or our images of same. Uncle Jenk, founder of
the nationally known All Souls Church on Chicago's South Side. Uncle
Jenk, key figure of the Western Unitarian Conference in its mission to
spread the Unitarian word across the Mississippi to the next ocean.
Uncle Jenk, espouser of all things liberal and humane and decent and
dovish. (The blood of the Civil War had turned Jenkin Lloyd Jones
forever against armed conflict.) Uncle Jenk, poet of the common man.
Uncle Jenk, the Wright relation who took in and put up at the All Souls
parsonage, at the start of those myth-laden Chicago years, that long-ago
Madison hick (with the shag hair and toothpick shoes—remember?)
bent on conquering the world. Uncle Jenk—who, in this context is, of
course, Daddy Jenk—is without doubt a great and charismatic figure in
the history of Unitarianism in America. But he was apparently an emotionally distant father, often a sad truism of great men. So how would an
only son hope to cut his own identity, ever get enough approval, in such
a shadow? By overcompensating? By developing early a kind of absolutist frame of mind, as a way of masking his fears and insecurities? By
one day needing to kill off in the psychic sense his famed father and to
become his seeming exact opposite in philosophies and beliefs? But that
is sounding way too close to psychoanalysis, and I am not a psychiatrist.
The only son, unlike his much smaller and older first cousin Frank
Wright, grew up a 185-pound athlete, skilled at tennis and swimming
and horsemanship. The only son (like his older cousin) was a failure at

college and (as with his older relation) was happy to dissemble about it ever after. He didn't finish undergraduate work at Madison—in fact, he seems to have been kicked out. He invented for himself a law degree at the University of Chicago, and then doubled down with the fiction of having gotten a master of law degree there. On his U of C transcript, such as it is, there is a note that says he was dismissed from the University of Wisconsin, and that at Chicago, in the winter of 1895, he was enrolled in three undergraduate classes, in one of which he was caught "cribbing," resulting in a suspension for the next six academic quarters, starting in the spring quarter of 1895.* It wasn't too long after this that he apparently said the hell with school and went east and took up a career in journalism. If you check his various writings and entries about himself through the decades, in speeches and essays and *Who's Who* listings and so forth, you'll find Jones blithely announcing, as if having been tutored by Frank himself: "After I got my Master of Laws degree . . ."

What isn't a lie is that Uncle Jenk's son, somewhere in and around his failed college period, spent a year out west on a Nevada ranch, and this was among the happiest periods of his life. He'd gone west, he once wrote, "full of uncertainty and indecision. . . . Had not my family felt that in some fashion I should follow a white collar life I think I would be out there now riding the Humbolt basin." Surely that's wishful thinking, but there might be more going on between the lines of those words— namely, rage at his parents—than first meets the eye. (His parents were both long dead when he misspelled Humboldt.) In any case, the flat fact is that he was always far too competitive and ego-driven to herd sheep for a lifetime in a pair of chaps.

On the idea of lifelong temper: Years after Jones himself was dead, one of his sons (he had three children, and all would be involved as adults in the running of the *Tulsa Tribune*), was quoted as saying: "He was very opinionated and argumentative. We often clashed. Or he would run over people. It's hard to describe that as a clash. He had a strong temper. You can never out-argue people with a strong temper." People who worked for him through the years testified to his capacity for an erupting King Lear–ish anger. Then the charm would flood back.

---

* The paper trail in Wisconsin is less complete. His yellowed "directory file card" in the registrar's office at UW indicates that he took courses in the 1893–1894 academic year. The single word "withdrew" is handwritten in ink next to "November 1894."

Going east. The only son took with him all of his ingrained Unitarian and liberal values, taught at home, at the dinner table, in the front pew on Sunday, at extended Lloyd Jones summer reunions. His career in East Coast journalism, where he worked primarily as an editor, was not insignificant. He worked on some papers and then got on with some magazines—notably *Cosmopolitan* and *Collier's Weekly*—during some of their greatest muckraking moments. He came in contact, if not became intimate friends, with such iconic American journalists as Ida Tarbell and Lincoln Steffens and Samuel Hopkins Adams. These liberal crusaders and reformers hated Standard Oil, political machines, robber barons, the railroad monopolies. In a way, they were inventing the idea of investigative journalism in America. And editor Jones seems to have been right there with them.

After something like fourteen years of toil in eastern fields, he came back home to the true fields of Wisconsin with his wife, Georgia, and their one small child. Wisconsin was considered one of the most progressive states in the union. While still in New York, Jones had heard that there was a chance to acquire the *Wisconsin State Journal*, which he instantly foresaw as the leading liberal daily in the state. His patron in obtaining the business was one of the greatest Republican progressive names in America, possibly the most admired man in all of Wisconsin: Robert Marion La Follette. He'd earlier been governor and he now was a United States senator. Jones needed something like $100,000 to buy the *State Journal* and La Follette prevailed on wealthier friends to stake him to $85,000 in loans. (Jones got the paper from Amos Parker Wilder, a distinguished name in Wisconsin journalism history, but who would mostly be remembered now for being the father of three-time Pulitzer Prize–winning novelist and playwright Thornton Wilder.) It wouldn't quite be accurate to say that the younger and lanky Jones felt hero-worship, surrogate father-worship, for the older and almost comically short-statured and fist-shaking and flush-faced firebrand, "Fighting Bob"—but close enough.

Fighting Bob stood for women's suffrage and the worth of black people—so did Dick Jones. He was against child labor—ditto. He loathed predatory wealth and political machines—ditto again. He campaigned for the dignity of a working wage for every person in America. He saw his native state as "the laboratory of democracy." It was part of something called the "Wisconsin Idea," which had to do with harnessing the intellectual firepower of the University of Wisconsin (right in Madison's backyard) into helping improve the lives of every citizen. With a powerful news outlet in the state capital, now controlled by a man instinctively aligned with his own populist sympathies, La Follette could further his not-secret presidential aspirations. (To kick that dream along, he'd also recently begun his own nationally distributed magazine, *La Follette's Weekly*.) Among all the things the younger man had in common with the older (the two were not quite eighteen years apart), self-regard wasn't the least.

Jones took over the paper on July 29, 1911. There was a huge photograph of him on page one—the hair poofed up and winged out at either end far more ridiculously than what you see in the picture here. He ran his first editorial (a fortnight later) in a two-column width. It was headlined LET'S GO TO IT. Six days later he was going to it in an editorial about an "unholy alliance composed of the Santa Fe Railroad, the Southern Pacific Railroad . . . the ever present Guggenheims." Soon there were contests, and jingles, and crazy headlines on crazy stories designed to lure new readers, and some of them were being set in 96-point type, as if William Randolph Hearst himself were breathing on the operation. "WHY DID MY SON JACK THROW HIMSELF AWAY ON THAT SOCIETY GAL?" ASKS HIS MOTHER. He seemed to be trying to turn the *WSJ* into some odd combination of Hearstian tabloid rag and serious broadsheet news outlet for progressivism and civic good, albeit shrilly proclaimed. This included his attacks against local vice, liquor, loitering. From the outset you can track his editorials and find not just the doctrinaire, ego-driven views, but almost a weird, rigid, bifurcated way of thinking. It was as if there were no middle ground, or seldom anyway. There was good in the world, and there was evil in the world, and the preacher's son would tell you the difference.*

Not long after he took control, there was a sensational murder-kidnapping story. It involved a seven-year-old girl named Annie Lemberger. The police put bloodhounds on the trail. The *State Journal* ran

---

* The best scholarship on the history of the *Wisconsin State Journal* remains a 221-page (in typescript) unpublished thesis for a master of arts degree in journalism in 1951 at the University of Wisconsin by a graduate student named Norman Weissman, and entitled "A History of the Wisconsin State Journal Since 1900." I am deeply indebted to its research, even as I have tried to add my own.

front-page boxes, late bulletins. On the third day of the running story, in his editorial, sounding like Arthur Conan Doyle, the editor wrote: "In the stillness and darkness of night a ghastly devil hand slips through the window, lifts the child from its slumber and carries it away." Later that day they found the child's body in Lake Monona. Her killer was still at large. The next day Jones headlined his editorial: THE FIEND MUST BE FOUND. "The dirtiest and most damnable kind of a murder has been committed here. . . . Revenge is the only motive that could possibly be the root-cause of this terrible crime. We none of us know what insane maniac may harbor a spirit of revenge for some real or imaginary cause against any of us." It's as if he was unwittingly writing pre-echoes of something three years off, at serene Spring Green.

The authorities charged a local ne'er-do-well who had served time in a state asylum. There was a forced confession. One of the judgments of history is that Richard Lloyd Jones's paper, with its lurid headlines, with its compulsively readable coverage, had helped railroad a false conviction. (In the middle of the fever, apparently worried at what he'd stoked, the editor had tried to back off, do damage control, expressing doubt about the convicted man's guilt. He'd flown his paper off the handle, and he knew it. And he never really apologized. This, too, one day, in a far-off state, would have its tragic echoes.)

He wrote an editorial that fall, and, suddenly, in the middle, lapsed into all caps: EVERY SCHOOL HOUSE IN AMERICA SHOULD BE OPENED AS A NEIGHBORHOOD CENTER WHERE THESE GANGS OF YOUNG FELLOWS CAN BE TRANSFORMED INTO SELF GOVERNING CLUBS OF CITIZENS IN TRAINING. It was as if his typewriter had run amok.

Actually, Dick Jones barely typed. He was known for striding up and down in the halls of his editorial offices, dictating his beliefs to his stenographer, nearly giddy at his turns of phrase.

That piece ran on Wednesday, October 25, 1911. In the same issue there was a story about the city denying housing to a newly transplanted black minister. Madison was a liberal place—but hardly free of racial anxiety. The small article, on page 3, in the news columns, seemed subtly to be taking up for the clergyman. The article was unbylined, but had sentences such as these: "Because of race prejudice in this city, the trustees of the church have been unable to secure a suitable residence for their pastor." The editor was taking a stand—the right moral one.

Morality? Jones had had the *State Journal* for something like five months when his older and world-famous first cousin—whose fame had always rankled—was revealed by the Chicago press boys to have installed his lover at the newly built Taliesin. You recall how Frank Lloyd Wright seemed only too happy at Christmastime 1911 to be making a naïve ass of himself by lecturing the out-of-town reporters on his and Mamah's moral integrity and higher purposes. At first, Cousin Richard seems to have tried to ignore the story, as did all of the pietistic relatives of the Helena and Wyoming valleys. But on the day after Christmas, on page 2, feeling pressure to report something, Jones's paper ran a medium-sized piece headlined WRIGHT DEFIES SOCIAL CODE ON ELOPEMENT. There was no direct mention that the two were related. At the end the editor couldn't resist a personal rebuke, which he personally drafted:

> It is a source of very grave and deep humiliation to all his relatives . . . that he should have chosen to bring his scandal into their midst. They have repudiated him absolutely and none but his own sister, who lives in the vicinity, gives him any recognition whatever. His attitude is one of defiance against all the established social codes which have been found to best conserve the best interests of society. . . . He returned from Europe and his wife and children accepted him back in the home. But he did not remain there long. He slipped out of sight again, and though he has been living in this bungalow with the woman, much to the mortification of his friends and family, for several months, the Chicago newspapers have just learned of his "new life" in this bungalow.

A bit of backstory. The two had known each other all their lives, if it was also true they'd never spent huge amounts of time together. (When Wright first came to Chicago, at the end of 1886 or early in 1887, to work for J. Lyman Silsbee, he and Richard slept in the same bedroom, perhaps in the same double bed—until Frank found his own rooming house.) Growing up, their six-year difference would have been large. (In Chicago that first spring, Frank was nineteen, so Richard would have been twelve, soon to be thirteen.) Richard seemed to have looked up to his far-shorter cousin even as he tried to compete intellectually with him. As the years went on, and their veiled antagonisms grew, they were able to catch up to each other in their emotional ages—but the journalist had never been able to draw alongside in the fame category. Not even close. Now, running his own newspaper, and with his money-hurting cousin bringing major scandal, Jones could happily stick in the shiv, to wit the paragraph just quoted.

In that same edition, on December 26, 1911, in a two-column-wide editorial headlined ONWARD, he wrote: "If we are to be honest, if we are to be true, if we are to be disciples of the lowly Nazarene, whose birthday we make our greatest holiday, we must ever be morally alive."

A day later, with the Wisconsin adulterers still making tawdry headlines in Chicago, all of it still deeply humiliating the maternal relatives, Cousin Richard came in from a night at the theater in downtown Madison with his wife. There was a telegram from Wright on the hall table. Wright wanted to make a statement in his defense and hoped that his cousin—despite what he'd just written in his paper—would be willing to publish it. Yet another opportunity for Jones to twist the knife, since Wright more or less had his hat in his hand. The next day, the 28th, at his office the editor dictated a two-page, single-spaced, typed letter. It dripped not just with his wordiness but with his moral condescension, his pinched-ness, his abstemiousness. Sentences like this one: "Whatever your own school of philosophy may be and however much you may be impatient with what you may regard as obsolete standards of morality and conservative social codes, you must remember that society as a mass still believes in and holds to the social standards that have in the course of centuries seemed to best conserve society." He remonstrated Wright on the so-called "virtue of your experiment." He wanted his cousin to know that "I do regard it as most unfortunate in every possible way that you should have brought what you must have known would be inevitable publicity of an undesirable kind" into the decent lives of the Lloyd Joneses. He signed it, with a great flourish (he loved underlining his name and also exaggerating the loop in the "L" in "Lloyd"), "Very truly yours, Richard Lloyd Jones."

Was the editor by now secretly sleeping with his secretarial hire,

Amy Comstock? Doubtful. She was too new at the paper. Soon he would be, though. And no doubt of it.

And Wright's reaction to this letter? A few days after the New Year, he wrote a rather amazing letter of his own to Francis Little, who, with his spouse, had been a client since the early 1900s. Wright was in the midst of trying to design a new home for the Littles on Lake Minnetonka in the exurbs of Minneapolis, and was fretful about the commission falling through. (You'll recall that this house, or the restored living room of it, is now sitting in the Metropolitan Museum of Art.) The letter is disdainful and arrogant and rationalizing—some of Wright's worst tendencies—even as it's piercing with its own kind of honesty. It's also eloquent, even (or especially) if many of the sentences don't track. It's also full of the old winning and artful Wrightian guile. He wrote the letter in longhand from Taliesin. He dated it "Jan 3, 1912." He put it on engraved stationery bearing the address of Orchestra Hall in Chicago. ("Telephone: Harrison 457.") He addressed it to "Mr and Mrs Little."

> The long expected news paper outbreak has come—and the situa-
> tion has no doubt reached you—in bad line and false colors—the
> usual caricature of anything touching sex or family. . . . My chil-
> dren as are other children were infected by the idea that father and
> mother existed solely for them. . . . Mrs. Wright and I only angered
> and stultified one another. The children were demoralized by that
> depressing consciousness in the atmosphere. . . . [N]o one can judge
> those situations but myself—So you see I am as Mr. Little said, "a
> hopelessly selfish piece."

He says: "I am the fool now—but honest—at least: A barnyard foul I never was!" And: "I may be no more than a peacock destined to feathers and a strut but—as *one is*: to be the best one sees: in that is manliness & heaven enough for me—and may God be merciful to me for what lies I told and lived to get there and credit given for those I would not tell." Of his children? "I don't care to whittle away at them and sandpaper them to *my* ideas in the idiotic fashion of 'good' fatherhood—but I love them all—I love my work—my mother and sisters, my aunts here and the few friends I possess—I had very few—fewer than most men."

As for Cousin Richard himself? Wright doesn't score Jones by name, but surely he must have him directly in mind when he says this, as if to nail his essential character: "The animosity of current morality hisses like a snake in my ears. The 'Jones conscience' of which I once stood in awe manifests itself chiefly as *fear;* the *dread* of wills sick with ambition. . . ."

Jump ahead—to an overshadowing year. The morally hissing journalist, with his dread will and do-gooding ambition, kept pasting the citizenry of Madison with his ego and progressive-thinking editorials. In the spring of 1914, the great black educator and reformer Booker T. Washington came to Madison to give a talk at a Congregational church. Earlier, I referenced Booker T. Washingon with the unexplained comment that he has an uncannily large role to play in the tragedy of Tulsa. Cusseta, Alabama, is about forty minutes by car up the road from what had been established by Washington in 1881 (so about seven years before Julian seems to have been born) as the Tuskegee Normal School for Colored Teachers. As was noted earlier, it's almost impossible to say the words "Booker T. Washington" without thinking of the word "Tuskegee." (In the popular imagination we know this iconic Alabama place-name in the history of black higher education as Tuskegee Institute, but it is properly now Tuskegee University.)

By the same token, it is also almost not possible to say "Booker T. Washington" without wanting to say "W. E. B. Du Bois," and the over-simplified truth is that, nearly always, the first name, the first life, will suffer in regard to the second. (They were and were not contemporaries. Washington was born in 1856 and died in 1915. Du Bois was born in 1868 and died in 1963.) The legacies of these two great leaders of late-nineteenth-century and early-twentieth-century black America—whose most important work was essentially done before the term "civil rights" had entered the lexicon—seem inextricably bound. And as that dual legacy has shaved itself down through the decades, Washington is thought of, not wrongly, as the great accommodationist, who preached a philosophy of racial solidarity and self-help and what he regarded as a realistic acceptance by his people of the evils of discrimination. While Du Bois, a founder of the NAACP, with his Harvard doctorate and prolific writing (he tried his hand at fiction and poetry, among all his other works), stands in the collective imagination for the principle of proclaiming "Never." For Du Bois, discrimination toward blacks had to be met at the battlements. If the earlier leader wanted to work inside the system that got handed to him, the later one wanted to tear it down, maybe even burn it down, if that's what it took, except that the tearing down of segregation would be mainly through force of his intellectual thought. To use another metaphor, Washington didn't wish to make waves so much as to try to calm them, while Du Bois stood for capsizing the vessel. The good Negro, the go-along Negro, the hardworking and self-respecting Negro, as against the overthrowing Negro: a great oversimplification of the thought and work of two giants, but not a wholly incorrect one.

The editor of the *Wisconsin State Journal* was in the audience on the warming Saturday evening in late April 1914 when Booker T. Washington lectured in Madison. There is a much-traveled story in the Lloyd Jones family about Jones having afterward brought Washington into his home and put him up for the rest of that weekend when it was discovered that no Madison hotel would have him. This story has passed down through at least three generations of Richard Lloyd Joneses, which is to say to his grandchildren and great-grandchildren. I have personally heard variations of it from four of Jones's grandchildren—all in their upper age now and, as you might expect, in various stages of denial about the terrible thing that happened in their native city a decade or more before they were born. What they have said to me, each in his or her way, is: *But how could Grandfather be the awful person history has made him out to be, you're making him out to be, if he stepped forward and did that for Booker T. Washington? Doesn't that alone prove he wasn't a racist?*

Actually, to me it proves just the opposite of the point they are longing to make. And I say that deeply grateful to each of these septuagenarian descendants for not having slammed down the phone when I called to ask if I might come over to speak to them.

The theme of Washington's address that Madison evening was that the American Negro "is not in the ditch." There would always be the drunkards and the loafers and the misfits. But the Negro, despite his

---

* I don't believe the story to be exactly accurate—but, more crucially, neither does a Wright scholar named Mary Jane Hamilton, who has given over something like forty years of her professional career to an extended study of the Lloyd Jones clan. What might be true here is that there was a paler version of the "hosting," namely, that Jones and his wife put on a luncheon for Washington at their home on Harvey Terrace that weekend.

weaknesses, was supporting himself, and the evidence was everywhere. In the downward turn of lynching statistics alone, you could almost chart the progress, the hope. No transcript of the talk appears to exist. But from the several papers, in Madison and beyond Madison, that reported on it, a reader almost can't help get the feeling—or I couldn't help get the feeling—that what he was politely talking of to his capacity mixed-race audience in the pews was the fundamental difference between a "good Negro" and a "bad nigger."

The next morning, Jones's newspaper ran a modest story. It was the Sunday edition and they had to shoehorn it in on page 3. Jones himself may have gone back to the office to write it. It was headlined BOOKER T. WASHINGTON TELLS OF NEW ERA FOR THE NEGRO.

Not quite four months later, a very bad man, claimed to be from the West Indies, went berserk and burned down the home of Frank Lloyd Wright, although that isn't all he did.

———

Isn't history in some sense driven by all the small ironies? On the Saturday before the igniting of the so-called Tulsa Race Riot (which is to say, something like a little more than forty-eight hours before the first can of gasoline got emptied and the first matchstick got struck), the editor and owner of the *Tulsa Tribune*—which was always trying to compete against its better financed and larger-in-circulation competitor a few blocks away, the *Tulsa World*—published on the "church page" one of his regular installments of the "Saturday Sermonette." In effect, these were secular homilies, offered and bylined by a preacher's son, on how to live your life with decency and propriety. The sermonette on May 28, 1921, on page 3, was entitled "Conscience." This was its third paragraph: "The voice of conscience was never silenced without retribution. No man knows a greater glory than the testimony of a strong, clear conscience."

The man who wrote that was going regularly by then to room 500 of the Tulsa Hotel for assignations with his much younger secretary and assistant editor. He told associates that he was keeping an office in the hotel to get away from the distractions of the newsroom, that he could go over there with the hardworking Amy Comstock to polish off some editorials and correspondence, and then return to work later in the afternoon. Work did get done over there, at the hotel, but so did a lot of raw sex, at least if some later sworn depositions (by about a half-dozen private detectives and others spying on the two through keyholes in an adjoining room) are to be believed. According to the documents, the lovers had a fetish for standing in the doorway and watching each other on the toilet.

Irony. The front page of the *Tribune*'s city edition of Tuesday, May 31—the one carrying, in column eight, far down on the right side of the page, the six-paragraph article headlined NAB NEGRO FOR ATTACKING GIRL IN AN ELEVATOR—featured ten local women who'd made it to the last round of a *Tribune*-sponsored beauty pageant. The city (or at least the *Tribune*'s readers) had been avidly following the contest. This was the day's main story. The beauty editor wrote the piece, and the paper ran snapshots of the finalists: RACE NARROWS, HOUSEWIVES, TYPISTS LEAD. The lead on the story: "Oh, please, Mr. Christy, who's going to win The Beauty Contest?" Mr. Christy was a local civic official who'd get to make the announcement the following Sunday. But the beauty contest, and Mr. Christy's announcement, were going to get wiped out by something else history had in mind.

The paper that day, the 31st, on the streets as usual by a little after three, ran to sixteen pages. It cost five cents. The editors had a little box up at the top right that announced the average daily paid circulation was 26,642, with seventy-five percent of it paid in advance. "A circulation good as gold" were the words inside the box. As said above, if you go to the microfilm reels of this edition (because that's all we have), what you'll see is the jagged hole where the NAB NEGRO headline and story are supposed to be. Coming up from underneath is a rather sexy ad for ladies' silk hosiery.

On the editorial page of that edition: the even larger jagged hole. It's what we have.

But as was also noted above, there are existing copies—the actual newspaper itself—of the state edition of that day, with the front-page article intact, and, as I said, I have held a copy of that front page, fragile as parchment, in my hand. No matter how hard some parties may have wished it to be so, the article didn't get "disappeared," not in the state. But here is something that even close scholars of the riot have gotten confused about: the state edition of the May 31 paper is actually dated

June 1. Why? Because the newspaper had an eccentric (and damned confusing) habit of dating its overnight issue with the following day's date. By the time the state edition reached some of its in-state destinations, it really *was* the next day—even if it was essentially the same paper from the day before. Sometimes parts of the inside of the paper would be remade in the composing room in the late hours of the evening, and even into the first hours of the next morning. But most of the main stories remained the same. So it would be far more accurate to think of the state edition as the May 31/June 1 edition—and the editors could have just as easily double-dated it that way. In any case, this is the paper that has slipped through the webs of time. The beauty queen finalists are still there. Mr. Christy is still holding the readers in suspense. NAB NEGRO is there.

And by "now"—the real time of "now," middle of the night, when the state edition is being pitched off in tied bundles in darkness at various rail stops in Oklahoma—all of Greenwood is afire. The ludicrously slanted accounts of that wouldn't appear in the paper until Wednesday afternoon, in the city edition of the paper. That was the *real* June 1.

On page 6 of the overnight state edition, there was a two-column story with this headline: DICK ROWLAND IS SPIRITED OUT OF CITY. (Fearing a courthouse lynching, the sheriff had him taken out of the courthouse jail by a back door at two a.m.) So parts of the paper had to have been re-plated in the composing room into that next morning.

And the editorial page of the state edition, dated June 1 (but, really, to say again: it's the May 31 paper): Do we have it? Yes, but not with an editorial headlined TO LYNCH NEGRO TONIGHT. The main editorial in the state edition is headlined A DISARMAMENT DRIVE and has nothing to do with a city, or a section of a city, burning down. What happened? Apparently, what would one day be thought of as the missing holy grail of the Tulsa Race Riot got subbed out and the other got put in its place.

There are plenty of other things, though, that are fact and so don't need to be preceded by the word "apparently." By Wednesday, June 1, afternoon papers across America were starting to run bulletin accounts. Both of Tulsa's white-owned papers had scrapped everything to put out running stories, with extra editions. The editor of the *Tribune*, attempting to back and fill, ran a front-page editorial, decrying lawlessness.

"Lynch law leads not to law but to lawlessness and lawlessness is a repudiation of government," he wrote, as if with no shame. Second paragraph: "Whatever ground it may have had, a story starts that a negro in the county jail was to be lynched." *A story starts,* as if his paper had no involvement. He cried for calm. By the time those words would have appeared in the city edition of June 1, Greenwood was mostly rubble. Troops of the National Guard were standing over the ashes.

Roughly at the hour that those words would have made the street, that Wednesday, Richard Lloyd Jones was preoccupied with something else. The United News wire syndicate had reached him in his offices in either late morning or early afternoon and asked him to draft an at-the-scene report. He probably got it in to the New York offices of the wire service late in the afternoon, or at least by suppertime. Perhaps he was putting the first words on the story as the city edition of his own paper was streaming onto the corners of Tulsa. The next day, his first-person account appeared in cities across the country, including New York and Chicago. The *Chicago Tribune* gave his account major play, with graphics. The story was headlined POWDER OF RACE HATE LIGHTED BY SPARK OF CRIME. The byline: "By Richard Lloyd Jones," and under that, in brackets: "Former Editor of Collier's Weekly and Publisher of the Tulsa, Okla. Tribune. Written for the United News." The *Chicago Tribune* was buying in, uncritically.

His moral hypocrisy is hard to bear. The level of self-removal from blame is stomach-churning. The Manichaean way of thinking: on full display.

> It is the old story over again—ancient as time—race prejudice.
> A Negro rapes a white girl. Either a fool or an enemy of law and order spreads the story that a mob is going to lynch the Negro. Such a story spreads faster than a dry grass fire. . . .
> We find Negros who are good, bad, and indifferent. The good are respected; they are kind and courteous; they are helpful, and the southerner has an affection for them. The indifferent are in the twilight zone, and the white people are indifferent to them.
> But there is a bad black man who is a beast. The bad black man is a bad man. He drinks the cheapest and the vilest whisky. He breaks every law to get it. He is a dope fiend. He holds life lightly.

He is a bully and a brute. A dozen of such collect at the Tulsa county courthouse with firearms when they hear the lynching rumor. . . .

The fire department lent itself to keep the flames along the black border. They were not obedient flames and the white man in many instances has suffered along with the black man because some loose mouthed, shallow minded, blundering creature last evening spread the lynch alarm and twelve base, brutal black men set out to "show 'em" and if need be to shoot up the town.

"It has been a hideous thing," he wrote in the concluding paragraph. *Some loose mouthed, shallow minded, blundering creature last evening spread the lynch alarm.* A true statement, even if, as noted above, the word "lynch" does not appear in the six-paragraph story that ran on the bottom of column eight of his city edition of the day before. Actually, not really a true statement, come to think, because, whatever else you wish to say about him, or think about him, Richard Lloyd Jones was never shallow-minded.

His wire-service piece (surely he was paid) appeared in papers in America on Thursday, June 2. Two days later, in Tulsa, he essentially rewrote that article as an editorial for his editorial page—only now, in his own backyard, he could afford to say it all. It was as if the first piece had been the dry run for the second. (There's also the distinct possibility that the wire-service editors in New York had watered down his language, if not his beliefs.) The riot was major news throughout the country. On page one of the *Tribune,* an unbylined piece began: "The blood of Tulsa, shed in the race riot of Tuesday night and Wednesday morning, will wash the city to its deepest, darkest depth." It isn't possible to know who wrote that—but the sentence has his stylistic sound. On page 3, the editor published, under his own name, his regular Saturday Sermonette. This one was titled "Hypocrisy." He wrote: "Hypocrisy is the homage vice pays to virtue. Because it is the mask that hides all vice, it is the greatest vice. The bad man, at best, is bad, but when he pretends to be saintly he is vicious." And a few paragraphs later: "The hypocrite despises those whom he deceives. And, because he is untrue to others, he is untrue to himself and comes to despise himself."

The editorial of June 4 was unsigned, as was usually the case. But can there be any doubt the words are his? You need only compare them

to the words of the wire-syndicate piece. It's essentially the same story of the 2nd, just viler. The headline: IT MUST NOT BE AGAIN.

> Such a district as the old "Niggertown" must never be allowed in Tulsa again. It was a cesspool of iniquity and corruption. . . .
>
> In this old "Niggertown" were a lot of bad niggers and a bad nigger is about the lowest thing that walks on two feet. Give a bad nigger his booze and his dope and a gun and he thinks he can shoot up the world. And all these four things were to be found in "Niggertown"—booze, dope, bad niggers and guns. . . .
>
> The Tulsa Tribune makes no apology to the Police Commissioner or to the Mayor of this city for having plead with them to clean up the cesspools in this city.
>
> Well, the bad niggers started it. . . .
>
> These bad niggers must now be held, and what is more, the dope selling and booze selling and gun collecting must STOP.

The editorial ran to eight paragraphs. It's as if Richard Lloyd Jones had just written "Stop" on his life. For the rest of his life he would try to avert his eyes from that editorial. And so would his newspaper, and so would his family, long after Jones was dead.

By the way, you won't find that editorial in the state edition of Saturday, June 4, 1921. It appeared in the city edition, and then got disappeared. In its place was an editorial that Jones had run the day before, on Friday, headlined TULSA WILL. That one was about Tulsans needing to stand proud, work together, heal the terrible wounds of fratricide. It isn't possible to say who yanked the "bad nigger" piece from the city edition on the 4th, before it could get into the state, but all I can think is that cooler heads in Jones's employ must have momentarily prevailed on him.

Another *by the way*: A week later, on Saturday, June 11, with Greenwood pooling and incandescing, smoldering, his paper did it again, or a form of it. The editorial was headlined IT MUST BE STOPPED. Can I prove without doubt that Jones himself wrote it? I cannot. But I can say without doubt that he was known to write the great bulk of the editorials in his own newspaper, and the language and style here are once again his. The piece speaks of "the heroic defense by the white men who stood their ground and saved this city from a more serious disaster than that which we experienced." The piece speaks of how it is "well established that lawlessness was allowed to run unarrested in the old 'Niggertown.'" It attacks *The New York Times* for not understanding the situation and quoting one-sided reports that are "viciously untrue." The piece says that "the bad negroes will trump up the lie that the whites started it." The piece declares that "America is not going to submit to any attempt to shift responsibilities."

The *Tribune*'s readers get their bylined Saturday Sermonette that day, too.

That man on the station platform in the chaotic Spring Green midnight dark isn't standing there yet. He's in his corner office at Carroll and Doty in downtown Madison, directing coverage, trying to make first sense of a bewildering news flash. Because of all the 1914 war news flooding out of Europe, Dick Jones's *Wisconsin State Journal* is now appearing four times a day: an 8:30 a.m. early birder (even though he runs an afternoon daily, he's trying to go head to head with his rival, the *Democrat*), the noon paper, the city at 4 p.m., the final at suppertime.

Frank Lloyd Wright is on the South Side of Chicago, his knuckles going white against a table. Actually, maybe by the time a Linotypist begins to set the first line of type on a metal slug in the *Journal*'s first-floor composing room, a stricken man and his second boy are in a taxi, bolting toward Orchestra Hall, or have already reached the eighth floor of his Loop offices.

Was the *Wisconsin State Journal* the first paper in the country to get out the first printed word on August 15, 1914? I can't prove that, but I think so. It might have been somewhere around 2:45 p.m.

To read his newspaper's coverage that Saturday, and in the several days following, is to imagine, however rightly or wrongly, powerful things about Richard Lloyd Jones's state of mind. His paper's first paragraph under an **EXTRA!** that's huge and black: "A negro employed by Frank Lloyd Wright on his estate near Spring Green went insane today, killed three people with a hatchet, wounded several and then set fire to the Wright bungalow, which is now burning."

Actually, it *was* ongoing: Taliesin *was* burning as Madisonians were reading about it.

Mamah's son is "missing. It is not known whether he is kidnapped or killed."

The next day, in the Sunday paper, the same kind of continuousness, ongoingness: "Little Martha Cheney also unrecognizably cut . . ." But, of course, she had died the day before.

A few paragraphs later, a run-on sentence, which in its own way might suggest the run-on disbelief in his mind: "Carlton had been here about two months, he had been pleasant."

The next day, Monday, picking up from some error-riddled accounts in the Chicago papers, which had entrained their reporters to the scene: "The big negro Carlton stood at the door and with the frenzy of a fiend sunk a shingler's hatchet into their skulls as they rushed through. Not unlike the manner in which cattle are butchered in the stockyards."

This very bad man is being variously referred to in Jones's paper, over a run of days, until coverage dwindles, as "butcherer of seven people." "Negro fiend." "Maniac."

Sometime late that Saturday afternoon, or maybe early that evening, Dick Jones got into his car and drove the fifty or so minutes to Spring Green. (He seems to have gone alone.) And, as you've heard by now, some hours later, under the platform eave, with perhaps admixtures in him of sorrow and pity and rage and cousinly love but also a not-quite-concealed relish, he was reported to have taken by the coat collar a just-detrained and now fairly emotionally naked relative and said to him these twisting-in words: "Stand up, Frank! It couldn't be worse, get hold of yourself!" According to John Lloyd Wright, Cousin Richard "thundered" the words.

———

Here is what I contend. After August 15, 1914, what had been a predisposition in a hubristic man for an absolutist way of thinking became only more absolute. There were "good Negroes" in the universe, as exemplified by Booker T. Washington, and there were "bad niggers" in the universe, as exemplified by Julian Carlton. Did Jones ever write or say the latter such thing directly about Carlton? If so, I have never found a record of it. If he had, it would make everything direct and limpid. We'd have the smoking gun. I know for a fact he never wrote a "bad nigger" editorial in the *Wisconsin State Journal.* (Indeed he never wrote an editorial at all about the events of August 15—and that is astounding to me.) No, that kind of language, which would have never played in the enlightened university town of Madison, would have to wait for racist Tulsa. But the fact of the absence of such an editorial or other piece of signed writing in the aftermath of the events of Taliesin doesn't keep me from believing that he saw the worth of African Americans in precisely such stark, bifurcated terms. That's a word I earlier used: "bifurcated." I contend that long before he ever relocated to Oklahoma, and well before Julian Carlton's apparent madness, this kind of tragic and almost schizoid way of thinking had grown deeply into the head of Frank Lloyd Wright's first cousin—and that what occurred at Taliesin only solidified, heightened, the predilection in him.

There's another thing I contend in regard to Richard Lloyd Jones, and it is equally crucial to an understanding of him. And here, at least, there is more direct evidence. It is intimately bound up with the disposition to the Manichaean frame of mind: namely, that in the years after Taliesin's tragedy, Wright's cousin made a steady, hardening pivot away from the liberal values of his Unitarian family heritage toward something on the militant other side. In a word, he went from a progressive to a right-wing hawk. He went from pacifism to jingoism. He went from hatred of war to all-out support for war. It was the same dualistic thinking that permitted no room for argument or error. It's all there in his editorials in the *State Journal.* You can track it. It didn't happen in a swoop. It was a cumulative process. But when he went over, he ended up going over all the way. And the actions of Julian Carlton—or so I believe, if cannot stone-hard prove—were an inextricable part of his going.

The savagery at Taliesin doesn't represent cause and effect; no, it was in gear before then, and everything was of a piece, with the tragic fulfillment coming one day in a place far from Wisconsin. And what's more, in order to make this 180-degree turn from where he'd once been, politically, philosophically, humanely, Dick Jones was forced, in effect, to slay not just one but two fathers.

Go back to his photograph. I spoke of it as having been uncannily snapped at a hinge-point in his history. Broadly, I was referring to World War I and America's declared entry into it, which was eight months off. But particularly I was referring to his relationship with Robert M. La Follette, which was just about, at the moment of the closing of the lens, to sever for all time. You can't read the *State Journal* in this period, from mid-summer 1916 into mid-1917, certainly not its editorial page, without coming on words like "American" and "patriotism" and "Stars and Stripes" and "honor" and "duty" and "flag." On Jones's editorial page was a huge furling flag with the words "For Our Country" beside it. The editor had already broken with his own father over America's possible entry into the war. Jenkin Lloyd Jones had become the loudest voice in all of Unitarianism against going to war against Germany. (His spouse, Susan Lloyd Jones, Richard's mother, had died in 1911, and in 1915, the seventy-two-year-old preacher had married Edith Lackersteen, who'd long worked for him in his mission on the South Side. She was said to be an imperious woman much unloved in the Lloyd Jones Wisconsin clan. One theory is that Uncle Jenk's increasingly louder pacifism was driven by Edith. Almost certainly the stepmother, who had arrived in the family quite late, had something to do with the emotional estrangement of father and son.)

Fighting Bob, the second father, the anti-interventionist and self-proclaimed man of conscience? He became the scourge of the United States Senate. There were calls for his expulsion. Nationally, he was denounced in editorials and cartoons—but nothing in the way the editor of the *Wisconsin State Journal* denounced him, mocked him. It was personal. A few years before, Jones had told his readers: "Robert M. La Follette is the ablest and truest statesman America has produced in half a century." Now, he was a traitor, a pro-German agent. His conduct was treasonous, he was a moral coward. (La Follette would end up suing him for libel. At the 1918 trial, realizing he faced bankruptcy, the editor recanted, if not exactly apologized. The lawsuit went away.)

On February 13, 1917 (six months after the cook-an-egg-on-a-Madison-sidewalk photographic moment), the editor began an editorial that had neither his father's name nor La Follette's in it—but it was about them, in one echo or another: "It's about time that we began to fly the American flag, talk about the United States, think of our national honor, our national welfare and not like a lot of cowed creatures who plead so piteously for peace that we lose all sense of justice." Two months later, the editor who had once admired all things Teutonic wrote: "The Kaiser is the most cruel and arrogant creature with power that ever lived. He is the arch enemy of the world. He and the whole crew of Hohenzollerns must be CRUSHED."

The same either-or language of Tulsa.

Which Booker T. Washington didn't live to witness, even from afar. He had died on November 14, 1915 (nine months before Jones semi-leaned back in his editor's chair for the portrait photographer). The next day Jones had put the news of his death on page one (GREAT WORK IS ENDED), and on the next day wrote an editorial headlined THE FALLEN LEADER OF A RACE. The piece ran to more than a thousand empurpled words.

One week before Washington's death, D. W. Griffith's *Birth of a Nation* had opened in Madison. The editor of the *Wisconsin State Journal* can rightly be praised for attacking this racist work of pioneering film art—made by the Kentucky-born son of a slaveholder—the more so when other Madison officials were willing to register their seeming know-nothing admiration. Jones wrote a slashing front-page piece. But if you didn't know, you could also be fooled. The piece puts on view all of his split way of thinking. Yes, he is denouncing the movie—but for the wrong reasons, essentially. "The picture is wonderful," he says. "Its battle scenes are masterpieces of mimicry." The chief reason he hates it is that it desecrates the American flag and the boys in blue who fought to preserve the union. Griffith dishonors the name of Abraham Lincoln, whose cause the editor has personally championed throughout his journalistic life. He allows that the movie will help foment race hatred, but this seems not his driving concern. The name of the movie itself "is an insult to George Washington." At the back, he attacks the Ku Klux Klan. And yet, within a few years, in another state, a moral hypocrite will be all but promoting the Klan, defending their crusades for law and order. In racist Tulsa, that card will play, raise circulation.

(You can track the either-or thinking in regard to black people in other ways in these years. Five months before Booker T. Washington died, Jones ran a news piece about a supposed local den of iniquity on East Washington Street. It "was a loitering place for negroes." That word, "loitering," would have special resonance in the baiting-into-being of the Tulsa Race Riot.)

In the late summer of 1917, Jones's managing editor, a principled man named William T. Evjue, had had enough of slandering La Follette. He resigned and started his own paper. For a while *The Capital Times* seemed to have little chance. But slowly it won over its readers, even as Jones kept overplaying his hand with his continued abuse of Fighting Bob and, now, with his slurring of the supposedly pro-German University of Wisconsin. (Fighting Bob's wife, Belle Case La Follette, a national figure in her own right, came in for Jones's slandering as well.)

Uncle Jenk died on September 12, 1918—in the Lloyd Jones home valleys. He'd made nearly seventy-five. His son was with him for the last four days and announced the death to the Chicago press. The two had never been able to fully reconcile emotionally, let alone politically.

By 1919, losing the circulation war to the *Cap Times* (from nearly the start people were calling it this), Jones knew he had to unload his paper. On July 1, 1919, the new ownership (a chain of papers out of Davenport, Iowa) took over the *State Journal*. Within a few months Jones and his wife and three young children—with Amy Comstock and a few other loyalists figuratively and almost literally in a belching wake—motored toward the wide-open spaces of Oklahoma. (Years before, at *Collier's*, he had reported a piece on the nation's newest state and decided he liked it a lot.) He'd found a new paper down there, the *Tulsa Democrat*, which he'd soon rename the *Tulsa Tribune*. By December, full of beans, he had it up and going.

A year and a half later would come the overnight of gasoline frenzy.

Those months leading up to Memorial Day 1921 need not be told in full here. Essentially what happened is this: The new editor seized on a campaign of law and order that, as time went on, got increasingly whiffed, undertoned, with racial implication, tropes. Was it deliberate? It is difficult to conclude otherwise. The cynical view would be that a soulless man who really didn't stand for anything except his own gain had stepped figuratively from his dust-laden touring car upon arrival and decided that law and order would be the story that would play, and that he would use it to go about "dog-whistling" into existence a race riot. I don't believe the second part at all. Rather, he'd made the political turn. Rather, he'd hardened. Rather, he'd gone to a far other side from the ideals of his youth and earlier adulthood—and Tulsa is what came out of it. At bottom was the same kind of absolutist, either-or thinking that, back in Wisconsin and earlier, in New York, had been channeled toward liberal causes. Down here, anti-crime was the righteous cause. If the cause would also, conveniently, along its way, in a largely racist society, net him some racist readers, well, okay, in fact, better than okay. He sorely needed readers, of any stripe. He was in hock to his creditors. So the morally expedient man played a card. So the sorrow and catastrophe waiting to happen happened. And once it did, what did the editor do? Largely double down. Write some post-riot racist tracts that would follow him into eternity. More than anything, I believe, it was the hubris. It was the cursed Lloyd Jones pride. It was the inability to say *I made a grievous mistake.*

You can't read Jones's editorials in the year and a half before Memorial Day weekend 1921 and not be aware of the drumbeating law-and-order theme: Let's catch the crooks, let's wipe out the vice in our city, let's clean up the damn place. There is a historian of the Tulsa Race Riot named Scott Ellsworth. He is white and grew up in Tulsa and loves the place much. (He teaches in the Department of Afroamerican and African Studies at the University of Michigan.) In 1982 Ellsworth wrote the first scholarly work of modern times on the riot: *Death in a Promised Land.* He held nothing back. He is also one of the main authors of the governor's 2001 riot commission report. He charts Jones's anti-crime editorial stance, with its increasing racial implications and undertones. In early February 1921—so roughly four months ahead of the riot—Jones ran a front-page news story about the possibility of the Ku Klux Klan spreading into Oklahoma. (It's a knotty question as to how much of a factor the Klan played in the actual riot itself, which is to say the burning and the looting and the killing of that night. In essence, the answer among historians seems to be that the Klan really didn't get started in Tulsa in serious ways until *after* the riot. Eventually the Tulsa Klan would grow so stuffed with membership that it would be able to build its own brick auditorium, Beno Hall. Beno, it was commonly said, stood for "Be No Nigger, Be No Jew, Be No Catholic.")

The *Tribune*'s February 4, 1921, piece, which featured a large photograph of hooded figures, was almost literally a Klan press release. It quoted the Imperial Wizard, who claimed, in effect, that violence was anathema to his organization. (Not quite a year later, on Christmas Day 1921, which is to say seven months after the riot, Jones would publish an editorial proclaiming: "The K.K.K. of Tulsa has promised to do the American thing in the American way.... There are many noble-minded, right-minded men working in the K.K.K., believing that the failure of our public officials warrants drastic action.")

In those months before the riot, the editor gave much coverage to lynching threats across the state. By mid-May 1921, his editorials were taking on a more ominous tone. "The people of Tulsa are becoming awake to conditions that are no longer tolerable." Two days later, a Jones editorial threatening that if the mayor and the city commission didn't get going, "an awakened community conscience will do it for them." Five days later, an in-depth front-page report about corruption in the police department and about the gambling, the loitering, the unchecked prostitution in Tulsa's black community. (In some areas of town, the piece alleged, there were whites and blacks doing sordid things together.) A judge was quoted: "We've got to get to the hotels. We've got to kick out the negro pimps if we want to stop this vice."

On Thursday, May 26, 1921, Jones published an editorial that began: "Lawlessness to fight lawlessness is never justified." It *seemed* as if he was suggesting that such a path was the wholly wrong way. But underneath it, the racial whiff? To my reading, that's the implication of the entire piece. Two days later, the morally hypocritical man—going almost daily to room 500 of the Tulsa Hotel for assignations with his secretary/associate editor—ran his Saturday Sermonette about the perils of conscience. It contained that pregnant line: "The voice of conscience was never silenced without retribution." To quote historian Ellsworth, in his riot commission narrative, it was about forty-eight hours later, "in this highly charged atmosphere, that two previously unheralded Tulsans, named Dick Rowland and Sarah Page, walked out of the shadows, and onto the stage of history."

And you know the rest.

———

There is a set of letters. They run to perhaps as many as 50,000 or 60,000 words. They are between Frank Lloyd Wright and his first cousin. The bulk of them—the ones that have survived—date from late 1928 into early 1933. Their ostensible subject is the huge, leaky, over-cost, glass-and-textile brick, artistically dead-ended, and—to my mind—ugly Tulsa home called Westhope that Frank Lloyd Wright designed for Richard Lloyd Jones and his wife roughly a decade after the Tulsa Race Riot. Wright scholars have made much of these letters. In many ways they are even richer than the exceedingly rich correspondence between Wright and Darwin Martin in Buffalo. Blood is ever thicker than water, and Lloyd Jones blood can pump hilariously with its vitriol and its love and its rankness of ego and pride. The letters are full of gorgeous insult. They are a hoot to read. Their constant subtext and overtext is that both men, the hubristic architect and his hubristic client, have each other's number. And yet I can't help reading them in another way. And the word "hoot" does not apply.

In these tens of thousands of words, the pogromming of Greenwood never comes up, not overtly, not by name, not once. But it's there. There are Wright's references to a "baptismal of fire and ashes—volcanic I would say." That sentence is followed by this one: "For those who can survive it it's swell." Again he's not talking of Tulsa, not per se. And yet. But still.

You hear things from him like: "Do not try to bang whang everything and everybody just because you are a damned 'printer'—, whenever we're in trouble there—See?" That letter ends with this sentence: "Now, what can I do to make you easier in your mind?"

You hear things from him like: "It is your fault that striking quick and hard as you do you must often miss. . . ."

You hear things from him like: "You have double the punch I have when you deal with the opposition—and are more ruthless. More power to the punch of your capable pen."

But then other kinds of notes, hidden and not hidden. From a letter quoted at the start of this book, only now to quote it at fuller length: "And what is a home anyway Richard? I'm not conscious of ever having had but one and I did give that up that I might be good friends to my children instead of a father and do something for their mother than nagging it out with her for the rest of our natural lives. . . . I've met with terrible misfortunes and accidents in trying to have another [home]. . . . There is a good deal of sadness back of all the bravado and though you may not know it, I too have fought a good fight." (The word "fought" was typed as "faught.")

From Wright's side of these double-boomeranging letters (every time I go back I feel and find something more, hiding in plain sight), there is generally an artful wheedling for more funds, at least once the contracts have been signed and the commission is actually under way. Ahead of that, and behind it, he can let out far more bluntly the central thing that he knows about his cousin. In my view, you can accuse Frank Lloyd Wright of just about any sin under the sun—but not of moral hypocrisy. He likes to put his so-called sinning right in your face.

This letter, about hypocrisy: written on November 6, 1928, when the talks about building a house on four sloping acres on South Birmingham Avenue in South Tulsa are seriously getting started and yet no money has been thus far exchanged. "You are not a bad fellow, Richard Lloyd Jones, and my affection for my cousin goes deeper than his prejudice or any predilection of his. . . . But you have a curse on you, old man, that your experience here will not dispel,—you are a Puritan and a publican of the worst stripe. The hypocrisy necessary to be these things is bred in the bone, dyed in the wool, and as natural to the man as the kink in his hair or the color of his eyes. But I know the 'righteousness' that moves a man to his characteristic acts, is usually the good in him, not the flower gone to seed. In your case, Richard, gone to seed too soon."

That letter prompted, three weeks later (he'd been away), a nine-page, single-spaced, typed response of hot denial—which only proved the arrow had arrowed straight to its mark.

Wright addresses him now and again as "my dear sermoneer." At one point he says, "Buck up, Richard." Is that a half-conscious and two-decade-old echo from words reportedly thundered at him on a train platform on the worst night of his life?

For his part, Cousin Richard can be brutal—in fact, more brutal than Wright, because he holds the purse strings. He knows that his architect is financially on his knees. On May 25, 1929, he tells his cousin: "You have no idea Frank how terribly ignorant you are. I mean just that, ignorant. . . . All you know is Japanese prints and tapestries and horizontal lines and angles to please the eye of the greatest artist in the world. To any man of sound sense, Frank, you are simply hideous."

Six months earlier, from sermoneer: "You covet attention. . . . Christ tried to teach us to love one another, to live generously, unselfishly, with thoughts of others. Would you like it if somebody, strutting, self-seeking, self-centered charmer came into your home and charmed your wife away? You would not. The lesson of the Golden Rule never reached Frank Lloyd Wright. . . . You are a house builder and a home wrecker. . . . You sneer at your own country. You call it ridiculous. You are essentially a man without a country. Like a chanticleer you strut around, thinking you are bigger than your country. . . . But your absurdly high visibility and self-seeking and self indulgence, self glorification set you off by yourself and you stand squarely before yourself blocking your own progress."

Maybe only the blooded sons of two ministers could talk to each other like this and somehow still remain so deeply involved with one another. In 1941, a decade after Westhope had been built, in another exchange that had to do with old lingering grievances about money, Wright wrote a three-point letter. It went like this: "ONE. How you stink!" He elaborated on the stink and then went to point "TWO. But for that, you and I might have done a great work together." He was talking about his cousin's envy of him. Which led him to point "THREE. And since when, but for that low-down cousinly jealousy, is the spread of my peacock's tail any skin off your fat old behind, my dear cousin?" He wasn't done, though. "IN CONCLUSION. Is the stink only to prove that instead of drying-up you are rotting-out?"

"Rotting out" is not a description you would think to attach to the baiter of the Tulsa Race Riot if you were tracking his life only from the outside in the forty two and a half years given to him past Memorial Day 1921. It was the hubris, principally. He kept right on with Amy Comstock, whom, as we know, he had put on his masthead as an associate editor, right next to the name of his own spouse, whom he'd also made an associate editor. Not even a year after the ashes of Tulsa, his political enemies in the town's white power structure—whom he had pilloried constantly in his pages—entrapped him (by spying through that hotel keyhole) while he was doing nasty things with Comstock. Let the details be spared here, but the sworn statements from hired private dicks are in an inch-thick set of documents donated to the archives of the Tulsa Historical

Society & Museum. (There is a rich irony attached to this fact: Descendants of Jones's family helped establish the society and its headquarters as a way of doing civic good for Tulsa.) To me, the most shocking thing is not the descriptions of some of the over-the-top sex but the snickering of the lovers about Georgia Lloyd Jones. They knew that she knew. Had long known. Georgia Lloyd Jones—whom everybody, including Frank Lloyd Wright, called "George"—was, by all accounts, a woman of great dignity. You can see it in the old photographs. She dresses beautifully, has a slender figure, at least till late age. George Jones wasn't going to let her marriage go under. She was a small-town Wisconsin girl whose own prominent father had kept a mistress, an open secret. At the time of the keyhole spying, George and her husband were raising three children, the oldest of whom, his father's namesake, was thirteen, and the youngest of whom, a girl, was eight.

At midday on March 21, 1922, the editor of the *Tribune*, having resuspendered his trousers and affixed his bow tie and having ridden the elevator to the hotel lobby, so that he could go back to his real office on East Archer Street, was confronted by some of the men who had the goods. It had to have been a shocking moment. What did he do? Doubled down once again. Rushed back to the paper and dictated a front-page editorial for the next day, denying it all: THE BULLIES ARE BUSY. He announced that he wouldn't be run out of town. He would "hurry to court any who libel or slander." He said: "We have edited this paper behind the typewriter. We can, and if need be WE WILL edit this paper behind the typewriter AND THE GUN."

The upshot? Although a city attorney issued warrants against the two for lewd conduct, the whole thing ultimately blew over. Jones owed the banks too much money for the *Tribune* to collapse. It is said that KKK members intervened to keep the warrants from being served. Jones apparently blew town for a while. So did Amy. She went to Milwaukee and stayed with her parents and wrote a pathetically sad letter of denial to her closest sister, Effie, who was married and lived in Detroit. She wrote on the top of that letter: "Please destroy this or lock it up, or return to me." She described how the whole thing was lies, how the enemies of "Mr. Jones" had stopped him in the lobby and "threatened him with some very unpleasant publicity." She spoke of a planted Dictaphone and of paid men who "reported seeing things."

(Amy died early—at age fifty-seven in 1944. She looked old-maidish by then. She'd never married. She'd been decorated with many awards as a pioneering female journalist. At her death no one mentioned the blame-shifting racist diatribe she had written a month after the riot for a New York social welfare magazine called the *Survey*. It was entitled "Over There: Another View of the Tulsa Riots." It had taken all its cues from the man for whom she had worked since 1911 on Carroll Street in Madison. It had passages like these: "It was in the sordid and neglected 'Niggertown' that the crooks found their best hiding place. It was a cesspool of crime. There were the low brothels where the low whites mixed with the low blacks. . . . There, for months past, the bad 'niggers,' the silk-shirted parasites of society, had been collecting guns and munitions. Tulsa was living on a Vesuvius that was ready to vomit fire at any time.")

In the years after the riot, the owner of the *Tribune* grew wealthy. He turned more staunchly Republican. He became a confidant of Herbert Hoover. He presided over the pre-convention campaign of Alfred M. Landon of Kansas in his landslide Republican loss to Franklin Roosevelt in 1936. He traveled widely. He established a vacation home back in his beloved Wisconsin. He took another mistress—or some of his descendants believe this. (She, too, was in his employ.) He ceded more and more editorial control of the paper to his children. He kept up his weekly sermonettes (and vanity-published them in hardback volumes through his own newspaper). Finally, in his eighties, he grew old and sickly. For the last seven years of his life he was mostly an invalid, keeping to a bedroom with tall windows in the ugly house (destined nonetheless for the National Register of Historic Places) that his first cousin had built for him. He was reduced mainly to nods and shakes of his head when grandchildren came over to splash in the pool and ask him something. Generally, they avoided him. Something about him was forbidding. His death, on December 4, 1963, at ninety, a fortnight after the death of JFK in Dealey Plaza in Dallas (he loathed Kennedy), made four columns of the *Tribune*'s front. The obituary perpetuated some of the more harmless and long-traveled lies—about college and so forth.

George Jones moved out of Westhope. She had never liked the old leaky place anyway. She wanted smaller quarters and so she traded places with a young restoration architect who was bowled over by the master's work. As she was packing up, the widow, who'd been married to her late husband for fifty-six years, surveyed some of the contents of the house. There was a giant framed oil painting of Dick Jones, unbearably full of himself. It wouldn't fit in the new place. She and her black maid, Helen Mae Jackson, who had served the family for so many years, carted it outside and cut it into pieces and set it on fire. They stood there watching it burn. Some years later George told one of her grown grandchildren that if she were ever to write a book about her marriage—which she wouldn't do—she at least had the title: *But Hath Not Love.*

In 1971, on the riot's fiftieth anniversary, the *Tulsa Tribune* produced on page 7a its first-ever article on the riot since the riot happened. It wasn't a large article. The deceased editor (whose middle child was now the editor and publisher and whose oldest child was president and board chairman) came out the hero of the riot, but perhaps just in the one small typo of the story (double use of "the") you can read the nervous lie of it all: "Richard Lloyd Jones, publisher of the The Tribune wrote a front page editorial in the June 1 issue, which did much to calm the stricken city. 'Lynch law leads not to law but to lawlessness and lawlessness to a repudiation of government,' Mr. Jones began." Yes, he had written that. This is how the 1971 so-called retrospective piece concludes: "For 50 years The Tribune did not rehash the story, but the week of the 50th anniversary seems a natural time to relate just what did happen when a city got out of hand." Out of hand. Hemingway would have called that an obscenity.

———

And so you wish to know how any of this long, interrupting, but not-interrupting fable connects directly to the life of Frank Lloyd Wright, other than the entirely self-evident fact (by now) that Wright was the close and complex blood relation of the morally catastrophic Richard Lloyd Jones? I can only meet your question with a question. It's the essential and basically unanswerable question I have been trying to ask out loud in one form or another from the first page of this book.

It's this: Is there some awful sense in which 1914 in Wisconsin led inexorably to (or maybe had to be avenged by) Oklahoma in 1921? Really, what I am driving at here is deeper, more far-reaching. Is it possible to think that if 1909 had never "happened" (the desertion of your family and the running away with another man's wife because the two of you in your love and giftedness and freethinking ways consider yourselves above the codes and sanctions that ordinary people try to live by and with), then 1914 might never have "happened," just as 1921 might never have "happened"? Does '09 lead to '14 and does '14 lead to '21?

I once tried out this hypothesis on a Wright scholar I admire. He laughed and said: "Pretty Catholic. Pretty Faulknerian."

But, actually, I am speaking of a chain of moral consequences that is even broader and more far-reaching and further-back-in-time than these lodestar events. You have barely heard in this narrative about Frank Lloyd Wright's father—or, more accurately, about what happened to Frank Lloyd Wright's father, in history, at the hands of Frank Lloyd Wright. But you will.

And why am I thinking in such unprovable directions at all? Because, as I've also tried to say in one form or another throughout this narrative, I believe Frank Lloyd Wright *himself* came to think in these directions—or at least to wonder about them: early on, for sure, and in the middle, but even more so toward the back end of his life. Again, as I've tried to say, and will keep on saying, keep on aiming to show, this not-quite-concealed wondering is something you have to search for in the margins, in the narrows, in the blue channels of an impossibly swirled life. A life, as Wright biographer Ada Louise Huxtable has succinctly said, you couldn't invent, because no one would believe it.

In one of his letters to his cousin, when he was building him his extravagant house, Wright said: "I could damn myself some damns that would make yours look like petting." In another, he said, putting the remark in quotes: "Perhaps 'a burnt child dreads the fire.'"

PART III

Shaking It from His Sleeve
The Year 1936

Design in art, is recognition of the relationship between various things, various elements in the creative flux. You can't invent a design. You recognize it, in the fourth dimension. That is, with your blood and your bones, as well as with your eyes.

—D. H. Lawrence, "Art and Morality"

There at the end, in his one-bulb cell, everything gone, or mostly, the killer cries, with what seems a tincture of redemption, self-awareness: "I didn't want to kill! . . . But what I killed for, I am! It must've been pretty deep in me to make me kill! I must have felt it awful hard to murder. . . . What I killed for must've been good! . . . When a man kills, it's for something. . . . I didn't know I was really alive in this world until I felt things hard enough to kill for 'em. . . ."

Julian Carlton? No. Bigger Thomas, in Richard Wright's 1940 hugely selling naturalistic and didactic novel, Native Son. *(It sold 215,000 copies in its first three weeks.) Bigger is a twenty-year-old emotionally stunted and desperately poor black man living on the South Side of 1930s Chicago, up from the Deep South, who goes to work for a rich white family. He commits rape and murder and decapitation and incineration with only the most limited understanding of what has made him act. That is, until the end, when the author has the condemned man (Bigger's going to get the chair) delivering his frenzied speech to his friend and communist lawyer, Boris Max. But some critics at the time didn't buy this scene, this speech, and doubtless more critics wouldn't buy it today, no matter how iconic the novel is in American literature. That was the trouble: it was a speech. It was unconvincing, unartistic. (Actually, many critics would doubtless say that about the whole sprawling work.) The sliver of seeming change in the brutalist man wasn't organic enough to all that had gone before. In 1949, James Baldwin, a fellow African American, newly arrived on the literary scene, with a need to slay the fathers, attacked Wright in a famous essay, "Everybody's Protest Novel." He said that "hatred smoulders through these pages like sulphur fire," but the hatred doesn't tell us anything about real life. He seemed to be asking rhetorically: How do you create an authentic story with such an opaque character at your core? How do you find someone's humanity when he seems all but sub-human?*

Blood and Bones

Taliesin, August 15, 1914

I t feels necessary to pick up from earlier pages some loose ends, dangled threads, not least the core question about Julian Carlton: Why did he do it? That won't be answered here, or anywhere else, by anyone, not ever, although a hedging theory will be offered. It may be as good as anybody's.

So: a last glimpse at the blood and bones—which is to say the actual life—of an opaque man, a seeming cipher, who was on earth for only a little more than two and a half decades. And in that time worked himself indelibly into a slice of American myth. In fact, maybe a couple.

Dangled threads. Julian's life in Chicago pre–August 15, 1914. We know so little of it.

Some of what we know, at least in regard to the period immediately before the 15th, we owe largely to the *Chicago Tribune*, which, in the days after the massacre, managed to get a lot of things wrong, even as the paper gave us material for history we wouldn't otherwise have.

As was said in a previous chapter, the contention here (if it cannot be proven) is that Julian had lived more or less invisibly in Chicago for at least several years prior to 1914, that indeed he may have arrived sometime after 1907 or 1908, which is the last trackable period of his Alabama life. His name appears in no Chicago directory or other kind of roll or listing (or none I could find him in) from 1907 through 1915, but that doesn't mean a lot in and of itself: thousands of itinerant black workers, without fixed addresses, up from Alabama or Mississippi or Georgia, moving in and around the South Side, in and around its famous "Black Belt," or, more accurately, what *became* the Black Belt, wouldn't necessarily have shown up on any 1907–1915 Chicago rolls or lists.

But is it possible, as I suggested earlier, that Julian, in his nineteenth or twentieth year, kissed Galon and Mariah goodbye and left Birmingham (maybe even in the company of an older sibling) and went somewhere else *first*? Perhaps, but my instincts say he headed straight north, toward the dream of Chicago, as part of what I've already described as the pre-wave of the Great Migration. I imagine him coming alone. Chicago is almost literally due north of Birmingham, 661 miles.

On the other hand, is it possible he came to Chicago in the company of the young woman—her age has never been substantiated, and we know almost nothing of what she looked like—who was already his wife, whether legally or in the common-law sense? If the world knows little about Julian Carlton, it knows a thimbleful about Gertrude Carlton.

On Monday, August 17, 1914, two days after the act, when a half-conscious man was carried to a chair in the passageway outside the grated door in his dugout Wisconsin cell for a preliminary arraignment (it took place in the early afternoon, and the prisoner was judged too weak by the jail physician to be brought into the courthouse next door, where half the county seemed to be waiting), the *Chicago Tribune,* purporting to be quoting Gertrude Carlton, at least indirectly, was telling its readers:

"The negress gave information tending to show her husband was insane. Carleton [*sic*] is a black, squat negro, and was once a Pullman porter besides recently being a servant to John Vogelsang, Chicago restaurateur. The Carletons were employed by Wright two months ago."

Gertrude was also being held in the county jail in Dodgeville, Wisconsin. (Dodgeville is the seat of Iowa County, which is where Taliesin is located. It's sixteen miles south of Taliesin. So many have gotten this wrong. The problem has to do with the Wisconsin River. Spring Green, on the north side of the river, is in another jurisdiction—Sauk County. So after his capture, the prisoner wouldn't have been taken there, even though Spring Green's jail was close by, and even though lawmen from Spring Green, and a lot of other places, had rushed in.)

Soon they'd let her go. Soon the authorities would put her on a train to Chicago with less than seven dollars in her pocket, at which point Gertrude Carlton, as more than one Wright chronicler has said, disappeared into the fine print of history. No one has ever been able to find a trace of her life after what happened at Taliesin. Did she marry and, if so, did she change her name? Did she bear children? What were those children told? It is conceivable one or more are alive. I am still searching that thread.

But regarding what Gertrude purportedly told the *Tribune*'s reporters, even if the words weren't placed inside quotation marks: her mate was hardly squat and he had never been a Pullman porter. He *had* worked for the Chicago restaurant owner John Z. Vogelsang as a kind of servant-butler-handyman in his home, for his family of four, up on the north side of the city, at 523 Deming Place. Gertrude had worked there, too, just as she worked at Taliesin before the fire and murders. Both Julian and his woman, or wife, seem to have lived at the Vogelsang residence for some months earlier in 1914, getting their room and board along with their wages. They may have worked for the Vogelsang family in parts of 1913, or even before that.

Vogelsang's Restaurant was on West Madison Street and was a name Loop lawyers and bankers and La Salle Street stock traders knew practically as well as they knew their own. It is my belief Julian had worked first in the celebrated noontime eatery itself (heavy German food, with the waiters in tuxes) and then up at the owner's ornate and forbidding-looking home. (More or less a stone hulk.) The second job followed the first. And why? Because he had done such a good job at the first—not as a waiter, but as a porter, or maybe even as a busboy or dishwasher. As for the relevance of such a fact, if it is a fact, it seems self-evident: even in a lowly position, in a large restaurant (maybe fifty or sixty staff), he had apparently impressed the owner enough that the owner asked him to come and work as a servant in his home. The masks of Julian.

After the massacre, the Vogelsang family would fall over itself to say what a fine employee and person he'd been. John A. Vogelsang—the restaurant owner's son, who was in his middle twenties and in business with his father—was quoted in several Midwest papers, particularly the *Milwaukee Sentinel,* as saying: "He was a good, honest servant and seemed rational at all times. He worked at our house with his wife and when he left his wife accompanied him. After he sought work with Mr. Wright he asked for a recommendation, which we gladly gave him." In early 1914, the elder Vogelsang had won the concession and catering contract for Midway Gardens. He became general manager. He and Wright saw a lot of each other in the winter and spring and early summer of 1914. Wright had apparently asked at some point: *Do you know a good Negro cook and butler?* (Wright alludes to this in his autobiography. Their friendship never really recovered. How could it have? As for Midway: by October 1914, with the gardens already facing bankruptcy, Vogelsang resigned, or was sacked.)

Julian's Pullman porter myth has gotten into any number of Wright books. The Pullman Car Company was headquartered in Chicago and had its own company town fourteen miles south of the city. Again, a Negro working as a porter on the railroad (just as with a Negro born in, say, Barbados or Haiti or some other exotic-sounding place) would have a certain worldly aura attached to his name, never mind that the working conditions for sleeping-car porters were exploitative and often humiliating. But, in any case, according to specialists in the Pullman archives I queried, there is no Julian Carlton who ever worked for the car company. So, again, was working for Pullman part of his many-layered self-invention? Or had one newspaper gotten it wrong, and then just the pass-along effect? The word "porter" in and of itself wouldn't necessarily have anything to do with the fact of being a porter on the railroad. In the second decade of the century, there must have been thousands of black porters around Chicago—at restaurants, hotels, offices, department stores—but only a relative handful who were the other kind of porter, turning down beds and shining shoes and rolling on steel to far places (while working a double-shift for lousy wages in a uniform that the company forced you to buy with your own money).

Earlier in that day's story (of the 17th), quoting Gertrude directly, this from the *Trib*: " 'We were well treated and liked the place,' the woman said [she is speaking of Taliesin], 'but my husband had the notion that he was being pursued. He recently got to waking me up in the night at our quarters in the bungalow to listen for noises.' " Those quotes sound half-invented.

She goes on: " 'They're trying to get me,' he kept saying. Then some times he would choke me and threaten to knock my brains out. He took that hatchet to bed with him. Two weeks ago he forced me to tell Mrs. Borthwick that we were going to quit because I was lonesome.' "

Acquaintances of the two, who knew them in Chicago, are quoted. They testify to his extreme excitability. There would be a whist party at somebody's house, and if he lost, Julian would erupt in fury. "He would leap around like a wild man. At other times he was morose and sullen, avoided other persons and gave every evidence of being a moron." In a way, it's almost as if the newspaper is describing a character named Bigger Thomas in a yet-unwritten fiction called *Native Son*.

A janitor at a South Side elementary school is found—at some point in 1914, Julian had worked as a kind of assistant janitor at Frances Willard School at St. Lawrence Avenue and Forty-Ninth Street. (The next day, on August 18, also in the *Tribune*, the janitor, John Keenan, would recall Julian's incessant smoking, and his "dopey" demeanor, and that he had to loan Julian a dollar for overalls on his first day on the job. But he showed up for the work.)

Also this, in the story of the 17th: "After they left the employ of Mr. Vogelsang the Carletons lived for a while at 4733 Evans Avenue. They shunned the neighbors and formed few acquaintances. Carleton's wife would flee from their home in terror of her life at times. . . ."

I've already spoken of 4733 Evans Avenue, but not of the larger significance of this address. It turns out to be an iconic, or near-iconic, spot, the epicenter of something that would someday get put into books. The neighborhood, that is.

To back up: Between 1910 and 1920, 50,000 Negroes from the Deep South came to Chicago. In 1910, 44,103 blacks were living in the city—and by the next census 109,458. The greatest part of this mass relocating occurred in the second half of the decade, when Julian was dead. But he was one of those 50,000 who came during the decade. In both literal and figurative ways, the Great Migration for the country and Chicago starts right here, or there.

The census numbers kept growing, exponentially, especially during the thirties. By 1944, 337,000 African Americans were living in Chicago. Almost all were confined to a city within a city. Which is to say a strip of land, a tongue, a kind of corridor that ultimately stretched itself out for something like seven miles, north to south. (At its greatest point, east to west, the tongue of land was said to be about a mile and a half in width.) This city within a city had a name: the Black Belt. It's what it was.

The "Black Metropolis"—which was the more dignified name that two sociologists affiliated with the University of Chicago, St. Clair Drake and Horace R. Cayton, gave to it in their landmark 1945 work of sociology and anthropology entitled *Black Metropolis: A Study of Negro Life in a Northern City*—became, in effect, the second-largest black city in the world. Only Harlem was larger and more renowned. By then, this belt was wearing another name, and its residents were damn proud of it: "Bronzeville." The words "South Side" had long taken on the status of myth among blacks in America. If Harlem was "Jazzonia," the South Side was Bronzeville. The Promised Land. Louis Armstrong and the poet Gwendolyn Brooks and the activist Ida B. Wells (who helped found the NAACP) and the baseballer Rube Foster (founder of the Negro National League)—to cite only four—lived for a time in Bronzeville. Lena Horne and Duke Ellington knew it. Sleek brown men with gold in their teeth curled nightly over silver horns in the low wattage of second-floor Bronzeville rooms. Gorgeously dressed women in impossible hats did the Saturday sidewalk stroll. The theaters and cafés and restaurants had dreamy names: The Dreamland. The Regal. The

Sunset. The Club DeLisa. The community throbbed not just with jazz, but with the blues and gospel, too. "Midnight was like day," Langston Hughes said. "The street was full of workers and gamblers, prostitutes and pimps, church folks and sinners." Was there grinding poverty and crime? Certainly. But all the glorious rest. A blue, hazy moment of history.

In its early years, the buckle on the belt of this invisibly roped off metropolis within a metropolis was the intersection of Thirty-Fifth Street and State Street. (That's the nightlife and commercial district Langston Hughes chiefly knew—and Richard Wright, too. His Bigger Thomas lived with his mother and sister at a made-up address that was quite close to Thirty-Fifth and State: 3721 Indiana Avenue. Wright, a sharecropper's son from Natchez, Mississippi, had come north to Chicago in December 1927 to experience "the warmth of other suns," which is the title the writer Isabel Wilkerson gave to her magisterial 2010 account of the Great Migration.)

In later years, from perhaps the late twenties onward, and into the thirties, the buckle on the belt began to shift southward, to Forty-Seventh Street. That's when Bronzeville became Bronzeville. There was a saying: "If you're trying to find a certain Negro in Chicago, stand on the corner of Forty-Seventh and South Park long enough and you're bound to see him." South Park was shorthand for South Parkway. (Today it is Dr. Martin Luther King Jr. Drive.)

In the early summer of 1914, two anonymous working people named Julian and Gertrude Carlton lived about three hundred feet from Forty-Seventh. All Julian had to do was exit the front door at 4733 Evans, turn right, and walk to the corner, and he would have been standing in the near heart of Bronzeville, except it wasn't yet Bronzeville. It doesn't matter. It's what I meant when I said earlier that I sometimes feel that this small, mysterious man had an uncanny gift for inserting himself into American myth. In this case, it would have been the mythic *pre*-place. But if anybody had wanted to find him, early that summer, he would have been right there. (Frank Lloyd Wright, early that summer, was due south—almost on a plumb line, as was said earlier—working at Midway Gardens. When he wasn't at home in Wisconsin.)

If you go to Julian's old neighborhood today, Forty-Seventh and Evans, you'll find some fast-food joints, including an Uncle Remus

Saucy Fried Chicken outlet with murals and civil rights history inscribed on its walls.*

———

Unsaucy, which is to say dark and rageful and mostly wordless: Julian in that almost lightless earthen cell at Dodgeville. Three times in the seven weeks before he dies, they bring him before the court. On Monday, August 17, the court comes to *him*. He is placed in the chair outside his door, seeming barely to be breathing. He whispers something that can't be understood. A formal plea of not guilty is entered for him. Reports the weekly *Dodgeville Chronicle,* the county's most important paper: "His seared throat is swelling. . . . He is unable to swallow. . . . He groans and tosses on his cell cot." Since Saturday he has been taking only milk from a spoon.

Ten days later, Thursday morning, August 27, nine o'clock: They get him into the courtroom. It's right next door. It takes the sheriff and five deputies. He has refused to walk, he keeps trying to fall down. The lawmen half-drag and half-carry him up the stairs and out onto the landing and into the courthouse and up to the second floor. You can't get a seat in that room today. Over five hundred people, including little kids riding in the saddle of their father's shoulders, are out on the lawn, hoping for a glimpse. They put him in a corner. He's in cuffs. He's moaning and mumbling. The deputies hand him slices of apple and bananas and orange peel—which he chews and spits out. He fidgets with a cup of water—will he knock it over? The *Chronicle,* reporting some of this on page one the following day, puts his weight loss at thirty pounds.

* Mysteries of his life: How is it he and Gertrude lived in a solidly built Victorian row house—cut up into rooms and flats—that seems to have been one of the houses on the street breaking the color line, at least if the 1910 and 1920 federal censuses are any evidence? In 1910, seven people are living at 4733 Evans, and all of them are listed as either black or mulatto. They are from Georgia, South Carolina, Tennessee, Kentucky, and Illinois. They list their jobs as porter on the railway or nurse or washwoman or streetcar conductor. Nearly every other residence on the block is white. Ten years later, in the next census, ten people are at 4733—most from the South (including Alabama). Again, all are black or mulatto. Julian's name appears on neither census (he is dead, of course, by the time of the second), but in the middle of that decade, for however long, he is in that house—I have no doubt. Which seems astonishing, because the "tongue" of black life on the South Side wasn't generally thought to have pushed nearly that far south by then. It was still up closer to downtown. Then the belt began to extend southward from, say, Eighteenth Street and State, eventually to Thirty-Fifth and State. But it would be a good while before the belt got as far down as virtually all-white Forty-Seventh. And yet, somehow, Julian was there, on Forty-Seventh, with a handful of others, in 1914, breaking the color barrier, in one conscious way or another. Just happenstance? And what kind of resistance might there have been to their presence?

Spring Green's *Weekly Home News* (they come out on Thursdays, so they're able to beat the *Chronicle* by a day) is also on hand, and they have him chewing the cut-up fruit and faking insanity and making faces at people as the charges are read. "He made no answer to the charges but 'Granted,' and Justice Arthur ordered a plea of not guilty to be entered to each charge."

(Time out: The *Weekly Home News,* a newspaper that Frank Lloyd Wright tended to read pretty faithfully throughout his life, and to carry issues with him in his suitcase when he had to leave town, covered the fire and murders extensively—no surprise. The surprise is that the paper accomplished some of the most convincing reporting of all, especially in the days right after August 15—that's the conclusion you reach when you go back and look at what its tiny staff turned in vis-à-vis many of their local competitors, not to say the gigantic *Chicago Tribune.* Not that the *Home News* didn't let its racism bleed blithely through. This sentence in its first report: "In the sweating process at Dodgeville the black brute said that the fire was an accident—that he lighted his pipe while cleaning a rug with gasoline." The further surprise is that the *Home News,* with which Wright sustained a long love-hate affair, was known for being one of his fierce critics. Its morally righteous editor, W. R. Purdy, had relished taking him on for his "insult to decency.")

At the conclusion of the event, and event is what it seems, the prisoner is formally bound over for trial to the circuit court, which won't convene in Dodgeville until late September. In the interim he is committed back to his cell. Incidentally, the day before, Wednesday, the sheriff of the county, John T. Williams, who's been professing his belief that his prisoner is not insane, and who has been trying to engage him in talk (it isn't really working), had decided to give him the freedom of the corridor outside his cell. But out there, Carlton had hurled a drinking cup at the lawman, and then a water pail, and then got hold of Williams's leg and wouldn't let it go. The officer, a burly man, had yelled for his deputy, who came bolting down the stairs. They had managed to get Carlton back in. Amid his weakness, these out-of-nowhere bursts of otherworldly power.

Two days after the August 27 appearance, the prisoner's wife, or woman, or ex-woman, for she claims to have renounced him completely, is put on a morning train for Chicago. *Gone.*

Now a month later. September 29, 1914. Tuesday afternoon, second day of the circuit court's fall term: seven divorce cases and a burglary also on the docket. His is the second case today—as if he's just taking his place with whatever legal matters have come to transpire in Iowa County, Wisconsin, since the last time Circuit Judge George Clementson came to town. (His authority in the case is superseding the local magistrate's.) Yesterday, the prisoner had been given a court-appointed attorney. (Ernest C. Fiedler is going to make fifty dollars for his efforts, paid to him by the county in the middle of the next month.) But the case doesn't proceed. The circuit judge, in consultation with two local doctors, and on the judgments of his own visit to the prisoner's cell, makes a last-minute decision that Carlton is too weak. However, a quick arraignment will be held and the charges read aloud. So, at 1:30 p.m., first business after the noon recess, they get him in, carry him in. They put him in a chair. He keeps sliding off the chair. They bring in a cot. He seems semi-catatonic. Against his refusal to speak, a plea is entered for him: not guilty.

(Time out again: I had long been told that no court records of all this exist—that, yes, some copies of things were available on microfilm, but that no actual documents have survived. But then, with some luck and the help of a generous county clerk, who got interested and registered her own great surprise at finding them, I was able to locate batches of the original documents. They were in big dusty books in a vault down in the unused portion of the courthouse complex—basically in the same area where Julian had been held, maybe thirty feet away. The long pages, cracking with age, are beautifully penned. As I've said before, to look at them now is to get a shivery feeling about how the bare *facts* of something can sometimes overpower almost anything you could ever make up: "It is remembered that at a regular term of the Circuit Court for Iowa County, began and held at the Court House in the city of Dodgeville in said county, commencing on the 28th day of September A.D. 1914. . . .") *It is remembered.*

CONDITION OF NEGRO CAUSES POSTPONEMENT is the *Chronicle*'s one-column headline, that Friday, October 2. Five days later, Wednesday the 7th, the accused is dead. Is anyone with him in his cell when he dies at about one p.m.? Isn't known. He is thought to have weighed less than ninety pounds. He had reportedly refused all food—

except once or twice when he had gorged from the tin plate the sheriff brought in. Two days after his death, a one-column story, accompanied by the one photograph that has survived: small man, denim shirt, close-cropped head, gazing down. "The negro has been dying for three days," the newspaper reports. "The sheriff told him so, and asked him to make an ante-mortem statement, but Carlton paid no attention." By then Sheriff Williams has filled in and signed the death certificate. Under *Cause of Death:* "Starvation—suicidal—following attempt at suicide by Hydrochloric acid."

The most famous occupant in the history of the Dodgeville, Iowa County, jail had lived for fifty-three days past his act. Had he spoken fifty-three words?

————

And so to circle back once again to the uncircumscribable question: Why did he do it? He did it because he was mad. Gone berserk. All the rest is anybody's argument, and has been, for a century. Some of the suppositions are daffy: he was put up to it, he was part of some kind of undefined conspiracy (possibly even involving Wright himself), he was overdue his back wages. (You attempt to destroy everyone and everything in sight because the master hasn't given you your pay envelope for a week or two? Doesn't parse, even for a madman, or a temporary madman.)

There is the long-running (and not quite parsable) theory that he had gotten it into his head that he was an "agent of the Lord," and thus must destroy these wanton adulterers. In 1965, in a brief memoir-history-biography entitled *The Valley of the God-Almighty Joneses,* Wright's adoring baby sister, Maginel Wright Barney, advanced this belief (those are her words, "agent of the Lord"), although she was hardly alone of his family with the theory. John Lloyd Wright, in the odd, crucial book that has been quoted several times, offered his own twist: "There were those of the clergy, too, who later from their pulpits used this tragedy as a moral lesson, calling forth endless expositions and quotations. I wonder if their previous criticism and prophecy of evil could have influenced the Barbados, who may have seen the possibilities for future glory for himself as the crime took shape in his warped mind." It's true that more than one Spring Green pulpit had railed against the sinners, although a lot of the railing had seemed to die down by the time Carlton struck. Wright biographer Robert C. Twombly addresses the pulpit-clergy-prompting theory in his 1979 book, *Frank Lloyd Wright: His Life and His Architecture.* Twombly's is an important and deeply researched study, with which I often enough find myself disagreeing. But not at all with this sentence: "And the rumor that the superstitious Barbadian emigre had taken it upon himself to punish Wright's 'immorality,' prodded by vindictive preaching at a local evangelical church, does not explain why he acted in the architect's absence." Precisely. And why would Julian have attended that church? He was black and possibly would not have been welcome. He was living out of town. He would have had to borrow a horse or a buggy, and that isn't likely, although it's more unlikely he would have gone in the first place—or have even known about such a church and service. And, besides, I don't picture him a churchgoer, even if he was descended from churchgoers.

On Monday, August 17, forty-eight hours from the rampage, the *Chicago Tribune* printed an exchange from the day before between one of its reporters and Edwin Cheney. The reporter has caught up to Mamah's former husband at the Spring Green rail depot. It's Sunday midday. He's going home, with the remains of his children in a little wooden box. *Reporter:* "Do you believe there could have been any other explanation of the crime? There have been rumors, you know." *Cheney:* "I am sure that he was insane and that there was no other reason." Conspiracy theorists love the word "rumors." What are the rumors the reporter has in mind?

The truth is that, in a century of looking, every theory comes up wanting, and yet two theories continue to bob over top of the rest. One can be done away with quick enough. Julian was enacting revenge because Mamah had dismissed him, and crudely. They'd gotten into an altercation. She'd mistrusted him from the start, and he had sensed it. She had used her power over him, over both of them, him and Gertrude, and it had driven him into a faceless rage. Firstly, that wouldn't have been in Mamah's character. She was a softer woman than that, albeit a softer woman with a great tensile strength. But a shouting episode doesn't quite fit, nor does an imperious manner. Secondly, there is convincing evidence to argue the case (just as Gertrude had said to the *Tribune*) that the couple had been intending to leave for at least several weeks, and had given notice to their employers. On the Wednesday and Thursday before the massacre, Richard Lloyd Jones's *Wisconsin State Journal* ran in its help-wanted sections a notice Wright seems to have placed there himself. The *Weekly Home News* had the same ad in its paper of August 13. The classifieds referred to a house in the country and the owner's need for "either two girls or married couple. Separate rooms with bath furnished. Forty dollars per month for two. Increase if satisfactory." Interested parties should apply to Frank Lloyd Wright at Taliesin. (Taliesin came out "Taliesen"—doubtless a typesetter error.)

So, again, this theory doesn't stand up to light. Even as it hangs around.*

Maybe part of the reason it does is because, roughly eight days before the murders, Julian had supposedly gone to Madison to see a dentist. (Would hired black help earning low wages and living in the country go nearly forty miles to the city of Madison for dental work?) But he went instead to Chicago (on the train, it seems) and apparently wired his wife from there that he would be gone longer than he thought. (How do you not get in trouble with your employers for such a sudden absence?) In Chicago, he seems to have stayed on the South Side with Maurice Dorsey, one of his few friends, who lived with his family on South Wabash Avenue. (It's close, but not *that* close to 4733 Evans.) Dorsey, older, apparently more stable (he's listed in Chicago directories for several years running), worked as a porter at Vogelsang's. (It's my thought that Julian would have originally found work at the restaurant through Dorsey. And this is also why I believe he would have been employed at the restaurant first, and while there caught the owner's eye for his hard work. And, by the way, when he was at the restaurant, did he ever bus Wright's table, their paths crossing even then? Wright frequented Vogelsang's.)

Why had Julian gone secretly to Chicago in that brief period before August 15? Perhaps to try to line up a job once he and Gertrude returned. (Back at Vogelsang's?) And yet, out of this bare fact—that he

---

* No Wright researcher has explored more fully—and, it has to be said, more pedantically—the dozens of theories than the late University of Wisconsin literature professor William R. Drennan, in his 2007 *Death in a Prairie House.* I am grateful for his research, even as I have sought to do my own. The book's tone is exceedingly odd—as if the author were conducting some kind of high-horsed and personal inquest.

had turned up in Chicago shortly before what happened—have arisen some laughable conspiracy theories. For instance, that he and Wright, down at Midway, had hatched the whole thing. But why? Oh, forget it.

Which essentially leaves one remaining theory, the most credible and widely held. It hangs on the name Emil Brodelle. He was the approximately thirty-year-old Wright draftsman from Milwaukee, known for both his drawing skills and his quick temper. *Had* Brodelle, two or three days before the act, ordered Julian to saddle his horse, and when Julian refused, called him a "black son of a bitch"? *Had* they gotten into another altercation on Friday the 14th, not twenty-four hours before it happened? Had there been earlier bad blood? No one knows for sure, but the legend is that Brodelle had so humiliated him that the servant had decided to take his revenge, but not just on the draftsman.

That Saturday night, in his Dodgeville cell, Julian had supposedly told a local man named Harper Harrison that Brodelle had insulted him and had even struck him and thus he'd made up his mind to get him. Harrison was a Spring Green harness maker and part-time deputy for Sauk County, one of the scores of lawmen and semi-lawmen and other volunteers who'd rushed in. At the preliminary hearing on August 27, Harper told this story. But how did he get into Julian's cell, and with apparently no one else there?

I can't buy the Brodelle theory. Not wholly. I can't buy the Harper Harrison. Not wholly.

Which is why I have spent a good deal of time, with only meager success, trying to understand things about the life of Sheriff John T. Williams. If you pore through the dozens of contradictory newspaper accounts, a hazy picture begins to emerge: of a good and decent and maybe even half-unwilling officer of the law standing up to his oath against lynch mobs. In those first hours after the killings, once Julian was in captivity, carloads of men were ganging at Taliesin with ropes and guns. Some would have been Williams's neighbors. He had spent his life in the area. He was in the Masonic lodge and was a deacon at his church. He was a farmer and a Congregationalist. (To move it out of time: He served as sheriff only once, from 1913 to 1915, and afterward went back to farming. For a time, he was an assemblyman. He died in a Madison-area nursing home in 1944, at seventy-eight, having lost his wife a few months before. For his last ten years he'd been stone-blind. His only son, who seems to have had no children of his own, got elected sheriff of the county a dozen years after his father had served.)

In his photographs, the sheriff looks blunt and blocky, maybe a 220-pounder, serious, although not unfriendly, and with a prominent ridgeline on his nose. On August 15, 1914, he was either forty-eight or forty-nine, his term in office was nearly done, and he'd be damned if he'd let his vigilante neighbors string up this madman before this madman got his moment of justice: this is the impression that seems to leak up through the old clippings. There are numerous stories about how he and his deputies with drawn guns had stood off the mob. "They'd better let me live if they expect to find out something," Julian had supposedly warned.

For the next seven weeks, no one was around Julian Carlton more in that dungeon-like space than the sheriff of Iowa County. He may have seen him daily. Williams and his family lived upstairs. Mrs. Williams cooked the jailhouse meals. Somehow, I can't help thinking of him as Julian Carlton's last friend on the earth—or semi-friend. I keep imagining him addressing his prisoner as "son." For certain he would have been trying to draw him out on what had happened, but I can't help feeling that he was also, in whatever way he was able, within the limits of his job and oath, trying to be kindly to someone who was clearly dying and hated by everyone in sight.*

Apparently, Julian acknowledged several times in those last days that he had killed Brodelle, but that he couldn't remember the rest of

---

* What seems remarkable is that it's all still there, more or less. You can go to Dodgeville today and stand outside the building where the old jail was—as was said earlier, it's right next door to the courthouse—and look at the bricked-up windows at ground level. Behind those windows, dug into the earth, are the old cells. On the front side, the wells have been filled in, and there's a huge Trane air-conditioning unit implanted there. In the rear, the bricked-up window wells are still in place, quite visible, and so are the bars across them. There are stories about Iowa Countians in 1914 trying to get a glimpse of the killer through the window-well bars. If you get *inside* the old jail annex, you'll feel everything in a much deeper way. Down a stairway, with the first step in need of re-nailing. On a hook: a flyswatter that could almost be vintage 1914. Then a double-thick wooden door with an iron clasp on it, and behind that door the narrow and dirt-floored passageway, almost like a catacomb, leading to a row of four or five cells. The light slants in through the windows at ground level, so not much light at all. This is what it was like for me the first time I saw Julian's stone cell, taken there by Tari Engels, the county's register in probate. The last time I stopped by the courthouse to say hello, they'd done a renovation and had connected the courthouse itself to the old jail and what had been the upstairs family quarters for the sheriff. By the way, this is the oldest courthouse complex in Wisconsin, made of beautiful native Galena limestone—with a plaque out front. What's down below is the unmarked historical artifact.

it. Apparently, the sheriff had persisted, and, again, I can only picture it as a gentle kind of persisting, parts manipulative but larger parts sincere, solicitous. *But why did you do it, son? He had disrespected you, is that it?*

According to the *Chronicle*, Julian, at one of these turns, had answered: "I guess you solved the question."

It doesn't quite parse. That he would have done all *that*? Because of Brodelle?

Sheriff Williams apparently never set down any written record of those conversations, although "conversation" seems like not the right word.

But a question: Could Julian have said it—"I guess you solved the question"—because the sheriff had wanted him to say it, and he knew it? To my ear, there is something wan in the words, something almost wishing to please. Just in that answer, maybe his last spoken sentence, a small feeling about his humanity. He was a monster—or he was a monster in his slaughtering moment. But his life had to have been other things, too. History prefers him to stay the cartoon of madness.

And so my theory, for what it's worth. Yes, it probably had to do with Emil Brodelle, but it was also something far larger and not definable, like the act itself. I believe a good part of it was rural paranoia, stoked by fear. I believe that old Alabama family ghosts had swarmed up inside. He'd arrived with his mate in the Wisconsin woods (well, Taliesin is not exactly in the woods, even if it's very rural) and everything came back— that life he had left behind as a boy, fled, with his family, when he was eleven or twelve, pre-Birmingham. (If only we knew more about that life.) All of it began speaking to him in his waking Wisconsin dreams, and in his sleeping ones, too. Some kind of *shining* overtook him. From testimony and reportage in the *Tribune* (in its long story of August 17), he was apparently already a moody person, prone to eruptions—that brief glimpse of him in Chicago, pre-Taliesin, bears it out. ("He would leap around like a wild man," if the trick-taking card game known as whist didn't go his way.) He must have worked very hard to keep this moody and erupting side out of sight of his employers. So, after some two months at Taliesin, the woods pressing in on him like a vise, the paranoid man gets a shingling hatchet, maybe from the toolshed, and sticks it under his pillow and begins proclaiming wild things to his partner. (On the death certificate, Sheriff Williams wrote in that the deceased was married, and yet Williams told the *Chronicle* that Julian had told him at the last that he and Gertrude were not married; that they'd been living together for two years.) In the end, whatever racist thing Brodelle may have sworn at him was almost immaterial. It only flint-struck the fuse. It might have happened anyway.

There must have been ten thousand things burning in his mind on August 15, 1914—I wrote this at the start of the chapter on Julian and his Alabama roots. But I do believe that swarming ghosts of a Deep South past are at least a part of the answer.

Let it be. All theories are suspect, in a sense.

———

In place of any real knowing, it's time to pivot. I will simply tell a different kind of story. It's about an ashen-faced and incredibly subdued man, late on Sunday afternoon now, about eighteen hours after it has happened. The early evening skies are threatening but holding off. All afternoon this man has been cutting down Mamah's garden—dahlias and nasturtiums and roses and zinnias and hydrangeas. He has put his carpenters to work fashioning a box with lengths of new-sawn pine, and the tenpenny nails hammered in clean.

In his own words, which are better than anyone's: "So I cut her garden down and with the flowers filled a strong, plain box of fresh, white pine to overflowing."

So often, Frank Lloyd Wright's writing can be obtuse, lofty, sententious, full of circumlocution, not to say ego. But at other times, as you've already encountered, he can drive the nail straight and true. In *An Autobiography* he gets into nine short paragraphs what no one else has ever come close to being able to register: all the sorrow of Mamah's burial. Vincent Scully, already quoted, once said: "The tragedy which occurred at Taliesin in 1914, more terrible than that which struck Oedipus, has been described by Wright in some of the most restrained and moving writing ever done in America." It's not an overstatement.

In both the 1932 and 1943 versions, the author kept the nine paragraphs nearly identical. To repeat: I nearly always prefer the 1932 version—but, in this case, the later edition has the tiniest improvements to make you feel it all even more deeply.

He tells how the men from Taliesin dig the grave in the family cemetery, under the trees, beside the Lloyd Jones family chapel. One of his uncles—Enos Lloyd Jones—has given consent for a non-family member to be placed among them.

Things are ready. Wright and his son John go over to his sister's house, at Tan-y-deri, where he has slept so badly last evening. He and John lift the body "and we let it down to rest among the flowers that had grown and bloomed for her." The next sentence, a gift of its own plainness: "The plain box lid was pressed down and fastened home." Workmen set the coffin on their shoulders and walk it a few feet and then place it on the back of a buckboard, a little spring wagon. It, too, is filled with flowers. He has cut down Mamah's entire garden, and the flowers are bowering and mattressing and lining not just the bottom of her box, but are serving as a blanket and cushion over top of her, inside the roof of the fastened box, while even more flowers are on the outside of the box, and all around the wagon, the petals spilling out onto the ground.

"We made the whole a mass of flowers," he writes. "It helped a little."

A little sorrel team—the horses' names are Darby and Joan, and they are almost ponies, whinnying—take the box in the wagon across the fields. Wright walks alongside the team. He has the reins loosely in his hands. His twenty-one-year-old son is behind. Two cousins wait at the churchyard gate. Then, "Together we lowered the flower-filled and flower-covered pine box to the bottom of the new-made grave. Then I asked them to leave me there alone." He wishes to fill the grave himself. The sun is starting to disappear down the backside of the valley's hills.

In these nine paragraphs, almost perfectly registered, there is one sentence that stands apart from the others. It's the only one that isn't direct, simple, unadorned. It's a very mysterious sentence, or is to me. You can't quite diagram it. The author seems to be speaking of some kind of force that he "dimly" perceives is "coming in far-off shadows of the ages," and that this force, or forces, are "struggling to escape from subconsciousness and utter themselves."

What is he saying?

It almost sounds as if he's talking about a hydra-headed monster let loose on the world.

Although I wouldn't presume to know Wright's true meaning, I think at least some of it might be this: he understands what has happened, and costs that will have to be paid, in his own life and elsewhere. Something he cannot control, but has nonetheless helped to set in motion, is out there, in the universe, having escaped the subconscious, wanting to utter itself, or themselves.

The next sentence, after the mysterious sentence, preceded by an ellipsis: "Then slowly came darkness."

Wright wrote these nine paragraphs in the mid- to late 1920s, about twelve or thirteen years after August 15, 1914 (about half a dozen years after the Tulsa Race Riot). Scully is right. The passage on Mamah's burial is its own little masterpiece, not only among the best words Wright ever put down, but almost rivaling in their economy of language what Ernest Hemingway was capable of in his finest moments. One of Hemingway's core writing values was to try to make the reader *feel* more than he or she necessarily understands.

The second-to-last sentence in the nine-paragraph passage is one that was quoted toward the start of this book, and it, too, is beautiful, even (or especially) with its quirkily placed comma: "All I had to show for the struggle for freedom of the five years past that had swept most of my former life away, had now been swept away."

Wright doesn't tell us so, but we know from other sources: the heavens afterward opened.

———

And those next days and nights, which stretched into weeks and deep into that fall? The sleeplessness, the boils, the fevers, the chills, the weight loss, the obsessive stalking of the grounds, the breakneck rides across moonlit fields, even as the rebuilding of his home was taking up and, in fact, going quite fast. Meryle Secrest's fine biography recounts a moment when he may have contemplated suicide. It was two days after the burial. The recent heavy rains, including a hailstorm, had burst the dam at the lake at the bottom of Taliesin. Wright was there when the breach happened. Water came whooshing down the creek and caught him at the bank. In those maybe ten seconds of not moving, or moving too slowly, was he like a man leaning out over a ledge of a New York skyscraper, wondering what it would feel like to take just one more small step? Billy Weston, survivor of the massacre, father of young Ernest

Weston, helped yank him to safety. Secrest: "He still, it seemed, wanted to live."

This was on Tuesday. That Thursday, August 20, just five days after, the *Weekly Home News* published a letter. It was headlined and boxed: FRANK LLOYD WRIGHT TO HIS NEIGHBORS. This letter has already been quoted—it's the one in which he writes about the black cunning face of Julian coming before him in his dreams. As was noted, he is by turns contrite and grieving and humble and haughty. He expresses his deep gratitude for the way the community has rallied around him. He has loathing for how the press, most especially the *Chicago Tribune,* has covered the catastrophe. ("The birds of prey were loosed upon her in death as well as in life. . . .") The life they'd known wasn't perfect. "Mamah and I have had our struggles, our differences, our moments of jealous fear for our ideals of each other—they are not lacking in any close human relationships—but they served only to bind us more closely together. We were more than merely happy even when momentarily miserable." And then, with sudden contempt for those whom he is thanking: "You wives with your certificate for loving—pray that you may love as much and be loved as well as was Mamah Borthwick." But his eloquence, too: "She was struck down by a tragedy that hangs by the slender thread of reason over the lives of all, a thread which may snap at any time. . . ." Ever the contradictory, cross-grained man.

Contradictory? Cross-grained? Not quite a month after the holocaust, the *Weekly Home News* has a report on the recent, annual, rural mail carriers' picnic. The idea is to get all of Sauk County's postal carriers together and to give them a late-summer salute. From the story: "A trip in automobiles to the Frank Lloyd Wright country home, 'Taliesin,' upon Mr. Wright's invitation, was participated in and enjoyed by the carriers and their friends, many of whom had never been south of Spring Green on the river road, across the big bridge in sight of the fertile valleys and hills of our neighboring county of Iowa." Next paragraph: "We are told that this was one of the most successful and enjoyable meetings the association has held."

Yes, a gay picnic for the mail gang, hosted at his still-charred property. Perhaps they sat out in the tall grasses of the nearby hills that afternoon, away from the traces of acrid scent. Was he walking around in suspenders and a summer white shirt, with a fat watermelon balanced on his shoulder, having plucked it himself from the garden, wanting to carve it up with a big butcher knife and personally hand out the slices? That was on September 7, 1914. Down in Dodgeville, the wasting man had exactly one month to live. The master of Taliesin had another four and a half decades to live. Some of his greatest professional triumphs—and eclipses—were still up ahead. And although you won't want to believe it, some of his greatest personal disasters as well. Yes, fire was going to be in the mix.

There was once a middlebrow culture and architecture critic named John Cushman Fistere. He wrote for Architectural Record *and* Ladies' Home Journal *and* The Saturday Evening Post. *He could turn a journalistic phrase, if nothing in the manner of Thurber or Mencken or A. J. Liebling. In December 1931, seeming to be sniffing some of his prose through his nose, he wrote a much-discussed appraisal of modern architecture for* Vanity Fair *entitled "Poets in Steel." The idea was to name the ten or so contemporary architects—of skyscrapers and other works—who had a chance of being remembered into the next century. He put Frank Lloyd Wright at the head of the list, but in a snarky way. What he was really saying was that the sixty-four-year-old was through. He called him an "aging individualist," the "idol of certain intellectuals," an artist with a "martyr complex," a builder "better known than his buildings," somebody who seemed "more genius than architect," and who, when you added it all up, had "designed comparatively few buildings to support his manifold theories." His dismissing final sentence about Wright, before he went on to handicap the chances of others on the list (Raymond Hood, Ralph Walker, William F. Lamb, Ralph Adams Cram, Harvey Wiley Corbett—and so on) was this: "As an architectural theorist, Mr. Wright has no superior; but as an architect he has little to contribute for comparison."*

The editors didn't even deign to use one of his drawings. They went with the renderings of his lessers, asnore now, like John Cushman Fistere, in their near-oblivion or even just plain oblivion, at least in terms of instantly recognizable American names. Uh, how about world names? Wright would have corrected that insult in a heartbeat.

Connective Tissue: Two

At Ocatilla, Chandler, Arizona, with Olgivanna and daughters, winter 1929

etween late 1914 and mid-1936, an interval of not quite twenty-two years, Frank Lloyd Wright got catastrophically involved with a mad morphine addict named Miriam Noel, built the Imperial Hotel in Tokyo, conceived a child out of wedlock, suffered Taliesin burning down again, spent a couple of nights in the Hennepin County jail in downtown Minneapolis on charges of moral turpitude, lost his house in foreclosure (the bankers even auctioned off his cattle), lost his beloved and no-longer-estranged *lieber meister* (he was there, in the last forty-eight hours or so, of Louis Sullivan's infinitely sad and squalid dying), experimented semi-successfully with textile block housing in California, got married for the third and final time, this time to a Montenegrin mystic three decades his junior (it was with her, Olgivanna, three and a half years before, that he had conceived that seventh child), gained Taliesin back, wrote his autobiography, built Westhope for his hotheaded first cousin in Oklahoma, went begging for work and clients, seethed at his professional obituaries, watched himself being replaced by lavishly embraced glass-and-steel European modernist darlings named Le Corbusier and Gropius and van der Rohe, began what he called the Taliesin Fellowship (as a wily way of trying to stave off both oblivion and further poverty), got his nose broken on Main Street in Madison courtesy of an enraged ex-employee to whom he owed $280 in back wages (the blood gushed out of him like an opened fire hydrant, and for a few days after he went around with a comic-looking plaster of paris holster riding down the ridge of his proboscis), and then, nearing the age of seventy and against all career and personal odds, came roaring back to something greater and even more arrogant than what he was before, if that can be imagined.

And that's only the half of it, what happened to Frank Lloyd Wright in these years. Incidentally, that monster sentence contains only the loosest chronology.

Baseball historians like to say that the greatest baseball team of all time—one of the greatest sports teams ever—was the 1927 New York Yankees. You know, Murderers' Row: Babe Ruth, Lou Gehrig, Tony Lazerri, Bob Meusel, Earle Combs—all the storied rest. (The team won an astounding 110 games on the way to a World Series sweep of the Pittsburgh Pirates.) Frank Lloyd Wright seems never to have given a bent T-square about the game of baseball, but in 1936 he had his own Murderers' Row at the plate. To name three: Fallingwater near Pittsburgh, the Johnson Wax administration building at Racine, and a little 1,550-square-foot, L-shaped, sandwich-walled, flat-roofed, slab-floored, radiant-heated, three-bedroom, $5,550 "Usonian" dream, on what was then the far western edge of Madison. It's there today, same spot, at the sloping northeast corner of Birch and Toepfer avenues, and it's known as the Herbert and Katherine Jacobs House. (More accurately, it's the Jacobs House I, but that will be explained.) The contention here is that the Jacobs—the "Jake," as I like to think of her—is the greatest of these wonderworks, even if most professional critics would surely disagree. The Jake is like a Russian hand-painted egg of a human shelter, in all her brick-and-wood simplicity. And within those 1,550 square feet are some profound implications for the world we inhabit now. The first time I caught sight of her lacquered beauty, I wanted to reach over, pluck her off her concrete pad, and nest her in my palm. The Jacobs will be the center of gravity for what I have to say about the miracle year 1936, Frank Lloyd Wright's '27 Yankees.

But I can't tell about that improbable season just yet, this improbable house just yet. Once again, a bridging and capsuling of some of the years in between needs to come first—in this case, it's a pretty large swath of years. It seems crucial for you to have some basic feeling for this period, if only as a context for further appreciating Wright in 1936. So again, I'll work somewhat in the pluperfect and stand on the shoulders of many predecessors (but with a few slants and discoveries and small detours of my own to offer).*

———

It was a three-page, handwritten letter on half-sized sheets, in a neat and clearly feminine hand, and it was dated December 12, 1914—which is to say four months, minus three days, from what Julian did. The first sentence was multi-clausal, with an ornate word or two, an unusual expression or two. The second sentence was a sort of command. You could almost imagine the letter being orated from a stage, the sheet being held aloft.

My dear Sir
　　Because I stand aghast at the immensity of your sorrow, because my own soul has been chastened by grief, and I know how desolate are anniversaries and fete days, I send to you my good wishes. Rejoice that you are worthy to bear so great affliction, that your strength is greater than human tragedy.

---

* I'll cite and quote some of my indebtedness as I go along, but to cite an overriding indebtedness right now, to two working Madison historian-biographers, the first of whom was referenced in an earlier footnote: Mary Jane Hamilton and David V. Mollenhoff. They've both given of their personal time to this project. But I refer even more to their co-authored chapter in a long book about Wright and Madison—it's entitled "An Old Madison Boy," and it can be found in their 1999 volume, *Frank Lloyd Wright's Monona Terrace*—which, in so many ways, was the open sesame for my basic grasping of Wright's life, from his birth up through his seventieth year. In forty-seven pages of beautifully illustrated prose, they even sketch in the family ancestry—on both sides. To quote just one sentence from "An Old Madison Boy," which goes a long way toward explaining much not only about Wright post-Julian but about Wright, period: "[He] was one of those people who seem to have a powerful steel spring that releases its energy only when they have been prostrated by life's worst blows." Yes, the will to survive, against all, always.

It was signed, "Sincerely, Madame Noel."

I've studied this letter. The word "immensity" could almost be "university." Maybe it is. It would fit with her looniness. The *university of your sorrow.*

He had taken the bait like a carp would take a night crawler.

Mad Miriam had just entered the picture. She was going to be in the picture for the better part of the next fourteen years. She was going to become Frank Lloyd Wright's second wife, although "become" is the operative word: it took the hideously mismatched pair almost nine years to get married—and only six months more for them to separate for good, although there had been frequent hysterical separations (on both their parts) and uncounted knock-down, drag-outs in between. (Mainly of the verbal kind.) But even after their final separation, in the spring of 1924, their joint misery was hardly over. In fact, that's when Mad Miriam went really off the rails, with her vindictive jealousy during the next several years seeming to know no earthly bound. Even after their divorce (more than three years from their separation), the misery had kept up. Okay, if Miriam may never have been mad in the way of Julian, burning and hatcheting everything and everyone in sight, she was figuratively that. She pursued him across the continent—literally.

"I suppose it's just a question of how much punishment one can stand," Wright had said at one point in the hot holy pitch of his misery, although he wasn't specifically referring to her just then. "Drowning men—they say so—clutch at straws" is the way he explains his instant, fatal attraction in *An Autobiography.*

Her real name was Maude Miriam Hicks Noel. She'd been forty-five then (six weeks older than Mamah). She'd been a supposed widow then. (Actually, she was a divorcee with three grown children, married at fifteen, though it's true her former husband was dead.) She'd worn a monocle dangling delicately from her neck on a string of white silk then. She'd worn turbans and crushed velvet and sealskin capes and long dresses with cloth of gold in them. She'd had the slightest head tremor then. She'd smoked skinny French cigarettes then. She'd consulted spiritualists and mediums then. She'd been a devotee of Mary Baker Eddy then. She'd just come from Paris then, where she is said (by her claiming) to have held salons and participated in sculpture competitions recognized by the Louvre and had sat talking the rain-slickened midnights away with Leon Trotsky and Mrs. Harry Payne Whitney, to say only two.

From *An Autobiography:* "A violet pallor. Mass of dark red-brown hair. Clear-seeing eyes with a green light in them."

One other alluring thing about her, and you could get it right off in her speech: she was out of the Deep South, from Memphis, daughter of a physician, Andrew Guthrie Hicks, a Civil War veteran, who graduated from Memphis Hospital Medical College and is said to have been the son of a great Tennessee slaveholder and plantation master.

Wait a minute. *Hicks?* That name is all over Chambers County, Alabama. If you were paying any kind of half-attention to all that confusing genealogy in the chapter on Julian's roots, you'll recall that Mariah Diana *Hicks* Frederick was the widowed plantation mistress from whom—I am convinced, if cannot nail—Julian's mother (Mariah Diana Frederick Carlton) derived her name. Julian's mom—I feel certain—was born a slave child on the Frederick plantation. Julian's mom didn't have Hicks in her own name, not that I know, but there is no question that that was the maiden name of the woman who was the mistress of the plantation after her physician husband had died early. There are numerous Hickses on tombstones in cemeteries in and around tiny Cusseta and in other parts of the county. So could any of those Hickses be traced up to Tennessee and to Memphis? Is it a million-to-one shot that Wright's second wife was somehow remotely related to the Frederick/Hicks slaveholding clan of Cusseta and environs, out of which Julian eventually emerged—could she be a fifth cousin, twice removed? Beats me. But far-fetchedness is what the life of Frank Lloyd Wright is about.

To return to traceable fact: Wright had replied two days later. (We have the dated letter and its postmark.) He had been living mostly in Chicago then, renting a small Georgian revival red-bricked townhouse on East Cedar Street immediately north of the Loop. He still had his office down on Michigan Avenue at Orchestra Hall. In Wisconsin, Taliesin II, as he called it, far grander than what had been destroyed, had been rising from its own ashes—in fact, with astonishing speed. It had been rising, you could guess, on OPM—other people's money, most notably the money of that great, good, exasperated, fool-able and yet still believing Buffalo soul, Darwin D. Martin.

From *An Autobiography:* "A horrible loneliness began to clutch me, but I longed for no one I ever loved or that I had ever known." And here was Miriam, her note to him seeming miraculously to have risen up out of the pile of unread or discarded condolences.

In his note of the 14th, he'd signed it "Gratefully." She'd replied almost immediately, on December 17. He'd written right back. (It was now six days from Christmas.) He'd spoken in that note of the 19th about how he'd been "so utterly flung back upon myself—damned at flood tide. . . ." He'd talked of the "weaknesses of the unquenchable ego of the individualist (to speak of myself in kindly terms). . . ." Three days later he was writing to her again (there seems to have been a note from her in between, but we don't have it), telling her that he had children "mostly grown who will spend Christmas eve with their mother, who is a stranger to me. . . ." He had assumed he'd spend Christmas alone. But now, possibly, they might spend it together, or at least meet at his office on Christmas Eve. "So—come—, you will be welcome here at my workroom at five on Thursday—we can plan our evening as we will."

She'd come, dressed to the exotic nines, in a taxi from the South Side, where she'd been staying with one of her daughters. From *An Autobiography*: " 'How do you like me?' she said." His answer: " 'I've never seen anyone like you,' I said."

The next morning, at 25 Cedar, she'd written him a note that had begun, "Lord of My Waking Dreams!" (They'd apparently gone from Orchestra Hall to his house that evening, where he is claimed by Miriam to have put on a black velvet jacket and Chinese trousers.) As she would write in her autobiography a decade and a half later, shortly before her death (a pathetically sad document, unreliable on the facts, and yet oddly moving), describing first sight of him at his studio: "In that one glance, I '. . . had fed in honeydew / And drunk the milk of paradise.' " In the waking-dreams note on Christmas morning, perhaps thrust at him while he'd still dozed on the storm-tossed bedsheets in his nightshirt: "Let me crown your head with a wreath of violets and bind your hair with fillets of gold. . . . I kiss your feet with my trembling lips—I am your prisoner."

And you can guess: It had all gone practically straight down from there. (She had tried, in her autobiography—it never got published in book form, but was serialized in five abridged installments in a Milwaukee newspaper in 1932, two years after her death—to make it seem as if the abandoning of herself to him, and vice versa, had taken place over the course of several months. Really, it had taken less than a few hours.)*

Within months, maybe weeks, of their having moved in together, there'd been ghastly scenes. They'd separated, come back together. She'd been allowed to go to the newly risen Taliesin II—only to encounter there a screech of a housekeeper Wright had hired some months before. Her name was Nellie Breen, an elderly and fiercely proprietary woman, who had turned out to be her own surreal piece of work. Wright had ended up firing her, in early October 1915, but not before the avenging housekeeper had purloined letters from Miriam to Wright out of a drawer in his private desk. She'd gotten them to federal authorities in Chicago, insisting they were proof her former employer had violated the Mann Act: escorting females across state lines for indecent purposes. Miriam's letters, which had also come into the delirious hands of the Chicago press, were of the same rhetorical quality of the letters just quoted, only from the other end of the telescope. Again, the lurid headlines. (Typical letter, appearing in the *Sunday Tribune*, November 7, 1915: "A dead woman whom you tortured [Miriam is speaking of Mamah] as you have tortured me and to whose memory you have given no real loyalty. . . . You are blind to God—veiled as I think mortal never was . . . a pathetic, bitter, angry man.")

Of Nellie Breen, the put-upon master of Taliesin had been quoted in the *Tribune* on November 8 as saying "But to get back to the homely, weazened, deaf little celtic nemesis who has set out to make my life miserable. . . ." He had informed Chicago readers of her "dried up figure and shriveled, unpleasant face. She is very deaf and uses an ear trumpet."

To review: Wright had Miriam. Wright still had his hell-on-wheels mother, Anna. Wright had a scorned ex-housekeeper of an old Irish bat with a horn up to her ear ratting on him to the feds. Weren't the gods outdoing themselves?

The upshot? He had hired his friend and thundering Chicago lawyer, Clarence Darrow, to make things go away. Darrow had made them go away. No formal charges ended up being brought under the Mann

---

* Because Miriam Noel Wright's life has been so ripe for ridicule by three generations of writers, I particularly admire biographer Meryle Secrest's portrait. She doesn't hold back on the unhingedness, but she also exhibits a keen and sympathetic female understanding.

Act, not this time. In fact, it all had passed over pretty quickly. And meantime he and Miriam would go on—for years and years. It was "the leading of the blind by the blind," he explains in his autobiography.

———

If, in the after-years of an unimaginable burning, you'd been "continually expecting some terrible blow" to strike again; if "waking or dreaming," the "sense of impending disaster" kept hanging over you, then might not the designs emerging from your drawing board reflect a bunkered frame of mind? What would these designs have ended up looking like on the outside after they were built? Fortresses?

The quotes above are from *An Autobiography.*

Wright scholar Neil Levine has a chapter in his *Architecture of Frank Lloyd Wright* entitled "Building Against Nature on the Pacific Rim." It's about the work in the years following what happened at Taliesin. Levine is chiefly concerned with the design and construction of two buildings: the massive and ornate Imperial Hotel in Tokyo and a massive residence in Los Angeles called Hollyhock House that almost looks like a vision of a twentieth-century Mayan temple. (Wright had worked on the Hollyhock project between 1917 and 1920, with the help of his son Lloyd Wright and some others, for yet another wild woman, a patroness of the arts named Aline Barnsdall.) Levine takes his chapter title from Wright himself. In the 1932 edition of his autobiography, Wright discussed the cantilevered engineering masterstroke that went into the design of the Imperial. He'd entitled the passage "Why the Great Earthquake Did Not Destroy the Imperial Hotel." (He is referring to the Great Kanto Earthquake of September 1, 1923—which struck on the very day that the hotel formally opened. And, it's true, the Imperial largely rode out that horrific quake and firestorm that killed 140,000 people and burned 300,000 buildings. But, as in all things Wrightian, it's a muddier story than that.) In the 1943 edition of the autobiography, perhaps only suggesting how much he was still haunted by August 15, 1914, Wright added this to the title line in his section about the hotel: "Building Against Doomsday." He was referring to seismic events, but surely he meant something more as well, even if not consciously.

Which is partly Levine's point—that these two major projects, post-Julian, the Imperial and the Hollyhock, were always connected in Wright's mind as an architectural response to what had happened. Levine: "In them he sought to work through the meaning of the tragedy and to counteract its effects through a transference of the idea of a 'natural architecture' onto the more remote plane of public, monumental expression. . . . No longer conceiving an architecture at one with a benevolent landscape, he imagined the process of building as a confrontation with the violent and irrational forces of nature embodied in the unstable, seismic conditions of the Pacific Rim." Not building *in* nature, but against.

Wright once noted that both the hotel and the Barnsdall house sat on the "red line of seismic convulsion." That's almost poetry, and, again, the image may have come to him as something more than only geologic. The vast Pacific was in between, but in both L.A. and Tokyo the architect had been trying to bunker his buildings against unforeseen eruptions of violence. The Hollyhock's basic material is hollow clay tile with a stucco exterior. The foundations are concrete and brick. The ornamentation is cast stone. The place sits on a hill and you can see Los Angeles forever. You walk up to it and you almost don't want to enter. (The early-twentieth-century architectural historian Henry-Russell Hitchcock, quoted previously, spoke of the Hollyhock's exterior feel of monstrous weight and "almost pyramidal gloom.") Unity Temple in 1905 seemed a forbidding monolith from the outside to nearly every Oak Park eye. And then you got inside. Everything changed. You were floating in a light-filtered cube. Still are.

Several things can be true at once: that is, if Frank Lloyd Wright may have been bunkering in and down during this period, he was also reinventing himself as an artist. A Wright scholar, Kathryn Smith, has written acutely of both the Imperial and the Hollyhock. Of the latter, she has noted that the house "was designed at a pivotal evolutionary moment in Wright's development. Turning his back on the Prairie house . . . he began to experiment with new ideas . . . to give form to meaning. . . . Even the awkwardness of his choice of the literal imagery of the pre-Columbian temple shows Wright grasping for the essential, searching for beginnings." In other words, even if he'd been waiting for the next terrible blow to strike from out of seeming nowhere, and even if the Hollyhock is far from a Wright masterwork, nothing like Unity or the Larkin Building or the Robie House, Picasso was in a new phase, almost as if Julian hadn't happened.

The Imperial project had taken up most of Wright's creative obsession from 1916 to 1922. His five percent commission on the nearly five-million-dollar contract had been a quarter of a million dollars. He'd made five exhausting trips to Japan in these six years (and gotten quite ill with something akin to malaria during a 1920 stay). In the almost four years between October 30, 1918 (when he and Miriam had departed for what was his third trip for the project), and late July 1922 (when they'd left Yokohama on the *President McKinley*), he'd been on Japanese soil for not quite three years. There'd been trips back home in between— but then the turning almost right around, as if pursued.

The key cantilevering principle at work in the Imperial (which has certain strong resemblances to Midway Gardens) had been one of balancing on floating foundations. "Why not then carry the floors as a waiter carries his tray on an upraised arm and fingers at the center— *balancing* the load," he says in *An Autobiography*. He had used reinforced concrete, and had set the load, like a waiter carrying his tray, on a series of thin concrete pins that were eight or nine feet deep and two feet apart: the building above had been connected to the mud cushion below, more or less riding on it. "Why not, then, a building made as the two hands thrust together palms inward, fingers interlocking and yielding to movement. . . . Why fight the quake? Why not sympathize with it and out-wit it?"

———

The sky above, the mud below. They could not have stayed together for so long had there not been ardor between them, real love, by their own enabling definitions. Their letters testify to it. Wright biographers have undervalued this point, in my view.

In his autobiography, Wright talks of how Miriam, in the plunges of her addictions, could just go off—"strange disturbances. Sometimes unnatural exaggeration, mental and emotional, spoiled life entirely for days at a time. I had hunted causes. Yes . . . I had looked into myself, too." (The ellipsis is his.) And then the peace would come.

As was said above, their altercations seem mostly to have been verbal, but at least once she'd apparently gotten a gun in her hand and had been weaving toward him. (It was over his flirtations with a Russian friend of hers—Madame Krynska.) Another time, Miriam had grabbed a knife and was coming at him. (It had only been a dull fruit knife, she'd claimed in her autobiography.) As for Wright's eruptions, there have long been undocumented stories about his striking her. Miriam had once told the Chicago press that he had broken two of her ribs.

He once said in a letter: "I loved her enough to kill her and myself."

In the early summer of 1919 (in Wisconsin, Cousin Richard is now selling out his business to a syndicate of papers and getting ready to take over another property in far-off Tulsa), there'd been another terrible row. It seems to have been the Madame Krynska business. His anxieties were working overtime. Miriam had packed up and fled to a summer resort named Ikao, a short day's travel from Tokyo. There'd been so many delays in starting the actual construction on the Imperial—it was now about to happen. He'd written her a stream of letters. Biographer Brendan Gill reproduces one of these letters at great length—more than a thousand words. Gill feels the letters are mainly about "self-abasement." Not to me. Rather, it was as if he'd suddenly seen himself clear, had realized what he'd given up for his art, how he'd lived a kind of half-life. (Not that any of this clarity and humility would stick.) "Instead of making the sacrifices myself I have been taking them from others as my *right*," he told her.

I took you as I take everything. . . . But then came the self-deception I have practiced always. . . . I did not know how to treat a companion as an equal. . . . Long ago there ceased to be any other face for me. No one ever seemed able to wear clothes; no one ever seemed so worth coming close to or doing things for as you. . . . Of course you don't love me now. I don't see how you could. . . . This inner chamber I call my heart has been very long neglected. . . . [I]n spite of the commotion the dust is on everything and blood stains are on the floor. The pictures are turned to the wall in regret and shame. . . .

It almost sounds in this last part as if he'd been trying to apologize for having gone at her with his fists. That word again: "shame."

A one-page note: "I will not write you of my loneliness here nor of my feelings."

At the bottom, a layered postscript, which he'd dated "June 9th": "A long, lonely but lovely ride home my face burned to a cinder—it scares me when I see it in the glass."

Another letter, on the thin stationery of the Miyako Hotel, Kyoto, two pages long, in a neat hand. He had dated it: "Friday June 11th," and, like the one above, he hadn't put in the year. But the internal evidence suggests that it had probably been written that same week, even if June 11, 1919, was a Wednesday in Japan. (He was quite capable of forgetting the day of the week and misdating his correspondence.) He'd addressed it "To the woman by my side—" and he'd ended it: "I feel that no words of mine can show my regret for what I am and shame for what I do." Next paragraph: "I guess my talent has screened me from myself all along—It is well that I have come face to face with myself unequivocally at last." Next paragraph: "And when my need is greatest I am alone."

They'd reconciled—and, soon, gone straight back to their mutual poisoning, his self-absorptions, her rages if another woman had so much as glanced his way. And yet there they were, end of that summer, on August 25, 1919, disembarking, arm in arm, at Vancouver, on the *Empress of Asia,* having sailed from Yokohama. On the passenger list, she'd identified herself as "Miriam L. Wright," even though they weren't married. (Kitty Wright, all this time, had never released him.) Miriam had made herself a year younger—claiming forty-nine on the manifest instead of fifty. He'd given his true age of fifty-two—but had then put his birth year as 1869. Oh, maybe the bursar couldn't add.

———

Finally, in 1922, Kitty *had* released him. They'd effectively been separated for thirteen years, and for how much of that time had she still held out ludicrous hope? They'd signed divorce papers in November, with a legal wait of twelve months before he could marry again. Three months after the papers, on February 10, 1923, Wright's mother had died. Anna was eighty-four. She'd been in a sanatorium not far from Madison. The *Chicago Tribune* had devoted three paragraphs. Her son seems not to have been at the service at the family burying ground at Unity Chapel. He was thought to have left for Los Angeles, where he'd more or less relocated since returning from Japan, working there (and fighting there) with his son Lloyd, trying to find jobs there, with patchy results.

In late November 1923, after waiting out the obligatory year, Frank Lloyd Wright married Maude Miriam Noel on a bridge over the Wisconsin River, at midnight, in a semi-secret ceremony. As was said above, the marriage as a marriage didn't last even six months. From *An Autobiography:* "But instead of improving with marriage, as I had hoped, our relationship became worse." Several sentences later: "To oppose her now in the slightest degree meant violence." By early May of 1924, Miriam had moved out of Taliesin, but not before, or so Wright claims in the autobiography, he'd consulted a famous Chicago doctor. Wright names him as "Dr. William Hixon," but he really meant Dr. William J. Hickson. The two knew each other, and Hickson had a distinguished career as a psychiatrist in Chicago. (He had a great interest in the arts.) According to Wright, Hickson had told him that he had to let her go, that to oppose her "would only be to burn her up more quickly." Did Hickson use that curious metaphor, or was it really coming from some half-conscious place inside of Wright? (How many dreams might he still have been having about people literally in flames? He would have drafted that sentence about twelve or thirteen years after Julian's act.) In any case, Wright doesn't try to put it all on his wife. Indeed, on the same page that he misspells Hickson's name, he speaks, yet again, of his own shame, and "an unfamiliar moral cowardice." That line was quoted toward the start of this book.

Wright's biographers have mostly thrown up their hands as to why they'd gotten married in the first place. Perhaps it isn't so much of a mystery. Perhaps they'd wanted only to prove to each other that they could do it, and they could then be free to find a way out as quickly as possible. But, to say again, things were not even close to over.

———

Miriam had moved out and Louis Sullivan had died in squalor—both events had occurred at roughly the same time. About six years previous, Wright and his *lieber meister* had come all the way back together. In his various writings, not just in the autobiography, Wright typically confuses the issue of how long they'd been estranged. He claims at one point that it was twelve years before he ever saw or spoke to Sullivan again; at another point he says that it was nearly twenty; at another he indicates it had been something like twenty-six. The closer truth, as biographers have gauged, is that they'd probably been fully apart for something like seven years from the moment when Wright, riding on his dignity, had thrown down his drafting tools and stalked out of Adler & Sullivan in 1893. And then, somewhere around 1900, the slow, awkward coming back together of master and former pupil, protégé, pencil. Until, that is, around 1918, when, after an apparently abject phone call to Taliesin from Sullivan, they more or less *rushed* back to each other, and stayed that way until the end of the master's life.

Abject? Sullivan, whose fame was international, could barely make his rent. He hadn't had real work for years. A midlife and ill-considered marriage had foundered.

He'd long been living alone in a room in an old brick pile of a hotel on the South Side of Chicago. To read the letters between Wright and Sullivan from 1918 to 1924, but especially from Sullivan's side, is to see a prodigiously proud man, a true genius of American architecture, reduced to nearly the level of begging. Far from disdaining, Wright had responded from the first in compassion. Again, the other Wright.

"With the future blank I am surely living in hell," the master had written to him, in one of their earliest exchanges, after they were fully back. (It's dated April 1, 1918.) "To think I should come to this, at 61." Seven months later, November 4, 1918: "Your letter, mailed at sea, reached me this morning. To find a cheque in it positively paralyzed me, for I was at the very end of my string." (Wright and Miriam are on the ocean for Japan.) Not quite three years later, on August 19, 1921: "I have just cabled you as follows: 'Am in trouble. What can you do in the shortest time.'" Later in this letter: "[T]he nervous strain has become unbearable. . . ."

Fifteen months later, from Wright's side: "I am going to tell you a secret, which I hope you will keep—I am extremely hard up, and not a job in sight in the world. . . . [But] you must know that I would share my last crust with you. . . . I enclose something of what I have left, to insure you something of Christmas. . . ." Wright has just signed divorce papers with Kitty. He's been lately home from Japan. Hoped-for work isn't coming.

Jump it forward to the second week of April 1924, to the dying, in that rattletrap room at the Warner Hotel at Thirty-Third Street and Cottage Grove Avenue. Wright is there, either the day before or two days before. Sullivan can barely breathe. He's suffering from a grossly dilated heart. He's got an acute case of neuritis in his right arm. His speech is slurring. In his checking account at the Corn Exchange National Bank there are $189, but only because friends have lately put the funds there. (He's been five or six weeks behind on his nine-dollar-a-week rent.) The room is all but bare—a few books on shelves in the bathroom, a few pictures torn or scissored from popular magazines stuck up on the walls. By the master's bed is one small piece of carved jade—memento from a lifetime in art. And, oh, yes, several advance bound copies of the life story Sullivan has been trying desperately to finish. It's titled *The Autobiography of an Idea*. His publisher has rushed the first copies to him.

From Wright's autobiography: "He wanted to get up, I helped him, put my coat round his shoulders as he sat on the bed with his covered-up feet on the floor. . . . I was sitting by him, my arm around him to keep him warm and steady him. I could feel every vertebra in his backbone as I rubbed my hand up and down his back to comfort him." Wright got him back into bed, "covered him up—and sat there beside him on the edge of the bed. . . . He seemed to sleep well. . . . The nurse had stepped out for a moment."

Wright had left. (There'd been an "imperative call from Taliesin"— Miriam?) This was either on Saturday or Sunday, April 12 or 13. On Monday, early in the day, Louis Sullivan had died in his sleep. Wright got word after he was home. Let this be said: If others had given more than Wright in those last weeks and days, Wright had still given much, and maybe something indispensable. In any case, he'd been there, in and amid his own personal turmoil. He'd heard the master gently address him as "Frank."

———

Fire!

He's up on the roof, with buckets, like Ahab atop his whale, roaring, cursing, fighting to stop the thing, his legs burned, his lungs seared, his wild hair catching sparks: "From Hell's heart I stab at thee." That's from *Moby-Dick*. From *An Autobiography:* " 'No, fight the fire. Fight! Fight I tell you! Save Taliesin or let it all go!' I shouted. . . ."

It's futile. The place is gone again. It's April 20, 1925. It had started in his bedroom, at suppertime, something to do with bad wiring in the telephone just at the head of his bed. No one had died, but another devastating loss. In the midst of fighting it, he had more or less said to himself: "The place seemed doomed now—even to me."

To back up: After Miriam had left (she'd gone to California, where she intended to start a cinema career), Wright, veering on fifty-seven, and with the work momentarily seeming to be looking up (it would turn out to be a false god; he was entering one of the most desolate periods of his working life), had taken up with twenty-two-year-old Mary Hurlbut, French major at the University of Wisconsin. (She had straight dark hair and a plain, sober face and looked somewhat older than her classmates, at least judging from yearbook pictures. It isn't quite clear how they'd met.) The relationship had continued through the second half of 1924. Had he been using her? Perhaps the using had been mutual. According to his autobiography, he had continued to feel himself "lower down in my own estimation than I had ever been in my life. . . ." There'd be a reprieve—and then, before he knew, he would have "dropped back into the aching void."

Then, in late November of that year, he had been staying for a night or two at the Congress Hotel on Michigan Avenue. (It was his preferred Chicago address. In the years after he and *lieber meister* had come back together, he would sometimes book two rooms at the Congress, side by side, one for Sullivan, one for himself. Across the street was Sullivan's masterpiece, the Auditorium Building.) Wright and an artist friend had gone to the ballet. It was a Sunday matinee at the Eighth Street Theater. They'd scored two balcony seats by the rail. The third seat had remained empty—until just as the performance was beginning an usher had led in a tall, thin, hatless woman with hair parted in the middle and brushed down over her ears: it was Olgivanna Lazovich Hinzenberg, with whom he'd be destined to spend the rest of his life. As said above, she was twenty-six then, born in Montenegro, educated in czarist Russia, daughter of a supreme court justice, separated from her husband, with a seven-year-old daughter named Svetlana. She had studied in

Paris with the famed philosopher-poet and spiritual guru of mind-body consciousness, Georgi Gurdjieff. Right off: something mystic.

To the burning point here (in several senses): By February of 1925, the married Wright had moved the married Olgivanna and her child into Taliesin. He'd fallen wildly in love again. By early March, she'd become pregnant. And the next month: Taliesin burning to the ground—if not all of it. In the pictures taken the next morning, you can see the stone piers and chimneys standing up from the ashes. In the ashes are melted heads and other pieces of stone figures that Wright had collected in Japan. "Another savage blow struck" is the way he puts it in the autobiography, no need to say the name "Julian." Four lines earlier: "The living half of Taliesin—gone—again."*

He and the handful of others who were at Taliesin that night, as well as neighbors who'd rushed in, had fought it in vain for two and a half hours. And then "a tremendous pealing roll of thunder and the storm broke with a violent change of wind that rolled the mass of flame up the valley. It recoiled upon itself—as the rain fell hissing into the roaring furnace." *Furnace.* Then, too, the lurid bystanders "sneering at the fool who imagined Taliesin could 'come back' after all that had happened before."

Was his grandfather's Old Testament prophet rebuking him for his sins? He despises Isaiah. "Isaiah is the vengeful prophet of an antique wrath." A page earlier: "If the angry prophet had struck twice he could strike again." Maybe the most compelling sentence in the entire fire passage: "Again searching causes, I wondered." *I wondered.* A leitmotif

---

* On the falling wildly in love again: It needs to be pointed out that, despite Olgivanna, Mary Hurlbut was apparently still somewhat in the picture, at least into the early winter of 1925. There's a diary entry testifying to it. The diary is by Richard Neutra, who was then a young Austrian architect who'd come to work briefly as a draftsman for Wright at Taliesin (and who would go on to become a landmark modernist architect, working for most of his life in southern California). In an entry dated January 1925, Neutra writes of "Mary," who was "Wright's present sweetheart," and of how Wright and his chauffeur had picked her up at Madison the day before in his Cadillac. This fact flies in the face of what has been the general historical view, promulgated not least by Wright himself: that it had been pretty much swoon-time for him the second he had met Olgivanna. Perhaps the truth once again is in the middle. I am thinking of the early summer of 1907, when a forty-year-old architect seems to have begun his no-going-back sexual relationship with Mamah Cheney—which was about the same moment when construction began on the Edward Boynton House in Rochester, and when Wright, no matter his deep involvement with Mamah, may or may not have also gotten involved with twenty-one-year-old Beulah Boynton. And then, of course, there's the Ida Heller story . . .

of the semi-secret life. Never mind. By the next day the rebuilding had begun.

The New York Times gave the fire four paragraphs. "Crossed wires," it explained, with no apparent irony. The *Chicago Tribune* could only stomp with factually inaccurate glee, writing once more of the "love nest" that had "won him notoriety in every civilized nation." Wright and Kitty had "signed a compact by which he was allowed to make Mrs. Cheney his common law wife." Mamah and her children were "buried on the sunny hillside." And then, his "grief assuaged, Wright strolled in from across the world one morning with a new queen for his kingdom of love—one Mrs. Maud Miriam Noel, Parisian sculptor." The *Tribune* apparently had no clue that Olgivanna had become the new strolled-in—and expectant—queen. You can read this account and, again, fairly wish to take *his* side. As for local coverage: The *Wisconsin State Journal* ran a seven-column headline across the front page: FRANK LLOYD WRIGHT'S HOME BURNS. The story began in column one. In column five was an entirely unrelated story—the headline of which might still have made Wright choke, had he happened to have glanced at the paper: FIND NEGRO SLAYER GUILTY OF MURDER IN FIRST DEGREE.

———

That crossed-wire fire of 1925 had been like a cymbal-clash for a Wagnerian opera that had all but put Wright's career out of business, that had all but put his *life* out of business, for at least the next three and a half years.

Enter Mad Miriam again.

Not long before the '25 fire, Olgivanna had obtained a divorce from her Russian architect husband, Vlademar Hinzenberg. Later that summer, Wright had filed for his own divorce, charging Miriam with desertion. (All he really wanted was to get her out of his life, because he had a new life now.) It looked for a time as if things might proceed, once they'd agreed on financial terms. But then Miriam had found out the true story, and this had sent her into paroxysms of fury. Late in November, she had traced the pair to a Chicago hotel. On December 2, 1925, Iovanna Wright had come into the world. Miriam had discovered the

Chicago hospital and had gone there for a scene. It had begun to occur to Miriam that she might have Olgivanna deported.

Right before Olgivanna presented Wright with his seventh child, Miriam had held a press conference—of sorts—in her room at the Southmoor Hotel in Chicago. She had just entered her own "bill of divorce." Actually, the Chicago press hadn't been aware until now that Wright and Miriam had even been married. The *Tribune* had quoted her: "Just two months after Mamah Borthwick died, when the sod was still green on her grave, Mr. Wright met me. He hadn't been with me ten minutes before he said, 'You're mine.'" Earlier in this story, published on November 27: "He told me that if I made trouble I never would get the money settlement I was supposed to get. But I don't care. I don't care if I starve to death and freeze. My life is over." She had talked about his physical abuse. She'd stalked the room. She'd cried. Oh, he was such a cad, even if she'd once loved him so deeply. Why, he had once worn brown knickerbockers to the opera.

(The day before, to another Chicago reporter, she had said: "Mine was a greater tragedy than Mamah Borthwick's. She is dead, but I live on. O, how I loved him.")

Six months later, on June 3, 1926, Miriam had tried to storm Taliesin. The good gray lady—not Miriam, but *The New York Times*—gave the storming a poker-faced four paragraphs, describing how Miriam had stopped in Dodgeville for warrants. She had found the front gate of her former home locked. She had tried to force her way in through a back entry but a truck had been wedged across the drive and several men had been standing guard there. She had stomped back to the front to rip up a "No Visitors" sign. Another sign was behind glass, set in a wood frame. She had smashed it with a rock. Wright hadn't been there that day.

The April 1925 fire had destroyed a claimed $300,000 worth of Wright's Asian art—tapestries, screens, sculpture, and prints. But it had spared an even larger and more precious trove of Japanese prints— Wright had had the foresight to store the art in a vault. He owned a $39,000 insurance policy on his house, but it wasn't nearly enough to rebuild, and besides, there were all his living expenses, legal expenses. So he'd been forced to mortgage the entirety of Taliesin with the Bank of Wisconsin. He owed the bank $43,000. By September 1926, seventeen months from the fire, having failed on the payments (had he made a single one?), the bank had foreclosed.

But meanwhile, Miriam had teamed up legally with Olgivanna's former husband. His principal objective was to get custody of his daughter, Svetlana. All Miriam had cared about was making Wright's life more miserable and Olgivanna's, too, and if the custody battle could help that cause, fine. In August 1926 (not long before the Bank of Wisconsin had foreclosed), Miriam had both refused to grant Wright a divorce and had sued Olgivanna for $100,000. Double whammy of vengeance.

Wright and Olgivanna had become alarmed that the courts might try to take her daughter. So the four—Wright, Olgivanna, nine-year-old Svetlana, and baby Iovanna—had gone into hiding. "Fugitives," according to the midwestern press. Not quite under the cover of darkness or an alias (but sort of), he had driven the family to Minnesota, where he'd rented a cottage on the shore of Lake Minnetonka, south of Minneapolis. (It was here that Wright, at Olgivanna's urging, started work on the first sections of *An Autobiography*. How would he have found the concentration?) They'd been at Lake Minnetonka for approximately six weeks, end of the first week of September to the third week of October. That's when Hennepin County sheriff's deputies, tipped, had come to the kitchen door on a Wednesday night and had arrested Wright and brought him to the hoosegow in Minneapolis. They'd then returned for Olgivanna. In the *Chicago Tribune* (page one, October 22, 1926) the story was all about the "love nest" that had been "raided" by lawmen "last night," with formal federal warrants for arrest under the Mann Act currently in hand for their "debauchery." Wright's bail had been set at $12,500 and Olgivanna's at $5,000. According to the newspaper, Olgivanna had gone nearly into hysterics upon being led into court. (She and her children had been put in the women's ward.) And Miriam? She was in the Southmoor in Chicago, deliciously following developments. "I will never divorce Frank Wright as long as I live, but if my attorney wants me to help press charges against him, I most certainly will," she had told the paper. On the back page, the *Trib* ran photographs: of the reprobate, in his high white collar and cheeky hat and cane crooked in an arm; of his lover, looking shyly seductive (it was an old photograph, from European days) in a nearly sleeveless dress and sidelong glance. The caption had described how she, too, had been "captured" at the cottage.

The upshot? The lawyers had mostly made it all go away again. By Saturday evening it was announced that, in exchange for generous visitation rights with Svetlana for Olgivanna's ex-husband, adultery charges would be dropped. Mann Act charges were still pending against Wright, but they, too, had a good chance of dissipating. Miriam Noel Wright, however, had no intention of dissipating, not yet.

Early January 1927: Wright in Manhattan. The Anderson Galleries on Park Avenue are auctioning off 346 of his Japanese prints—by order of the Bank of Wisconsin. The auction catalog costs a dollar and is beautifully illustrated; he has written the introduction. That week he'd had lunch at the Plaza Hotel with the young and rising cultural critic Lewis Mumford. (They'd corresponded a bit, but this had been their first meeting. For the next three decades their relationship would go through many turns.) Wright had not seemed the least shy about narrating his crazed life. Mumford, twenty-eight years younger, had been moved by the "curious softness about Wright's face," but even more by how none of what was happening to him had apparently "corroded his spirit or sapped his energies: his face was unseamed, his air assured, indeed jaunty."

On the auction's first night, 155 items were sold for $23,295—the prints had been expected to bring at least $50,000. Onward.

That same month, back in Wisconsin, friends, relatives, patrons, and business associates had begun forming something called Frank Lloyd Wright, Inc. It was a "rescue corporation." In effect, a man no longer able to control his own life and finances had hit upon a brilliant idea: sell shares in himself. The thing was being put together by Philip La Follette, son of Fighting Bob. Philip La Follette was a well-known Madison lawyer (and future Wisconsin governor). The idea was that the governing board of FLW, Inc., would henceforth make all money decisions, and pay the child-man at the center a salary so that he could proceed with his artistic genius. The shareholders would be reimbursed against future commissions. The corporation would attend to the lapsed mortgage and all else.

The centerpiece of the incorporating brainstorm had tried to enlist some of his old touches: Darwin Martin in Buffalo, for instance. Up there also was another longtime friend, client, believer, and exasperater: William R. Heath. He was a lawyer and, like Martin, a high executive of the Larkin Soap Company. A year or so after Wright had built a Buffalo house for Martin, he had designed one for Heath—this had been circa 1904. Now, more than two decades later, here was Frank Lloyd Wright, sixty, of unseamed face, of uncorroded spirit, father of a baby girl, blithely pinning a note on the door of Heath's current Buffalo home (designed by someone other than Wright), trying to enlist "Billy" as a shareholder in himself—FLW, Inc., that is. He had pinned it there because Heath and his wife hadn't come to the door. (Were they hiding behind the stair?) Characteristically he had forgotten to date the letter—so we don't know the exact period, but it seems to have been in the late fall of 1927. In any case, he had promised Heath that, were he to agree to sign up and become a member of FLW, Inc., he'd be able to get out of the arrangement if he felt it wasn't working. ("I will promise to find release for you whenever you need it or want it.") The note, full of the old Wrightian guile and charm, had the other elements, too. "I have been so badly whipped for my ignorance and willful disregard of the facts," he had said. "Too many fairy tales when a boy maybe—Too gushing a fountain of creative-energy to be safe. . . ." Despite the guile and charm and momentary humility, Heath had declined to part with $7,500 to be a shareholder, although the faithfully exasperated D. D. Martin did, and Wright's sister Jennie, and Alexander Woollcott of *The New Yorker* (a longtime Wright friend), and various others.

In late August 1927, the corporation now officially registered with the state, Wright's divorce had gone through. Miriam had relented—well, momentarily. She had gotten the loot: $6,000 in cash and a trust fund of $30,000. She had been living at the Claremont Apartments in San Francisco. Shortly, the San Francisco Bureau of International Newsreel had a photograph out on the wires: fifty-eight-year-old Miriam, in white gloves, cape, scarf, fur topper, on the back platform of a train, gesturing, smiling, looking youthful and alive again. (In many other photographs of her in these years, you can't miss the sadness and sickness in her eyes.) The caption: "Good-bye trouble; Hello Art. Admitting cinema ambitions and hinting at movie offers, Mrs. Frank Lloyd Wright quietly left San Francisco for Hollywood, Chicago, Paris and points East. The divorced wife of the famous Chicago architect who has filled columns of newspaper space in her legal tilt with her noted husband, has been in San Francisco for more than six months. For a time she was penniless, hungry sometimes, and unable to pay her rent, she said."

That slightly surreal photo and caption had run in various papers on September 21 and 22, 1927. Exactly seven months earlier, at Taliesin, on Tuesday evening, February 22, something else slightly surreal had happened: another fire. But this one had been fairly small—about $3,000 in damage. It had been contained quickly, but on the other hand if there'd been a big wind up, or if the bucket brigade hadn't vaulted into work, who knows: Would the whole shebang have gone up again? Again, the papers spoke of "crossed wires."

Surreal? In the fall of 1927, not too long before Wright would have been pinning a note on a prospective shareholder's Buffalo door, and only about six weeks after her divorce, Miriam Wright had been arrested in the lobby of the Lorain Hotel in Madison for having posted through the mails an obscene letter to her former husband. After she had made bail, she is claimed to have gone back to Chicago and drafted a letter about her ex-husband and his shameful lover to every member of the United States Senate.

At the end of 1927, the Bank of Wisconsin had discovered that Wright was living at Taliesin with Olgivanna. He'd been ordered out, bag and baggage. But just when it seemed he'd become homeless again, there was an offer to spend the winter in Arizona. The offer was from Albert Chase McArthur, who'd once been a Wright apprentice, and was now engaged, with his businessmen brothers, in building the Arizona Biltmore Hotel in Phoenix.* Wright was being brought in as a consultant on the use of textile blocks for the ultra resort. Unforeseen port in a storm: Arizona had just entered Wright's life and would be a deep part of him until his last breath, literally, more than three decades hence.

In July 1928, the Bank of Wisconsin had sold Taliesin at a sheriff's sale—and the bank itself had been the high bidder. Wright's lawyer, Phil La Follette, had then worked out arrangements for FLW, Inc., to come in and relieve the bank of something it hadn't wanted in the first place.

---

* Albert Chase McArthur was the eldest son of Warren McArthur, for whom—back in 1892, at Forty-Ninth and South Kenwood, on the South Side—Wright had built, as you'll recall, one of his earliest bootleg houses, with its gambrel roof, next door to another boot, the even finer hipped-roof George W. Blossom House, and all of this having come about when he was still working for Louis Sullivan. With old pal Cecil Corwin serving as beard.

This had happened in September. It had happened just a little while after Wright and Olgivanna had gotten married at midnight in Rancho Santa Fe, California. After the textile-block consulting work, the family had taken a cottage in La Jolla, just north of San Diego.

About six weeks before their August 25, 1928, wedding, Miriam, in Los Angeles for dental work, and having learned of the whereabouts of her former husband, had boarded a train to San Diego. There, she had hired a taxi to take her to La Jolla. In about ten or twelve or fourteen minutes of chaos, she had gleefully trashed everything in sight having to do with Frank Lloyd Wright—who, along with his family, wasn't home that afternoon. In her posthumously published autobiography (in *The Milwaukee Journal* in 1932), she wrote: "I went to the back door and found it open . . . I decided to get on the front page of the newspapers and see what effect publicity would have upon the situation." In a letter to a female friend in Milwaukee, Helen Raab, after she'd been sprung from jail, Miriam had said: "As a wreck it was a great success. If I had had fifteen minutes more it would have been a perfect success. I wrecked the whole house inside. Smashed Chinese porcelains, tore valuable pictures and prints from the walls, cut their clothes up with big studio shears, broke to powder, valuable china and the love nest looked like hell."

And yet, amid all this hell-hath-no-fury, things had finally begun to settle out and down for Miriam's former husband. The upper-aged married man and his itinerant young family, moving like gypsies, had been able to come back home to Wisconsin—Phil La Follette and the rescue corporation had worked it out. And Miriam? On January 3, 1930, which was about fourteen months after Wright had moved back into Taliesin, she had died in a Milwaukee hospital, where she'd been recovering from abdominal surgery. She'd been brought there from a sanatorium for the mentally ill. She was sixty. She'd been buried the next day at Forest Home Cemetery. A Unitarian minister had said a few graveside words. Her three children hadn't attended. She'd left nearly everything she had, including the manuscript of her autobiography, to Helen H. Raab, who was her closest friend in her last two or three years.

A few typescript copies of her 145-page life story exist; one has come into my possession. Title page: "MY LIFE WITH FRANK LLOYD WRIGHT." Under it: "THE STORY OF AN UNDISCIPLINED

SOUL—" Also typed there, in the upper left: "Motion picture rights reserved." The last delusion.

This is how her book closes: "On the day my husband married Olga Hinzenberg, I had thought I could go no farther into the depths of suffering, but that day was my Gethsemane. I was crucified all over again. I knew there was nothing more left in the world for me to live for." Next paragraph: "For me the day is done, and I am in the dark."

At one point, late in her inexplicable life, Miriam had gotten dressed up and gone to a Madison portrait photographer. The DeLonge gallery made a series of large-format, soft-focus prints. Several of those prints, in their original studio-engraved, softbound covers, are still around. There she is, pearls and pursed lips and a chaste dress, looking downward. In her round face, such a brown-toned loveliness. She doesn't look loony in the least.

By late 1928, Maude Miriam Noel Wright's ex-husband, having regained an emotional footing and his beloved home that had now burned down twice (almost a third time, before the fire was averted) in his ancestral valley, had been trying to figure out what he was going to do with the rest of his life. He was only sixty-one. Already, too many wise men of the earth had been saying he was all washed up. That's what they thought.

About the proboscis. The one that was referenced earlier. The one that got kicked in with a boot on Main Street in Madison and spurted blood like a broken water main and got decorated for a few days with a plaster of paris cast. The one that earned another embarrassing page-one treatment in Richard Lloyd Jones's Wisconsin State Journal: *FRANK LLOYD WRIGHT'S NOSE BROKEN IN FIST FIGHT HERE. Just that headline would have been so consternating. It implies the other party got the better of him. When he told the story himself, in the 1943 edition of the autobiography, he adjusted the facts, naturally. As to what really happened, it can sort of be pieced together from court documents and various news accounts. (The* Chicago Tribune *also had the story on page one.) Chiefly, the schnozzola saga is about getting what's coming to you at the hands (or foot) of an unstable former employee who is owed back wages and who's come to loathe the very sight of you. It can be read as its own little bright red Wrightian parable. And it seems clear that Wright himself understood it that way—the deserved retribution—even if he had to put that part (in the autobiography) in code. For this reason, the story seems worth elaborating on, small as it may be in the scheme. Why? Because it's suggestive once again of that other man, mostly hidden man, the Frank Lloyd Wright bent, in spite of himself, on giving himself away.*

It happened on Halloween in 1932. Perfect. If five or ten minutes of non-life-threatening gore is going to splatter all over the place, why not have the event occur on the night of goblins and tricks and treats? Wright's broker than broke in this period of his life (and that's saying something), and yet here he comes this afternoon, about five o'clock on October 31, tooling into town with one of his apprentices in his Cord L-29 Phaeton sedan, which he's paying for, theoretically, on the installment plan. (He has missed many payments and the threat of repossession is always upon him.) Maybe it's the sight of the car alone—those swooping seven-foot-long fenders, those custom Spanish leather seats, that snout of a hood that looks long as a sexy cigarette racing boat—that drives Claude Richard Sechrest over the top. C. R. Sechrest and his wife, Myrtle, are late employees of Taliesin. He is known as a rough customer. He's seven years younger

*than Wright. He may have Native American blood in him. Wright owes
Mrs. Sechrest, who had worked inside the house (while Sechrest had done
labor outside), something like $280. Back in the spring, Sechrest got so
enraged that he went around nailing doors and windows shut at Taliesin.
Eventually he got put off the place. His wife was supposed to stay on in
her job, but left soon after and never got her money. Apparently, once or
twice the Spring Green law had to be called when Sechrest tried to force
himself back into Wright's presence. The back pay issue has never been
resolved. And now the Sechrest family—so it will be claimed to the courts
in the aftermath of the incident—is stone broke. And here comes Wright
with his damn rich man's car, putting it all in his face. Oh, yeah?*

*The architect and his apprentice, who is chauffeuring the master
today, slide into a long parking slot outside of the Wisconsin Foundry
and Machine Company. Wright's in town to collect some provisions at
local stores. (This is another problem: he has outstanding accounts all
over Madison with merchants. Wouldn't the effrontery of the Cord have
driven them a little bonkers, too?) What happens next remains cloudy.
One of the Sechrest grown sons is said to have spotted Wright going into a
store. He fetches his father. The son holds back the apprentice-driver while
Sechrest the elder jumps in front of Wright, just as he's emerging with a
sack of something or other. He demands his money. The battle ensues.
Hard to say who's getting the better of whom, but then the attacker, physically much larger than Wright, slips off the curb and tumbles backward.
The man who's always trying to duck his bills comes right down on top
of him. A second later Sechrest frees a foot and lurches upward with his
boot, catching the deadbeat clean in the chops. But let's let the deadbeat
take over, in his self-serving way, because no matter the self-servingness,
it's his typically damn good read:*

> *So I clinched with him and he went down into the gutter on his
> back. I held him down there until he said he had enough. But, in
> the split second when getting off him I stepped back to let him up,
> he kicked backward and up at me with his heavy boot, caught me
> on the bridge of the nose with his boot heel. . . . Blood spurted all
> over him. . . . While holding him down there I deliberately aimed
> the torrent of blood with a broken nose full in his face. His own
> nose, his mouth, too, clotted with blood, he gagged and gasped for*

breath. . . . "God damn it, men, take him off," he shrieked. "Take the man off me, for Christ's sake! He's killing me!"

This was on a Monday. Two evenings later, four or five of Wright's apprentices (the Taliesin Fellowship has begun this fall, and a gang of new recruits and artist-acolytes have lately arrived) come hunting for Sechrest at his home at 1036 Williamson Street in Madison. They bring a black-snake whip. Supposedly, they crack him a couple of times. Supposedly, one of the kids socks him in the face. Sechrest grabs a big knife from the kitchen drawer and drives them off. (Recounting this part in his autobiography, Wright, who wasn't there, and claims he was unaware the apprentices had gone to town looking for Sechrest, has the "assassin" wielding the weapon from behind his screaming spouse, whom he's using as his shield.)

The next day, a pair of warrants get sworn out—one set for the apprentices, another for Sechrest, who'll end up in the hoosegow for the next two months until the thing sort of peters out and the case gets dismissed on New Year's Eve. (The kids get off far lighter.) All of this makes for wonderful headlines and copy (HORSEWHIPPED BY WRIGHT STUDENTS FAMED ARCHITECT'S ASSAILANT CHARGES). The AP photo that goes out across the wires has Wright sitting in court on the day of the issued warrant, looking slightly dazed and with the plaster cast on his beak and with his arm draped around the chair of one of his apprentices, who is in a suit and tie. What almost doesn't parse is not the cast riding on the ridge of his nose or the gash in his forehead, but how undandi-fied Wright looks: wrinkled shirt with mussed hair and a scarf around his shoulders. In the several thousand photographs that must exist of Frank Lloyd Wright, in drawers and our imaginations, he is almost never looking less than a million puffed-up bucks. Here, he seems momentarily exposed.

In An Autobiography, *at the end of the Sechrest telling, he seems momentarily exposed. The author sets off the passage with this headline: "A Coarse Incident." The first time I read the account, I was certain he had included it because he wanted history to know, no matter all the stories about the fire hydrant gush of his blood, that he had come out on top—literally. Now I don't think that, or at least not entirely. I think he wishes also to impart something else, albeit in semi-concealed ways. "That boot was a symbol," he writes. Next sentence: "So was the nose." Next sentence, set off in its own paragraph: "Never mind. dearest . . . I know what the moral is." He is addressing his unnamed wife, Olgivanna. (The typesetters have goofed. There's supposed to be a comma after "mind.") What he is saying is that Olgivanna would never have to tell him that he had it coming, because he understands it himself. Accepts it himself.*

And what happened to Claude R. Sechrest? He lived to be eighty-nine, with great-grandkids. He spent years farming land north of Madison. He died of a coronary thrombosis in an ambulance on the way to a hospital one Saturday in 1963. His obit in the Wisconsin State Journal *made no mention of the great "street battle," which is what the paper had gleefully termed it at the time.*

In the first-day story about the incident, there was this: "Mr. and Mrs. Sechrest were employed by Wright at Taliesin several months ago. Some difficulty arose and Sechrest left Wright's employment." I saw that and shivered: Julian. Could Wright have seen it? Wouldn't he have seen it? And were all the ghosts of August 15, 1914, before him again in his dreams?

In the Fourth Dimension

Herbert and Katherine Jacobs House, 441 Toepfer Avenue, Madison,
Wisconsin, commonly thought of as Jacobs I

I t's a kind of mouse-house. It's like being inside a wood-and-brick-and-glass haiku. She's so airy and light. She's so mitered and mortared and tight. She's so functional and spare and exquisitely livable. Here she sits, these eight decades later, as if floating imperceptibly on her concrete base of tamped-down sand, in her board-and-batten butternut glow. I have been privileged to sit on a sofa in the living room of the Herbert and Katherine Jacobs House, at dusk, when her current and carefully caretaking owner—his name is Jim Dennis, and he's had her far longer than anyone else—has turned on the lamps and lit the fifteen-watt ceiling bulbs, watching a Wisconsin summer evening roll up from the blue lakes somewhere down below. "This house is like a piece of furniture, like a big wooden cabinet," Dennis said the first time he had invited me in. In the time since, my respect and wonder have only grown. The careful owner, retired from a long career of teaching art history at the University of Wisconsin, had set out the pistachios and put on the piano jazz. For a lot of that evening, we had just sat in a semi-silence. Somehow, rather than a piece of furniture or a big wooden cabinet, I kept thinking that by some Wrightian sleight-of-hand I had been turned into a Lilliputian and then deposited in the well of an oversized custom-made guitar. Even though, in entirely another sense, the "Jake" is so small and seemingly delicate that you almost feel you could place her in your palm and still have room there for something else, as I've elsewhere said.

Actually, she's not delicate at all. She's hardy as hell. She's had to be to survive so many hard Wisconsin winters.

Frank Lloyd Wright designed something like 308 Usonian houses in his lifetime—and something like 140 got built, from New York to Alabama to Silverton, Oregon. But this is "Usonia 1." She gets pride of place. Usonia: a melodious word that Frank Lloyd Wright said he took from the writings of English novelist Samuel Butler, specifically a work called *Erewhon*. He said it stood for "United States of North America," with the "i" stuck in to make it easier to roll off the tongue. He said he meant the word to refer to a particular kind of practical and artistic and simple dwelling that would speak uniquely to the landscape and character and people of the United States. The only problem is that no Wright scholar, and apparently no Butler scholar, either, has ever been able to find the word "Usonia" or "Usonian" in Butler—or anywhere else, other than in the writings of Wright himself. Again, let it be.

Is there a dark side of the moon here? There is, although no fault of the house, and perhaps that card should be laid on the table at the outset, to think about through the rest of this. You could make a case, and historians have, that the tract developers of postwar America— picture Levittown as the shorthand example—saw the ingenious thing Frank Lloyd Wright did in the middle of the Depression, appropriated it to their own fashion, and ended up giving us what we think of as the banality, the conformity, the great cookie-cutter sprawl and rancher-drear of the American suburb. So is this the house that spawned the nightmare vision of our late-twentieth-century selves? Is 441 Toepfer Avenue in Madison where it all begins, those little pink houses all in a row, what one critic (he's a Brit, William J. R. Curtis, and perhaps saw it the more clearly) has referred to as the "all too often clumsy 'ranch-style' shoe boxes, laid out in jerry-built monotony on the boom tracts of the 1950s"?

That's a vast oversimplification, of course, and probably fundamentally unfair, but let us allow there is a grain, even more than a grain, of truth in it: something along the lines of the law of unintended consequences. Okay, but can Wright be held accountable for all the paltrier design-and-building imaginations that came along in his wake, after he—inadvertently—had shown the way? Isn't that a little like saying Shakespeare should never have written *King Lear* because someday, somewhere, someone was going to come up with *The Texas Chainsaw Massacre*? (Which, incidentally, is now regarded as one of the best horror films in history.) And here's the thing: The old shaman himself foresaw the dilemma. The mortar was barely dry on the blades of the tradesmen doing the troweling on the beyond-magical Jacobs House when Wright wrote prophetically in the January 1938 issue of *Architectural Forum* (not quite the entirety of which the editors gave over to his work, down to letting him basically assume the duties of an editor in chief): "As a matter of course a home like this is an architect's creation. It is not a builder's nor an amateur's effort and there is considerable risk in exposing the scheme to that sort of imitation or emulation. This is true because it could not be built except as the architect oversees the building and the building would fail of proper effect unless the furnishing and planting were done by the architect."

Considerable risk in exposing the scheme. The building would fail otherwise. That's his ego talking. Even as it's his utter truth talking.

In that same issue of the *Forum*—his first sentence—he said: "The house of moderate cost is not only America's major architectural problem but the problem most difficult for her major architects. As for me, I would rather solve it with satisfaction to myself . . . than build anything I can think of at the moment. . . ." And then, right into his hectoring and haughty mode: "In our country the chief obstacle to any real solution of the moderate-cost house-problem is the fact that our people do not really know how to live, imagining their idiosyncrasies to be their 'tastes,' their prejudices to be their predilections and their ignorance to be the virtue where any beauty of living is concerned."

But you had to keep forgiving him his superiority. Because his heart was in the right place. Because he wanted to create something for the common man—a dignified shelter for ordinary Americans that would provide not only shelter but beauty at the same time. Art and economy wrapped into an elevating one, so as to raise up the lives of its occupants in both conscious and unconscious ways.

Put your mind for a second back on all those magnificent Prairies at the turn of the century. They were American buildings, all right, and he had cracked the mold right in two when he'd built them. But they weren't democratic houses, especially. By and large they were rich people's dwellings, with their servants' quarters and spindled stairs and ribbon-glass windows and quarter-sawn-oak astonishments. No matter their radical designs, they still spoke, at least in terms of social hier-archies, to Victorian American domestic life. He went after the com-missions, avidly—it was a path to his fame, he wanted the money, he wanted the designing challenges. But did he always want something else besides, secretly and not so secretly? How to create for hard economic times, in a changing world, something that might turn out to be both American *and* democratic? Something that would have its own beauty, and perhaps the more so for its very bare-bonedness, for the seeming humility of its design and materials? How to bust wide open that mold? How to build the Everyman Prairie?*

He went on in that same issue of the *Forum:* "I am certain that any approach to the new house needed by indigenous culture—why worry about the house wanted by provincial ignorance—is fundamentally dif-ferent. The house must be a pattern for more simple and, at the same

---

* Although numerous Wright historians have made the point, in one way or another, about Amer-ican *and* democratic, the first Wright chronicler who helped me to understand the concept in crystalline ways was William Allin Storrer, author of many Wright texts, but not least his *The Architecture of Frank Lloyd Wright: A Complete Catalog,* which has been around for four and a half decades and is now in its fourth edition and has served almost two generations of Wright-goers as a kind of field guide, not unlike what Roger Tory Peterson, starting in the 1930s, began doing for bird lovers with his seminal hind-pocket field guides. There are other fine Wright field guides as well, and no slight is meant to them, but it was Storrer, in just a few introductory pages to the *Catalog,* and in our subsequent face-to-face talks, who made so much come clear. A separate point: There was never anything wrong per se with the houses of Levittown. In their own right, and on their own terms, many of them were pleasing models of efficiency and practicality, perhaps never more so than in the original Levittown houses on Long Island in the late 1940s. The problem came in the packing of them together, numbingly, in relatively dense suburban tracts. Until I saw a Levittown for myself, and then began to consult the work of some historians and critics on the matter, I had a kind of knee-jerk reaction about the word "Levittown." It simply meant "bad." Not at all. Again, I need cite the writing of critic-historian Paul Goldberger, previously referenced, for helping to set me straight.

time, more gracious living: new, but suitable to living conditions as they might so well be in the country we live in today."

At the end, he spoke of the new ideas of "freedom of movement, and privacy too, afforded by the general arrangement here, unknown to the current boxment. . . . I think a cultured American housewife will look well in it. The now inevitable car will seem part of it. Where does the garden leave off and the house begin? Where the garden begins and the house leaves off. Withal, it seems a thing loving the ground with the new sense of space—light—and freedom to which our U.S.A. is entitled."

Freedom of movement. A thing loving the ground. The country we live in today. But privacy, too. And informality, and spontaneity, much of it achieved by the mobility of the now inevitable car. In a sense, the soothsayer of architecture is preaching the same gospel he's always preached: openness and flow and freedom in this great Emersonian and Whitmanesque and Jeffersonian and Thoreauvian experiment called America. But he's also defining, nailing, so it seems to me, exactly what so much of postwar United States society and culture would turn into: the great arrived middle class, with its emphasis on an informal way of living. He peered into his ball and saw the changing dynamics and lifestyles of the American family. And he, uniquely, was here to serve it, build for it, proselytize it. It would only add to his myth. A plus-sum game. Everybody wins, not least himself.

By the way, that issue of the *Forum*—published by Time, Inc., and now regarded as a collector's item—ran to 179 pages. Magazines in the thirties were chockablock with advertising and seemed long as your arm. There were 32 pages of front matter. Then his 102-page special insert, which amounted to a magazine within a magazine, since they packaged it with its own soft front and back cover. Then a final 38 pages of this-and-architectural-that. At the very front—essentially on page one, 31 pages before the start of his insert—there's a hoot of a photograph of him. He's seated at a desk. He's shooting his French cuffs. You can see his pocket square. He's got his iron-gray hair swept back past his ears. He's Bogarting his unlit Lucky. Oh, maybe it's a Chesterfield. In the freckled fingertips of his joined and weathered-looking hands, he's fiddling with what seems like a matchbook—apparently he's just about to light up. (It's sort of a prop—in general, he's against smoking.) Beneath the photograph, taken by noted Time, Inc., staffer Peter Stackpole, the editors have written, in all caps, blocky type, miming something of his own lettering style: "TO HAVE WORKED IN CLOSE ASSOCIATION WITH MR. WRIGHT IN THE DEVELOPMENT OF THIS ISSUE, WHICH WAS DESIGNED AND WRITTEN BY HIM, HAS BEEN A STIMULATING EXPERIENCE. . . ." Surely, that was editor code-speak in the halls of Henry Luce for *Damn, if we aren't glad this baby has gone to bed.*

But, really, this story of the Jake has started in the wrong place. Isn't it always finally about the people? Wright biographers and historians, referencing the medicine man himself, love to speak of how he spent seven decades shaking his designs out of his sleeve. (It's an entertaining legend, and I, too, am more than willing to fall for it.) But what about shaking the *people* out of his sleeve? How did he pull that off?

———

American studies: In the late summer of 1936, Jesse Owens was driving Adolf Hitler mad at the Berlin Olympics (a gold medal on August 3, another on the 4th, a third on the 5th, a fourth on the 9th). Edward Hopper was finishing a painting called *Cape Cod Afternoon.* A New Jersey quartet called the Hoboken Four was admiring itself on page 45 of the new issue of *McCall's* magazine—the crooners had won first place on the Major Bowes Amateur Hour radio show, and the editors were showcasing them in a smallish photo feature. (The skinny guy at the right of the frame was named Frank Sinatra.) In Hale County, Alabama, James Agee, a writer for *Fortune* magazine, was living on a slab of washed-out plateau, among three appallingly damaged white cotton tenant farm families, trying to decode their lives. (The documentary photographer Walker Evans was there, too, freeze-framing in his box what Agee was trying simultaneously to capture in words.)

And in Madison, Wisconsin, a Harvard-educated and semi-bohemian reporter for one of the two local dailies climbed into his secondhand beater (possibly it was thirdhand) and drove himself and his wife semi-nervously out Highway 14 to Spring Green to keep an appointment with someone they imagined would have scant time for them or their request. His name was Herbert Austin Jacobs. He was thirty-three years old. He had big bony hands and a shock of grin and a cowlick of hair and a kind of unfailing optimism. He liked to roll his own cigarettes and buy wine in gallon jugs. He and his nine-years-younger wife, Katherine (she was quieter but no less adventurous and frugal), had a small daughter and $1,600 in the bank. (It had come from a great-aunt's inheritance.) At *The Capital Times,* rival of the better-off *Wisconsin State Journal,* they were paying Herb Jacobs two dollars a week more than his age. Thirty-five bucks. The family was managing to live on twenty-two, and salt away the other thirteen.

Here were two ordinary citizens of the United States, making a life and a living in the belly of the Depression, who, in another sense, were anything but ordinary. It was as if, without really knowing, they owned the oddest combination of all the right-seeming ingredients for what was going to turn out to be a landmark moment of building history. But what they also couldn't have understood was that the equation went both ways: the man they were driving out to meet needed them as much as they were hoping for him.*

The Jacobses had this goofy idea—they'd more or less rehearsed what they were going to say on the hour's drive out from town—that the most famous architect in America might be willing to pause in all of his important projects just then and design for them a small and sensible and low-cost and, not least, beautiful house. The hazy figure they had in mind, including the prospective lot that their prospective house might be built on, was, gulp, five thousand dollars, which to them, in another way, was a sum as big as the earth. They decided to go bold and put the request to the great man as a challenge: "What this country needs, sir, is a decent five-thousand-dollar house. Can you build it?"

" 'Will you walk into my parlor?' said the spider to the fly," their host

---

* History has lost the exact date and time of this meeting, but we do know that it happened the week of Monday, August 3, 1936, and apparently in the hour or so before supper. They hadn't been invited to stay on for dinner, which was okay by them, since they'd left baby Susan Jacobs, who wasn't quite two, in the care of friends back in town and told them they'd try to be home before dark. Home was a rented apartment with three sticks of furniture at 1143 Sherman Avenue on the near east side of Madison. I've wondered how Herb got off from work, since he was a newbie at the paper. Only weeks before, he'd come over from *The Milwaukee Journal,* where he'd worked for the previous five years in a variety of reporting jobs, having started out on what that old newsfolk call "late cops"—he was the night police reporter, hanging around the desk sergeant at headquarters and trying to steal looks at the blotter for a possible story to run down. When he could, the Harvard grad would go over to a greasy spoon where there was a sign in the window: "Two eggs, any style, 5 cents. Limit 8 to a customer." He tells some of these stories in his 1978 illustrated memoir, written with his wife's contributions: *Building with Frank Lloyd Wright.* It's a charming and rather brief book, but it's almost unavoidably hagiographic, as are most memoirs by people, clients or otherwise, who once intersected with Wright. But doesn't that fact alone tell us something: that in a sense his ego is always easier to take from the inside than from the out? The charm wins out—mostly.

said, grinning, after they'd shaken hands, after he'd heard their request
(Herb was the one who'd more or less stammered out the so-called
bold challenge), after the host had taken twenty-four-year-old Katherine lightly by the elbow and steered her in a kind of half-seductive
waltz toward one of his beautiful and uncomfortable straight-backed
chairs in the low-lit inner sanctums of Taliesin. Or at least this is how
I am picturing things.

A minute before this, Wright apparently said something like: Would
you really be satisfied with a five-thousand-dollar house? Most people
want a ten-thousand-dollar house for five thousand dollars. No, no,
they assured him. Wright told them he'd had such an idea in his mind
for at least twenty years, and they were the first two to ever come along
and ask. It was a lie to their faces, which in the larger scheme didn't
matter much. Suspend the Jacobses here, in the spider's parlor, while I
relay a little of who they were, how they came to this moment.

———

The word "Harvard" possibly threw it off. Harvard had come about for
Herb Jacobs (in 1922) through a scholarship from a Harvard alumni club
in Milwaukee, and that's because the club admired the work of Herbert
Jacobs senior and had wished to help out his children. Herbert Jacobs
the elder, along with his wife—she had a background as a teacher—ran a
Milwaukee settlement house. Jacobs the father was a secret socialist and
an ordained Congregational minister, who'd given up the latter work to
minister in secular ways to deprived people. There must have been some
deep anger in him about the injustices of the world. He and his spouse
are said to have never made more than $2,500 a year in their entire lives.
The settlement house, of which Herbert H. Jacobs had been appointed
"warden," was affiliated with the University of Wisconsin. (It is thought
to be the pioneering place of organized social work in the state.) It was
on the south side of Milwaukee, in the heavily Polish Fourteenth Ward
(but Germans and Slavs and other ethnic groups crowded there as well),
in the dirtiest, most industrial quarter of the city. So Jacobs the son
learned early on about privation. He learned to think of it somehow
as a virtue—an embraced aesthetic rather than a given-in-to fate. His
boyhood "home" was a three-story, twenty-seven-room, repurposed
building where the "clients" or "guests"—people sometimes brought

in from the streets that afternoon—often got to experience sit-down dinners at candlelit tables covered with linen. The boy was surrounded by people with bad teeth, bad luck, grime under their nails, too much rotgut liquor in their past. The snoring alone in that house of twenty-seven rooms must have been something.

Herb Jacobs (he was born, the second of four Jacobs children, in 1903, so, to keep the measuring stick in your mind, Frank Lloyd Wright was a little more than twice his age) used to wait those graciously set tables every night with his kid brother Ralph (after they'd eaten in another room, at the kids' table). They'd bring the seconds, they'd refold the cloth napkins after the diners had bellied away from the table. From the time he was about twelve, Herb was shoveling forty tons of bituminous coal every winter into the settlement house's boiler. It was what was expected of him. His father was a good and spiritual man—and also a stern and moody and sharp-tongued and somewhat distant man.

If the son knew about hardship and social injustice from almost the time he could walk, he knew about family death, too—before he'd gone to first grade. First, his older sister died. A few years later, Herb's youngest brother died. As an adult—and he was going to live to be eighty-four—he seldom talked about this blunt fact: four kids in the family, and two of his siblings dead before they could get out of their childhoods. I have asked the three children of Herb Jacobs—who are now septuagenarians and octogenarians themselves—why it was so (that their father could never really talk about it), and their answer is mostly: Well, it was how men of that era coped, behaved. "He wasn't one to dwell on his inner feelings," the middle Jacobs child, Elizabeth Aitken, who is something of the family historian (and an extremely nice person), told me. Her father wrote several of what can be thought of as loose autobiographies. (He was nothing if not prolific—as a journalist, as an author, as a letter-writer, as a diarist, as a newsletter-keeper. His better-known works, in book form, center around his and his family's long association with Frank Lloyd Wright.) But you can comb all of his books and what you'll find is literally one sentence about the loss of two of his siblings in his childhood—or that is all I could find. It's in a book entitled *We Chose the Country,* and this is the sentence: "When I was five, our own family was reduced when my older sister died of tuberculosis and when my youngest brother died a few years later, after a speechless paralysis that lasted three years." What would it have been like to witness that TB death, the little brother's frozen face? *Reduced*, he says.

The impression you could form is one of way too much seriousness. Mirthlessness. But the more you peer into Herb Jacobs's contradictory-seeming life, as it intersects with Frank Lloyd Wright's contradictory life, the more you'll find an under-running theme of what might be termed whimsy by way of insatiable curiosity.

On the whimsy: He had a great weakness for limericks (bawdier the better in most instances), and loved spouting them at dinner parties. (His children got the sanitized versions.) And he was also a lifelong and pathetically bad and corny—and in that sense terrific—doggerel-maker. When he was in his eighties and struggling with a recently diagnosed cancer (this was in California, when he was retired from teaching journalism at Berkeley, far away in time and distance from the northeast sloping corner of Toepfer and Birch), he sent out a mimeo-graphed "poem" of three stanzas to friends with these lines: "This is no letter / But just a note till I'm much better / Right now I clutch my fake diploma / Five months in that cancer school, lymphoma / But set out an easy chair for me / They've stopped my chemotherapy." (The blood cancer would kill him almost exactly a year later, but not before he'd composed his own sizable obituary. A lot of papers picked it up. *The New York Times* incorporated some of it in its own staff-written obitu-ary, under this headline: HERBERT JACOBS, 30'S REPORTER WHO RESHAPED ARCHITECTURE. That was and was not true.)

On the unslakable curiosity. Really, it's one of the prerequisites for being a great reporter. In Jacobs's case, it was a muscle that had flexed itself to absurd-seeming proportions. Again, Elizabeth Aitken, middle child: "This was a man who read the *Encyclopaedia Britannica* for plea-sure. The old onion-skinned volumes—all twenty-four of them, or how-ever many it was. He would use a magnifying glass. He started with 'A' and he went all the way through. More than once."

Curiosity? He once had a flat tire at night and pulled off to the side of the road outside Madison. This was in the late summer of 1951. Beastly hot out. He and his wife were at the edge of a cornfield. They sat there. He said, "Damn, honey, I think I can hear the corn growing. Maybe it's true, that old saw." He got out of his car and walked into the cornfield.

He cupped his ear. Herb was then working as the farm editor of the *Cap Times*. (Just in charting the number of jobs he had at the paper in his twenty-six years on staff, you can get a sense of the restless and up-for-trying-new-things kind of person he was: editorial writer, farm reporter, farm editor, feature writer, city editor, news editor, photographer, a columnist banging out 750 words six and seven days a week. In a sense, he was always *too* facile. His kids remember him sitting after supper with his battered portable on his knees and rolling a piece of newsprint into the carriage and just typing the next day's column straight through.)

The old farmer's saw: "It's so hot out you can almost hear the corn growing." The next week Herb organized a team of agronomists from the university to accompany him into the same field with recording devices. Damn, if the experts didn't claim they, too, could hear snapping and crackling noises, or at least could hear them once they got back to their labs and had bent over the reel-to-reel tapes with their earphones. Herb's story in the paper went out nationally. The *Globe Gazette* in Mason City, Iowa, had just opened its big North Iowa Fair, and so put the great snapping news on page one.

His whole life, he seems to have been a tinkerer, a tweaker, an experimentalist, a can-doer, a back-of-an-envelope kind of quixotic contemplater. (He once explained his life as the phenomenon of "aggressive drift.") His literary bone was far larger, but there was definitely an applied science gene somewhere in there. Curiosity? You can go to Wikipedia and look up something called "Jacobs's Method." The method has to do with crowd counting. It's still in use, at least to some degree. In the spring of 1967, the lecturer in journalism at the University of California, Berkeley, used to watch the student-strike voters massing below his tower-window office at Sproul Hall Plaza. (What history knows as the Berkeley Free Speech Movement had started three years before.) Herb got an enlarged aerial photograph. He ruled it off in one-inch squares. He got a magnifying glass—perhaps the same one with which he used to read the *Britannica* on frozen nights back in Madison—and began counting heads. He came up with a formula which is too complicated to explain here, but it had to do with how many square feet a single person will occupy in various crowds, from tightly packed to loosely knit. *Time* magazine did a feature on Herb, holding up his aerial photograph, in his bow tie, amid all the free-speech heads in the picture, with this caption: "The squares have it." He loved the joke.

Because, in fact, he *was* something of a square, and he knew it. There was a kind of prudishness to him in and amid the bawdy limerick-making. It was as if he knew time was short on this earth, and you'd better account. (He thought movies were a waste of time—this didn't go over large with his teenaged children.) He was about conserving what you have, making much of little. Again, his middle daughter: "It wasn't appropriate to want things that cost money." I've spoken on the telephone with Elizabeth Aitken (she lives in Oregon) for more than several hours on several occasions, and we've kept in loose touch by email, and I keep waiting for the other shoe of parental bitterness to drop. It hasn't. Nor have I heard it in the voices of the other two Jacobs children.* (I have only been able to hear their voices; the circumstances have never worked out to meet them.) In fact, what appears to have sifted down in all their lives are most of the values their parents preached, by direction and indirection: the less you have to take with you in this world, the better off you are. Too many material possessions are an unhealthy thing.

So this one final story of the dozen more that might be told. It has to do with the way Herb found his wife—to whom he was married, and apparently in happiness, for fifty-three years. (They'd been married for two and a half years on the day they drove to Spring Green.) It was almost as if he did it by lottery. From one of his books: "I know the procedure I followed is not orthodox, but it seemed to work out all right for me. I simply looked over the list of my female friends and acquaintances of suitable age, picked one that I thought I would most enjoy living with, put on a strenuous courtship campaign, and married her, all in less than four months." (There was a chocolate cake involved, too—she killed him with her baking skills.)

---

* The eldest Jacobs child, Susan Jacobs Lockhart, grew up to be an artist and also to have a long career in Wright-related activities, including serving on the board (and then as president) of the Frank Lloyd Wright Building Conservancy. As a child, she wore hand-me-downs from relatives or homemade clothes that tended on the drab side—grays, mostly. She had to wait until her last year of high school before getting her first-ever new coat—from a store. Her parents bought it, but she got to pick it out. "Lipstick red," she said, cackling. "And you were okay, having to wait that long?" I nudged. "Yes," she said. "Well, mostly." I thought I could hear the smallest rueful laugh on the other end of the phone line. But no bitterness came through.

So now you're wondering who *she* was. She, too, seems the sum of her own wonderful contradictions. Katherine Jacobs's maiden name was Wescott. She grew up, the youngest of six, on a series of hardscrabble farms in what's known as the kettle moraine region of Wisconsin. It's glacial-drift country west and north of Milwaukee. Lives there are not necessarily known to be cosmopolitan. The dirt-poor family produced all of its food, made its own clothes. How is it then that all six Wescott kids got to college? (Katherine had walked to a one-room schoolhouse.) How is it then that Katherine's big brother, Glenway Wescott, left that lean country and, eventually, become one of the Paris expats of the twenties, right there on the Left Bank of myth and memory with Hemingway and Fitzgerald and Joyce and Djuna Barnes and Gerald and Sara Murphy and all the rest? (Hemingway loathed him, and not the least of it was that Glenway was pronouncedly gay. Hemingway wrote him into a hilarious if cruelly homophobic scene in *The Sun Also Rises*. In the original version of the scene at the *bal musette,* in the Rue de la Montagne Sainte Geneviève, the character's name is "Robert Prescott." Max Perkins, Hemingway's famed editor at Scribner's, fearing libel, made him change the name to "Robert Prentiss." Still, everyone in Montparnasse knew it was Wescott, whose name has slipped increasingly into literary oblivion. Sic transit. Hemingway keeps eating whole most of his onetime competitors.)

Never the intellectual her husband was, but loving to be around books and book people (she was clerking in a Milwaukee bookstore when she met Herb), Katherine Wescott Jacobs seems chiefly to have been about the purpose-driven life. More than her husband, she was the anchor of the family—spiritually and morally. To paraphrase an old song lyric: If Herb made the living, Katherine made the living worthwhile. (And, in fact, she contributed to the family income through the years, with clerical and other jobs.) She could work all day long—it was the farmgirl heritage. She was a thin, small, bespectacled woman, not what you'd call beautiful (you can see it in all of the old family pictures, and, almost astonishingly, her husband more or less said it himself in one of his books), but she apparently had something far deeper than mere looks. She was content to let him have the limelight after their house (and somewhat their own lives) became famous. In her last years, in their joint retirement in California, she tapped a vein she didn't know she had. She became a sculptor. Her work got into galleries. The art seemed to have come out of nowhere, but it was rooted down there all along, deceptively out of sight.

Is it possible that Frank Lloyd Wright had already built a new kind of American dwelling in his mind that was an inanimate extension and expression of two people named Jacobs whom he didn't yet know but knew all the same? Simplicity as their aesthetic. Art in their DNA. Frugality as a value. Hard work as an ethic. Openness to experimental things almost as a matter of course. The doctrine that less will always be more, if you know how to make good and artistic use of the less. "We were a bit outside the American pattern, anyway," Herb Jacobs says halfway through *Building with Frank Lloyd Wright,* an understatement that could also stand as a definition of the home that he and his wife and their family were destined to occupy for barely five years.

Well, Wright did meet them, on a sultry afternoon in early August 1936. And at that meeting it almost seems as if he had understood, maybe in the first two minutes of sitting down, and maybe in his glands far more than in his intellect, that they were almost perfectly right. As if God himself had sent them. Maybe he did.

Robert Frost's poem "The Gift Outright" begins: "The land was ours before we were the land's. / She was our land more than a hundred years / Before we were her people." It was as if Herb and Katherine Jacobs were their house, and their house was them, long before they ever physically came to be joined with her.

––––––––––

Joinery? That's a building word. Some words here about "the thing itself," meaning the architecture, the construction, the design. "The thing itself," Walker Evans once said, speaking about the illusive nature of photography. "The thing itself is such a secret and so unapproachable." As regards 441 Toepfer Avenue, that line seems both apt and not true.

She was described earlier as a 1,550-square-foot, L-shaped, sandwich-walled, flat-roofed, slab-floored, radiant-heated, three-bedroom Usonian dream. Go back, if you will, to the photograph at the top of this chapter. Perhaps the idea of fourth dimension ("You can't invent a design. You recognize it, in the fourth dimension") starts with the fact that the entire house is just more or less sitting there, as if without real anchoring to the earth. To quote historian Paul Sprague: "There is no true basement nor are there foundations. The concrete pad that supports everything above it was poured over a tamped sand base." Another way of framing this thought: All the walls, whether of brick or wood or glass, inside and out, rest, as if precariously, on a simple sheet of concrete laid atop sand fill.*

Why hasn't the big wooden cabinet just blown away?

The second improbable thought (and fact): You're looking at her almost inside out. Meaning: her rear is her front, and her front is her rear. As has been said by many chroniclers, the Jacobs has turned her back to the street, has given Toepfer Avenue the cold shoulder. What you see is her backside, meaning her front, at least in terms of family functions. All the living is intended to take place back here, out of sight of the public eye.

That might be said of almost any house, by any architect—the essential living out of sight of the public eye—except that in the Jacobs the idea approaches the next dimension. All the living—in the living room, dining area, and bedrooms—is meant in some way to face out and toward nature, into a garden and modest expanse of yard. It's not quite literally possible—but it almost is—to open up the entire back side of this house, converting her into an outdoor living room, thanks to a series of glazed floor-to-ceiling doors of plate glass set into narrow rectangular frames. (To keep costs down, the windows and doors, every other set of which can be opened, were made by machine at a local planing mill, and fitted into their frames built on site—and the glass was similarly installed.)

---

* I'm drawing gratefully on what are recognized as the two definitive pieces of writing about the house. Both are in lengthy article form, the first being Donald G. Kalec's "The Jacobs House I," published in 1990, and the second, written in 2001, by Paul Sprague, which doesn't bear a title per se. (It was part of an application to get the house designated a National Historic Landmark—successfully so, in 2003.) Both authors are esteemed architectural historians. Kalec, who knew the Jacobses personally and was able to interview them extensively, made available his research files. We were once talking over lunch about the house. He is a small, modest man, who has taught for years at the School of the Art Institute of Chicago. He had known the Jake for half a century. He sighed. "I guess it comes down to the mystery of how so much is made of so little." He paused. "I mean, she has such long legs." Pause again. "Such artful artlessness." God bless Herb Jacobs himself for saving so much paper—and placing it, before he died, in several important repositories. He had a wonderful archival sense. As his middle daughter told me: "He knew what was interesting about his own life." Amen.

Again, quoting Sprague: "When opened in summer, the barrier between inside and out is dissolved and the two realms made one."

Another way to think about this dissolving effect: If the architect parsimoniously gave his clients few electrical outlets—in the original plans, there were no more than two wall outlets (four sockets) in the entire house, one for the family radio, one for a clock, the other two for lamps—then he gave the family a profusion, a luxuriance, almost an absurdity of ways to get in and get out. At least on the back side—er, the front side.

It's as if Wright made the house the lot, and the lot the house, each folding into the other, even if the house takes up only a portion of the lot.

The glass used for the original windows and doors was cut from old Madison store windows, with the gold leaf or other lettering taken off before installation at the site. (The glass has long since been replaced with insulating double panes.)

L-shape: There are two separate wings, and you can get a sense of it by studying the photograph, even if the wing over on the right can only partially be seen. To orient you: That wing faces south, the other east, both to catch the sun at good times. One wing—it's the one you see in full—is made deliberately grand. (I know: it sounds entirely funny to be using the word "wing," as if she were a mansion, but, in fact, the architect created two distinct identities in 1,550 square feet.) The deliberately modest wing is where the sleeping occurs. No need for a sense of grand on this leg of the L. Sleeping is for sleeping. The bedroom you're able to get a glimpse of on the right is the second bedroom, which is really the first one as you come down the hall. Next to it (out of sight here) is the so-called master bedroom, but by any modern standard, pretty small (roughly twelve feet by sixteen feet). The ceilings in the bedrooms are low and snug: seven feet, three inches. At the end of this wing there's a small third bedroom, which for unclear reasons Wright kept wanting to call in his plans a study. (The addition of this study/bedroom is why the price of the house climbed to $5,500.) All three bedrooms face the garden, with the foot of the beds in each room about six feet from the rectangular frames of glass. The first bedroom (again the one you're able to see) has three glass doors facing the garden, and the master alongside of it has six: so theoretically, nine ways to get outside in just those two rooms. But a question: If you weren't coming in from the outside, how would you enter each bedroom? Via a narrow hallway that runs along the outside edge of the sleeping wing. The effect is something like a Pullman railroad car in the golden age of rail travel—or maybe three staterooms on a lower deck of a miniature ocean liner. (The steward tells you to go along the hallway and find the door to the compartment that's yours.) Except never one to do anything ordinary, Wright decided to jog the hallway around the master bedroom, and then to widen it at the far end. Apparently, he wanted to break up the monotony of a long hallway, give the hallway itself some pizzazz.

Flat roof: yes, but no. You have to think in multiples, plurals. To quote historian Donald Kalec: The Jake rises "vertically into a series of layered roof planes." In fact, there are three levels of flat roof. (You can see two here, the one tucked in beneath the other.) Wright built his roofs with two-by-fours covered with asphalt and gravel. But what happens when it rains? Simple: The flat roofs aren't quite flat. Wright gave an almost imperceptible rise to the surfaces by placing wedges in the center, thereby forcing water to seek the edges and not sit in the middle. Thus the water can drain off the sides without need of gutters or downspouts: such disfiguring things. Not a problem, because the eaves are so wide and overhanging. The overflow will fall far enough from the sides of the house so that the owners never need worry about water getting into the foundations—

Of which there are none. Because she's built on a concrete slab—remember?

Move your eye one blink to the left of the bedroom that you can see. You're at the juncture of the L, the pivot point of the house, where some real Wrightian genius lay, even though there's genius everywhere in this house.

There's a masonry core at the juncture of the L, a brick mass, inside of which are one wall of a hearth, a kitchen, and a bathroom. This brick core helps hold up the house. But aside from the engineering aspects, the mass gathered at the L allows the kitchen to be placed at the approximate center of the house. Except that it's not called a kitchen any longer. In the new lexicon, this tiny room—seven feet by eight feet, with an open floor space of just four feet by five feet, although with a luxuriously high ceiling and generous counter space and tall cupboards—is to be thought of as the "workspace." The important person busying herself to prepare the family evening meal will no longer be in an inconvenient spot. She'll be in the heart of the flow, literally and metaphorically. (Isn't it a kind of feminist manifesto from a notorious lothario?) This person will be able to keep an eye on the children emerging from a nap in one wing, and at the same time will be only a short distance from her spouse, who, on the other side of the fireplace, might be composing on his lap a story for tomorrow's paper—in one take.

Say it this way: The housewife, from her pilot's perch, in the not-quite-center of the house, has far larger control of the enterprise, the moment, the new dynamic of living.

You can't see the kitchen in this photograph. But it's there, at the heart of the L.

The dining room: Again, it's really a kind of alcove, an eating nook. It's right across from the kitchen. It's set into a bay—you can see the window. Fitted below: a skinny, oblong, no-frills, custom-made, modernist table, able to seat at least eight.

The single bathroom. It's next to the kitchen. It's six feet square. Like the rest of the house, it's made of bricks and boards. No tiling. Tiling is too costly for this kind of living. Okay, but instead of a rectangular tub placed along the wall, how about a not-quite-square tub that will fit into a corner? Critical space can be saved, and the tight little box of a bathroom will get some extra pizzazz, and, hey, won't all the neighbor kids soon be begging to come over to try out the tub? (They did. It's true that the custom-made tub cost some extra dough, but the architect deemed it worthwhile, and Ma and Pa Jacobs, whose family grew to four while they lived in the mouse-house, readily came to agree.)

A word about the garage. There isn't one. Instead there's a "carport." A word, an idea, that Frank Lloyd Wright claims to have invented—and built here for the first time. It's a roofed, cantilevered space, open on two and a half sides, with a floor of gravel, its own small engineering marvel.

A word about the masonry. If there is wood everywhere in this house, there's plenty of brick, too. The architect specified that the masons lay the bricks, both inside and out, conforming to a system he'd first devised for his Prairies. He had the bricklayers trowel the horizontal joints with pale-colored mortar, and then rake, or recess, them to produce a shadow line, between brick and mortar, thus accentuating the stretch-out effect: the flat line of the American prairie. For the vertical joints, Wright specified that the mortar be the reddish color of the bricks themselves, and that the masons trowel it flush, so as to blur things optically. The old sleight-of-hand.

Last stop on this virtual tour, grandest room of all, the one that takes up the bulk of this photograph—and the bulk of the mouse-house, period. In square footage, the living room is about one-third of the whole. The room, with its specially designed furniture, some of it built in, can be said to have an inner and an outer focus. The inner is the huge hearth at the north end, the outer is what extends beyond the glazed glass, toward you, as you're looking. In other words, the idea of winter and summer as almost inherent properties of the room itself. The room is approximately eighteen feet wide by thirty feet long, but because everything else is so spare and utilitarian, because one thing flows into the next, the space has almost an opulent feel. (It's what Wright meant when he told the Jacobses: "In this house, you will have the sense of space—not space itself, but the sense of space—that most people pay ten thousand dollars for.")

The ceilings are nine feet, four inches high—a relative extravagance.

And yet the wall you can't see: It's on the opposite side of the glazed panels. It's board-and-batten, tongue-and-groove, redwood-and-ponderosa-pine. It's the famous Frank Lloyd Wright "sandwich wall," possibly used here for the first time anywhere in America.

To break this down: The wood here consists first of rows of vertical pine boards. They are standing on end. They are seven-eighths-of-an-inch thick. This thin first layer is wrapped on both sides with special paper to make it airtight. Next come nine-and-a-half-inch-wide pine boards placed horizontally along both sides of the vertical boards. They're the slices of bread, held in place by horizontal wood strips known as battens. The battens, recessed by a quarter of an inch, are three and a quarter inches wide, and they've been screwed in, not nailed. The edges of the wide horizontal boards and the smaller horizontal battens are specially milled so that they interlock, to expand and contract with weather. Ah, the big wooden cabinet. With the sandwich walls. Sealed tight with #10 flathead wood screws.

Inside, the walls look pretty much the same as they do on the outside, in the way one side of your ham-and-Swiss looks pretty much like the other side. Except that the pine on the inside has been treated with many coats of wax, to give it its transparent gleam. Outside the house, the pine has been given many coats of linseed oil. Both inside and out, the natural grain of the wood has come deeply through, the more so with age.

There are twenty-six-foot-long bookshelves inside—they fortify the wall.

Wright wanted to use cypress—its natural shine. The cost wasn't feasible. But he had an inspired idea: redwood for the battens. (He paid the extra cost himself.) Thus, there is a beautiful banding effect both inside and out: the burnished red of the battens set against the yellow-orange glow of the waxed pine. It's a duotone effect, a shadow line, inside and out, like a pinstriping on a sports car, except that the pinstripe here is three inches wide. Maybe a better image is rows of red ribbon on a very large present, waiting to be opened. The added cost, Wright decided, was like fitting a not-quite-square tub into a nook of a tiny bathroom: pizzazz. Overall, the woody feel of this house far outweighs the sense of brick and glass. How did he do that?

The overhead lighting. Think of it as an early form of track lighting. Wright dropped U-shaped metal channels four inches from the ceiling. To the sides and bottoms of these channels he placed sockets for low-watt bulbs. The wire for the sockets was stripped along the inside of the channels. Result? A suffused glow coming down. Strings of bare-bulbed light, like something at a summer backyard picnic. Primitively beautiful.

And, finally, the most radical idea of all, not just in this room, but also across the entire house: the heating system. Wright used radiant heat, only he preferred calling it "gravity heat." In his autobiography he said, "It was simply 'gravity heat'—heat coming up from beneath as naturally as heat rises." Remember, the house has no foundation—she rests on a concrete slab, sitting on a tamped sand base. So: Wright had one-and-a-half-inch pipes sunk into the sand fill. He had four rows of the pipes laid around the perimeter of the living room, and three rows around the bedroom wing. Then he had the mat poured directly over top of the pipes that had been sunk into the sand. To quote Donald Kalec: "When steam was forced under pressure through the pipes, the whole floor became the heating element." To quote Paul Sprague: "The heated pipes [would] chase any frost from the sand and warm the house by heating the slab." The fill below the floor would never freeze, even in Wisconsin winters of twenty below, because it would always be warm down there. And atop the floor? Well, according to the laws of gravity, hot air must rise, while colder air will be pulled down to the floor—to get warmed and to rise again. The convection principle: Warmed by contact with the floor, the colder air, no longer cold, rises to continue to heat the house and its occupants. Floor as a heating pad.

But where is the steam for the pipes coming from? A small boiler. The architect had to house the furnace somewhere, and so he grudgingly gave the Jacobs the smallest basement possible. Wright loathed basements—just repositories for clutter. He placed the mouse-basement directly below the kitchen and the bathroom. The dimensions are six feet by seventeen feet. Except for this rude below-ground intrusion in his ingenious house (and he did think of it as *his* house, as much or more than it would ever be *their* house), the Jacobs sits flat on the earth, even as she organically emerges from it.

According to Herb Jacobs, in that first meeting at Taliesin late on that mid-week afternoon in the first week of August 1936, Wright asked if they'd be willing to try out a heated floor. He told them he had become acquainted with the idea when he was living in Japan. He said theirs would be the first residence in America to have such a system. The adventurers said, sure, they'd be willing to try. Odd thing, though. He didn't use the term "radiant heat" or "gravity heat." He called it "holocaust heating."

I've talked to many people in the Wright universe about the Herbert and Katherine Jacobs House. I've done a good amount of primary and secondary research. But I've yet to come across anyone, in print or in person, remarking on the savage-seeming irony of those words. To me, they're like a baseball bat to the side of the head.

———

Now to a cliffhanger (almost literally) of a weekend house in a rhododendron forest over a waterfall some sixty-eight miles southeast of Pittsburgh, and to a so-called cathedral of clerical office space at 1525 Howe Street in Racine, Wisconsin. Namely: Fallingwater and the Johnson Wax administration building (their popular names), two of the most famous pieces of architecture of the twentieth century. Their histories, too, are intimately bound up with the miracle comeback year of 1936. How is it that Edgar J. Kaufmann and Herbert F. Johnson, with their money and sensibilities and secret stirrings, should have shown up on the client doorstep—as if God himself had sent them—at the moment that Frank Lloyd Wright needed them to show up, and thereby make possible in a midwifing way two buildings for the ages but, in the bargain, help a supreme egotist to rise from the architectural dead? If that can't be explained, maybe the smallest spool of the yarn can be nibbled at.*

Shaking them: Johnson's nickname was Hib, which was a shortening of his christened name, Hibbard. He was the grandson of the founder of the company, and he had come into the kingdom in 1928, when he was barely twenty-eight. (He was born in the last year of the old century.) The kingdom was S. C. Johnson & Son, a privately held, family-centric, money-pouring-in maker of waxes and paints on the shores of Lake Michigan. The firm was located in a small industrial city between Chicago and Milwaukee. If it was an international concern (plants in England, Australia, and France and Canada), there was something essentially hometown and middle-western and benevolent and paternalistic and yet at the same time surprisingly forward thinking about the company. It held a philosophy of "enlightened selfishness": you treat your employee right, and the treatment will come back to you in spades. The firm apparently didn't need or want a corporate headquarters in New York City; pint-sized Racine was just fine. It believed (when a lot of its corporate peers didn't) in the eight-hour workday, in Christmas bonuses, in paid vacations. It believed in closing up shop if the thermostat on the factory floor ever got above ninety degrees in the middle of the summer. It believed in advertising its wares on the radio: in the middle of the Depression (and for many years afterward), it served as the official sponsor of the *Fibber McGee and Molly* show, which grew

* The fact is, it's hardly something that happened only here. Time and again, the phenomenon pops up. Ada Huxtable, in *Frank Lloyd Wright*, uses words and phrases like "providentially." And "As luck and fate would have it." And "The client who appeared fortuitously at this time. . . ." She'll say things such as: "in which serendipity, as usual, played a notable part." It's as if she's shrugging. Me, too. A Jungian psychologist might call it the riddle of synchronicity, luck based on huge desire. The mystical idea of wishing something so badly to happen that you almost will it into happening.

into a kind of corny national institution. (The truth-bending Fibber and his forbearing wife, Molly, were from Wistful Vista, which could almost describe lake-hugging Racine itself.)

The Depression had hit the company hard. Profit-sharing ceased. But layoffs were avoided. At the nadir point, somewhere in 1932, the firm's research chemists had come up with a new product, a self-polishing floor wax given the catchy name "Glo-Coat." Presto, back in the money. So much so that by mid-summer 1936 serious talk was again in the works for the design of a new central headquarters. The new building would sit in the middle of the plant, amid the smokestacked factories and warehouses. But let it be something eye-catching. Something artistic and modern and yet efficient and corporate-like. Only problem: The competent Racine architect who'd been commissioned for the job was just that: competent. His submitted ideas didn't *pop*. Frankly, they were boring.

Wouldn't this long-view history and short-term reversal of fortune have made things next to perfect for the strutting arrival of an anything-but-boring self-proclaimed genius who, for all the strut, hadn't had a successful commercial project in a decade, and was secretly looking for almost any work he could find? It was as if he'd custom-fitted the gestalt of S. C. Johnson & Son to his own needs and decentralized view of the world.

Hib: In a sense, *he* was something artistic and modern and yet efficient and corporate-like. As an undergraduate at Cornell he had majored in chemistry (knowing he'd come home to the company), but, crucial to note, he'd also taken art history and drawing classes. He seems to have thought of himself throughout his life as a kind of artist manqué. In another life, he might have taken a dare and tried to become a real artist, the hell with chemistry and manufacturing. Anyway, he'd ended up marrying the daughter of his art professor soon after college. The marriage would fail after a decade. When the divorce came, in 1934, Hib and his wife, Gertrude, had a ten-year-old daughter and a six-year-old son (who would one day succeed him at the company, while sustaining a lifelong difficult relationship with his father). There was another child, a daughter, in the middle of those two, who died a hard death at four. All that's being said is the CEO's personal life was far more complex than might meet the eye—or than has generally been portrayed. (His second wife, to whom he was married for not even a year and a half, succumbed to alcoholism and depression and other ills.) It would all have its resonance.

Hib was cocky—how could you not be if you'd become head of a multinational family business while still in your twenties? (His father had served as president before him. When Herbert Johnson, Sr., died, at not quite sixty, in 1928, Hib—who had changed his first name to Herbert—got control.) Hib was handsome—he liked straw boaters and three-piece suits that tended to fit him like envelopes. He had a dazzling grin—you can see it in so many of the old photographs—and a need for speed, which his streamlined Lincoln-Zephyr, with its low-raked windscreen, didn't wholly satisfy. Turns out Frank Lloyd Wright had the same car.

In 1986, the architectural historian Jonathan Lipman published *Frank Lloyd Wright and the Johnson Wax Buildings;* it remains the definitive account. "His path differed from the typical president of a corporation," Lipman told me. "It's not necessarily the same profile. In a sense, Hib's ruthless ambition and drive had never been tested. He was more willing to take risks with the company money, more open to new ideas, even if he had a board to consider. He would have shared Wright's belief in the power of architecture to touch people deeply. So it all just lined up. For both of them."

The skeleton of it: On Friday, July 17, 1936, two company higher-ups, although not yet Hib, had motored over to Taliesin to meet Wright for afternoon tea. (It would have been a drive of about 143 miles, heading northwest out of Racine.) Ground was soon to be broken on the more-or-less approved (and boring) designs of the aforesaid Racine architect, whose name was J. Mandor Matson. At Taliesin, the stops had been pulled out—the apprentices had raked the grounds and polished the floors and filled all the vases with new-cut flowers—and not least had Taliesin's master laid on the charm like clotted cream. Through the rest of that weekend, the general manager of the company (his name was Jack Ramsey, and his wife was in the Johnson family) had paced. On Sunday morning, before church, he'd gone to his office at SCJ (as the firm shorthanded itself) and written by hand a ten-page letter/memorandum to the boss. Hib was in far northern Wisconsin, fishing, at the Johnson summer cottage on Lake Owen. Ramsey told Hib he'd had to force himself not to send wild telegrams. "Honest Hib I haven't had such an inspiration from a person in years," he wrote. Yes, the guy was a bit of an artist: weird clothes and his goofy Windsor tie. "Don't think of newspaper publicity on his matrimonial troubles and all that right away, as I did." Crazy to say, he could "tell us what we were after when we couldn't explain it to ourselves." As for the $300,000 that the board had generally approved for the new project—why, Wright had all but snorted. He said he'd doubtless be able to lop a hundred grand right off the top of that number, while creating something the world would beat a path to Racine to see.

Ramsey seems to have handed his fevered letter to Hib on Monday morning. (The chief must have come down from the lake on Sunday night.) That was July 20. The next day, Johnson was at Taliesin for lunch. He drove over in the Lincoln-Zephyr. It would have taken about three hours. (It's not entirely clear whether he went alone.) About this lunch, there has been much mythologizing, and many of Wright's biographers seem to have fallen for it. Hib was not quite thirty-seven, thirty-three years younger than Wright. Supposedly, the two insulted each other left and right, as if not giving a damn. I don't believe the half of it, not even in terms of a reverse psychology on Wright's part. What I believe occurred was that they both badly wanted it to happen, if for different reasons. And in fact, it did happen. The so-called hardheaded business-man, with his secret soul of art, found himself in his Wrightian thrall. The architect? He'd scored his newest touch.

Two days later, the president wrote to say that he was axing J. Mandor Matson ($4,460 had already been ponied up) and was now commissioning Wright as his new architect. He sent a $1,000 check as earnest money. A day later, the addressee slit open the morning mail and held up the dough and shouted across the drafting room to his apprentices: "It's all right boys, we got the job." This was Friday, July 24, 1936. Which is to say about eleven or twelve days before a young Madison couple drove out to Taliesin in their beater.*

---

* In the 1943 edition of his autobiography, Wright told of the arriving $1,000 and of how "the pie thus opened, the birds began to sing again below the house at Taliesin; dry grass on the hillside turned green, and the hollyhocks went gaily into a second blooming." In a later edition (not published until after his death), he upped the retainer to $10,000. It couldn't have been a printing mistake—if you examine the two editions, you'll see that the truth-twister had made subtle tweaking to his sentences throughout that paragraph. He knew.

Did it all go beautifully from there? Hardly. Wicked cost overruns, ungodly delays, all kinds of ego fights with zoning officials, permit grantors, contractors, subcontractors. And that original $200,000 estimate (shortly revised upward, to $250,000, to include the cost of furnishings)? Well, it went about ten times as high—to $2.1 million. On New Year's Eve 1936 (five months after the mythologized lunch at Taliesin), the *Racine Journal Times* splashed a story across the entire top of page one—with a rendering of what the building would look like. WILL COMPLETE BIG STRUCTURE NEXT SUMMER was the story's subhead. Wright told the paper (he would repeat versions of this line for years to come): "This new building will be simply and sincerely an interpretation of modern business conditions designed to be as inspiring to live in and work in as any cathedral ever was to worship in."

It wasn't completed by the next summer. (A joke to begin with.) The building opened in May 1939, concurrent with the opening of the New York World's Fair at Flushing Meadows. *Life* magazine did a feature: "'The World of Tomorrow' was officially born . . . on a onetime dump in New York City. . . . But future historians may well decide that a truer glimpse of the shape of things to come was given last week by a single structure, built strictly for business, which was opened in a drab section of Racine, Wis." Next paragraph: "The new administration building of S. C. Johnson & Son (wax polish) was designed by the master architect, Frank Lloyd Wright. It is genuine American architecture, owing nothing to foreign inspiration, different from anything ever built in the world before." Did he write the piece?

Did the roofs leak? In the early years, SCJ office staff were known to keep five-gallon buckets by their desks on rainy days. They'd greet each other at the water cooler: "So do you think today's going to be a one- or a two-bucket rain?"

In 2014, the family member running the empire (Hib's grandson, whose name is Herbert Fisk Johnson III) told *The New York Times* that the building's cost "was close to half the net worth of the entire company when it was done." But who was counting?

Because Wright was right: The world beat a path to Racine to see what he'd made, and it still does. What you find on the outside is a curvilinear, streamlined, red-brick face, looking vaguely like some Art Deco moon station. What you find on the inside of the half-acre "Great

Workroom" is a forest of slender "dendriform" columns of concrete and steel mesh that widen at the top like plates to hold up the ceiling. Depending on your imagination, these tapering columns might make you think of gigantic mushrooms or lily pads or Brobdingnagian golf tees. In the original design, there were some forty-three miles of layered Pyrex translucent glass tubing, creating a natural light free of shadow—not so helpful on cloudy days, of which there are almost too many to count in Racine, Wisconsin, from October to April. The creator grudgingly agreed to add artificial light to his cathedral, and further modifications have been made through the decades, and surely he is yet cursing every one of them from his grave.

When I saw it for the first time, the experience surpassed expectations. Such a vaulted grace, in an American workspace. Rows of seeming Lilliputians, in Cherokee-red ergnonomic chairs, tapped away on keyboards, or whispered into their iPhones. It almost felt like a diorama—of galactic proportion.

———

On to Fallingwater, to "E.J.," as Wright called him. To the mystery of how he, too—this brilliant and vulgar and rich and adulterous and grudge-nursing and art-minded and lederhosen-wearing Jewish merchant prince of Pittsburgh—got wriggled out from the underside of a sleeve to subsidize one of the most recognized buildings in the history of architecture. Hang on to the grudge-nursing idea. And the Jewish merchant theme. They're intertwined, and key.

First, the thing itself. If a shelf of books has been written about Fallingwater, let a paragraph of description be ventured here. She (yes, let her have the feminine gender) seems to hover there at her death-defying thrusts. And "thrust" is the word. On her fiftieth anniversary, in 1986, Paul Goldberger wrote in *The New York Times:* "This is a house that summed up the twentieth century and then thrust it forward still further." The critic called it Wright's "greatest essay in horizontal space." The essay in thrust stone has to do with how the main floor cantilevers itself beyond its supports straight into midair. Except that there are *three* layers of concrete terraces leaping out into space. In effect, the house, like the stream over top of which she hangs, is her own cascading thing of terraces and balconies, if not quite pure projections into thin mountain oxygenated mist, then appearing so. Wright's own favorite meta-phor (I referenced it in regard to the Imperial Hotel) might again be helpful: Imagine a large tray, laden with platters of steaming food, held aloft on the fingertips of a velvet-hipped, tuxedoed waiter as he swivels between tight tables. Everything depends on an intricate, interlocking, three-dimensional balance.

Next, the timelines. It's firmer if more prosaic narrative ground. We have real *dates* for Fallingwater. In all likelihood she got conceived, more or less, seven days before Christmas, in 1934, and then got drawn up, on three sheets of tracing paper, in different colors, in a supposed two hours, before a crew of jaw-dropped apprentices, almost exactly nine gestating months later, on Sunday morning, September 22, 1935.

About these two dates, especially the second, so much has been written. The first: December 18, 1934. This is the day Frank Lloyd Wright walked the property for the first time with Edgar J. Kaufmann. (They'd met just a month before.) I have heard it figuratively said that the greatest service any architect can provide for his client comes in the first fifteen minutes of standing at the site: he sees something that people with normal eyes cannot see. Wright saw Bear Run that day, its darkly wooded grounds, its boulders and rock ledges and waterfalls and stream. (The place is invariably described in relation to Pittsburgh, but in point of geographical fact its location in southwestern Pennsylvania is much closer to West Virginia.) And something happened. Eight days later (the day after Christmas), he said in a letter to Kaufmann that was mailed in care of his huge department store in downtown Pittsburgh (they called it "The Big Store," and it took up a city block, with twelve retail floors encompassing 750,000 square feet): "Visit to the waterfall in the woods stays with me and a domicile has taken vague shape in my mind to the music of the stream. When contours come you will see it."

The second date: September 22, 1935: Could it have really hap-pened that way? Had nothing been put on paper in the intervening nine months and then it all shot out, thrust itself out, the plans, the elevations, the basement, the first floor, the second floor, sketched to a perfect scale of one-eighth of an inch equaling one foot, while at least seven apprentices stood around him at the sloping board in the morn-ing sun, as if he were Jesus at the Last Supper, making water into wine (actually, that was at the wedding at Cana), as if he were Houdini doing the greatest trunk trick of his career? Or, to use another image: Could it have all happened "like Athena popping full-grown from the brow of Zeus"? Those are the words of an art historian from the University of Pittsburgh named Franklin Toker, who, in 2003, published a trouble-making and debunking and, to my mind, altogether excellent book entitled *Fallingwater Rising.**

And, incidentally, why that Sunday? Because of pressure from his client, the new touch of touches, who'd already written a goodly amount of checks, who dare not be lost, and who was now motoring toward Taliesin. (He'd been in Milwaukee for a powwow of retailers.) Part of the legend is that Wright took the call and boomed: "Come along, E.J., we're ready for you." And, meanwhile, not a pencil lick of work had been done.

Probably it didn't happen that way at all. Probably the truth is in the middle.

Namely, that the architect had worked on rudimentary plans, more or less privately, in his bedroom or another place. And then on that September Sunday, nine months after he'd first seen the site, with E.J. on the way, he'd ambled to the board, no further need of anything, because it was all inside him, committed to memory. He took up the tools before the boys. The newborn arrived, spanking wet and beautiful. This is Toker's belief.

And how does 1936 figure into all this, no less the late summer of 1936? The year 1936 is the year when construction finally began on Fall-ingwater. It's the year—and specifically it was August—when all of her was in danger of collapsing into the stream.

The cantilevered balconies were cracking and groaning and heaving and sagging. Wright's head apprentice, on site, at the direction of the client, and under the collaboration of a Pittsburgh firm of registered engineers, allowed for more steel to be added than had been called for in the master's drawings. The master didn't know. The reinforcing was done before he could stop it. The extra steel arrived on August 15; it was set in place when the floor slab got poured on August 19. The architect

---

* The book seems to be hated by some in the professional Wright universe, including folk at the Frank Lloyd Wright Foundation. Which might only suggest how true it cuts to the bone, slicing away at long-held Wright-related myths. I admire his book—it's the scholarship, it's the writing, it's the deep spoiling for a fight.

was kept in the dark. By the time he *was* informed, there was nothing he could do. A titanic ego had to face one of its greatest structural stresses on record, at least in terms of a building project. (It is more than evident to you by now that it's my belief that the greatest ego stress Frank Lloyd Wright ever suffered happened on another August 15—August 15, 1914.)

To read the letters and wires would put you in mind of those earlier exchanges between Wright and his first cousin in Tulsa. He talks of "treacherous interference." (This is to the on-site contractor.) He wires his head apprentice, Bob Mosher, to DROP WORK AND COME BACK IMMEDIATELY. (STOP) WE ARE THROUGH UNTIL KAUFMANN AND I ARRIVE AT SOME BASIS OF MUTUAL RESPECT. He says to the client: "I thought I had found a man and a client." Next paragraph: "But is this your usual method in dealing with men?" Next paragraph: "If so I will make a prophecy—in ten years time no one will work for you for either love or money."

And it all blew over. Wright still fumed that the steel had been "inserted over my head" (that's from a long letter of August 31 to Kaufmann, and he's already cooling, regretting to some degree his outbursts), but in a deeper way he knew that, to quote Toker, the "house might have collapsed in months" had the furtive adding not been done.

And, finally, the man himself. Who *was* Edgar Kaufmann? This needs bow again to Toker, who has done Kaufmann a lasting service: by humanizing him. His great humanity lay in his great vulnerability. Apparently, there was always something deeply inferior-feeling in this profane, swaggering, oversexed, art-literate, wealthy Pittsburgh retailer. The semi-secret insecurity seems to have been tied up with his Jewishness and his line of work. Out of this sandpapery rub came the beautiful grit of Fallingwater.

On one hand, E.J. seems not to have given a damn what the world thought of him: he married his first cousin; he kept mistresses in open display; he fathered a child with a model in his department store and named her Betty Jo, after his mother. Et cetera.

On the other hand, he longed for acceptance. "He was always keenly aware on some deep down level that he was a *merchant,*" Toker told me. So it didn't matter he had one of the most beautiful department stores in the world—literally. It didn't matter he'd built other buildings in and around Pittsburgh. It didn't matter he was a civic-minded philanthropist. It didn't matter he'd studied at Yale. Toker: "He felt it. Even his own people, the Jews, subtly put him down. In Pittsburgh the great Jewish families were industrial—in steel, in copper, in concrete. He had a *store*. He wanted to make an architectural monument. Think of it this way: Edgar had the money and he had clear title to the site. He didn't have the rest. He didn't have the genius. That was Wright."

He'd been born into a German-Jewish family dynasty of merchants. The Kaufmanns lived on the North Side, which was then its own town of Allegheny City. It was the core of Pittsburgh cultural life. Gertrude Stein came from there. The Carnegies and Heinzes, the composer Stephen Foster, the Impressionist Mary Cassatt, the poet Robinson Jeffers, the dance master Martha Graham—they'd known the North Side.

He'd just turned forty-nine when he and Wright met—and that's another part of the debunking. It has to do with Edgar Kaufmann, Jr., who, in late 1934 and early 1935, was a Wright apprentice. But it didn't go well. Wright may have "hounded" (Toker's word) the son out of Taliesin because of suspected homosexual activity. He later had a rich role in New York cultural life—as a professor at Columbia, as a curator of design at the Museum of Modern Art. Toker is a little hard on him, in my view. His grievance is that "Junior," after his father's death in 1955, began subtly to usurp most of the credit for Fallingwater, for the conjoining of Wright and Kaufmann, and that a generation of arts journalists bought too willingly in. In essence, the son wanted the world to believe he had led his father to Wright, and that without *him* Fallingwater wouldn't have otherwise existed. Again, the truth might be somewhere in the middle. Isn't it nearly always?*

At the end of his prologue, Toker writes two beautiful, fell-swooping sentences: "What made the house so radical, I believe, was the urgent need of its designer and of its patron to redress the wrongs the world

---

* The Kaufmann father-son story is its own great Oedipal tale. Edgar junior's gayness, even his artistic refinements, could not have been the least of E.J.'s many disappointments in his only son. It seems a deeply tragic family. Kaufmann's spouse-cousin, Liliane (she was Edgar junior's mother), who had her own affairs, who suffered for forty years at the flagrant infidelities of her husband, died in 1952 of what may have been a lethal mix of alcohol and the sleeping pill Seconal. History will doubtless never sort out whether it was an accident, or a half-suicide, or even a full one. But as Toker notes, the rumor of death by her own hand has always swirled.

had done them. For Wright, this meant the mockery of the German modernists who had outflanked him; for Kaufmann, it meant the anti-Jewish snobbery of Pittsburgh."

Something needs to be said about those outflanking European modernists, and all they represented. Again, it's necessary context—call it crucial—for appreciating the miraculous-seeming comeback Frank Lloyd Wright made in 1936.

———

Do you recall how he was regaining an emotional footing, or seemed to be, in late 1928? The upper-middle-aged man and his all-but-homeless young family had been yo-yoing themselves from one coast to another. But now he'd momentarily beaten back the bankers and managed to move back into the beloved (if flea-bitten-looking) Taliesin.

He'd been able to get married legally to Olgivanna—on August 25, out at Rancho Santa Fe, near San Diego. Six weeks before that (remember?), Mad Miriam (between sessions in an L.A. dentistry chair) had hailed a hack and stolen into his rented house in La Jolla to smash Oriental porcelains, to cut up Olgivanna's dresses and his black capes with some kind of garden shears. (Torching the premises was perhaps a match too far, even for her.)

Even in the teeth of such chaos, and even with no work to speak of, he'd found a certain kind of separate peace, and a lot of that was tied up with being able to go home, a married man again, to Wisconsin, to enjoy some autumn picnics with his family on the tawny riverbanks of his ancestral Lloyd Joneses.

Yes, but no. He was seething at his professional obituaries. This terribly proud man had been all but left behind. He was regarded, at least by much of the eastern cognoscenti, as belonging to another age. Again, Meryle Secrest summarizes it well: "The very qualities now seemingly outmoded in Wright's work, the respect for materials, the reverence for place, the organic quality of the building's design, and the architect's attempt to satisfy the emotional and spiritual needs of the occupants"— these things were thought musty and fusty except by a relative critical few. The new "truth" in architecture seemed to have little to do with the romance of the earth or a love for nature. It had to do with a kind of steel-and-glass ruthlessness, sleekness, minimalism, efficiency. This aesthetic had been preached for a good while, and lately much of it had been coming out of a small German design school started after World War I and known commonly as Bauhaus. New design prophets named Le Corbusier and Walter Gropius and Hannes Meyer and J. J. P. Oud and Ludwig Mies van der Rohe (not all of them associated with Bauhaus) were holding architecture's sway and imagination, or much of it. A house "is a machine for living in" was the famous dictum of Charles-Édouard Jeanneret, better known as Le Corbusier, the severe-looking Swiss-born French architect and urbanist and writer, born in 1887, two decades after Wright. (A little too famous: The statement, made in 1923, was to trail him for the rest of his life.) It was as if the very architectural coldness and rigid-seeming mechanistic ways of these brave new European modernists were their very virtue, at least in the eyes of the tastemakers. Never mind that most of them had cut their aesthetic molars on what Wright was doing at the turn of the century, and into its first decade.

Numbers can't graph the humiliating quotient of all this, but here are several: Once he had left the mixed success of his Los Angeles phase—and he had left it for all intents and purposes in the spring of 1924—Wright was able to get built only three works for the rest of the decade. These were a minor job for the Martin family of Buffalo (his oldest touch); the contentious project for his ruinous cousin in Tulsa; and a short-term encampment for himself outside Phoenix. This last he named Ocatilla, after the prickly cactus plant in the Sonoran Desert. (The accepted spelling is Ocotillo; through the years he futzed with the spelling.) Prickly: it fit the mood. More about that temporary camp in a minute, which essentially was the forerunner of what we know today as Taliesin West, and that burned away, or a lot of it, not five months after Wright built it. Yes, once again the fire story.

But the numbers story. Wright biographer Robert Twombly, previously referenced, has computed that from 1915 to 1932 (roughly from the time he was forty-eight until he was sixty-five, which should have been the prime work years of his life), the greatest architect in America had been able to execute only thirty-four commissions: roughly two a year. Twenty-nine of those thirty-four had come before 1925. So many others, started and stopped, and some with great promise, had found the shelf.

The word "obituary" keeps showing up in his letters. He was sick of reading his obits. Who were these people, to treat him like this? Didn't they know? Here he is, in May 1928 (so about five months before being able to move back into Taliesin), writing to critic Lewis Mumford, who he felt was on his side. To remind you, the two had met for the first time a year and a half before, in January 1927, and of that initial meeting (lunch at the Plaza, with Wright sweeping in), the far younger Mumford would say, decades later, in an autobiography, that Wright's "planet was in all but total eclipse."

The eccentric punctuation is fully intact.

My obituaries are all of such nature as to make me want to arise and fight. Indeed, I feel that for the sake of the cause,— 'Architecture',—to which I am so deeply committed, I must 'come back'. The 'come back' seems to be a favored American institution. From now on you are to find me actively engaged in that performance. So far as your clear head, good pen and good heart will go in the matter I hope to see you standing by.

This was May 3, 1928. What seems to make this letter the more poignant is its attempted lightness—and implicit begging for help. Three days before, on April 30, he had written Mumford and dropped any pretense of levity. He talked of "grave-robbing." He said he was "heartily sick of the historical falsifying" of the truth. Along with the letter he sent a carbon copy of yet another letter that he had written (on the same day) to a tastemaker named Fiske Kimball, director of the Philadelphia Museum of Art, who had just published a history of architecture in the United States. Actually, Kimball's treatment of him had been kind, and yet in a kind of past-tense way. In the letter to Kimball (folded up and put into the envelope to Mumford), Wright told Kimball he didn't need someone using him to dress up his moral and leave "me in exile. Yours was no donkey's kick at a 'dying lion'. Nor am I lion, nor dying, nor am I in exile."

Except that he was in exile, and knew it. Still, there were some projects, not that they were destined to come to fruition. After the fall stay at Taliesin, Wright, in mid-January 1929, had returned to Arizona— his second grateful and thawing-out winter there. He'd worked on two hopeful commercial and large-scale commissions. One was a high-rise apartment project in lower Manhattan at what was then called St. Mark's-in-the-Bouwerie. (One of the oldest church sites in the city.) It was destined to stay on paper.

As was an Arizona commission called the San Marcos-in-the-Desert Hotel. It was envisioned as a luxury winter resort of 110 rooms in the South Mountains below Phoenix. The client was a large-scale dreamer who'd named an Arizona town after himself: Chandler. (It's southeast of Phoenix.) He was Dr. Alexander J. Chandler, son of a minister, born in Canada, a veterinarian by training, eight years older than Wright. Chandler had migrated to the Phoenix area in 1887, in the same year that a nineteen-year-old tracer-draftsman was shooting ahead at J. Lyman Silsbee's in Chicago.

In Arizona, for the next four months, Wright and his family and a small crew of draftsmen-apprentices, along with their families (about fifteen people in all), camped out. Almost literally. With cheap canvas and rough lumber, Wright and his followers had constructed nearly overnight what he called "box-board cabins" on land provided rent-free by Dr. Chandler. The structures were built so that natural light filtered through the translucent canvas fabric roofs. "We put it together with nails, screws, hinges, and rigged it with ship cord," he says of Ocatilla in *An Autobiography*. To quote Neil Levine, who writes at length about it in *The Architecture of Frank Lloyd Wright:* "Wright meant Ocatilla to capture the essence of impermanence and represent it architecturally in organic terms." In his autobiography, Wright says: "'Ocatilla'—the camp—is ephemera. To drop a seed or two, itself? Who knows?" And: "The desert is prostrate to the sun. All life here is sun-life: and dies a sun-death." It almost sounds as if he's talking about *fire*.

Was he? It's part of the lore that Ocatilla just blew away. That after Wright and crew departed again for Wisconsin the camp was permitted to go back into the washes and arroyos. And, supposedly, what didn't disintegrate got carted off by local Native Americans. But not true. About a decade ago, an architect and dedicated Wright scholar named Brian Spencer came on a letter buried in the archives. Wright and his followers had left Arizona in late May 1929, and about a week later a caretaker wrote to him care of Taliesin: "I am sorry to report that we had some hard luck yesterday—about 2 o'clock I discovered a fire in camp." Further down: "The kitchen, dining room, cooks' dormitory and the Weston cottage burned, and the garage caught fire but we put it out." Some local toughs, who'd come out from town that Sunday, may have helped themselves to whatever they could steal. And then, driving off, had perhaps tossed a match.

Wright's reaction isn't known. This is. In four years, he'd known three burnings of places where he'd laid his head: the near-total one at Taliesin in 1925; the averted one at Taliesin in 1927; now Ocatilla. Sun-death, fire-death. Prostrate to its mercies.

San Marcos-in-the-Desert never got built. Chandler couldn't raise the estimated $750,000 for the project. That fall, the financial inferno on Wall Street known as Black Monday had set off the Depression. The bleak prospects had grown bleaker.

With no real work in sight, the rejected prophet, who tried hard to pretend otherwise, had turned to lecturing. In the spring of 1930, he'd given the prestigious Kahn Lectures at Princeton. That fall, he'd given back-to-back lectures on his old home ground—the Art Institute of Chicago. Had these invitations paid the rent? Not even close.

All but left behind, all but left out: In late 1931 plans were intensely in the works to mount an architecture show at the new Museum of Modern Art in midtown Manhattan. (The museum, not yet with its own building, had opened in late 1929.) A young and cocky intellectual out of Harvard named Philip Johnson, only in his mid-twenties, without architectural training or background, was curating the show with the critic Henry-Russell Hitchcock. It was all about the thrilling new "International Style." This was the name taking hold (after some previous abortive labels like "New Pioneers") to celebrate these thrilling European modernists—Gropius and Mies and all the rest. As was said above, so many of the new truthsayers were identified with a German art school, combining crafts and the fine arts, started in postwar Weimar in 1919. Bauhaus would exist for only fourteen years, and would operate in three cities—Weimar, Dessau, and Berlin—before shutting down in 1933, new enemy of the Third Reich. By the time of the MOMA show in New York, the legend of Bauhaus had migrated nearly to myth.

Modern Architecture: International Exhibition, said to be the most important architecture exhibit ever mounted up to that point, opened in February 1932. Wright was in it, all right—but barely. (At the last minute, knowing he was upstaged, he decided to pull out; it was only by the interceding of Lewis Mumford that he relented.) In the exhibition catalog, and also in a follow-up book, they more or less entombed him in a marble vault. (The curators declined to place him among the sixty-five most important architects in the world.) To Mumford, Johnson had earlier said in a letter: "Wright was a great pioneer but he is a romantic and has nothing more to do with architecture today." (Johnson would later say that Wright was "the greatest architect of the nineteenth century," an endlessly quoted line.) This upstart, good at quips, much on the make, was almost forty years younger than Wright; it was to be love-hate for the rest of their lives.

The following month (on March 30, 1932), *An Autobiography* appeared. As noted previously, the book sold out its first printing right away (albeit a small first printing). Wright's pal, Alexander Woollcott of *The New Yorker*, supplied a quote for the newspaper ads: "If I were suffered to apply the word 'genius' to only one living American, I would save it up for FRANK LLOYD WRIGHT." *The New York Times* ran a large Sunday review, blithely retailing so many of the old fabrications: "Scorning to use the influence of his uncle, the famous Jenkin Lloyd Jones, he achieved the miracle of getting himself a job with the architect of his uncle's new church, J.L. Silsbee." Ha.

Not that he was realizing any instant cash. It's saying something to suggest that 1932 may have been about the most broke year of Wright's perennially strapped life. The country was financially broke, of course. On May 19, Olgivanna, owner of her own high pride and pridefulness, sent a letter to Wright's baby sister. It was three pages, handwritten. It's as if the characters themselves on the page were stricken—slashing, jerky. There's a name in this letter you will instantly recognize. (Hint: Think proboscis—that event hasn't quite happened yet.) "Dear Maginel," she begins:

> We are in desperate condition. The Sechrests have shut us out of the hill—nailed all the doors leading to their part, dining rooms, kitchens, storerooms, waiting for the money we owe them three months salary. We cannot go to Parsons [local grocer and butcher] before we bring them a little money and we have 5 dollars cash. . . . For God sake, Maginel, can you help us? Frank has not been sleeping past two nights. . . . We need money as we never needed it before.

We are destitute at the present moment and I can hardly collect my wits. . . . Can you send us $300. . . . I cannot sleep or eat. I am simply sick over it all. Can you help us? Frank is in despair—repeating— 'what can we do, what shall we do when our last dollar goes?' Try to do something. Please, it is more terrible humiliation than I can tell you.

She signed it, as if nothing at all was wrong: "Love to you, Olga."

There is a story, possibly apocryphal, that Wright was so cash-desperate in the late spring of 1932 that he tried to hawk a copy of his book for five dollars to his old draftsman, Herb Fritz—buck and a half over retail price. (To remind you: on August 15, 1914, Fritz was the one who crashed through a window and crushed his arm and then went rolling down the hill toward dammed-up water.) Fritz lived in Madison with his family. He was in middle age now, still associated with Wright, as was a namesake son. He said he couldn't afford to buy the book. (The Wrights had come into town for dinner at the Fritzes'.) Reportedly, Wright said something like "Okay, well how about three, Herb?" He said he wished to take Olgivanna to a movie. Fritz hung his head again. Wright is said to have shrugged and inscribed the book and given it over for free.

The will to survive, always that. A bold idea had struck. Actually, it had been hatching for several years: Why not start a work-school for aspiring architects (or other kinds of would-be artists) who would learn at the master's feet—all the while milking his cows and chopping his wood and painting his barns? Was it a cynical try at forestalling penury on the backs of some youthful Wright worshippers—or a heroic humanistic experiment? Probably portions of both. Books have been written about the Taliesin Fellowship. To say this much here: The fee was $675, and in 1933 it got raised to $1,100, which was more than Harvard's tuition. To read the one-page admission form is to hear the clink of money: "This application is to be accompanied by check for two hundred dollars payable to Frank Lloyd Wright. . . . Note: The total tuition fee of $1100.00 includes participation in all the activities of the Fellowship and includes living expenses. Clothing, personal laundry and drawing materials are excluded. Both men and women will be required to work four hours each day at whatever work may be assigned to them, as a feature of their training. This is considered an essential feature of the tuition fee."

The fellowship was announced to open in late October 1932. By the end of the year, a couple dozen candidates from all over the country (and a few foreign countries), some fresh out of high school, others with graduate degrees, had shown up for sweat and glory at Taliesin. Momentarily, the beast of bankruptcy had been thrust from the door.

Came Halloween of 1932—you know that story. (The proboscis.) But here is what happened next: The hubristic man went on a short book-and-lecture tour. He entrained for the East six or seven days after he'd appeared in court in the Sechrest matter—the plaster of paris was apparently off. For the first talk, at the Albright Art Gallery in Buffalo on November 9, he semi-behaved. Reminder: Cecil Corwin's kid sister, Marquita, and her son, and maybe her husband, had come to this event; there'd been a small reunion. Which led to the Damon and Pythias reunion, at least by letter, after so many years. Soon Cecil, who worked as a draftsman in an architectural decorating firm at Times Square, would be writing to Frank with quiet dignity about how their "ways had been diverse and divergent. You have made a name for yourself of inestimable value. I have only made friends and a living." And Wright would answer, gentleness in his voice, about how "those old days were romance."

Two days later, he was at the Institute of Art at Brown University. He insulted his audience. (While he was at it, he ridiculed the majestic Gothic architecture of Yale.) He left Rhode Island and trained back to New York to stop over at the Hotel Lafayette. (It was downtown; he and Cecil were about a ten-minute taxi ride from each other, not that they knew.) A couple days later: Rochester. The director of the Memorial Art Gallery met him at the train station. They drove around town in a cab while he dismissed everything in sight. They went by the beautiful Prairie on East Boulevard that he'd built a quarter of a century before for Edward Boynton and his daughter, Beulah. He'd not been back since. The house had gutters and downspouts on it. He rose straight up in the back of the cab and smashed his head. "They have destroyed my house!" It didn't go so well that night at the talk. He cut off questioners. He'd neglected to bring the lantern slides he'd promised and said that exhibiting slides was for little people. The gallery decided to withhold his fee. (A couple weeks later would come a note of apology "for such pessimism as crept into the talk." Probably it was some real guilt, but also a bid to collect the loot.)

From Rochester he trained back to the city and then a couple days later on to Cambridge, Massachusetts, for a fresh round of insults— but also with a few pearls tossed to the swine: "Organic architecture is based on the interior content, which we call the life of the thing. When architecture ceases to express the life of the people, what is it?"

All during this zigzagging of the East, the sixty-five-year-old writes letters, some to be typed up by his secretary once he's back home. He dashes them by hand early in the morning and late at night and on the way to the talks themselves. Money is constantly on his mind. To a Chicago publisher he's known for years: "Dear William Kittredge: Alas! and Alack! where could I raise any money now to buy anything?"

On stationery of the Lafayette, he tallies his expenses and the take at each stop: "Buffalo—150. Providence—150." In about ten days, he has pulled in something like a thousand dollars, minus his expenses. Near the end, Olgivanna wires: YOUR FAMILY LONESOME FOR YOU SEND US WIRE HOW YOU ARE WHEN EXPECT YOU.

Well, he'd gotten home safe. And it was onward from there, the usual zig, the arrogant zag. It was late 1932. Within four years, a man who didn't think of himself as an American failure, not ever, no matter how the world might be misinformed, was in the process of creating an office cathedral, a backwoods Shangri-La leaping from a rock, a mouse-house on the western edge of Madison. And being thought a god again. Historians would one day say that if Frank Lloyd Wright had conceived nothing but these three buildings, if his career had somehow been able to know only the single year 1936, it would have been enough to secure him his lasting place.

———

When Herb and Katherine, not quite a pair of innocents in the world (but something along those lines), entered the spider's parlor on that August afternoon, certain currents and schemes were operating above their heads. It was said earlier that Wright told them a lie to their faces but that, ultimately, the lie didn't affect them much. That's true, in a qualified sense. The lie was that no one had ever come to him asking for a moderate-cost house, and that he'd been hoping for such a thing for years. In fact, he'd been much in touch over the previous year or so with two likely-seeming American families—the Lusks and the Hoults—who'd asked for precisely the same kind of house. Both families were destined to slip into the footnotes of Usonian history, and the reason, principally, was money: neither could find financing, after Wright had made detailed preliminary designs for them. If either one of their houses had been built, *they* would have been the occupiers of Usonia I. Which is why, in both a technical and an historical sense, it's accurate to think of the Jacobs House as the first *built* Usonian.

So Wright's need to have it go right this time was large, and that was operating over top of some of what the Jacobses understood. They were just the beneficiaries, in the right place at the right time.*

I am further convinced he was determined to do it for $5,000 because that number was in the air of the architectural world. It was a kind of mystical benchmark figure in the middle of the Depression. Indeed, in April 1936 (five months before he met the Jacobses), *Architectural Forum* had devoted an entire issue to the subject. On the bare cover just this: "The Five Thousand Dollar House." Inside, the editors wrote: "If, in an effort to produce a good house for $5,000, you should take a $10,000

---

* A footnote *about* the "footnotes": the Lusks and the Hoults. It's fascinating to see how much Wright adapted *their* plans to what rose at 441 Toepfer Avenue. In a real sense, what Wright drew up for Mr. and Mrs. Robert D. Lusk of Huron, South Dakota (he was the editor of *The Evening Huronite,* which promoted itself as "The Newspaper for Central South Dakota"), and for Mr. and Mrs. Charles H. Hoult of Wichita, Kansas (he became the president of the United Sash and Door Company, which had been co-founded by his wife's grandfather late in the same year, 1886, that the Madison bumpkin was striking off for the Eternal City of the West), are the remarkably close paper constructions of the wood-and-brick-and-glass reality. Wright never threw anything away. No matter the legend of Sunday, September 22, 1935, in his studio regarding the falling out of Fallingwater, it was usually a process of refining and erasing and drawing over top of the first thought—and sometimes the fifteenth thought. In any case, I confess to having gotten semi-obsessed with the Lusks and the Hoults. What was driving it, I suppose, was the old journalistic question: Whatever happened to the ones who got away? The names alone, the towns alone, the middle of the American middle: Huron, South Dakota, and Wichita, Kansas. The United Sash and Door Company. *The Evening Huronite.* It sounds like pure Norman Rockwell. But as in almost everything else connected with Frank Lloyd Wright, there turns out to be more than enough mystery and paradox to go around right *here.* I can't quite resist quoting a little of the correspondence. To Mrs. Louise Hoult of 302 North Broadway in Wichita (she was the family point person for the house that never came to fruition), Wright says on March 17, 1936 (not quite five months before meeting the Jacobses): "The wood is used in a simple construction of wide boards and battens outside—stained for protection and banding the house into rhythmical patterns." A month later, on April 24: "The Kitchen and Dining are really one and sunlit from above. The Kitchen is deliberately small to make work easy and would be a kind of modern laboratory. . . . The foundation is only the concrete mat on which the whole house rests." In a sense, these two families await their doctoral dissertation.

house and reduce it to half the size, you would uncover two pertinent facts. In the first place, your half-house would cost considerably more than $5,000. In the second place, it would be too small to attract a buyer. With $5,000 to spend on a house, you must concentrate more on your effort on stretching the dollar than on shrinking the house."

It's as if they'd thrown down the dare to somebody who wished to consume the competition with his morning bacon. Except that he had no competition. In his mind.

Years later, Wright told Herb their house was the first in his career he had ever agreed to build under a fixed-price contract. By damn, he was going to hold it to $5,000 (actually, as was noted earlier, the contract they signed went to $5,500 because of the third bedroom), and, by further damn, he was going to hold his fee to $450.

On August 24, 1936, Herb and Katherine went out to Taliesin for dinner—an invite had come by telephone. At Fallingwater, Wright was in the fuming middle of the great cantilever crisis, but the Jacobses apparently knew nothing of this. Before going out, Herb had typed a list of particulars on newsprint from his paper. He'd entitled it, all caps: GENERAL CONSIDERATIONS ON HOUSE. Then, underlining the word, "Personnel," as if this were an inner-office memo, he'd begun: "Man, wife, small child. Provision should be made for future additions of bedrooms, to allow for increase in family." Wright probably put the sheet in the inner pocket of his coat and tried to keep a straight face. Again, Elizabeth Aitken, middle Jacobs child (two years from being born at that point): "See, he would have been intrigued by this family that just didn't have a lot of money. I think he was attracted to that, in and of itself. It made him like them right off."

Things got going, more or less. Plans were worked up. (Wright would produce a total of seventy drawings, all told.) On November 15, Herb and Katherine's architect made a great ceremony of signing the one-page contract. He dictated the document, and Katherine wrote it out in her beautiful penmanship on another piece of Herb's filched cheap newsprint from the *Cap Times*. Two apprentices signed their names as witnesses. Two weeks later, on December 1 (again, they were out to Spring Green for dinner), the preliminary drawings had been converted into working drawings, and these also were signed, each sheet, in a ceremonial flourish, and backdated to November 15.

And then the architect got sick. Bad sick. A cold turned to pneumonia. He'd been making almost weekly trips to Racine. The problems with Fallingwater had kept up. Finally, he himself couldn't get up. His fever spiked; he had deliriums. For about a week, it looked truly bad. As always, he rallied; his wife and the doctor (whose bill didn't get paid, at least not for weeks that stretched into months) had helped get him through.

The Jacobses sold back their first lot and bought a double lot on the other side of Toepfer Avenue—really, they had no choice, if Wright's design was to be realized. (Their first lot had been on the west side of the street, but Wright's plan was that the house would be as wide as the lot itself. The subdivision company, which owned the lots, balked at this.) If, by January 1937, Herb and Katherine had a much larger piece of ground, on the better side of Toepfer, with a better siting for the house, they were now also seriously reduced in cash. How would they find financing, with almost nothing to put down? The Federal Housing Administration rejected them for a mortgage, at least partially because of Wright's plan for a flat roof. (In the judgment of the FHA, resale considerations would be too poor.) But then, as if sent by heaven, a Madison man with a good heart and grateful memory came forth. He was a building-and-loan guy, in business with his brothers. His name was Harry Haley. He'd read in the local paper about what Wright was up to. (This is another part of the story: Herb's own paper got scooped—the *State Journal* had found out and run a piece first: WRIGHT TO ANSWER NEED FOR LOW COST HOUSING FOR MADISON RESIDENCE.) You see, as a boy growing up in Chicago, Harry Haley's folks used to take him on weekends to a fandango of an entertainment complex on the South Side called Midway Gardens. He'd never quite gotten over that experience. Sure, he'd be glad to stake Herb and Katherine to $4,500.

(Time out. Who in America doesn't know Frank Capra's *It's a Wonderful Life*? George Bailey is the beautiful-hearted, small-town building-and-loan guy played by Jimmy Stewart. George gets into deep money trouble and wishes he'd never been born and tries to kill himself, only to get saved by his guardian angel, Clarence. Which means that he lives to save Bedford Falls itself from the evil Mr. Potter. "Harry Haley"— sounds a little like "George Bailey," doesn't it? What if he hadn't come forth at the critical moment? What if he'd never been born? What if, in despair, he'd thrown himself off a Madison bridge and there'd been no Clarence to jump in and save him? But that's a Christmas movie. As it turns out, in real life, two decades before, Harry had been a volunteer ambulance driver in World War I—little more than a kid when he'd gone over. He'd been assigned to the French army. He'd seen some of the biggest battles of the war, when the casualties in the French regiments had run as high as seventy percent. But he'd made it home, and home was now Madison, where his dad and big brothers had a real estate and insurance business. Page one, *Cap Times,* Monday, May 5, 1919: MADISON BOYS FROM OVERSEAS ARE ARRIVING. And below that, smaller type: HARRY HALEY, LAWRENCE CARROLL, "BINKS" MORGAN AMONG THOSE HERE. In a way, Harry's story, vis-à-vis the Jacobses, is its *own* Christmas movie.)

First of June, the contractor came in and graded off the topsoil. (His name was Bert Grove—again, just the names.) A few days later, they dug the mouse-sized basement. On July 2, they brought in the dirt and sand for the fill and wetted it down with hoses. The boiler was installed on July 22. Then the heating pipes laid in the sand fill. Then the great test of the iron pipes in the "holocaust heating" system. The date was August 3, 1937. There is a photograph—the master in a shirt and tie and floppy hat and a pair of goofy pants pegged at the ankles. He's in open-toed sandals. He's got his cane. He's staring down into the boiler, which is sending up puffs of steam. By damn, it's working. Two of the apprentices are in the frame—Jimmy Thompson and Bennie Dombar. And Bert Grove. And Hugh Peake, the plumber and steamfitter, who's a devoted Adventist. (These names are not being made up.) Herb can't get away from the paper, but Katherine's on hand to record what Herb will later describe in *Building with Frank Lloyd Wright* as "the historic scene of the first American floor heating project."

Construction speeds up, slows down. By mid-September, the brick walls are in. The legend is that Wright used "culled" bricks from what was in progress over in Racine. Some of the bricks were curved. This made the work a little harder for the trowelers on Toepfer. Did Hib Johnson know that Wright's apprentices were robbing from Peter to pay Paul? As Donald Kalec puts it in an arch endnote: "It is not clear whether the culled bricks from the Johnson Wax Building were carted off by Wright's apprentices as a 'donation' to the low cost of the Jacobs house or if the contractor paid for them." I'll go with the idea that they got carted off, out of sight of Hib.

On November 27, 1937, two days after Thanksgiving, Herb and Katherine rent a small van and move themselves and their baby daughter into their new home, which isn't quite finished. (At Bear Run, the Kaufmanns are beginning to spend weekends at the not-quite-done Fallingwater.) They don't have much in the way of furniture—that's okay. By Christmas of the next year, they still don't have a rug for the living room, but they've managed to acquire some beveled basswood roll-down screens for the glazed windows. A part of the slab in the living room has heaved up by about an inch, but Bert Grove comes by and fixes it. By now there's another child in the house, and her parents have paid for her delivery by selling their beater. (Fine by Herb to ride his bike the three and a half miles to work at the newspaper—in the winter months he dresses like an Eskimo.) By now, too, so many people wish to come through the house that her owners are charging admission. They've thumb-tacked to a fulcrum post out near the garage a ticket-like sign made of brown cardboard: "Visitors. There is a charge of 50 cts to visit the house." (Within a couple years, the accumulated take surpasses their architect's commission.) They still have no charge accounts or anything else on the installment plan, save their mortgage. At the paper, Herb's up to $42 a week.

Two years in, some changes. The truth is, the house is uncomfortably cold in the cold months. The gravity heat works a lot better in some spots than in others. Herb puts a radiator in the bathroom. (This pulls on the electric bill, to their chagrin.) At Wright's suggestion, a switch is made from steam heat to forced hot water. Herb installs a small coal bin (he builds it himself) and an outside chute. Still, they sometimes have to wear snow caps indoors, and nightly the kids huddle at the hearth with their homework. But they love their house almost *for* those realities. In the heat of summer, the neighborhood kids come over, and then Susan Jacobs and her baby sister, Elizabeth, demonstrate the way to the perfect cool-off: spread-eagling on the concrete floor with a wetted-down sheet over top of you.

A funny thing happened. Like most things in our lives, it seemed to happen incrementally. It was some sort of feeling, as Herb later wrote, of "beginning to be vaguely dissatisfied, without knowing just why." Next sentence: "Our life in the Wright house probably contributed to this unrest." Why? How? It was as if their home was so much a part of nature—the outside coming in; the inside going out—that Herb and Katherine couldn't get out of their minds the idea of moving to a farm. Herb: "The banks of floor-to-ceiling windows on the garden side made nature a great part of the house, letting in the sun, the moon and the stars, adding the changing landscape as a permanent part of our daily life." It was almost as if the architect had inadvertently cut off his nose to spite his face. In September 1942, Herb and Katherine found a fifty-two-acre farm further west of the city. Two months later, the family was gone from 441 Toepfer. They'd lived in the house almost exactly five years. And Wright's reaction? The Jacobses had committed a traitorous act. But the hard feelings cooled. Eventually, he'd design a whole new house for them, which they would also grow to love. And this is where Jacobs II comes in. By the end of the forties, the Jacobses (now a family of five) were living in something called the "Solar Hemicycle." It featured passive solar construction and a windfoil design. It would be the family's home until after the children had grown up and left to pursue their own professional lives. Eventually, the parents themselves forsook Wisconsin for California (where grandchildren lived). The Solar Hemicycle is still there.

Jacobs I endured some not-great keepers in the decades after Herb and Katherine. There was a deaf dentist. There was a wholesale beverage dealer. There was a civil engineer. There was a medical student from the university (with a dog)—who rented the house out to other grad students. In all, there were about six sets of owners and renters over the next four decades who treated her with various levels of respect and disrespect. In her worst moments, you could drive by and wish to keep on driving by. The exterior was creosoted (think of blackened railroad ties) and the roof was caked with so many layers of asphalt that the joists were sagging—and leaking. The carport was listing. The garden crawled with weeds.

And then, in 1982, a UW art history professor, Jim Dennis, came suddenly into her life. The professor paid $105,000 for her and began repairs with two restoration architects based in Chicago. It took several years. The restorers and their workers jackhammered up the living room floor and replaced the old iron heating pipes with new plastic-tubed ones. They added structural steel for reinforcement. They put on a membrane roof. (Essentially, it's rubber.) They shored up the carport. They painstakingly removed the creosote and replaced some of the pine and redwood. "The rule," Jim Dennis told me, "was to try hard not to violate the spirit of a single thing Wright did." You could say she's more artful and solid today than at any point in her eight-decade history. Many pages back, I expressed a similar thought about the Frank Lloyd Wright Prairie house of my Kankakee childhood—the B. Harley Bradley at 701 South Harrison Avenue. It, too, *she*, too, had to wait many years to find her true believers after her original believers.

For a good while now, history and historians have been aware of a rich irony: that in the miracle comeback year of 1936 a washed-up man essentially beat the European modernists at their own game. In the previous ten years, the architectural has-been named Frank Lloyd Wright had not executed more than five buildings, but here he was now, in the second half of '36, working on the Jake, the SCJ, and Fallingwater, all at once. He was more than back—he was pulverizing his would-be peers. The metabolizer and world-class assimilator had stolen out from under Le Corbusier and Mies slices of their own vision—and converted them to his. He married his own ideas about the romantic and the organic to their ideas about the functional machine, and the result was greater than the sum of the parts. He'd been watching them all along, even as he'd scorned them. In *Sketches from a Life*, published in 1982 (the same year that Jim Dennis drove up Birch Avenue with a former student and turned right on Toepfer to gasp at a forlorn jewel), Lewis Mumford wrote: "In Fallingwater, designed for Edgar Kaufmann, he had created a dynamic multi-dimensional composition that made Le Corbusier's buildings seem flat cardboard compositions." Ditto an interior forest of corporate office space. Ditto a $5,500 family dwelling. The modernist influence of Gropius and all the rest is discernibly present in each work, but the end product is uniquely his. You know my bias, which is far from any kind of true scholar's architectural judgment: in the geometric interlocking of her horizontals and verticals—the brick pillars, the banded wood walls, the rectilinear frames of floor-to-ceiling glass—

the American *and* democratic mouse-masterpiece called Usonia I is as complex a work of art as what leans out over a waterfall at Bear Run, as what stands on the industrial south side of Racine. For me, this supposedly simple home on its ordinary semi-suburban lot will always be the first among equals. And, to say again, her influence and implications seem vaster.

But to end this with another idea, an unprovable proposition. It goes straight to the heart of American *and* democratic. To repeat: I believe that in achieving what he achieved at 441 Toepfer Avenue, Frank Lloyd Wright got back in touch with his true architectural and personal self. In Greek mythology, the hero's journey is the journey of return. In the Jacobs House, an impossibly haughty man had found a way home, and not just figuratively. Had found a way home to the small-town and common-man values from which he'd sprung. He'd come, after all, out of ordinary citizens of the United States—never mind that they thought of themselves (on his mother's side, but on his father's too) as better than everyone around them. He certainly had no wish ever to be thought of as part of the common man, and yet one way to understand Frank Lloyd Wright's contradictory life is that he spent practically all of it running from the very thing, idea, ethic, he could never really escape: middle-class values and morals. He mocked them, despised them, defied them, even as those values and morals kept pursuing him, coursing through his veins. Not for nothing did he think of himself as "an old Madison boy." He was that, at bottom, no matter what else he also was. The architectural critic Michael Kimmelman has said it simply: "His abiding subject was America's middle class. Wright's architecture anticipated, and, in its way, even hastened the evolution of the nation from an agrarian to an urban and suburban society. . . . [H]is architecture made the middle class the centerpiece of a new concept of American democracy."

Wouldn't the impulse to build worthy shelters for un-elitist Americans argue, in its own way, for his fundamental decency as a human being, the hell with all his dross and refuse? It's only partly what I meant toward the start of this chapter when I wrote: "But did he always want something else besides, secretly and not so secretly?"

With the Jake, he'd again touched his roots, whether he exactly understood it that way or not. On some level, or so I believe, the deep touching gave him psychic strength for all the work that followed. What followed, for a seventy-year-old, over the next two decades, was a late-life explosion of creative energy that no one, doubtless not even he, saw coming. (Some of what got produced had almost nothing to do with the American middle.) This improbable burst—call it fire—took him, more or less, right up to the end, never mind the setbacks and sorrows (and flames) waiting along the way. American-cum-democratic, and coming back: T. S. Eliot could be quoted here, those beautiful lines from *Four Quartets* about how "the end of all our exploring / Will be to arrive where we started / And know the place for the first time." Arrive where we started? That's a good segue for bringing on stage William Carey Wright, Frank Lloyd Wright's terribly misunderstood father. In a way, he's the emotional linchpin. It's such a complex and deeply sad tale, which nonetheless might be thought of as a ballad. Because music is very much in it. And so is the theme of return.

PART IV

At His Father's Stone

There are only two or three human stories, and they go on repeating themselves as fiercely as if they had never happened before.

—Willa Cather, *O Pioneers!*

———

It's almost not possible to peer deeply into the life of Frank Lloyd Wright and not hear stories about visits he made, solitary and otherwise, toward the back of his life, to his father's grave. What is the meaning of those visits, however few or many there actually were? After all, wasn't this the parent who was rebuked and cast off and never spoken to again for having so long ago deserted his family, walked out on them, leaving them to their collective shame and grief and virtual poverty?

Except he didn't. If anything, the real story of the bitter family breakup back there in Madison in 1885 was exactly the other way around. Was exactly the opposite of the impression you would have formed from reading An Autobiography.

The Sad Ballad of William Carey Wright (1)

W. C. Wright, circa 1890

The grave is in a place called Bear Valley, Wisconsin. It isn't hard to find. From Taliesin, it's about a thirty-minute drive northward. You cross the Wisconsin River and go to Spring Green and turn west on U.S. 14 and then, at the village of Lone Rock, you turn onto state route 130, which is a two-lane blacktop, and head north again. That'll take you up into the valley. At first the road is straight as a string. It's almost as if you're riding on the ocean floor—it feels that flat. You won't see many cars. The rich fields are on either side—it's as if the loam is edging right up to your wheel wells. Off in the distance is a line of greenish-blue forested bluffs. You'll pass Rushing Waters Lane. You'll see Cold Spring Farm, with its registered Holsteins and shelterbelt of trees.

In geological terms, Bear Valley is regarded as an ancient Wisconsin valley "because of its wide flat plain, and because it is U-shaped, as compared with newer valleys, which are narrower, steeper sided and V-shaped." That's from a local history. The next sentence, which isn't trying to be lyrical and thus is all the more lyrical for the not trying: "Thousands of years of flooding have washed a layer of rich, deep black alluvial loam onto the floor of the valley, and it is this soil which is the basis for the economy of the valley today." It seems like a good spot to lie down in for eternity.

The little country churchyard sits right at the elbow of County B and 130. There's a farmer's fence and a double-gate, with a lift-latch. The graves spread themselves out on both sides of a small church with a belfry and an unusually tall spire. It's an elegant-looking building, with a simple name: Brown Church. That is its color, that is its name. There are some trees and shrubs. Mostly what you'll be aware of is the quiet.

His father's marker, slender, of brownish-red marble, not low to the ground but rising up, like a pillar or small column, is over on the left as you go in. He's here among Carswells and Goodriches and Burnhams and Jensens and Winterburns. He's here beside his first wife. Her name was Permelia. She died in April 1864, in the aftermath of giving birth to their fifth child, who was a stillborn. That double sorrow happened three years before Frank Lloyd Wright appeared on the earth, first child of another marriage, first child of what now seems to have been a doomed union from practically its first day. Except that if there had been no such union, the world would have never had the architecture of Frank Lloyd Wright. Well, it may have had it in a far lesser form. Because it seems unarguable now that, no matter what influence from the mother's side, the true artistic genius of Wright lay in the genes of the failed father. Those are the headwaters: William Carey Wright, a man so prodigiously gifted, who lost at life. Why? That seems not possible to know, at least not fully. Some kind of incurable restlessness, some misplaced dreaminess, some fundamental impracticability and maddening lack of being able to stick in any one place or to any one thing, or at least to any one thing that might have provided a reasonable living. Perhaps if there'd been just one more tick of the clock, quarter turn of the wheel, *he* might have been the world's Frank Lloyd Wright. Instead, it was a life, for all its talents and charismatic qualities, which went slowly toward oblivion. A life with more than its share of seeming bad fortune in it. How do you explain bad fortune? You don't.

No one knows how many times Wright came to this elegiac spot in the last several decades of his life. Was it three, five, ten? There are stories he started showing up here as early as the 1920s. The problem is, what we mainly have are the stories—or, maybe more accurately, the hearsay of the stories. There is very little solid documentation that has passed down. I have been able to find solid documentation for one apparently impromptu visit, and a kind of half-solid documentation for another. One visit seems to have occurred in the mid-fifties, and the other in the last year or so of Wright's life—so he was over ninety then, and his face often had a strange roundedness and small puffiness and redness to it. In that instance, he couldn't have gone to Bear Valley alone. (His son-in-law drove him.) On both, he was apparently deeply moved. Was he overheard to say, Father, I am sorry? Did he break down and weep? No, nothing so dramatic, or at least not that I know anything about. But it doesn't matter. He was here. He came. The barefaced fact of his coming, even if only twice, and I'm pretty sure it was far more than that, seems its own charged testimony, wordless witness. To what?

Well, doubtless to all kinds of unsayable regrets, but not least to the terrible lie a son once told in his autobiography against his father. A lie made more insidious for the cunning way it was told. Which is to say by insinuation and implication more than by outright statement.

For a good while, history believed this lie. Even after history knew better (Wright himself was dead almost a decade by then), there still seemed some perverse inclination on the part of so many people in the Wright universe—not least some serious biographers and scholars and journalists—to think of things in the prior way, or at least to slip almost unawares into the old language. About the father's "desertion," his cruel abandonment. The cultural critic Neil Postman once wrote: "A myth is a way of thinking so deeply embedded in our consciousness that it is invisible." Mark Twain once supposedly said that "a lie can travel halfway around the world while the truth is putting on its shoes."

Actually, the case will be made here that the prideful Frank Lloyd Wright, toward the back of his life, with his semi-concealed conscience and greatly underestimated capacity for regret, was paying emotionally charged visits to Bear Valley, Wisconsin, to stand at the stone of his spurned and so wrongly blamed father, even when he was nowhere close to Bear Valley.

———

The story of the family deserter—who wasn't, who didn't—can't be told without, in effect, going back to the future. That is, to Frank Lloyd Wright's origins, and his pre-origins. Basically, we're flashing back—selectively. Returning to where we've never quite been.

To say it plain, to say it legally: He didn't desert *her* and destroy the family as a family; she deserted *him*. The legal facts, legal judgments, on this point are unambiguous and incontestable. *He* was the plaintiff. *She* was the defendant. It was the *father* in this family who sued the *mother* for divorce on the grounds of emotional cruelty and physical violence and spousal abandonment. It was the mother who had left the marriage in every way except by her physical removal from it—and, in a way, she had done precisely that. And it was a circuit court, in the spring of 1885, after a four-month, fairly open-and-shut case, that ruled in the plaintiff's favor, concluding that "all the allegations of the complaint are true." In fact, the defendant never even showed up in court. She didn't dispute a single charge. It was part of her strategy. She just wanted it over.

For the almost neurasthenically attuned oldest child of this doomed union not to have known the real story—even if he didn't know every particular—flies in the face of all reason. But to try to tell it as a *story,* not as any kind of cold legal brief:

On December 13, 1884—a cold, cruddy Saturday in the upper Midwest—Frank Lloyd Wright's fifty-nine-year-old father went to a lawyer's office in downtown Madison near Capitol Square and reluctantly began divorce proceedings against his forty-six-year-old spouse. For most of the last eighteen years, William C. Wright—whose professional life to that point would have defined the words "itinerant" and "underpaid"—had been miserably married to Anna Lloyd Jones Wright.

From all the available evidence, "miserably" is putting it lightly, but let's go with that for the moment. Three days later, on Tuesday the 16th, nine days before Christmas, William's attorney personally served three copies of a summons to the Wright home on Gorham Street, along with a copy of the three-page complaint for "willful and unjust desertion." Living with their mother in that small, unfestive home (but who knows, maybe they had decorated for the holidays anyway) were seventeen-year-old Frank, fifteen-year-old Jennie, seven-year-old Maginel. (Their father, a lapsed clergyman who was eking a living as a music teacher and sporadic lecturer, had recently moved out, and seems to have been rooming with Madison friends.) Anna was aware that the suit was coming. Aware? It seems safe to say it couldn't get there fast enough for her, Christmastime or otherwise. Good riddance to bad rubbish.

On wanting it over: In late November or early December—so just before William filed his complaint and his spouse got served—Anna, without a lawyer, but in the company of two of her brothers, had come to the law office of William's attorney for what had to have been an incredibly strained meeting. William was present. Damn, how she must have towered over him figuratively and physically in that moment, never mind the towering over of the heavy-bearded, huge-shouldered, farmer-boned Lloyd Jones brothers, next to whom, in family gatherings, poor William, with his pale skin and fine features, had usually seemed so much smaller and frailer than he actually was. It isn't accurate to say that Anna was half a head taller than her husband, although you hear that a lot. Apparently, he stood something like about three hairs over five-foot-five, while she was about five-foot-eight in her bare feet. There are few photographs of the two together, but in the ones we have he seems jammed down into himself, while she is mannish and serene (except when she's looking almost terrifyingly mad). Did she outweigh him by twenty pounds? As a younger woman, Anna used to ride a horse across the Lloyd Jones valleys, squared tall in the saddle, not sidesaddle, but in the manly way her brothers did, with her long legs hugging the animal's flanks, in her blue military cape with its hood and brass buttons, hair tossed in the wind. Or this is part of the Lloyd Jones family lore.

The gist of the strained meeting in attorney J. H. Carpenter's office was to see if there was any possibility of a last-minute reconciliation;

and, if not, and the case was to go forward, then to see whether William would agree to make good on an earlier verbal promise to deed over to Anna his share in the family home, and also to give her almost all of its contents. The two Lloyd Jones brothers who were present had pledged to the attorney that if William would surrender the house and its goods, they would see to it that the children were looked after, and their sibling as well.

The answer to the first question was moot: there was no chance of a last-minute reconciliation. Anna would never again live with William as his wife. She hadn't had intercourse with him for more than two years. She didn't love him. Actually, she loathed him. She just wished him to get out. She had already made this plain. But, for the record, she was willing to say it out loud once more that day to the four other people in the room. From all that can be known, this is the last legal thing she uttered in the case.

The second question—the deeding of house and home—was agreed upon, if the divorce should take up. Which it promptly did.

On January 24 (the new year now, obviously), the defendant, having failed to answer the delivered summons in the legal time period, was declared in default. Two and a half months later, on April 6, 1885, the plaintiff gave an eight-page affidavit-deposition. The document was a fuller reporting of what he'd stated in his December 13 complaint. For such a proud, bantam, churchly, formal man, descended from a long line of proud, bantam New England preachers, this had to have been a humiliating moment, to hang out the marital laundry like this, if only before his lawyer and the court "Referee."

In pen and ink, the recorder took down the sworn-to words. From the evidence of the document, William seems to have been coached a little by his attorney. (There are instances where the deponent seems to be going back and asking to add a sentence or two; the recorder puts in the scratch-outs and additions and elaborations and strike-throughs, sometimes writing between the lines, with an arrow, or down the side of the page. It's possible William came to these insertions and stops and starts on his own.)

At least six times in the eight pages, William speaks of his wife's "temper," her "outburst," her "personal violence" against him. Of how "ungovernable" she could become at unexpected moments. He never quite declares that she has struck him in the face with her fists, but you almost can't help picturing that.

He testifies that for approximately three years—going back to February 1882—she has refused to "occupy the same bed with me." Apparently, they'd kept sleeping in the same room downstairs, but she wouldn't have him near her bed. He would often ask and be rejected. A year went by. It was now February 1883, and she was refusing him to be in the bedroom itself, which was not far from the hearth. He had to go upstairs at night, to one of the coldest rooms in the house. Summer or winter, if he so much as tried to enter what had previously been their bedroom, even if in the daylight hours, she'd "drive me out. This was for the two years last spent."

Here is a large chunk of the deposition, as it appears on the page, some of the sentences not tracking in their spelling and grammar, and with some faulty punctuation, and more than a little repetition, and maybe all of the document being much more credible just because of these things. (The indentations for paragraphs are hard to make out.) The word "reluctantly" was used up above—that he had finally come to the conclusion he had no other choice but to bring a divorce suit. That's my overwhelming reading not only of these eight pages, but of the entire story.

She sometimes said she did not love me and sometimes she said she hated me she told me on March 4, 1883. I hate the very ground you tread on. If you will give me the place you may go when you please. I don't care what becomes of you. She has twice said she would never live with me as a wife and for two years has protested against and refused me intercourse as between husband & wife.

Her language during the last three years has not been kind and I do not know of any thing kind word or expression that she has used toward me. . . .

I have made special effort during the last two years to have her reconciled to me. . . . I made such an effort in August 1883, she was then visiting among her friends. I went to see her. I tried to have a pleasant visit with her. . . . I went intending to overlook every thing. . . .

She treated me said I had blackened her to her people. . . . I have sought both by interviews and letters a reconciliation. I have written letters three different times seeking reconciliation. . . .

I have never intentionally blackened her character. I had once confidentially inquired of one of her relations if there had been insanity in the family. I did not suppose this was ever to be spoken of. It was communicated to her and she complained of it. . . .

~~It was~~ It is now several months since I have lived in the same house with her. For more than two years last that I trid to be with her, I was compelled to go upstairs and sleep alone. . . .

The reason I inquired if there had been any insanity in the family was on account of her violent conduct towards me. . . .

At last her brothers came to me and spoke about the necessity of peace in the family. I said there was nothing I wanted more, that I had been outrageously abused. . . . I told them I had suffered a good many years that I was entitled to a divorce for cruelty, personal violence, and refusal of my marital rights. . . . Many times before I had thought on the subject of a divorce but had made up my mind that for the sake of our children . . . but when after suffering violence indignity and abuse for years I was represented as being prime offender I could endure it no longer. . . . Very many times I had to make my own bed, though I paid a hired girl at the time. . . . a larger part of my mending I did myself or carried away because when I requested her to do anything it was often neglected, never ~~chearfully~~ cheerfully done, and when it was done, often threwn in my face or on the floor. . . .

I left at last because comfort and peace were out of the question and I did not deem it safe to stay.

Our married life had been unhappy from the start. She was jealous of the three children by my first wife. . . . She wanted more money than I could furnish and constantly blamed me for not having more. . . . She would be violently angry if I remonstrated against her course, would resent any suggestions about economy.

On April 24, 1885, the court rendered its ruling. It found that "the defendant deserted the plaintiff," that all of the charges were true, and that the plaintiff was "entitled to the divorce for which he prays." The defendant got custody of the children, the oldest of whom was due to turn eighteen in another six weeks. She also got almost all the contents and property in "Lot one Block one hundred thirty nine in the city of Madison." It doesn't say so in the documents, but the legend is that the whipped and impecunious and surely relieved little man—who was sixty years old now—went away with the clothes on his back, some books, a couple of violins, a small instrument called a melodeon, his sheet music, and one mahogany bookcase. It can't be said what he owed his lawyer, whom he had known for twenty years. It can be reported what the clerk's fees were, which were filed the next day and that, presumably, William had to pay: $5.75. Probably just that amount would have pinched him.

The legend is he never saw any of them again—his ex-wife, his son, his two daughters. (Like most legends, it leaks just the tiniest bit. But it's spiritually true.)

He had nineteen years remaining to him. When you try to trace those nineteen years it almost seems as if Frank Lloyd Wright's father never stayed in one place for more than five minutes. If moving from one town and state to the next was already the pattern of his life, he doubled down on the compulsion in the years after his family broke up.

———

You haven't heard the half yet about fits of alleged physical violence and a screaming hysteria in this family on the mother's part, a hysteria and violence (with the aid of a two-tined carving fork and a wooden roller for the pounding of meat) that were enacted chiefly on the youngest stepchild. If these things actually happened (or even fifty percent happened), it would have been impossible for everyone living in the house not to have known about them, on some level. But I'd like to flip it, the story, in another direction. Flip it even further back in time, to far quieter things. The wronged man you're hearing about was washed in the blood of a New England religiosity. From all that can be known, it was a world of believers on their knees, with music in their bones. It was the Lord every day and three times on Sunday. Old-time Christians like to say that the playing of an organ in church, or the beauty of voices raised in song to God, is a form of praying twice. This was the family of William Wright, whose mother once said of him in a letter, in May 1844, when he was still a young man, casting about, trying to find himself:

"As for William, he is all Music, Music. I think he will make something if he tries. I feel troubled on his account at times as well as the rest. I have felt very desirous that my sons should occupy useful stations in the Church of God."

He came from many Protestant clergymen and a few poets. The family liked to claim its roots to European kings and queens in the Middle Ages. As for American poets, James Russell Lowell was somewhere in his family line—a distant half-cousin or so of roughly William's same age. He was born on January 2, 1825, in a little town just outside of Springfield, Massachusetts, the fourth of five children. His father, the Reverend David Wright, who had been to Yale, was said to have been so diminutive that he couldn't preach from his Baptist pulpit—the congregation would never be able to see him over the pulpit's transom. (He would stand beside the pulpit, on a box or little stepladder.) For much of his growing up, the family lived in and around Hartford (down the road from Springfield), which in some ways still thinks of itself as second only to Boston in terms of New England importance.

He went to college at fourteen, enrolling at Amherst in 1839. (Martin Van Buren was the eighth president of the United States; Emily Dickinson, about to turn nine, was with her parents in the Dickinson Homestead on Main Street.) Much has been made of this—his precociousness. But perhaps even more should be made of the fact that he didn't finish. That he dropped out. There is a rather amazing, small cache of his letters as a young man, to family members, that seems to reveal much about how the child was the father to the man. In these fourteen letters, on watermarked stationery, in blue ink, with big curvy characters, you get the drift, the pride, the bantam ego, the wit, the whimsy, the loner aspect, the melancholy, the extraordinary intelligence, the indolence, the pretension, the dreaminess, the charm, the dandy quality, the more-than-slight superiority complex, the deep and abiding love for music: the playing of it, and the composing of it.

For instance, to his older brother, Thomas G. Wright, who is studying for the ministry and is his instructor on the piano and the organ, William writes on February 25, 1841, from his college room at Amherst, where he is a semi-slacking sophomore, that it's a fasting day and "so we have some leisure; for all we have to do to day is to go in and hear a sermon this afternoon." He's studying Oedipus Tyrannus (he spells it this way), which he judges to be Sophocles's best work. Hard, but he gets the stuff. "They were not very rigid in examining me at the commencement of the term; and notwithstanding my previous laziness, told me when it was over, that he (for I was examined by one tutor only) thought I had been pretty diligent while absent." Of his lodging, some distance from the college grounds: "I have a tolerably good room; and when I am not too lazy to keep myself in wood I make out to keep warm." He isn't much troubled with the "blues," even though "I *do* room alone. I like boarding myself very well, as long as have victuals inplenty, though I think it would be a great deal pleasanter to have some one to eat with. It is not probable that I shall board myself next summer if I *stay* here, as victuals will not keep so well then as they do now. I have had no one, yet jeer at me for boarding myself; nor have been called Sister Wright; and if I should be, such a combative fellow as you used to think me would not hesitate to de*fend* himself. I play on the violin at the Baptist church here; they appear to be pleased with my services."

He left school and went back home to live with his parents. The family was now in central New York State (the father's ministry had taken them there), in Waterville, which is close to Hamilton, where older brother Thomas was finishing seminary. Here he is, on April 5, 1842, starting a letter to his brother, but trailing off. His father finishes it: "My dear Tom, I hoped your brother would have written more particularly. He feels in a manner alone here . . . and I fear will sink down into stupidity and inaction."

Fifteen months later (it's July 11, 1843; he's eighteen and still living at home, still seemingly directionless), another letter to Tom, who's now been ordained into the ministry. Family members are adding tidbits to the fold-over. William enters two contributions, and in both he includes snippets of music he's lately composed. He artfully embeds the musical lines, with the notes and bars, into the body of the letter. "Letter No. 2. Dear Brother. As there is room for more writing in this letter, and as all have written what they wish rather than have this sheet go unfilled I will send you another piece of my music; worthless it may be, but—however I will send it—for dissection." He adds that "I composed this entirely without the piano, and it is not very melodious. I suppose that it is likely they will not either of them stand the test of so great a critic. However as I was your pupil in the Rudiments of Harmony I thought you would like to see the effect in part of your teachings." He provides the words for his composition, which opens in the form of a hymn/ prayer: "Great is the Lord, his works of might."

By 1848, a gap of seven years (very little of which is known), he is back at college, older now than most of his classmates. He's matriculated at Madison University in Hamilton (which will later change its name to Colgate University). Within two academic years, he has graduated, earning both a bachelor's and master's degree. He has read law and taken some medical courses (or at least pre-med courses), but it is music that still seizes his mind. He seems to have been at the top of his class, or classes (since he was apparently an undergraduate and graduate student at the same time). The university has asked him to give the commencement speech. He has titled it "Efficiency, How Attained." The school prints his name and the title in the commencement program for August 15, 1849—but at the last minute the valedictorian comes down sick. Letter to brother Tom four days later, August 19: "Of course I was used up so that I could not 'sprout' commencement day, but it matters little, for I have had the mental discipline of *writing* my speech without the *excitement* of its delivery." Tom Wright has been ministering in Claremont, New Hampshire, and his kid brother has lived on and off with Tom's family. Tom and his wife are expecting. "So I am *again* an uncle," William says, in the same letter in which he has reported on his not-delivered commencement speech. "A fertile soil that of Claremont. Dear me how old I am getting. I really believe I shall do something desperate in five or six years, or I shall not catch up with my brothers."

In 1850, William, now twenty-five, took a job teaching music at Utica Female Academy in Utica, New York. (It isn't far from Hamilton.) It was a boarding school for proper young ladies. (Pew rental for the chapel was seventy-five cents a quarter.) He taught piano, voice, and violin. He composed deep into the night. Some of his works had already been published as sheet music by well-regarded music publishing houses in Boston and New York. They were tuneful piano parlor works, essentially. (If you think of the Americana music of Stephen Foster, his musical contemporary, you'll have the idea of William's basic style and sound. His pieces often have gay staccato bounces or little purling runs of harmonic chords.) He wasn't trying to be Bach or Beethoven, his largest symphonic heroes, but it was clear he was growing confident of his powers. He gave these published compositions evocative and jaunty titles, like "The Hemlock Ridge Quick Step," or "O Linger Not Love." To listen now, more than a century and a half since these pieces were composed, is to hear all of the antebellum nineteenth-century bounciness, yes, but also something laced deep with melancholy. Is that just a retroactive reading in, given what is known about how his life turned out? Perhaps, but I don't think so.*

On love, and its lingering: "You ask if I do not feel tempted sometimes to commit matrimony!" he says in a letter to his sister-in-law in New Hampshire in early 1851. "I sometimes feel tempted to *want* to—but I choked down such an absorbing emotion whenever I find it rising." Next paragraph: "You and Thos. are really well started on the road to ancestral glory with one son and one daughter. . . . I have given up the idea of overtaking you, in despair, unless you should be disposed to halt and wait for your left-behind, wifeless bachelor brother, to take *himself* a partner and set out on this highway to a *marital immortality.*" He asks for family news. "I have none myself. You will excuse brevity for I really have no time to write more. My love to Thomas. Tell him that his last letter was too short, like himself." (Thomas was apparently even shorter than William.)

But love did linger. That letter to his sister-in-law was in January 1851—and by August he had committed matrimony to Permelia Holcomb. She was one of his piano students at Utica, seven months younger. Her father was a farmer in Litchfield, which is in Herkimer County, east and southeast of Utica, with a rich agricultural history. William's father presided at the ceremony. William and his spouse moved to Hartford, his nominal hometown. He opened a music school. He became the organist at South Baptist Church. He wrote "L'Agreable Reverie," and described the work on the title page as a *Romance Originale avec Varia-*

---

* Until about eight or nine years ago, the wider world knew next to nothing about the music of William C. Wright. That's when a professional musicologist and independent Wright scholar from Oak Park named David Patterson began locating old sheet music and tracing the lost history. In 2013, he produced, on Permelia Records, *The Music of William C. Wright: Solo Piano and Vocal Works 1847–1893.* The CD comes with thirty-one pages of liner notes that include an expert analysis of the music as well as Patterson's thumbnail sketch of the life. I'm grateful for his research, and for the generosity of his time (even if we disagree on fundamental aspects of the life), not to say grateful for the pleasures of the recording itself, which seems to bring the man right back from the dead. Patterson found contemporary musicians and vocalists to perform the twenty-one tracks.

tions pour le Piano Forte. He provided a formal opus number: *Opus 10*. You can sense him starting to think of himself more grandly.

And yet . . . the questing, the desultory aspects. The last surviving letter in this cache of fourteen is datelined "Hartford Dec. 10, 1851." Again, it's to his brother Tom. He's been married to Permelia since August 4. Permelia sends her love, but she has a "'crying cold' at present and does not feel very well." At the top of the final page, with a double underline: "Thomas I do not know what to write." A few lines down: "With much love to you both. I will close now before anything happens."

Children came along—with difficulty. Three years after the marriage, a stillborn. (Had they been trying for these three years to start a family?) That same grieving year, 1854, William, twenty-nine, published his first book; it must have given him some large pride and small solace. It was closer to a bookette: eighty-two pages, beautifully bound and printed in small format. There are probably not a dozen copies extant in America of *The Piano Forte Manual*. The book feels as delicate and fine-featured as William himself looks in every surviving photograph. It fits right in the palm. There are chapters on melody and dynamics and rhythm. Even taking into account the formal qualities of nineteenth-century prose, you can sense something of his own character in the way he writes—both with modesty and not. From the preface: "That this little book will prove a *perfect* desideratum, it is not our wish to assert; but that it will be found far nearer what is desired, than anything of the kind before it, we hope a candid and thorough examination of its pages will evince." And: "Trusting that this book will meet the wants of teacher and pupils, and that a thorough trial of its merits will commend it to general favor, we resign it to their consideration. With love for the art. Wm. C. Wright." (There are passages in the tiny book where you can almost imagine him conducting a lesson with a pointer with one of his more promising students: "Unless otherwise indicated, the first note should be accented with a strong pressure of the finger, while the second note is to be closely connected with the first, but must be pressed lightly, and shortly. . . . One must especially avoid the detestable habit of striking the Base notes invariably a little before the Treble.")

Something happened—the man with such love for the art seems not to have published another note of his own work for almost twenty years.

Was it, as some have suggested, the realities of being a husband and the need to earn a living? Was it a creative paralysis? In any case, he seems to have taken up the law in earnest now. (Or semi-earnest—did he ever truly wish a life in law?) He was admitted to the Connecticut bar in 1857 and practiced in Hartford for the next two years, while not giving up his music school. The year before, his first son, Charles William, had been born. The year following his admission to the bar, a second son, George Irving, arrived.

But then, in 1859, eight years after his marriage, a passage point: he and Permelia and their small sons moved west, to Wisconsin, and specifically to a little shipping town on the north bank of the Wisconsin River called Lone Rock. Wisconsin had been admitted to the union eleven years before. Lone Rock, founded three years before, was on the major rail lines of Richland County. Bear Valley was just up the way. Why the relocation to this frontier spot? The best explanation seems to be that whole extended families from Herkimer County, New York (home ground of many of Permelia Holcomb Wright's people), were resettling themselves in the rich valleys of southwestern Wisconsin— like European immigrants, one branch had pulled out the next. Over a period of years, some of Permelia's family, immediate and extended, would make the journey to Richland County: the lure of western migration. *O Pioneers!*, to reference Willa Cather.

William, not quite dreaming of life behind a plow, set himself up in a law practice in a tiny stone building in Lone Rock. He also taught music. In July 1860, a daughter—Elizabeth Amelia, known almost right from the start as Lizzie—came into the family. Within a year, William was appointed commissioner of the Richland County Circuit Court. He ran for county superintendent of schools, losing on his first try, but gaining office on the second. The Civil War was on, and he was drafted, but—reportedly—he engaged in the not-uncommon practice of paying for a substitute. (He is said to have sold one of his prize violins for twenty-eight dollars, which bought the deferral.)

He was a pedigreed man from the East, and by now he had developed a rich baritone-bass singing and speaking voice. Despite his shyness and formalness in some matters, he is said to have been able to make friends almost effortlessly. He is known to have given stirring speeches on public occasions, and these were reported on in the local press. Perhaps this ability as an emerging orator, almost in spite of his natural inclinations, had something to do with the decision to go back to God—that is, to the family business. On August 5, 1863, William was ordained to the Baptist ministry. He worked as a pastor in both Lone Rock and the county seat, Richland Center. The legend is that he rode a horse between the two towns, which are sixteen miles apart, toting his knapsack and a red, leather-encased melodeon. He'd play for himself along the way, and at the services lead his congregation in song. The circuit rider for God wasn't a horseman, but he had taught himself to ride appreciably well in that rough country. His hair hadn't yet gone shock-white but it streamed backward from his domed forehead. For such a small man, he had an unusually large head, testament no doubt to his braininess.

In late March of 1864, Permelia gave birth to another stillborn. In less than two weeks, Permelia herself was dead, at thirty-eight. She and William had had not quite thirteen years together. The thirty-nine-year-old minister, always pressed to make a living, was now the dazed, single parent of three children under the age of eight. (Permelia's mother, who'd migrated to Wisconsin, is said to have moved in to help out with the caretaking.) In a little more than two years, the widower would be married again, this time to an area schoolteacher thirteen years his junior. It has been said in various books that the schoolteacher had once boarded in the Wright home. (Permelia is known to have taken in boarders as a way of trying to help out with the family income.) It has also been said that, nearly right from the start, the schoolteacher had been angling secretly for William—or, if not angling, then dreaming (or at least silently fantasizing, perhaps in her nightgown on her pillow) that someday, some way, William might be hers. So far as I know, no one has ever been able to confirm the first of these stories (that she was once a boarder in the Wright household, and thus would have come to know him, or at least observe him, up close, and Permelia, too), much less the second: the secret lusting for the faithful and highly educated man of God. (That will doubtless never be confirmed.) But what can be said with conviction is that, on August 17, 1866, in Wyoming, Wisconsin, which is a township outside of Spring Green, on the south side of the river, William C. Wright made the worst mistake of his life. It's the day he married erstwhile schoolmarm Hanna Lloyd Jones. You could say it was the worst mistake of Anna's life, too. (She hadn't yet lopped off the "H" in her first name.) It's part of the lore that the stiff-necked Lloyd Jones clan, who were there in number, didn't really cotton to the man from the East. He wasn't Unitarian and, despite all his education, he seemed to have no practical knack for making a living. Then, too, he was so damn small, not that they would have gone about saying that aloud to someone other than their own kind.

———————

Comes now some tales of gothic horror on a stepmother's part. As was rhetorically asked before: Did these events actually take place? I can't prove it, but I utterly believe they did.

On the general idea of "step": Nowhere in *An Autobiography* will a reader encounter the fact that Frank Lloyd Wright had three half-siblings. Wright was actually the sixth-born child (and third son) of William C. Wright. His half-brother Charlie was eleven years older. His half-brother George was nine years older. His half-sister Lizzie was seven years older. Wright grew up with all of them, or at least spent large chunks of his growing up with them. But they're not there in *An Autobiography*. He wrote them out. And yet, in a real sense, they managed to write themselves back in.

But to tell it as a *story:* Anna got pregnant in something like six weeks. In her eighth month, which is to say in early May 1867, William relocated himself and his family from Lone Rock to the county seat. The Richland Center Baptist Society was putting up a new building (on Church Street). Their son was born the following month, on June 8. Anna's universe had a new fixed star. Actually, the star had been fixed from the moment she knew she was going to have a child, and, in another sense, perhaps fixed from the instant she had said *I do.* William's salary was $300 a year, and he tried to supplement it, but not well, with his abiding love, music. Parishioners held "donation parties" for the family. From newspaper accounts, it's easy to discern what a popular figure William was in the community—but this must not have been enough, neither the money nor the esteem. (The donation parties had to have been their own small humiliation.) The old lures were obtaining: to go somewhere else.

He gave his farewell sermon on March 13, 1869—a little less than two years since the move to town. By then, a newspaper on the Iowa side of the Mississippi, in a ferry town called McGregor, fifty-seven miles from Richland Center, had welcomed him to *its* community. "Rev. Mr. Wright," wrote the editor of *The North Iowa Times*, on March 3, on page 3, with less than razor accuracy, and yet in another sense with perfect accuracy, "is not professionally a clergyman though he preaches very acceptably when requested to do so. His business is with Music, the tuning of pianos, organs, melodeons, etc. R. Hubbard & Co. have sold Mr. Wright an interest in their extensive Musical department; he can be found at head quarters, Bank Block. Our city has reason to be glad that so valuable a gentleman has been added to its religious, musical and social list."*

It should be noted that the move from Wisconsin to Iowa took place when Anna was again in her eighth month. It was as if William had a talent for uprooting his family at lousy times. (Mary Jane Wright, Frank's little sister, was born on April 26, 1869. Among the things that Jennie Wright would suffer in her adulthood from the brother she generally adored was that of having her birth year blithely co-opted by him.)

McGregor, Iowa: the new dream, where there might be more income. The town, larger than Richland Center, sat in a kind of slit, or trough, between steep, rocky bluffs. French traders named it "Coulée des Sioux"—the gulch of the Sioux. White settlers named it "the Pocket City." The sidewalks were made of planks. Muddy Main Street (the town emptied into the river, and so all of its dirt streets tended to be sloughs of mud, from rising water) was lined with buildings with false fronts. The place looked like nothing you'd think of in wide, flat, fertile Iowa. It looked like something in the Wild West. On the other hand, the setting could have almost been something in the Swiss Alps.

He came, supposedly, as the Baptist Society's temporary and part-time pastor. But the money wasn't there in Rodolphus Hubbard's music

---

* Regarding newspaper and other kinds of contemporaneous accounts: Numerous Wright biographers before me have dug out documentary evidence of William's life in the almost too-many-to-count places he lived in before and after Anna—but special mention has to be made of the work of Robert C. Twombly, in his joint Wright biographies of 1973 and 1979. The earlier book is entitled *Frank Lloyd Wright: An Interpretive Biography*. The second, which amounts to a kind of do-over (by his own acknowledgment), in which he made corrections and added new material, is entitled *Frank Lloyd Wright: His Life and His Architecture*. (Twombly, and this second work, have been referenced previously.)

store, and so he slowly migrated back to the pulpit as his full-time work. His church was a lowly affair—on the upper end of town, in the second ward, a block off Main. It looked like a dinky firehouse (which, in fact, is what it became—a firehouse—in the later years of the nineteenth century, when its membership dried up and the Wrights were long gone). The biggest church in town was the United Methodist—catty-cornered from William's: a red-brick building, twin-steepled, far more imposing. But William set himself to work. In no time, he was a major figure in town, and his preaching and public speaking (and some of his local concertizing) got write-ups in the paper. The Wrights seem to have lived next door to the church—it wasn't a real parsonage, because the congregation was too poor and small to afford one.

On the 1870 federal census, he lists himself as "clergyman." He puts the value of his real estate at $300, and the value of his personal estate at $250. (Today, that would have been a cumulative worth of about $10,000.) Anna is listed in this census as "Keeping house." The household consists of Charles, fourteen; George, twelve; Lizzie, ten; Frank, three; and baby Jane, who is one. A servant named Nellie Conner is also in the household. So the restless man of God isn't doing half badly—at least for now. (No doubt that listed net worth represented Anna's dowry as well, from her schoolteaching days.)

Listen to his voice. Reverend Wright is delivering a funeral eulogy. It's December 1870. He's been in McGregor for not quite two years. The editor of the paper, Colonel A. P. Richardson, who's a member of his church and has become a good friend, has suddenly died. The orator is orating: "Colonel Richardson was a man of more than usual talent and wit, and had abilities which he might, no doubt, have used to signal advantage. He seems, however, to have been in the main contented with his sphere, and not very much disturbed by ambitious aspiration. In his temperament he was highly social and sympathetic, and possessed to more than an ordinary degree the faculty of making friends among those with whom he was wont to mingle. In his manner he was unostentatious and outspoken, with an evident dislike to all airy pretensions and pompous parade." These things could almost be said about William—yes, but no. In seven more months, he and his family will be gone. "Ambitious aspiration," or something, will have overtaken him.

But listen to another voice.

[S]he was very sweet to us children till after they were married. Then she grew worse and worse each year. She had a terrible temper and seemed to make no effort to control it. She vented it upon me mostly, because she was jealous of Father's affection for me, and the boys could keep out of her sight, but she wouldn't allow me to. As I grew older she used to tell me often that she hated me, and all my Mother's people. . . . She told me many a time that she hated me and all my mother's people and I had no reason to doubt it. She told us we could call her Mama or Mother, as we chose, and as "Mamma" was sacred to our own mother, we chose to call her "Mother." . . . I am sure that I would have loved her if she had been kind to me or at all affectionate; for I was hungry for love. . . . While we lived in McGregor I was very much afraid of my stepmother. She not only beat me till I was black and blue all over, but threatened me with some terrible things, and especially if I should tell my father about her treatment. I had no wish to make him any more trouble than he had already, so I kept things to myself, for I was ashamed of it. Once one of the girls [from school] saw some of my bruises and asked the cause and I told her I fell down. But I grew more and more afraid to be left alone with her. When father was around she never treated me so badly as he would not allow it and she didn't want him to know, anyway.

This is Elizabeth Wright Heller speaking—in the guise of her childhood self. This is Lizzie, William's youngest child by Permelia, remembering her life from the vantage point of her relative old age. *The Story of My Life* is a 132-page, single-spaced typewritten document that was begun in Portland, Oregon, in April 1929, when its author was nearing sixty-nine. Its author wasn't a professional writer—she'd worked as a young woman in a Midwest newspaper office, she'd been a farm wife, she'd raised a family, she'd lived in numerous places (although mostly in Iowa). She just wanted to set things down in a memoir fashion. Over a period of about eleven years, she did exactly that, taking up her "book" manuscript again whenever there was time. So you find lots of moseying around and disarming sentences in *The Story of My Life,* such as this: "Today I have written two pages of retrospection which can be inserted in this most anywhere, and though I have a lot of work to get done, I must try and finish this history, for I think it will be quite interesting to my children, and may possibly do them some good in some way. Anyway, I would like to finish it, since I began it, and it seems to me quite interesting."

Such disarming-ness is only one reason why I greatly trust this document, which, it goes without saying, carries nothing even close to the legal weight or force of an 1885 Dane County divorce document.

A double-spaced typed copy of Lizzie's original manuscript is at the State Historical Society of Iowa at Iowa City. (Her family put the story there some while after her death, which was on March 3, 1950; she'd made it nearly to ninety.) The Elizabeth Wright Heller Collection contains many valuable items relating to her father's life (not least family photo albums and some of William's old, fragile sheet music), but nothing as valuable as this unpublished autobiography. Except that "unpublished" isn't quite right. Wright scholars became aware of the manuscript some years ago, thanks in part to Brendan Gill. So far as I know, he was the first biographer or historian to make slices of the work available to a national readership. Gill included excerpts in his 1987 *Many Masks*. In the scheme of Wright studies, that's a fairly late date—or, to say it another way, a fairly late moment in respect to some cemented (and baldly wrong) impressions about Wright's background. In Iowa, the descendants of Permelia and William Wright still say Gill's name with something like reverence.

But *story*. Once again, something happened in McGregor. Was William no longer "contented with his sphere"? But why? Money must certainly have been a part of it. But did he feel his gifts were larger than McGregor could appreciate? (In the papers, the town seems to be doing nothing but adoring him.) In April 1871, he announced his impending departure. He'd been the town's Baptist pastor for just over two years. The community begged him to stay; the church membership voted not to accept the resignation. At first, it looked like he'd relent. ("The Rev. W.C. Wright has been prevailed upon by the Baptist society to remain . . . to the evident gratification of all the people of McGregor," reported *The North Iowa Times*.) But no go. From the July 5, 1871, edition of the *NIT*: "The Rev. W.C. Wright has closed his connection with the Baptist Church. . . . The people of McGregor have not submitted willingly to the decision. . . . They love him, the church, of which he has been the pastor, loves him and separate from him with regret, and will ever follow him with their kindest wishes to whatever field of labor he may be called."

The next field of labor—still in the Lord's service—was Pawtucket, Rhode Island, although the family didn't immediately go there. He told the *Times* that he had a few business matters to attend to in Spring Green, Wisconsin, and that these might take several weeks, and that he and his family would then entrain for the East to spend the summer and fall with his relatives, before taking up the new mission to which God had called him. But as it worked out, the family spent the next five months with Anna's folk in the Lloyd Jones valleys. There must have been some awkwardness in that. For one thing, William wouldn't have had any real income. Actually, the whole family *didn't* stay with Anna's people. Lizzie—she was eleven now, a tiny thing, prone to sickness— was put with Permelia's mother up in Bear Valley. The only explanation seems to be that William was desperate to get his daughter away, at least for a time, from Anna's rages and clutches, which were semi-out in the open by then. Grandma Holcomb had apparently become aware of what seemed to be going on in the house—some demonic need to take things out on the youngest and frailest of William's three by Permelia.

From *The Story of My Life*: "I heard Grandma tell Aunt Nellie that she saw my stepmother knock me down once and that was all she could stand."

Pawtucket: an old hulking, smoky, eighteenth-century manufacturing city of muskets, linseed oil, shipbuilding, potash. But at least it was a *city*. And furthermore it was in the East. In December 1871, William took over at impoverished High Street Baptist Church. It was his third pastorate and the third family relocation in the five and a half years since his marriage to Anna. The original High Street church had burned down three years before, and, if anything, the new congregation was in far worse financial shape than McGregor's had been when William started there. No matter: The idealistic pastor plunged in, hell with the money aspects. Again, everyone seemed to love him. The family lived in nearby Central Falls. Lizzie Heller's memory in her old age of the rented house is visceral: the big basement kitchen with the cistern, the glossy floor painted green with a spatter-paint of white over top. Her memory is visceral about some other things, too.

From *The Story of My Life:*

> I remember one time in the winter [if this was the second winter in Rhode Island, which it seems to have been, then she would have been twelve, going on thirteen, and her baby half-brother Frank, who hadn't started school yet and so was at home, would have been five, going on six] when Mother was in one of her tantrums, she got mad about something and as usual vented it on me; she jumped up and down and pumped water as fast as she could and threw it over me and yelled with every jump. Father had his study on the third floor but he heard the racket, and came down to see what was up. He told me to go upstairs but I was afraid to go past her to the stairway and my clothes were dripping wet, but I slipped out the front door and went around to the back and up the outside stairs. My clothes froze on me before I could get in the house.

Next paragraph:

> One other time when he was at home and up in his study, she was frying meat at the stove with a long two tined fork that goes with a carving set. She got mad at me for something or nothing, and grabbed me by the hair and held my head back and jabbed that fork at my face, and said she would put my eyes out. I screamed "Papa!" with all my might, and he came running down and stopped her, but I had the worst fright of my life. I believe she would have done so if she had dared to, she seemed so full of venom and hate. I think those were the only two times when Father was home.

Next paragraph:

> I remember once when we had a hired girl for [a] while, Mother got mad and grabbed me by the hair and yanked me back and forth all over the kitchen. After she went upstairs I combed my hair and it came out by the double handfuls, and the girl looked at me, aghast.

She seemed to think that was awful, but it was not nearly so bad as some other things she did to me.

Next paragraph:

When Mother and I were out together, which was seldom, or if anyone was with us, she was very sweet to me and called me pet names, just for effect. It made me despise her for being such a hypocrite, but I never gave her away or told Father the things she did to me when he was away. I remember one time she was pounding beefsteak with a heavy hardwood roller with sharp ridges all over it, made for the purpose, and she pounded me all over my back with it until I was black and blue and sore, but not bleeding. I suppose those things relieved her feelings, but they certainly did not relieve mine any.

Three paragraphs down:

I never could please her, no matter how hard I tried. She admitted sometimes that she hated me and all my mother's relatives; she said she would like to have all our heads laid over a log and take an ax and chop them off. I do not know whether her mind was just right or not. She seemed to have periodical spells when she got the "Mad Hysterics" and raved like a maniac. Then she would be sick in bed for a day or two and I would have peace. I did not mind the work or taking care of the children if she was not around.

And this paragraph, which is just below the Mad Hysterics paragraph. Lizzie is telling how William has decided he must send his child away, to his own people, lest something irreversible should happen. His two sons by Permelia, not quite grown, are still living in the house, and, of course, little Frank and Jennie.

Mother embraced me in parting and kissed and wept over me, so that my heart melted toward her. But whether she thought it would make a better impression on my memory, or her tears were tears of joy of getting rid of me, or of contrition for her treatment of me, I never knew. But I felt like forgiving her all her unkindness, and did, in a way, but I was never able to forget.

And then these three paragraphs from *The Story of My Life*. It is about half a dozen years later, in Madison. (Yes, I am skipping briefly out of time.) Lizzie has rejoined the family. Her father has decided it is safe for her to come back. She is a young woman now, in high school, older than most of those around her. She seems to be nineteen, with perhaps a year of school left before she earns a diploma. So it must be 1879, roughly six years before the divorce. She's living with her half-siblings and one of her full brothers in the Wright home on Gorham Street.

I took the course for Normal and special students. I liked the school very much and my teachers, as usual, but did not enjoy my stepmother any, nor my half brother Frank who was his mother's idol and badly spoiled by her.

Frank was twelve at that time and Jennie was ten and dear little Maggie-Nell was a darling about two years old. I loved her dearly and Jennie too. But my stepmother had not improved and still disliked me and all my mother's relatives and talked for the hour against them and about her own hard lot. . . .

She had her usual spells of mad hysterics and acted like a raving maniac and told father to send for the officers and take her to the Asylum and I used to wish he would. Poor man, he led a wretched existence. She was always sick in bed for a day or two after these attacks and then we had peace, like a calm after a storm.

I said above I highly trust this work, even if it's finally just a memoir, far from any kind of legal document. The trust is founded on an inherent *sound* in the writing itself. That sound is akin to something like innocence—no matter what suffering is in the story. But she's hardly a pushover. *The Story of My Life* is a book of about ninety thousand words. Probably less than five percent of it is devoted to Anna, and to what Lizzie reports that Anna did to her. The great bulk of the narrative is about Lizzie's raising her own kids, about living through hard economic times, about trying to be a good wife, about trying to find time to get daily on her knees, about her own flaws and failings. The writing is episodic and informal, as if she's talking over the back fence with her apron on and her nylons rolled down past her kneecaps. The writing can also be unintentionally hilarious. She tells you about her dentures. ("But every once in a while I had to have some of my lower ones out. I have often said that my teeth were a lot of trouble to me from the time I first began to get them until they were all gone, and then some. I parted with them all with pleasure.") She tells you about the hired girl—actually, she forgets to tell you about the hired girl when the hired girl came. (So that paragraph begins: "I forgot to tell about May.") She tells you about her son Paul. ("But Paul was born with kidney trouble and an acid condition and had to have the doctor before he was a week old, and he was a prey to rheumatic troubles until after he grew up, the same as I was. . . . He was a delicate baby and never got fat like the rest of them, but he never had a chance. The children had the whooping cough that summer and Paul was hardly three months old when he took it, and it seemed as if he could never live through it.") She'll tell you plenty about her own sins as a mother and a spouse and a Christian and a neighbor. ("But when I lost my temper and became angry and said things I shouldn't, as I sometimes did when it seemed I could endure no more, I always felt badly afterwards on account of my religion. I felt that I had disgraced the name of Christian, and that might have a disastrous effect on others. I knew God would forgive me, for He knew my heart, but others didn't and I couldn't forgive myself. . . . I never cried when I was mad, though some do. I cried when I was so tired and worn out in body and nerves and brain and felt blue and discouraged and some little things upset me and I broke down and wept.")

And in the midst of all this, she tells you about Anna's blind hatred of her.

But she doesn't neglect to tell of those isolated moments when Anna turned surprisingly kind, motherly. The child craved them. There was that bout, on the long journey to Pawtucket (there were stops with family in Philadelphia), with what she calls "inflammatory rheumatism." She tells of how "Mother treated me with the water cure method. . . . She carried me down two flights of stairs and put me in a tub of hot water beside the cook stove with my feet in a pail of hot water and covered me all up with blankets and kept me steaming for about half an hour, afterwards putting me to bed." Anna tended her day and night for maybe as much as a week, the author remembers.

So did Lizzie put this in as a sop? It's impossible for me to believe that. Again, it's the *sound* of her book, the sound of her stories. They just ring true. They lack guile.

But let it be said, or maybe admitted: Although I've searched long and hard to try to find any kind of written corroboration among her siblings—all decades dead—I've never found it. Does this change my opinion? No. It just doesn't make sense that Lizzie could have been making all this stuff up. Or, for that matter, wildly exaggerating it. (I keep wondering about her older brothers. Didn't they want to knock Anna cold?)

Toward the back, Lizzie writes: "Poor Father. What a life she led him so many years. It must have been a veritable Hell on Earth. But maybe she was better after she got rid of me and my brothers. I suppose she was afraid I would tell about her. But I was always ashamed to let folks know about her for it seemed a sort of disgrace to father to have a wife like that. But she could be very nice when strangers were around. I guess I have always hated a hypocrite ever since."

The idea of shame, the victim's shame, makes the book ring that much truer.

Three paragraphs down: "I don't know why it is, but I've had so many memories of her lately that I wanted to forget and they have made me feel blue. I don't like to get all stirred up over such things, but I have always hated injustice anywhere. . . . She hated me, and often said so, and never wanted any one else to like me because she was so jealous. But enough of her, too much in fact."

At the end of her book (we are somewhere in the early 1940s, and her own husband, John Heller, has been dead for decades), speaking of her favorite grandchild (she has a slew of them), she says: "I think I will have Hope typewrite the 'Story of My Life' and make several copies to distribute among my children. She is taking a business course and paying for it herself, besides her high school course. She has got several prizes in music this year on the saxophone, getting First in the State and Second Rating in the National Music Contest at Minneapolis, Minnesota."

Quick cut—to the tense of modern times. In an overbright and overheated parlor, on a gray November day, in a little Iowa town up from Cedar Rapids, a former high school typist and award-winning saxophonist—who has topped ninety herself—is talking about her long-gone grandmother. I've come to talk with Hope Rogers, to try to further assure myself of what I already feel certain of in my bones: that Lizzie told the truth. (It was Hope, along with family members, who eventually placed the manuscript in the State Historical Society of Iowa.) She's a tough prairie woman, a lifelong Iowan, nobody's fool. She's a bit of a hoot. She's got two canes and a walker. She'll talk your damn head off. She's a voracious reader and the author of two self-published books. In 1976, a quarter century after her grandmother died, Hope Rogers wrote her own book about William and Permelia and Lizzie and some others on her side of the family. It's entitled *Grandpa Wright*. (Grandpa Wright, whom she never knew, was really her great-grandfather—but she was speaking metaphorically. To all of William's descendants in Iowa, or the ones I've talked to, William seems to be "Grandpa Wright.") On page 4 of Hope's own book, which had a modest run in her region of Iowa, with some praising press coverage, there is this: "Inevitably, however, as I interrupted the writing of her memoirs on my way home from school, grandma's memories dwelt upon the cruelty of her stepmother, details of which were so vivid that even in her seventies, my grandmother still woke in terror that her stepmother was chasing her again with the butcher knife."

I've just asked about the butcher knife—or the dream of the butcher knife. And Hope says: "I'd stop at Grandma's. I was coming from school. I'd come in and put my books down. I might be hoping for a snack. She'd be usually sitting reading a paper or a magazine. Sometimes I'd go in and she'd just be trembling. Just shaking. Maybe she had just wakened up from a nap. She had had the nightmare again."

"Did you ask her what the nightmare was?"

"No. I didn't have to. It was always the same one. Anna chasing her around the room with the big knife again."

(Let it be noted that there is no section of the manuscript that has Anna chasing Lizzie with a butcher knife. All those awful other things, yes. But, as we know, dreams have a way of folding in, blurring, trans-forming, reimagining, our childhood traumas.)

This is my second visit to Vinton, Iowa—to ask the same questions. The first time, four years earlier, Hope, recuperating from a pelvic fracture, had said: "Oh, if anything, Grandma didn't tell it half as bad as it was. It wasn't in her character. I'm absolutely sure she held things back." She paused. "Now me, I wouldn't have held a single thing back. If you want to know, I kind of believe Anna was a witch. Literally. They were all from Wales, you know. They were descended from the Druids."

We had looked at some old family albums. There were yellow-tinted photographs of Lizzie Heller in advanced age sitting on a summer porch swing with bushes blooming behind her. She seemed so ladylike—big round glasses, short hair, collared dress, string of beads. (Was it a Sunday midday, and they were all home from church?) She looked so tiny. There was another photograph of Lizzie in the yard of a farmhouse wearing a big winter coat. Her hands were clasped behind her. Her lace-up shoes looked to have a fresh coat of chalky white on them. She wore a brooch at the locked collar of her simple countrywoman's dress. She was looking off, pensively. She couldn't have weighed more than ninety pounds.

In that first visit, I had asked Lizzie Heller's granddaughter a question I already considered rhetorical: "Is it somehow possible Frank didn't know what was going on?"

"Yes," Hope had said instantly, half cackling. "In the way Jupiter could be made out of green cheese."

I've since talked to others in this widely populated family, with its numerous branches. I've talked to a few *great-great-great*s of William. I've spent time with Hope's own children, who are *great-great*s and upper-aged people themselves, with their own children and grandchildren. None of them is unbiased, of course. One Rogers daughter, whose name is Jeanne Swift, said: "We were the ones they tried to leave out of the story—but we've got the same blood." Another of Hope's daughters—her name is Mary Catherine Rogers—said: "See, we've had to listen to William called just a deadbeat and a drifter. There are still people in the Frank Lloyd Wright world who no doubt think that, or have that impression."

———

In January 1874, William departed Pawtucket. He'd been the shepherd of High Street Baptist barely two years. (Again, as in McGregor, the congregation had voted not to accept the resignation.) The next stop, but again not immediately, was Weymouth, Massachusetts. (There was a seven-month stay in Essex, Connecticut, where William's widowed father was now living.) Same pattern as before—except not quite. In Weymouth, which is sixteen miles southeast of Boston, it almost seemed as if William—from the start—was trying to work himself out of a job. In a congregation of strict adherents to the Bible, the new pastor instituted a singing school and musical programs on Sunday evenings. That was anathema to some. A decade and a half before, the Weymouth Baptists had banned from their religious presence any kind of music and theatricals. It was as if their new shepherd was acting on his principles—self-destructively. But maybe there is another explanation. It's a fact that, after a fallow period of nearly two decades, William had begun to write and publish music again with several respected Boston publishing houses. (He'd begun in the Pawtucket tenure, actually.) In 1874 alone, four of his works got into printed circulation in Boston and New York. It had to have brought tremendous pride. And perhaps it was this overweening pride, even selfish pride, at least in terms of putting the welfare of his family above all else, which instilled in him a false sense of security about his Weymouth pastorate. It couldn't have helped that a member of the congregation donated a pipe organ to the church. (He must have been one of the few liberal-minded folk amid those rigid believers.) The pastor played it with all the stops out, head tossed back. Meanwhile, as usual, the family finances were close to perilous.

In June 1877, William and Anna's third child, Margaret Ellen (soon enough to be known as Maginel), was born, and this had to have brought its own new strains, economic and otherwise. By that October, Reverend Wright was out of a job. Was he fired, or did he resign under pressure? History has never quite been able to figure it out.

The family stayed in the East for about another six months. The head of the house tried to make a living as he could, lecturing, performing in a few public musical events. (They seem to have brought in virtual pennies.) He apparently was now starting to turn away from the Baptist faith. His wife's religion was Unitarian, and they embraced music. To quote historian Mary Jane Hamilton, previously referenced, regarded as a premier authority on Wright family history (and who, not incidentally, considers Elizabeth Wright Heller's manuscript to be a trustworthy document): "With no prospects for employment in the ministry and with virtually no cash in hand, William and his family returned to Wisconsin."

In those few words, you can sense the beginnings of a defeated man. And surely in some sense, deep down, he had to know. Since his ordination in 1863, the charming and supremely gifted William Wright had been a parson in five towns. Less than a decade before, he'd gone east with much hope, if with darkening family problems. But now, in April 1878, a fifty-three-year-old with diminished professional prospects and a wife who'd begun to loathe him openly was going back to the valleys of his wife's people. In less than four years (according to a Dane County divorce document), this man's wife would be refusing to have him in her bed in their modest home on Gorham Street in Madison, if still, apparently, allowing him to sleep in their bedroom. (There must have been two beds in there.) In less than five years, this man's wife would be refusing to let him even cross the threshold of their bedroom, never mind any absurd fantasy on his part about marital intercourse. At various points through here, apparently, this man's wife was subject to spells in which she raved like a maniac and told her husband to please for God's sake get the officers from the asylum to come and cart her away. In less than seven years—the date was December 13, 1884, a cold, cruddy Saturday in the upper Midwest—this man, now fifty-nine, having recently moved out of his home, in fear of his physical safety, would trudge to his lawyer's office in downtown Madison just off Capitol Square and reluctantly initiate divorce proceedings. To remind you, this man's eldest child from his wretched and at-last-ending second marriage was seventeen and a half. The boy hadn't yet struck off for the Eternal City of the West to make his world name in architecture: mother-fueled, father-ghosted. That would be a few years after.

Father-ghosted. It's apparently the last photograph ever taken of him, or at least the last that has survived. William Carey Wright is in his eldest son's parlor in Pittsburgh. In two or three or five more weeks he'll be gone. (Someone has typed "May 1904" on the back of the original print, which is in the archives of the University of Wisconsin. William died on June 15, 1904.) What is it about this photograph that seems so moving? Is it something to do with the way he's playing the upright piano, with such concentration, as if sealed off from everything else around him? Even his grandchild, in the foreground, holding her doll with such a solemn expression, is turned away from him, as if figuratively to suggest his aloneness. Her name was Alma Hazel Wright. She was the youngest child of Charlie and Sophia Wright. She's nine. (Seems a little odd for her to be holding a doll at this age. Is that belt that's cinched loosely around her waist her dad's belt? There's a bow in her hair, and her dress seems a dress-up dress, suggesting that this could be a holiday or a church day. Might it be Memorial Day weekend, in which case Grandpa Wright is only two weeks from his sudden collapse?) Alma Wright, who never married, and lived to be eighty-five, died in a nursing home in 1980 in nearby Greensburg, Pennsylvania. Frank Lloyd Wright was her uncle, or, more accurately, her half-uncle. It can't be said whether they ever met, but that seems highly doubtful. It seems highly doubtful Alma's famous uncle even knew of her existence.

But the solitary man. That long dark coat. Those stubby legs. Those short, blocky arms. The way he is seated toward the stool's forward edge, so that his hands can reach the keys and his feet the pedals. That straw-white brush of mustache. That long shelf of white hair reaching past the nape of his neck. That fixed concentration, with the semi-clenched jaw. (Perhaps the fixedness and seeming slight swollenness of his jaw has to do with the tooth loss and gum ache of old age.) If you peer closely, you'll see his small, poised hands reflected—ghostlike—in the mirror-like gleam of the piano's fallboard. This is a Victorian man in a Pennsylvania Victorian parlor, framed by a big potted plant and a tuned-out child, jammed down into himself, lost in the castles and dreams of his life's one true passion, with the reaper just around the corner.

The Sad Ballad of William Carey Wright (2)

William C. Wright, Pittsburgh, May 1904

Think of it as a kind of patricide, or maybe patricide after the fact, because William Carey Wright was long deceased by the time his son set it down in print.

The most malevolent, which is to say reverberating, which is to say boomeranging, lie of Frank Lloyd Wright's life is contained in a few pages—really, in a handful of paragraphs—in the early sections of *An Autobiography*. Earlier, I said it was a lie made all the more pernicious and insidious for the cunning way it was told—namely, by insinuation instead of overt statement. For instance, you never actually encounter the word "deserter," even if that's the exact implication, and even if that was the single great biographical takeaway about William for a whole first generation of Wright chroniclers. What you do encounter in overt ways is the monstrous fiction of Anna's sorrow over his leaving, Anna's victimhood intermixed with her hero-hood, her stubborn belief that her walking-out husband might someday return to her.

The following quotes are from the 1943 edition of the autobiography. (The 1932 edition is virtually the same. In this instance, the 1943 reads more smoothly because the author has yoked his sentences into longer paragraphs.) In the '43, the key passages begin toward the bottom of page 48 and run over to the middle of page 51. The header on the section: "The Father."

What seems remarkable is that even while he's weaving the lie, Wright, in another part of his writing self, is stringing fuses under the bridge, trying to blow up the whole thing. And, important to note, it isn't as if the son is saying he hates his father in these few astutely misdirecting paragraphs. No, it's a far more complicated and human thing. The pity and the sorrow and the pride and indeed the ambivalent love shine through—authentically. This is what makes the greatest lie of Wright's life so complex: the way he intertwines the truth of how their lives were back then with the terrible falsity of what ultimately happened.

Experience it for yourself:

"By now, family life was not so well at the small town house by the blue lake," he writes. "There was no longer much agreement between father and mother."

In the next paragraph: "Mother for some years had been ailing. Poverty pinched."

Next paragraph: "The youth would see her self-denial at table. See her eating only what the others did not want. Drinking her tea without sugar and not because she preferred it so: when, rarely, a chicken from the small coop in the back yard would be killed and come to the table—pretending to prefer the neck of the roast chicken so well you almost believed she did."

Next paragraph: "Provisions often arrived from the farm [he means the Lloyd Jones farms out in the Helena Valley and the Wyoming Valley]—potatoes, vegetables, barrels of apples. The father's earnings were small and shrinking. Music wasn't much of a livelihood in Madison. Irregular preaching there and in surrounding towns less so. And the father grew irascible over this and cross-currents of family feeling. The Joneses didn't much approve of Anna's privations. And he, being a proud man, resented their provisions. His helplessness irritated him."

Next paragraph: "The lad was his mother's adoration. She lived much in him. Probably that didn't help either."

Two paragraphs down: "The son had sympathy for his talented father as well as admiration. Something of that vain struggle of superior talents with untoward circumstance that was his father's got to him, and he was touched by it—never knowing how to show Father. Something— you see—had never been established that was needed to make them father and son. Perhaps the father never loved the son at any time."

The next sentence, with its ellipsis, with its boomeranging and multi-layered shadings, is one that's been quoted previously by me, although now in its full context: "Memories would haunt the youth as they haunt the man. . . ." I believe they were *already* haunting the man who had just put down that beautiful, trailing-off sentence.

He describes himself listening late at night at the door of his father's study. His father is pacing, preparing for a public reading. He remembers his father declaiming aloud Edgar Allan Poe's "The Raven," experimenting with the intonation, the dramatic pauses. He says: "Sometimes, after all had gone to bed he would hear that nocturnal rehearsal and the walking—was it evermore?—would fill a tender boyish heart with sadness and a head would bury itself in the pillow to shut it out."

(Is he really putting a pillow over his ears to try to shut out something else—two parents screaming at each other from another place in the house? Although screaming doesn't seem to jibe, exactly, with William's character.)

A space break at this point. The author is preparing the reader for the heart of the heart of the heart of his deception.

"One day when difficulties between father and mother had grown unbearable the mother having borne all she could—probably the father had borne all he could bear too—said quietly, 'Well, Mr. Wright'— always she spoke of him and to him so—'leave us. I will manage with the children. Go your way. We will never ask you for anything except this home. The savings of my earnings as a teacher have gone into this, and I have put into it so many years of my life.

" 'No—we will never ask you for help.'

"'If ever you can send us anything, send it. If you cannot we will do the best we can.'"

Next paragraph: "Who can know what, in the eighteen years preceding, gradually and inevitably led to the heartbreak under simple words—spoken so quietly?"

Three paragraphs down: "The father disappeared and never was seen again by his wife and children. Judge Carpenter quietly dissolved the marriage contract." (No. As you already know, J. H. Carpenter was William's attorney. The judge who presided over the case was Alva Stewart.)

Next paragraph: "The mother's people deeply grieved, shamed because of her 'disgrace.'"

Next paragraph: "She herself bowed down in grief. Although believing in the rightness of separation for the children's sake, she had not believed in her heart—it seems—their father would take advantage of her offer to release him."

Next paragraph: "And until he died fifteen years later [no: nineteen], she never ceased to believe he would come back. There was never a thought of another man in her life, nor thought of another woman in his. Perhaps it was that their life together had worn its soul away in the strife of failure after failure added to failure: the inveterate and desperate withdrawal on his part into the arid life of his studies, his books and his music, where he was oblivious to all else."

Next paragraph: "So the boy himself, supersensitive, soon became aware of her 'disgrace.' His mother was a 'divorced woman.' His faith in her goodness and rightness did not waver. Therefore there was injustice to her. Did this injustice to her serve some social purpose?"

Next paragraph: "The wondering resentment grew in him. It became a subconscious sense of false judgment entered against himself, his sisters, Jennie and Maginel, innocent of all wrong-doing. His mother's unhappiness—was it a social crime? Why must she, as well as they, be punished. Just what had they all done?"

And then the next sentence, a part of which was quoted previously, and which has probably been quoted in hundreds of Frank Lloyd Wright books, and which contains, possibly, the single most meaning-laden and quite beautiful seven words that he ever wrote, spoking themselves out in so many directions of possibility:

"He never got the heavy thing straight."

Actually, those are the first seven words of what is a longer sentence. The rest of it is this: ". . . and just accepted it as one more handicap— grew more sensitive and shy than ever." In the 1932 edition, that sentence is followed by "And a little distrustful." In the 1943 edition, the author massaged his subconscious a little and wrote: "And he began to be distrustful—of what he could not have told you then."

———

History took the bait. The phrase "walked out" became a kind of reflexive refrain among biographers, especially early ones, many of whom were inept at the overall job.

In 1958, a year before Wright's death, Grant Carpenter Manson (a scholar from Harvard, previously referenced) wrote in his generally admired *Frank Lloyd Wright to 1910: The First Golden Age:* "Also in the year 1885 William Wright walked out on his family, never to return." That appears on page 2 of the biography. (It's clear that Wright read Manson's book. Because he made some layered comments about it.)

Another early biographer, Finis Farr, wrote in his 1961 *Frank Lloyd Wright:*

"Whereupon William Wright took his violin under his arm, put on his hat, and walked out. His wife and children never saw him again."

Another early biographer wrote, in his hagiographic 1965 biography, which is entitled *Frank Lloyd Wright: America's Greatest Architect:* "The long succession of failures—as preacher, teacher, musician, and perhaps also as parent, had eaten away at the marriage of eighteen years. . . . Without a word, he stepped to the hatrack, picked up his hat, and walked out of his family's life forever."

Herbert Jacobs, by then no longer living in Madison but rather a journalism lecturer at the University of California, Berkeley, wrote those words.

In 1972, biographer Charlotte Willard, in her *Frank Lloyd Wright: American Architect*, wrote: "William walked out of the house without a word and was not seen again by his wife and children. The marriage contract was dissolved by a local judge. Mrs. Wright was hurt that her husband could leave without any attempt to win her back. It was many years before she got over the blow to her pride and the 'disgrace' of her divorce." (The last five words of that passage—"the 'disgrace' of her divorce"—might be an unarguable proposition.)

In 1979, well after the facts were known, well after the bit about Anna being "bowed down in her grief" had been exposed for its bogusness, a Wright apprentice named Edgar Tafel (he'd been one of the first Taliesin Fellows, arriving in the fall of 1932 and staying until 1941) wrote in a memoir-biography entitled *Years with Frank Lloyd Wright: Apprentice to Genius:* "William Wright led his family to Massachusetts, where he was minister of a Baptist church in Weymouth for a few years, then back to the Midwest, to Madison, where he tried to organize a private music school in addition to his church work and public-speaking engagements. In 1885, after increasing discord, William Wright left his family, obtained a divorce, and never returned."

Along with "walked out," *left his family* became a stock phrase.

The record didn't get corrected, or start to get corrected, until about a decade after Wright's death. To reprise: In the late sixties, which is to say some three and a half decades after the publication of the first version of *An Autobiography,* a University of Wisconsin doctoral student from Mississippi, who was working part-time in the university archive, got an assignment from his superiors to prepare a research memorandum about Wright's growing-up years in Madison. His name is Thomas S. Hines, Jr. (Some years back, I had a wonderful telephone conversation with him at his home in California.) What Hines did was the simple and time-consuming shoe-leather thing, the basic reporting thing: namely, to go looking for documents, legal and otherwise, so many of which turned out to be hiding locally more or less in plain sight. (Essentially, the documents were in Madison drawers of various kinds.) The grad student published the results of his reporting in the winter 1967 issue of the *Wisconsin Magazine of History,* under the milquetoast-sounding title "Frank Lloyd Wright—the Madison Years: Records versus Recollections." And, as was said previously, it was a red-faced and crossing-over moment for the Wright universe, since so much bilge—about Wright's true age, his schooling, his parents' breakup—had been previously swallowed and put out as the truth. Well, if not entirely swallowed up to that point, then about ninety percent so.

But even after history woke up, the old tropes had a perverse way of sticking, or at least slipping back in. Even some of the more scholarly scholars—by now into the second and third wave of Wright studies— were susceptible. For instance, Robert Twombly, referenced admiringly earlier. No question that in both his 1973 and 1979 biographies Twombly is aware of the real story—and tells it well and economically. (His Wright biographies, in my view, represent the pioneering in-depth biographical work of modern times.) In the '79 edition, the material about the breakup appears principally between pages 12 and 16. And yet the awareness of the true facts didn't keep Twombly, at the back of his book, eleven or so pages from the end, when he was (rather brilliantly and even lyrically) evaluating Frank Lloyd Wright's place in history, from writing a long summarizing sentence, the middle part of which contained this: "for when William Wright deserted the family and left it impoverished. . . ."

William left the family, yes. But only in the narrowest, most literal, and almost technical sense of the word. The word "deserted" does no justice to the truth, and surely Twombly himself would agree. It's as if, for all his research, the scholar had momentarily lapsed into historical amnesia. William moved out because he'd been all but shoved out the door by Anna, and, for all I know, literally so. For all I know, for all anybody knows, the not-figurative but *actual* shoving out the door involved Anna's fists, or even a two-tined carving fork or a roller for pounding meat.

One more example: In 1994, the Museum of Modern Art mounted a comprehensive retrospective exhibition entitled *Frank Lloyd Wright: Architect*. It was thirty-five years after the artist's death. The museum published a large companion book by the same title. The first essay was by William Cronon, a hugely admired American historian from whose spoken and written work on Wright I have learned much. (In 2012, he was president of the American Historical Association.) Nonetheless, Professor Cronon wrote: "Wright's father emerges from the record as a rather pathetic figure, a charming, personable, footloose spendthrift, talented but unfulfilled, who could never satisfy his demanding wife. William Wright finally walked out on his family, much as his son would do a quarter of a century later."

In fairness to that passage, here is the clause that follows "a quarter of a century later": Cronon inserted a dash and finished the sentence with "though William's wife was eager for his departure and Frank's was not." (He was referring to Kitty Wright, obviously.) But that clause does not correct the incorrect impression that "walked out" would leave with the unsuspecting reader.

Did Frank Lloyd Wright, who'd never live to see these books get written, understand in his cells that they *would* get written? He was far too aware not to know.

Mark Twain had it right: A lie can encircle half the globe while truth is still trying to get its boots on. To again reference cultural historian Neil Postman: The insidious thing about false myths is the way they can take root inside our collective unconscious. In a real sense, we're still trying, six decades on, to de-weed the Wrightian garden, still trying to get our shoelaces tied half right. The Wright universe knows, has long known, the truth about Anna and William's breakup. Only it doesn't. Or maybe to better say it: History is still trying to remember what it fully knows.

Was William innocent in the ruin of his marriage? Not even close. And did history tar him unjustly? Absolutely. And can you trace the tarring to what his son set down in print starting in 1932? There seems no other way to understand the story.

———

So, two critical questions. First, if the son knew the truth about his parents (even if he might not have known every particular), if he witnessed what he witnessed as a child and then later as a teenager and young adult (it's not possible to believe he could have been in ignorance of the kind of things that went on in that house over so many years), then why did he do what he did? Like the mystery of Julian Carlton doing what he did on that August afternoon, it's anybody's argument. Various latter-day biographers and historians have wrestled with this question (although not enough, in my view). The biographer who may come closest to a shrewd psychological explanation is the one who was just being criticized a little: Robert Twombly.

In 1926, when he wrote the sections of his autobiography dealing with his parents, Wright was a fugitive from the law avoiding arrest under the Mann Act. . . . Since 1909 he had been involved in a series

of highly publicized love affairs. He had been divorced once, married twice, lived with three women, and was linked with yet a fourth
companion. Far from apologizing or feeling remorse for his behavior, he believed himself persecuted by an intolerant society. . . . Just
as Anna had suffered through her "persecution," so he had been
publicly condemned for doing what he felt was right. Just as she
had been "punished" for her courage, so had he been ostracized
for acting openly and honestly. As Wright saw it, he and his mother
had suffered similar, unjust fates, and the parallel between their lives
was a certain solace. Identifying with Anna's interpretation of her
marital difficulties gave him a crutch to lean on during his own.

In other words, Wright did it, at least in part, for the basest of reasons: because it was useful to him. It served his needs. It was expedient.
He didn't take his mother's side out of love and loyalty so much as to
further his own cause in the public's eye at his father's expense.

Is that it? We'll never know for sure. But let's say it's exactly what
happened: he made a self-justifying and cynical calculation.

And so the second question, interlocking with the first: What would
be the internal cost of something like that, that is, if you possessed a
conscience, and not an insignificant one? As you quite know by now,
it's the question, essentially unanswerable, that I've been seeking to ask,
in one form or another, since this narrative began.

———

*Paying emotionally charged visits to Bear Valley, Wisconsin, even when
he was nowhere close to Bear Valley.* I do not wish to try to make
the claim here that his father is on the tip of Frank Lloyd Wright's
tongue—lovingly, longingly, ambivalently, affectionately, achingly, half-
apologetically, wholly apologetically—in the last ten years or so of his
life. But I almost wish to claim that.

Once you start looking and listening in this context, the phenomenon seems hard to miss. So many of the references are veiled—except
when they're not. Everything's there by indirection—until it isn't. Sometimes the actual mention is fleeting—a sentence, a few swallowed words
within a sentence. But if you're listening carefully, bending down and
cupping your ear, you'll begin to hear all the undernotes. It's as if the

shade of William Carey Wright, like a telltale heart, is beating quietly beneath the floorboards of whatever else it is his son is purportedly saying.

These references, ghostly and otherwise, come up in his interviews for broadcast, in recounted dreams, in authored pieces for publication, although perhaps most tellingly the phenomenon seems to appear in his free-associating remarks before the apprentices at Taliesin, when he is exhorting them about morals, about life.

Curiously, or not so curiously, the word "sublimated" also tends to show up. Wright almost always brings up this word in reference to the idea of music and architecture—how both arts are really "sublimated mathematics," and how his father had taught him to understand a symphony as an "edifice of sound." He'd been using the latter metaphor since at least the late 1920s. (The edifice-of-sound idea shows up at least twice in both the 1932 and 1943 editions of *An Autobiography*.) But in the last decade or so of Wright's life, the metaphor was almost a hobbyhorse: music as an edifice of sound, and how he first learned to listen at his father's knee, perhaps at the age of ten, and how implicitly grateful he is, and how architecture is essentially the same thing as great symphonic music, the two arts just "sublimated" mathematics, taken to a higher plane.

Sublimating is all about channeling, transferring, redirecting, diverting.

He brought this idea into a talk on April 15, 1958, at the University of Arkansas in Fayetteville, for instance. He gave brief prepared remarks and then took questions from the student architects. When you study the transcript, it sounds as if the layered word "sublimating" is tripping him up a bit: "Architecture and music are like this—architecture is sublimated . . . let's see now, music is sublimated mathematics and the architecture is also. . . . Beethoven was probably the greatest architect who ever lived—Beethoven. My father taught me to see a symphony as an edifice of sound and I never listen to a symphony now that I don't see a building—see how it was built—see them proceed to lay the foundation, to make the edifice out of the sound."

A year earlier, in the spring of 1957, he spoke warmly of his father at the University of California, Berkeley. A student had asked a question about legacies, and the word "spawn" came into his mind. He said, "First of all, my father was a preacher and his father was a preacher—my own grandfather." And then it was on to the other side of his family. But then his father was back, and what his father gave him: "My family, of course, my father being a preacher and teacher of music, we were desperately poor and so I had to go to the Madison university." (He means UW.)

At Christmas 1956, he was in his suite at the Plaza Hotel in Manhattan. (He'd redecorated it floridly and had come to think of it as his Taliesin East. Not quite daily, the great egoist would march the twenty-nine blocks up Fifth Avenue to inspect the job site at the Guggenheim Museum, one of his last great projects, which he wouldn't live to see completed.) This day, he'd had a dream. His baby sister recounts it, in his words:

> "Strange . . . I dreamed of Father during my nap. Just this afternoon. I was in a dark place, at first I had no idea where it was. Then I knew: the little chamber behind the organ in the Weymouth Church, the chamber for the organ bellows. I was pumping away and pumping away. Father was playing Bach. I heard it, Sis, in the dream, very distinctly, every note as he used to play it. My God, Bach required a lot of air! I had to pump like the devil, and woke up tired."

The bellows and pipe organ memory is a well-traveled Wright story—it's in *An Autobiography,* for instance. But usually it's a much darker memory. Most times it's about his father's harshness—William had apparently made his child pump the bellows past the point of exhaustion and had brought Frank to tears (and also brought Anna to rage at her husband, when she found out). But that doesn't seem the tone or the point here. The son has had a daytime dream of his father, and is recounting it to his baby sister, Maginel, with what seems like an urgency, even small panic. "I heard it, Sis, in the dream, very distinctly, every note as he used to play it." Panic? Yes, as if he suddenly has his lost father back, every beautiful note, just the way he used to play it. *I heard it, Sis. I heard it.*

Maginel Wright Barney tells this story rather blankly on page 12 of her adulatory *The Valley of the God-Almighty Joneses.* The book, as previously noted, is a brief memoir-biography, published in 1965 (so six years after Wright's death). It's only a bit more reliable on the facts than John Lloyd Wright's *My Father Who Is on Earth,* published two decades earlier. Maginel has ridden the elevator to his suite with a steaming baked potato in a paper bag. Her big brother is sick of New York's fancy-shmancy cuisine. He wants plain Wisconsin fare. He has importuned her to bring the potato. She gets inside the door and he is telling her about the dream, as if wishing to seize her by the lapels of her fur overcoat.

Six months earlier. Summertime in New York City. Again, his suite at the Plaza. Are the windows open? Are the stacked taxis honking below Bergdorf's? It's June 5, 1956. An editor from Horizon Press, with two female producers from Caedmon Records, are interviewing him for what will be distributed to the public on a long-play recording entitled *Frank Lloyd Wright on Record.* He's boasting on himself and architecture. It's the mother of all arts. All the arts, writing, painting, sculpture, are inferior to the mother art, architecture. Architecture is moribund now, too—except for his own, naturally.

One of the female interviewers, who isn't shy: "Can we elaborate a little bit on this parallel between music and architecture?" The interview is about five minutes old.

"Yes," he says, "I've always felt . . ."

His mind has gone to William. (Is it because two strong females are in the room?)

"My father taught me, he was a preacher, but he was first of all a musician and made his living, or tried to, teaching music later on. He never was able to support his—"

It seems the next word will be "family." It isn't. There is no direct object to the thought. Instead, he says: "He was never able to support his—uh, by way of it, and his life was a kind of tragedy." The words "his life was a kind of tragedy" have come out in a lighter tone, as if he wishes to say the thought and get rid of it. The stumble has lasted a second. Then, regaining: "But he taught me that a symphony was an edifice—of sound. And that it was built, and I learned pretty soon that it was built by the same kind of mind in much the way that a building is built." And then he's on to Beethoven. And his gratitude to his father who'd taught him how to listen to Beethoven, all of those structural repetitions and undernotes, and how they relate to the art of architecture, if you know how to build on a grid, if you know how to listen to the depths of your soul. He's back in charge.

In the fall of 1957, the editors of *Saturday Review* asked him to write a piece on his love of music. (The editors were planning on devoting much of the issue of September 28, 1957, to what they called "The Vinyl Sound Decade.") It isn't a long piece. It's one of the last things Wright ever published in a popular magazine. He wrote a couple of introductory paragraphs about how music and architecture blossom on the same stem—both "sublimated mathematics." And then he cribbed the rest of it verbatim from his autobiography. Perhaps he had just slapped out the introduction in three minutes, and the hell with the piece, he'll just collect the money. Except I don't think so. Here is the last sentence of the first paragraph of the lead-in, which, although not quite able to be diagrammed, seems, to my ear anyway, to wish to parse and diagram everything:

"My father, a preacher and music-teacher, taught me to see—to listen—to a symphony as an edifice of sound."

Yes, it's the hobbyhorse. With a twist.

Sometimes, the most revealing things Wright ever has to say are contained in and around the dashes—spoken or written. Consider the single dashed phrase here. If you remove it, the sentence, not wonderfully clear to begin with, has no direct object and makes almost no sense at all. It would read "taught me to see to a symphony. . . ." It would contain one too many prepositions. Only when you restore the dashed phrase do you get his meaning. The magazine's copyeditors surely recognized the grammatical weakness, but must have let the sentence stand as written because, well, Wright was Wright.

But is it possible, in both a psychological and literal sense, that Wright was really saying, and maybe without even realizing: *My father, a preacher and music-teacher, taught me to see*? Period. Full stop. He is expressing his deep gratitude, in a three-letter word. His father, so long gone, and whom he had betrayed, and possibly for the basest of reasons, and for at least several generations' worth of histories and biographies, had taught him how to *see*. Which, in terms of the artistic life, meant only everything. In that three-letter word, in that semi-clumsy sentence, did Wright understand it all and say it on paper: the unpayable debt he owed? Did he recognize he could not have become the world artist he became had not his father opened for him all the beautiful ways and doors of seeing?

And maybe the seeming stand-aloneness of the word "see" was just due to the quick top he'd slapped on what was essentially a canned piece of writing.

The last paragraph of the *Saturday Review* piece: "Sometimes it was as though a door would open, and he could get the beautiful meaning clear. Then it would close and the meaning would be dim or far away. But always there was some meaning. Father taught him to see a symphony as an edifice—of sound!" Again, that's straight from *An Autobiography*. And the door imagery is beautiful. And maybe more laden here.

But nowhere do you encounter the rubbings and tracings and shadings and seeming sublimations of a man with a pricking conscience more hauntingly than in his off-the-cuff and almost stream-of-consciousness talks to his apprentices. In Wright circles, these Sunday morning sermonettes—which by and large have not been closely examined by scholars—are known as the "Talks to the Taliesin Fellowship." They took place over several decades in both Wisconsin and Arizona. There are scores of them, and many have been preserved on audiotape. They were mainly recorded on old reel-to-reel machines. You sometimes hear the crackling and the static and the buzzing. By no means am I steeped in them all. But I am still willing to bet that you could put the transcripts into one large pile, stack all the tapes on top of one another (there are said to be something like 250 hours of tape, covering the years 1949–1959), close your eyes, and just reach in for one— and, likely as not, William C. Wright will be there, as subtext, on the page or on the tape, in some form or manner, veiled or unveiled, direct or indirect, disguised or undisguised, fleeting or otherwise, named or not named. His father's there when he's not there at all. When his father does come onstage, directly, it is *never*, at least from the inspecting I've done, with his son's anger or recrimination. What you encounter is the gratitude, the soft longing, and occasionally something way past that.

In Arizona, at Taliesin West, Wright sometimes gave the sermonettes in the drafting room, after breakfast. In Wisconsin, he almost always gave the talks at Hillside, which has long been part of the Taliesin complex. (Wright built the original Hillside Home School in 1887 as one of his earliest works. It was a small private academy run by his maiden aunts, Ellen and Jane Lloyd Jones, who dedicated much of their lives to teaching. A decade and a half later would come Hillside Home School II. Eventually, it was to merge with Taliesin itself.)

On Sunday, about nine o'clock, at Hillside, in what is commonly referred to as the living room, the master would appear, turned out in a tailored suit, perhaps a custom-made blousy dress shirt from Budd of New York, one of his porkpie hats shaped to order in Paris. The living room remains a beautiful space, two stories tall, with a huge hearth, and four stone piers supporting a balcony. (In many ways, it resembles the Oak Park drafting room—that large, square, vaulted space with its octagonal balcony—that Wright hinged onto the east side of his home in 1898.) Carved into the bottom of the balcony are words from chapter 40 in the Book of Isaiah, his grandfather's unforgiving Old Testament prophet. Carved into the fireplace mantel is a verse from the eighteenth-century English poet Thomas Gray's "Elegy Written in a Country Churchyard."

"I think it is a natural human tendency to talk about the thing that is uppermost in your mind," Wright said in one of these Sunday morning talks. (It was April 25, 1954.)

September 12, 1954:

How many have already learned that there's a price you have to pay for everything? You may think you're getting away with something, you may think that well, God, I got free that way, but that time is never finished. . . . A man in this life never does anything that doesn't add up in the end to having him. He is that which he does. . . . Well, now of course in confession, they say confession is good for the soul. I think it is. And maybe there is something in that cleansing process. . . . So it's a fine thing to develop within your own selves a good conscience. And when you do a thing that's wrong, and you know it's wrong, and you come to know it's wrong, the finest thing for your own souls is lay it on the table . . . admit to yourselves, yes, that was a mistake, never again.

But couldn't these be just general remarks? Yes, except that about a minute and a half later, his father is in the room, if not by name: "I've been a minister's son, brought up in the midst of religious action all my life—generations, generation on generation. . . ."

January 5, 1958: "Who's going to preach the sermon this morning? Anybody? What is the problem? What is the deepest trouble anybody in the Fellowship is conscious of—let him now break down, weep and confess. I think Sunday morning is for confession, not profession."

October 3, 1954: "It's these little unconsidered things, like a leak in the bottom of a pin pan that would soon empty the pan. And it's so with a life like ours if we don't give heed and have a conscience concerning all these little things which might contribute and add up to a tremendous thing in the end."

Less than three minutes later, William is present, if not by name: "Well, anyway, let's have Sunday morning among us. I hate the guise of a preacher. You know, I am the tail end of a great long line of them. On my father's side going back to the days of the Reformation. . . ."

May 27, 1956: He's on the hobbyhorse of Beethoven and sublimated mathematics. Then, five minutes later: "There you are. So that's very largely the reason why we're all confused, we're all wandering about here with no place to go like Jephthah without a father. There seems to be no home. No spiritual home." (In scripture, courageous Jephthah led the Israelites in battle against the Ammonites.)

March 24, 1957: It's one of his more celebrated Sunday talks. He's reflecting on art, culture, architecture, the Bible. He's reflecting on the "master architect" of them all: Jesus Christ. Then, a fair way in: "'The truth will make you free.' Did you ever stop to think of that? What's the meaning of 'The truth will make you free'?"

Several minutes later: "What if a man has done wrong, and he comes to the realization of the fact that he has done wrong. If he is wrong, he will come up and take his medicine and his punishment and start again."

But it's as if he's getting lost in his thoughts. His voice weakens. "So where are we now?" he asks, about a half-minute later.

Next sentence: "There is no substitute for intrinsic responsibility, innate responsibility for your own acts, for your own character and for your own self." He moseys on this theme for several more minutes. He tells a story about a bad child on a recent airplane trip. It's a pretty funny story, actually.

It seems as if he may be winding up: no direct reference to William rising in him, apparently. Until suddenly: "Well, you see, it is all wider than a church door and it is all deeper than a well."

Has "church" clanged his father invisibly into the room? About forty seconds later: "The Fellowship, as we call it, and we are a Fellowship, is a family." Is "family" triggering something? A few seconds later: "Go back to the Bible again, back to Jesus, who said, 'As ye mete it out, so shall it be meted unto you.'" Still, no William, at least by overt reference. Until the next sentence: "And the older I grow, and the son of ministers after minister after minister, on both sides, mother and father. I never used to think too much about the Bible. I had heard so much about it. I was in it. I used to get it for breakfast, dinner and supper." Get what? The idea of sin, of guilt?

One more example, some of it perhaps sublimated and other of it right out in the open. To my ear, it is the most telling Sunday Fellowship talk of all, one of the most revealing moments of all. It's September 7, 1958, almost seven months to the day before his death. He starts right in with his father. It seems a rather trivial story. He describes how he and Olgivanna were walking along to Hillside from Taliesin just a little bit ago, and somehow the walking along itself must have tripped something in him that had happened when he was about seven. The family lived in Massachusetts then. His mother and father would walk along with the children to church. Everyone would be dressed up. Their rented house was about three blocks away. His father discovered that he'd forgotten to put on a necktie. A Baptist preacher cannot preach without a necktie. Unthinkable. So his father got the house key from his mother and rushed back home, only to discover that she had taken the wrong key from her purse. He had no choice but to break through a window. He got the tie, put it on, rushed back to catch up with the family. But now he's got a bleeding finger from the broken glass. His mother fixes it up. At church, the family always sits in the first pew, looking up at the small, charismatic figure in the pulpit. Today, with a ribbon or piece of gauze around his red finger, the man of God up above doesn't seem so "formidable" to his son. He almost doesn't seem like a preacher. He seems like an ordinary man with a nicked finger and the crimson showing through. And yet, damnedest thing, the son is able to hear his father's sermon more clearly than he has ever heard it.

On the old staticky tape, his voice has begun to drop and slow. It's as if the story about the necktie and the cut finger in Weymouth has given way to something else.

"Now is that right or wrong?" Are *right* and *wrong* doing their cunning work? What is the antecedent of "that"? It isn't clear. He is stream-of-consciousness-ing.

A moment later: "Is that fair?"

Suddenly, he seems weary. His voice has fallen not quite a full register. "Anyway, I don't know. I was thinking of it as we came along this morning."

Is he finished? (Can't be; just started the talk.) "So what would you like to . . ." He has stopped in the middle of his sentence, as if he's gazing somewhere else. The pause is only two or three seconds, but seems twice that. ". . . touch upon this morning? Has anybody any doubts, fears, qualms of conscience, let him confess them now."

You can hear the smallest titter or clearing of a throat in the room—not his.

"How many of you have committed crimes since I last saw you?"

Small laughter from the apprentices, as if they're not quite sure how to react.

"How many of you would *like* to commit crimes?"

Much louder laughter now. The relief is palpable. He's joshing—that must be it.

"Well, you see, the old preacher blood comes surging to the front every so often. . . . It's been leaking all these years, little by little, until now I have none of it left."

Leaking out. Bleeding through. At the margins. All these little hidden and not-so-hidden unconsidered things, like something sitting practically invisible in the bottom of a pin pan. But, of course, this is stealing from his own metaphor.

———

But what about the paying of *literal* visits to Bear Valley, Wisconsin, to stand at the stone of your wronged father? Earlier, I said I've been able to find documentation for two such visits (one that I consider rock-solid in its trustworthiness and the other less so), but that I have to believe there were many more than that. Does it matter in the end how many there were, alone or in the company of others? Wouldn't just one be enough? I'll start with the testimony that is less than rock-solid:

His name was Henry Herold. He was a Taliesin Fellow for two one-year periods in the mid-fifties, when he was in his mid-twenties. (His first stay was from November 1954 to the following November; and his second from May 1956 to June of the following year. So Wright would have been within three or four years of his death.) One afternoon in the drafting room at Taliesin, Wright came up and stood behind him. He didn't speak. He just looked down on what the apprentice was working on. Wright nudged him over and sat down beside him on the bench. He must have seen something promising in the cub's renderings. He took a pencil from his coat pocket. Such one-on-one teaching moments occurred when they occurred. Very possibly Wright didn't even know Herold's name, or at least he might not have been able to summon it just then if he were asked.

Something possessed Henry Herold to say, and almost in a blurt:

"Mr. Wright, I was down at your family's cemetery at Unity Chapel on my lunch break, and I was kind of looking at the headstones, and I saw your mother's stone, but not your father's. I was just curious. Is your father buried somewhere else?"

A slow leaning back. A poising of the pencil. This faraway look.

"Oh, yes, my father, well, you see, he's up in Bear Valley. It's a cemetery not very far from here. His life, was, you know, a tragedy."

There seemed the barest breath of something between the "you know" and "a tragedy." Nothing more was said. There was now an awkwardness between them. Soon Wright got up and walked away.

This moment is touched on in a long oral history that two Taliesin archivists did with Henry Herold toward the end of his life. It's where I first encountered it. What you've just read is my own account of the moment—from my own interview with Herold. I was after something different from what the Taliesin archivists were after. Herold died in 2015, at not quite eighty-six, after a long and successful architectural career in Marin County, California. In the summer of 2014, on hearing he wasn't doing so well, I called him up without any prior warning and spoke with him for almost an hour on the telephone. As it turned out, little massaging was needed to get him to remember.

"Oh," he said. "Well. Unforgettable. I remember the faraway look.

And the slow moving back from the bench or the seat. And the soft-ness of his voice. And the half-turning. And the pause before he said 'tragedy.' He had this great wreath of silvery hair, you know. I think he may have had a double-breasted tweed coat on. You nearly always saw him dressed up like that. I think he would have produced the pencil from his right pocket of the sport coat or the suit jacket. I think what happened was that my question just caught him out. We were sitting side by side. I think we were touching, just barely. It wasn't a whisper, exactly. But here's what I'm thinking as I'm telling you this: Why did I ask him that thing in the first place? It was so damned impertinent of me. I almost feel ashamed now. Maybe because he sat down beside me and I felt some kind of sudden rush of deep intimacy. I can't say. Maybe I was thinking about my own father, whose life also turned out tragic. Except I didn't know about the tragic part until he said it. I was just curious about why his father didn't have a headstone there in the family cemetery at Unity Chapel. Anyway, I just asked him. It came out of me. And I've never forgotten."

A little later in our conversation, Henry Herold said something else: "Now that you've made me think back on all this, I'm pretty sure he said he'd just been to Bear Valley. Maybe the day before or a couple days before. Yes, pretty sure he'd just gone."

I tried to press him for more details—he couldn't pry them loose.

Here is someone else remembering things related to Wright and his father—except that there's a lot more of Bear Valley itself in the remem-brance. A long swatch of an oral history is worth quoting at length, with its pauses and repetitions and verbal tics. The oral history was with Wil-liam Wesley Peters. Two Taliesin archivists recorded it on videotape in Arizona in May 1990. He was in his late seventies and would be dead of a stroke about a year later. As even casual Wright students know, Peters is an extremely notable person in the Wright universe, not least for the fact that he was Wright's son-in-law. (Except that you never hear him on the tape or anywhere else that I know of referring to his father-in-law as anything other than "Mr. Wright.") He arrived at Taliesin in 1932 as one of the very first apprentices. (If you turn back to the very beginning of this book, and look at the first image that leads into "Out of the Old Testament," you'll see Peters. He's two in from the right, in the first row, with his raised right arm supporting his jaw.)

He had a nearly six-decade history at Taliesin. He was from southern Indiana. He was studying at the Massachusetts Institute of Technology, but the famous university wasn't giving him what he was seeking. He came to Spring Green and met the great man (who would become his father-in-law a few years later when the apprentice married Svetlana, Wright's adopted daughter by Olgivanna—but not without some family turmoil in the interim). For decades, Wes Peters served as one of the legs of the "three-legged stool" that Wright said he needed to squat upon in order to be able to do his work. He possessed a native engineering brilliance. He was slow-talking, if quick-witted. He was at least six-foot-four and could eat two lunches and go back to work. He was a person of whom you could take emotional advantage. He wasn't built for introspection or emotion. He liked crude jokes and wore big clunky Navajo jewelry and was a disaster with money and was loyal to the Wrightian cause until the day he died.

Wes Peters is remembering the day he drove "Mr. Wright" to Bear Valley.

On the videotape he's in a short-sleeved western shirt. Every once in a while he pokes up his glasses. He keeps crossing and uncrossing his long legs and arms, which have gone slack and skinny. In the first seven or eight minutes of the tape, he's having a good time remembering cross-country railroad trips, and of how his father-in-law, to pass the hours, would help himself to somebody's book and begin writing in it. He once did that with a volume of poems by D. H. Lawrence—told his son-in-law to hand the thing over, he was going to improve D.H.'s poetry.

Still on the subject of traveling with Wright, Peters says, as if a lost memory has just bubbled up out of nowhere:

> One day, this was not long before his, oh, it was about a year before his death, I guess, he got very much interested in his father. And we were driving around in the car and he said that he had always felt his father, he'd always seen his father from the things his mother told him. And he was approximately nine years old, I think, I believe that's right, when his father and his mother separated. And Mr. Wright had always said that he'd gotten the story of his father from his mother, and that now he felt that it was a little bit slanted.

And his father, he thought more and more of the things he owed his father. As he told in his autobiography, he spoke how his father had actually taught him many things. For instance, he emphasized the fact that his father had taught him to think of music as structure, as a structure. And it was really a form of architecture. And it taught him many things, and of course he got to be very interested about his father's life, because he didn't know much about his life, he said he didn't really know much about his father's life, after he left his mother. Actually, his father was a person who apparently had tremendous gifts in many different directions, but never became a real master of any one of them. But he turned his hand to law, the law and the ministry. And he actually ran for a while for political office, and he was even for a while, I understand, took part in medicine, considered taking, studying medicine for a while. And he was also a musician and a composer. And once we went over to the cemetery where his father is buried. And Mr. Wright, I don't know that Mr. Wright had ever been to his father's grave, I've forgotten whether he had. But we went over there and we hunted up his father's grave and hunted up the thing. It was in the Coon Valley, or Bear Valley, I guess it's the Bear Valley Cemetery, I guess it was the Bear Valley Cemetery, the first one you come to from Lone Rock. And we hunted around the thing until Mr. Wright found it. And he told, after, on the way back after he had looked at it, he said that he had—

Peters looks away from the camera. A sound emits from his throat. It sounds like "oomh." It's something between a swallow and a gulp.

—really he kept reminiscing about how his father had not only taught him to love music, but Mr. Wright became very interested in looking up his father's old books, where he had actually written some of the music in the books. And he said he realized his father was really a great influence on him. And where he'd never learned this, he'd always been taught by his mother that his father was necessarily bad. Her life with him was a closed book, and she would never talk with Mr. Wright about any qualities good, bad, or otherwise. And Mr. Wright felt very sad about this, really, in a way. And after his mother and he were separated or eventually he went

back to the children of his wife, I mean his former wife, and they
supported him. And he also gave music lessons and things. It was
a lonely life. I don't know how old he was when he died, but Mr.
Wright was really suddenly very moved . . .

Suddenly very moved. It's not possible to know if Peters is misremembering the business of Wright supposedly being nine years old
when his parents split up—or rather if Wright had deceived him on that
part. It doesn't matter, nor do other inaccuracies, because the emotion
on the tape trumps it all. The "oomh" makes you imagine, or makes me
imagine, by extension, some of what Wright's emotion must have been
like that afternoon, about a year before he died, when he went to Bear
Valley. I'll never be able to prove it, but I have to believe that at least
some of the "suddenly very moved" was intimately related to the terrible
lie he'd once told the world about his father.

————

William Carey Wright lived on the earth nineteen years after April 24,
1885 (the date of the divorce decree). It's as if all a former man of the
cloth wanted to do, was able to do, was to go somewhere else. (As for
former man of the cloth: there was virtually no chance a divorced minister could assume a pastorate again, not at that time in America.) As was
said above, if this compulsion for going to the next place was already
the basic script of his life, William, in his final years, seemed to turn
the compulsion into a kind of grim art form. Did his son know? I have
to believe on some level he knew it all, even if he was aware of practically none of the details. And as for the motion: Must not some of it,
or even whole large portions of it, have been tied up with a sense of
family failure?

There were moments in those nearly two decades when Wright
and his father were practically within handshakes of each other—in
the same way of Frank and his old pal Cecil in their separate after-
years. There were a few occasions, around the turn of the century, when
Wright was giving a public address, and, I am fairly certain, William
was in that vicinity on that same day. It's not beyond imagining that he
saw a posted notice and slipped into a back row to hear his boy speak.

At Thanksgiving 1884, about ten days or so before he formally instituted proceedings against Anna, William had gone out to Wahoo, Nebraska, to be with his second son, George Irving Wright, who was a lawyer and a local judge. There was a railroad price war on, and tickets from Chicago to Omaha could be had for a dollar, round-trip. He probably couldn't have afforded to go otherwise. Lizzie Heller and her husband, John, had also come for the holiday. Lizzie describes this in her life story: "Father told us how things were getting worse and worse with him and we all wanted him to leave her. John said it was bad enough to run the risk of hell in the next world without living in it in this and George gave him a lot of advice. He told him to come out and practice law with him." It seems to have been this visit that gave William the courage to return to Madison and divorce his wife.

Story: For a little while after the divorce, William remained in Madison. He had a music studio above a store at 23 Pinckney Street on the east side of Capitol Square. The building was called the Ellsworth Block, and it's still there, not much changed in 130 years. (You can get a wonderful feel about his life just by entering that old building.) His rented space was directly across from the statehouse. When the family was together, he'd walk or take a horse-drawn streetcar from the Wright home on the lake at Gorham and Livingston—it was about eight blocks on a diagonal. It can't be said where he lived after the divorce, but it must have been fairly close by. One day later that spring, William encountered his youngest child on the street. Maginel was coming from school. According to Maginel, her father picked her up and brought her to his shoulder and kissed her and tried to pull her into talk and then led her to the best clothing store in town, where he bought her new shoes and a straw hat. He then walked her home, saying goodbye perhaps a block or two away. When she discovered what William had done, Anna took the things off the child and burned them in the big wood range in the kitchen.

For about five years, from 1885 to 1890, in Wahoo, which is just west of Omaha, William read the law again. It was a living. His composing gift returned. He wrote a tune called "Floating on the Bay." It's easily one of his most beautiful, with soft chord repetitions. It is said the piece came to him from memories of Lake Mendota in Madison. He'd go down the steep bank from the house on Gorham and pull up the anchor of the family rowboat and go out alone on the water. "Floating on the

Bay" has a little couplet attached as a prologue to the music: "While o'er moonlit bay I float / Gentle wavelets strike the boat."

The half-hearted lawyer, practicing with his son, was no longer in touch with eastern music publishers—so he formed his own imprint. Henceforth, all his compositions would bear the publishing stamp: *Wahoo Neb. Nebraska Music Co.*

The sense of his own importance, despite everything: He published a *Series of Musical Pieces Composed Expressly for the Cabinet Organ*. He called the suite "The Starry Cluster," and he invented names for some of the composers of the five pieces. In addition to himself, there was the noted Russian "K. Erduikshek," the noted Frenchman "C. Ouvrier," and, not least, the noted German "Wilhelm Kehri." The grandiloquent-sounding *Wahoo Neb. Nebraska Music Co.*—which, in effect, must have had its offices in the top of William's hat—brought out the work. The cover of the sheet music was Victorian-scrolled, curlicued.

After Wahoo, it was Omaha. He listed himself as "music teacher" with his residence and studio at 1716 Sherman. He self-published another small book, *The Golden Monitor,* and sold it by mail order, postpaid, for a dollar. He joined the Royal Order of Masons and worked himself up to an "H.P." designate: High Priest. Again, the undoubted charisma and ability to make friends.

By 1892, he was in Stromsburg, Nebraska, which is about ninety miles west of Omaha, in Polk County, corn and milo and soybean country, out where fierce winds blow, in the "Swede Capital of Nebraska." Article from *The Stromsburg Headlight,* April 7, 1892: "Prof. Wm. C. Wright, A.M., has been secured by Prof. Bryant, to take charge of a conservatory of music, to be known as the Central Normal Conservatory of Music, of Stromsburg. Prof Wright is an author and composer of music; and a teacher with years of experience. He is a graduate of several prominent conservatories, and a man of modern ideas and methods. The conservatory department of the College will be based upon the New England conservatory plan; and our people will rejoice to know that they are to have advantages in music, second to none in the state. The work will begin at once." From subsequent write-ups, he seems to have thrilled the citizenry with local performances—but the Stromsburg citizenry couldn't hold him. Within a couple of years he was gone, but not before penning (was it late at night, in his second-floor room,

The Sad Ballad of William Carey Wright (2) | 453

after pacing, after reciting aloud "The Raven"?) a piece called "The Hour of Melancholy." Once again, he supplied a poetic prologue, not part of the music itself: " 'Twas evening's weary, pensive hour; / I heard it tolled from belfry tower, / And yearnings sad, and bodings dim / Woke in my soul a plaintive hymn."

When he was a child, William's son used to watch his father composing at the square-legged piano, a pen held crosswise in his teeth, the black ink dripping into his white beard and down his shirtfront, his face growing fearful with blotches and smudges. The fevered composer, bent over the keys, would rush to a nearby desk to scribble down more chords, and then back to the instrument to try them out, oblivious to all else.

In Stromsburg, William composed another piece. It was a march, jaunty, but with unmistakable sadness and yet a kind of defiance in it. He titled it "The Fallen Hero's Triumph." It seems to have been his last completed composition.

After Stromsburg, it was Atchison, Kansas, on the west bank of the Missouri River. And then it was upstream and across the river to St. Joseph, Missouri ("William C. Wright, music teacher," in a local directory). It was 1896 now. And almost before the next set of directories could catch up to him, he had relocated to Des Moines, Iowa. He's there by at least the back end of 1896. In the following year's directory, page 608: "Wright's School of Music and Oratory." Next line: "Wm C. Wright, Director, 954 6th Ave." Which is also where he's living. (Earlier on that page: "res. same.")

If no longer composing, he had begun to publish in these years a series of essays in a nationally regarded music magazine called *Etude*. There would be eight altogether, in the last decade or so of his life, with such titles as " 'Playing by Ear'—A Bane or Benefit?" And "Which Hand First?" And "From a New Standpoint." That one, published in August 1895, is about music, even as it's about other things. "A prime element of success is *will*," the author says. "Will is more than wish, more than fitful resolve."

He's in Des Moines—until he isn't. From the 1898–1899 directory: "Wright Wm C. removed to Perry, Ia." It's as if a poet is working for the city directories of Des Moines. That word: "removed." As if to limn his life in seven characters.

He stays in Perry (a little burg northwest of Des Moines) for the next two years or so. In the federal census of 1900 he's listed as "widowed." (Well, he *is* the widower of Permelia.) He's renting. He's seventy-five. He's teaching music.

But sometime that same year, back out to Nebraska, to live with his lawyer son, George, and his family in a small town named York. George is still doing the law but he has also turned to the ministry. William is still trying to teach music, but you get the strong sense that all of it is now in steep decline, and that the money is mostly gone and the health going. He seems to be alternating long stays with either George and his wife, Cordelia, and their family, or with Lizzie Heller and her family. The Hellers are in Ladora, Iowa. Lizzie has told her father (it's in *The Story of My Life*) that he is welcome to move in permanently with them. Perhaps this is why William, before moving to Lizzie's, makes one long trip back east. (Are his Nebraska and Iowa children paying for it?) His eldest son, Charlie, is in Pennsylvania, with his wife and children. He hasn't seen Charlie in a good while. Charlie has made his life as a machinist. In the fall of 1903, William travels to Pittsburgh for an extended stay with his working-class son and his family. It is in this red-brick house, at 7324 Bennett Avenue, with its small frame porch off the back, in the Homewood section of Pittsburgh, early on Wednesday, June 15, 1904, apparently having just come back from the drugstore at the corner with the morning paper under his arm, that Frank Lloyd Wright's father collapses and dies within two or three minutes. (I picture him as having risen early in his upstairs room, and having bathed and trimmed his straw-white mustache, and having put on a tie.) Has the dying happened in the same downstairs room where he had been photographed, perhaps by Charlie, a week or two weeks or three weeks before, playing an upright piano, in his long dark coat, with little Alma Hazel, in the foreground, seeming to tune her grandpa out? Has it happened on the same day that a black photographic box on a tripod, about 468 miles west, on a sunny veranda in Oak Park, is making a series of small white puffing noises? (Many pages ago, you'll remember, I was imagining that it happened this way, just for the synchronistic hell of it—the day Wright got photographed with his family.)

On the city's Registry of Deaths, it is reported that the deceased, who had been feeling poorly for the previous few days, has lived for seventy-nine years, five months, and thirteen days. Again, he is put down as a "widower." He has expired of "old age" and "cardiac insufficiency." Homer E. Leslie's funeral home, in the neighborhood, prepares the body. There's no notice of his death in any of the four or five Pittsburgh dailies. (I have never been able to find a death notice in any newspaper anywhere.)

His will is a one-page document, its language lawyerly, but somewhat confusing all the same, poorly typed, single-spaced. It starts off "In the name of God, Amen." He wishes to give what he has in equal measure to his six children. "The intention of this will is to make all my children equal sharers of my estate." Primarily what he has at the time of the drafting of the will is Life Insurance Policy No. 150.694 with Connecticut Mutual Life Insurance Company, worth $577. He recognizes that the dreaded Anna—who was, during the marriage, the chief beneficiary of the policy—might try to interfere with equal distribution, along with some of the children from his second family, or indeed succeed in having his wishes ignored altogether on the insurance policy. In that event, "I direct that one dollar be paid to each of my children out of my personal estate." (He made out the will in January 1890, in Wahoo, five years after the divorce. How it all worked out can't be said. I've never been able to find the probate papers.)

Son Charlie rode with the coffin back to Wisconsin. Lizzie and others in the family came from Iowa and Nebraska and other places, and some of them were there to meet the train when it pulled into Lone Rock. The funeral at Brown Church, up at Bear Valley, and the internment afterward in the little churchyard cemetery were on June 18, 1904. The loamy fields had been newly planted. It was a pleasant early summer morning, with a small body of mourners. The following week, in Spring Green's *Weekly Home News,* this tiny item: "Mrs. Anna Ll Wright and daughter Maginel returned to their home in Oak Park, Illinois, after a visit of ten days in the valley." Which means that she was in the immediate vicinity when the man she hated with all her heart was put into the ground beside Permelia. In the years to follow, the Wright family, which is to say the second Wright family, including its world-famous member, will claim that they had no idea about the death. It doesn't matter if it isn't the truth. They wouldn't have attended his funeral. He was the cast-out man.

Not quite ninety-two years after that Saturday service, on another Saturday morning, a priest said a mass and performed a ceremony at Saint Matthew's Catholic Church in Cedar Rapids, Iowa. William's great-great-great-granddaughter, Alecia Colleen Swift, got married on that March day in 1996 to a local boy. The bride got to choose the music. She wanted Brahms Opus 39, but mostly she wanted "Grandpa Wright." And the piece of his she wanted most was "Floating on the Bay," with its gentle, repeating, sad, wave-like chord progressions. For some reason, the man bringing the flowers was late, so the family instructed the organist to keep on playing the piece. And then the flowers arrived. And everything was beautiful.

The contemporary American novelist Claire Messud comes to mind. Her mother, suffering from dementia, once said to her daughter: "There's so much of life to get through after you realize that none of your dreams will come true." A variation of that line found its way into Messud's great novel, *The Woman Upstairs*.

When I began peering into William's life, I had imagined him as more or less innocent in the bargain. He wasn't. He was wronged terribly, but he wasn't blameless. I can almost feel tinges of sympathy for Anna. (They tend to dissolve quickly.) There *was* something close to foolish and infuriating about William, no matter all his gifts and, yes, accomplishments. What I now believe happened was that Anna, with her awful and inborn ("ungovernable") temper, with her terrifying will, suffered a prolonged siege of mental illness, brought on, at least in part, by the realization that none of her own dreams for personal fulfillment would ever come true as William's spouse. Those dreams would all have to be sublimated and diverted and channeled and redirected into her firstborn. Did anyone in Frank Lloyd Wright's life ever love him more, believe in him more? God knows she was never an easy woman. Her life was pioneer-hard, before William, and during William, and for large parts after. If the vote here will always be cast for William, and against the cruel Anna, it must nonetheless be acknowledged she gave her son something in terms of a will and inner strength that seems unquantifiable. And the world reaped the benefit. And that's something hard to argue against, even if you can argue against Anna herself till kingdom come.

And that conflicted firstborn? I can only think that, in some real sense, he spent the rest of his life after the 1885 family breakup—but most especially after the publication of the 1932 autobiography—searching for the father he had metaphorically murdered for posterity. On one of my reporting trips to Iowa, Hope Rogers's daughter, Mary Catherine Rogers, a decent and frank and thoughtful and searching person, just like her hoot of a mom, said to me in a phone conversation: "Didn't you ever wonder about Frank and all those pianos? It was as if he was trying to have one in almost every room. What is that about? He's trying to fill up all the empty spaces left by his father with all his Baby Grands. I mean, isn't it kind of obvious?"

Isn't it kind of obvious? There is a story that spooks me and seems so limpid in its meanings. It's about a fire—and a piano. It was yet another fire on Frank Lloyd Wright's property at Taliesin—which he himself accidentally started. Afterward, he went into the part of the building that hadn't been destroyed, and, with the acrid smells all around him, and little licks of flame breaking out here and there, sat down at a Steinway and played for a long time. Beethoven and Bach and some Brahms. Everyone left him alone. The sound lilted out over the Lloyd Jones valleys. I'll come to more details of that fire.

PART V

End Story
1950–1959

A good plan is the beginning and the end, because every good plan is organic.
　　　—Frank Lloyd Wright, in *Architectural Record*, January 1928

Take care of the terminals, Wright! The rest will take care of itself.
　　　—Louis Sullivan to his pupil, Frank Lloyd Wright

MIKE WALLACE: Are you afraid of death?
FRANK LLOYD WRIGHT: Not at all. Walt Whitman has the guard
　　　on that. If you want to consult him, read him. Death is a
　　　great friend.
MIKE WALLACE: Do you believe in your personal mortality?
FRANK LLOYD WRIGHT: Yes, insofar as I am immortal, I will be
　　　immortal. To me "young" has no meaning. It's something
　　　you can do nothing about, nothing at all. But youth is a
　　　quality, and if you have it, you never lose it. And when they
　　　put you into the box, that's your immortality.
　　　　　　　—*The Mike Wallace Interview*, ABC Television,
　　　　　　　　　　　　　　　　September 28, 1957

So long, Frank Lloyd Wright
I can't believe your song is gone so soon
I barely learned the tune
　　　—Simon & Garfunkel, from "So Long, Frank Lloyd Wright"

The kinescope saved it, caught it: the night (it was October 29, 1957) when Frank Lloyd Wright and Carl Sandburg appeared on a grainy, black-and-white, local, live TV show called Chicago Dynamic, *and Wright, the once and ever narcissistic child, kept trying to throw off, disconcert, his old friend by poking surreptitiously at his shoe tops with his long-handled cane. It's fairly hilarious to get hold of a tape now and watch him doing it. On the other hand, maybe fairly pathetic.*

The two oracles and native midwestern sons are sitting across from each other, their knees nearly touching. They've known each other for something like half a century, but don't manage to get together very often. The set is wonderfully primitive. The ultra-suave Alistair Cooke is serving as moderator. The program is originating from the east wing of the cavernous Museum of Science and Industry on South Lake Shore Drive in Hyde Park. That's where Chicago's educational television station, WTTW ("Window to the World"), Channel 11, has its studios. The idea is that the station and its doings will be a "working exhibit" for Chicagoland.

At first, it looks like he's drawing circles on the floor. The cane snakes over. He pokes Sandburg. The cane withdraws. It goes back again. You can just catch it on the bottom of the screen. But why is he doing it at all? Because he wants to gain the upper hand in the show, naturally. And he does.

Their part of the program is scheduled to run from nine thirty to ten o'clock, which is when the station normally signs off the air and either puts on a test pattern or fades to total black. But someone in the control room apparently signals: Hey, this thing's going great, let's extend sign-off an extra ten minutes or so. *And they do.*

The poker is ninety. The pokee (who has won three Pulitzer Prizes and is the author of that greatly beloved folk-poem about Chicago being "Hog Butcher for the World") is seventy-nine. Wright is the far more dapper-looking. He's got on a high effete collar and a silky scarf and sits at a forty-five-degree list. Sandburg, his carriage erect, has his string-mop of white hair that's parted almost exactly in the middle of his head and flops down around his large ears. There's something appealingly boyish and meaty about his face. You can almost imagine him having come in from some nearby field and climbing into his town duds and hustling over to the museum to get his pancake applied. (Actually, Sandburg lives these days far from Illinois—on a small farm named Connemara at Flat Rock, North Carolina.) Around the neck of his shirt, which looks more like a work shirt than a dress shirt, the biographer of Abraham Lincoln has lassoed a tie. He's wearing a dark, baggy, double-breasted suit. Lying across his knees like a shawl is a tan overcoat. Maybe it's chilly in the museum.

At first, Sandburg doesn't seem to be aware of what Wright's doing. He's listening to Cooke's introduction. The moderator is mellifluously saying how absurd it is for an Englishman, even an ex-Englishman, to be asked to present to a Chicago viewing audience two of the most recognizable faces in contemporary Illinois history—"rather like importing a Russian peasant to explain Bing Crosby to Bob Hope."

The poking has registered. Sandburg looks down. He studies the cane. It's as if his face is caught between slight disbelief and a silent would-you-please-stop-doing-that-Frank. *After a bit, Frank does. He'll try to resume later.*

Like his dress, Sandburg's speech is mostly plainspoken and tinged with modesty, while Wright's is full of his usual bombast and outrageous pronouncements. He's tossing sound bites, although America doesn't even really know that term yet.

The Lincoln Memorial? "It's one of the most ridiculous, most asinine miscarriages of building material that ever happened."

The Jefferson Memorial? Ha, "a public comfort station."

The Washington Monument? ". . . positively the act of an ignoramus unaware of the dignity and beauty of the shaft that he was finishing when he made it pointed. . . ."

At one point he addresses Cooke as "my dear Alistair," as if to an earnest but slow-grasping child. At another he says to Sandburg: "And you're a poet, my dear boy."

There was a sixteen-year-old schoolgirl named Louisa Michael working on the set that night—except that when she was reliving the memory of all this for me a few years ago her name was Louisa McPharlin and she was a successful and longtime Chicago realtor. She was almost six decades removed from that night. But she could squint and see the poking.

In 1957, Louisa Michael was a junior at Hyde Park High School, and she'd convinced her parents that it wouldn't interfere with her schoolwork if she took a part-time job at the ETV station, which was only a short bus ride away from where her family lived, in the Kenwood neighborhood of the South Side. Chicago was a pioneering broadcast center for America, and the independent-minded schoolgirl was in semi-thrall to the bright lights of live television. She got to do things like move props around and fetch snacks for guests and even help with makeup. That day, after school (it was a Tuesday), she got dressed up in her fancy yellow cashmere dress and yellow sweater and yellow heels, and over she went. She rode the bus to the museum with more than her usual anticipation, because it turns out that the Kenwood house Louisa Michael lived in with her parents, David and Ruth Michael, was a Frank Lloyd Wright house.

And not just any Frank Lloyd Wright house, either. It was the afore-mentioned, dormered, gambrel-roofed Warren McArthur House at 4852 South Kenwood Avenue, an early bootleg from 1892 with Cecil Corwin's name on it as architect of record.

As she was helping apply the cosmetics, the schoolgirl sort of blurted: "Oh, Mr. Wright, I've been growing up in one of your houses."

Beat. "Yes, and which one is that?"

She told him.

"How do you like the sideboard in the dining room?"

The whole house, with its art glass and diamond-paned windows in the octagonal bays, is a gorgeous thing. There's California quarter-sawn oak throughout. On the outside, the architect used Roman brick, to accen-tuate the horizontal. On the interior, he banished all paint and wallpaper: a symphony of wood. He drew the house in the Dutch Colonial Revival style. There are six bedrooms and five thousand square feet of floor space. There's a mild cantilevering effect, anticipating the real Prairies to come. This is another proto-Prairie, a harbinger, an 1892 signal point.

About eight years after he designed the house, Wright, his fame now ticking toward high noon, came back and did some additions. One of them was the sideboard.

McPharlin: "I had my sixteenth birthday party in that dining room. I had the rehearsal dinner for my wedding in that room. How in the world did he remember the sideboard?"

Louisa McPharlin's family moved into the Warren McArthur House in

1954, when she was thirteen. The Michaels were just the third owners. Her parents paid $26,500 for the property—an enormous sum for them. At the point when McPharlin and I met, she had just put the house up for sale for her nearly one-hundred-year-old mom. It had been in her family for close to six decades. She was very sad to put it on the market. McPharlin co-listed the property with Coldwell Banker for $1.48 million. Did it go in a finger-snap? In the summer of 2014, after not quite two years, and after a drop in price of half a million, her treasure of a girlhood home sold for $925,000. A large uptick from where things had started for her family, but in another sense a disappointment. (There'd been renovation problems and some other issues, not an uncommon fate for Wright homes, especially the early ones.)

But, actually, there is another story about that flickery TV night, and in a way it's probably the real reason why I'm dwelling on this in the first place. It's about another kind of poking, and who knows its true meaning. Wright seemed to be going out of his way to tell the viewing audience about the time at Taliesin he had dressed up Carl Sandburg in velveteen bloomers, the two of them having a fine old campy time. It was in the early twenties, apparently. Sandburg had come for a weeklong visit or so and to work on the first volume of what would become his six-volume Lincoln biography.

From the transcript of the show:

Sandburg: "I believe he had dressed me in a velveteen jacket like an artist."

Wright: "Remember, I used to put one on you, Carl?"

Sandburg: "Yes, yes, I have photographs."

Wright: "Bloomers with all the rest. We'd sit before the fire and talk about art and we rode around the countryside and had a nice time together. Carl wrote the first two chapters of his Lincoln at Taliesin. Didn't you?"

Sandburg: "Ya, ya."

Wright: "And we had a good time and I enjoyed myself in front of the fireplace when we were talking about art. And then said Carl to me when we went away, 'Frank,' he said, 'you've been an ideal companion, we've had a fine time together when we'd go out in the countryside and ride around. I said you're an ideal companion. But when you put those damn clothes on me and put me before the fire and talked about art, God, I said, you made me sick.'"

If you turn to pages 486 and 487 of the 1943 edition of An Autobi-ography, *you'll come on a similar kind of seeming impromptu remark about getting into velveteen pantaloons with Sandburg. Wright is tell-ing his readers about breakfast on the veranda at Taliesin. He's waxing purple. "Ribbons of the white mist into which the morning sun has already resolved the dew are lifting, going up to ride as clouds in the blue while the shadows are still wide and long."*

He's telling what folks have on, including his wife and daughter. Next paragraph:

"Me? Oh, I have on raw linen. Loose wide-sleeved jacket buttoned at the wrist, wide baggy trousers tied close around the ankles. Carl (Sand-burg) once visited me when he was working on his 'Lincoln.' I dressed him up in similar style. Lloyd Lewis [a Chicago newspaperman and client and great friend of both Sandburg and Wright] was there and got a good 'shot' of us in the artistic semi-elegant negligee. For years Carl has been trying to buy that picture from Lloyd for fear someone will see it! Well, anyway, that is what I have on."

Negligee? By the way, that parenthesis in the text is Wright's. It's as if he wanted to emphasize to the reader who exactly the Carl was.

A theory about why such seeming stream-of-consciousness might have arisen at all: Sandburg is recognized as one of the first Lincoln historians or biographers to have suggested, just barely, the possibility of Lincoln's homosexuality, or bisexuality. Among Lincoln scholars, this has long been a matter of hot dispute. One of Lincoln's deepest friends from his early days in Springfield, Illinois, was Joshua Speed, partner in a local gen-eral store. In Abraham Lincoln: The Prairie Years, *volume 1, published in 1926—which is the same year that Wright, in hiding with Olgivanna and the children at a lake in Minnesota, began working on his own life story—Sandburg wrote:*

Joshua Speed was a deep-chested man of large sockets, with broad measurement between the ears. A streak of lavender ran through him; he had spots soft as May violets. And he and Abraham Lincoln told each other their secrets about women. Lincoln too had tough *physical shanks and large sockets, also a streak of lavender, and spots soft as May violets.*

In the preface to that volume, Sandburg wrote: "[M]onth by month in stacks and bundles of fact and legend, I found invisible companionships that surprised me. Perhaps a few of those presences lurk and murmur in this book."

There isn't any question that Wright knew Sandburg's biography. Indeed, it seems all but unarguable that he cribbed from Sandburg's mannered-cum-folksy style and tone (just as he metabolized some of the third-person style and tone of his mentor Louis Sullivan's 1924 The Autobiography of an Idea) in creating his own (in my view) far superior prose work. The old pattern: assimilating the work of others and making it more brilliantly into your own bold new thing.

But what gives with the pantaloons, and the seeming urge to talk about them?

Could it be that a lifelong florid impulse in Wright—in speech, in dress, and sometimes in what came off the drawing board—sensed a sympathetic level of comfort vis-à-vis Sandburg? And, thus, he could find himself spontaneously talking out loud, laughing out loud, writing out loud, about his own streaks of lavender and patches that were dewy as spring violets. His own capacities and sometimes even predilections for lavender, lurking and murmuring in the shadows—and sometimes no shadow at all. A way of poking at Carl, a way of poking at himself.

Oh, just a theory, and possibly all dewy.

Terminals (1)

Frank Lloyd Wright with his eight-year-old grandson,
Brandoch Peters, June 1, 1950

n 1950, Frank Lloyd Wright turned eighty-three. Had he lived to
early summer 1959 (instead of dying suddenly two months before),
he would have made ninety-two. In that yardstick of years, nine years,
taking him across the transom of his tenth decade, when he seemed to
transform himself from America's most famous architect into a kind of
pop fixture and phenomenon in our national consciousness, something
like Hemingway or Elvis, he designed or worked on 346 projects—
almost a third of his life's entire output. An almost incredible number.
Some of the projects were brilliant beyond brilliant and daring beyond
daring (the spiral-ramped Guggenheim Museum on a wedge of Fifth

Avenue opposite Central Park springs to mind), and others seem almost loony beyond loony and egocentric beyond egocentric. (Think of a mile-high skyscraper proposed for Chicago's lakefront, 528 floors tall, with a "taproot" foundation going as far into the ground as the Empire State Building goes into the air.)

But let me start elsewhere—with another tragedy erupting up out of a seeming nowhere, as if insisted upon by the gods. This gothic-ism, for want of a better word, involved not fire but water, the freakish drowning of two people, a mother and a child, in what may have been less than three feet of water. It happened on a calm, sunlit, early autumn Taliesin morning. And the photograph on the previous page, so grandfatherly at first glance, homely, in the best sense of that word, locks right into that terrible incident.

It was taken on June 1, 1950, in a portrait studio in Dodgeville, Wisconsin—which is to say eight days before Wright's eighty-third birthday. In terms of the date alone, the image could serve as one end of a pair of chronological bookends for the period 1950–1959, but that fact—its date—is almost incidental. Study the picture a little more closely for a moment. A photograph can sometimes seem to have the strange power to almost bypass thought, short-circuit it. Which is to say that your subconscious can be registering something instantaneous and visceral (and not necessarily false), while your conscious mind is still standing in the doorway, reaching for a cigarette. That happened to me the first time I looked at this photograph—and perhaps the eighth or ninth time, too. Somehow, my conscious mind didn't want to latch on to the truest thing about the image. I was too enamored of those identical-looking herringbone jackets. The two heads of luxuriant hair. (Yes, the boy's is less vainly swept and coiffed than the old man's, but it's been patted pretty neatly into place all the same for the shoot.) The matching silky ties. And what is that confidence being whispered, or getting set to be whispered, into the child's ear—wouldn't you wish to know that most of all? In its goodness, probity, intimacy, the picture flew right in the face of that distinctly unlikable man, call him distinctly detestable man, who had written, with such seeming blitheness, in his autobiography: "Is it a quality? Fatherhood? If so, I seemed born without it. And yet a building was a child. I have had the father-feeling, I am sure, when coming back, after a long time, to one of my buildings. That must be the true feeling of fatherhood? But I never had it for my children." It may be the most indicting thing Wright ever said about himself.

I must have *wanted* it to fly right in the face.

The truest thing about this photograph, I think, is the profoundly sad eyes of Brandoch Peters. (It's a Welsh name—you pronounce it BRAN-doc. Wright preferred "Beau," a name he'd begun calling the boy when he was barely out of infanthood. In turn, Brandoch used to call Wright "Gra," which is about all he could manage of "Grandfather," when he was first learning to talk.)

If you look up "thousand-yard stare" in a dictionary, it will say something like this: "The thousand-yard stare or two-thousand-yard stare is a phrase often used to describe the blank, unfocused gaze of soldiers who have become emotionally detached from the horrors around them. It is also sometimes used more generally to describe the look of dissociation among victims of other types of trauma." The disassociating fact here, horror floating in the background, is that the eight-year-old peach-fuzzed boy, with the right point of his dark shirt collar sticking so boyishly out, possessed of his one-thousand-yard stare, is a survivor, lone survivor, of a fatal car accident four years before. It's the hole in his life that will never be filled up.

Effectively, Brandoch Peters watched his mom and his two-year-old brother die in front of him. If he perhaps didn't see the actual dying, in the time-fractions of its happening (there was a lot of chaotic sudden violence), his cells had to have seen it, experienced it, sealed it.

To say it plain: A car overturned, and he was in it, riding in the front seat, with his mom and little brother. It happened about a mile and a quarter as the crow flies from the Taliesin property line. Car isn't right. The vehicle was a rag-topped, steel-framed jeep, with open sides, hard to control if you're not watching your business. It seems not to have overturned so much as somersaulted into a slough just past the Wisconsin River, on its north shore. It was headed into town when something went horribly awry. The one who survived was not quite five.

It happened on September 30, 1946 (so, to be precise, three years and eight months and two days from the instant of this shutter-snap). It happened about ten o'clock in the morning. Early that day—it was a Monday—Wright and his wife were headed for Chicago. They'd had weekend guests, including some out-of-town family, and people were said to be in a fine mood. The Wrights had left Taliesin perhaps about eight thirty or nine o'clock and were apparently on a train maybe fifteen miles out of Madison when the first word came. A conductor apparently rushed through the car waving a piece of paper and shouting, "Frank Lloyd Wright! Frank Lloyd Wright!" That is how Olgivanna Lloyd Wright remembered it, when she told the story in her autobiography. She worked on her autobiography fitfully over many years, and it didn't end up getting published until just a few years ago. (Olgivanna died in 1985.) But the idea of getting a first fractured report from a train conductor as you're settling yourself into a three- or four-hour ride to Chicago: yes, that has its echoes, distantly.

"Here I am," Wright is supposed to have called out to the trainman.

On the sheet of paper was a scribbled message from a phone operator that may have been handed through a window at the previous stop. According to Olgivanna, it said something like: "Frank Lloyd Wright get off the train your daughter was in an automobile accident."

She was his adopted daughter—who, as many Wright chroniclers have noted, was as close or even closer to him than any of his seven biological children. Her name was Svetlana Wright Peters, whom everyone knew as "Svet." She had shoulder-length raven black hair and a hot-tempered personality, but also a great vivacity and an ability to charm the socks off almost any male in sight, not least her adoptive father, whom she called "Daddy Frank." Svet was the wife of Wes Peters, Wright's right-hand engineering marvel and perhaps his always too-loyal and sublimating man. Svet was Olgivanna's child from her long-ago first marriage (to Russian architect Vlademar Hinzenberg). To remind you of the basic thread: When Wright and twenty-six-year-old Olgivanna met—in Chicago, in late November 1924, at a Sunday matinee of a ballet—Svet was seven. Olgivanna was separated from Hinzenberg and seeking a divorce. Fifty-seven-year-old Wright was separated from (although hardly rid of) Mad Miriam.

Svet and Wes were expecting their third child sometime after the first of the year—so, really, three lives lost that morning. She'd just begun to wear billowy clothes. Meryle Secrest wrote in her Wright biography that it was after the accident that people began to notice that

Wes Peters, who'd always stood a head taller than anyone around him, began to stoop.

The child who died with Svet was named Daniel Peters. He was two. His big brother, "Brandy," as some knew him, was thrown clean and climbed up the bank and started running back toward Taliesin. He may not have been running so much as walking in a kind of dazed zigzag.

At that moment, Svet's husband, along with some apprentices, was up on a roof at Taliesin, starting some shingling. Again, just that shivery word, as if to lock it all back in, distantly: Julian Carlton and his shingling hatchet.

It's known that the mother and her boys had left the property that morning and made a quick stop at a little combination diner and filling station and repair garage that sat on the south bank of the river, just down the hill from the Wright home. They went into the Bridge Lunch, where Daniel and Brandoch returned some empty soda pop bottles, happily pocketing the pennies. (Their mom said they could spend them in town.) They climbed back in and proceeded toward Spring Green, where Svet intended to run some errands. They crossed the steel-girder bridge spanning the river itself. On the north side, there are some marshes. Little Daniel, a squirmy kid, may have been sitting on the lap of his older brother. Svet, fearful that the two might fall out of the jeep, may have reached over with her right arm to take hold of Daniel and position him in between herself and Brandy. There were no seat belts in the jeep. They would have now been approaching the small concrete bridge over the slough. In trying to reach over with her right hand and hold the wheel with her left, Svet must have lost control. The jeep skittered leftward across the macadam, hit the abutment and flipped over on itself, into the water.

Was a kitten involved? The boys may have brought along one of their favorite kittens from Taliesin. Did the kitten climb up on the back of the seat and distract the driver? For years after, Olgivanna was said to fly into a rage at the sight of a cat. We'll never know.

It is believed Svet snapped her neck in the eight- or ten-foot flip into the water, and so she probably died more or less instantly, even before hitting the water. There doesn't seem to have been an official coroner's report (in any event, coroner's reports no longer exist from 1946 in Sauk County). The death certificates for both Svet and Daniel have the word

DROWNING written in large letters in the box for "Immediate cause of death." Next to that entry, under "Duration," the county coroner wrote: "few minutes."

Fifteen minutes before the accident, Glenn Richardson, who owned the Bridge Lunch and the garage attached to it, had been headed into town in the wrecker with his mechanic, Donnie Fogel. Richardson, having forgotten something, turned around and went back to the garage. He started out again. That's when he came on a little boy, his clothes drenched, walking (or half-running) along the road. Richardson and his mechanic pulled over. Brandoch cried, or so it has been reported in several oral histories and in the various newspaper accounts, something like *Won't you please help me? My mommy went in the water.* The two men grabbed the child and drove quickly to the scene, which couldn't have been more than a couple hundred yards up the road. They ran down the bank. They managed to lift out Daniel. But they couldn't free Svet—she was pinned behind the wheel. The garage owner and his mechanic got the wrecker and backed it up and used a cable to raise the jeep several feet. They carried Svet to the bank. She was white and inert. According to his grandmother, Brandoch said: "I saw my mother lying on the lawn with her eyes open."

Sirens now and a state trooper on the scene and an ambulance from town and people jumping out of cars arriving from all directions. (Again, Brandoch: ". . . and then daddy came and many people came.") A Spring Green doctor directed the ambulance driver to take Svet and Daniel to an emergency room in Madison. There, at the hospital, maybe forty-five minutes later, police and medical personnel tried— uselessly—some resuscitation efforts. A doctor pronounced the two dead, and later in the afternoon the bodies were brought back to a funeral home in Spring Green. By then, the *Capital Times* in Madison had out a front-page story, with a seven-column headline. Once more, as if in faintest echo: MRS. PETERS AND SON, FRANK LLOYD WRIGHT KIN, KILLED. A few days later, the *Weekly Home News* in Spring Green wrote in a boxed piece on the front page that was slugged MEMORIAL: ". . . it didn't seem real—as it never does when a mother and child die suddenly together. Folks had to go to the bridge, had to see the little farm jeep lying upside down in the waters of the slough. Then they could believe."

The funeral was at five o'clock the next afternoon, Tuesday, October 1. The Taliesin Fellows chorus sang on the terrace outside the garden room. (Svet had been the director of the chorus.) A Fellow tolled an ancient Chinese bell. Frank Lloyd Wright read a poem composed that morning by his daughter Iovanna, Svet's sister, younger by almost eight years and who had pretty much always lived painfully in her big sister's shadow. The burial was in the family churchyard cemetery, next to Unity Chapel, under the trees, where Mamah Borthwick had lain since the rainy evening of August 16, 1914. Again, a profusion of flowers, lining the plain pine casket, wild purple asters and clematis and roses. Several of the Fellows made a path of red maple leaves from the chapel gate to the grave. Earlier that day, Wes Peters had dug the grave almost entirely by himself. In an interview filmed in 2007, his sixty-seven-year-old son—who by then had suffered a stroke and was enduring other maladies—talked about getting himself over to the chapel yard by himself while his father was doing the digging. All Brandoch could see was the top of his father's head. Shovelfuls of earth were being flung out of the hole. The child leaned into the hole and asked his father something about whether it was true that mother and Daniel were getting buried today. Brandoch's father stopped his work and wiped his brow and grinned broadly. "Yes," he said. In the film (you can find it on the internet), Brandoch shakes his head and says: "What that smile must have cost him." He lets it trail off.

They didn't let Brandoch attend the service. His grandparents and his father felt he was too young. Somebody minded him up at the house.

In 1992, in an oral history conducted by a Taliesin archivist, Brandoch, who was fifty, said of the accident, as if to explain his life in a sentence: "And I can't give you the exact year for that, but the reasons for it are quite obvious."

For five years after the accident, Olgivanna renounced alcohol, meat, coffee, tea, jewelry, anything with sugar, makeup. In Arizona, she moved into a tent. Her husband kept saying: "The only way you can get back is not to stop your work."

The hole that could never be filled: cruelly, although the intention was the opposite, his elders tried to make the survivor into a cello prodigy. It's not that Brandoch didn't have talent, even a gift, as a musician—but he was hardly a prodigy. For five years, he got to study at the Juilliard

School in New York. (His grandfather had used his connections.) He played with an orchestra in Munich. And eventually he came back to Wisconsin. For the next thirty or so years, he was a local sheep farmer. (He had tried to learn the futures business on the Chicago Board of Trade—and lost his shirt.) He stayed to himself, mostly. He never married. He gained a reputation as something of the township crank, the local malcontent. He worked on a book manuscript entitled *Frank Lloyd Wright and His Inner Circle: A Grandson's View*—but couldn't find a publisher. (Some of it was made into a 2008 documentary film, with Brandoch as narrator. Near the open is a fleeting reconstruction of the accident. The film is available on DVD.) On March 1, 2004, he suffered the stroke referenced above. Seven years later, there was a bad car accident. (Yes, another one.) By then signs of a creeping dementia were evident to anyone who knew Brandoch well, and one of those was a decent and no-nonsense and generous woman named Sue Schuetz. For a time, they'd been romantically involved. Eventually, Schuetz agreed to take over his affairs and to serve as his power of attorney. On December 15, 2017, Brandoch, whose dementia was now Alzheimer's, about to turn seventy-six, no longer able to live on his own, entered a Dane County nursing home. That's where he was, as of this writing. Visited two or three times a week by Sue Schuetz.

We've had conversations about Brandoch, on the telephone and in person and via email, and she has made me understand things about him in ways for which I am grateful.

"He's never had good self-esteem, he's avoided people," Schuetz said. She said his father was trying hard to be a father, but the truth is Wes Peters was so often away, working on a new site as Wright's head engineering man. Schuetz: "You hear all this talk, even from Brandoch himself, in oral histories and so forth, about how close he was to his grandparents. But, really, he got left behind. That's the story, as I can put it together. Wright was always too self-absorbed. He didn't really love kids, or he didn't love them enough. Olgivanna may have tried, but she was off dealing with her own grief. He had to take a back seat. He *did* grow up and become a cranky old bachelor whom people didn't understand and wanted more or less to avoid."

A question I knew the answer to: Why was she going out of her way to take care of him?

Quietly: "Because his life is important. Because there really isn't anybody else."

In another conversation, Schuetz said: "He's been letting it out for these last six or seven years—wanting his mother. He's been crying for his mom for the last six or seven years. He gets confused. He thinks she's still alive. He thinks his father's still alive. And his grandparents."

Of the photograph in Dodgeville on June 1, 1950, Schuetz said that Brandoch had once told her, in a moment of clarity, that Olgivanna had more or less stage-managed the shoot. "It wasn't the original pose, apparently." They were trying different things, and Olgivanna saw the two of them like that and said: "There. That's the one I want!"

"So then the photograph is a lie," I said, a little too self-righteously.

"Not exactly," she said.

To quote the complicator himself, from *An Autobiography:* "Again searching causes I wondered." An odd, beautiful sentence. Against any true knowing: the wondering, the searching.

———

The yardstick of years, elliptically, selectively:

In January 1951, Henry R. Luce's editors at *Architectural Forum* again devoted a great chunk of their large-format monthly to Wright's work. Again, as in 1938, they let him design it. They turned over thirty-four pages in the well of the magazine—a four-color portfolio insert with its own front and back cover, of soft, yellowish, cardboardish paper. The insert was a beautiful thing, a piece of art in itself, showcasing seven groups of his work, including what is known as the research tower at S. C. Johnson & Son. In the mid-forties, Wright had come back to Racine—and to Hib Johnson—to construct the building that would serve as the company's research and development division. Once again Hib had proven the willing and enlightened if often exasperated building partner. Wright didn't do it small—he'd go big or he'd go home. He designed the complex something like a tree, with reinforced concrete slabs cantilevering from the building's central core. The fourteen stories alternated between square floors and circular balconies. The walls weren't supported from the outside; rather from inside out. A central shaft, or spine, or "trunk," held the elevator and the mechanical systems. Naturally, the thing went over budget, and over time, but there it is today, a stunning architectural modernist work, sheathed in its brick and translucent glass, sitting alongside the cathedral-like administration building. The American Institute of Architects has designated the buildings at SCJ as among the core seventeen Wright works representative of his contribution to American culture. (*Only seventeen?* you can hear him stamping from heaven.)

The cover of the *Forum* featured the research tower, taken at night, glowing in its translucence. Inside, the architect's ego glowed translucently. He wrote: "It is no exaggeration to say that we have had little or no organic character in our Democracy. . . . We came over in buckled shoes, knee breeches, lace around our wrists and around our necks, Colonials with a nostalgia for things left behind. So Democracy has remained largely our empty boast." A couple of pages over: "The Machine has so far produced for us only the weeds of a Civilization."

At the back of the insert was an odd color portrait of him (by noted architectural photographer Ezra Stoller) that almost looked like a painting more than a photograph. He's in his Taliesin bedroom, with big windows and a hint of hills behind. He almost looks embalmed, mummified—or, maybe better, as if it's not him but a wax figure of himself, in a diorama. Beneath the picture: "Frank Lloyd Wright, 81, is now in the 56th year of an architectural practice which has changed the shape of building throughout the western world." (Er, he's eighty-three.)

Four months from that issue, he got named. The Red Scare was on, and its most hateful and sweaty-seeming face was Wisconsin's junior senator, Joseph McCarthy. In 1949 Wright had signed his name to a list of distinguished Americans supporting a New York City conference for world peace. A year later the event's sponsors got cited as a "Communist front" by the House Un-American Activities Committee. A year after that—on April 4, 1951—the House released a lengthy list of people alleged to have been "affiliated with from five to ten Communist-front organizations." Among the named: Langston Hughes, Albert Einstein, Dorothy Parker, Artie Shaw, Judy Holliday, José Ferrer (they'd both just won Oscars), Dashiell Hammett, Lillian Hellman, Paul Robeson. It was like an honor roll. In the *Cap Times* seventeen days later, Wright penned a front-page piece: "I would like to ask my fellow citizens which they feel to be most dangerous to our system of the free life: A sociologic idiot like a Communist or a political charlatan like a McCarthy." That fall he used that text to address an audience at the University of Wisconsin, just salting up his prose a bit. In place of "political charlatan like a McCarthy," he said "political pervert like a McCarthy." (Actually, maybe he had written "pervert" in the April 21 *Cap Times,* and its editor—his good friend Bill Evjue—had gotten him to tone it down.)

A year later, almost exactly, from the naming: a burning. It's the Taliesin fire that was referenced at the end of the last chapter—when Wright went into the ruins, with other parts of the building still smoldering, and sat down at the piano and played for a long time. It happened on April 26, 1952, a Saturday afternoon. Wright had caused it. He was burning some rubbish about thirty feet from the building. He'd run out of matches and gasoline and had sent one of his apprentices to get more of both. He walked away. The flames got up under the eaves.

Two days before, Wright and his wife and daughter Iovanna had arrived back from Paris. Many of the Fellows were still in transit from the winter stay in Arizona.

This fire didn't burn Taliesin per se, which is to say the main house. Rather, it burnt what everyone knows (now as well as then) as Hillside. Hillside, referenced earlier, is the third of the three main complexes that make up the greater Taliesin. As was noted, Wright had first built the structure in 1887, as an academy, for his mother's maiden sisters, Ellen and Jane Lloyd Jones. In 1901, Hillside Home School having outgrown itself, Aunt Ellen and Aunt Jane commissioned their nephew to design a new building. He made it of native stone and oak timbers, and it featured many Prairie forms, including low-hipped roofs and casement windows and great hearths. In 1915, Hillside—which is about three-quarters of a mile across the knobs of green from Wright's home—closed its academy doors for good. In 1933, Wright made the structure a part of the Fellowship, with dormitories and dining room and a theater and a drafting room and the great space referred to as the living room.

And about half of Hillside was taken down that Saturday. But no one died. The next day, trying to sound insouciant, Wright told a reporter for the *Weekly Home News:* "I lit that rubbish fire myself." From the front-page account in the *Wisconsin State Journal* (it was a wire story, and *The New York Times* picked it up as well): " 'The oak mill construc-

tion was considered fireproof,' the 82-year-old architect said. [He was eighty-four.] 'But we lit a fire outside, burning leaves and grass. . . . We went away and the wind shifted. It shipped the fire into the building.'"

Three fire companies fought the blaze for about two hours. When their pumpers went dry, around suppertime, the firemen tried to run water up from a small pond between Hillside and the highway. Farmers came with milk cans in their pickups and organized relays. (Many others from the town and the county stood on the fringe to watch: not-so-secret schadenfreude.)

Wright had no insurance on the structure.

In the photographs, the fire looks like something no rural fire company in the world could have hoped to extinguish. But, in fact, the firemen did get it out, eventually.

From the *Home News* report: "Sunday morning, while his students worked to shovel the wreakage [*sic*] from what was once the second floor of the wing, and while orange flames still licked the smoking debris of the theater, Wright led the Home News reporters into the fellowship living room and sat down at a 49-year-old Steinway piano which had been salvaged from one of his early houses." Next paragraph:

"Somewhat as he had played, alone, to comfort himself after the much more tragic Taliesin fire of 1914, Wright softly played the old piano. . . . The old Steinway, blackened with smoke, stood against the wall. On the other side was the burned office, and above the piano, windows connecting the two rooms had been smashed by the heat."

In a letter to friends several months later, a Taliesin Fellow from China named Ling Po described how Wright had stood at the edge of the flames, "giving orders to the firemen, who ignored him completely." Po wrote of the surreality: how the day darkened and the half-dozen or so fire trucks fought on in vain just as the master himself kept shouting in vain. The apprentice told of how the following day, Sunday, in a family meal at Taliesin, with Wright seeming in an almost weirdly buoyant mood, he had promised to start rebuilding immediately. According to Po, he said: "We always had been tested by fire, not to say purified by it. But, tested to the last minute is a little too much. From now on let's have no more fire. I'll set no more." At that meal, there was a box of rhubarb pies. Herb Fritz, Jr., and his wife had come to offer sympathies, and had brought the pies. Fritz, a Spring Green architect, had once been a Taliesin Fellow. He was the son of Herb Fritz, Sr., Wright's old draftsman, who, you'll recall, was one of the two survivors of the 1914 massacre. At the lunch, Wright, who was gigging young Fritz on the quality of his architecture, had said to Fritz's wife: "We will forgive your husband for his house on account of your pie."

But there is another eyewitness account of the 1952 fire, by a Taliesin Fellow named Frances Nemtin, and this is the one that tells of how Wright went into the building not on Sunday morning, when the fire was perhaps ninety-eight percent out, but on Saturday evening, when there was still some real danger, not to say acrid air. Nemtin, in a two-page reminiscence written years later, said: "When the livingroom [sic] was safe Mr. Wright insisted on going there to survey the damage. Shortly I heard him playing the piano there, in consolation? He had lost a valued concert-grand Bechstein in the theater as well. . . ."

Nemtin spent seven decades in the Wright universe. She died at age ninety-six in 2015. In the spring of 2014, about eleven months before her death, on a reporting trip to Taliesin West, I got to speak with her. She invited me into her tiny quarters. She was in a wheelchair, but her mind was wonderfully alert. I brought up the fire and the going in. Was it true, as I had been told, that she and some others in the Fellowship had stood some safe distance off, listening, attending?

"Yes," she said. They didn't know what else to do.

I asked if one of the pieces he played was Beethoven's Sonata no. 8 in C Minor, Op. 13, commonly known as the *Pathetique,* with its lilting repetitions, especially in the transcendently beautiful and sad second movement. (I had been told this by several others. The sonata was a favorite piece.) She said she couldn't be sure, but it sounded right.

"How long did it go on—his playing?"

"I don't know, hard to say, maybe an hour."

"It was his defiance?"

"No, consolation."

"His grief?"

"Okay, yes. But consolation, I think. That's the word I'd use."

"Could it have had anything to do with his father—going in there to play like that?"

"I've never thought about that," she said. She didn't seem to regard it as something coming from the moon.

A few months after the fire, Wright wrote by hand to the chief of the Spring Green Fire Department, Lawrence Larson, enclosing a check for $100. "Dear Chief," he said, "I want to give a little testament of appreciation for what the boys did for Taliesin in the fire at the school buildings. It isn't much but I wish it spent for a party for the boys. I would like them to have as good a time as they can have on $100. Yours with thanks. Frank Lloyd Wright."

For someone so locally notorious for stiffing people, the gift must have been its own small shock. (The chief wrote back to say the money was going to be used for a new firehouse.)

————

The Wrights had been in Paris (and, as I said, had returned home two days before the fire) to view the largest exhibit of Wright's work ever shown. As Wright historians have written, the show that came to be known eventually as *Sixty Years of Living Architecture* was possibly the largest one-man career retrospective ever mounted for any architect in history to that date. At the fire moment, spring 1952, the show was in the midst of a big European run. The previous June, the exhibit, with its drawings and photographs and three-dimensional models, had opened in the Strozzi Palace in Florence. Between February and August 1952, the show, an aesthetic festival on wheels, was going to travel to Zurich, Paris, Munich, and Rotterdam. Then it was going to go to Mexico. And then, triumphantly, in the fall of 1953, it was going to roll into America, to New York City.

Actually, this ego extravaganza had started in the States—with a preview of sorts in Philadelphia in the latter part of January and in February 1951. The unveiling was at Gimbel Brothers Department Store, part of the huge Gimbels chain. (The thirty-four-page insert from *Architectural Forum* was reprinted and distributed as a special "offprint" for the crowds in both Philadelphia and Florence.) The show's financial sponsor was Arthur C. Kaufmann, who was executive head of the Philadelphia store, and also a less flamboyant but quite wealthy cousin of Edgar J. Kaufmann of Fallingwater fame. (Like E.J., Arthur had grown up in Pittsburgh, and had worked in retailing, but then, in 1934, had moved across the state, to its even larger metropolis, to take over Gimbels. In Philadelphia, he would develop a national reputation for his civic do-gooding and cultural-mindedness.)

So Wright had a new money angel. Kaufmann would help back the traveling exhibit, provided that the first stop was in Philadelphia, in the wide halls of his own gilded department store. The retrospective was organized by a German-born architect and sculptor named Oscar Stonorov, who'd done much cultural work in Philadelphia. On January 25, 1951, the head of Gimbels hosted an opening-night black-tie dinner in Philadelphia, which Wright attended. In 2017, longtime Wright scholar Kathryn Smith published an astute book about all this entitled *Wright on Exhibit*. It is one of those studies that are so much wider than their seemingly esoteric focus: really, a kind of biography disguised as a technical treatise. The author uses the structural device of telling the history of Wright's many exhibitions to produce insights like this, regarding the Prairie house: "[H]e broke the wall down into a series of elements such as piers, flat planes, and window bands—all geometrically organized by dark wood strips. The wall was now defined as an enclosure of space. Windows were no longer holes punched through a mass, but a light screen filtering sunlight into the interior."

The New York version of the show, which Wright titled *Sixty Years of Living Architecture: In the Realm of Ideas,* opened in late October 1953. It opened in two temporary structures erected on the northeast corner of the secured site for the headache-plagued Guggenheim Museum. One of the things Smith sheds light on is the interrelationship between the exhibit itself and Wright's battle to get the Solomon R. Guggenheim Museum built. He'd been battling to get it built since 1943. A decade had elapsed since he received the commission, and a first ceremonial spade had yet to go into the ground. He was now facing more code restrictions. He was now facing redesign necessities. He was now going through an appeals process. And one of the things he apparently began to sense, in the summer and fall of 1953, was that *Sixty Years*—which would be by far the largest exhibit of his work held in Manhattan in his lifetime—could be a public relations instrument in his marathon battle. Smith: The exhibition "could serve another vital purpose: to affect public opinion through the press, draw high attendance, and inspire positive newspaper reviews in an effort to influence city officials to grant him permission to build the Guggenheim Museum." In other words, the limelight he so craved could be put to beautiful use: win-win all around. Was this the point in history that Frank Lloyd Wright seemed to take up residence on the back of America's cultural eyeball? Critic Paul Goldberger has expressed it well: "This nineteenth-century man became the twentieth century's first architecture media star. Wright, who loved nothing more than being talked about, did not believe his fifteen minutes would be up, in his lifetime or in any other."

No question that the still-new black-and-white magical thing called television had much to do with the almost imperceptible shift from being merely a famous architect. It was love at first sight between Wright and the silvery patch. Two Wright scholars, Jane King Hession and Debra Pickrel, in their carefully reported 2007 book, *Frank Lloyd Wright in New York: The Plaza Years, 1954–1959,* calculated that, between 1953 and 1958, Wright appeared on something like two dozen television shows. Only a very few are findable today. Some were never recorded. Others, even if captured on kinescope, eventually got tossed, probably due to storage reasons.

Still, some nuggets got saved. We've seen the 1957 Wright-Sandburg joust on Channel 11 in Chicago. In May 1953 (so five months in advance of the New York unveiling of *Sixty Years*), the eighty-five-year-old (soon to be eighty-six) sat for a nationally televised half-hour conversation (it wasn't live; it had been filmed a week or so earlier) with Hugh Downs. "Sat" could be the operative word. Downs was then a thirty-two-year-old little-known staff announcer at WMAQ, the NBC affiliate in Chicago. The interview was done in Wright's bedroom at Taliesin, with Downs seated in what looked like an especially low-to-the-floor easy chair on the left, and Wright in a much higher padded chair to the right. He was already in place when the cameras rolled. "Come in, lad," he says. Downs enters, stage left, and takes the low-cushioned chair, the soft padding of which seems to sink him even deeper downward.

The interview is fairly wonderful. Wright's in a three-piece suit, and he has his legs crossed (you can see his stacked-heel shoes), and he's holding a big book of his work. He fiddles with his fingertips, with the buttons on his vest. He speaks softly, in singsong cadences. His hair is a little mussed. In a couple of sentences, he drills home again how Anna Wright had made him the centerpiece of her life. She had decided on her son's destined profession before he was even born. (From all that can be determined, this is true.) "My mother was a teacher and she wanted an architect for a son. I happened to be the son and, of course, naturally an architect. . . . The room into which I was born was hung with the wood engravings of the English cathedrals. . . . So I was born into architecture." He tells of how he just missed getting his undergraduate degree at the University of Wisconsin, that old fib about if he had only "stayed three months longer I would have been given a degree as an engineer." He explains Fallingwater: "Well, there was a rock ledge bank beside the waterfall and the natural thing seemed to be to cantilever the house from that rock bank over the fall." He describes how "early in life I had to choose between honest arrogance and hypocritical humility. I chose honest arrogance, and have seen no occasion to change—even now." (It's a line he will use in letters and talks and interviews throughout the fifties.) His most satisfactory achievement? "Oh, my dear boy—the next one, of course, the next building I build." His greatest disappointment? Probably that so many people have copied him brainlessly: "imitation of imitation by the imitator." Downs asks why he has not always been treated kindly in the press or by his fellow architects. "Well, I don't see why they should have treated me kindly. I was entirely contrary to everything they believed in and if I was right, they were wrong. Why should they treat me kindly? It was a question of time, I suppose, of their survival or mine."

(The show went so well in Wright's mind that he decided to insert it into one of his latest books, *The Future of Architecture*. The work was soon to come off the press. He got hold of a transcript and reworked it, to make himself sound even better than he had in the real thing.)

That program aired on May 17, 1953. Two days earlier, at Rockefeller Center in Manhattan, Wright was a guest on NBC's *Today* show, hosted by Dave Garroway. To the soundtrack of Dinah Shore and Tony Martin singing "I'll Take Manhattan," the cameras closed in on a headline from the *New York Herald Tribune* of the day before. It was a three-column story above the fold with a three-decker head on page one: SAYS FRANK LLOYD WRIGHT: GRASS IN THE STREETS OF N.Y. IN 25 YEARS. It was written by Judith Crist (later to become a famous American film critic). First paragraph: "Twenty-five years from now grass will be growing in the streets of New York City and flowers blooming on its sidewalks." Next paragraph: "This prediction was made yesterday by Frank Lloyd Wright following an announcement by Marc Connelly, president of the National Institute of Arts and Letters, that the eighty-four-year-old [nope] architect had been selected by the institute's 250 members to receive its Gold Medal for Architecture on May 27." Last paragraph (readers would have had to turn to the jump, on page 40): "Mr. Wright grinned reminiscently. 'You know, once I was told that Winston Churchill said I had one of the two best brains in this country. But I'll never know if it was a compliment until I know whose is the other brain.'"

Possibly Churchill said something like that once.

In four days, the new colonizer of American media had appeared on two coast-to-coast TV shows, and in the newspaper considered the favorite of the Manhattan literati.

Sixty Years, the New York edition of it, opened its doors on October 22, 1953. Regarding the two temporary structures for the show: One was a full-sized house, an *actual* house, erected on the proposed Guggenheim site. Which is to say a 1,700-square-foot and completely furnished two-bedroom home that almost could have been transplanted, lock, stock, and custom cabinetry, from, say, the northeast sloping corner of Birch and Toepfer avenues in Madison. You could pay your fifty cents admission to the show and walk right in and plop yourself down in the twenty-six-by-thirty-two-foot living room, trip on a low-lit lamp, take in a gorgeous Japanese screen, stare up at the twelve-and-a-half-foot-high ceiling. It was all glass and brick and gleaming wood: a perfect little Usonian dream having found temporary domicile on a corner of Manhattan, fronting Fifth Avenue, at East Eighty-Ninth Street, across from Central Park.

The other structure was a pavilion, or gallery, to hold the show's more than eight hundred drawings and artifacts; the scale models; the large-format photographs, the potted plants. Wright erected a kind of elaborate, translucent tent, 145 feet long and 50 feet wide, using canvas and indirect lighting and pipe scaffolding. The structure, with its angled roof, seemed as impermanent as it did unorthodox. There are numerous photographs of him that were taken while the pavilion and the Usonian house were being built, all in a rush, in the days before the opening. Here he is one day in early or mid-October, no rush at all, with his cane, in his tweed overcoat, with his watch fob, with his porkpie lid. Around him, New York workingmen—plasterers and bricklayers and electricians and carpenters—are going about their jobs. There is one particular photo. It was taken by his longtime personal photographer, Pedro Guerrero. He stands, head tilted upward, as if posing for sculpture, with the cane at his side like a long forefinger, while Guerrero snaps the picture and somebody from the press films him from four feet away with an eight-millimeter camera. It's meta: the shooter is shooting the shooter, both of them making a record of Wright at the same instant. (To the left, behind his gramps, in an overcoat, in a dress shirt and tie, with slightly mussed hair, looking glum, or at least distracted, is eleven-year-old Brandoch Peters.)

The show was a smash—running seven days a week for fifty-three days (they extended the run into the second week of December), drawing (according to the Guggenheim Foundation) 60,000 visitors. (*The New York Times* reported about half that figure.) On October 20, two days before the opening, there'd been a preview for the press. Wrote the *Times* (the story was well inside the paper, but still . . .): "A white-haired 84-year-old [nope again] architect moved quietly around his living room yesterday, helping to arrange large bronze chrysanthemums and greenery in flower holders." Next paragraph: "He was Frank Lloyd Wright, widely acclaimed architectural genius, putting the last decorative touches to his Usonian house on Fifth Avenue. . . ." Two paragraphs down: "In a navy-blue suit, a dotted Windsor tie and an individualistic tan felt hat, Mr. Wright was the focal point as he veered from courteous attention to his guests to the last-minute problems of the exhibition." Next paragraph: "The fieriness that has become legend was not in evidence, and the equally renowned humor showed only occasionally. In the great living room, Mr. Wright waved his cane and said, 'I think this has the old Colonial on the run.'"

The critical praise ran fairly undiluted—with the exception of the one critic who mattered most to Wright: Lewis Mumford of *The New Yorker*. The two had known each other, gotten cross with each other, for not quite thirty years. Both men were possessed of their flinty independence and seriously inflated sense of self. The subset story of Frank Lloyd Wright and Lewis Mumford is its own father-son tale, and none of Wright's biographers, or Mumford's, either, has ever captured the full length of it. The exhibitionist on exhibit decided to give the critic his personal tour of *Sixty Years*. There seem to be no photographs of that day, but you can imagine Wright, peacock-clad, taking the far younger Mumford (he, too, a bit of a clotheshorse) by the elbow and steering him suffocatingly through. Mumford suggests this in his autobiography, *Sketches from a Life*, which was published in 1982, two decades after Wright was dead. Wrote Mumford, remembering that guided tour: "But in seeing his life, so to say, spread before me, with his voice as a persistent undertone, I realized as never before how the insolence of his genius sometimes repelled me." (A version of that could be chiseled on Wright's tombstone: *Here lies Frank Lloyd Wright. The insolence of his genius was so often repellent.*) In his autobiography Mumford noted how, despite their long mutual affection (punctuated by estrangements), they'd never found time to be a guest in the other's home. In their lengthy correspondence, Wright is often beseeching Mumford to come to Taliesin and experience the wonder of it. But the critic understood viscerally that would be a bad idea. From *Sketches:* "But Wright could not understand my unwillingness to abandon my vocation as a writer to have the honor of serving his genius; and he was puzzled, almost nettled, over my unreadiness to break into my own work at any given moment to be his guest."

Mumford's critical response to *Sixty Years* came in the form of a long two-parter. It appeared in *The New Yorker* in the issues of November 28 and December 12. It was as if he knew he had to rise to every writing thing that was in him. The two pieces may be the single best piece of long-form journalistic criticism ever written about Wright—no question the single best thing ever done on him up to that point. To me, the pieces are a kind of mash note masquerading as a tour-de-force put-down. And, of course, Mumford knew how Wright was going to take it, or at least take it initially, which is why, just before the first of the two articles appeared, on November 23, he wrote by hand a two-page letter: "Dear Frank: Yesterday I finished one of the most difficult tasks I have ever attempted: a criticism of your life & work in architecture. The first article will appear in The New Yorker this week." He said that "in fear and trembling and admiration and love I dared write the article about your work that no one else, friendly or hostile, has yet dared to write."

Wright, who was in Arizona, but about to make his way to New York, wired on November 29: YOU ARE THE ONLY ONE REALLY QUALIFIED TO CRITISIZE STOP IT IS THE PSYCHOLOGICAL MOMENT AND WILL PROBABLY BE USED AS MY EPITAPH.

The pieces were titled "A Phoenix Too Infrequent." They appeared toward the back of the magazine, where Mumford's column, "The Sky Line," regularly ran. I'll quote here from only the first one, to my mind the more brilliant of the two. (It's also the more favorable.) In that issue, the author was up against E. B. White and Vladimir Nabokov (he had a short story) and William Carlos Williams (he had a poem) and A. J. Liebling—to name only four contributors, both staff and non-staff.

His lead: "New York is finally, to its past discredit and its present honor, harboring its first building by Frank Lloyd Wright, the last and greatest of the trio of master builders that began with Henry Hobson Richardson and Louis Henri Sullivan." In the next paragraph: "By almost universal acclaim, Frank Lloyd Wright is the most original architect the United States has produced, and—what is even more important—he is one of the most creative architectural geniuses of all time."

He explained how Wright, if not singlehandedly, helped bring about a "change in our attitude toward American art, a change from colonial dependence upon European models to faith in our native abilities." A few sentences later: "But Wright, magician though he is, was not alone in producing this transformation. . . . Even the open plan was not Wright's singlehanded creation. . . . The fact that these precedents existed in a diffused, inchoate form while Wright was still an apprentice points up the real measure of his contribution."

Further on:

> His strong individual feelings and convictions dominate his con-structions; by intention they are neither reticent nor anonymous, for his buildings are corporeal extensions of his personality. This means that to love his buildings, and especially his houses, you must love the man and accept his philosophy of life; you must love him to the point of surrendering to him. . . . In return for this surrender, he will charm and entrance you. . . . Speaking with all reverence for a great master, I must confess that Wright's dwelling houses sometimes put me off by persuading me that he is thinking not of the client's needs but of the architect's own desires and delights. . . . Wright, fully aware of his own arrogance, has gaily defended it on the ground that arrogance is more decent than simulated humility.

The close, or at least the start of the long final paragraph: "For all his towering genius, Frank Lloyd Wright is, by his own philosophy and practice, an Isolato, to use the word Melville applied in 'Moby Dick' to his spokesman Ishmael. Each building by Wright stands in self-imposed isolation—a monument to his own greatness, towering defiantly above the works of his contemporaries. Though it dazzles us by its brilliance, it sometimes fails to invite our love, because it offers no halfway place between rejection and abject surrender."

In his autobiography, Mumford told of how Wright had read the piece on an airplane coming in from Arizona, and that he became so exercised that "he then and there wrote me a letter that trembled with rage as if from some mechanical vibration. His references to me were all in the third person—'He says that'—as if it were a Letter to an Editor." This myth has appeared in many books (Mumford's own biographer passed it along), but, alas, it turns out to be just another good Wright story ruined by the facts. He was enraged, but he didn't write the letter as the airliner was descending through choppy darkness into LaGuardia. He wrote it the next morning on two pages of hotel stationery from his suite in the Plaza, and the handwriting wasn't shaky. It began, without a date, and in large lettering: "Dear Lewis—Read your 'appreciation' in the plane coming in last night—both glad and furious—." Yes, some of it addresses Mumford in a kind of weird third-person way that's hard to parse. But, overall, there was more passivity in his aggression—which perhaps only gave away how truly angry he was. And yet, he was able to close: "But love to you just the same. You will learn better now—Affection no end Frank."

Mumford wrote right back, on December 3: "I grieve that you have taken my *New Yorker* criticism so ill; for the best praise of a man's work is not that which is unqualified, but that which remains after all qualifications." He ended: "With deep respect and warm love still, as from one Master to another—Lewis." In *Sketches from a Life,* Mumford said that something "impish" had seized him to write that sign-off—but it seems doubtful. His own ego was at work. (Let it be added here that, for all his self-regard and prowess as a writer, Mumford was capable of sloppy errors. The mistake about writing the letter on the airplane is just one example. He can misquote his own letters; he can get dates and simple facts wrong.)

In time, the wound healed over. In a letter that seems to have been written two or three days later, Wright began: "I love you just the same." Not that he didn't continue to seethe and to lecture. In fact, a couple weeks later, on December 18, he wrote a long letter and kept adding postscripts ("Llewis! What really hurts is to know that you—to whom I have looked with hope and love should understand my work so much in reverse"), but ended up not mailing it off.

On June 17, 1954, Rocky Marciano won a decision over Ezzard Charles in a fifteen-round heavyweight championship fight in Yankee Stadium. (It was on a Thursday night, and the thing was a bloodfest.) In the Midwest, but especially in Chicago, people were staggering under the blows of an eight-day heat wave. On June 18, at three p.m., the mercury registered 98.1 degrees. Two hours later on that Friday afternoon,

Frank Lloyd Wright's troubled last child got wed at Holy Trinity Russian Orthodox Cathedral on the near northwest side of the city. (It's a Louis Sullivan landmark—he'd worked on the church between 1899 and 1903.)

Iovanna Lloyd Wright was twenty-eight, and this was already her second marriage. She was going to be married three more times in her life—badly. If all of Wright's children, in one measure or another, had not-easy lives, there seems not much question that Iovanna's life was the hardest and saddest of all. It was drinking and sexual hungering and depression and bipolar disease, and not least was it a fearsome anger. She lived to be eighty-nine, dying in September 2015. She spent roughly her last twenty-five years in several Southern California nursing-homes-cum-sanatoriums. She was probably mentally ill for more than half of her life.

At that hopeful wedding in that ornate Sullivan church on that broiler afternoon, her father, who'd turned eighty-seven ten days earlier, was in a white suit and white shoes—he looked like a Kentucky colonel or maybe an ice cream man trying to enter heaven. The bridegroom was a lanky Taliesin apprentice named Arthur Pieper. Several dozen Taliesin Fellows attended. There were no pews in the church—during worship, the congregation stood in a square space dominated by an octagonal dome. The members of the Fellowship formed themselves in a quarter circle around the priest and the wedding couple and both sets of parents. The couple was facing the sanctuary. The celebrant had his incense boat on a gold chain, and he intoned prayers and swung the chain back and forth. He also had a small brazier with glowing coals. He walked around the couple several times, blessing them. On one of his passes, either the brazier or the incense bowl or perhaps it was a candle came too close to the bride's lace gown and silky white veil, which trailed nearly to the floor. The fabric burst into flame. Several Fellows leapt forward and batted out the fire with their feet and arms. The commotion may have lasted about a minute and a half before the calm was regained and the rites eventually taken up again, through the pungent smell of something newly burnt.

"All my life I have been plagued by fire. All my life I have been plagued by fire," the man in the ice cream suit was heard muttering to himself at the rear of the church. He is said to have been walking back and forth along a wall, tapping his cane softly on the Byzantine flooring.

They keep it under lock and key, in what is known as the "Classics Cage." The document is hardly the Magna Carta, but a Wright researcher could be forgiven for thinking so. It felt a bit like that to me the first time I held it: an annotated copy in Wright's own penciled hand of a first edition of John Lloyd Wright's My Father Who Is on Earth. You get to experience, as if in real time, the father's reactions to what the son had to say about him to the world: his anger, self-pity, recrimination, but also a surprising degree of acceptance and self-awareness.

This rare book, in the truest sense of that word, is part of the special collections at Avery Architectural and Fine Arts Library at Columbia University. If you have the proper credentials and fill out the proper forms, an archivist will bring out a gray box on a rolling cart. The box, known in the archive world as a "clamshell," folds outward. It's made of thin, stiff board, and is covered with a linen-like fabric known as buckram. Inside lies the treasure.

On the day of the publication of My Father Who Is on Earth, March 29, 1946, the deeply conflicted fifty-three-year-old son, with a quaking in his heart, sent his father a copy by parcel post. His father had not seen the book up until then. As has been said elsewhere in this narrative: the book is full of factual error, and the author's filial neediness on the page in places is almost painful to experience, and yet it's an absolutely necessary read for anyone hoping to gain fractions of insight into Frank Lloyd Wright. John Wright was there, beside his father, at crucial moments, not least at that moment of first shock on that August midday at Midway Gardens in 1914. And that makes him unique for history's sake.

On April 11, 1946, the marked-up copy of My Father came back to its author. Wright seems to have read and annotated the book in something like twenty-four hours (even if it didn't come back right away). There was a typed note. It was on a half-sheet of stationery, in the trademark Taliesin buff and Cherokee-red colors. "Dear John," the note said. "Herewith ungracious comments marked on the opus—itself—as I read." Next paragraph: "Kindly send me another one—will you?" Next paragraph: "Hope you and Frances are happy and get some money as well as fun *out of it all." There was a big swirl down to the signature line—almost as if Wright was making a rendering of something at his drawing board. It was signed: "Love—Dad." Beneath the "Dad" was his typed full name. So affectionate, so oddly formal.*

On the top left corner of the dust jacket of the book, John wrote in ink: "Author's Copy from Dad."

And inside? As was just said, Wright's anger, self-pity, ego—but, overall, his remarkably restrained response, a glimpse once again of his humanness, his vulnerability, the underestimated capacity for regret and self-awareness. Two examples will suffice:

On page 195, the publisher (it was G. P. Putnam's Sons) had printed a black-and-white photograph of Wright, but it came out in stark shadows. It looked like something in a badly inked Sunday rotogravure. It could almost have been a shot of Bela Lugosi as Count Dracula. Wright wrote beside it: "What a horrible looking monster! . . . serves me right? Dad." It's the question mark that's telling.

Then, on page 117. It's the end of a weird little chapter entitled "Frankie and Johnnie." John is trying to sum up his father. He's trying to soar: "I can think of him too as Don Quixote, to whom every windmill was a woman in distress. . . . I can think of him in his ball game with life never waiting for a base on balls. . . . Then again, I think of him in his great burst for freedom, jolting against the world at large with actions, at times, of shocking boldness; driving through life in chase of his own ideals, oblivious of the road signs, skidding from shoulder to shoulder. . . ." The passage winds up: "My impression of my whole life with him is one of comedy, tragedy, the sublime, the ridiculous, and I never knew where one left off and the other began."

Wright wrote thirty-eight words beneath, and on the left he drew a kind of parenthesis. His handwriting is light on the page—until the end. But all of the words are very legible, as if he was writing slowly and thinking things through. He wrote: "The man apparently was a sort of clever-confidence-man—winning by sheer dexterity over those of more solid worth and greater attainments—tho not 'unique.' Many suffered in silence that he might glitter . . . I know! I know!"

The exclamation point after the first "I know" is thick and black. He must have been pressing down very hard.

To time-frame things: Five months later, Svet and Daniel and Brandoch Peters somersaulted into three feet of swampy water.

Terminals (2)

Frank Lloyd Wright, March 1959, about a
month before his death

A gain, the yardstick of years, 1950–1959, elliptically, esoterically.
The Guggenheim, it has to start there.

No project dominated and plagued Frank Lloyd Wright's
last decade like the building of the Solomon R. Guggenheim Museum.
The basic plans had come into being between 1943 and 1945. Construction didn't start until 1956. The opening wasn't until October 21, 1959,
six months after Wright died. There is a Wright scholar named Bruce
Brooks Pfeiffer. He died on Christmas Eve in 2017, at age eighty-seven,
after serving for decades as the founding director of the Frank Lloyd

Wright Foundation Archives in Arizona. He wrote or edited or collabo-
rated on dozens of Wright books, including a volume of Wright's Guggenheim correspondence. In the preface to the letters book, Pfeiffer said
that the Guggenheim "is the story of a struggle that lasted seventeen
years. In the course of it the curator who commissioned the building
was fired, the donor died, a host of lesser protagonists came and went,
and the architect who created it never lived to see it in its finished form."

Neil Levine has also put things in focus. Fairly or unfairly, the structure that fronts Fifth Avenue, between East Eighty-Eighth and Eighty-
Ninth streets, facing Central Park, "came to be seen as the summation
of Wright's architectural thought and thus, to all intents and purposes,
the building by which his ultimate significance for modern architecture would generally be judged." Numerous books, and parts of books,
have been written about the museum, and more will come. Speaking
just from here, Levine's sixty-three-page chapter, "The Guggenheim
Museum's Logic of Inversion," in his *The Architecture of Frank Lloyd
Wright,* is *the* essential and readable treatment, while Ada Huxtable's
overview in her brief biography, *Frank Lloyd Wright,* is its own lyrical
summation. (The reader is aware by now of how much this narrative
is indebted to these two Wright scholars.) Huxtable defines the Guggenheim as Wright's "search for a plastic, sculptural architecture that
would be unbroken by conventional walls and floors, where mass and
space were one." To my way of thinking, that sentence could almost
be applied—even or especially with the word "plastic" in it—to all his
Prairie houses, to Unity Temple, to Fallingwater, to the Johnson Wax
buildings, to every Usonian. Wasn't it the same effort to have mass and
space somehow come out as a free-flowing one? In the Guggenheim—
again to quote Huxtable—the aim was to create a "continuous spiral
surrounding a great unitary space." And he did it, although not without
much compromise and accommodation, gnashing of his teeth.

What a strange-looking building, even now, after our collective eye
has long adjusted. Is there any other structure in Manhattan—or, really,
in the rest of America—that looks quite like the cream-colored and
smooth-spiraling stacked cylinder known universally by its shorthand
name? You can go to the Guggenheim, on any day of the week, summer
or winter, and someone will be standing outside on the sidewalk taking
photographs. As many chroniclers have said, the block-long building

itself (it's a very short block, about 250 feet) seems to wish to trump anything inside it. *His* art was going to be better than any art on the walls. Surely, that was one of his not-so-secret drivers all along.

The better shot of the exterior is from across the street, with one's back up against a retaining wall of Central Park. Is it a big white ice cream freezer? Is it a washing machine out of *Gulliver's Travels*? There is a famous *New Yorker* cartoon from 1958 (there have been many *New Yorker* cartoons about the Guggenheim), published about eleven months before the opening. A man and a woman are pictured from behind. They're in a sports car with the top down. Apparently, they're stopped in traffic. They're gazing over at the vaguely ominous moonship taking shape. You can't quite tell who's talking, although it seems to be the female. "Are they allowed to do that on Fifth Avenue?" she asks.

As the exterior, so the interior: the spiral serves as a single, overlapping gallery of reinforced concrete, rising six stories along its ascending ramps. But Wright didn't wish people to climb up through the galleries; he wanted them to descend *through* the art. The museumgoers would come into his vast atrium-lobby, take in his ramps and giant skylight overhead, be overwhelmed at the structural magnificence, ride an elevator to the sixth floor, step out, and then begin a slow, winding come-down through space, through time, through art, through—so he must have figured—Frank Lloyd Wright himself. His genius, that is.

The spiral as a form had long fascinated Wright, and there are clear antecedents to what became the unique phenomenon of the Guggenheim. He claimed to have gotten the basic idea from the ancient ziggurats of the Assyrians and Babylonians. Ziggurats were temples taking the form of terraced pyramids, of successively receding stories, approached by ramps. But his ziggurat would grow wider as it wound toward the top. (An "outward slant to the top," in Huxtable's words.) An inverted spiral, he claimed, was something "optimistic," not "pessimistic," which is what he had decided the pyramidal ziggurats of Mesopotamia were: pessimistic. What did he mean, exactly? If you go upward, narrowing as you go, toward a point, you're being essentially closed off to life and the world, whereas if you go upward, widening as you go, you're being essentially open to life and the world? Yes, except he didn't want you to climb upward; he wanted you to stroll downward. But, by that logic, you'd be going from wide to narrow—and so isn't that

"pessimistic"? Whatever. It sounds a little like the old snake-oil salesman in the heat of his pitch. In late September 1945, unveiling an early
model of the museum at the Plaza Hotel, the salesman had told sixty-
eight assembled reporters, some of whom were not quite convinced:
"Democracy demands this type of building. The thing you can't get any
more in church you ought to get here." William Carey Wright's son, in
his secular pulpit.

If the building is its own iconic and nearly inexpressible thing, then
the story of some of the people connected to the museum, to the long
trek of getting it built, lines up with some very mad-seeming folk. Even
a casual student of the Guggenheim would likely know that this is a reference first and foremost to the Baroness Hilla von Rebay, the museum's
curator and founding director. All you have to do is study Hilla's pictures. The queenliness, the exotica, the obduracy, the artiste-ness, the
great stylishness, the vanity, the intelligence, the gift for dramatization
and complication: they come almost instantly across. Even her full
name was operatic: Hildegard Anna Augusta Elizabeth Frelin Rebay
von Ehrenwiesen. She was born into the aristocracy of Germany and
had become a reputable abstract artist herself. She'd been a day away
from her fifty-third birthday when—on June 1, 1943, with the consent
of the "copper king," old Mr. Solomon Guggenheim, who had all the
money and who was her patron and employer—she'd sat down and
written by hand, on blue paper in blue ink, a letter to Wright at Taliesin.

"Could you ever come to New York and discuss with me a building
for our collection of non-objective paintings," she'd asked. "I feel that
each of these great masterpieces should be organized into space and
only you or so it seems to me would test the possibilities to do so." Three
times in the relatively brief letter she'd used the word "space." (Had
she divined it?) She'd closed by saying she wanted a "temple of spirit, a
monument!" It was a little like Mad Miriam standing aghast, in that first
letter to the reeling man, at the "immensity" (or was it "university") of
his sorrow. How did Frank Lloyd Wright find these women?

Except he thought that Hilla was a man. "I appreciate your appreciation," he'd responded nine days later, on the 10th, yes, he would be
interested, in principle, in accepting such a commission. "Why don't
you run down here for a week end? Bring your wife," he said.

The idea of "non-objective" art, or at least the concept of it in the baroness's head, was that it was capable of creating a different world order. Again, Huxtable: "They [the practitioners] claimed to have created a new kind of reality that extended pictorial space beyond the picture frame into real space, and that any division between the two ceased to exist." The inner peace one got from looking at the work of, say, Wassily Kandinsky or Max Ernst or Hans Richter was capable of solving mankind's problems. No more war, maybe no more hunger. Look at the pictures. Float with them. Be with them. S. R. Guggenheim, who was eighty-two when Hilla wrote to Wright, and who'd come to his passion for abstract art late in life, had established, with his wife, Irene, and under Hilla's seductive guidance, a temporary museum in a townhouse on Fifty-Fourth Street. There, the non-objective art wafted, as if free of material constraints, to the strains of Bach. The paintings were hung close to the floor, on pleated gray fabric.

Wright had ended up going to New York, and had met the baroness and Guggenheim, and by the end of June they'd entered into an agreement. By then, too, Wright was in his own sway to Hilla. Among her theories about life, never mind art, was that bloodletting was especially good for the constitution, and having all your teeth pulled wasn't a bad idea, either. Within weeks she had somehow convinced Wright and Olgivanna to submit themselves to a German physician in New York named Meyers. The doctor, reportedly, had them recline on hard leather sofas while he applied huge black leeches to their throats. (Was the Bach on?) By the middle of August, Wright had had three rounds of leeching. He'd also had all his teeth yanked and had been fitted with dentures. (There was a lifelong pattern in Wright for falling for bizarre medical and nutritional ideas. For a while, he was mad about consuming raw eggs at teatime.)

Soon enough, he and Hilla would be at each other's throats, forget the leeches. For the next nine years, or close to it, until Hilla got sacked (it was a forced resignation, in March 1952), the two would know their own kind of intractable marriage and war of the roses. It's all there in the letters. On December 18, 1943 (so six months after the initial contact, and the site not yet secured), Wright, still on the client honeymoon, had written his coming antagonist: "We are going west sometime late in January if all goes well—I hope we can get a plot before that time as I am so full of ideas for our museum that I am likely to blow up or commit suicide unless I can let them out on paper. That building ought to show how to show a painting." In six months, on July 6, 1944 (they'd gotten the site now, and the concept of a spiral was fully in his head), he'd be firing off this missive: "Dear Hilla: I wonder to whom have you been listening again." Next paragraph: "I foresee I am to have no client but am to have instead only a group of small critics whispering to you concerning something about which they can really know nothing. . . ." Four paragraphs down: "You see you are giving me a bad quarter of an hour, a sort of nightmare: because where I thought I had an appreciative, understanding strong and reliable client your note says to me that I have only a frustrated, vacillating prey. . . ." Second-to-last paragraph: "You know nothing about screens. . . ." He'd signed it "Sincerely, Frank Lloyd Wright."

By the time Hilla Rebay was finally out of the picture, Guggenheim himself had been dead for two and a half years (he had died on November 3, 1949), and his nephew Harry had come in as the chairman of the foundation's board of trustees. By then, too, the Museum of Non-Objective Painting had broadened its focus and had been renamed the Solomon R. Guggenheim Museum. There was now a whole new cast of antagonists. But, same story: on and on, the perfect storm of trouble and complication, out of the forties, rolling on into the fifties. In 1952, the New York Building Commission had denied a permit because of an alleged thirty-two code violations to the plans. It was sometime after this that arguably the most powerful man in all of New York, Robert Moses—who, just to thicken the plot, was distantly related to Frank Lloyd Wright by marriage; and who, as head of the city (and state) park systems, and as the city construction coordinator, and as a member of the city planning commission, could pretty much work his will at will—reportedly said at a meeting of the building commission: "Damn it, get a permit for Frank. I don't care how many laws you have to break." Not that Robert Moses had any real love for modern art, much less for the building that his roundabout cousin was planning to erect. Still, it would be almost another four years before a permit would finally get issued and construction started. "I will have a building permit on my desk by 8 a.m. tomorrow or there will be a new building commissioner," Moses reportedly said in a phone call to the department commissioner in late March 1956. It was there the next morning, or that is the legend.

Demolition work began on May 7, 1956. That morning, on page 29, *The New York Times* ran a story, with a sketch of the museum. (The story was alongside a piece about President Eisenhower having selected a new and rather boring official portrait of himself: yin to the yang.) The next day, the *Times* published an editorial entitled "The Hot Cross Bun." "With due respect for the talents and audacity of Frank Lloyd Wright, we must say that we were somewhat aghast at the sketch published in this newspaper yesterday," the editors wrote. "The net effect, if we may say so, will be precisely that of an oversized and indigestible hot cross bun." Not quite three years before, on September 5, 1953, in a piece running to more than three hundred words, "Mr. Wright's Architecture," the editorial page had taken up for him entirely: "New York still has no building by America's most renowned architect. Will New York continue to be rigid in its refusal to give him a chance to demonstrate his genius in our town?" That was then.

Construction started later in the spring. The contract went for $2.5 million, but the final cost would exceed that figure by another million. It was the middle of 1956. At Christmastime, in his empurpled suite at the Plaza (call it heavily streaked with lavender, more about which soon), an eighty-nine-year-old would be telling his baby sis about a dream he'd just had that afternoon. About his father. About playing the organ in the Weymouth church. About pumping the bellows. "I heard it, Sis, in the dream, very distinctly, every note as he used to play it."

————

Wishes were fishes, there would have been a lot more in this narrative about some of Frank Lloyd Wright's old apprentices—Kamal Amin, for instance, a courtly and elegant and extremely intelligent man, a native of Egypt (his name is pronounced Kah-MALL Ah-MEN), who is living, as this is written, in an assisted living facility in Scottsdale, Arizona. He came to work at Taliesin from Cairo in 1951 at age twenty-one, spurning his family's wealth and position. He got to observe Wright, and sometimes at arm's length, for almost the entirety of his final decade. (Yes, Kamal was there, on that late Friday afternoon, in Chicago, in the Orthodox cathedral, to hear the cane's soft tapping on the Byzantine flooring, and, a little earlier, to leap forward with his mates and help put out the burning bridal veil. He recounted it for me brilliantly.)

"Without Mr. Wright, I wouldn't have had a life," Kamal once said. It was in one of our earliest conversations. He hadn't yet entered assisted living. We were driving around Phoenix looking at some of the master's work as well as some of his own. I asked if he had a small case of hero worship? "Oh, a large case," he answered, laughing. Then he said, "God must have done a lot of work to produce this human being. An accident like that just doesn't happen." Then he said, "Everybody born one hundred and forty-seven years ago is now dead. Except for Frank Lloyd Wright. He can make you as mad today as he could one hundred years ago."

Another time, he talked about Wright's hands. (We were at lunch, and the then octogenarian, twice divorced, with his daily bouts of vertigo, was flirting madly with the female server.) He held up the slender, parchment-like fingers of his own right hand. He spread them wide. Then, with the thumb and forefinger of his other hand, he began tracing a kind of invisible sheath, or sleeve, down the first two fingers on his right hand. He did this several times without looking up. He almost seemed no longer there. It was as if the sheathing motion, tracing motion, beautiful to witness, was helping him to remember. It was as if it was some kind of tactile mnemonic device. Then, in a speech still laced with the cadences of his native ground, he said:

His hands. Oh, my goodness, his hands. You couldn't believe his hands. Magic sprang out of his hands. He'd sit down beside me at the drawing board. He'd scoot me over. Or even before he sat down, he'd walk along and tap you on the shoulder. That was just magic. That was the magical moment. He was scooting you over or tapping you on the shoulder, and then you knew: he was going to sit down beside you for a little while in the drafting room. He was going to look at your work. You'd get him all to yourself. He'd take up one of my pencils. His line, such a strong, quick line. How did he do that? It was flowing right out of his fingertips. The way he would maneuver the triangle on the paper, like a surgeon with his knife. The triangle would become part of his left hand. In his other hand was the pencil. His right hand was in a dance with his left hand. Sometimes, he'd be humming to himself. Sometimes, as he'd turn the triangle on the sheet, make a quick new line down the straight edge, the tools would catch the light, bounce it. I'd be holding my breath. In the next half hour, you were the luckiest person in the world. Getting to watch those magic hands at work.

I looked up from my scribbling. "Damn, your heart must have been pounding at some of those moments."

"It's pounding now," he said.

———

It doesn't quite seem possible—except it's true—that the elderly man waging his near-constant battles through the fifties with the Guggenheim should also have been at work with his apprentices and associates on the design for the Anderton Court Shops in Beverly Hills. And the Kalita Humphreys Theater in Dallas. And the Marin County Civic Center in San Rafael, California. And Herman T. Fasbender's medical clinic in Hastings, Minnesota. And the Pilgrim Congregational Church in Redding, California. And the Juvenile Cultural Center at Wichita State University in Kansas. And the Dudley Spencer residence at 619 Shipley Road in Wilmington, Delaware. And the Wyoming Valley Grammar School in Wyoming Valley, Wisconsin. And Seamour and Gerte Shavin's house on Missionary Ridge in Chattanooga. And the Robert and Elizabeth Muirhead Farmhouse in Plato Center, Illinois. And the R. W. Lindholm service station at the edge of the Fond du Lac Indian Reservation in Cloquet, Minnesota. And (speaking of cars), the luxury showroom at 430 Park Avenue in Manhattan for European importer Maximilian Hoffman. That's an even dozen Wright works (in more or less random listing), and there were so many others: conceived, commissioned, semi-drawn, fully drawn, realized, never realized. Sometimes, the list of Wright's fifties projects and the places where the projects were located begins to sound like a gazetteer of America itself.

Another *how-is-it-possible*. Namely, how is it possible that Frank Lloyd Wright has had his work built in three centuries: nineteenth, twentieth, and twenty-first? It sounds like a typo. It isn't. The Blue Sky Mausoleum in Buffalo—completed in 2004, holding twenty-four crypts, the conception for which he first began talking about with his old friend and usually exasperated client, Darwin Martin, in 1925, and whose cascading marble design he drew in 1928—is among the handful of posthumous Wright structures, large and small, realized in the current century. It's getting its own special mention here almost for the name itself. Blue Sky Mausoleum: the heavens above, the green earth below. Fitting in perfectly with the gospel of the organic. The structure, open-aired, on the brow of a hill, is located in the city's Forest Lawn Cemetery. In a way, a pity the man himself can't lie there.

Three Wright scholars on the complicated subject of his fifties work, some of which was temporary in nature and is long gone.

Ada Huxtable:

> It has never been possible to deny the power and original-ity of Wright's architectural imagination, no matter what form it assumed, but much of his late work has remained a subject of controversy. He increasingly created a world of his own, full of bright color, exotic references, and futuristic imagery, with flying saucers, screens, spires, statues, and polychrome, jewel-like decora-tion, that is a curious mélange of Buck Rogers, the *Arabian Nights,* and Native-American sources. Critics and historians who lavishly praised his earlier work found this decorative exuberance over the top. . . . Two of the most respected architectural writers of the 1970s, Manfredo Tafuri and Francesco dal Co, saw it as all downhill: a kind of "science fiction architecture" in which a "selfconscious exoticism" deteriorated to the level of "ultrakitsch."

Robert McCarter, whose work has been instrumental to getting this book done (he is a practicing architect as well as a university professor and a prolific author):

> Every sketch from Wright's hand was now, by definition, a stroke of genius. Apprentices recall Wright, after dashing off a drawing at his board, saying to himself, *sotto voce* but still loud enough so all could hear, 'I'm a genius this morning.' Genius of this sort does not feel compelled to explain itself, nor is it accountable or responsible to anything except its own whims. . . . As a result, the integration of space, function, construction, human scale and landscape that had always been Wright's unifying and primary principle of design

now began to disappear from his work, and a kind of disintegration began to dominate many of his larger designs.

Neil Levine: "One of the reasons for the difficulty of Wright's work in the fifties is its sheer quantity; another is its variety; still another, and undoubtedly the most important, is its apparent eccentricity in comparison with the rest of contemporary production."

Levine has an intriguing word for much of the late work: "unassimilable." Something not to be metabolized. Could it be that we're still too close, that it will take another fifty or seventy-five years as a culture for us to understand what Wright was really up to in his final decade?

In the meantime, to speak of five:

He designed Annunciation Greek Orthodox Church in Wauwatosa, Wisconsin, in 1956, but the building wasn't completed until 1961, two years after his death. It has been called a wonderwork of form and structure, with a geometrically exact floor plan and a concrete-dome shell set ingeniously on thousands of steel bearings, so that it can expand and contract in Wisconsin's extreme weather. At the top of this flying saucer (as Wauwatosans are known to refer to it), there is a series of semicircular windows. They look like eyeballs, from a hydra-headed alien. As more than one critic has said, the bejeweled saucer-church seems to be lifting off the ground, not arising out of it, which would seem to be against every organic preachment.

The H. C. Price Company Tower in Bartlesville, Oklahoma, has won major architectural awards. Wright built it between 1952 and 1956 for the owner of a Bartlesville pipeline construction firm. It's nineteen stories tall, with 37,000 square feet, and was designed as a multi-use structure, to house corporate headquarters and apartment residences and other professional offices. It stands, as if a strange greenish-blue tree, having been taken from its forest and replanted into the middle of a small city (or large town) in the northeastern Oklahoma oil fields. Something about it feels naked. Something about it feels gaudy. Four central shafts of steel-reinforced concrete support the building, like the trunk of a tree. Its concrete floor slabs are cantilevered, like branches. The tower is sheathed in copper and tinted glass. (Its turquoise color derives from the oxidized copper.) Wright is said to have modeled the structure on his unrealized 1929 design for an apartment tower at St. Mark's-in-the-Bouwerie in lower Manhattan. I remember the Sunday I drove there from Tulsa to take the tour. The building felt airless and cramped. Wright's custom furniture, much of it in red hexagonal patterns, seemed straight out of the Jetsons. I couldn't wait to get away.

Beth Sholom Synagogue on the outskirts of Philadelphia, in Elkins Park, Pennsylvania. Advocates, and they are not few, have called this structure—which Wright didn't live long enough to see open its doors, and that overran its cost by nearly three times the original estimate—the definition of holy light. The building is a kind of triangular pyramid sitting on a six-sided base. A 160-ton steel tripod frame holds everything in place. The sloping main sanctuary seats 1,100 people. Wright said the design of the interior was meant to suggest hands cupped together: a people "resting in the very hands of God." The roof over the sanctuary is 100 feet tall and is held up by three 117-foot-long steel beams, allowing the inside to seem to float free of all internal support. The main place of worship is one large room, with overhead translucent panels made of corrugated wire glass and plastic. It's as if you're praying in a gigantic light-infused teepee. When I drove over on a late spring afternoon, the sunlight filtering through the corrugated wire-glass panels was striking. But the building as a whole left me even colder than I had anticipated. It seemed out of scale, too massive for its leafy residential neighborhood. It was as if Mount Sinai had come to the near suburbs. The architecture, at least to my eye, was ugly, even garish. In the main room, I counted at least thirty rain buckets, along with two plastic wading pools, the kind that three-year-olds love to splash around in when it's ninety degrees in the backyard. "All these years, it's never stopped leaking," the docent said. "We can't seem to fix it. We put up with it for the magnificence." But, actually, the buckets and wading pools (all had small puddles in them) were the best part of the tour, for it was as if they were bringing the humanness right back.

His "Taliesin East," or "Taliesin the Third": students of Wright know that this refers to a suite of rooms, numbers 223–225, at New York's Plaza Hotel, which Wright took over in the summer of 1954, on a semi-permanent basis, as both office and home away from home, so as to be closer to the Guggenheim struggles. Through the years, he had stayed often at the Plaza, and he and his wife were in various rooms and suites there earlier in the fifties, but by August of '54, the evidence suggests that he had claimed 223–225 as his own and had begun to redecorate the space outlandishly. The suite was on the northeast corner, on the second floor. These were the best rooms in the hotel, affording panoramas of both Fifth Avenue and Central Park. Christian Dior had once lived in this suite, as had Diamond Jim Brady, or this is the legend. Wright loved telling people he'd turned the joint into "Diamond Jim Brady Modern"—which, according to the descriptions I've read, and the photographs and film snippets I've seen, would almost understate the case. To quote again Wright scholars Jane King Hession and Debra Pickrel, in their excellent *Frank Lloyd Wright in New York: The Plaza Years, 1954–1959:* "In the living room, Wright employed a sophisticated color palette of gold, rose, deep purple/red, peach, and black. The wall surfaces . . . were covered with Japanese rice paper flecked with gold leaf, set within frames of gilded wood molding on rose colored walls. . . . He detailed the windows in four layers, adding floor-to-near-ceiling drapes in a rich purple/red velvet. . . . The hassocks were topped with peach velvet cushions, which Wright specified were to be secured with 'black cord tipped with scarlet balls.' " What on earth did the architect have in mind? A Nob Hill bordello in Victorian San Francisco? One of those storied brothels on Basin Street in Storyville in turn-of-the-century New Orleans?

One more work of the final decade—meant to go against everything said in the previous four paragraphs. The Seth Peterson Cottage at Wisconsin's Mirror Lake State Park. In her bare organic beauties (yes, let her be endowed with the feminine gender), in her tininess, in her out-of-the-wayness, I believe that this simple-seeming structure can be thought of as one of Wright's greatest works, bar none. The building is Wright's smallest residential design: 880 square feet. The building is his last Wisconsin commission. The building is a variation on the Usonian form, constructed of locally quarried sandstone and Douglas-fir-faced plywood and cedar shingles and glass. A fireplace separates the main dining and living area from the Lilliputian kitchen, which connects to a single bedroom and bath. The flagstone floors are radiant heated, and the stone projects outward under the interior walls to create a terrace. As with other Usonians, you almost don't know where the inside ends and the outside begins, and part of this is due to the floor-to-ceiling glass in the main room. The place is a kind of wood-and-glass hutch, with a steeply pitched roof. Except that there's also a kind of monumentality, and possibly that's because of the great chimney and walls, which rise almost two stories over the bathroom and kitchen. Best of all, the Seth Peterson (as those who know the building often refer to it, without needing to add the word "cottage") appears to hang on the edge of a steep bank that dives down through the trees to undisturbed Mirror Lake: despite her height, she's nestled in there, a part of the landscape. This is the first Frank Lloyd Wright home ever to be rented out to Wright-goers for overnight stays. (Not cheaply.) Rentals have been permitted since 1992, the year of her little-publicized comeback.

Long before I got to experience in the flesh this tiny jewel on a narrow lake in the Wisconsin woods, I got curious about her namesake and original owner, principally because the words "untimely death" kept showing up in the various official Wright-sponsored writings about the work. What did that mean? There are many spooky things about the namesake's life and death, and only one of them is that Seth Peterson and Frank Lloyd Wright shared the same birthday: sixty-nine years apart in age, exactly. Peterson was an asthmatic child, with a soft and almost effeminate side. He grew up not particularly good with girls. He loved art. He was a talented pianist. He was from Black Earth, Wisconsin, which is west of Madison, on the way to Spring Green. While still in boyhood, he got on to the houses of Frank Lloyd Wright. In high school in Black Earth, he and one of his best friends, Bert Goderstad, used to do whatever they could to connect to the great man's architecture. More than once, they rode the train down to Chicago and then a commuter out to Oak Park just to stand on the sidewalk and look at Wright houses. Other times, they would drive out toward Spring Green in the Peterson family DeSoto, hoping to catch a glimpse of Wright. Once, they got an impromptu tour of Taliesin.

In early 1954, when he was seventeen, Seth applied for an apprenticeship at Taliesin, but he was too young and besides couldn't afford the tuition. Over the next few years, he seems to have applied again, unsuccessfully. Meanwhile, Bert Goderstad had gone on to St. Olaf College in Minnesota, while Seth had become an IBM computer operator at the state's motor vehicles department. In the summer of 1957, now twenty-one, having been rejected yet again for an apprenticeship, he enlisted in the army and was sent to Europe. But his asthma worsened and he received a discharge nine months after his enlistment. He came back to Wisconsin and got his old job back with the state. He dreamed of being able to live in his own specially designed Wright house. Two or three times, he is said to have approached Wright. No go. Finally, Seth mailed him a retainer. (It is said to have been as much as a thousand dollars; there seems no documentary record of it.) Wright, being Wright, apparently cashed the money. Now he was stuck. Seth, meanwhile, had acquired a ledge of land up near Wisconsin Dells, about fifty miles northwest of Madison. Seth, meanwhile, had fallen in love. Over the next year, the plans for a Wright cottage at Mirror Lake got developed. Construction began in mid-1959. Wright had suddenly died that April. The work continued. On and off for the next year, on weekends, Seth and his fiancée camped out in sleeping bags as their castle rose around them.

And something went wrong. He broke up with his fiancée. There are stories about his having gotten into financial trouble with construction loans. There are other and unconfirmed stories of a darker kind. What can be said is that on Easter Sunday, April 17, 1960, Seth Condon Peterson hanged himself in his family's basement. He'd been living with his parents. His mother found him about 3:15 that afternoon. He didn't leave a note. He was twenty-three, less than two months from turning twenty-four. The coroner ruled it "a suicide as a result of general despondency." That was in the next day's paper. The funeral was at the family Lutheran church.

In the years after, the house spiraled downward. In 1966, the state of Wisconsin took over the property. The cottage got neglected and then boarded up. For about twenty years, she stood empty and deteriorating. And then in 1989, some dedicated preservationists and Wright-lovers formed the nonprofit Seth Peterson Cottage Conservancy. It took three years and something like $300,000 to bring her back. She's there now, renewed, pristine, like the lake she perches above.

Bert Goderstad is in his eighties and lives in Hastings, Minnesota. In a long telephone conversation, he said he's never been able to figure it out, the suicide. "If I had been there that afternoon, it wouldn't have happened, no, it would not have happened, I would have somehow kept it from happening," he said. Of the cottage at Mirror Lake, he said: "It's beautiful, and quiet, and modest, like Seth's own life." He added: "It's just a mystery." Had he ever heard stories of other tragedies connected to Wright houses? He'd heard of a few. Then: "Why do you think that is, the tragedies?" I didn't really answer, but the word "unassimilable" was in my head.

———

Yardstick of years: On March 31, 1956 (so just when the building permit for the Guggenheim was finally going through), an eighty-eight-year-old said in a letter that he "would consider myself in my dotage if I were to in the least go out of my way to institute comparisons with those who are comparative children in the realm I spiritually inhabit." Forty-six Marches before, same date, writing from his "little cream white villa" in Fiesole, Italy, a forty-two-year-old had said in a three-page seemingly shame-filled letter to his British friend, C. R. Ashbee: "I have believed a terrible thing to be right and have sacrificed to it those who loved me and my work in what must seem a selfish, cruel waste of life and purpose. . . . I want to live true as I would build true." That letter was quoted several hundred pages ago. Wright had fled America with Mamah, leaving Kitty Wright and his family behind, as Mamah had left Edwin and her children behind. If his March 31, 1910, letter is shame-filled, fear-filled, and it is, it's also full of his ego and arrogance. To get it all, you must study what's beneath each sentence.

As that, so this: The March 31, 1956, letter with the "dotage" sentence was written to fellow architect Oscar Stonorov, who'd helped arrange the European tour of *Sixty Years of Living Architecture*. You can read the stylized language and perhaps hear only the ego. But in truth a great anxiety is under this remark. Beneath this sentence is Wright's fear of being replaced by those hated glass-box makers of the International Style—like Ludwig Mies van der Rohe. It doesn't matter that he is everywhere on television, that he pops up in *Look, Esquire, The Saturday Evening Post, Holiday, Time, Life*. It doesn't matter how many commissions. (In just 1949–1950, Wright's office received more than sixty commissions.) It doesn't matter how many awards and honorary degrees. (In 1949, the American Institute of Architects awarded him its highest honor, the Gold Medal, for a lifetime's achievement.) The fear of being a has-been, that the Internationalists are superseding him, is alive and real.

Two months after the dotage sentence, Wright appeared as a mystery guest on the hugely popular Sunday night TV game panel show, *What's My Line?** You can watch the old footage and feel a certain sympathy for him—not that he's in his dotage, no, no. He's the evening's first challenger. (Liberace will sign in later.) The celebrities on the panel don their blindfolds. He enters from the left and chalks his name slowly but with a grandness on the blackboard. He starts to turn in the opposite direction of where he's supposed to go. "Uh, right here, if you will, please, sir," says urbane and bow-tied moderator John Daly, showing him to the desk. "World Famous Architect" appears in large white letters on the screen for the viewing audience. He acknowledges he's not an expert on the format. "Somewhat," he says to Daly. "I've watched one of the shows with interest." Daly's job is to rule on the questions and to flip the cards when a line of query goes wrong. The guest is having trouble hearing some of the questions. Daly is helping him along, interceding. Soon enough, though, the old charm and wit emerge.

"You have a very impressive speaking voice," says Dorothy Kilgallen, behind her fold.

"This service that you perform, sir, do you use your hands?" asks Peter Lawford.

About ten minutes in, and having used up just four of the allotted ten wrong questions, the panel is able to identify him. (Put it down as just another proof of his fame.)

"Have you built anything recently, or are you active now in some new designs?" Daly asks, after the masks are off, doing chitchat before the commercial break and next guest.

"Did you say active? I'm in harness." (How dare Daly ask a question like that.)

This was at the beginning of the summer. At the end of that summer, and continuing into the fall, something else happened that put Frank Lloyd Wright's insecurity and ego neediness on far greater display: his

---

* The date was June 3, 1956. Another time frame: Seven days earlier, in Wisconsin, before flying east for the show and other business, he'd said in his Sunday Talk to the Taliesin Fellowship: "There you are. So that's very largely the reason why we're all confused, we're all wandering about here with no place to go like Jephthah without a father. There seems to be no home. No spiritual home."

straight-faced promotion of his supposed Mile High Skyscraper. He
debased himself with this stunt, and on some fundamental level he had
to know. On August 25, at Taliesin, he gave an audience to a reporter
for the *Chicago Tribune*. The reporter's story (there was no byline on it),
published the next morning in two columns of page one of the Sunday
paper, had him "reclined" as he gave the interview. The Empire State
Building "would be a mouse by comparison," he said. The structure was
to be a government office building for Chicago, and he saw it rising on
the lakefront, near the Adler Planetarium. The reporter noted that the
Board of Trade building, the city's tallest structure, was forty-four stories and rose 612 feet off the ground, so that Wright's proposed building,
at 5,280 feet, would exceed it by more than eight times. "It's feasible,"
Wright was quoted as saying. "It's thoroughly scientific. It's Chicago's if
Chicago wants it." He said there were "several prominent Chicagoans"
seriously interested. He wasn't at liberty to say their names.

But didn't he despise cities? Wasn't he a fierce advocate of decentral-
ization? Wasn't he contradicting himself? His ready answer: "If we're
going to have centralization, why not quit fooling around and have it,
because it looks like it will take a century to decentralize as it is."

He'd calculated right: Papers around the country picked up the story
and rolled with it.

That fall, he rolled into Chicago for a three-day blitz. (*Sixty Years
of Living Architecture* was also on exhibit.) On October 16, he held a
midday press conference in the ballroom of the Sherman House Hotel.
By now, he had refined and elaborated on his idea. Not only would his
528-story "Mile High Illinois" hold 100,000 people, but there also would
be room in it for 15,000 cars and 100 helicopters. The cost was probably going to exceed $100 million, so some visionaries would have to
be willing to get behind him. The structure was going to have elevators
that weren't really elevators, suspended on cables, but something closer
to atomic-powered vertical trains, five cars tall, running on ratchets, as
in a cog railway. His "taproot" foundation would consist of sinking a
central concrete mast deep into bedrock. Unlike the ordinary and boring skyscraper, with floors the same size stacked one on top of the other,
his bold bid was to allow floors to be of various sizes and to cantilever
from the central mast.

Maybe fifteen reporters and a couple TV crews and some others who had wandered in were present at the event. (One attendee had not wandered in at all. He'd driven down from Wisconsin early that morning: Seth Peterson.)

Wright stood at a microphone. Behind him was a twenty-two-foot-high rendering on canvas, colored in shades of gold and silver and blue. "This is the Illinois, gentlemen," he announced. "In it will be consolidated all government offices now scattered around Chicago." The drawing showed a needle-like structure growing narrower as it climbed. The story in the next day's *Tribune* (SKY CITY PLAN NO IDLE DREAM, SAYS WRIGHT) was pretty much buried on page 8 in section 4. By now the editors must have sensed a need to back off. (The piece ran alongside a story about a man named Stanley Greak who'd climbed up 120 feet on the Van Buren Street Bridge the morning before. He'd refused to come down until the firemen brought him a pint of wine. He'd tried this before. By the time they'd lured him down, a high-wire artist over at the Sherman House was in full oratorical mode. The headline on the piece about the bridge-climber was REPEAT STUNT.) There were half a dozen Wrightian quotes in the piece. The most revealing remark in the story: "I detest seeing the boys fooling around and making their buildings look like boxes. Why not design a building that really is tall?" The boys? That was a reference to the Internationalists, and perhaps specifically to Mies van der Rohe, whose monolithic twin pair of glass-and-steel apartment towers, at 860–880 North Lake Shore Drive, had won praise, and not just in Chicago, when completed five years earlier. The boys? Mies was not quite nineteen years younger than the man standing at the microphone.

This was on October 17. Chicago mayor Richard J. Daley had proclaimed it "Frank Lloyd Wright Day." That evening, also at the Sherman House, there was a benefit banquet in Wright's honor. The mayor attended and presented a plaque. Eight hundred people are said to have paid $25 a plate. The raised money was going to be put toward perpetuating the Taliesin Fellowship. Olgivanna Wright was there on her husband's arm. When her husband took the podium, he denounced nearly everything, including the state of education, cities, American culture, his fellow architects. On cars: "The automobile makers ought to be ashamed of themselves. The modern automobile is a designed monstrosity." *Ashamed of themselves?*

Perhaps the real cause of his dyspepsia was the no-shows. He had asked Robert Moses to be the main speaker, but Moses had begged off. He had then asked Lewis Mumford. Mumford didn't want to break away from his work and fly out to Chicago for a one-nighter, but thought he might do it, as a way of helping to repair past ill feelings. But then, studying the invite more closely, he realized he was being asked to be a party to something essentially circusy. Years later, in *Sketches from a Life*, recalling Wright's publicity ploy, which was the only way he could view the Mile High, Mumford wrote: "In that project all of Wright's egocentric weaknesses were crystallized in an ultimate fantasy, conceived as if by a lineal descendant of Kublai Khan. What a monument of futility. . . . Naturally, I could not lend myself to a proposal that violated every canon of Wright's own conception of an organic architecture, as well as my own. If this was what old age had done to Wright, I had no desire to exalt his mummified remains."

No one ever took Wright up on his gimmick—er, idea. No one ever came close.

———

You have read relatively little in this narrative about Wright's Madison boyhood—a fuller account kept giving way to other material, and so the story had to be picked up largely by osmosis. But here, near the end, are two documented and interrelated facts about his boyhood. First: From his sixth grade (in 1878) through his junior year of high school (1884), Wright spent part of every late spring and early summer working—much against his will—on the Wyoming Valley farms of his maternal uncles, particularly the farm of his uncle James Lloyd Jones. It was dawn-to-dusk labor, six days a week, of "adding tired to tired," as Wright said in his autobiography (and repeated through the rest of his life, after he had come to understand and honor, not despise, the experience). Anna Wright had put him to this agricultural sweat for several reasons, not least her fear that her long-tressed, mama-adored, intellectually bent son was turning into a sissy.

Fact two: In Madison, on or near the playground of Second Ward School (it was a block away from the unhappy home on Gorham Street), probably in the autumn of 1879 (so he would have been twelve then), Wright met Robie Lamp, destined to become, almost immediately, his best boyhood friend. It might be more accurate to say his only true boyhood friend. In a sense, Robie (it was pronounced ROW-bee) Lamp was Wright's pre–Cecil Corwin. His Cecil before Cecil was exactly a year older than Wright (born on June 8, 1866), and would live only to age forty-nine. Robie had red hair and blue eyes and freckles—and badly withered legs. They "were shriveled, and dangled dead," Wright wrote in *An Autobiography*. He moved along on crutches. His upper body was extra strong, "because the legs were helpless." In the way of kids anywhere, the neighborhood kids could be awful. They called him "Cripple." They waited for him after school. "The schoolboys teased the cripple—unmercifully," Wright wrote, and from what the scholarship on Robert M. Lamp has since shown, he wasn't, at least for once, exaggerating.

From *An Autobiography*: "Savagely, squat-on-the-ground, he would strike out at them, those powerful arms of his swinging the brass-shod crutches. The tormentors were careful to keep out of reach but enough of them together could get him and in this autumn . . . they would bury him in the leaves until he was all but smothered, wherefrom he would finally emerge, raging, sputtering and crying."

Next paragraph: "Plucked up by his farm training of a season, the boy rescued him. Drove off the boys cruelly picking on him; got the crutches they had wisely thrown so far out of his reach; dusted him off; got him up on them and on his smile again." If even fractions of this actually happened, wouldn't it be just one more reason to be willing to reassess all that we think we know about the obnoxiously self-absorbed Frank Lloyd Wright? In any case, they apparently became fast friends from that moment, sharing their passions for inventing, drawing, designing, letterpress printing. (They built an iceboat and went out on Lake Mendota's 9,740 acres.)

From the first paragraph in which Robie appears, exactly as with Cecil, the author of *An Autobiography* seems to be guiding us to think of the relationship between the two as having been something deeper than the word "friendship" can convey—or at least this is my reading of it. In that first paragraph of Robie's introduction, Wright says, again speaking of himself in the third person: "More than ever shy, the boy had need of few friends but somehow always needed one intimate companion. He couldn't live, move and have his being, so it seemed, without a heart-to-heart comrade. Even then." (This is from the 1932 edition. In the 1943 edition, he kept the same passage, and in the next paragraph spoke of him as "that inseparable companion.")

Earlier, I wrote: "The guess is that Wright's feelings toward Cecil, right from the start, were something powerful and equivocal and disconcerting all at once, but not quite acted upon." The reason I felt able to write that sentence was because of what Wright himself seemed to wish me as a reader to know—or I could only take it that way. I also wrote, as regards the possibility of an actual physical relationship: "Anything is possible. Human beings can be hard-wired in their sexuality in unknowable ways—and thank God for it." I also wrote, as regards the sexually freighted language that Wright employs in so many of the Cecil passages, especially at the start: "Far from being unaware of what he's doing, he's absolutely aware. And at the core of the awareness is something decent. It's his own form of homage, his own expression of solidarity and kinship and gratitude. Gratitude for all that Cecil gave him, back there, when he'd been so young and inexperienced and know-nothing hungry."

I can only apologize for quoting myself.

But why bring up any of this now? Because I believe (if cannot prove) that Frank Lloyd Wright, that notorious American lothario (which is what I called him in the Cecil chapter), with his many tabloid sexual scandals, possessed of what seems to have been, from everything that can be determined, a heterosexual libido almost on the order of Chaplin's or Valentino's, always had in him a capacity for an equivocal something else.

Is this to suggest that the high-sexed man was probably bisexual, or had bisexual leanings? Yes. Do I have any real proof? I do not. Do I have any notion that he ever once acted on his bisexuality, if that indeed is what it was? I do not.

And why would any of it really matter? Because I believe that there is a connection to be made, and not an overreaching one, between what I have just said and the seemingly hard-to-reckon work of the fifties, or at least a lot of the work. Indeed, I think there is a connection to be made to the "artistic semi-elegant negligee" into which an unhappy Carl Sandburg was apparently fitted at least once in his life. I think that all of this, and more, every bit of it, is trying to show us the person that

Frank Lloyd Wright really was. And, to his immense credit, he wished us to know. At the end of his life, he was consciously and unconsciously allowing a deeper, fuller portrait of himself to appear, to come forth, in edges and pieces, and one way he showed it was in some of the built work itself. This, from the same person (as I have tried to show) who was so deeply worried in his last years about his architectural legacy. Only another piece of the impossible puzzle palace.

To quote Huxtable again: "[I]n old age, the work tends to become freer and more experimental, less caring about expectations and conventions. When Picasso reworked the old masters in bold, personal interpretations, the paintings were considered by many to be a disappointing coda to his career. Late work is often treated as a form of senile decadence. Almost always problematic, it is often dismissed or discreetly ignored."

So I wonder—with full apology to both Levine and Huxtable—if the word "unassimilable" isn't right at all, and whether the work *is* so "problematic." Perhaps we don't need another fifty or seventy-five years as a culture to figure out what historians and critics call "late Wright." Perhaps the meanings, some of them, have long been right there, hiding from us in plain sight.

On the excessively healthy heterosexual libido that was apparently at full rage nearly right up to the end: It's known that Olgivanna Wright was prone to tell intimates how her husband wanted to have sex with her two and three times a day in the mid- and late fifties. Sometimes she'd bring it up without warning to apprentices at Taliesin. "I just can't do it," she'd say. I have talked to three former apprentices who told me that she had told them that. Was Olgivanna protesting a bit too loudly? I would guess not. I would bet he *was* a randy old goat, if not to the very end, then close to it. (They'd long had separate bedrooms, but that wouldn't have stopped anything.) And yet, at the same time, I wonder if Olgivanna wasn't secretly fretting about masculinity "optics," no less than Anna Wright had once fretted that her prize son, marked for his immortality, was in danger of turning into a teenage sissy. Was Olgivanna worried about, say, late-life, off-the-cuff remarks on Chicago television sets about velvet pantaloons? Worried about what some visitors might make of an effeminate-seeming suite of rooms at the Plaza? And so she'd stoke the other side a little? Oh, maybe just dewy theories.

Robert M. Lamp, who appears in *An Autobiography* in a much smaller way than Cecil Corwin, had a distinguished career in Madison, both in state and city government and in private business. Wright built him a kind of blocky Prairie foursquare and also a lake cottage called Rocky Roost. He stayed a bachelor nearly all of his life, until 1913, when he quickly married his housekeeper, who was half his age, and who had a five-year-old son. He was said to have been a happily married man and a fine stepfather, the more so because these gifts had arrived late. But that child died of pneumonia in little more than a year. The Lamps adopted another child, and, again, Robie was said to be struck at so much luck. But in not even a year from the adoption, he fell ill with kidney and heart problems (probably the lifelong withered limbs had a role, too), and he died quickly, on March 6, 1916, in a local sanatorium.

———

Wasn't he too indestructible to die? He'd had at least one stroke a year or so earlier, and was taking an anticoagulant called dicumarol. These days he was apt to stand with his mouth sagged open a little, staring into middle space. The dizziness could come and go without warning. Still, the neurons fired, or mostly. And almost always he was up early, at the work.

Frances, his second-youngest by Catherine, just sixty, had died that February on the East Coast. A shock. A month later, on March 24, 1959, his long-ago first wife died on the West Coast. Catherine had been in a sanatorium for a long while, since a fall. She'd had a marriage after her marriage to Wright, but it hadn't worked out. Kitty was eighty-seven, a day away from her eighty-eighth birthday. Meryle Secrest reports that Wright's fourth child brought his father the news in person. David Wright had been with his mother in California at the last, and then the next day flew to Arizona, which was his home. David told Secrest that his father's eyes began to water when he got the word. "Why didn't you tell me?" Wright asked his son. Why hadn't David alerted him while he was still on the coast that she was close to dying? "You never showed any interest," the son answered.

A few days later, it was Easter Sunday. The Scottsdale morning was very fine and bright. The desert didn't yet have its heat. At the festive meal, Wright and his wife were dressed all in white and sat under umbrellas, amid the balloons and the dyed eggs. He liked calling her "Mother," no matter that she was so much younger. She called him "Fraanck," drawing it out in the Montenegrin accent that had never left her. (In front of the apprentices, it was always "Mr. Wright.") They'd been through some very nasty times, and in the mid-fifties more than once she had threatened to leave him. But they'd made it to here, not quite thirty-five years together. After the Easter breakfast on the terraces, he said, "Come along, Mother," and arm in arm they passed through all the bright young faces of the Fellowship and went back to their rooms to lie down.

On Saturday morning, April 4, in the drafting room, he stopped at three or four boards to look at projects. At Kamal Amin's table, at about eleven, he sat down, having nudged Kamal over. The two had been working on something that he was calling the "Donahoe Triptych." It was for a rich Texas lady who wanted a second home in Paradise Valley, Arizona. A few weeks earlier, he'd signed off on preliminary designs, but he had a suggestion or two now. Humming, he took up one of Kamal's pencils. His hands were sure, although it was hard for him to see. It may be the last architectural drawing to which Frank Lloyd Wright ever gave his attention.

Olgivanna came in and called him to lunch. The apprentice from Cairo, who'd been around for eight years, got up and thanked him and then went back to the work, glad he'd get to see him later, for the usual Saturday night dress-up and dinner and movie or other entertainment.

Sometime after lunch Wright's nose began to spurt blood. Through the afternoon he felt increasingly sick to his stomach. Toward evening, he began to throw up blood. They got him dressed and into the car and drove to Phoenix. He was in the back seat, with his head on his wife's lap, his stomach swelling like a bowling ball. At St. Joseph's Hospital, the doctors quickly determined he was suffering from an acute abdominal blockage. Surgery would be a large risk, but it was probably his only chance. But they didn't operate until Monday evening, the sixth. No malignancy was found. There seemed cause for hope. He went in and out of lucidity. A bed, in a solarium, was fixed up for his wife. In the intensive care unit, from inside his oxygen tent, he said to Olgivanna, or so she would recount years later in her autobiography: "So this is the way you treat me—and all those doctors of yours. You have a plot conceived to kill me." But that was almost a cause for joy, that he could talk to her like that. At another point, calmed, no longer moaning (they had been administering sedatives), he said: "My dear little wife, you are doing your best, aren't you?" She promised him that he would pull through. "Olgivanna, when the tree is dying cut it. Nothing can save it," he said, or so she would remember.

On Wednesday evening, some good sleep, apparently. But early the next morning—on the death certificate, the time would be registered as 4:45 a.m.—he suffered a thrombosis. The night-duty nurse had just been in to check on him. She seems to have left and then returned. "He just sighed—and died," Mrs. Jessie Boganno was quoted as saying. It was April 9, 1959.

Two of his grandchildren were at Taliesin West. Brandoch Peters, who was seventeen, was living there, attending school. Later in the morning, Olgivanna took him in to see the body. She also led in Tim Wright, twenty, who was baby Llewellyn's son. He just happened to be in Arizona, visiting. He had spent three teenage summers at Taliesin in Wisconsin, getting to ride around on big tractors. He was at Taliesin West now, because he was more or less at loose ends with himself. (He'd come across the country to Arizona in a junker station wagon he'd bought in Florida for $50.) Tim Wright is a soft-spoken and well-read and highly educated man with a wry sense of humor, who has topped eighty. He told me he has no memory of any real conversations with his grandfather in those last days, but he has an indelible memory of getting to see what Frank Lloyd Wright looked like in death. "This little shrunken old man in this hospital gown," he said. "I think he probably wasn't even five-foot-five at that point. He was just this little shriveled thing."

On the death certificate (filled out later that morning), "Acute coronary insufficiency" was listed as the immediate cause. "Acute hemorrhagic infarction of the small bowel" was given as the underlying and unbridgeable cause. Wes Peters and several others drove the body in a coffin to Wisconsin in a panel pickup truck. It was 1,668 miles, and they made the curving driveway of Taliesin in twenty-eight hours, no stopping, save for hamburgers and the fill-ups. The funeral was on Sunday, the 12th, at five o'clock. In the chill early April weather, a farm wagon, hitched to a team, and filled with petunias, with the mourners behind, clip-clopped the box to the family cemetery down the hill and across the road from the place that in Welsh means Shining Brow.

In the last interview he ever gave—it was on Friday, April 3, 1959, the day before he fell into his fatal sickness—Frank Lloyd Wright said that there could never be great art "unless it possessed a spiritual quality. If there were no spiritual quality in architecture, it would just be plain lumber."

Last Word

For the Two Taliesins

To get to the one in the desert, you drive up out of the metropolitan sprawl of greater Phoenix and Scottsdale. That sprawl comes closer by the year. Ahead, to the northeast, are the McDowell Mountains, modest in size, nothing like the Tetons or the Sawtooth or the High Sierra. But they have their own grandeur. As you make the winding ascent up to the mesa, you see more and more cactuses—the prickly pear, the buckhorn cholla, the staghorn, and most especially the not incorrectly named giant saguaro. But you don't see Taliesin West, not yet. It's too flat to the land.

Then you begin to get glimpses. First, the fins that jut up from the roof. They are red, and they run in a row, slanted at an angle. They are like spars on a great sailing vessel, on this desert of the ocean, on this ocean of the desert. You're almost right on top of the complex before you can see it more fully. Even more then does Taliesin West begin to seem like something constructed not for land, but for water, except what is the desert but a kind of tideless, inland sea? One of the earliest architectural images in his head, when he first began building in Arizona, was of a little fleet of boats sailing out on the open water—"desert ships." At the same time, he wanted something that would belong "to the desert as though it had stood there for centuries." And that's what he worked to create at Taliesin West, over the passage of years, using indigenous materials, using rocks and boulders hauled up out of the arroyos, set into wooden forms and anchored with concrete, always revising, always playing to the desert's gift of light, its stark geometric forms, building his many-terraced and brightly colored and low-slung maritime "camp," with its sloping stone walls and turned-up beams, all of it in homage to and in harmony with the parched and thirsty-seeming mountains behind.

If you were fortunate enough to see Taliesin West for the very first time at the end of winter and the start of spring, just when the Sonoran Desert has begun to bloom, you could sustain these watery and bone-dry illusions almost effortlessly. In late afternoon, the temperature starts to fall fast. Just a bit ago, it was so warm, the sky so ragingly blue. But now you want to put on a sweater. The saguaros climbing up the southern slope of the mountains are picking up the light. Everything, even your wristwatch, is picking up the light. The little desert birds—they're quail—that run so fast, with their quick little steps and bobbing heads, seem to be seeking their nighttime shelter. The yellowing and bluing and pinking and watermeloning of the world are happening faster than you can keep track. In minutes, the mountains, like papier-mâché, with shadows in their folds, having turned four or five shades of pink and watermelon and raspberry, are growing dark. The saltless sea begins to seem so becalmed that you almost don't want to speak above a whisper. The sun sinks below the horizon. The mountains begin to look themselves again. Everything is now fading to black, except, that is, for Phoenix and Scottsdale, which are behind you, to the west, down the mesa. Their lights are winking on, by the millions, and that, too, is something beautiful to witness, like "a look over the rim of the world," to quote him again.

And yet, let the other Taliesin, the first Taliesin, have the last word. If Arizona by day is a scape that looks brown beyond brown, then southwestern Wisconsin by day, in high summer, seems preternaturally green. A green that will almost hurt your eyes. He seems to have loved Arizona from the first moment he saw it in the late twenties, but his soul belonged to the Midwest, and specifically to rural southwestern Wisconsin, to its wooded bluffs and loamy fields and ledges of outcropping rock. His maternal people came into these deeply carved river valleys in the decade before the Civil War, led by his Old Testament grandfather, who, back in Wales, had been a farmer and a minister and a maker of tall black hats. At first, the family farmed on rented land on the north side of the river. But by 1864 the Lloyd Joneses had found their way to the even lusher valleys on the south side, where they acquired their own farms, acquired their own political and spiritual and moral superiority.

"Wisconsin soil has put the sap into my veins," the patriarch's morally superior grandson once wrote in an essay, after he'd become world famous, about why he loved his native state, and particularly, this neck of it, and why he could never be very long away from it before the old longings to be home set in.

I've traveled to Taliesin often in the course of this book. I never fail to feel a sense of the timeless when I'm on the brow of the hill, his hill. He found the best location in the valley, no question. I was at Taliesin on August 14, 2014, and somehow forgot what the date meant. Then it struck: it was the 100th anniversary, if anniversary is the word, of what Julian Carlton did. Well, the 100th anniversary, minus a day. All that week, I had been in Wisconsin, in Madison and in other places, doing other reporting work for this book, and the date had just slipped by me. Now it came back like a sucker punch: *Julian and the shingling hatchet. One hundred years ago tomorrow.*

I was standing with my back to the house and to the Wisconsin River. I was looking down and across the valley, to the south. It was almost a 360-degree view. I could see Tan-y-deri, the foursquare Prairie he built for his sister, where the sheeted bodies were laid out that night. I could see the ribbon of two-lane asphalt, which is state route 23, where it makes its swerve to the right, and where County T comes in on the left. I could just make out, or thought I could, the lines of the brown-shingled family chapel. The heat seemed to be rising up from the valley floor in visible electric waves. The hayfields and rows of corn down there were baking, no doubt. It was very hot, and still, and humid. Even on this hill, you couldn't buy a breeze.

In the quiet, it was hard to imagine the screaming and burning of that day. But it was necessary to imagine it. Because it had once happened.

Keiran Murphy was standing beside me. She was made mention of many pages ago. She is Taliesin's cultural historian. She knows so much about the house's history, and yet always constructs her answers to my infernal questions with something provisional in her voice. It's her fundamental modesty.

I brought up Julian and the fact that it happened one hundred years ago tomorrow.

I didn't have my notebook with me, so this will be a reconstruction of our conversation. I said something to the effect of: *I'm in as much doubt as I ever was, maybe more, about why he did it.* And she said something to the effect of: *Isn't it almost better that way?* And I replied: *You mean the mystery itself is the more powerful thing?* And she said: *Yes, just like Wright himself. Who would ever really want to get to the bottom of the mystery of Frank Lloyd Wright? If you did that, you might not ever have a need to come back.*

After a while I said goodbye and got into the shuttle bus that takes tourists down the hill and across the road to the parking lot at the visitor's center. I got into my rental car and drove away, northward, across the river, certain I'd be back, and also thinking to myself, almost saying it aloud: *You can never get to the end of the knowing.*

Acknowledgments

In the Essay on Sources, which follows, I will name as many individuals as I can, in the relevant places, who helped on this project. Here, though, I'll express a special gratitude to a core of individuals, several of whose names have already appeared in the text. (They are not all Wright authorities, but each was critical to the research then in progress.) I would also like to use this space to thank another category of people who, each in his or her own way, to smaller and larger degree, helped to get this seven-year project across the ending line. For someone who has come into his mid-seventies, it was never a given it would get across.

First, among the Wright professionals: Tim Samuelson. It's nearly inconceivable to me this book could have been done without him. I stood on his wide shoulders all the way through. We have become good friends—the professional relationship long ago eased into a personal one. As I said in the text, if we have had one conversation about Frank Lloyd Wright, we have had one hundred. I became his pupil. Why this generous man—who is known to every serious or even halfway-serious researcher on Chicago and its cultural history—decided to invest so much time and trust in me, I don't know, and don't wish to. He is the ambling encyclopedia (and also the eccentric *New Yorker* profile-in-waiting) of almost anything to do with Chicago and its glorious, gaudy history. His official title is a mouthful: cultural historian for the City of Chicago and the Department of Cultural Affairs and Special Events. Tim and I met in the summer of 2012, not quite a year into the research. He had just put together a landmark exhibit at the Chicago Cultural Center entitled *Wright's Roots*. I was just then trying to learn about FLW and his origins: serendipity from the gods. I called up Tim and said I was coming to Chicago, and might we meet? Of course, he said, but then quickly suggested I see the exhibit on my own first, to form my own impressions and questions. Then we might go through it again together. He's ever been like that: guiding, suggesting, pointing, never once instructing or insisting. We've pedaled bikes around Hyde Park (where he lives in a Mies van der Rohe high-rise apartment building with a killer view of Lake

Michigan), looking not just at FLW stuff, but at stuff too laughably obscure to mention. It was Tim—to reference what I wrote in the book's dedication line—who took me one steaming afternoon six or seven years ago to the now-gone stone that became the book's keystone, its literal *touch*stone. I have a treasured photograph of Tim in his baggy shorts and sandals and yellow T-shirt and mostly bald head leaning halfway over and pointing impishly between the weeds at the chipped wedge of worthless-seeming concrete that marked the unrecognized spot where a part of fabled Midway Gardens once stood. I didn't want to go see it that afternoon. Too arcane, I told myself. Wouldn't help with what I was doing. Just a damn rock. "Okay, but I think it might do something for you," he said gently. We've disagreed on some major and minor points of interpretation of FLW's life and work, exactly as it should be.

Keiran Murphy, cultural historian of Taliesin at Spring Green. As Tim, so with Keiran: showing principally by *indirection.*

Indira Berndtson, administrator in historic studies, in the collections and exhibitions department of the Frank Lloyd Wright Foundation at Taliesin West. Again, for reasons I can't quite say, she seemed to have just decided, early on, to take a chance on me. Indira literally grew up in the Wright universe: her mom, Cornelia Brierly, who lived to be ninety-nine, was one of the first female Fellows at Taliesin. There are pictures of Indira as a child sitting in close proximity to FLW. She unfailingly calls him, as do so many others who work at either Taliesin, "Mr. Wright."

David Bagnall, curator and director of interpretation at Frank Lloyd Wright Trust in Chicago. Nearly every time I went to the Home and Studio on Chicago Avenue in Oak Park, this genial Britisher would come down from his office to offer to help. I have been traveling to Oak Park now for about a decade and a half, over the length of two long books. I should invest in real estate there, except I don't have those kinds of resources. I'm not even speaking of FLW houses.

I cannot cite all the staff historians and archivists and reference librarians and genealogists at all the archives and museums and research libraries—from local institutions to federal and university and semi-private ones—who went out of their way to help, but these two dozen or so individuals need to be singled out, if in no particular order: Margo Stipe, director and curator of collections at the Frank Lloyd Wright Foundation in Arizona. Shelley Hayreh, archivist at Avery Architectural and Fine Arts Library at Columbia University. (I am indebted to the entire staff at Avery, including the former curator of drawings and archives, Janet Parks.) Sally McKay, head of special collections services at the research library at the Getty Research Institute in Los Angeles. Oskar Munos and the late Bruce Brooks Pfeiffer at the Frank Lloyd Wright Foundation Archives. (Every Wright researcher in the world knows

Pfeiffer's name.) Marc Carlson, librarian of special collections and university archives at the University of Tulsa. Ian Swart, former archivist and curator of collections at the Tulsa Historical Society & Museum. Robin Brown and Mary Hamilton and the late Miriam Syler at the Chambers County Library and the Cobb Memorial Archives in Valley, Alabama. Jim Baggett, head of archives and manuscripts at the Birmingham Public Library. Mary Bennett, special collections coordinator at the State Historical Society of Iowa. Gary Johnson and Arlene Balkansky, reference specialists at the Library of Congress. Hollis L. Gentry, genealogy specialist at the library of the National Museum of African American History and Culture. Leigh Tarullo, curator of special collections, and her assistant, Emily Reiher, at the Oak Park Public Library. John Pollack, curator, research services, at the Kislak Center for special collections in rare books and manuscripts at the University of Pennsylvania. Laura Surtees of the Rhys Carpenter Library at Bryn Mawr College. And last but not least, five other library specialists at UPenn: Ed Deegan, Patty Lynn, Kirby Bell, Lapis Cohen, and Catherine Rutan.

I feel special gratitude to the staff of the library-archives division of the Wisconsin Historical Society in Madison. And to David Null and Katie Nash of university archives at UW.

Too, this small number of scholars and journalists (as well as one Wright grandson) need get special mention for a willingness to go above and beyond: Mary Jane Hamilton, David Mollenhoff, Ron McCrea, Scott Ellsworth, Brian Spencer, Mark Hertzberg, Bill Martinelli, William Storrer, and Tim Wright. (Ellsworth is the outlier here: he isn't a Wright authority, rather a premier Tulsa authority.)

With particular thanks: my longtime agent, Kathy Robbins, and her associate, David Halpern, wise counselors, never pushing me to hurry and finish, but always there, along with the superb staff.

At the University of Pennsylvania, where I have had the privilege of conducting writing workshops for more than two decades, I wish to acknowledge for their friendship and support the following colleagues (in some cases they are former colleagues), if in no strict order: Al Filreis, Julia Bloch, Jessica Lowenthal, Gregory Djankian, Witold Rybczynski, David Brownlee, Larry Silver, Bill Whitaker, Allie Katz, Zach Carduner, Jim English, Wendy Steiner, Jed Esty, Amy Kaplan, Buzz Bissinger, Michael Gamer, Deb Burnham, Zach Lesser, Paul Saint-Amour, Emily Steiner, Peter Stallybrass, Herman Beavers, Rebecca Bushnell, Tim Corrigan, Peter Conn, Dave Espey, Margreta de Grazia, Jamie-Lee Josselyn, Loretta Williams, Elizabegh Lunger, Ann Marie Pitts, Stephanie Palmer, and James Trumbo. Except that three more names have to be added to this list: Brian Kirk, Rich King, and Nicolo Marziani. They are more than computer specialists for the English Department—they keep giving moral, never mind tech, support. Not for nothing is my office next door to theirs. I tend to run in with my tongue out, afraid that the world (or at least my machine) is about to blow up. Brian, perhaps my best friend at the university, is always there to soothe things. I departed daily journalism a long time ago, after some thirty glad years at it, and scarcely dreamed, at the back end of my life, of finding a new work home among such good people.

These, too—former students, old *Washington Post* colleagues, friends from first grade (it's true), newer friends, fellow authors, siblings, a stray relative or two, some world-class physicians, some professional associates—all of whom have "tended" me in one way or another, and without whom this book likely wouldn't have gotten done. Again, in no special order: Mike Woyahn, Chris McConnell, David Maraniss, Douglas Brinkley, Melissa Faye Greene, John Baskin, David von Drehle, Robert Kaiser, Shelby Coffee, John McDonnell, Suzanne Radl-McDonnell, Howell Raines, Pat Toomay, Jess Yu, Elaine Wong, Michael Morse, Naomi Shavin, Gabe Oppenheim, John Moffatt, Tom Hayes, Sandra Tedeschi, Sunita Nasta, Richard Toof, Robert and Susan Frye, Elaine Chiang, Ed Woehling, Tom Rankin, Hiram Rogers, Dan Collins, Charlie Clements, Gigi Wizowaty, Tina Hinkle, James Godsil, John Coyne, Talmage Boston, Wil Haygood, Patrick Keegan, Tari Engels, Eric Hendrickson, Mark Hendrickson, Jeanne Snider, Marty Hendrickson, Ed Murphy, Burma Mathews, Cherie Curran, Ed Lynch, Alfie Wilkes, Jack Ryder, Voula Yurick, David J. Singer, Lynn McClellan, Stephen Solotoff, Neenah Ellis, Noah Adams, Bobbye Pratt.

At Alfred A. Knopf, I wish to express deepest respect and gratitude to a host of dedicated book people, but especially to Sonny Mehta, Carol Devine Carson, Cassandra Pappas, Paul Bogaards, Dan Novack, Nimra Chohan, Nicholas Latimer, Sam Aber, Ellen Feldman, Katie Schoder, Gabrielle Brooks, but, most of all, as I have said on the acknowledgment page of previous books, my editor, Jonathan Segal. It is now a relationship of almost forty years. My previous book was dedicated to Jon. All the endurance, all the closeness, all the other as well. (It's not precisely true we can go to war over what *he* regards as one too many adverbs—in this sentence, for instance.)

For the British edition of this book, I am deeply grateful for the careful attentions of campaigns manager Hannah Shorten and, in particular, Stuart Williams, publishing director at The Bodley Head.

And then my family: last but first on this list. Nothing would work without them. That's Ceil, my wife and believer of forty years, who more than anyone knows the emotional cost of living with a book. ("Sister wife," she calls it.) That's sons Matt and John, men of accomplishment in their thirties of whom I am undyingly proud. Our beautiful and professionally soaring daughter-in-law, Jennie. And, not least, our grandson, three-and-a-half-year-old Jackson, prince of the city, emperor of joy.

Essay on Sources

In the source notes for my previous book, I said I've long felt projects find their authors, and not the reverse, and that often enough the finding can be a half-aware thing traveling on for years—or decades. I'll repeat that assertion here, and almost with a vengeance: I think Frank Lloyd Wright and this book found me circa late 1953 and early 1954. That was the Christmas, 1953, best I recall, when Santa left under a tree for a middle-class nine-year-old in the living room of 230 South Harrison Avenue in Kankakee, Illinois, a maroon-colored J.C. Higgins three-speed. By early spring I was sailing down Harrison, headed to Riverview Park (now known as Cobb Park), with the wrist strap of my Spalding ball glove hooked to the handlebars of my new bike. Harrison slopes gently downhill toward the river, and at the very bottom of my old street—as I've told in the text—stand the seminal B. Harley Bradley and War-ren R. Hickox houses. Usually, I'd blur by and catch them in the peripheral vision of my right eye, but I can recall more than once putting on the brakes and staring over at these immense and strange-looking objects. (As was told in the text, the Bradley, seeming the far more immense and seductive of the two, had just become a glitteringly rich restaurant called Yesteryear.) I'd drink in a look from the sidewalk and then turn left and continue the several blocks over and down to Riverview. But what's startling to me now is to realize that there were Prairie forms and echoes and traces all over my childhood home-town, not just at the tail end of my own street. Indeed, our own rented home, five blocks northward (only a vacant lot there now), had overhanging eaves and other Prairie touches—you can see them in the photographs. There was a Prairie, or at least proto-Prairie, around the corner, just past the alley, on Merchant Street, maybe one hundred yards from our house. There was, and is, a moderately famous Prairie, the Charles E. Swannell House, designed in 1911 by the firm of Talmadge and Watson (they were successful if derivative Prairie School practitioners), at 901 South Chicago Avenue. That house, still there, with its own Wikipedia page, was practically right at the park, and I had to have pedaled past it scores of times. What I am saying is that all of that unique Prairie look and feel, in a downstate prairie town, must have been working on me, by osmosis. Isn't a gradual and sloping and unconscious assimilation of ideas the best way we learn?

As with my previous books, all nonfiction, the material for *Plagued by Fire* has been gathered in three ways. First, from my own reporting and interviewing. As I have said in the notes to previous books, I come proudly from a journalistic tradition, and so the notion of being able to go out into the world and talk to people who have something stored inside them about the central subject has always been its own anchoring comfort. I just don't mean the seeking out of scholars or architects or authors or critics, but of individuals who actually *knew* Wright, to one degree or another. At first thought, it might seem improbable there could be anybody still alive who knew him. After all, he was born just a little more than two years after Lincoln's assassination. Part of the explanation, of course, is because he lived so damn long and cut across and through so many swaths of society. (Consider, by contrast, Ernest Hemingway: he was born in 1899, thirty-two years after FLW, a whole generation behind. But in 2004, when I began working seriously on a book about his life, there weren't but about five people on the earth, outside his surviving son, who could truly claim to have known him in any close-up way.) As FLW's grandson, Tim Wright (who barely appears in this book, but who has added much to it), once said to me: "My grandfather contained within himself one hundred years of midwestern American cultural history." Yes, like a spreading oak, five-foot-seven in height. There is another circumstance that pertains here: namely, that idealistic young people, sometimes seventy years younger than himself, were finding their way to FLW's doorway right up to the end of his life, as would-be Taliesin apprentices and fellows. In the fifties, when they applied, many were still in their early twenties, while Wright was crowding ninety (or already beyond it). Those still alive are old themselves now. It's true that not every one of them knew him well, or even reasonably well. Still, enough did. I doubt that there are too many other instances in American artistic history where this May-December age-difference phenomenon has played itself out so prominently. In any case, I wish I could say I tracked down everyone who ever intersected with him, from old apprentices to relatives to potential clients to creaky journalists to the stray surviving Wisconsin creditor or two (or at least the offspring of same, who might have witnessed him in artful-dodger mode). I talked with as many as I could. (See notes further on re some of the artful dodging.)

The second way I obtained information was from documentary material— letters, manuscripts, photographs, drawings, newsreels, audio recordings, old kinescopes. I have written books in one guise or another having to do with the Great Depression, Vietnam, civil rights, Hemingway, but the ocean of Wright-related archival material felt just about as swamping as those. There are Wright-related archives across this country (including at my own university in Philadelphia). The goal was always to try to fight my way *out* of the library, out of the archive. The places where I have spent the most time in the last seven years are at Avery/Columbia; the Wisconsin Historical Society in Madison; the local history room of the Oak Park Public Library; Taliesin West in Scottsdale; and the department of special collections and archives at the University of Tulsa. Other repositories and libraries will be noted as this goes along.

There is another kind of "documentary material," though. As was said in the text, FLW designed over 1,100 works, and not quite half were realized, and about 400 still stand. They are in forty states, Japan, and Canada; some seventy-odd are accessible to the public via tours, with or without admission fees. I have seen somewhere over one hundred Wright buildings—often enough from the inside, but sometimes from just out on the sidewalk, gazing, like a nine-year-old without his J.C. Higgins.

The third way I obtained information was from so-called secondary source material, which became primary in its own way, at least some of it did. I am referring principally to books and monographs on architecture, and then to several works essentially biographical in nature. Some of it, especially the for-mer, represents a scholarship I can only marvel at. It is evident I am not any kind of bona fide architectural writer, and so I did a lot of grateful standing on shoulders. But I know what I know and like what I like. As was said in the pro-logue, there is just so damn much out there on Wright, and it runs the gamut: biographies, histories, theses and dissertations, journalism, critical studies in academic journals, historical fictions, websites (not to say chat rooms, which can be a trip through the looking glass). I had, first of all, to learn not to be afraid. And then in a sense to throw away everything I'd tried to absorb. And then to remind myself that if I could offer anything, it would have to be in the realm of the unconventional, finding my own way (to Tulsa, to his largely ignored father, to Cecil Corwin, to Julian Carlton), aiming for an evocation, an interpretation, a portrait, a *story*. Another experiment in group-biography.

There was also the material in private hands. In some cases, it turned out to be primary in nature: letters, entries in journals, handwritten scraps in an album. The chapter on Cecil Corwin, for instance: I am the beneficiary of the generosity of Cynthia Beach-Smeltzer in Rochester, New York, and Andy Haynes in Tryon, North Carolina, both of whom opened the family drawers of memorabilia. In Clinton, Iowa, an esteemed architect and letterpress artist named Phil Feddersen, in his nineties, gave me invaluable items related to the life of Miriam Noel Wright. Donald Kalec (I noted this in the text) loaned his research files on the Jacobs House in Madison; that included correspondence of Herbert and Katherine Jacobs not in any public repository. And so forth.

Biographies: As noted in the text, Meryle Secrest's 1992 FLW work is the most thoroughly researched full-record life available; I had it admiringly close at hand all the way through. Robert Twombly's 1973 and 1979 bios (as was noted, the latter being a reworking of the former) are vital contributions. Ditto Brendan Gill's 1987 impressionistic and more personal and sometimes criticized portrait—for which I wish to stick up. If it has factual errors in too many places, the work nonetheless achieves things other FLW bios do not, and I am personally grateful for avenues of exploration that the book suggested to me. (For full citations of these and many other works in this essay, see the selected bibliography.)

On factual error: This book is doubtless not free of it, no matter how hard I tried to make it be otherwise. I will say this and be done with it: I have yet to encounter a single work on FLW without factual error. I am convinced it just has something to do with the quicksilver nature of the subject. Dealing with Wright and the truth is like trying to hold mercury in your fist. So much error has gotten passed along. Julian Carlton was never from Barbados.

As is evident, the two FLW works—one brief; one almost literally monumental in its physical size, never mind its scholarly heft—that I kept in my spiritual hind pocket, start to finish, are Ada Huxtable's condensed life and Neil Levine's study of the architecture as filtered through the storytelling blocks of the life. One is the excellent overview (if, as said in the text, too unsuspectingly reliant on the mistruths), while the other is the academic deep dive without ever reading as if it were something academic. But there are other architectural-cum-biographical book-length works that were crucial, and perhaps first among these is Anthony Alofsin's *Frank Lloyd Wright—the Lost Years, 1910–1922: A Study of Influence.* A close second would be Kathryn Smith's recently published (2017) and almost deceptively titled *Wright on Exhibit.*

Every long-form researcher of nonfiction has his hind-pocket rabbit's feet. In addition to the above-named works (but most especially the Levine, the Huxtable, and the Secrest), the following *brief* pieces were invaluable for providing a line of thinking and feeling. They are essays and reviews and introductions and chapters from larger works. To use a metaphor from the last project, they amount to my own portable FLW satchel-library. Pride of place goes to William V. Mollenhoff and Mary Jane Hamilton's "An Old Madison Boy," to which I've paid tribute in the text. ("OMB" is chapter 2 of their book, *Frank Lloyd Wright's Monona Terrace.*) Second pride of place: "The Dreams of Frank Lloyd Wright," by Michael Kimmelman, in the August 11, 2005, *New York Review of Books.* The others, in no particular order: " 'Shaking Houses Out of His Sleeve,'" by William Allin Storrer, in the third edition of his *The Architecture of Frank Lloyd Wright*; "The Romance of the Horizontal" and "Roof, Cantilever and Rift," both of these being chapters in Donald Hoffmann's *Understanding Frank Lloyd Wright's Architecture*; Paul Goldberger's "Not an Urbanist, Only a Genius," in the February 13, 1994, *New York Times Magazine*; "The Domestic Architecture of Frank Lloyd Wright," by Norris Smith, collected in *Writings on Wright*; Bruce Brooks Pfeiffer's introduction to his *Frank Lloyd Wright*; Robert L. Sweeney's introduction to his *Frank Lloyd Wright: An Annotated Bibliography*; Jack Quinan's introduction in the most recent edition (2017) of *Wright Sites*; Martin Filler's "Frank Lloyd Wright" in his *Makers of Modern Architecture*; William J. R. Curtis's "Wright and Le Corbusier in the 1930s," in his *Modern Architecture Since 1900*. And, last but not least, Malcolm Cowley's "Rebels, Artists, and Scoundrels," in his *—And I Worked at the Writer's Trade*. That piece doesn't contain the words "Frank Lloyd Wright," but it's nonetheless all about him, spiritually speaking. This is the baker's dozen of take-alongs I returned to, whenever I began to feel lost.

Except that the most thumbed take-along was always *An Autobiography*. As was said in the text, for all of its deceptions and distortions and elisions, it is the most revealing and honest written Wright there is. The artist is always bent on giving himself away.

What follows isn't meant to be an all-inclusive source-noting. As in previous books, I will offer a kind of prose-form route map of my own devising, both essay and citation, not every cite, no, but rather the ones I judge the reader will be interested in knowing. Essentially, these notes are trying to combine sourcing with some of the rich backstory: book within the book. I will use "FLW" in most instances, and other abbreviations will be self-evident. To emphasize a point made in the text: When giving page numbers for quoted passages from *An Autobiography*, I am always referring, *except* where otherwise specifically indicated, to the 1932 edition. In general, page numbers are supplied for book-length works only. Newspaper and magazines, no. Re FLW's letters: Microfiche copies are at both Avery Library at Columbia and the Getty Center in Los Angeles, and I have logged some hours bent over the microfiche reader in both places. (See my acknowledgments for formal names of both of these institutions located on opposite coasts.) Not every letter FLW ever wrote or received is in these two repositories, no—but the great bulk. The indispensable index to the letters—the original copies of which were formerly at Taliesin West but are now at Avery—is *Frank Lloyd Wright: An Index to the Taliesin Correspondence*, edited and with an introduction by Anthony Alofsin, produced by Garland Publishing in 1988. The "Garland," as I've often heard it called. Every serious FLW researcher knows this guide. Again, it's not an index to *every* letter written or received by FLW, but a heroic accomplishment nonetheless: an outsized set of books, five volumes, bound in soft blue, that has helped sustain psychologically—and *actually*—this long journey.

In 2012, FLW's vast archive came east. Under an agreement with the FLW Foundation, Avery at Columbia and the Museum of Modern Art jointly acquired the trove. At Avery are 23,000 architectural drawings, 44,000 historical photographs, transcripts, films, interview tapes. One could spend half a lifetime in that comfortable space, and never get a word written.

PROLOGUE Out of the Old Testament: August 15, 1914

PRECEDE. My historical-cum-imaginative reconstruction of what it must have been like that night, after a lot of thinking and reading and going to the scene(s). (Yes, it was a buffet parlor car, and he sat in a compartment, and newsboys did stick sheets through the windows at various stops.) Cowley's epigraph quote is in "Rebels, Artists, and Scoundrels," referenced above. Ali Smith's epigraph quote is in a November 26, 2014, profile in *The New York Times.* In that same piece, Smith said, "Every great narrative is at least two narratives, if not more—the thing that is on the surface and then the things underneath which are invisible."

CHAPTER. Re newspaper quotes pertaining to the massacre: I tried to embed in the text itself where and when the quote, however real or bogus-sounding, appeared, with these exceptions: Gertrude's "I dunno what took him" is in the August 21, 1914, *Dodgeville Chronicle,* the editors having picked it up from other papers. Julian's "altercation" quote is in the August 17, 1914, *Milwaukee Sentinel,* and the full quote is worth reproducing here, in contrast to his Stepin-Fetchit-sounding remarks in other papers. ("We had an altercation on Saturday morning during which Brodelle abused me for more than an hour.") The "It's muriatic acid, boys" is in the August 17, 1914, *Chicago Herald.* The "head cleft in twain" re Mamah was in various papers, including the August 16, 1914, *Milwaukee Sentinel.* The "O Mama, look at Julian," supposedly cried by John Cheney (except that there were no surviving witnesses), is in that same *Sentinel.* The "Three wounds back of right ear" (re Martha Cheney's death) is in *Weekly Home News* of Spring Green, August 20, 1914.

Re Martha's death, the hardest (at least for me) to have tried to imagine and reconstruct: it has been written in enough places that Julian caught and killed her out in the sunlight on the rough stones of the loggia—but I don't think so, because the workers in the second eating space would have witnessed it through the windows and then bolted up themselves. As was said in the text, I think the child did bolt up and take off running from the terrace, but that he caught her somewhere still in the house, and killed her, or thought he did, out of sight of the workers. Later, she crawled outside. Meanwhile, the killer raced to where the workers were. But we'll never really know. I emphasize this small point only for that reason: the never quite knowing.

Re FLW quotes in this chapter from *An Autobiography:* The "blow had fallen" is on p. 188. The "shaken itself out of my sleeve" is on p. 179. The "All I had to show" is on p. 190. The "what it means to be an artist" is on p. 157 of the '43 edition. The "memories would haunt" is on p. 48. The "heavy thing straight" is on p. 51. The "Shame to me too" is on p. 260 of the '43. "Dissension and discord" is on p. 261 of the '43.

Re FLW quotes from his letters and other places, not otherwise evident from text: The "no being lonesome after that" is in a talk to the Taliesin Fellowship on January 5, 1958. The "In my own life" quote is December 8, 1908, to Darwin Martin. The "wish I had been less taking" is December 6, 1935, to Darwin's widow. The "Ugly things happen" is December 22, 1943, to Hilla Rebay. The "I have found that when a scheme develops" is from *Architectural Forum,* January 1938.

Others: The Boyle passage is on p. 437 of the paper edition of *The Women.* Huxtable's quote about being unable to invent FLW's life is on p. xv of her intro to the paper edition of her bio. J. L. Wright's description of his father getting word is on pp. 80–81 of a 1992 edition of his memoir-cum-autobio. (The original 1946 title was *My Father Who Is on Earth.* He later retitled it *My Father, Frank Lloyd Wright.* In itself, the retitling might or might not say something about his lifelong conflicts.) My *Washington Post* story on Loren Pope was February 25, 1997. Lewis Mumford's "He lived from first to last like a God" is on p. 433 of his *Sketches from a Life.* Scully talking of FLW never looking back (not true, which is my whole thesis) is in the 1998 PBS film documentary *Frank Lloyd Wright,* by Ken Burns and Lynn Novick. FLW's remark about reaching too high is on p. 147 of Maginel Wright Barney's *The Valley of the God-Almighty Joneses.*

Paul Kruty, author of the definitive work on Midway Gardens (*Frank Lloyd Wright and Midway Gardens*), helped me to plot out the spot, or vicinity of the spot, where FLW was standing when the news came—as did Tim Samuelson.

Essentially, the effort was to reconcile the irreconcilable: the event itself. A futile act, I knew, before starting, because there are so many interpretations and supposed true versions. I pored over acres of conflicting newspaper accounts. Keiran Murphy was invaluable—we examined old drawings and latter-day computer reconstructions of Taliesin in 1914. The late Robert Drennan's *Death in a Prairie House* was particularly helpful, although, as is noted in a later part of the text, his tone is disconcerting, something like a district attorney conducting an inquest. Important point: I say Mamah, in running away with FLW, had forsaken her own spouse and two little children—true. Except that her adopted niece was living in the Oak Park house as well. I was referring to her biological children and didn't want to confuse the issue for the reader at this very early point. This is made clear in the later chapter "Unity and Mamah."

Finally, the South Side parking lot that, until recently, held the stone where Midway Gardens stood is a private lot, serving the residential buildings I described. The reason the stone is no longer there is because developers came in and built a supermarket on the property immediately adjoining. In the process, they eventually bulldozed the stone. Tim Samuelson couldn't get there in time. It broke his heart. I like to think, though, that the developers didn't bulldoze the stone so much as return it, disappear it, back into the earth. At any rate, not a trace left. (For more comments on this, see p. 574.)

PART I Longing on a Large Scale: 1887–1909

DeLillo's quote is at the opening of *Underworld.*

The Enigma of Arrival

PRECEDE. Historian Andrew Saint wrote of some of these details in *Frank Lloyd Wright: Europe and Beyond*, pp. 136–37, edited by Anthony Alofsin. The author puts the year as 1950. He had gathered the personal reminiscences of the British architect-author Colin Penn and also of Sir John Summerson, who was one of the leading British architectural historians of the twentieth century. However, at an architectural symposium held in Chicago in the early seventies, on the so-called Chicago School, Summerson remembered that FLW had made his poetic "long grass of the Prairies" remark on an *earlier* London visit, in 1937. (See *The Prairie School Review* 9, no. 2, 1972, p. 35.) In all likelihood, Summerson was misremembering.

CHAPTER. The figure of destroyed buildings in the Great Fire, as well as the city's doubling of population from 1880 to 1890, are from a first-rate condensed cultural-cum-architectural history of Chicago, "The Shaping of Chicago," by Perry R. Duis, in the *AIA* [American Institute of Architects] *Guide to Chicago*, pp. 3–24. FLW's fanciful narrative of his arrival and first days and of meeting Cecil is essentially between pp. 63 and 70 in *An Autobiography*. (He seems, as is typical, to be spelling many Chicago place-names by memory, and is generally accurate on both spellings and location. One example of a misspelling: the famous bakery-café he discovered on his supposed second night was Kohlsaat's, not Kohlsatt's.) The "Is it a quality?" is on p. 111 of the autobio. Secrest's elided quotes about "Exactly when" he came are on p. 83 of the paper edition of her bio. FLW's "To cut ambiguity" quote is on p. 205 of *Frank Lloyd Wright: A Testament*. A copy of the typed transcript of his May 14, 1951, Detroit talk, with his penciled-in "edits," was given to me by Kamal Amin (for more on Amin, see chapter "Terminals (2)," and also my notes to that chapter). The elided quotes beginning with "So the university training" are between pp. 56 and 59 of the autobio. My conversations, both email and phone, with Thomas S. Hines were in August 2014. The elided quotes from Garland's *Rose* are between pp. 183 and 191. Kitty Wright quoted in *Tribune* re Garland and only a few others "able to understand him": November 7, 1909.

The division of archives at Steenbock Memorial Library at UW Madison has FLW's registration cards and skeletal transcript (just two posted grades), and also evidence (in old yearbook) of his fleeting membership in Phi Delta Theta. I combined what I found there with research at the Wisconsin Historical Society (also on the UW campus) and then joined it with Professor Hines's findings of so many years before—to which every FLW researcher is indebted.

The dates of *Sieba*'s run were in the Chicago papers of 1886.

Re Uncle Jenk and his All Souls church and its completion date vis-à-vis trying to pin down when FLW came to town: Meadville Lombard Theological School in Chicago has crucial materials in its library-archives, and I am indebted to the help of archivist John Leeker. Not least of these is the church annual (*All Souls Church, Fourth Annual, 1887*) covering the events of the church year 1886 and into early 1887, which shows FLW as a church member and boarding with a local family by *at least* January 6, 1887. My belief is he probably came right after Christmas 1886, stayed briefly with Cecil, moved in briefly with his uncle, and then began rooming with the church family nearby. As said in the text, the *Fourth Annual* also contains what seems to be FLW's earliest known published drawing—of Unity Chapel. For more on this, see "The Earliest Work of Frank Lloyd Wright," by Wilbert R. Hasbrouck, *Prairie School Review* 7, no. 4 (1970). The late Hasbrouck was the *Review*'s founding editor and publisher. This is an informed and scholarly piece. He places FLW's Chicago arrival in the early spring of 1887. I respectfully disagree, wishing to move up the arrival by at least two months. And why is that possibility/fact important at all? Because, or so I contend, of the emotional pull on the young Madison hayseed (who'd earlier visited Chicago, to scout out a job) of Cecil S. Corwin—drawing FLW back to the city in ways he didn't quite understand. Only a theory, with some corroborating facts to help it out.

The "boy architect belonging to the family" is in *Unity* magazine, August 28, 1886.

As said in the text, Aunt Nell's letter to FLW was March 9, 1887. Anna

Wright wrote to her son the next day. ("My Dear Frank, I have been looking for a letter from you. . . .")

The word "supposedly" was used a handful of times in the chapter—for instance, in regard to whether FLW had ever seen electric arc lights before, or had ever been on a cable car. He'd have us believe this from the autobio—it heightens the drama of the lone boy coming to the great city. But I believe he would have *had* to have earlier seen arc lights and ridden cable cars. It's known that his father had preached at Uncle Jenk's church in 1884, and the family seems to have been with him. Additionally, Rev. William Wright and family would have come through Chicago on trains on various eastward and westward journeys. So I think the "I had never seen electric lights before" at the start of the Chicago telling is just one more part of the mythmaking.

Many histories and maps and guidebooks, among them *History of the Development of Building Construction in Chicago* (long considered the premier catalog of the city's architecture); *Chicago: Growth of a Metropolis; Chicago and Its Makers; Rail City Chicago, USA; AIA Guide to Chicago; Chicago, the Marvelous City of the West;* and *Rand, McNally & Co's Bird's-Eye Views and Guide to Chicago*. Above them all: *City of the Century,* by Donald Miller, not quoted from till the chapter "Ships on the Prairie," but consulted all through these early chapters.

The chapter's title is my homage to the late V. S. Naipaul's great book of the same name.

And, finally: Was FLW's middle name originally Lincoln? It seems so, but nonetheless there has long been argument among scholars. It seems that his father, a great Lincoln admirer, bequeathed the name. Neither birth certificate nor family Bible has ever surfaced. Various biographers have had it one way or the other. If he was born Frank Lincoln Wright, which is what I believe, when did Lincoln turn to Lloyd? (See the text in the chapter "Ships on the Prairie" re Tim Samuelson's research on the 1897 Heller House, and how, in the course of doing the drawings, "Frank L. Wright" seems to have become more or less permanently "Frank Lloyd Wright." But that doesn't speak to the question of Lincoln vs. Lloyd.) The 1880 federal census lists thirteen-year-old "Wright, Frank L." as a nephew and "servant" (really a family hired hand) on the farm of Uncle James Lloyd Jones. My own belief is that his middle name was *just then* in the process of morphing in his mind from Lincoln to Lloyd, and part of the reason was the tearing fabric of his parents' marriage: he was henceforth going to put his lot with the Lloyd Joneses. It would take a while for the transformation to become complete. As for possible doubt about whether he *was* christened Frank *Lincoln* Wright, I will take the nearly unimpeachable word of scholar Mary Jane Hamilton. She has him as Frank Lincoln at birth.

The Lost Architect

PRECEDE. The "end of the present social order" quote was in *Washington Post,* October 26, 1938, reporting on his talk to the Federal Architects Association of the day before. The "He was brutal" quote is in *Pedro Guerrero: A Photographer's Journey,* p. 81.

CHAPTER. It's a source of not-small mystery to me why more book-length FLW biographers and historians haven't tried to peer more deeply into Cecil's life. From the start, I was curious about him. He was like a figure in the borderland between shadow and myth, and I just sensed that his own story would illumine FLW's. This isn't to say Cecil doesn't come up in practically every long-form FLW work—he does. But just not at the depth I believe he deserves. Very late in the research (when I was long past the Cecil chapter) I found FLW saying this of Cecil in a talk to the Fellowship (it was on December 14, 1958, so just four months before his death): "One of the first acquaintances of mine and the dearest friend perhaps I've had." As with so much of the content of his Fellowship talks (see "The Sad Ballad of William Carey Wright 2"), the remark had just seemed to fall out of him unbidden. To be blunt: I have wondered whether previous book-length chroniclers have wished largely to avoid Cecil because of the difficult sexual ambiguities.

The chapter is primarily a product of my own reporting and research, although, again, Tim Samuelson—who had thought about Cecil for years and done some informal work of his own on Cecil's mysteries—was invaluable. An architectural historian, Donald M. Aucutt, former editor of a no-longer-published journal entitled *Prairie,* has offered important biographical work in print—and ahead of me. I discovered it somewhat belatedly in my Cecil travels and was glad to compare my findings with some of his. (Aucutt published a series of articles and entries about Cecil in his magazine between 2005 and 2012; he and I have never met.) Some Cecil materials are in the McCormick Library of Special Collections at Northwestern University. Mark Hertzberg's *Wright in Racine* (the author became a friend during the writing of this book) adds to the record. Mostly, I just dug out on my own what I could from newspapers, from various directories and family histories and local histories and church histories and census records and real estate records and cemetery records and university records, not to say records such as Cecil's death certificate and probated will from Erie County, New York (which is to say Buffalo). I am grateful to an Illinois genealogist and author, Gene Meier, who helped with research on the family. The largest trove of personal family material came from Cynthia Beach-Smeltzer and Andy Haynes, mentioned above, and more about each of them in a moment.

As said in the text, Cecil's presence in the autobio runs essentially from pp. 67 to 128 in the '32 edition. He comes in and out of the narrative as FLW does a great many other things. The reader can find almost all of the Cecil-related quotes between those pages, and no need to cite them individually here. Except for this: the reference to "loving concerts" is on p. 75 of the '43; that two-word sentence doesn't appear in the '32. Again, I have tried whenever feasible to embed in the text the dates and names of publications of journalism having to do with Cecil, re later events in his life.

Goldberger's quote is on p. 51 of the companion book to the 2013 PBS special, *10 Buildings That Changed America*. FLW's "To say the house planted by myself": I first came across this apparently not-well-known quote in the booklet "The Usonian House: Souvenir of the Exhibition, 60 Years of Living Architecture," which was produced in conjunction with the opening of the *Sixty Years* show in Manhattan. (It's in the archives of the Guggenheim. For *Sixty*, see chapter "Terminals 1.") FLW quote "So long as we had the luxuries" is on p. 115 of the autobio. The "Swallowing my shame hard" is on p. 67 of *Genius and the Mobocracy*. The Maxwell "I had inadvertently walked" is on p. 9 paper edition of his novella *So Long, See You Tomorrow*.

Cecil's letter to the Miles family is August 7, 1899. *Morning Telegraph* p. 1 story is April 7, 1902. *Boston Daily Globe* is April 7. Ditto *New York Daily Tribune*. Kenneth Cobb at the New York City Department of Records and Information Services found the 2nd District court docket.

Details of purchase of Oak Park lot are in endnotes, p. 276, of "An Old Madison Boy."

Re arc of a life. First, Cecil's family: seven children in a minister's family, spread over approximately eighteen years, with Cecil, the semi-closeted gay child, in the approximate middle. To say three overachieving siblings: his eldest brother (mentioned in the text): John Howard, prominent Manhattan lawyer. His older brother, Charles Abel, painter and muralist. His younger brother, Arthur Mills, poet and renowned physician. All these Corwin kids, competing for family position—as said in the text, it must have brought its own terrible pressures. I have to think the family knew, eventually, or maybe earlier, of Cecil's semi-secret about himself.

Cecil and college: As said in the text, he attended three and apparently graduated from none—Illinois College in Jacksonville, Ill.; Beloit College in Beloit, Wis.; and the University of Illinois (then known as the Illinois Industrial University), where he was in the architecture curriculum until 1883. (That would have been only a few years before he and FLW met.) In a 1916 directory of alumni, there is an asterisk by his name, which seems to question whether he did, in fact, graduate. It appears he left UI a few credits short of the requisite for graduation. (Aucutt's research guided me to my college inquiries.)

Re glimpses of Cecil's surviving work: If you go to the South Side, to the Kenwood district, to South Dorchester Avenue, between East Fiftieth Street and Hyde Park Boulevard, there are five attached Cecil row houses from no. 5027 to no. 5035. They hardly compare to FLW houses, but they are there. In the summer of 2015, I got inside one. It was being offered for $865,000. I introduced myself to the realtor. She had no idea who Cecil Corwin was. The owners, too, had never heard of him.

Cecil's scant death notice is in the February 1, 1941, *Buffalo Courier-Express.*

Re the seemingly loaded photo of FLW and Cecil, and its own ambiguous history: You can find it sliced in half in the back of the autobio. FLW cropped it. You see only the edge of his shoulder and Cecil looking admiringly (homo-erotically?) toward him, except the uninitiated would never know this. Next to the sliced photo is a different photo of FLW, gazing out at the world. (It's close in kind and texture to the photo at the start of "The Enigma of Arrival.") So doesn't this fact alone suggest on some level that FLW was uncomfortable with the picture of himself and Cecil because of what it seemed to connote? But where did FLW get this picture? At the end of 1931, when the autobio was in production, FLW dashed a wire to Cecil's brother Arthur, asking if he could send a photo of Cecil "in his early or middle years" ASAP. Arthur replied the next day that he didn't have a picture but that he would reach Cecil to ask him. He did. Cecil sent a photo, but it was returned because of a wrong mailing address. (We know this from Cecil's "reunion" letter to FLW, quoted extensively in the text.) My guess is that the equivocal photo is *not* the one Cecil sent, and anyway it apparently didn't reach FLW in time for publication. So FLW used his own photo—the one we know; the one at the start of the chapter—but sliced it in half, because of his unease. To me, this seems the only plausible explanation.

Re Cecil and the autobio: We also know from the coming-back-together letter that an NYC architect named Chester Holmes Aldrich gave Cecil what seems to have been an early copy, and that Cecil read it, and of course saw all the protective stuff between the lines. Aldrich, as noted in the text, was an upper-crust society architect. His career would have represented everything that Cecil's did not. I wonder if Cecil had drafted for him, although I could find no record.

Finally, Andy Haynes and Cynthia Beach-Smeltzer. I have spoken above of their generosity. But two stories. While I was in N.C., Haynes said he was going to put me on the phone with someone who actually knew Cecil. This can't be possible, I said. Someone alive who knew Cecil? (Born, to remind you, in 1860.) Haynes dialed up a relative named Carroll Pickens Rogers, Jr., who was born in 1912, and who was 102 and absolutely clearheaded on that day in October 2014 when we spoke. He kept pronouncing Cecil's name "SESS-ill," which further threw me, for I had always assumed it as "CEE-cill." Carroll Pickens (he was the grandson of Emma, Cecil's late-life spouse) said: "There was some unfair criticism of him. I think some people in the town and in the family thought he was fortune hunting. My grandmother didn't take kindly to that. The truth is, there wasn't all that much money left by then anyway."

Beach-Smeltzer: In a way, *she* is the story, or at least somebody else's whole other Cecil story. We have known each other from almost the start of this book. Her grandmother, whom she never knew, was Cecil's kid sister, Marquita Beach. The legend that Cynthia Beach-Smeltzer grew up with is that her great-uncle Cecil (who died before Cynthia was born) had come home to Buffalo a broken man, and that it was somehow FLW's fault. He had stolen something vital from Cecil. FLW was just a subject avoided in the family, she told me. No matter her deep interest in genealogy, she'd never let herself read FLW's autobio. I went to Rochester, and slowly she began to change her mind. Cecil wasn't embittered in regard to FLW. (Despite her researches, she had never seen their coming-back-together letter.) Cecil was entirely proud of what they once had—and so was FLW. The real fate was that the two had met at all. Cecil came to see how inferior his gift was next to FLW's. Inferior, okay, but worthy all the same. That is the true tragedy of the story—he couldn't see it, or lost sight of it. One day, in an email, Cecil's great-niece said: "I have been giving this much thought. We have to go back to square one. . . . [W]e need to forget the Beach family myth passed to me . . . as completely false." There's some beauty.

Ships on the Prairie

PRECEDE. The James Agee quote from *Let Us Now Praise Famous Men* is near the start of the chapter "Near a Church." FLW's claim for the Winslow as the first prairie (lowercase) is in "Recollections: United States, 1893–1920," published in the weekly British periodical *Architects' Journal*, July 16, 1936. (Between July 16, '36 and August 6, '36, the magazine ran four Wright reminiscences, all under the title "Recollections." See *AJ* reference at the end of my chapter "Attended by the Gothic.") "Horizontal line" quote as the line of domesticity and "the only one here worthy of respect," with its quirkily placed comma, are both in an essay in the famous *Ausgefuhrte Bauten und Entwurfe von Frank Lloyd Wright*, published in two folios in Berlin in 1910–11 by Ernst Wasmuth Verlag—and known in shorthand among Wright scholars as the "Wasmuth Portfolio." (See "Connective Tissue: One" chapter.) He wrote the Wasmuth essay—it's entitled "Studies and Executed Buildings by Frank Lloyd Wright"—in June 1910 from Florence. In 1998, Rizzoli brought out an English translation, and it is from this edition and translation that I took the quotes. The "loved the prairie by instinct" quote is in *AJ*, July 16, '36, and also in *An Autobiography*, p. 137. Indeed, an early version of that *AJ* article can be found in the autobiography, starting on p. 136. The "born an American child" and the "should begin *on* the ground" and the "rooted deep in racial instinct" and the "not as a cave" quotes are all from the same July 16 *AJ* issue. (In the manuscript division of the Library of Congress, in the Frank Lloyd Wright Papers, under "Speeches and Articles, 1933–35," there is a nineteen-page typed manuscript of what turned into the four *AJ* pieces in the summer of 1936. It's on yellow onionskin and contains handwritten revisions. At the top, in his precise hand, FLW wrote: "Final Revision December 15, 1935." It's interesting to compare this manuscript to the published *AJ* pieces and to see how few changes the editors made; maybe it was part of the bargain.) Faulkner spoke immortally of "the last ding-dong of doom" in his Nobel Prize acceptance speech, in Stockholm, December 10, 1950.

CHAPTER. A copy of Llewellyn's "Letters to His Children" is in the research center of what used to be known as the Frank Lloyd Wright Home and Studio Foundation in Oak Park. (This has been a point of confusion. The Home and Studio Foundation, established in 1974, became, in 2000, the Frank Lloyd Wright Preservation Trust. In 2013, the organization changed its name to Frank Lloyd Wright Trust. The streamlined-named Trust now preserves and cares for the Robie House in Hyde Park; the Rookery, a landmark office building in the Loop; the Emil Bach House in Rogers Park on the North Side; Unity Temple; and the Home and Studio.)

Robert Llewellyn's children—Thomas Wright, Elizabeth Catherine Wright, and Tim Wright—remembered their father for me. Elizabeth's 2011 lovingly annotated book of letters between her parents, written during the Depression, *Dear Bob, Dear Betty,* was valuable.

Miller's "This is what is amazing" quote is on p. 304 of the hardback edition of *City.* His "making history" is on p. 303, and the "world center" is on p. 305. Levine's "For someone with virtually" quote is on p. 3 of *Architecture.* FLW's Wainwright as "first human expression" quote is in *Modern Architecture: being the Kahn lectures for 1930,* p. 85. His "left him like any tramp" is on p. 92 of the autobio. The "heavy-bodied, short-legged" quote is on p. 100. The "toady" quote is on p. 99. Elmslie's letter to FLW is October 30, 1932. His undated letter to his partner circa fourteen years later is in the William Gray Purcell Papers in the Northwest Architectural Archives, University of Minnesota Libraries, Minneapolis. *Life* piece is August 12, 1946, and *Reader's Digest* reprint is November 1946. Gill's "Sullivan's graphic work" quote is on p. 77 of the paper edition of his bio. Sullivan's "every inch" quote is in *Lippincott's Monthly Magazine,* March 1896. FLW's "Ah, that erotic supreme adventure" quote is on p. 269 of the autobio. Secrest's "One of the most difficult aspects" quote is on p. 139 of her bio. FLW's "first sensed the definitely decorative" quote is on p. 106 of the autobio. The Robie as a "steamship at anchor" is on p. 433 of the *AIA Guide to Chicago*. Miller's "drew an estimated 27 million" quote is on p. 488 of *City*. Levine's "new urban vision" quote is on p. 6 of *Architecture*. Sullivan's "lewd exhibit" quote is on p. 322 of his *The Autobiography of an Idea*. FLW's quote re the Winslow "had burst on the view" is on p. 125 of the autobio. Hitchcock's quotes re the Heller are on pp. 27–28 of his *In the Nature of Materials*.

The fiction of the handmade shoes that cost the impecunious draftsman $20 to $25 is in Elmslie's circa 1946 letter to his partner, Purcell. Ottenheimer's whipping a child not his own is in the August 22, 1885 *NYT*. Re the barrel-vaulted playroom atop the Oak Park home, and its mural inspired by *Arabian Nights:* Cecil's brother Charles painted it. (One more Corwin connection.) Re FLW taking credit for LHS's Wainwright (and *other*): In a letter of circa March 20, 1903, from D. D. Martin to John Larkin, there is this: "The $500,000 Wainwright Building and the Union Trust Building of St. Louis; the Schiller Theatre and the Stock Exchange in Chicago; the Seattle and Pueblo Opera Houses, all Adler & Sullivan's work, were, I inferred from Mr. Wright, largely his creations." (This letter is reproduced on pp. 131–33 in Jack Quinan's *Frank Lloyd Wright's Larkin Building*.) The hugely important FLW/Martin correspondence is held at university archives, State University of New York at Buffalo—and not indexed in the Garland. Ida Heller: My talk with her great-granddaughter was in March 2016. As noted in the text, the Illinois state archives has a coroner's report. But I couldn't locate an official death certificate. Fortunately, a repro-duced copy (from the Office of the Cook County Coroner) is in the appendix of Zana Wolf's 2000 doctoral dissertation on the Heller. Data is where you find it.

Among many works consulted, particularly helpful was an essay by Patrick Pinnell, "Academic Tradition and the Individual Talent: Similarity and Dif-ference in Wright's Formation," in *On and By Frank Lloyd Wright,* ed. Robert McCarter (Phaidon, 2005).

Attended by the Gothic

PRECEDE. My own memory and imagination.

CHAPTER. A labor of love, not to say gratitude, to be able to go back to my childhood hometown and try to reconstruct the byzantine life and unlikely survival of the B. Harley Bradley. To repeat what was said in the text: there are just some FLW works that seem bent on rewriting FLW's own history and unlikely survival, and this is one, perhaps *the* one, not that I had any real idea about that when I started revisiting Kankakee, much less when I lived there. (What I principally knew about in the years long after I had moved away was the ghastly murder of Stephen Small.) Among the local preservationists and genealogy researchers who came crucially to my aid were Norman Strasma, Mardene Hinton, Laura Golowski, and Mary Schatz. They possessed varying amounts of paper (archival material) and much personal lore; my job was to try to separate the fact from the myths. Sharon and Gaines Hall, who brought the house so beautifully back up to shine, were welcoming—and allowed me to interview them several times. Among FLW scholars, Thomas A. Heinz knows much about the house, and has shared some of it with me in email and phone conversations. (He's long had a work-in-progress on the Bradley; he keeps trying to find a photo of Bradley himself.) In his *The Vision of Frank Lloyd Wright*, he calls the house "[t]he building that signifies the beginning of the first great period of Wright's career." Among other contributions Heinz (an architect as well as a prolific author) has made to the scholarship is to tease out the connections between FLW and the Bradley/Hickox families, and how FLW came to get the commissions. (It has to do with the Roberts family of Oak Park, for whom Wright did work. Mrs. Roberts was a relative of the Bradley/Hickox clan.) There is a first-rate documentary on the house, "An American Home," released in 2017 by Chicago filmmaker Tom Desch. The adopted son of Yesteryear proprietors Marvin Hammack and Ray Schimel—Tonino Dessolis— provided insights on the phone about both men. Essentially, I put the Bradley's story together by hanging in the house, by consulting FLW histories, talking to the experts, reading local histories, and, not least, combing newspaper files. For this last: I've tried again to embed in the text whenever feasible the general time frames and names of publications regarding the house and its (*her*) specific tragedies and turns—B. Harley's 1914 suicide and Stephen Small's 1987 kidnapping, for instance. So no need to itemize the many publications here, except for these several that may be of interest: *Newsweek* story on the house (re Barbra Streisand and desk) is February 1, 1988. *Tribune* piece about the house having "deteriorated into a vacant, cold and musty-smelling building" is October 20, 1985. The *Kankakee Daily Journal* "Wrong on Wright" editorial, which seems to have marked a preservation turning point, is December 2, 2001.

At the back of this chapter: Spencer and the Prairie School and Steinway Hall, all of these being rich myths, and all of them a subspecialty of Tim Samuelson. Easy to know why: it's because so many Prairie Schoolers have faded into obscurity, except among aesthetes, and Tim wishes to speak for the forgotten. So I am the beneficiary of many conversations about the Prairie School and of the legend of Steinway. At the same time, debt to other Prairie scholars, and perhaps first among these are the works of H. Allen Brooks. (His lengthy introduction in his 1984 *Frank Lloyd Wright and the Prairie School* is the best condensed summary I've seen of what the so-called school was.) Richard Guy Wilson's "a movement about style as much as" quote is on p. 94 of his long, important essay, "Prairie School Works in the Department of Architecture at the Art Institute of Chicago," in *Art Institute of Chicago Museum Studies* vol. 21, no. 2 (1995). Levine quote about *Ladies' Home Journal* designs is on p. 30 of his *Architecture*.

Finally, re FLW's age and birth year: When did he begin to shave off two years? I am not sure anyone knows. I think the real answer may be that he did it in dribs and drabs (sort of like slowly morphing "Lincoln" into "Lloyd" as his middle name), starting in the middle or late teens of the century, but not always sticking to the fib. As noted in the text, passport applications and ship manifests are a documentary help. But they are inconsistent. The earliest fudging I can find is on his August 1919 sailing homeward from Japan on the *Empress of Asia*. But that was sort of a split fudging—see my chapter "Connective Tissue: Two." And two years later, in 1921, he—momentarily—reverted to the truth: i.e., stating on the passenger list he was born in 1867, not 1869. (Re this sailing, and its importance, see notes for chapter "The Man on the Station Platform.")

Unity and Mamah: The Sacred Against the Profane

PRECEDE. FLW's quotes in the two successive paras of my text beginning with "This absorbing, consuming phrase" are on pp. 165–66 of the autobio. The "I, too, sought shelter" quote is on p. 168. Re uttering Mamah's name just once: as noted in the text, it's on p. 190. (In the next edition of the autobio, the '43, I also can find just one mention, but it's a different passage: on p. 188.) The "So, when family-life" quote is on p. 170. The "I loved my children": p. 166. The "architect absorbed the father": p. 111. The hard-to-believe Warren McArthur story is on p. 110.

CHAPTER. First, re the many quotes in this long chapter: again, I tried when not cumbersome to the story to embed the source (and date and publication name if the quote was from a piece of journalism). But here are some other citations, including several journalistic ones not otherwise identified, going in order: "If the artist will only open" is on p. 57 of *Frank Lloyd Wright: Essential Texts*, and the "primitive river bed" is on p. 48. The review in *American Architect and Building* is in the April 26, 1902, issue. FLW's "simple cliff of brick" is on p. 151 of the autobio. Huxtable's "futuristic and old-fashioned" quote is on p. 100 of the paper edition of her bio. Report of Frank Borthwick's accident is in the October 10, 1888 *Dixon* (Ill.) *Sun*. The "Death was caused" re Jessie Borthwick is in the April 19, 1901, *Oak Park Times*. My talk with Meredith d'Ambrosio was in June 2016. Levine's "Inside, it is low, dark, snug" quote is on p. 49 of *Architecture*. The quoted Charles White letters are in an expert piece in the autumn 1971 (no. 4) *Journal of Architectural Education*, by Nancy K. Morris

Smith and Charles E. White, Jr. The FLW quote "No, my dear Mrs. Gablemore" is in the July 16, 1936, *Architects' Journal*. His oft-quoted line that Unity Temple "is where you will find the first" is in a 1952 address, "The Destruction of the Box," to the Junior Chapter of the AIA of NYC. (The line is quoted everywhere, but the source seems seldom noted by chroniclers.) The "looks easy enough now" is on p. 160 of the autobio. Hemingway's "dignity of movement" quote re icebergs is on p. 192 of the 1932 edition of *Death in the Afternoon*. Scully's "not a big building" and Levine's "raised platform" and "space dropping away" are from their on-air interviews in the '98 Burns-Novick FLW documentary. Levine's "free of material" quote is on p. 43 of *Architecture*. My interview with Lesniak was in November 2013. The "[I]t may amuse you" comment is in the Elmslie letter of October 30, 1932. The "How had she come to a point" quote is on p. 32 of *Loving Frank*. Allen's quotes are on p. 25 of her *Family Memories*. Twombly quote is on p. 126 of paper edition of his 1979 bio. Janet Ashbee's December 21 journal entry is in the Papers of Charles Robert Ashbee, Archives Centre, King's College, Cambridge. (It has been reproduced in several books, notably Felicity Ashbee's *Janet Ashbee: Love, Marriage, and the Arts & Crafts Movement*, but to read a copy of the entry in her own hand, mailed to me from the archives, was a powerful experience in trying to get a sense of the breakup of the FLW family.) *Oak Leaves* report of FLW ornament talk is in its edition of January 16, 1909. Handwritten minutes of Unity's meeting of March 9, 1909, are in Unity's archives in Oak Park. Levine's quote re the Robie is on p. 52 of *Architecture*. FLW's remark re Robie as "source of world-wide" is in a letter of March 20, 1941, to Mrs. Julius Weil (she was Dankmar Adler's daughter). *Oak Leaves* coverage of Unity's September 26 opening is in its edition of October 2, 1909. *Oak Leaves* editorial re slaughter of August 15, 1914, is in its August 22, 1914, edition.

Other: *Oak Leaves* ran J. L. Wright's 1904 picture of the family in its August 6, 1969, edition. For Mamah's bio and that of her family and also of Edwin Cheney, I consulted census records, cemetery records, city directories, local histories, university records, corporate records, newspaper files. Re the great myth grown up around the "Yellow Devil" in Oak Park. Many chroniclers have fallen for the false legends about FLW and cars. But a prolific latter-day researcher named Richie Herink has tracked down information (and in some cases the registrations) of almost every vehicle FLW ever owned, and he generously shared his time and research. See his *The Car Is Architecture: A Visual History of Frank Lloyd Wright's 85 Cars and One Motorcycle*. (Mary Jane Hamilton wrote a lengthy piece about FLW and his cars in the winter 2010 *Frank Lloyd Wright Quarterly*, but she, too, defers to the astonishing work of Herink.) The depressive FLW photo, which I have identified as being taken circa mid-

1909, just a few months before he fled: no absolute proof of the date, but David Bagnall, curator at FLW Trust, hedgingly agrees. Other researchers have dated the picture from 1904 and 1905 and even earlier. Alofsin has it as a frontispiece in his *Lost Years* and puts the date as "circa 1909." (The FLW archives has it as 1907; I believe '09.) Re Bagnall and the Oak Park home: he allowed me free roam on various days when tours were in progress, and I remain grateful. The most thorough overview guide on the house remains—for me—a 48-page 1988 illustrated publication (with floor plans and photos), published by the Home and Studio, *The Oak Park Home and Studio of Frank Lloyd Wright.*

Finally, on the thorny question of numbers, which is to say trying to get precise counts for how many projects, realized and unrealized, FLW accomplished in specific periods (not to say in the whole of his career). What a researcher soon discovers is that the numbers vary, and years overlap. Different scholars have come up with different counts, and the FLW Foundation itself, in various publications and writings, has produced conflicting figures. The reader will note (in the passage in the text beginning "Data alone could never tell this story") that I am hedging my bets in the sentence itself. (I hedge them elsewhere in the text re supposed counts for specific time periods.) The numbers that I've provided here are from high authorities, and I gladly defer. The 1899–1909 figure (114 built works out of 208 projects) is from Robert McCarter, who is thought to have published the first-ever comprehensive list of FLW works in his 1997 *Frank Lloyd Wright.* The list was assembled at McCarter's request by Bruce Brooks Pfeiffer, founding director of the FLW Foundation archives at Taliesin West. (Both men appear in the narrative in the chapter, "Terminals 2.") The figure cited here (114 executed; 208 accomplished) can be found on p. 90 in McCarter's brief bio, *Frank Lloyd Wright,* published in 2006, in a Critical Lives series from Reaktion Books. The figure that, between 1902 and '06, FLW and draftsmen worked on 75 projects: this is from author Patrick F. Cannon, who has had a long association with the (as-now-named) FLW Trust in Oak Park. (See p. 88 in his *Hometown Architect.*) Finally, Levine, on p. 46 of *Architecture,* cites the figure of 45 houses, and 25 others between 1903 and 1909 that went unbuilt. To repeat: I am more than happy to go with the tallies of these authorities, but let it also be said that I have tried several times to do my own counting, based on published lists from the foundation, and in consultation with the archivists in Arizona, and then comparing them with the figures from the scholars, and damn if I can get nearly anything to reconcile precisely. It's like a checkbook that refuses to balance. Finally, you throw up your hands. FLW must be chortling.

PART II Chains of Moral Consequence: 1914–1921

The Ellison quote is in the novel's prologue. Morrison's is on p. 17 of her novel. FLW quote is in a talk to the fellowship, December 17, 1950.

Coming Before Him in His Dreams: Notes on an Alabama Native Son

PRECEDE. Again, it was put together from conflicting news accounts, as well as from conflicting accounts in numerous books and journalism these decades later, as well as from old directories and census records and a handful of oral histories: the best obtainable version of the truth, as I could perceive it. Again, Keiran Murphy was crucial. We got out the floor plans, walked the spaces, tried to imagine. The *Weekly Home News* letter is in its August 21, 1914, edition.

CHAPTER. As said in the text, it was a lightly inked (or penciled) question mark beside "Alabama" on Julian's death certificate (copy on file in the Iowa County courthouse in Dodgeville, Wis.) that took me south. The vital clue hiding in plain sight, seemingly ignored by predecessors. I worked with local historians and genealogists in Alabama as well as with statewide archivists. Census records and county courthouse records were pathfinders. Slowly, a skeletal picture of the skeletal-looking man (in the only photo we have) began to emerge. Large help came from the archivists at Cobb Memorial Archives in the Chambers County Library—amazing local resource.

Hollis L. Gentry, mentioned in the text, genealogy specialist at the Smithsonian's National Museum of African American History and Culture, helped me locate Galon Carlton's probated will and other documents. As to that will: I'm still in wonder it could slip through the nets of time. I'm still in wonder it existed at all. I'm still thanking Gentry.

Du Bois quote is on p. 30 of his *Black Reconstruction in America*. The interview with Bert Frederick is on pp. 126–27 of the Alabama portion of *Born in Slavery: Slave Narratives from the Federal Writers' Project, 1936–1938*.

Chambers County coda. An amateur Alabama genealogist whose hobby is hunting for lost family cemeteries took me one day into a deep wood off county road 187, which in turn is off a larger road that locals refer to as the Cusseta-to-Huguley Road. Don Clark had been hunting for a good while for the Frederick family cemetery. It wasn't marked on many local maps, and those that did have it marked had its location wrong. The spot is about three and a half miles east of Cusseta. Other Chamber Countians with no connection to the Fredericks have long held this land.

I happened to be along that afternoon. We went in Clark's pickup. We climbed a padlocked fence and went into the wood. The plot of stones, prob-ably untended for decades, was in a thicket of old pines and poplars and sweetgums. Carved on Mariah Diana Frederick's toppling and mossy stone was "Good bye Mother. We hope to meet you in heaven." This was the matri-arch—I feel certain, if cannot prove—to whom Julian Carlton's mother once belonged as property. According to Clark and others to whom I've spoken, family cemeteries on old Chambers County plantations were often located within a brief distance from the main house. The slave shacks would have been nearby. So the mother of the twenty-six-year-old who did what he did that August midday may have been born a slingshot or so away from where I stood. Or at least I wished to think of it that way. Not that it shed any light whatever on Julian's riddles.

Connective Tissue: One

PRECEDE. The "Cantilever slabs overhanging" quote appears as a caption (he wrote it) in his January 1938 *Architectural Forum* piece (and the piece is dis-cussed in the later chapter "In the Fourth Dimension"). The figure of circa 200,000 visitors per year comes from the Conservancy.

CHAPTER. First, re quotes, and their sources: again, as above, the ones that are cited here are those that are not otherwise readily identifiable from the text itself. FLW's "I remember" meditations are on p. 364 of the autobio. His daugh-ter Frances's letter re "champ Elysees and "Louver": It must have been written in January 1910, because the note was mailed to her father in Paris—where he apparently was. Atop the letter is something that looks like "Thursday '10 1910." That makes no real sense. (January 10 of that year was a Monday.) Pos-sibly the child was putting the new year down twice? Dinesen's oft-quoted "all sorrows": she seems to have said it, spontaneously, in a phone interview, and the line was then published in *The New York Times Book Review*, November 3, 1957. Huxtable quote re "romantic passion" is on p. 112 of the paper edition of her bio. Mamah's letter to Key re "Trying to live": as said, the letter is undated, but Alice Friedman, referenced in text, believes it to be circa May 1910, and that is important re FLW and his state of mind. (See additional comment below on this.) FLW's "little cream white villa" line is on p. 168 of the autobio.

Re the FLW-Ashbee letters: The letters quoted are from three sources. Alof-sin's *Lost Years* (see pp. 52–56), Gill's bio (see pp. 210–11). But the correspon-dence is more elaborately discussed and reproduced in Alan Crawford's 1970 piece (vol. 13) in the journal *Architectural History*, "Ten Letters from Frank Lloyd Wright to Charles Robert Ashbee." For FLW's March 31, 1910, letter, I was able to examine a copy of the original—which makes all the difference, given

FLW's always quirky punctuation and sentence structure and underlining of words. Quoting an FLW letter that has been reproduced in a book or article, no matter how scholarly, comes with its risks.

FLW's July 4, 1910, extremely long letter to Anna Wright: Keiran Murphy supplied a transcription copy of the original. (I have been unable to find this letter indexed in any FLW repository. But William Drennan, in his *Death in a Prairie House*, p. 182, has this source note, in quotes; "Typed FLLW/Porter ALLW4016" folder, FLW Archive, Taliesin West. That file appears to be no longer active.)

Other: The details of FLW's return home from Chicago papers, notably the *Tribune*. W. E. Martin's letter to his brother D.D. is October 10, 1910, and is quoted on p. 212 of Gill bio. Kitty's letter to Janet Ashbee is quoted on p. 213 of Gill. Alofsin quote re "double life" is on p. 67 of *Lost Years*. FLW's "At least I will know" letter to D. D. Martin is October 25, 1910 (and is reproduced in full on p. 17 in the not-heretofore-mentioned *Letters to Clients: Frank Lloyd Wright*, edited by B. B. Pfeiffer). FLW's wire to Martin re "tight real estate situation" is April 3, 1911, and follow-up letter is April 12.

Re number of commissions for 1909 and 1912: Again, this figure is based on the comprehensive list published by Robert McCarter in back of his 1997 *Frank Lloyd Wright* (referenced above), the list having been compiled by Pfeiffer of the FLW Foundation.

Re the Boynton House and Beulah and the rumor of a relationship with FLW, and right at the time of Mamah, and whether all of it may be a leaky vessel: See Prof. Leonard K. Eaton's *Two Chicago Architects and Their Clients*, pp. 112–17. See story in *Rochester Democrat and Chronicle*, April 11, 1959, and also a story by Bill Ringle of *Rochester Times-Union* in its January 22, 1955, edition. (Ringle donated his research notes to the local history and genealogy division of the Rochester Public Library.) None of these overtly suggest a romantic relationship (Eaton's has the nearest whiff, if perhaps inadvertently), but my guess is that these works must have had *something* to do with stories you still hear in Rochester about Beulah and FLW, although perhaps the real source was gossip at the time. To me, the relevance of it has only to do with Mamah.

Finally, re Mamah's letters to Ellen Key as they assume added import in trying to gauge FLW and his own doubts: As said in text, the letters were found only in modern times in Stockholm. They brought Mamah's mute voice to life. European scholar Lena Johannesson wrote of them in 1995 in *Nora: Nordic Journal of Women's Studies*. Then American scholar Friedman brought the story further along in 2002 in the *Journal of the Society of Architectural Historians*. A third scholar, Barbara Miller Lane, again discussed the letters (the first six of which, as noted in text, are undated) in a 2008 book, *Modern Swedish Design: Three Founding Texts*. Lane disagreed with Friedman as to the dates of the early letters, and also re the timing and details of Mamah's and FLW's contacts with Key. But if Friedman is correct, and I think she is, then Mamah's very first letter ("Trying to live"), written in May 1910 (a sizable extract appears in Friedman's *JSAH* piece, "Frank Lloyd Wright and Feminism"), lines right up with when FLW was revealing some of his own great doubts about their sojourn in Europe. An inverted window to the man, so to speak. So the letters are beautiful for their own sake—and much more.

The Man on the Station Platform

PRECEDE. Just one more try to square the unsquarable. I've walked the upstairs and downstairs of Tan-y-deri, trying to imagine. Re FLW and the sobbing and the piano: As noted in text, the story has traveled much by word of mouth. It has come up in several oral histories, including a 1995 interview, conducted by historians at Taliesin West, with John S. Christensen, who is the grandson of a long-deceased eyewitness: Frances Inglis Thayer. She was a young Chicago girl who was visiting at Spring Green on the night of August 15—and is said to have seen the dead bodies and heard FLW playing Bach over and over. Secrest's account of Franklin Porter is told on pp. 221–22 of her bio. The circa-1917 veranda photo is in the files at Taliesin. J. L. Wright's description of the depot and R. L. Jones's "Stand up" to FLW is on pp. 81–82 of his *My Father*.

CHAPTER. There's a clutch of good books (most listed in the bibliography) about the still woefully unknown American tragedy known incorrectly as the Tulsa Race Riot. (In Tulsa and elsewhere, there has been a concerted push in the last several years among people of color to have the name formally changed to Tulsa Race Massacre. I wholeheartedly support the push.) But, as said in the text, none of these good books has sought to explore any connection between Tulsa's biblical fire and Taliesin's biblical fire, and indeed almost none even makes the connection that RLJ and FLW were cousins, let alone intimate and contentious first cousins. When FLW does come up, it's only in passing. This is wholly understandable—the chroniclers weren't engaged in a work about FLW. His history was peripheral—except it wasn't, which is my whole point. I will say quickly that I, too, might never have stumbled on this mother lode of hidden story were it not for a former Wisconsin newspaperman and FLW author named Ron McCrea. He pointed me toward RLJ, as a way of possibly understanding something more about FLW; my gratitude is everlasting. (McCrea's illustrated study, *Building Taliesin,* which takes the form of a closely detailed narrative album, has been valuable across great swaths of this book.)

Again, I've sought to embed in the text the source of major quotes, including the ones from newspapers (many quotes from newspapers in the story, which, of course, has much to do with newspapers and a newspaperman), but I've done that *especially* here so as to go into some important background. (A ton of background, but I'll restrain myself.) But first, re quotes, in newspapers and otherwise, the sources (or pub dates) of which aren't readily identifiable from the text, and going in order: "History knows no fences" is, in fact, the title of one of the key essays in the 2001 governor's *Final Report*. (The report, scholarly and minutely detailed, runs to nearly 200 pages, counting maps and graphs and endnotes; it's available online and can be downloaded in its entirety.) The essay is by Scott Ellsworth, referenced in the text, and the late John Hope Franklin, one of the country's greatest historians of twentieth-century black history. The Blanche Cole oral history ("we had lost everything") is in a document entitled "Survivor's Remembrances" at the Greenwood Cultural Center, which is a remembrance museum and memorial located in the heart of where the slaughter happened. (A moving experience to visit.) Re "Where's my baby" cry from unidentified mother: recounted on p. 104 of James S. Hirsch's *Riot and Remembrance,* one of the better books about the riot. (FLW's name does not appear in it.) Adjutant General of Oklahoma National Guard's quote re "fantastic write-up" is on p. 59 of the *Final Report* (and appears in various books). RLJ's fiction of earning a master's in law and also his quote re "full of uncertainty" are in a long celebratory piece in the *Tribune* he wrote about himself to mark his 20th anniversary of owning the paper: October 8, 1939. "He was very opinionated" is on p. 274 of Tim Madigan's *The Burning,* another good riot book. RLJ's first editorial in *WSJ* is August 10, 1911. B. T. Washington spoke in Madison April 26, 1914. RLJ's front-page review of *Birth* is November 7, 1915. Re the letters between RLJ and FLW: These are the ones not identified in the chapter by date: FLW's "baptism of fire" is November 18, 1929. His "bang whang everything" is December 22, 1930. His "striking quick and hard" is undated, but seems from May or June 1930. His "double the punch" is April 7, 1933. His "what is a home anyway" is December 5, 1928. RLJ's "You covet attention" is November 26, 1928. FLW's "How you stink" is May 29, 1941.

Other: Comstock's article in *Survey* is July 2, 1921, and her letter to her sister is April 18, 1922. (I found it at the Wisconsin Historical Society.) *Tribune*'s 50th anniversary piece, seeking to cleanse itself and the deceased man who baited it into being, is June 2, 1971. FLW's "could damn myself" is April 27, 1929, and his "burnt child" is July 10, 1930.

Other: A retired Tulsa dentist-turned-investigative-journalist, Steve Gerkin, who became a friend, has published important work on Dick Rowland, the instant scapegoat of the Tulsa tragedy. Gerkin's work appeared in 2013 in a now-defunct and wholly beautiful alternative broadsheet magazine in Tulsa, *This Land;* the stories are at thislandpress.com and are also in Gerkin's *Hidden History of Tulsa.* As said in the text, some of the parallels between Rowland

and Julian Carlton are striking (their mysterious origins, physical size, the layered self-invention).

Other: Since 2000, Marc Carlson of the University of Tulsa, mentioned in acknowledgments, has maintained a web link to the riot, including timelines, photographs, list of known victims, comparisons with other so-called riots in America; this living organism can be accessed at tulsaraceriot.wordpress.com. The research center of the Tulsa Public Library has an *actual* copy of the state edition of the *Tribune* with the NAB NEGRO on the front page: history didn't disappear it. Sheri Perkins, history and digital collections librarian, let me hold it. Ian Swart, mentioned in the acknowledgments, at the Tulsa Historical Society, has all kinds of riot-related documents and Jones family memorabilia—and, as with the two just mentioned, great amounts of Tulsa lore in his head. Frances Jordan-Rakestraw and Hannibal B. Johnson are two Tulsa authorities without whose knowledge and help (and writings, in Johnson's case) I couldn't have done this chapter. That goes double for Scott Ellsworth, mentioned above. He lives in Ann Arbor, but he's always humming "Take Me Back to Tulsa."

Other: There were three crucial works in my trying to understand RLJ in Wisconsin as a newspaperman before the relocating to Oklahoma: the Weissman master's thesis, referenced in the text; W. T. Evjue's *A Fighting Editor;* David Mollenhoff's *Madison: A History of the Formative Years*, notably chap. 6, which deals entirely with the years RLJ was editor of the *WSJ*. Mollenhoff (as indicated in the text) has been an occasional writing partner of M. J. Hamilton.

Other: There is a letter from FLW to his sister Jane Porter, dated March 7, 1929, in which he says: "I am dreadfully sorry for Dick. He is meeting the fate of all negatively good people." This would have been roughly eight years past the riot, and seems to suggest the degree to which the denying RLJ must have realized how he'd never escape what he'd done. But the more I study the letter and its background (FLW was answering a letter from his sister written the month before), the more I have grown convinced that this "Dick" is not RLJ, but another member of the Lloyd Jones clan. I am not positive, though, and that's what makes it haunting. (Secrest references the letter on p. 368 of her bio and believes it is indeed about RLJ, but she is making no connection to the riot. That never comes up in her text.)

Which leads to another crucial question: How much did people in the family who lived far away from Oklahoma know about Tulsa and of what RLJ did and how much did they talk about it among themselves? It's inconceivable to me that they didn't know—they were too close a clan. And yet I have never found an overt reference in a Lloyd Jones letter. It's all coded, exactly like the correspondence I quote from in the text between FLW and his cousin. Something else: I said in the notes for "Attended by the Gothic" that the passenger list for the *Empress of Asia* and its arrival from Japan at Vancouver in the spring of 1921 with FLW aboard was of special importance—and here is why: it places him back in America a whole month before Tulsa's ashes. He was home. He had to have been aware, even if he didn't know the particulars, not then, or maybe even ever. The family had to have been aware, and the shame and embarrassment—not to say the coded silence—only grew in the years after. Precisely, you might say, like the shame and embarrassment and coded silence of Tulsa itself only grew in the years after. A fact: The riot was taught formally for the first time in the Tulsa public schools only in the academic year 2012–13—and it is still, as is my point, an event tragically underrecognized in the country at large.

Finally, squaring it all back home. Irony is where you find it, or take it. There was no room to go into this in the text, and there is hardly any room for it here, and it could make its own separate story, but in my five reporting trips to Tulsa, over three years, I met or talked on the phone to a number of RLJ's descendants. I talked to four of his grandchildren. The irony is that each was unfailingly pleasant, and even generous. Did they have every motive to be? Maybe, and maybe not. These grandchildren understood—the more so as it went along—that I was writing a piece for a book that was going to condemn their grandparent. And yet the four of them talked to me. Each of these descendants, who were in advanced years, has had a professional career, and in a few cases that career is ongoing and distinguished. They've all grown up in one way or another in the newspaper business. Of the grandkids, the one I was most reluctant to see was RLJ's granddaughter, Georgia Lloyd Jones Snoke. Why? Because I had heard she was the most defiant, the most defensive, the most argumentative. Her position has long been that it's entirely too convenient to blame it all on her grandfather. The tragedy has many parents. So I went nervously to see her. So, queerly, we got along famously. It was as if I had walked into the camp of the enemy and found, if not a friend, then someone I could talk to with utter frankness—and vice versa. She is intellectually rigorous. We have traded many emails. Neither of us convinced the other, not even close, but we've heard each other out. I'll leave it there.

PART III Shaking It from His Sleeve: The Year 1936

Lawrence's quote is in a 1925 essay, "Art and Morality."

Blood and Bones

PRECEDE. Bigger quote is on p. 429 of the Harper Perennial Modern Classics edition. "Everybody's Protest Novel" is really an essay about Harriet Beecher

Stowe and *Uncle Tom's Cabin*. Wright's novel and Baldwin's attack come in only to underscore his points.

CHAPTER. Again, an effort to reconcile the unreconcilable, and I did it by as much cross-checking as I could of the dozens and dozens of news accounts at the time—and of books and articles written since, combined with going to the various places, trying to imagine. Also, the court records and transcripts. No one has ever solved the mystery of why; no one will. Perhaps more than any other single thing, being able to get down into the old dark Dodgeville cell helped me to get the chapter done.

Comment re Julian in *Milwaukee Sentinel* by J. A. Vogelsang (the father was J. Z., but historians tend to goof their different middle names) is August 16, 1914. Re Julian and myth of Pullman porter: Although archivists at the Newberry Library in Chicago (where the Pullman archives are) did a thorough check and couldn't find his name, they caveated that the records have small gaps in places, so it's theoretically possible he did work for the company—but doubtful in their opinion. Figures on black population in Chicago are from *Black Metropolis*, 1962 updated edition, pp. 8 and 12. I used the term "promised land" as homage to Nicholas Lemann's *The Promised Land: The Great Black Migration and How It Changed America*. Hughes quote ("Midnight was like day") is on p. 33 of his *The Big Sea*. *Chronicle's* "seared throat" is August 21, 1914. Death certificate is on file in Iowa County Office of Register of Deeds. Barney's "agent of the Lord" is on pp. 145–46 of her memoir-bio. J. L. Wright's "those of the clergy" is on p. 82 of his bio. Twombly's "And the rumor that the superstitious" quote is on p. 167 of his bio. The "guess you solved" quote is October 9, 1914. FLW's nine paras on the funeral are on pp. 185–86 of the autobio. Scully's "tragedy which occurred" is on p. 22 of his *Frank Lloyd Wright*. Secrest's "wanted to live" is on p. 222 of her bio, though not Weston's name as the one who pulled FLW to safety. (I verified that elsewhere.) Re FLW and the mail carriers: in *Home News* of September 10, 1914. In the same issue, there's a story about the art exhibits at the recent Inter-County Fair and of how FLW was grousing he didn't get more exhibit space. Wait a minute. Wasn't he wild in his grief?

Connective Tissue: Two

PRECEDE. Secrest (p. 391 her bio) has dug out an FLW letter to the great photographer Edward Steichen (December 9, 1931) in which he is trying to enlist him for a portrait in the magazine "and a come-back by me" as a way of refuting Fistere's article. Either it didn't take (with Steichen) or FLW gave up on the gambit.

CHAPTER. Again, I tried to identify within the text the source/dates for many of the quotes, journalistic and otherwise, but for ones not identified, see immediately below. My portrait of Miriam comes from her autobiography (more on that below), from FLW's autobio, from newspapers, from various biographies and histories, and, not least (and a bit more reliably in this case), from directories and genealogies and cemetery records and census reports. An example of the constant confusion-fog: Miriam is said in many books to have been a widow when she met FLW (she presents herself this way in her life story), but from what conflicting records I could obtain she was apparently divorced. And her former husband had died in 1912, not in 1911, as is commonly claimed, and as she apparently told people. In her autobio, she gives his name as Emil, but on his gravestone and in plenty of other records it is Ewel Noel. As said in the text, I admire Secrest's portrait (even though the above apparent "facts" are in conflict with hers). In too many other hands, Miriam has been the subject of brilliant cruelty (sometimes not so brilliant). As said in the text, her autobio never got published as a book, but much of it appeared four months after her death in five installments in the Sunday magazine of *Milwaukee Journal,* May–June 1932.

Sentence quoted in footnote from "Old Madison Boy" is on p. 72. FLW's "question of how much punishment" was a comment made to a friend after the 1925 fire (citations re the fire are covered later in this section), and the comment is quoted in article in the *Independent,* March 8, 2009. FLW's "Drowning men" is on p. 201 of the autobio. The "violet pallor": same page. His "horrible loneliness" is on p. 191. The "How do you like" and "never seen": p. 201. Miriam's "that one glance" is on p. 14 of her autobio and in May 15, 1932, *Milwaukee Journal* installment. FLW's "continually expecting" and "waking or dreaming" and "impending disaster": p. 194 of the autobio. Levine's quotes are on pp. 113–14 of his *Architecture.* Hitchcock's "pyramidal gloom" quote is on p. 116 of his *Modern Architecture: Romanticism and Reintegration.* Smith's quote re FLW "Turning his back" etc., is on p. 202 of her *Frank Lloyd Wright, Hollyhock House and Olive Hill.* Re FLW's constant travel to and from Japan: Alofsin, in Appendix A of his *Lost Years,* has once again done us the service of figuring out the dates. FLW's cantilevering quotes are on pp. 214–15 of the autobio. His "strange disturbances" is on p. 203. His "I loved her enough" seems to be from a letter in early summer 1919, and quoted on p. 275 of Secrest. For the long FLW letter, quoted extensively in Gill ("Instead of making the sacrifices"): it's undated, but almost certainly is from beginning of June 1919 (see below for more). FLW quote "But instead of improving" is on p. 257 of the autobio. The "burn her up more quickly" is on p. 258. Re FLW and LHS coming back together: as said in text, FLW confuses the issue all over the place. In the autobio (p. 107), he says it was twelve years. (If he walked off from the firm in 1893, that would mean 1905.) But on p. 260, he suggests it was circa 1913—which would mean 21 years. In his *Genius* book on LHS, he says (on p. 67) that it was "nearly twenty," but on next page indicates it was 26 years ("about 1919"). As said in text, the *true* time frame of the slow coming back seems to have been somewhere around 1900—i.e., after 7 years of estrangement. Again, this is only worth going into for emphasizing that FLW can never be trusted on the math or on most facts, even if you have to pay close attention for the deeper spiritual truths, which are always there.

His "I am going to tell you a secret" letter is on November 30, 1922. His "wanted to get up," etc., is on pp. 264–65 of the autobio. His "No, fight the fire" is on p. 261 of the '43 edition of the autobio. His "Place seemed doomed" is on p. 259. His "lower down in my own" and "aching void" are on pp. 508 and 511 of the '43 autobio. His "Another savage" and "living half" and "tremendous pealing" and "sneering fool": pp. 259–60. Re my footnote and Hurlbut and Neutra: Diary entry is quoted on p. 135 of *Richard Neutra: Promise and Fulfillment, 1919–1932*. FLW Isaiah quotes are on pp. 273–74 of the '43 autobio. The "searching causes" is on p. 259. *NYT* and *Tribune* reports: both April 22, 1925. *WSJ* is April 21. Mumford's FLW memories are on pp. 432–33 of his *Sketches from a Life*. FLW's pinned note on door of Heath in Buffalo: as said in text, no date, but almost certainly October or November 1927—letter is in the FLW collection at Library of Congress. Re Miriam's trashing of FLW's rented house in La Jolla: told in June 5, 1932, serialization of her autobio in *Milwaukee Journal* and also on p. 129 of the manuscript itself. Letter describing the trashing ("As a wreck") is on p. 142 of her manuscript.

And, finally, about that never-published manuscript, at least never published in full as a book. The document is absurdly embellished and factually wrong in so many places. Far worse, the author is guilty of changing and transposing large chunks of the texts of letters between herself and FLW, so as to suit her purposes. One example: The nakedly vulnerable and very long letter FLW wrote to her in the early summer of 1919, in which he speaks of how the "pictures are turned to the wall in regret and shame." Gill has the letter on pp. 254–56 of his bio. Miriam has it on pp. 77–78 of her ms. But she wholesale rearranges FLW's paragraphs and reworks sentences, at least from the copy that Gill reproduces. I worked hard to find a copy of the original. The letter is not indexed in the Garland. (Only seven letters between FLW and Miriam are in the Garland, and they are mainly in the 1914–15 period, with one dating to 1918.) I couldn't locate it elsewhere. In Gill's notes, he refers to it as an "unpublished letter" from June 1919. Miriam has it as August 10, 1919, but the letter was almost assuredly written in close proximity to his short and shame-filled notes to her of June 9 and 11 (both of which I was able to study in their handwritten form). So one of the most self-exposing letters he ever wrote remains a mystery—for me. I felt sure it might be among Gill's papers at the Beinecke Rare Book & Manuscript Library at Yale, but no. (Gill left boxes and boxes of his work at his alma mater, but nothing of substance related to his FLW bio.) Just one more FLW riddle. The mere existence of Miriam's self-deluding life story seems a not-small treasure. Indeed, if the work (a full copy of which has come into my hand) must be distrusted on every page, it can nonetheless, just like FLW's autobio, reveal essential and almost unwitting truths. It can also make you wince. In that estranged summer of 1919 in Japan, she reproduces in full what purports to be a letter to him, in which she says: "I see your jeering, sneering, mocking face, livid and distorted with anger and revenge, your grandiloquent gyrations, hell bent on making a false impression. I hear your ribald laugh, jeering at my misery." In an appendix to her manuscript, Miriam reproduces some plaintive letters to her final friend, Helen Raab, and in one she speaks of how "I can't find a publisher for my book which is the only true story of Taliesin." Perhaps she'll find one yet, who'll annotate it all. I've begun to hope so.

In the Fourth Dimension

PRECEDE. The tale of the proboscis was put together from newspaper accounts and court records, in the main. WSJ first report is November 1, 1932, and Tribune's is November 4. FLW's account is on pp. 432–33 of the '43 autobio ("A Coarse Incident"). Instead of naming Sechrest, he refers to him as an "Indian farmer." I wished to tell the story in the first place as a small parable of seeming to get your bloody deserts when you go around trying to stiff people, not least local folk, your neighbors, your employees—even a cardiologist who comes out from Madison to tend you in the middle of a winter night. (His name was Dr. Hugh Payne Greeley, and that particular stiffing, which Greeley set down years later in a kind of unpublished family memoir, happened in '38 or '39.) I have come on a couple dozen such FLW stiffing stories, easy. In the country, among good country folk, skinflint memories die hard, no matter who you were. Smallest recap of yet another: The Spring Green and Wyoming Telephone Company supplied phone service from Dodgeville up to Spring Green, and the master of Taliesin was chronically late (even when he did pay) on his bills. The secretary-treasurer of the association was a no-nonsense farmer named Wesley Eugene Walker. One day in the thirties, he got up on a utility pole and began to cut the wire that led to FLW's home. (Supposedly, the unpaid bill had gotten up to $1,000.) FLW came rushing down the hill. There was a standoff that may or may not have involved a pistol. No violence, and some worked-out terms—except that the stiffing started right up again. W. E. Walker is long dead, but his daughter, Margaret Peat, still lived in the Iowa County farmhouse where she was born and her parents raised her. I went to see her one day a few years ago. She was eighty-six, packing a delicious grin. She told me the above, as well as this: She was a ten-year-old home from school one day—so it must have been '41 or '42—and who's there sitting in the driveway in a big red car with one of his apprentices but FLW? He'd come to negotiate a bill. Her parents weren't home. She invited him in. He took the best seat in the parlor and said he'd wait. It was a rocker, a family heirloom. "Mr. Wright, we're not allowed to sit in that chair," she said. He ignored her and began to rock—and the thing tipped him ass over teakettle. Rocker was saved; FLW's dignity, not so much.

CHAPTER. Many FLW experts gave of their time, and key ones named below. First, though, re some quotes and sources, not otherwise embedded in text: Curtis's "all too clumsy" is on p. 203 of his *Modern Architecture Since 1900.* Herb's story re the "decent" $5,000 house and FLW response is told on first page of his *Building,* cited in footnote. His "When I was five" is on p. 7 of his *We Chose. NYT* obit of Jacobs is May 27, 1987. My talks with Elizabeth Aitken and her two siblings, Will Jacobs and Susan Jacobs Lockhart, were in the spring and fall of 2017 on the phone. (I regret not being able to meet them. Of the three, Elizabeth by far gave the most time, and we seemed to get along from the start. She is the informal family historian and provided some published family histories.) *Time* piece on Jacobs is April 7, 1967. Hemingway sketch of Wescott is in chap. 3 of *Sun.* (On February 14, 1925, EH wrote a letter to a childhood Michigan pal, Bill Smith, in which he said unguarded vile homophobic things about Wescott—classic EH, the devil always the measure of his angel.) On the Wescotts: Katherine Wescott Jacobs had a cousin, Harold Wescott, who'd been a student briefly at Taliesin, and this was yet another connection for how it all eventually came to be: the Jake as Usonia I.

Other: Herb's "outside the American pattern" is on p. 59 of *Building.* Evans spoke of "the thing itself" in an interview at Yale in 1974. The Kalec and Sprague quotes in this chapter are from their seminal pieces, spoken of in a footnote in text (and cited fully in the selected bibliography). Re FLW's use of term "holocaust heating": Herb tells of this on p. 4 of *Building,* and puts the words in quotes, but seems unaware of what I can only think of as savage ironies. My phone talks with Lipman were in fall 2017. *Life* "World of Tomorrow" is May 8, 1939. Re SCJ cost ended up "close to half the net worth" quote is April 29, 2014, in *NYT.* Goldberger quote in *NYT* on Fallingwater ("thrust it forward") is November 30, 1986. Toker's "popping full-grown" quote is on p. 7 of his *Rising.* (Our phone talks were in fall 2017.) FLW wire to Mosher is August 27, 1936. His "thought I had found" to Kaufmann is August 30. Toker's "What made the house" is on pp. 11–12 of *Rising.* Secrest's "very qualities" quote is on p. 389 of her bio. Twombly's computation of projects in period 1915–32 is on p. 192 of '79 edition of his bio. Mumford's "total eclipse" quote is on p. 431 of his *Sketches*. FLW's "put it together" is on p. 306 of the autobio. Levine's "Wright meant Ocatilla" quote is on p. 205 of *Architecture*. FLW's "ephemera" and "prostrate to the sun" quotes are on pp. 306 and 305 of the autobio. Caretaker's "am sorry to report" letter to FLW is June 3, 1929. (His name was George Weldon, and he might be otherwise lost to history were it not for Brian Spencer, referenced in text.) Johnson letter to Mumford re FLW ("nothing to do with architecture") is January 3, 1931. *NYTBR* review of the autobio is April 3, 1932. FLW apology to organizers of Rochester talk ("for such pessimism") is December 2, 1932. His letter to Kittredge is November 10, 1932. Olga's night-letter wire to FLW (YOUR FAMILY LONESOME) is November 16, 1932. Herb's "beginning to be vaguely" quote is on p. 64 of *Building*. Mumford's "In Fallingwater . . . had created a dynamic" is on p. 438 of *Sketches*. Kimmelman's "His abiding subject" quote is from his August 11, 2005, *New York Review of Books* essay.

From the start, I had envisioned the story as kind of an isosceles triangle, with the Jacobs at the top and Fallingwater and the SCJ representing the two equal sides: the Jake as first among equals—or my first. I kept trying out the thesis on a number of architectural critics and historians; they didn't hoot it out of town. As is evident, the two historians whose work I relied on most are Kalec and Sprague, and my in-depth talks with Kalec, in person and on the phone, further helped me to get the story done. Re files: The Jacobs papers— formally titled the Herbert and Katherine Jacobs Residence and Frank Lloyd Wright Records, 1924–1974—are at the Ryerson Burnham Archives at the Ryerson Burnham Libraries of the Art Institute of Chicago. Herb, the obsessive documentarian, left many treasures behind, including photos of the house-in-progress, of the house when completed, of the family at leisure in various seasons. He left letters. He left memos. He even left that ticket-like sign printed in large letters in his own hand, advising would-be visitors to the house that they'd have to pay 50 cents to get in.

There is an independently produced online radio program, *99 Percent Invisible*, devoted to design and architecture, and in episode #246, on February 7, 2017, Jacobs I is featured. (It's archived on the web.) Herb's voice, from an old NBC interview in the fifties, comes across loud and strong—you get his essential character. For the house itself, there is a wonderful website (www.usonia1.com) that will bring you right inside.

On Herb: It wasn't said in the text, but he had actually met FLW— fleetingly—once before he and his wife drove out in their beater in late August 1936. He tells of this in *Building*. It was two years earlier. He was still at *The Milwaukee Journal*. He drove the 118 miles in bad weather and got maybe 10 minutes of a walk-down-the-hall interview. From *Building*: "He was wearing baggy pants of his own design, gathered at the ankle, with a long woolen scarf wrapped around his neck, and a floppy French beret atop his head. The beret kept falling forward."

Re the restoration of the house, which began in 1983: Chicago restoration architect John Eifler—who has a national reputation for his work on FLW houses—was the key figure, along with project manager Bradley Lynch. Eifler gave much time to my reporting and made available drawings and plans and photographs. Others: Jim Draeger, state historic preservation officer at the Wisconsin Historical Society, and Bill Martinellli, a Madison Wrightophile, who has had a long role in helping to preserve the Jake, were generous with their time. Jim Dennis, longest owner in the house's history, allowed me in— graciously—three times over several years.

For the SCJ: Teri Boesel, archivist at the closely held company archives, opened those archives to me (albeit with her looking on). Mark Hertzberg, previously referenced, an author and old newspaper photographer, is a repository of Racine cultural lore.

Re the Lusks and the Hoults, referenced in the text and in a footnote: Somehow, all the chess pieces on the board weren't quite right for either of their FLW-drawn projects to become the world's first Usonian. As said in the text, neither family could find financing, but I think it's a larger story than that, a more mysterious story: It was as if their whole histories were just one beat off. They were adventurers, yes. But they didn't have what you might call the fourth dimension. That had to wait for Herb and Katherine. I am still pondering how they came along at precisely the moment in time when FLW needed them to come along. Shaking them from his sleeve. A very fine short work on the Hoults and their involvement with FLW is *Frank Lloyd Wright and Wichita: The First Usonian Design,* by Pamela D. Kingsbury, published by the Wichita–Sedgwick County Historical Museum in conjunction with a 1992–93 exhibition.

Finally, on the point of the house's legacy in terms of the world we now inhabit; on the point of American *and* democratic; on the point of building commonsense housing for the common man; on the idea of "return." My contention is that *all* of these things came together in the Jake. Three years before he died (it was in a taped interview at the Plaza in New York, and it was later put out as an LP recording, *Frank Lloyd Wright on Record*), FLW said: "You hear it asserted that that's what our country meant, that the common man was free to be common. Well, he wasn't. He was free to become *uncommon.*" I said in the text that William Allin Storrer is the first FLW scholar who helped me to understand the concept of American-cum-democratic, but my thinking has been shaped by the work of others as well. Paul Goldberger wrote a small, brilliant piece (April 2, 1981) in *NYT* on the worthiness of Levittown housing. In a 2007 work, *Last Harvest,* architect and historian (and emeritus professor at Penn, the university where I teach writing) Witold Rybczynski explores the link between FLW and the Levitt brothers, Alfred and William. (When he was twenty-five, the younger Levitt, Alfred, took a leave from the family business to watch the day-to-day construction of an FLW Usonian-type residence in Great Neck, Long Island.) Rybczynski allowed me to try out on him some of my earliest and hazy-formed FLW ideas.

The fact is, you can go back through FLW's career and find a steady pattern of wanting to design low-cost or relatively low-cost housing. We don't tend to think of him this way—but the buildings are there, if not in huge number, there all the same, as early as his own home of 1889, or the Francisco Terrace Apartments and the Waller Apartments of 1895, or the Joseph Walser House of 1903, or the American System-Built Homes Project of 1916. What I am saying is that, even while he was building on the large scale for the wealthy, or at least well-to-do, he was also always trying to get in a different kind of work for the ordinary citizen. On the American System-Built Homes: This project was and was not an early form of prefabricated housing. He'd aligned himself with a midwestern builder and had begun working on designs as early as 1912. The plan was to have the materials cut at the mill and brought to the site and erected fast. On July 8, 1917, the *Tribune* in Chicago ran a full-page ad: YOU CAN OWN AN AMERICAN HOME. From the text: "American Homes reflect American spirit. They are the most recent triumph of Frank Lloyd Wright, recognized at home and abroad as America's greatest architect. His fame is world-wide, though his most important work has been to teach the American people at home how they can live in homes that are beautiful, convenient, and enduring." The ad promised houses as low as $3,000. Yes, there was something patronizing about the ad's tone, but still: It was the impulse to give shelter to those who might be made *uncommon* by his art. Again, it goes back to one of the central themes of this narrative: a fundamental decency, in spite of all. Oh, by the way: His association with the building company went sour; the thing got into lawsuits. And, besides, World War I had come along and made materials scarce.

PART IV At His Father's Stone

Cather's quote is on p. 119 of her novel.

The Sad Ballad of William Carey Wright (1)

PRECEDE. However few or many visits: As said in the text, no one knows. Gill, on p. 38 of his bio, says that he came once in the 1920s, shortly after Anna's death, and again in the 1940s, but he provides no documentation. Other writers have suggested other time frames. My own feeling is that he may have gone six or eight times before he died—but, again, does the number itself matter? No.

CHAPTER. My portrait of William, in this chapter and in the one that follows, represents much combing of census records, city and state directories, family histories, genealogy charts, county histories, state histories, birth and death records, property records, college records, church records, church bulletins, local newspapers, court records—and, of course, reading what has been previously written and then going to some of the places to talk to folks. I went to as many places as I could in search of WCW and his obsessively restless and downward-sloping journey in America. Each time out, in the field or in the archives, offered a brushstroke of who he seemed to be. Twombly, referenced several times in these notes (with a footnote in the chapter itself), needs to get special mention here—and my admiration from a distance, since we've never met. Nearly every WCW place I went to, he had been there decades earlier. I am grateful for his research, even as I have tried to rely on my own.

In a real sense, the most fertile WCW reporting trip—which I made about a half-dozen times—was no further away than a football toss from my office in the English Department at the University of Pennsylvania. The rare books and manuscript library at Penn is the repository of the Wright Family Papers, 1833–1892 (its formal name), and within the collection, as was said in the text, are fourteen of WCW's letters, written between 1841, when he was a kid of sixteen, and 1851, when he was twenty-six and newly married to Permelia. (They're in box 2, folder 26.) Treasure beyond treasure. They are perfectly preserved and thin as parchment. This is where I first began to perceive FLW's father as the melancholy ascetic, possessed of his great charm and wit and intellect but destined nonetheless to be misunderstood by the world. Whenever I felt stuck in the writing, I would go back to WCW's early letters. I have embedded in the text where he was when he wrote them, and their dates. (Incidentally, one of the things the letters prove is that WCW was still attending Amherst College in 1840. It's been passed along in many places that he'd dropped out by then. A minor point, yes.)

Gratitude to David Patterson of Oak Park (also referenced in a footnote in the text). A true music scholar. We've spent a fair amount of time together, and not all of it has concerned WCW. He knows large amounts about FLW and the Oak Park buildings. (He once took me on an extensive guided tour of Unity Temple.) And yet, as said in my footnote, he and I fundamentally disagree on WCW. He doesn't regard the life tragically. I can only see it tragically.

On that point: WCW's descendants in Iowa—chiefly Hope Rogers, Jeanne Swift, Mary Catherine Rogers—just took me in, on faith and Iowa decency.

They plied me with kindness and family photos and many kinds of written documents—and their own not-shy feelings about their maligned ancestor. It's very hard for them to think of him as a tragedy. The family gave me a single-spaced copy of the original typescript of Lizzie's memoir, which is the one I have quoted from in the text; I will cite the page references for it below. (As said in the text, the copy on file in the State Historical Society of Iowa is a retyped double-spaced copy; there are small but important differences between the two.) If not for Gill's bio, the Iowa part of WCW's life might not have even been on my radar. He searched parts of it out long ago; I followed.

Local librarians were sometimes of almost astonishing help. For instance, in McGregor, Iowa, Michelle Pettit, director of the McGregor Public Library, had dug out for me in advance of my visit all kinds of clips and photos about WCW's time there with his family. I told her I was hoping to get things as right as I could, and Pettit said, in an email, after I was back home: "It is wonderful to see a place that I hold in my heart reflected in such a way." It was the same at the state level. It was as if Mary Bennett at the SHSI was on a mission to help me to understand.

Again, I have tried whenever possible to identify sources and dates in the text, but here, going in order, is additional info (primarily in regard to Lizzie's memoir): Description of Bear Valley is in chap. 1 of Judith Redline Coopey's *Herkimers, Holsteins & Cheese*. Postman quote ("A myth is a way") is on p. 79 of the paper edition of his *Amusing Ourselves to Death*. Extract of WCW's deposition on April 6, 1885: It's part of the divorce papers of Anna and William, and the entire case is in the FLW collection at Steenbock Library at UW. (For reasons I can't figure out, the Steenbock holding appears to be an *original* court document, not a copy.) As said in the text, the deposition is eight pages long, and the clerk's penmanship is difficult to read in places, and so my transcription of it varies minutely from that of several other FLW researchers, including that of Jerome Klinkowitz, who has reproduced the full case record as an appendix in his *Frank Lloyd Wright and His Manner of Thought*. Quote by WCW's mother (her name was Abigail Goddard Wright) is in a letter of May 9–10, 1844. WCW's "Unless otherwise indicated, the first note" quote is on p. 66 of his *Manual*. Extract from Lizzie's *My Life* ("was very sweet . . . till after") is on pp. 2 and 4. Her "Today I have written" is on p. 92. Her "saw my stepmother knock me down" is on p. 4. Successive extracts of "I remember one time" and "One other time" and "I remember" and "When Mother and I" and "I never could please her": These are on pp. 6–7. The "Mother embraced me" extract is on p. 8. Extract re "I took the course for Normal" is on p. 18. Her denture story is on p. 80, and the hired girl quote is on p. 83, and her son Paul as delicate baby is also on that same page, and her talking of her own sins as a mother is on p. 82. Anna's sudden kindness (the "water cure") is told on pp. 4–5. Lizzie's "Poor Father" passage is on p. 121, as is the "I don't know why it is." Her "I think I will have Hope typewrite" is on p. 130. My in-person talks with Hope Rogers and family were in 2013 and 2017 (and I have stayed in touch with the family in the time since). M. J. Hamilton's quote re WCW with "no prospects" is on p. 1 of an essay entitled "Frank Lloyd Wright's Madison Networks," which is in a volume entitled *Frank Lloyd Wright and Madison: Eight Decades of Artistic and Social Interaction*. (Hamilton's co-authors are Anne E. Biebel and John O. Holzheuter.)

Finally, this: Was WCW's middle name "Carey" or "Cary"? You find it both ways. The problem is exacerbated because WCW himself seems never to have spelled out his middle name, signing himself alternately as "William C. Wright" or "Wm. C. Wright." (On his tombstone it's William C.) Genealogy charts (the most reliable one compiled by his older sister, Abby Wright Whittaker) tend to insert the "e." Which is how I believe it should be—but who knows (or, maybe, who really cares?). The question seems a tad more trivial than trying to know when WCW's son became Frank Lloyd rather than Frank Lincoln. But you can find great threads about it in the FLW chat rooms, as if an idea for a doctoral dissertation might erupt at any second.

The Sad Ballad of William Carey Wright (2)

PRECEDE. In his book *The Weather of Words*, which is a slim, poetic meditation on photography and art and poetry itself, Mark Strand says, in reference to an old and unremarkable family photograph: "I have stared and stared at this photograph, and each time I have felt a deep and inexpressible rush of sadness." *This* unremarkable photo. The same rush. All I can think is that it's the way he's playing the piano, as if in his deep loneliness and agedness, and his grandchild facing away with her doll. I have stood on the walk outside the house in Pittsburgh where it was taken and let the rush do its rushing over. Have stood there trying to hear the tune.

CHAPTER. Sources (and dates, if applicable) of most of the quotes are embedded in the text, but again additional info: Finis Farr's "Whereupon" quote re the supposed walking out is on p. 21 of his bio. Herb Jacobs's "walked out" passage is on p. 30 of his bio. Willard's "walked out" is on p. 22 of her bio. Tafel's "never returned" is on p. 30 of his *Years With*. Twombly's "deserted the family" is on p. 408 of his '79 bio. Cronon's "walked out" is on p. 10 of his essay, "Inconstant Unity: The Passion of Frank Lloyd Wright," in *Frank Lloyd Wright: Architect*. Twombly extract ("In 1926, when he") is on p. 14 of his '79 bio. Transcript of FLW's talk at University of Arkansas is printed in *The Master Architect: Conversations with Frank Lloyd Wright*, edited by Patrick Meehan, and the quote in question is on p. 238. (On the audiotape, the momentary tripping up is more pronounced.) His talk at Cal-Berkeley was on April 17, 1957, and transcript is in same Meehan volume and quotes are on pp. 215 and 217. (Again, I have heard the audio, and the emotion is even clearer.) Henry Herold's oral history was in March 2000, on audiotape made by Taliesin archivists. (To repeat what was said in the text: this is my own account of the moment, taken from my conversation with Herold not long before he died; the account in the oral history is on p. 58 and is substantively the same, if briefer.) Lizzie Heller's quote re "Father told us how things" is on p. 46 of *My Life*. Item re Anna and Maginel in the area when WCW's body brought back to Wisconsin from Pittsburgh is in the June 23, 1904, *Weekly Home News*. Claire Messud's "There's so much of life" quote is in *NYT Magazine*, August 10, 2017.

PART V End Story: 1950–1959

The LHS quote, told by FLW, is on p. 55 of his *Genius* book.

Terminals (1)

PRECEDE. Sandburg's "lavender" passage is on p. 264 of first volume of his Lincoln bio. His "month by month" comment is on p. xii of the preface to that volume.

Wrightophiles tend to regard the two-part Mike Wallace interviews, broadcast in September 1957, as a kind of pinnacle TV moment for FLW—you see so much of his protean personality. (Wallace's too.) The neurons—at ninety—are firing. But for my money, the FLW-Sandburg tilt, a month later, on the home turf of Chicago, does the Wallace show one better. I had long been familiar with a transcript (it's produced in full in the work just cited, *Master Architect*). On YouTube and other places, there are snippets of the live 40-minute show (which, as said in the text, was only supposed to go for half an hour). But I couldn't find the whole thing, not until Julia Maish, a publicity manager at WTTW, got someone to dig deep in the station's library and cut a copy—again, much gratitude.

Backstory. Six months before, in April 1957, FLW and Sandburg had *also* sat for a joint interview, in print. Alicia Patterson, editor and publisher of *Newsday* on Long Island, conducted it. She was the daughter of Joseph Medill Patterson, founder of the *Daily News* in New York, and also the third wife of Harry Guggenheim, with whom FLW was so deeply engaged in the building of the Guggenheim. FLW and Sandburg met in FLW's florid suite at the Plaza. (Patterson published the piece in *Newsday* on April 20, 1957, under the title "Meeting of the Titans," and it, too, is reproduced in *Master Architect*, pp. 243–53.) The two men hadn't been in each other's presence in twenty years, although their friendship had stayed intact. Damned if FLW, in this earlier session, too, doesn't bring up the bit about the bloomers. Shortly into the talk, Sandburg says: "About time we were meeting up again." And FLW replies, as if from nowhere: "I used to put bloomer pants on you, Carl, tied around the ankle. And a short velveteen jacket, and we would sit by the fire and talk about art." Later, there's another curious exchange, or curious to my ear. Patterson asks FLW about Le Corbusier and Mies van der Rohe. And he answers: "I think they are two very pretty men in the wrong place." Pretty? Then he slices and dices them.

CHAPTER. The photo of Brandoch and his grandfather was made by Edgar L. Obma, whom FLW came to like and trust as a photographer. The fact that he was local—just down in Dodgeville—made it the better. (For a small-town artist, the full body of his work seems remarkable; the FLW negatives now are part of the archives at Taliesin West.) The figure of 346 projects in FLW's last decade (1950–1959) comes from McCarter's *Frank Lloyd Wright*, p. 171. (Note: This is the 2006 Critical Lives series bio from Reaktion Books, not to be confused with McCarter's far larger work of the same title, published by Phaidon in 1997. In the latter work, as noted above, McCarter published the first comprehensive list of FLW's entire output, executed and not executed. Prof. McCarter and I have exchanged emails re the thorniness of the numbers, and he says he feels confident of this figure, and I am happy to go with it.)

The story of the jeep accident comes from my sifting through many conflicting sources—oral histories, newspaper reports, published memoirs, several video memoirs, official documents (the death certificates principally). Again, the best obtainable version of the truth as I could find it. As said in the text, Olgivanna writes of the tragedy (pp. 143–46) in her autobiography, *The Life of Olgivanna Lloyd Wright*, published only in 2017, long after her death. The book cannot be trusted on many levels (absurd factual errors, in some instances, and long passages of talk, as if transcribed from a tape recorder, which wasn't the case), and so whether it can be trusted here is an open question. It *does* seem that the Wrights were on a train shortly out of Madison when word came (even though there are other accounts contradicting it), but in any case it is why I used caveating words like "apparently." As said in the text, I was able to find death certificates for Svet and Daniel, but not a coroner's report. As was also said, reports no longer exist for '46 in Sauk County, and whether a coroner's report was even done is an open question. If one had been done, it would have doubtless said more about the cause of death, in addition to drowning. (The broken-neck story and thus almost instantaneous death for the mother is part of the folklore. As noted, the county coroner did fill out the certificates and wrote the words "few minutes" in the box for "Duration.") The *Weekly Home News* report is October 3, 1946. Oral histories by Kay Rattenbury and John deKoven Hill (Taliesin Fellows) and Wes Peters and Mrs. Glenn Richardson; a memoir by Curtis Besinger (*Working with Mr. Wright*, pp. 158–59); and Secrest's bio (pp. 518–19): *all* of these and more shed light, if contradictory light. (For instance, Secrest has the Wrights in Chicago when they got the word.) As is the case with most oral histories, the ones cited here were conducted well after the fact. But in a letter to his parents two days after the accident, Johnny Hill, as folks called him, wrote: "It seems as if it had happened long ago. And also as if it hadn't happened at all." That seems real. For me, though, the *most* real sentence is Brandoch's, in his oral history forty-six years onward from the accident: "And I can't give you the exact year for that, but the reasons for it are quite obvious." Of the people I talked to re this sad event, and about Brandoch, who'd become afflicted with Alzheimer's disease, Sue Schuetz was easily the most helpful. Also: I said in the text that Brandoch wrote a manuscript some years ago that he could not get published (although parts of it were made into a documentary film). But the happy news here is that, as this is being written, plans are in the works for an abridgment of the book.

I spoke of an interview filmed with Brandoch in 2007. It's in several brief parts and was made by his cousin, Tim Wright, and is available on YouTube. A moving portrayal.

My talks with Sue Schuetz, by mail, phone, and in person, were in spring–summer 2018.

For quotes in the rest of chapter: I've embedded most of the sources (and dates when applicable) within the text. The others: *Home News* account of the '52 fire is May 1; the *WSJ*'s is April 27; Ling Po's letter is September 1; and FLW's note to the chief is undated but was probably early or mid-August, because Chief Lawrence Larson wrote back, thanking him, on August 15. Smith's quote re "he broke the wall down" is on p. 16 of her *Exhibit*. Her "could serve another vital" passage is on pp. 202 and 204. Goldberger's "nineteenth-century man became" is in his February 13, 1994, *NYT Magazine* FLW portrait. Re the Downs broadcast: Meehan, in his *Conversations*, relates the anecdote about FLW reworking what he actually said before printing it in his own book. Hession and Pickrel in their *Plaza Years* have a good synopsis of FLW's three-day broadcast media blitz, May 15–17. *NYT* story re open of *Sixty* ("white-haired 84-year-old") is October 21, 1953. Mumford's "But in seeing his life" and "could not understand my unwillingness" quotes are on pp. 437 and 433 of his *Sketches*. Re their exchange following the *New Yorker* pieces: in the FLW letter that starts "I love you just the same," you get his anger just by the handwriting—jerkier than usual and with a long sentence written at the top that he meant for the body of the letter. (He drew a line down into the text where he meant it to go.)

Re fire. Re Iovanna's wedding veil and FLW's quoted remark that became the shortened title of this book: As soon as I saw that quote and heard that story, I knew. I first encountered it at the end of Tafel's *About Wright,* which is a kind of album and scrapbook, serving as both memoir and oral history. (I was able to fill in other details of June 18, 1954, from talks with several living apprentices—and from archival research.) Tafel's own time at Taliesin went from 1932 to 1941. He had a good career in architecture and died in 2011, about a year before I began this book. He tells the fire-at-the-wedding story on p. 316, as part of a final chapter, "The Fires." That chapter itself is just six pages long. He relates the Iovanna story in two or three paragraphs. He tells of some other fires, through the years and from his own time at Taliesin, including the following one, in late 1932, of which you've heard nothing about in this text. (I left it out, principally for space reasons.) I'll quote Tafel, since he was there as eyewitness: "[A] fire started within a two-by-four stud wall. We all acted with dispatch. The dinner bell was kept ringing and a bucket brigade was immediately put into action. From the second floor of the students' rooms Mr. Wright directed the operation. He had us break through partitions from opposite sides with axes. At one point an axe pierced through a wall a foot from me. He thought nothing of that. 'Keep chopping away . . . from both sides,' he exclaimed. When the flames were extinguished, he stated again, as he had many times before, that the hollow stud wall was 'the invention of the devil.'"

To use an image that was employed earlier in this narrative, that description makes FLW sound like Ahab atop his whale. Defiant, more than slightly mad. Actually, I tend not to take much stock in this image. I think FLW suffered profound shock from nearly all of his large fires, and that all the seeming insouciance afterward was only that—insouciance. Brandoch Peters, in his book about his grandfather, says that Olgivanna once told him that after the shocking 1925 fire—in which FLW lost not just Taliesin for the second time, almost in its entirety, but also so many irreplaceable works of art—he just sat facing the wall for days. For me, this is the truer image. Facing a wall, almost catatonic. Or, perhaps, going into a charred space and trying to console yourself with your father's music.

I must thank Edgar Tafel, in his grave, with all my heart, and not just for providing me with the inspiration for a title. But even as I am thanking him, for a title as well as a leitmotif for a whole book, I'll register my puzzlement. The author speaks of these fires, the handful of them that he personally remembers or had heard of through the years, in his six pages at the end of his *About Wright,* with very little or no wondering in his voice. He more or less just counts them off, at face value, as if they were some kind of phenomenon. Well, that's exactly what they were. And yet. But still.

Terminals (2)

PRECEDE. About half a dozen times in this narrative I have more or less taken the name of J. L. Wright in vain—and not wrongly, I'll add. It was his inattention to fact, principally in his *My Father* book. But here I must flip that around. I have told of my trip to Avery to see FLW's annotated copy of John's memoir, and have traced the general background of the book's publication. But there is a much richer background, and all of it is told in a carefully documented *full* edition of *My Father*, published in 1994 (fourteen years after John's death) by Southern Illinois University Press (which has done a great deal of FLW-related publishing). The volume is edited by FLW scholar Narciso G. Menocal. He wouldn't have been able to do so had John himself not kept a close record of what had happened between his father and himself in terms of the writing and publishing of the book. It's a complicated history. Roughly a year before publication, on March 6, 1945, FLW had written his son: "What is this talk of a book? Of all that I don't need and dread is more exploitation. Can't you drop it?" A week later, on March 12, John wrote back and said: "Need I recall that your Oak Park batch of children have never exploited you, rather, perhaps, because they have been exploited [?]" So the son went ahead, tremblingly, and, as was told, sent his father a copy on the day of publication. In the archives at Avery, in the clamshell box, are *three* copies of John's memoir. The key one is the volume that came back from FLW with his penciled comments on April 11, 1946. FLW asked for another copy. John sent it to him, with his dad's comments transcribed in the margins (from the copy that had come back) along with John's replies. (He transcribed FLW's remarks in black pencil, and his replies in red.) But before sending the book off, John yet again transcribed all the comments into a separate volume, again differentiating with different colored pencils. Such attention to detail, for future historians, from a son who could invent and misremember and baldly misstate fact in his original ms. At any rate, all of this is in the '94 SIU edition. As Menocal says: "The book, then, is about an unresolved conflict, about the anger of a son toward a father who imposed his own idea of perfection upon his children, as an extension of his ego." At the back of the SIU volume, there's an essay by John's daughter, Elizabeth Wright Ingram, who says: "As I read from a few passages in my father's book, I noticed that Frank Lloyd Wright was quick to lash out at anything that suggests that he was grasping the full glory." I agree—and I don't. For as I have tried to show, there is, to my reading, some surprising restraint in his comments. It's the business about many who "suffered in silence," it's the business of "I know! I know!" Once again, so I contend, the man's humanity was trying to give itself away, especially toward the back of his life.

CHAPTER. Again, as many quoted sources (and dates) embedded in text as was possible. But: Levine's "came to be seen" is on p. 300 of his *Architecture*. Huxtable's "search for a plastic" is on p. 230 of her bio. Alan Dunn's Guggenheim cartoon is in the November 8, 1958, *New Yorker*. FLW "Democracy demands" quote is in October 1, 1945, *Time*. Quote re "Damn it, get a permit for Frank" is in a retrospective piece re Moses, six years after his death, in May 11, 1987, *NYT*. Moses quote re "I will have a building permit" is on p. 43 of Tafel's *About Wright*. (Note: In both these quotes, there is weak sourcing—the first being a building commissioner's recall, the other being Tafel's own editorial comment; it's why I use "reportedly.") Huxtable's "It has never been possible" is on p. 241 of her bio. McCarter's "Every sketch" is on pp. 192–93 of his Critical Lives bio. Levine's "One of the reasons" is on p. 365 of his *Architecture*, and his "unassimilable" comment ("But what is more interesting is what would remain eccentric and unassimilable") is on p. 366. The description of the Plaza suite is on p. 24 of Hession and Pickrel's *In New York*. My talks with Bert Goderstad were in spring 2018. FLW's rhapsodizing (in hindsight) on the value of "adding tired to tired" is on pp. 16–25 of the autobio. FLW's reminiscence of meeting Lamp is on pp. 29–30 of the autobio. Huxtable's quote re "in old age" is on pp. 241–42 of her bio. Secrest's account of David Wright telling FLW of Kitty's death is on p. 563 of her bio. Olgivanna's quoting FLW re "So this is the way" is on p. 80, as is his quote "My dear little wife" and the "when the tree is dying." Tim Wright's comment to me re "shriveled thing" was in our first in-person talk, fall of 2016. FLW's last interview is in *School Arts*, June 1959.

Re Seth Peterson: The life is still in shroud. It wasn't said in the text, but I spoke to his older sister, Carolyn Royster, who was in Kansas City. She was close to ninety. "My parents never got over it, never understood it," she said of the suicide in a clear voice one night late on the phone. What also wasn't detailed in the text is the degree to which many preservationists came together to save the cottage, and, again, not the least of these were esteemed restoration architect, John Eifler, and all-around-hand, Bill Martinelli, both of whom were cited above in connection with the Jacobs House. There is a beautiful little book, befitting the size of the house herself, *Frank Lloyd Wright's Seth Peterson Cottage*, co-authored by Eifler and Kristin Visser.

Re Robie Lamp: Wisconsin historian John O. Holzhueter published a long and scholarly piece in the winter 1988–89 *Wisconsin Magazine of History* entitled "Frank Lloyd Wright's Designs for Robert Lamp." He detailed the home and other projects that FLW built or designed for Robie (chief among them the Prairie foursquare, still standing, on a recessed lot on Butler Street near the capitol building in Madison), and went into the life as well. I submit, however, there is a full book yet to be written, and not just on Robie, but on Robie and Cecil both. Lamp and Corwin: the two best male friends a loner and egotist ever had.

Re Kamal Amin: I feel there is a whole book, an unvarnished telling, yet to be written about Olgivanna Lloyd Wright. In a sense, that book has already been written, and Amin is its author. It's entitled *Reflections from the Shining Brow*. It is a memoir of his years at Taliesin published in 2004 by a small California press. The slim book is a tightrope rarity: able to hang out the unclean linen without ever once sounding vulgar or untrue. The memoir is about FLW, of course, but even more it is about Olgivanna, and about the way she could employ her "Gestapo-like tactics" in her need for total control of the Taliesin Fellowship, even more so in the years after her husband was gone. It is not the entire life, however; it is Kamal's glimpse of Olgivanna, as he knew her and feared her and loved her and sometimes loathed her. That fuller book, objectively told and researched, is the one the world awaits.

LAST WORD. The "as though it had stood there for centuries" is on p. 454 of the '43 autobio, and the "over the rim of the world" is on p. 452. The "sap into my veins" is from a brief essay originally published in the journal *Industrial Wisconsin*, April 1930. One of the most lyrical things Wright ever wrote.

———

It was as if even in death, fire wouldn't leave him alone. In the early sixties, there were three fires at Taliesin in Arizona in less than three years. One, in the fall of 1964, destroyed a 150-seat pavilion. The damage was something like $100,000. Before this, there'd been successive dormitory fires in the same dormitory, within a year of each other. The apprentices got out safe.

It was never my intention to try to spreadsheet every fire. Just as I was finishing this manuscript, someone sent me a copy of an AP wire from September 18, 1937, page 3, in the *Daily Tribune* of Wisconsin Rapids, Wisconsin: FRANK LLOYD WRIGHT ESTATE THREATENED BY FIRE. The one-paragrapher beneath: "The Spring Green and Arena fire departments last night subdued a fire which threatened the Taliesin estate of Frank Lloyd Wright, prominent architect. The firemen confined the blaze to a small frame build- ing where gasoline was stored. Loss was estimated at several hundred dollars. Officials said the fire was caused by gas fumes when an employee lit a match in the building."

I never knew a thing about this fire. But there it was, there it is, licking at his history.

And yet I have in my mind a different four-letter word. Turn back to the photograph of a dining table and chairs at the very start of the book. This is the dining room of the Meyer May House (1908) in Grand Rapids, Michigan. A piece of Frank Lloyd Wright's core architectural idea can be glimpsed here. The idea is embodied in the word "home." With those (uncomfortable) high-backed chairs, with those posts of soft lamplight glowing at the four corners of the table, he is making the room within the room, the protected space amid the great flowing space. Even if there aren't any people in this photograph, what you nonetheless grasp is the "communion" of families sitting down to the simple and profound act of taking a meal together. I persist in believing that such feelings of probity and homeness are something he wished dearly to have in his own life but could find only in patches. It's one of the saddest things I know about him.

And, finally, the stone, the one at the site where Midway Gardens stood.

The last time I went to take a look at it, make sure the stone was still there, was after Thanksgiving 2018. I had hoped to get out to Chicago early in the new year, but that didn't work out. Tim Samuelson and I both worried about what the developers next door were doing, Tim a little less so than I. Worst case, he figured that if someone was going to commit a sacrilege and dig up the worthless-seeming thing, he could run over and salvage a slice, cart it home in a bag for his coffee table. Hell, he'd bribe someone if he had to, take over a roll of twenties and fifties.

But it was a bad winter. Tim got busy with other things. One day in early March, when there was a break in the weather, he pedaled over on his bicycle from his home on South Shore Drive. (He's never learned to drive.) It was a shock. The site looked entirely different. They'd installed a new fence, and graded the ground on both sides of the fence. The stone was nowhere to be seen. Tim was heartbroken, yes, but after a little while he was also something else, and the something else, I think, had to do with both his gratitude and his acceptance of how all things ultimately leave the earth. That evening, in an email subject-headed "Sigh," he said:

"I still think it's poignant and ironic that that small broken-up fragment of Midway Gardens brick made an appearance for us. You could still see the bulldozer tracks in the earth all around it. With the site now totally buttoned up with new construction that will last awhile, that little chunk of brick is likely the last bit of Midway Gardens that will ever reveal itself under the sun at 60th and Cottage Grove in our lifetimes and far beyond. And if the earth ever stirs there again into the far distance future, it's a safe bet that nobody else will be looking."

Amen.

Selected Bibliography

Along with this list, readers are invited to consult the Essay on Sources, since not everything cited there is included here, and vice versa. Also: Not every full-length work named here is the most recent edition of that book. In many cases (as with FLW's autobiography), I was working deliberately from the original edition, but comparing it to subsequent editions. (In numerous instances, there was *only* an original edition of a work, whether FLW's or another's.) When there was an edition of a work that I was heavily indebted to (so, for instance, the third edition of W. A. Storrer's field guide to FLW's buildings, with its epiphany-seeming introduction), I have listed it here, and signified it as such.

Alofsin, Anthony. *Frank Lloyd Wright—the Lost Years, 1910–1922: A Study of Influence.* Chicago: University of Chicago Press, 1993.
_____, ed. *Frank Lloyd Wright: Europe and Beyond.* Berkeley: University of California Press, 1999.
_____, ed. *Frank Lloyd Wright: An Index to the Taliesin Correspondence.* New York: Garland Publishing, 1988.
Amin, Kamal. *Reflections from the Shining Brow: My Years with Frank Lloyd Wright and Olgivanna Lazovich.* Santa Barbara, CA.: Fifthian Press, 2004.
Ashbee, Felicity. *Janet Ashbee: Love, Marriage, and the Arts & Crafts Movement.* Syracuse, NY: Syracuse University Press, 2002.
Barney, Maginel Wright. *The Valley of the God-Almighty Joneses.* New York: Appleton-Century, 1965.
Boyle, T. Coraghessan. *The Women.* New York: Viking Press, 2009.
Brooks, H. Allen. *Frank Lloyd Wright and the Prairie School.* New York: Braziller, 1984.
_____. *The Prairie School: Frank Lloyd Wright and His Midwest Contemporaries.* Toronto: University of Toronto Press, 1972.
_____, ed, *Writings on Wright: Selected Comment on Frank Lloyd Wright.* Cambridge, MA: MIT Press, 1985.
Brophy, Alfred L. *Reconstructing the Dreamland: The Tulsa Riot of 1921.* New York: Oxford University Press, 2002.
Cowley, Malcolm. *—And I Worked at the Writer's Trade: Chapters of Literary History, 1918–1978.* New York: Viking Press, 1978.

Curtis, William J. R. *Modern Architecture Since 1900.* Englewood Cliffs, NJ: Prentice Hall, 1983.

Drake, St. Clair, and Horace R. Cayton. *Black Metropolis: A Study of Negro Life in a Northern City.* New York: Harper & Row, 1962.

Drennan, William R. *Death in a Prairie House.* Madison: Terrace Books, University of Wisconsin Press, 2007.

Eaton, Leonard K. *Two Chicago Architects and Their Clients: Frank Lloyd Wright and Howard Van Doren Shaw.* Cambridge, MA: MIT Press, 1969.

Eifler, John, and Kristin Visser. *Frank Lloyd Wright's Seth Peterson Cottage: Rescuing a Lost Masterwork.* Madison, WI: Prairie Oak Press, 1997.

Ellsworth, Scott. *Death in a Promised Land: The Tulsa Race Riot of 1921.* Baton Rouge: Louisiana State University Press, 1982.

Evjue, William T. *A Fighting Editor.* Madison, WI: Wells Print, 1968.

Farr, Finnis. *Frank Lloyd Wright: A Biography.* New York: Charles Scribner's Sons, 1961.

Filler, Martin. *Makers of Modern Architecture: From Frank Lloyd Wright to Frank Gehry.* New York: New York Review Books, 2007.

Final Report of the Oklahoma Commission to Study the Tulsa Race Riot of 1921. Tulsa, OK, 2001.

Friedman, Alice T. "Frank Lloyd Wright and Feminism: Mamah Borthwick's Letters to Ellen Key." *Society of Architectural Historians* 2, no. 2 (June 2002).

Fritz, Herbert. "At Taliesin." In *An Uplands Reader,* ed. Edna Meudt. Dodgeville, WI: Uplands Writers, April 1979.

Gerkin, Steve. *Hidden History of Tulsa.* Charleston, SC: History Press, 2014.

Gill, Brendan. *Many Masks: A Life of Frank Lloyd Wright.* New York: G. P. Putnam's Sons, 1987.

Goldberger, Paul. "Design Notebook." *New York Times,* April 2, 1981.

Guerrero, Pedro E. *Picturing Wright: An Album from Frank Lloyd Wright's Photographer.* New York: Monacelli Press, 2015.

Heinz, Thomas A. *Frank Lloyd Wright Field Guide.* Evanston, IL: Northwestern University Press, 2005.

———. *The Vision of Frank Lloyd Wright.* Edison, NJ: Chartwell Books, 2000.

Hertzberg, Mark. *Wright in Racine.* San Francisco: Pomegranate Publications, 2004.

Hession, Jane King, and Debra Pickrel. *Frank Lloyd Wright in New York.* Layton, UT: Gibbs Smith, 2010.

Hirsch, James S. *Riot and Remembrance: The Tulsa Race War and Its Legacy.* Boston: Houghton Mifflin, 2002.

Hitchcock, Henry-Russell. *In the Nature of Materials: The Buildings of Frank Lloyd Wright, 1887–1941.* New York: Da Capo Press, 1986.

———. *Modern Architecture: Romanticism and Reintegration.* New York: Da Capo Press, 1993.

Hoffmann, Donald. *Frank Lloyd Wright's Fallingwater: The House and Its History.* New York: Dover Publications, 1978.

———. *Understanding Frank Lloyd Wright's Architecture.* New York: Dover Publications, 1995.

Horan, Nancy. *Loving Frank.* New York: Ballantine Books, 2007.

Huxtable, Ada Louise. *Frank Lloyd Wright.* New York: Viking Penguin, 2004.

Jacobs, Herbert, with Katherine Jacobs. *Building with Frank Lloyd Wright.* San Francisco: Chronicle Books, 1978.

Johnson, Hannibal B. *Black Wall Street: From Riot to Renaissance in Tulsa's Historic Greenwood District.* Woodway, TX: Eakin Press, 1998.

Kalec, Donald G. "The Jacobs House I." In *Frank Lloyd Wright and Madison: Eight Decades of Artistic and Social Interaction,* ed. Paul E. Sprague. Madison: Elvehjem Museum of Art, University of Wisconsin, 1990.

Klinkowitz, Jerome. *Frank Lloyd Wright and His Manner of Thought.* Madison: University of Wisconsin Press, 2014.

Kruty, Paul. *Frank Lloyd Wright and Midway Gardens.* Urbana: University of Illinois Press, 1988.

Lemann, Nicholas. *The Promised Land: The Great Black Migration and How It Changed America.* New York: Alfred A. Knopf, 1991.

Levine, Neil. *The Architecture of Frank Lloyd Wright.* Princeton, NJ: Princeton University Press, 1996.

―――――. *The Urbanism of Frank Lloyd Wright.* Princeton, NJ: Princeton University Press, 2015.

Lipman, Jonathan. *Frank Lloyd Wright and the Johnson Wax Buildings.* New York: Rizzoli, 1986.

Madigan, Tim. *The Burning: Massacre, Destruction, and the Tulsa Race Riot of 1921.* New York: Thomas Dunne Books, 2001.

Manson, Grant Carpenter. *Frank Lloyd Wright to 1910: The First Golden Age.* New York: Van Nostrand Reinhold, 1958.

McCarter, Robert. *Frank Lloyd Wright.* London: Phaidon Press, 1997.

―――――. *Frank Lloyd Wright.* London: Reaktion Books, 2006.

―――――, ed. *On and By Frank Lloyd Wright: A Primer of Architectural Principles.* London: Phaidon Press, 2005.

McCrea, Ron. *Building Taliesin: Frank Lloyd Wright's Home of Love and Loss.* Madison: Wisconsin Historical Society Press, 2012.

Meehan, Patrick J., ed. *The Master Architect: Conversations with Frank Lloyd Wright.* New York: John Wiley & Sons, 1984.

―――――, ed. *Truth Against the World: Frank Lloyd Wright Speaks for an Organic Architecture.* Washington, DC: Preservation Press, National Trust for Historic Preservation, 1987.

Miller, Donald L. *City of the Century: The Epic of Chicago and the Making of America.* New York: Simon & Schuster, 1996.

Mollenhoff, David V. *Madison: A History of the Formative Years.* Madison: University of Wisconsin Press, 2003.

Mollenhoff, David V., and Mary Jane Hamilton. *Frank Lloyd Wright's Monona Terrace: The Enduring Power of a Civic Vision.* Madison: University of Wisconsin Press, 1999.

Morrison, Hugh. *Louis Sullivan: Prophet of Modern Architecture.* New York: W. W. Norton, 1998.

Patterson, David W. "Frank Lloyd Wright's Musical Origins." *Frank Lloyd Wright Quarterly* 24, no. 4 (Fall 2013).

―――――. "William C. Wright: A Biographical and Musical Overview." Liner notes for *The Music of William C. Wright.* Oak Park, IL: Permelia Records.

Pfeiffer, Bruce Brooks, ed. *Frank Lloyd Wright: Collected Writings.* Vols. 1–5. New York: Rizzoli, 1992 [in association with the Frank Lloyd Wright Foundation, Scottsdale].

―――――, ed. *Frank Lloyd Wright: The Guggenheim Correspondence.* Carbondale: Southern Illinois University Press, 1986.

_____, ed. *Frank Lloyd Wright: His Living Voice*. Fresno: The Press at California State University, 1987.

_____, ed. *Frank Lloyd Wright in the Realm of Ideas*. Carbondale: Southern Illinois University Press, 1988.

_____, ed. *Frank Lloyd Wright: Letters to Apprentices*. Fresno: The Press at California State University, 1982.

_____, ed. *Frank Lloyd Wright: Letters to Architects*. Fresno: The Press at California State University, 1984.

_____, ed. *Frank Lloyd Wright: Letters to Clients*. Fresno: The Press at California State University, 1986.

_____. *Frank Lloyd Wright, 1867–1959: Building for Democracy*. Los Angeles: Taschen, 2006.

Quinan, Jack. *Frank Lloyd Wright's Larkin Building: Myth and Fact*. New edition. Chicago: University of Chicago Press, 2006.

_____. "Introduction." *Wright Sites: A Guide to Frank Lloyd Wright Public Places*. New York: Princeton Architectural Press, 2017.

Randall, Frank A. *History of the Development of Building Construction in Chicago*. Urbana: University of Illinois Press, 1949.

Riley, Terence, ed., with Peter Reed. *Frank Lloyd Wright: Architect*. New York: Museum of Modern Art, 1994.

Scully, Vincent, Jr. *Frank Lloyd Wright*. New York: Braziller, 1960.

Secrest, Meryle. *Frank Lloyd Wright: A Biography*. Chicago: University of Chicago Press, 1992.

Sergeant, John A. *Frank Lloyd Wright's Usonian Houses*. New York: Watson-Guptill Publications, 1984.

Smith, Kathryn. *Frank Lloyd Wright, Hollyhock House and Olive Hill: Buildings and Projects for Aline Barnsdall*. New York: Rizzoli International, 1992.

_____. *Wright on Exhibit: Frank Lloyd Wright's Architectural Exhibitions*. Princeton, NJ: Princeton University Press, 2017.

Smith, Norris Kelly. *Frank Lloyd Wright: A Study in Architectural Content*. Englewood Cliffs, NJ: Prentice Hall, 1966.

Sprague, Paul. "National Historic Landmark Nomination. Jacobs, Herbert and Katherine, First House." Washington, DC: National Park Service, National Historic Landmarks Survey, 2001.

Storrer, William Allin. *The Architecture of Frank Lloyd Wright: A Complete Catalog*. 3rd ed. Chicago: University of Chicago Press, 2002.

_____. *The Frank Lloyd Wright Companion*. Chicago: University of Chicago Press, 2006.

_____. *Frank Lloyd Wright: Designing Democratic America*. Traverse City, MI: Wine-Wright Media, 2015.

Sweeney, Robert L. *Frank Lloyd Wright: An Annotated Bibliography*. Los Angeles: Hennessey & Ingalls, 1978.

Tafel, Edgar, *About Wright: An Album of Recollections by Those Who Knew Frank Lloyd Wright*. New York: John Wiley & Sons, 1993.

_____. *Years with Frank Lloyd Wright: Apprentice to Genius*. New York: Dover, 1979.

Toker, Franklin. *Fallingwater Rising: Frank Lloyd Wright, E. J. Kaufmann, and America's Most Extraordinary House*. New York: Alfred A. Knopf, 2003.

Twombly, Robert C. *Frank Lloyd Wright: An Interpretive Biography.* New York: Harper & Row, 1973.

———. *Frank Lloyd Wright: His Life and His Architecture.* New York: John Wiley & Sons, 1979.

———. *Louis Sullivan: His Life & Work.* Chicago: University of Chicago Press, 1986.

———, ed. *Frank Lloyd Wright: Essential Texts.* New York: W. W. Norton, 2009.

Weil, Zarine, Cheryl Bachand, and Brian Reis, with introduction by Paul Goldberger. *Frank Lloyd Wright's Robie House.* Seattle: Frank Lloyd Wright Preservation Trust in association with Marquand Books, 2010.

Wilkerson, Isabel. *The Warmth of Other Suns: The Epic Story of America's Great Migration.* New York: Random House, 2010.

Wright, Frank Lloyd. *An Autobiography.* New York: Longmans, Green, 1932.

———. *An Autobiography.* Revised ed. New York: Duell, Sloan and Pearce, 1943.

———. *An Autobiography.* New York: Horizon Press, 1977.

———. *The Future of Architecture.* New York: Horizon Press, 1953.

———. *Genius and the Mobocracy.* New York: Horizon Press, 1971.

———. *The Living City.* New York: New American Library, 1958.

———. *The Natural House.* New York: Horizon Press, 1954.

———. *A Testament.* New York: Horizon Press, 1957.

Wright, John Lloyd. *My Father Who Is on Earth.* New York: G. P. Putnam's Sons, 1946.

Wright, Olgivanna Lloyd. *Frank Lloyd Wright: His Life, His Work, His Words.* New York: Horizon Press, 1966.

———. *The Life of Olgivanna Lloyd Wright: From Crna Gora to Taliesin, Black Mountain to Shining Brow.* Ed. Bruce Brooks Pfeiffer and Maxine Fawcett-Yeske. Novato, CA: Oro Editions, 2017.

———. *The Shining Brow.* New York: Horizon Press, 1960.

Index

Page numbers in *italics* refer to photographs.

Illustration Credits

ii   Used with permission of Frank Lloyd Wright Foundation and Marvin Koner Archive

xi   Balthazar Korab courtesy of the Library of Congress

4   Chicago History Museum, Hedrich-Blessing Collection

36   Courtesy Tim Samuelson; David Bagnall and Frank Lloyd Wright Trust

56   Frank Lloyd Wright Foundation Archives (The Museum of Modern Art/ Avery Architectural & Fine Arts Library, Columbia University, New York) #6002.0009

96   James Caulfield © 2018

108   Courtesy David Bagnall and Frank Lloyd Wright Trust

122   Courtesy Robert G. Bohlmann, AIA, and Wright in Kankakee

146   Courtesy Oak Park (Illinois) Public Library Special Collections

156   Bettmann Archive

166   James Caulfield © 2018

175   Frank Lloyd Wright Foundation Archives (The Museum of Modern Art/ Avery Architectural & Fine Arts Library, Columbia University, New York) # 6002.0002

190   *Dodgeville Chronicle*

220   Courtesy David Bagnall and Frank Lloyd Wright Trust

246   Wisconsin Historical Society WHI-3879

292   Wisconsin Historical Society WHI-55870

314   Frank Lloyd Wright Foundation Archives (The Museum of Modern Art/ Avery Architectural & Fine Arts Library, Columbia University, New York) #2702.0037

343   David Heald, courtesy of the Solomon R. Guggenheim Museum, New York

396   Courtesy family of Hope Rogers and Marion (Iowa) Heritage Center & Museum

428   Courtesy University of Wisconsin, Madison, Archives and Special Collections

467   Frank Lloyd Wright Foundation Archives (The Museum of Modern Art/ Avery Architectural & Fine Arts Library, Columbia University, New York) #6404.0001

478   Frank Lloyd Wright Foundation Archives (The Museum of Modern Art/ Avery Architectural & Fine Arts Library, Columbia University, New York)

493   © 2018 Pedro E. Guerrero Archives

Permissions Acknowledgments

Grateful acknowledgment is made to the following for permission to reprint previously published material:

The Frank Lloyd Wright Foundation: Speeches, writings, and letters of Frank Lloyd Wright and Olgivanna Wright copyright © 2019 by Frank Lloyd Wright Foundation, Scottsdale, Arizona. The Frank Lloyd Wright Foundation Archives (The Museum of Modern Art, Avery Architectural & Fine Arts Library, Columbia University, New York). All rights reserved. The Frank Lloyd Wright signature is a registered trademark of the Frank Lloyd Wright Foundation. Reprinted by permission of Frank Lloyd Wright Foundation.

King's College, Cambridge: Unpublished writings of Janet Ashbee copyright © 2019 by The Provost and Scholars of King's College, Cambridge. Reprinted by permission of King's College, Cambridge, on behalf of the estate of Janet Ashbee.

State Historical Society of Iowa: Excerpt from "The Story of My Life" by Elizabeth Wright Heller, from the Elizabeth Wright Heller Collection. Reprinted by permission of State Historical Society of Iowa.